PRINCIPLES OF
MICROECONOMICS
SIXTH CANADIAN EDITION

N. GREGORY MANKIW
HARVARD UNIVERSITY

RONALD D. KNEEBONE
UNIVERSITY OF CALGARY

KENNETH J. McKENZIE
UNIVERSITY OF CALGARY

NELSON / EDUCATION

NELSON / EDUCATION

Principles of Microeconomics, Sixth Canadian Edition
by N. Gregory Mankiw, Ronald D. Kneebone, and Kenneth J. McKenzie

**Vice President, Editorial
Higher Education:**
Anne Williams

Executive Editor:
Amie Plourde

Executive Marketing Manager:
Sean Chamberland

Technical Reviewer:
Ross Meacher

Developmental Editor:
My Editor, Inc.

**Photo Researcher and Permissions
Coordinator:**
Natalie Russell

**Content Production
Manager:**
Jennifer Hare

Production Service:
MPS Limited

Copy Editor:
June Trusty

Proofreader:
MPS Limited

Indexer:
MPS Limited

Design Director:
Ken Phipps

Managing Designer:
Franca Amore

**Interior Design
Modifications:**
Peter Papayanakis

Cover Design:
Trinh Truong

Cover Image:
Andy Roberts/Getty Images

Compositor:
MPS Limited

**Library and Archives Canada
Cataloguing in Publication Data**

Mankiw, N. Gregory, author
  Principles of microeconomics/
N. Gregory Mankiw, Ronald D.
Kneebone, Kenneth J. McK-
enzie.—Sixth Canadian edition.

Includes bibliographical references
and index.
ISBN 978-0-17-653086-0 (pbk.)

  1. Microeconomics—Textbooks.
2. Microeconomics—Canada—
Textbooks. I. Kneebone, Ronald
D. (Ronald David), 1955–, author
II. McKenzie, Kenneth J. (Kenneth
James), 1959–, author III. Title.

HB172.P744 2013   338.5
C2013-903552-4

ISBN-13: 978-0-17-653086-0
ISBN-10: 0-17-653086-X

To Catherine, Nicholas, and Peter,
my other contributions to the next generation

To our parents
and
Cindy,
Kathleen, and Janetta—
thanks for your support and patience

BRIEF CONTENTS

TABLE OF CONTENTS

Creativei/iStockphoto

PART 1
INTRODUCTION 1

Dusit/Shutterstock

PART 2
SUPPLY AND DEMAND I: HOW MARKETS WORK 65

Thinkstock

PART 3
SUPPLY AND DEMAND II:
MARKETS AND WELFARE 147

PART 4
THE ECONOMICS OF
THE PUBLIC SECTOR 209

Chad Mcdermott/Dreamstime.com

PART 5
FIRM BEHAVIOUR AND THE ORGANIZATION OF INDUSTRY 273

whethervain/iStockphoto

PART 6
THE ECONOMICS
OF LABOUR MARKETS 393

Sean Gladwell/GetStock.com

PART 7
TOPICS FOR FURTHER STUDY 461

PREFACE

As soon as we got our hands on the first U.S. edition of *Principles of Microeconomics*, it was clear to us that "this one is different." If other first-year economics textbooks are encyclopedias, Gregory Mankiw's was, and still is, a handbook.

Between us, we have many years of experience teaching first-year economics. Like many instructors, we found it harder and harder to teach with each new edition of the thick, standard textbooks. It was simply impossible to cover all of the material. Of course, we could have skipped sections, features, or whole chapters, but then, apart from the sheer hassle of telling students which bits to read and not to read, and worries about the consistencies and completeness of the remaining material, we ran the risk of leaving students with the philosophy that what matters is only what's on the exam.

We do not believe that the writers of these other books set out with the intention of cramming so much material into them. It is a difficult task to put together the perfect textbook—one that all instructors would approve of and that all students would enjoy using. Therefore, to please all potential users, most of the books end up covering a wide range of topics. And so the books grow and grow.

Professor Mankiw made a fresh start in the first U.S. edition. He included all the important topics and presented them in order of importance. And in the sixth U.S. edition, he has resisted the temptation to add more and more material. We have, in adapting the text for Canadian students, taken a minimalist approach: "If it isn't broken, don't fix it!" While the book is easily recognizable as Mankiw's, we have made changes that increase its relevance to Canadian students. Some of these changes reflect important differences between the Canadian and U.S. economies. For example, the Canadian economy is much smaller and more open than the U.S. economy, and this fact is explicitly recognized in this edition. Other changes reflect important institutional differences between the two countries, including the structure of the tax system and the nature of competition policy. Finally, the Canadian edition focuses on issues and includes examples that are more familiar and relevant to a Canadian audience.

We would not have agreed to participate in the Canadian edition if we were not extremely impressed with the U.S. edition. Professor Mankiw has done an outstanding job of identifying the key concepts and principles that every first-year student should learn.

It was truly a pleasure to work with such a well-thought-out and well-written book. We have enjoyed teaching from the earlier Canadian editions and we look forward to using the sixth Canadian edition. We hope you do, too.

HOW THE BOOK IS ORGANIZED

To write a brief and student-friendly book, Mankiw considered new ways to organize familiar material. What follows is a whirlwind tour of this text. The tour, we hope, will give you a sense of how the pieces fit together.

Introductory Material

Chapter 1, "Ten Principles of Economics," introduces students to the economist's view of the world. It previews some of the big ideas that recur throughout economics, such as opportunity costs, marginal decision making, the role of incentives, the gain from trade, and the efficiency of market allocations. Throughout the text an effort is made to relate the discussion back to the ten principles of economics introduced in Chapter 1. The interconnections of the material with the ten principles are clearly identified throughout the text.

Chapter 2, "Thinking Like an Economist," examines how economists approach their field of study, discussing the role of assumptions in developing a theory and introducing the concepts of an economic model. It also discusses the role of economists in making policy. The appendix to this chapter offers a brief refresher course on how graphs are used and how they can be abused.

Chapter 3, "Interdependence and the Gains from Trade," presents the theory of comparative advantage. This theory explains why individuals trade with their neighbours, as well as why nations trade with other nations. Much of economics is about how market forces coordinate many individual production and consumption decisions. As a starting point for this analysis, students see in this chapter why specialization, interdependence, and trade can benefit everyone.

The Fundamental Tools of Supply and Demand

The next three chapters introduce the basic tools of supply and demand. Chapter 4, "The Market Forces of Supply and Demand," develops the supply curve, the demand curve, and the notion of market equilibrium. Chapter 5, "Elasticity and Its Application," introduces the concept of elasticity and uses it to analyze events in three different markets. Chapter 6, "Supply, Demand, and Government Policies," uses these tools to examine price controls, such as rent-control and minimum-wage laws, and tax incidence.

Chapter 7, "Consumers, Producers, and the Efficiency of Markets," extends the analysis of supply and demand using the concepts of consumer surplus and producer surplus. It begins by developing the link between consumers' willingness to pay and the demand curve, and the link between producers' costs of production and the supply curve. It then shows that the market equilibrium maximizes the sum of the producer and consumer surplus. Thus, students learn early about the efficiency of market allocations.

The next two chapters apply the concepts of producer and consumer surplus to questions of policy. Chapter 8, "Application: The Costs of Taxation," shows why taxation results in deadweight losses and what determines the size of those losses. Chapter 9, "Application: International Trade," considers who wins and who loses from international trade and presents the debate over protectionist trade policies.

More Microeconomics

Having examined why market allocations are often desirable, the book then considers how the government can sometimes improve on them. Chapter 10,

"Externalities," explains how external effects such as pollution can render market outcomes inefficient and discusses the possible public and private solutions to those inefficiencies. Chapter 11, "Public Goods and Common Resources," considers the problems that arise when goods, such as national defence, have no market price. Chapter 12, "The Design of the Tax System," describes how the government raises the revenue necessary to pay for public goods. It presents some institutional background about the Canadian tax system and then discusses how the goals of efficiency and equity come into play when designing a tax system.

The next five chapters examine firm behaviour and industrial organization. Chapter 13, "The Costs of Production," discusses what to include in a firm's costs and introduces cost curves. Chapter 14, "Firms in Competitive Markets," analyzes the behaviour of price-taking firms and derives the market supply curve. Chapter 15, "Monopoly," discusses the behaviour of a firm that is the sole seller in its market, the inefficiency of monopoly pricing, the possible policy responses, and the attempts by monopolies to price-discriminate. Chapter 16, "Monopolistic Competition," looks at behaviour in a market in which many sellers offer similar but differentiated products. It also discusses the debate over the effects of advertising. Chapter 17, "Oligopoly," covers markets in which there are only a few sellers, using the prisoners' dilemma as the model for examining strategic interaction.

The next three chapters present issues related to labour markets. Chapter 18, "The Markets for the Factors of Production," emphasizes the link between factor prices and marginal productivity. Chapter 19, "Earnings and Discrimination," discusses the determinants of equilibrium wages, including compensating differentials, human capital, and discrimination. Chapter 20, "Income Inequality and Poverty," examines the degree of inequality in Canadian society, alternative views about the government's role in changing the distribution of income, and various policies aimed at helping society's poorest members.

The final two chapters present optional material. Chapter 21, "The Theory of Consumer Choice," analyzes individual decision making using budget constraints and indifference curves. Chapter 22, "Frontiers of Microeconomics," introduces the topics of asymmetric information, political economy, and behavioural economics. Some instructors may skip all or some of this material. Instructors who do cover these topics may choose to assign these chapters earlier than they are presented in this text, and they have been written to give that flexibility.

WALK-THROUGH

The purpose of this textbook is to help students learn the fundamental lessons of economics and to show how such lessons can be applied to the world in which they live. Toward that end, various learning tools recur throughout the book.

Chapter Openers Well-designed chapter openers act as previews that summarize the major concepts to be learned in each chapter.

Case Studies Economic theory is useful and interesting only if it can be applied to understanding actual events and policies. Updated or replaced with more current Canadian examples, the numerous case studies apply the theory that has just been developed.

Figures and Tables Colourful and eye-catching visuals are used to make important economic points and to clarify Canadian and other key economic concepts. They have also proved to be valuable and memorable teaching aids.

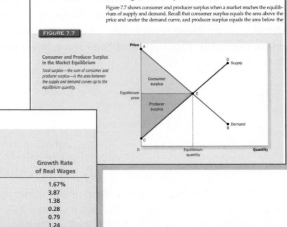

TABLE 18.2

Productivity and Wage Growth in Canada

Time Period	Growth Rate of Productivity	Growth Rate of Real Wages
1961–2007	1.73%	1.67%
1961–1973	3.00	3.87
1973–1981	1.29	1.38
1981–1989	1.15	0.28
1989–2000	1.54	0.79
2000–2007	1.03	1.24

Note: Sub-periods are chosen to be cyclically neutral (peak to peak). Real wages and labour share are calculated with the labour compensation series from the *Canadian Productivity Accounts*.
Source: Reprinted by permission of the Centre for the Study of Living Standards.

Updated Canadian "In the News" Features

One benefit that students gain from studying economics is a new perspective and greater understanding about news from Canada and around the world. To highlight this benefit, excerpts from many Canadian news articles, including opinion columns written by prominent economists, show how basic economic theory can be applied.

"FYI" Features

These features provide additional material "for your information." Some of them offer a glimpse into the history of economic thought. Others clarify technical issues. Still others discuss supplementary topics that instructors might choose either to discuss or skip in their lectures.

Key Concept Definitions

When key concepts are introduced in the chapter, they are presented in **bold** typeface. In addition, their definitions are placed in the margin and in the "Glossary" at the back of the book. This treatment helps students learn and review the material.

QuickQuizzes

After each major section, students are offered a quick quiz to check their comprehension of what they have just learned. If students cannot readily answer these quizzes, they should stop and reread the material before continuing.

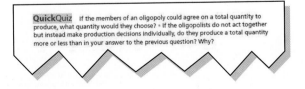

Chapter Summaries   Each chapter ends with a brief summary that reminds students of the most important lessons that they have just learned. Later in their study, it offers an efficient way to review for exams.

List of Key Concepts   A list of key concepts at the end of each chapter offers students a way to test their understanding of the new terms that have been introduced. Page references are included so that students can review terms they do not understand in the original context.

SUMMARY

- A price ceiling is a legal maximum on the price of a good or service. An example is rent control. If the price ceiling is below the equilibrium price, so the price ceiling is binding, the quantity demanded exceeds the quantity supplied. Because of the resulting shortage, sellers must in some way ration the good or service among buyers.
- A price floor is a legal minimum on the price of a good or service. An example is the minimum wage. If the price floor is above the equilibrium price, so the price floor is binding the quantity supplied exceeds the quantity demanded. Because of the resulting surplus, buyers' demands for the good or service must in some way be rationed among sellers.
- When the government levies a tax on a good, the equilibrium quantity of the good falls. That is, a tax on a market shrinks the size of the market.
- A tax on a good places a wedge between the price paid by buyers and the price received by sellers. When the market moves to the new equilibrium, buyers pay more for the good and sellers receive less for it. In this sense, buyers and sellers share the tax burden. The incidence of a tax (that is, the division of the tax burden) does not depend on whether the tax is levied on buyers or sellers.
- The incidence of a tax depends on the price elasticities of supply and demand. The burden tends to fall on the side of the market that is less elastic because that side of the market can respond less easily to the tax by changing the quantity bought or sold.

KEY CONCEPTS

price ceiling, p. 122   price floor, p. 122   tax incidence, p. 133

Questions for Review   At the end of each chapter are questions for review that cover the chapter's primary lessons. Students can use these questions to check their comprehension and to prepare for exams.

Problems and Applications   Each chapter also contains a variety of problems and applications that ask students to apply the material they have learned. Some instructors may use these questions for homework assignments. Others may use them as a starting point for classroom discussion.

QUESTIONS FOR REVIEW

1. Define the price elasticity of demand and the income elasticity of demand.
2. List and explain the four determinants of the price elasticity of demand discussed in the chapter.
3. What is the main advantage of using the midpoint method for calculating elasticity?
4. If the elasticity is greater than 1, is demand elastic or inelastic? If the elasticity equals 0, is demand perfectly elastic or perfectly inelastic?
5. On a supply-and-demand diagram, show equilibrium price, equilibrium quantity, and the total revenue received by producers.
6. If demand is elastic, how will an increase in price change total revenue? Explain.
7. What do we call a good whose income elasticity is less than 0?
8. How is the price elasticity of supply calculated? Explain what this measures.
9. What is the price elasticity of supply of Picasso paintings?
10. Is the price elasticity of supply usually larger in the short run or in the long run? Why?
11. How can elasticity help explain why drug interdiction could reduce the supply of drugs, yet possibly increase drug-related crime?

PROBLEMS AND APPLICATIONS

1. For each of the following pairs of goods, which good would you expect to have more elastic demand and why?
   a. required textbooks or mystery novels
   b. Beethoven recordings or classical music recordings in general
   c. heating oil during the next six months or heating oil during the next five years
   d. root beer or water
2. Suppose that business travellers and vacationers have the following demand for airline tickets from Toronto to Montreal:

(Use the midpoint method in your calculations.)
   b. Why might vacationers have a different elasticity than business travellers?
3. Suppose that your demand schedule for DVDs is as follows:

Price	Quantity Demanded (income $ $10 000)	Quantity Demanded (income $ $12 000)
$ 8	40	50
10	32	45
12	24	30
14	16	20
16	8	12

NEW IN THIS SIXTH CANADIAN EDITION

The sixth Canadian edition of *Principles of Microeconomics* has been carefully revised to ensure its contents are current and its examples reflect the interests and concerns of the student market. Responding to reviewers who requested additional but unobtrusive mathematics support, we have supplemented four chapters with new appendices: "The Mathematics of Market Equilibrium" (Chapter 4), "The Mathematics of Market Equilibrium with Taxes" (Chapter 6), "The Mathematics of Consumer and Producer Surplus" (Chapter 7), and "The Mathematics of Deadweight Loss" (Chapter 8). We have also included more technical questions in the end-of-chapter assignments to raise the difficulty level, and provided online math problems developed by Hannah Holmes, Subject Matter Coordinator, of McMaster University so students can practice their skills (see www.nelson.com/mankiwmicro6e). New sections were added to Chapter 2 to address such questions as, Why is the advice of economists not always followed? and What are the propositions with which most economists agree? Twelve new In the News boxes were added. Case Studies and FYI boxes have been revised and updated to reflect current world trends. Examples throughout the text were updated: for example, comparative advantage is illustrated by Sidney Crosby, monopoly is explained by the Windsor–Detroit bridge, and the disruption of a supply chain is discussed with reference to the 2011 tsunami in Japan. Key figures and graphs have been updated throughout the text, and the illustration program has been refreshed through the replacement of any dated-looking photographs.

Here is a chapter-by-chapter list of significant changes:

Chapter 1   A new In the News feature discusses the Olympic lineups and opportunity cost.

Chapter 2   A new section has been added on "Why Economists' Advice Is Not Always Followed." In the "Why Economists Disagree" section, a revised table lists "Propositions about Which Most Economists Agree."

Chapter 3   The "Applications of Comparative Advantage" section has been expanded and uses Sidney Crosby as an example. A new In the News feature questions whether free trade creates jobs.

Chapter 4   A significant addition to this edition is the new appendix "The Mathematics of Market Equilibrium," which guides the student through the process of solving for market equilibrium for linear demand and supply curves.

Chapter 5   A new FYI feature has been added on "A Few Real-World Elasticities."

Chapter 6   A new In the News feature discusses "Price Controls on Beer (and Milk)?" The new appendix "The Mathematics of Market Equilibrium with Taxes" builds on the Chapter 4 appendix on the mathematics of market equilibrium. This appendix shows the student how to include taxes in solving for market equilibrium.

Chapter 7   A new In the News feature examines "RockOn-ometrics."

Chapter 8   A new In the News feature looks at "Weight Loss vs. Deadweight Loss." The new appendix "The Mathematics of Deadweight Loss" builds on the new Chapters 4 and 6 appendices and shows the student how to calculate the deadweight loss of a tax.

Chapter 10   Two new In the News features have been added: "British Columbia Carbon Tax" and "British Columbia Leads the Way."

Chapter 11   This chapter includes the introduction of club goods. A new In the News feature asks, "Are Economics Students Grinches?"

Chapter 12   Tables and figures have been updated throughout this chapter.

Chapter 13   The new In the News feature discusses "The Economics of Very Big Ships."

Chapter 14   This chapter includes an expanded discussion of an upward-sloping long-run industry supply curve.

Chapter 15   New examples in this chapter include the Japan tsunami disruption of supply chain, the Windsor–Detroit bridge as a near monopoly, and price differentials between generic and brand-name drugs.

Chapter 16   A new Case Study focuses on a successful Canadian company, Canada Goose.

Chapter 17   The new In the News feature explains why "Bid-Rigging in Sewers Is Dirty Business."

Chapter 18   A new In the News feature analyses "Demographics and Labour Markets," while a new FYI feature asks, "What is Capital Income?"

Chapter 19   "Language and Wages in Canada" is the topic of a new In the News feature.

Chapter 20   Tables and figures have been updated in this chapter, and an extensive discussion has been added on income distribution and intergenerational mobility. A new In the News box proclaims, "The American Dream Is in Canada."

Chapter 21   A new In the News box discusses "Backward-Sloping Labour Supply in Kiribati."

Chapter 22   The new In the News feature reviews "Behavioural Economics and Facebook."

ANCILLARIES

For the Instructor

engagement | assessment | success
NELSON EDUCATION TEACHING ADVANTAGE

The **Nelson Education Teaching Advantage (NETA) program** delivers research-based instructor's resources that promote student engagement and higher-order thinking to enable the success of Canadian students and educators. Whether your course is offered in class, online, or both, Nelson is pleased to provide pedagogically driven, research-based resources to support you. Be sure to visit Nelson Education's **Inspired Instruction** website at www.nelson.com/inspired to find out more about NETA. Don't miss the testimonials of instructors who have used NETA supplements and seen student engagement increase!

The four NETA programs that accompany *Principles of Microeconomics* are NETA Engagement (the instructor's manual, including teaching tips for promoting student engagement), NETA Assessment (for testing and quizzing), NETA Presentation (for PowerPoint lectures), and NETA Digital (the framework that underlies all online offerings). Details of the supplements prepared specifically for use with *Principles of Microeconomics* follow the general NETA program notes below; see the heading for the **Instructor's Resource CD.** Instructor supplements can also be downloaded from the dedicated website at www.nelson.com/mankiwmicro6e.

NETA Engagement presents materials that help instructors deliver engaging content and activities to their classes. Instead of instructor's manuals that regurgitate chapter outlines and key terms from the text, NETA *Enriched Instructor's Manuals* (EIMs) provide genuine assistance to teachers. The EIMs answer questions such as: *What should students learn? Why should students care?* and *What are some common student misconceptions and stumbling blocks?* EIMs not only identify the topics that cause students the most difficulty, but also describe techniques and resources to help students master these concepts. Dr. Roger Fisher's *Instructor's Guide to Classroom Engagement* (IGCE) accompanies every *Enriched Instructor's Manual.*

NETA Assessment relates to testing materials. Under *NETA Assessment,* Nelson's authors create multiple-choice questions that reflect research-based best practices for constructing effective questions and testing not just recall but also higher-order thinking. Our guidelines were developed by David DiBattista, a 3M National Teaching Fellow whose recent research as a professor of psychology at Brock University has focused on multiple-choice testing. All Test Bank authors receive training at workshops conducted by Prof. DiBattista, as do the copyeditors assigned to each Test Bank. A copy of *Multiple Choice Tests: Getting Beyond Remembering,* Prof. DiBattista's guide to writing effective tests, is included with every Nelson Test Bank/Computerized Test Bank package.

NETA Presentation has been developed to help instructors make the best use of PowerPoint® in their classrooms. With a clean and uncluttered design developed by Maureen Stone of StoneSoup Consulting, *NETA Presentation* features slides with improved readability, more multimedia and graphic materials, activities to use in class, and tips for instructors on the Notes page. A copy of *NETA Guidelines for Classroom Presentations* by Maureen Stone is included with each set of PowerPoint slides.

NETA Digital is a framework based on Arthur Chickering and Zelda Gamson's seminal work "Seven Principles of Good Practice In Undergraduate Education" (*AAHE Bulletin*, 1987) and the follow-up work by Chickering and Stephen C. Ehrmann, "Implementing the Seven Principles: Technology as Lever" (*AAHE Bulletin*, 1996). This aspect of the NETA program guides the writing and development of our digital products to ensure that they appropriately reflect the core goals of contact, collaboration, multimodal learning, time on task, prompt feedback, active learning, and high expectations. The resulting focus on pedagogical utility, rather than technological wizardry, ensures that all of our technology supports better outcomes for students.

Instructor's Resource CD Key instructor ancillaries are provided on the *Instructor's Resource CD* (IRCD) (ISBN 0176554394), giving instructors the ultimate tool for customizing lectures and presentations. (Downloadable Web versions are also available to instructors at www.nelson.com/mankiwmicro6e) The IRCD includes

- *NETA Engagement:* The Enriched Instructor's Manual was revised by Constantin Colonescu, MacEwan University. It is organized according to the textbook chapters and addresses eight key educational concerns, such as typical stumbling blocks that students face and how to address them. Other features include the solutions to the in-text QuickQuizzes, Questions for Review, and Problems and Applications.
- *NETA Assessment:* The Test Bank was revised by Amy Peng, Ryerson University, technically checked by Ross Meacher, CA, and reviewed by David DiBattista for adherence to the NETA program of effective question construction and development of higher-order questions. It includes approximately 2800 multiple-choice, 340 true/false, and 170 short-answer questions, as well as 120 problems. Test Bank files are provided in Word format for easy editing and in PDF format for convenient printing whatever your system.

   The Computerized Test Bank by ExamView® includes all of the questions from the Test Bank. The easy-to-use ExamView software is compatible with Microsoft Windows and Mac OS. Create tests by selecting questions from the question bank, modifying these questions as desired, and adding new questions you write yourself. You can administer quizzes online and export tests to WebCT, Blackboard, and other formats.
- *NETA Presentation:* Microsoft® PowerPoint® lecture slides for every chapter have been revised by Marc Prud'Homme, University of Ottawa. There is an average of 35–45 slides per chapter, many featuring key figures, tables, and photographs from *Principles of Microeconomics*, Sixth Canadian Edition, as well as suggested classroom activities and links to videos and news articles for classroom discussion. NETA principles of clear design and engaging content have been incorporated throughout.
- *Image Library:* This resource consists of digital copies of figures, short tables, and photographs used in the book. Instructors may use these images to create their own PowerPoint presentations.
- *DayOne: Day One—Prof InClass* is a PowerPoint presentation that you can customize to orient your students to the class and the textbook at the beginning of the course.

Aplia™   Aplia™ is a dynamic homework system dedicated to improving students' learning by increasing their effort and engagement with your course. Founded by an instructor for other instructors, Aplia offers students premium, automatically graded assignments with detailed explanations that ensure they put forth effort on a regular basis. The Aplia™ for *Principles of Microeconomics* has been analyzed to ensure that it reflects the Canadian economics landscape.

Aplia™ saves instructors valuable time they'd otherwise spend on routine grading, while giving students an easy way to stay on top of coursework with regularly scheduled assignments.

More information can be found at www.aplia.com. Please contact your Nelson representative to package Aplia™ with your book.

For the Student

Study Guide   Revised by Shahram Manouchehri, MacEwan University, and Peter Fortura, Algonquin College, the Study Guide was prepared to enhance student success. Each chapter includes learning objectives, a description of the chapter's context and purpose, a chapter review, key terms and definitions, advanced critical-thinking questions, and helpful hints for understanding difficult concepts. Students can develop their understanding by doing practical problems and short-answer questions, and then assess theory mastery of the key concepts with the self-test, which includes true/false and multiple-choice questions. Solutions to all problems are included in the Study Guide (ISBN 0176560629).

Aplia™   Founded in 2000 by economist and Stanford professor Paul Romer, Aplia™ is an educational technology company dedicated to improving learning by increasing student effort and engagement. Currently, Aplia™ products have been used by more than a million students at over 1300 institutions.

For students, Aplia™ offers a way to stay on top of coursework with regularly scheduled homework assignments that increase their time on task and give them prompt feedback. Interactive tools and additional content are provided to further increase engagement and understanding.

Mankiw Website   Valuable resources for students can be found on the Internet at the Mankiw textbook support site at www.nelson.com/mankiwmicro6e. Updated and revised by Eric Moon, University of Toronto, the sixth Canadian edition website provides students with additional true/false, multiple-choice, and short-answer questions, crosswords, links to economics-related Internet sites, and much more. The multiple-choice quizzes were checked for compliance with the NETA program to ensure questions were clearly and effectively constructed.

In addition, online Math Problems were written specifically for the sixth Canadian edition by Subject Matter Coordinator Hannah Holmes, McMaster University.

Courtesy N. Gregory Mankiw

N. Gregory Mankiw is Professor of Economics at Harvard University. As a student, he studied economics at Princeton University and MIT. As a teacher, he has taught macroeconomics, microeconomics, statistics, and principles of economics. He even spent one summer long ago as a sailing instructor on Long Beach Island.

Professor Mankiw is a prolific writer and a regular participant in academic and policy debates. His work has been published in scholarly journals such as the *American Economic Review, Journal of Political Economy*, and *Quarterly Journal of Economics*, and in more popular forums such as *The New York Times, The Financial Times, The Wall Street Journal*, and *Fortune*. He is also author of the best-selling intermediate-level textbook *Macroeconomics* (Worth Publishing). In addition to his teaching, research, and writing, Professor Mankiw has been a research associate of the National Bureau of Economic Research, an adviser to the Federal Reserve Bank of Boston and the Congressional Budget Office, and a member of the Educational Testing Service (ETS) test development committee for the advanced placement exam in economics. From 2003 to 2005, he served as Chairman of the President's Council of Economic Advisers.

Courtesy Ronald D. Kneebone

Ronald D. Kneebone is Professor of Economics at the University of Calgary. He received his Ph.D. from McMaster University. Professor Kneebone has taught courses in public finance and in macroeconomics from principles through to the Ph.D. level, and he is a two-time winner of the Faculty of Social Sciences Distinguished Teacher Award at the University of Calgary. His research interests are primarily in the areas of public sector finances and fiscal federalism. He shared with Ken McKenzie the Douglas Purvis Memorial Prize for the best published work in Canadian public policy in 1999. Since 2008 he has been Director of Economic and Social Policy Research in The School of Public Policy at the University of Calgary.

Courtesy Kenneth J. McKenzie

Kenneth J. McKenzie is a professor in the Department of Economics and The School of Public Policy at the University of Calgary. He received his Ph.D. from Queen's University. Specializing in public economics with an emphasis on taxation and political economy, Professor McKenzie has published extensively in these areas. He is the winner of the 1996 Harry Johnson Prize (with University of Calgary colleague Herb Emery) for the best article in the *Canadian Journal of Economics*, the 1999 Douglas Purvis Memorial Prize (with Ron Kneebone) for a published work relating to Canadian public policy, and the 2000 Faculty of Social Sciences Distinguished Researcher Award at the University of Calgary. Professor McKenzie has taught microeconomics and public economics from the principles to the graduate level, and has received several departmental teaching awards.

ACKNOWLEDGMENTS

The success of each Canadian edition of *Principles of Microeconomics* and *Principles of Macroeconomics* has been due, in part, to the reviewers who helped us shape this text, edition after edition. We have benefited enormously from their advice and suggestions.

Collins Ayoo,
  Carleton University
James Wishart,
  College of the Rockies
Menouar Boulahfa,
  Dawson College
Weili Ding,
  Queen's University
Steven Lehrer,
  Queen's University
Kien Tran,
  University of Lethbridge
David Gray,
  University of Ottawa
Maurice Tugwell,
  Acadia University
Kevin Clinton,
  Bank of Canada
Keith Baxter,
  Bishop's University
Nancy Churchman,
  Carleton University
Aurelia Best,
  Centennial College
Bogdan Buduru,
  Concordia University
Stephen Rakocsy,
  Humber College
Byron Eastman,
  Laurentian University
Chris McDonnell,
  Malaspina University-College
Martin Dooley,
  McMaster University
Peter McCabe,
  McMaster University
Ernie Jacobson,
  Northern Alberta Institute of Technology
Ugurhan G. Berkok,
  Queen's University
Gregor Smith,
  Queen's University
Ibrahim Hayania,
  Seneca College
Ather H. Akbari,
  St. Mary's University

Herb Emery,
  University of Calgary
Costas Nicolau,
  University of Manitoba
Robin Neill,
  University of Prince Edward Island and
  Carleton University
Pierre Fortin,
  University of Quebec at Montreal
Michael Hare,
  University of Toronto
Hannah Holmes,
  McMaster University
Iris Au,
  University of Toronto
Peter Dungan,
  University of Toronto
Neil Roberts,
  Kwantlen Polytechnic University
Paul Hobson,
  Acadia University
Michael Francis,
  Carleton University
Mike Tucker,
  Fanshawe College
Xueda Song,
  York University
Bruce Cater,
  Trent University
Amy Peng,
  Ryerson University
Scott Skjei,
  Acadia University
Jyh-Yaw Joseph Chen,
  Kwantlen Polytechnic University
Troy Joseph,
  Carleton University
Lavinia Moldovan,
  Mount Royal University
Eric Kam,
  Ryerson University
Colin Mang,
  Nipissing University
Rauf Azhar,
  University of Guelph

Special thanks go to Bill Scarth of McMaster University, who offered invaluable advice regarding the structure and emphasis of the Canadian editions. Dr. Scarth is an award-winning teacher and author, and to ignore his advice would have been perilous indeed. His extensive comments were instrumental in helping us formulate our approach to the Canadian editions.

Our thanks to Ross Meacher, CA, for the technical check to ensure the accuracy of content throughout this sixth Canadian edition text and relevant supplements.

We would also like to thank our colleagues at the University of Calgary who provided invaluable informal input and useful examples and applications. We, of course, bear full responsibility for any misinterpretations and errors.

The student and instructor ancillaries are a key component of this book and we gratefully acknowledge the work of the authors:

Constantin Colonescu, MacEwan University (Enriched Instructor's Manual)

Peter Fortura, Algonquin College (co-author, Study Guide)

Hannah Holmes, McMaster University, Subject Matter Coodinator (student website Math Problems)

Shahram Manouchehri, MacEwan University (co-author, Study Guide)

Ross Meacher, CA (Study Guide and Test Bank technical checker)

Eric Moon, University of Toronto (student website Test Yourself questions)

Amy Peng, Ryerson University (Test Bank)

Marc Prud'Homme, University of Ottawa (Microsoft® PowerPoint® Presentations)

Russell Turner, Fleming College (Aplia consultant)

Canadianizing this book has been a team effort from the very start. We would like to acknowledge the editorial, production, and marketing teams at Nelson for their professionalism, advice, and encouragement throughout the process. Deserving special attention are executive editor Amie Plourde, consulting editor Rod Banister, and developmental editor Katherine Goodes to ensure the timely completion of our work.

Finally, we are grateful to our families for their indulgence and encouragement throughout the research and writing process. Their patience and understanding are greatly appreciated.

Ronald D. Kneebone   Kenneth J. McKenzie
October 2013

→ Time is another cost

INTRODUCTION

TEN PRINCIPLES OF ECONOMICS

The word *economy* comes from the Greek word for "one who manages a household." At first, this origin might seem peculiar. But, in fact, households and economies have much in common.

A household faces many decisions. It must decide which members of the household do which tasks and what each member gets in return: Who cooks dinner? Who does the laundry? Who gets the extra dessert at dinner? Who gets to choose what TV show to watch? In short, the household must allocate its scarce resources among its various members, taking into account each member's abilities, efforts, and desires.

Like a household, a society faces many decisions. A society must decide what jobs will be done and who will do them. It needs some people to grow food, other people to make clothing, and still others to design computer software. Once society has allocated people (as well as land, buildings, and machines) to various jobs, it must also allocate the output of goods and services that they produce. It must decide who will eat caviar and who will eat potatoes. It must decide who will drive a Ferrari and who will take the bus.

Learning Objectives

In this chapter, you will ...

- Learn that economics is about the allocation of scarce resources
- Examine some of the tradeoffs that people face
- Learn the meaning of *opportunity cost*
- See how to use marginal reasoning when making decisions
- Discuss how incentives affect people's behaviour
- Consider why trade among people or nations can be good for everyone
- Discuss why markets are a good, but not perfect, way to allocate resources
- Learn what determines some trends in the overall economy

scarcity
the limited nature
of society's resources

economics
the study of how society
manages its scarce resources

→ Buyers + Sellers interact to set
price points, Supply + Demand

The management of society's resources (e.g., people, land, buildings, and machinery) is important because resources are scarce. **Scarcity** means that society has limited resources and therefore cannot produce all the goods and services people wish to have. Just as each member of a household cannot get everything he or she wants, each individual in a society cannot attain the highest standard of living to which he or she might aspire.

Economics is the study of how society manages its scarce resources. In most societies, resources are allocated not by a single central planner but through the combined actions of millions of households and firms. Economists, therefore, study how people make decisions: how much they work, what they buy, how much they save, and how they invest their savings. Economists also study how people interact with one another. For instance, they examine how the multitude of buyers and sellers of a good together determine the price at which the good is sold and the quantity that is sold. Finally, economists analyze forces and trends that affect the economy as a whole, including the growth in average income, the fraction of the population that cannot find work, and the rate at which prices are rising.

The study of economics has many facets but it is unified by several central ideas. In the rest of this chapter, we look at ten principles of economics. Don't worry if you don't understand them all at first, or if you don't find them completely convincing. In the coming chapters we will explore these ideas in more detail. The ten principles are introduced here just to give you an overview of what economics is all about. You can think of this chapter as a "preview of coming attractions."

HOW PEOPLE MAKE DECISIONS

There is no mystery to what an "economy" is. Whether we are talking about the economy of Vancouver, of Canada, or of the whole world, an economy is just a group of people interacting with one another as they go about their lives. Because the behaviour of an economy reflects the behaviour of the individuals who make up the economy, we start our study of economics with four principles of individual decision making.

Principle #1: People Face Tradeoffs

The first lesson about making decisions is summarized in the adage "There is no such thing as a free lunch." Grammar aside, there is much truth to this adage. To get one thing that we like, we usually have to give up another thing that we like. Making decisions requires trading off one goal against another.

Consider a student who must decide how to allocate her most valuable resource—her time. She can spend all of her time studying economics; she can spend all of her time studying psychology; or she can divide her time between the two fields. For every hour she studies one subject, she gives up an hour she could have used studying the other. And for every hour she spends studying, she gives up an hour that she could have spent napping, bike riding, watching TV, or working at her part-time job for some extra spending money.

Or consider parents deciding how to spend their family income. They can buy food, clothing, or a family vacation. Or they can save some of the family income for retirement or the children's college or university education. When they choose to spend an extra dollar on one of these goods, they have one less dollar to spend on some other good.

When people are grouped into societies, they face different kinds of tradeoffs. Important in modern society is the tradeoff between a clean environment and a high level of income. Laws that require firms to reduce pollution raise the cost of producing goods and services. Because of the higher costs, these firms end up earning smaller profits, paying lower wages, charging higher prices, or some combination of these three. Thus, while pollution regulations give us the benefit of a cleaner environment and the improved health that comes with it, they have the cost of reducing the incomes of the regulated firms' owners, workers, and customers.

Another tradeoff society faces is between efficiency and equity. **Efficiency** means that society is getting the most it can from its scarce resources. **Equity** means that the benefits of those resources are distributed fairly among society's members. In other words, efficiency refers to the size of the economic pie, and equity refers to how the pie is divided into individual slices.

When government policies are designed, these two goals often conflict. Consider, for instance, policies aimed at achieving a more equal distribution of economic well-being. Some of these policies, such as the welfare system or Employment Insurance, try to help those members of society who are most in need. Others, such as the individual income tax, ask the financially successful to contribute more than others to support the government. Although these policies have the benefit of achieving greater equity, they have a cost in terms of reduced efficiency. When the government redistributes income from the rich to the poor, it reduces the reward for working hard; as a result, people work less and produce fewer goods and services. In other words, when the government tries to cut the economic pie into more equal slices, the pie gets smaller.

Recognizing that people face tradeoffs does not by itself tell us what decisions they will or should make. A student should not abandon the study of psychology just because doing so would increase the time available for the study of economics. Society should not stop protecting the environment just because environmental regulations reduce our material standard of living. The poor should not be ignored just because helping them distorts work incentives. Nonetheless, people are likely to make good decisions only if they understand the options that they have available. Our study of economics, therefore, starts by acknowledging life's tradeoffs.

efficiency
the property of society getting the most it can from its scarce resources

equity
the property of distributing economic prosperity fairly among the members of society

→ Market economy incentive : if you work hard, there is a high reward. Income redistribution reduces this reward.

Principle #2: The Cost of Something Is What You Give Up to Get It

Because people face tradeoffs, making decisions requires comparing the costs and benefits of alternative courses of action. In many cases, however, the cost of some action is not as obvious as it might first appear.

Consider the decision whether to go to college or university. The main benefits are intellectual enrichment and a lifetime of better job opportunities. But what are the costs? To answer this question, you might be tempted to add up the money you spend on tuition, books, room, and board. Yet this total does not truly represent what you give up to spend a year in college or university.

There are two problems with the calculation. First, it includes some things that are not really costs of going to college or university. Even if you quit school, you would

IN THE NEWS

OLYMPIC LINEUPS AND OPPORTUNITY COST

Principle #2—the cost of something is what you give to get it—is based on the concept of opportunity cost. The following newspaper article highlights one of the most important opportunity costs—the value of your time—and the role that prices can play in reflecting that cost.

There's No Such Thing as a Free Lunch, Pavilion or Zip Line

By Don Cayo

How much is your time really worth? Long lineups at Olympic attractions are a good way to understand cost–benefit ratios.

Vanoc is to be commended for both the quantity and quality of the Olympic freebies it has managed to orchestrate in Vancouver and Whistler for the duration of the Games.

As the lines at so many free sites clearly attest, many locals and visitors alike think this stuff is great.

But the lineups also suggest an irony—that, odd as this may sound, all these free sites and activities might provide better value if we had to pay to get in.

If this doesn't make sense then I'm guessing you don't value your time very highly. But I'm sure folks who place a premium on every hour—either because time is money, or so they can squeeze every drop of fun from their limited time off—will be quicker to grasp the point.

If you had to pay, the lines would almost certainly be shorter, either because fewer people would want to partake, or because the provider would feel compelled to offer better service. Conversely, the price of "free" admission can add up to several hours of your time.

Take the zip line over Robson Square as a case in point.

The concept of an urban zip line is a neat one. It offers a unique view of the heart of the city at its best. And I'd be on it in a flash if I were the premier.

But I'm not the premier, and I'm not zipping across Robson Square.

Why? Because he didn't need to line up, and I do. And I won't spend four hours—or five, or six—in the tedium of a line for a few moderately thrilling seconds.

We all make our own "cost–benefit" calculations according to individual criteria, of course. So some will stand one hour, but not two, in a lineup in order to drink a cold beer in a cool place.

Others will tough it out for as long as it takes. And still others will simply head home, turn on the telly and crack a brew from the fridge.

The need to balance the cost in time with the cost in money isn't unique to the Olympics, of course. It was on my mind, for example, this past Christmas Eve when I took my daughter's family to Grouse Mountain for "free" holiday stuff. My son-in-law stood almost two hours in line to hold our place for what turned out to be a short, lame sleigh ride. We agreed that we'd have cheerfully paid a reasonable ticket price for a better ride at the end of a shorter line.

Some companies—every busy grocery store, coffee shop or night club, for example—must factor customers' tolerance for lines into their business plans.

My observation is that young people seem more willing to wait. My guess is they are less curmudgeonly than my generation, and perhaps more tolerant of demands on their time. But a colleague suggests a more credible reason.

In his nightclubbing days, he recalled, the lineup at the door was as much a social experience as the club itself.

"We'd start the process of hitting on girls in the line," he said. "Then, when we got inside, it was easy to strike up a conversation."

So perhaps if I were young and single, I'd be queued up at Robson Square. But I'm not, and I'm not.

I've talked to a surprising number of people of all ages who seem to agree. And so for us, the main nonspectator event of the Olympics is milling around, wandering the downtown streets. We'll get our bunions walking, not standing.

Personally, given the neat people and cheery ambience, I enjoy it a lot.

And the price is right. It's free of both admission cost and what economists call the opportunity cost of lineups—the time we could spend doing other things.

Source: From "There's no such thing as a free lunch, pavillion or zip line; how much is your time really worth? Long lineups at Olympic attractions are a good way to understand cost-benefit ratios" by Don Cayo, *Vancouver Sun*, February 23, 2010, p. F3. Material reprinted with the express permission of: *The Vancouver Sun*, a division of Postmedia Network Inc.

→ Time is another cost

need a place to sleep and food to eat. Room and board are costs of going to college or university only to the extent that they are more expensive there than elsewhere. Second, this calculation ignores the largest cost of going to college or university—your time. When you spend a year listening to lectures, reading textbooks, and writing papers, you cannot spend that time working at a job. For most students, the wages given up to attend school are the largest single cost of their education.

The **opportunity cost** of an item is what you give up to get that item. When making any decision, such as whether to attend college or university, decision makers should be aware of the opportunity costs that accompany each possible action. In fact, they usually are. College- or university-age athletes who can earn millions if they drop out of school and play professional sports are well aware that their opportunity cost of a postsecondary education is very high. It is not surprising that they often decide that the benefit of this education is not worth the cost.

opportunity cost
whatever must be given up to obtain some item

Principle #3: Rational People Think at the Margin

Economists normally assume that people are rational. **Rational people** systematically and purposefully do the best they can to achieve their objectives, given the opportunities they have. As you study economics, you will encounter firms that decide how many workers to hire and how much of their product to manufacture and sell to maximize profits. You will also encounter individuals who decide how much time to spend working and what goods and services to buy with the resulting income to achieve the highest possible level of satisfaction.

Rational people know that decisions in life are rarely black and white, but usually involve shades of gray. At dinnertime, the decision you face is not between fasting or eating like a pig, but whether to take that extra spoonful of mashed potatoes. When exams roll around, your decision is not between blowing them off or studying 24 hours a day, but whether to spend an extra hour reviewing your notes instead of watching TV. Economists use the term **marginal changes** to describe small incremental adjustments to an existing plan of action. Keep in mind that "margin" means "edge," so marginal changes are adjustments around the edges of what you are doing. Rational people often make decisions by comparing *marginal benefits* and *marginal costs*.

For example, consider an airline deciding how much to charge passengers who fly standby. Suppose that flying a 200-seat plane across the country costs the airline $100 000. In this case, the average cost of each seat is $100 000/200, which is $500. One might be tempted to conclude that the airline should never sell a ticket for less than $500. Actually, a rational airline can often find ways to raise its profits by thinking at the margin. Imagine that a plane is about to take off with ten empty seats, and a standby passenger is waiting at the gate willing to pay $300 for a seat. Should the airline sell it to him? Of course it should. If the plane has empty seats, the cost of adding one more passenger is minuscule. Although the *average* cost of flying a passenger is $500, the *marginal* cost is merely the cost of the bag of peanuts and can of soda that the extra passenger will consume. As long as the standby passenger pays more than the marginal cost, selling him a ticket is profitable.

Marginal decision making can help explain some otherwise puzzling economic phenomena. Here is a classic question: Why is water so cheap, while diamonds are so expensive? Humans need water to survive, while diamonds are unnecessary; but, for some reason, people are willing to pay much more for a diamond than for a cup of water. The reason is that a person's willingness to pay for a good is based

rational people
people who systematically and purposefully do the best they can to achieve their objectives

marginal changes
small incremental adjustments to a plan of action

→ The cost of selling the passenger the ticket is simply the cost of having an extra passenger on the plane. The profits from selling a cheaper ticket strongly outweighs this.

on the marginal benefit that an extra unit of the good will yield. The marginal benefit, in turn, depends on how many units a person already has. Water is essential but the marginal benefit of an extra cup is small because water is plentiful. By contrast, no one needs diamonds to survive, but because diamonds are so rare, people consider the marginal benefit of an extra diamond to be large.

A rational decision maker takes an action if and only if the marginal benefit of the action exceeds the marginal cost. This principle can explain why airlines are willing to sell a ticket below average cost and why people are willing to pay more for diamonds than for water. It can take some time to get used to the logic of marginal thinking, but the study of economics will give you ample opportunity to practise.

Principle #4: People Respond to Incentives

An **incentive** is something (such as the prospect of a punishment or a reward) that induces a person to act. Because rational people make decisions by comparing costs and benefits, they respond to incentives. You will see that incentives play a central role in the study of economics. One economist went so far as to suggest that the entire field could be summarized simply: "People respond to incentives. The rest is commentary."

Incentives are crucial to analyzing how markets work. For example, when the price of an apple rises, people decide to eat more pears and fewer apples because the cost of buying an apple is higher. At the same time, apple orchards decide to hire more workers and harvest more apples because the benefit of selling an apple is also higher. As we will see, the effect of a good's price on the behaviour of buyers and sellers in a market—in this case, the market for apples—is crucial for understanding how the economy allocates scarce resources.

Public policymakers should never forget about incentives because many policies change the costs or benefits that people face and, therefore, alter behaviour. A tax on gasoline, for instance, encourages people to drive smaller, more fuel-efficient cars. It also encourages people to take public transportation rather than drive, and to live closer to where they work. If the tax was large enough, people would switch to driving electric cars.

When policymakers fail to consider how their policies affect incentives, they often end up with results they did not intend. For example, consider public policy regarding auto safety. Today all cars have seat belts, but that was not true 50 years ago. In the 1960s, Ralph Nader's book *Unsafe at Any Speed* generated much public concern over auto safety. Parliament responded with laws requiring seat belts as standard equipment on new cars.

How does a seat belt law affect auto safety? The direct effect is obvious: When a person wears a seat belt, the probability of surviving a major auto accident rises. But that's not the end of the story because the law also affects behaviour by altering incentives. The relevant behaviour here is the speed and care with which drivers operate their cars. Driving slowly and carefully is costly because it uses the driver's time and energy. When deciding how safely to drive, rational people compare the marginal benefit from safer driving to the marginal cost. They drive more slowly and carefully when the benefit of increased safety is high. It is no surprise, for instance, that people drive more slowly and carefully when roads are icy than when roads are clear.

→ Market dynamics, price of one goes up, more buy a competing product. Price changes act as incentives

incentive
something that induces a person to act

© Rick Friedman/Corbis

Mark Zuckerberg understood opportunity costs and incentives. In 2002, he entered Harvard University to study psychology and computer programming. While at Harvard, he launched Facebook from his dorm room in 2004, after which he dropped out to pursue the development of the company full-time. The rest, of course, is history.

Consider how a seat belt law alters a driver's cost–benefit calculation. Seat belts make accidents less costly because they reduce the likelihood of injury or death. In other words, seat belts reduce the benefits to slow and careful driving. People respond to seat belts as they would to an improvement in road conditions—by faster and less careful driving. The end result of a seat belt law, therefore, is a larger number of accidents. The decline in safe driving has a clear, adverse impact on pedestrians, who are more likely to find themselves in an accident but (unlike the drivers) don't have the benefit of added protection.

At first, this discussion of incentives and seat belts might seem like idle speculation. Yet, in a 1975 study, economist Sam Peltzman showed that the auto-safety laws have had many of these effects. According to Peltzman's evidence, these laws produce both fewer deaths per accident and more accidents. The net result is little change in the number of driver deaths and an increase in the number of pedestrian deaths.

Peltzman's analysis of auto safety is an offbeat and controversial example of the general principle that people respond to incentives. When analyzing any policy, we must consider not only the direct effects but also the indirect effects that work through incentives. If the policy changes incentives, it will cause people to alter their behaviour.

QuickQuiz   Describe an important tradeoff you recently faced. • Give an example of some action that has both a monetary and nonmonetary opportunity cost. • Describe an incentive your parents offered to you in an effort to influence your behaviour.

HOW PEOPLE INTERACT

The first four principles discussed how individuals make decisions. As we go about our lives, many of our decisions affect not only ourselves but other people as well. The next three principles concern how people interact with one another.

Principle #5: Trade Can Make Everyone Better Off

You may have heard on the news that the Americans are our competitors in the world economy. In some ways this is true, for Canadian and U.S. firms do produce many of the same goods. BlackBerry and Apple compete for the same customers in the market for smart phones. Inniskillin and Gallo compete for the same customers in the market for wine.

Yet it is easy to be misled when thinking about competition among countries. Trade between Canada and the United States is not like a sports contest, where one side wins and the other side loses. In fact, the opposite is true: Trade between two countries can make each country better off.

To see why, consider how trade affects your family. When a member of your family looks for a job, he or she competes against members of other families who are looking for jobs. Families also compete against one another when they go shopping because each family wants to buy the best goods at the lowest prices. So, in a sense, each family in the economy is competing with all other families.

Handwritten margin notes:
→ Cost-Benefit Calculation: How an individual weighs the marginal costs and benefits of a decision.

→ People think they're safer with a seatbelt, so they drive faster

→ Countries/people competing can be a good thing

→ In isolation, everyone is for themselves. In a society, we can complement each other's skills

Despite this competition, your family would not be better off isolating itself from all other families. If it did, your family would need to grow its own food, make its own clothes, and build its own home. Clearly, your family gains much from its ability to trade with others. Trade allows each person to specialize in the activities he or she does best, whether it is farming, sewing, or home building. By trading with others, people can buy a greater variety of goods and services at lower cost.

Countries as well as families benefit from the ability to trade with one another. Trade allows countries to specialize in what they do best and to enjoy a greater variety of goods and services. The Americans, as well as the French and the Egyptians and the Brazilians, are as much our partners in the world economy as they are our competitors.

Principle #6: Markets Are Usually a Good Way to Organize Economic Activity

→ The inherent competition of a market economy creates more success than a gov't run economy

The collapse of communism in the Soviet Union and Eastern Europe in the 1980s may be the most important change in the world during the past half-century. Communist countries worked on the premise that central planners in the government were in the best position to guide economic activity. These planners decided what goods and services were produced, how much was produced, and who produced and consumed these goods and services. The theory behind central planning was that only the government could organize economic activity in a way that promoted economic well-being for the country as a whole.

market economy
an economy that allocates resources through the decentralized decisions of many firms and households as they interact in markets for goods and services

Most countries that once had centrally planned economies have abandoned this system and are trying to develop market economies. In a **market economy,** the decisions of a central planner are replaced by the decisions of millions of firms and households. Firms decide whom to hire and what to make. Households decide which firms to work for and what to buy with their incomes. These firms and households interact in the marketplace, where prices and self-interest guide their decisions.

At first glance, the success of market economies is puzzling. After all, in a market economy, no one is looking out for the economic well-being of society as a whole. Free markets contain many buyers and sellers of numerous goods and services, and all of them are interested primarily in their own well-being. Yet, despite decentralized decision making and self-interested decision makers, market economies have proven remarkably successful in organizing economic activity in a way that promotes overall economic well-being.

In his 1776 book *An Inquiry into the Nature and Causes of the Wealth of Nations*, economist Adam Smith made the most famous observation in all of economics: Households and firms interacting in markets act as if they are guided by an "invisible hand" that leads them to desirable market outcomes. One of our goals in this book is to understand how this invisible hand works its magic.

As you study economics, you will learn that prices are the instrument with which the invisible hand directs economic activity. In any market, buyers look at the price when determining how much to demand, and sellers look at the price when deciding how much to supply. As a result of the decisions that buyers and sellers make, market prices reflect both the value of a good to society and the cost to society of making the good. Smith's great insight was that prices adjust to guide these individual buyers and sellers to reach outcomes that, in many cases, maximize the welfare of society as a whole.

Smith's insight has an important corollary: When the government prevents prices from adjusting naturally to supply and demand, it impedes the invisible hand's ability to coordinate the millions of households and firms that make up the economy. This corollary explains why taxes adversely affect the allocation of resources: Taxes distort prices and thus the decisions of households and firms. It also explains the even greater harm caused by policies that directly control prices, such as rent control. And it explains the failure of communism. In communist countries, prices were not determined in the marketplace but were dictated by central planners. These planners lacked the information that is reflected in prices when prices are free to respond to market forces. Central planners failed because they tried to run the economy with one hand tied behind their backs—the invisible hand of the marketplace.

→ Prices must remain pure and natural (consumer set) in order to keep the economy stable

ADAM SMITH AND THE INVISIBLE HAND

It may be only a coincidence that Adam Smith's great book *The Wealth of Nations* was published in 1776, the same year American revolutionaries signed the *Declaration of Independence*. But the two documents do share a point of view that was prevalent at the time—that individuals are usually best left to their own devices, without the heavy hand of government guiding their actions. This political philosophy provides the intellectual basis for the market economy, and for free society more generally.

Why do decentralized market economies work so well? Is it because people can be counted on to treat one another with love and kindness? Not at all. Here is Adam Smith's description of how people interact in a market economy:

Man has almost constant occasion for the help of his brethren, and it is vain for him to expect it from their benevolence only. He will be more likely to prevail if he can interest their self-love in his favor, and show them that it is for their own advantage to do for him what he requires of them. . . . It is not from the benevolence of the butcher, the brewer, or

Adam Smith

the baker that we expect our dinner, but from their regard to their own interest. . . .

Every individual . . . neither intends to promote the public interest, nor knows how much he is promoting it. . . . He intends only his own gain, and he is in this, as in many other cases, led by an invisible hand to promote an end which was no part of his intention. Nor is it always the worse for the society that it was no part of it. By pursuing his own interest he frequently promotes that of the society more effectually than when he really intends to promote it.

Smith is saying that participants in the economy are motivated by self-interest and that the "invisible hand" of the marketplace guides this self-interest into promoting general economic well-being.

Many of Smith's insights remain at the centre of modern economics. Our analysis in the coming chapters will allow us to express Smith's conclusions more precisely and to analyze fully the strengths and weaknesses of the market's invisible hand.

Principle #7: Governments Can Sometimes Improve Market Outcomes

If the invisible hand of the market is so great, why do we need government? The study of economics will refine your view about the proper role and scope of government policy.

One reason we need government is that the invisible hand can work its magic only if the government enforces the rules and maintains the institutions that are key to a market economy. Most important, market economies need institutions to enforce **property rights** so individuals can own and control scarce resources. A farmer won't grow food if he expects his crop to be stolen, a restaurant won't serve meals unless it is assured that customers will pay before they leave, and an entertainment company won't produce DVDs if too many potential customers avoid paying by making illegal copies. We all rely on government-provided police services and courts to enforce our rights over the things we produce—and the invisible hand counts on our ability to enforce our rights.

Yet there is another, more profound reason that we need government: The invisible hand is powerful, but it is not omnipotent. Although markets are often a good way to organize economic activity, this rule has some important exceptions. There are two broad reasons for a government to intervene in the economy and change the allocation of resources that people would choose on their own: to promote efficiency and to promote equity. That is, most policies aim either to enlarge the economic pie or to change how the pie is divided.

Consider first the goal of efficiency. Although the invisible hand usually leads markets to maximize the size of the economic pie, this is not always the case. Economists use the term **market failure** to refer to a situation in which the market on its own fails to produce an efficient allocation of resources. As we will see, one possible cause of market failure is an **externality,** which is the impact of one person's actions on the well-being of a bystander. The classic example of an externality is pollution. Another possible cause of market failure is **market power,** which refers to the ability of a single person (or small group of people) to unduly influence market prices. For example, if everyone in town needs water but there is only one well, the owner of the well is not subject to the rigorous competition with which the invisible hand normally keeps self-interest in check. In the presence of externalities or market power, well-designed public policy can enhance economic efficiency.

Now consider the goal of equity. Even when the invisible hand is yielding efficient outcomes, it can nonetheless leave sizable disparities in economic well-being. A market economy rewards people according to their ability to produce things that other people are willing to pay for. The world's best basketball player earns more than the world's best chess player simply because people are willing to pay more to watch basketball than chess. The invisible hand does not ensure that everyone has sufficient food, decent clothing, and adequate health care. This inequality, depending on one's political philosophy, calls for government intervention. Many public policies, such as the income tax and welfare systems, aim to achieve a more equitable distribution of economic well-being.

To say that the government *can* improve on market outcomes at times does not mean that it always *will*. Public policy is made not by angels but by a political process that is far from perfect. Sometimes policies are designed simply to reward

property rights
the ability of an individual to own and exercise control over scarce resources

market failure
a situation in which a market left on its own fails to allocate resources efficiently

externality
the impact of one person's actions on the well-being of a bystander

market power
the ability of a single economic actor (or small group of actors) to have a substantial influence on market prices

the politically powerful. Sometimes they are made by well-intentioned leaders who are not fully informed. As you study economics, you will become a better judge of when a government policy is justifiable because it promotes efficiency or equity, and when it is not.

QuickQuiz   Why is a country better off not isolating itself from all other countries? • Why do we have markets and, according to economists, what roles should government play in them?

HOW THE ECONOMY AS A WHOLE WORKS

We started by discussing how individuals make decisions and then looked at how people interact with one another. All these decisions and interactions together make up "the economy." The last three principles concern the workings of the economy as a whole.

Principle #8: A Country's Standard of Living Depends on Its Ability to Produce Goods and Services

The differences in living standards around the world are staggering. In 2010, the average Canadian had an income of about $43 000. In the same year, the average Mexican earned about $10 000, and the average Nigerian earned only $1400. Not surprisingly, this large variation in average income is reflected in various measures of the quality of life. Citizens of high-income countries have more TV sets, more cars, better nutrition, better health care, and longer life expectancy than citizens of low-income countries.

Changes in living standards over time are also large. In Canada, individuals' incomes have historically grown about 2 percent per year (after adjusting for changes in the cost of living). At this rate, average income doubles every 35 years. Over the past century, average Canadian income has risen about eightfold.

What explains these large differences in living standards among countries and over time? The answer is surprisingly simple. Almost all variation in living standards is attributable to differences in countries' **productivity**—that is, the amount of goods and services produced from each hour of a worker's time. In nations where workers can produce a large quantity of goods and services per unit of time, most people enjoy a high standard of living; in nations where workers are less productive, most people must endure a more meagre existence. Similarly, the growth rate of a nation's productivity determines the growth rate of its average income.

The fundamental relationship between productivity and living standards is simple, but its implications are far-reaching. If productivity is the primary determinant of living standards, other explanations must be of secondary importance. For example, it might be tempting to credit labour unions or minimum-wage laws for the rise in living standards of Canadian workers over the past century. Yet the real hero of Canadian workers is their rising productivity. As another example, some commentators have claimed that increased competition from Japan and other countries explained the slow growth in Canadian incomes during the 1970s and 1980s. Yet the real villain was not competition from abroad but flagging productivity growth in Canada.

productivity
the quantity of goods and services produced from each hour of a worker's time

→ In a 3rd world sweatshop, workers put in lots of time on very few individual goods. Automized vs manual

The relationship between productivity and living standards also has profound implications for public policy. When thinking about how any policy will affect living standards, the key question is how it will affect our ability to produce goods and services. To boost living standards, policymakers need to raise productivity by ensuring that workers are well educated, have the tools needed to produce goods and services, and have access to the best available technology.

Principle #9: Prices Rise When the Government Prints Too Much Money

inflation
an increase in the overall level of prices in the economy

In Germany in January 1921, a daily newspaper cost 0.30 marks. Less than two years later, in November 1922, the same newspaper cost 70 000 000 marks. All other prices in the economy rose by similar amounts. This episode is one of history's most spectacular examples of **inflation,** an increase in the overall level of prices in the economy.

Although Canada has never experienced inflation even close to that in Germany in the 1920s, inflation has at times been an economic problem. During the 1970s, for instance, average inflation was 8 percent per year and the overall level of prices more than doubled. By contrast, inflation in the 1990s was about 2 percent per year; at this rate it would take 35 years for prices to double. Because high inflation imposes various costs on society, keeping inflation at a low level is a goal of economic policymakers around the world. $2 \to 3\%$.

What causes inflation? In almost all cases of large or persistent inflation, the culprit turns out to be the same—growth in the quantity of money. When a government creates large quantities of the nation's money, the value of the money falls. In Germany in the early 1920s, when prices were on average tripling every month, the quantity of money was also tripling every month. Although less dramatic, the economic history of Canada points to a similar conclusion: The high inflation of the 1970s was associated with rapid growth in the quantity of money, and the low inflation of the 1990s was associated with slow growth in the quantity of money.

Principle #10: Society Faces a Short-Run Tradeoff between Inflation and Unemployment

Although a higher level of prices is, in the long run, the primary effect of increasing the quantity of money, the short-run story is more complex and more controversial. Most economists describe the short-run effects of monetary injections as follows:

- Increasing the amount of money in the economy stimulates the overall level of spending and thus the demand for goods and services.
- Higher demand may, over time, cause firms to raise their prices, but in the meantime, it also encourages them to increase the quantity of goods and services they produce and to hire more workers to produce those goods and services.
- More hiring means lower unemployment.

This line of reasoning leads to one final economy-wide tradeoff: a short-run tradeoff between inflation and unemployment.

Although some economists still question these ideas, most accept that society faces a short-run tradeoff between inflation and unemployment. This simply means that, over a period of a year or two, many economic policies push inflation and unemployment in opposite directions. Policymakers face this tradeoff regardless of whether inflation and unemployment both start out at high levels (as they did in the early 1980s), at low levels (as they did in the late 1990s), or somewhere in between. This short-run tradeoff plays a key role in the analysis of the **business cycle**—the irregular and largely unpredictable fluctuations in economic activity, as measured by the production of goods and services or the number of people employed.

business cycle
fluctuations in economic activity, such as employment and production

Policymakers can exploit the short-run tradeoff between inflation and unemployment using various policy instruments. By changing the amount that the government spends, the amount it taxes, and the amount of money it prints, policymakers can influence the combination of inflation and unemployment that the economy experiences. Because these instruments of monetary and fiscal policy are potentially so powerful, how policymakers should use these instruments to control the economy, if at all, is a subject of continuing debate.

HOW TO READ THIS BOOK

Economics is fun, but it can also be hard to learn. Our aim in writing this text is to make it as fun and easy as possible. But you, the student, also have a role to play. Experience shows that if you are actively involved as you study this book, you will enjoy a better outcome, both on your exams and in the years that follow. Here are a few tips about how best to read this book.

1. *Summarize, don't highlight*. Running a yellow marker over the text is too passive an activity to keep your mind engaged. Instead, when you come to the end of a section, take a minute and summarize what you just learned in your own words, writing your summary in the wide margins we've provided. When you've finished the chapter, compare your summary with the one at the end of the chapter. Did you pick up the main points?

2. *Test yourself*. Throughout the book, QuickQuizzes offer instant feedback to find out if you've learned what you are supposed to. Take the opportunity. Write your answer in the book's margin. The quizzes are meant to test your basic comprehension. If you aren't sure your answer is right, you probably need to review the section.

3. *Practise, practise, practise*. At the end of each chapter, Questions for Review test your understanding, and Problems and Applications ask you to apply and extend the material. Perhaps your instructor will assign some of these exercises as homework. If so, do them. If not, do them anyway. The more you use your new knowledge, the more solid it becomes.

4. *Study in groups*. After you've read the book and worked the problems on your own, get together with classmates to discuss the material. You will learn from each other—an example of the gains from trade.

5. *Don't forget the real world*. In the midst of all the numbers, graphs, and strange new words, it is easy to lose sight of what economics is all about. The Case Studies and In the News features sprinkled throughout this book should help remind you. Don't skip them. They show how the theory is tied to events happening in all of our lives. If your study is successful, you won't be able to read a newspaper again without thinking about supply, demand, and the wonderful world of economics.

This debate heated up in 2008. In 2008 and 2009, the Canadian economy, as well as many other economies around the world, experienced a deep economic downturn. Problems in the financial system spilled over to the rest of the economy, causing incomes to fall and unemployment to soar. Policymakers responded in various ways to increase the overall demand for goods and services. The Canadian government introduced a major stimulus package of increased government spending. At the same time, the Bank of Canada increased the supply of money. The goal of these policies was to reduce unemployment. Some feared, however, that these policies might over time lead to an excessive level of inflation.

QuickQuiz   List and briefly explain the three principles that describe how the economy as a whole works.

CONCLUSION

You now have a taste of what economics is all about. In the coming chapters we will develop many specific insights about people, markets, and economies. Mastering these insights will take some effort, but it is not an overwhelming task. The field of economics is based on a few basic ideas that can be applied in many different situations.

Throughout this book we will refer back to the ten principles of economics highlighted in this chapter and summarized in Table 1.1. Keep these building blocks in mind: Even the most sophisticated economic analysis is founded on the ten principles introduced here.

TABLE 1.1

Ten Principles of Economics

How People Make Decisions	#1: People face tradeoffs.
	#2: The cost of something is what you give up to get it.
	#3: Rational people think at the margin.
	#4: People respond to incentives.
How People Interact	#5: Trade can make everyone better off.
	#6: Markets are usually a good way to organize economic activity.
	#7: Governments can sometimes improve market outcomes.
How the Economy as a Whole Works	#8: A country's standard of living depends on its ability to produce goods and services.
	#9: Prices rise when the government prints too much money.
	#10: Society faces a short-run tradeoff between inflation and unemployment.

SUMMARY

- The fundamental lessons about individual decision making are that people face tradeoffs among alternative goals, that the cost of any action is measured in terms of forgone opportunities, that rational people make decisions by comparing marginal costs and marginal benefits, and that people change their behaviour in response to the incentives they face.

- The fundamental lessons about interactions among people are that trade can be mutually beneficial, that markets are usually a good way of coordinating trade among people, and that the government can potentially improve market outcomes if there is some market failure or if the market outcome is inequitable.

- The fundamental lessons about the economy as a whole are that productivity is the ultimate source of living standards, that money growth is the ultimate source of inflation, and that society faces a short-run tradeoff between inflation and unemployment.

KEY CONCEPTS

scarcity, p. 4
economics, p. 4
efficiency, p. 5
equity, p. 5
opportunity cost, p. 7
rational people, p. 7

marginal changes, p. 7
incentive, p. 8
market economy, p. 10
property rights, p. 12
market failure, p. 12
externality, p. 12

market power, p. 12
productivity, p. 13
inflation, p. 14
business cycle, p. 15

QUESTIONS FOR REVIEW

1. Give three examples of important tradeoffs that you face in your life.

2. What is the opportunity cost of seeing a movie?

3. Water is necessary for life. Is the marginal benefit of a glass of water large or small?

4. Why should policymakers think about incentives?

5. Why isn't trade among countries like a game, with some winners and some losers?

6. What does the "invisible hand" of the marketplace do?

7. Explain the two main causes of market failure and give an example of each.

8. Why is productivity important?

9. What is inflation, and what causes it?

10. How are inflation and unemployment related in the short run?

PROBLEMS AND APPLICATIONS

1. Describe some of the tradeoffs faced by each of the following.
   a. a family deciding whether to buy a new car
   b. a member of Parliament deciding how much to spend on national parks
   c. a company president deciding whether to open a new factory
   d. a professor deciding how much to prepare for class

2. You are trying to decide whether to take a vacation. Most of the costs of the vacation (airfare, hotel, forgone wages) are measured in dollars, but the benefits of the vacation are psychological. How can you compare the benefits to the costs?

3. You were planning to spend Saturday working at your part-time job, but a friend asks you to go skiing. What is the true cost of going skiing? Now suppose that you had been planning to spend the day studying at the library. What is the cost of going skiing in this case? Explain.

4. You win $100 in a hockey pool. You have a choice between spending the money now or putting it away for a year in a bank account that pays 5 percent interest. What is the opportunity cost of spending the $100 now?

5. The company that you manage has invested $5 million in developing a new product, but the development is not quite finished. At a recent meeting, your salespeople report that the introduction of competing products has reduced the expected sales of your new product to $3 million. If it would cost $1 million to finish development and make the product, should you go ahead and do so? What is the most that you should pay to complete development?

6. The welfare system provides income for people who are very poor, with low incomes and few assets. If a recipient of welfare payments decides to work and earn some money, the amount he or she receives in welfare payments is reduced.

   a. How does the existence of the welfare system affect people's incentive to save money for the future?
   b. How does the reduction in welfare payments associated with higher earnings affect welfare recipients' incentive to work?

7. In 1997, the Government of Ontario reformed that province's welfare system. The reform reduced the amount of welfare payments to a person with no income, but also allowed welfare recipients to keep a larger part of their welfare payments if they did earn some income.

   a. How does this reform affect the incentive to work?
   b. How might this reform represent a tradeoff between equity and efficiency?

8. Your roommate is a better cook than you are, but you can clean more quickly than your roommate can. If your roommate did all of the cooking and you did all of the cleaning, would your chores take you more or less time than if you divided each task evenly? Give a similar example of how specialization and trade can make two countries both better off.

9. Nations with corrupt police and court systems typically have lower standards of living than nations with less corruption. Why might that be the case?

10. Explain whether each of the following government activities is motivated by a concern about equity or a concern about efficiency. In the case of efficiency, discuss the type of market failure involved.

    a. regulating cable TV prices
    b. providing some poor people with free prescription drugs
    c. prohibiting smoking in public places
    d. preventing mergers between major banks
    e. imposing higher personal income tax rates on people with higher incomes
    f. instituting laws against driving while intoxicated

11. Discuss each of the following statements from the standpoints of equity and efficiency.

    a. "Everyone in society should be guaranteed the best health care possible."
    b. "When workers are laid off, they should be able to collect unemployment benefits until they find a new job."

12. In what ways is your standard of living different from that of your parents or grandparents when they were your age? Why have these changes occurred?

13. Suppose Canadians decide to save more of their incomes. If banks lend this extra saving to businesses, which use the funds to build new factories, how might this lead to faster growth in productivity? Who do you suppose benefits from the higher productivity? Is society getting a free lunch?

14. Imagine that you are a policymaker trying to decide whether to reduce the rate of inflation. To make an intelligent decision, what would you need to know about inflation, unemployment, and the tradeoff between them?

15. A policymaker is deciding how to finance the construction of a new airport. He can either pay for it by increasing citizens' taxes or by printing more money. What are some of the short-run and long-run consequences of each option?

http://   For more study tools, please visit www.nelson.com/mankiwmicro6e.

THINKING LIKE AN ECONOMIST

© Creative/iStockphoto

Learning Objectives

In this chapter, you will ...

- See how economists apply the methods of science
- Consider how assumptions and models can shed light on the world
- Learn two simple models— the circular flow and the production possibilities frontier
- Distinguish between micro-economics and macroeconomics
- Learn the difference between positive and normative statements
- Examine the role of economists in making policy
- Consider why economists sometimes disagree with one another

Every field of study has its own language and its own way of thinking. Mathematicians talk about axioms, integrals, and vector spaces. Psychologists talk about ego, id, and cognitive dissonance. Lawyers talk about venue, torts, and promissory estoppel.

Economics is no different. Supply, demand, elasticity, comparative advantage, consumer surplus, deadweight loss—these terms are part of the economist's language. In the coming chapters, you will encounter many new terms and some familiar words that economists use in specialized ways. At first, this new language may seem needlessly arcane. But, as you will see, its value lies in its ability to provide you with a new and useful way of thinking about the world in which you live.

The purpose of this book is to help you learn the economist's way of thinking. Just as you cannot become a mathematician, psychologist, or lawyer overnight, learning to think like an economist will take some time. Yet with a combination of theory, case studies, and examples of economics in the news, this book will give you ample opportunity to develop and practise this skill.

Before delving into the substance and details of economics, it is helpful to have an overview of how economists approach the world. This chapter, therefore, discusses the field's methodology. What is distinctive about how economists confront a question? What does it mean to think like an economist?

THE ECONOMIST AS SCIENTIST

Economists try to address their subject with a scientist's objectivity. They approach the study of the economy in much the same way as a physicist approaches the study of matter and a biologist approaches the study of life: They devise theories, collect data, and then analyze these data in an attempt to verify or refute their theories.

To beginners, it can seem odd to claim that economics is a science. After all, economists do not work with test tubes or telescopes. The essence of science, however, is the *scientific method*—the dispassionate development and testing of theories about how the world works. This method of inquiry is as applicable to studying a nation's economy as it is to studying the earth's gravity or a species' evolution. As Albert Einstein once put it, "The whole of science is nothing more than a refinement of everyday thinking."

Although Einstein's comment is as true for social sciences such as economics as it is for natural sciences such as physics, most people are not accustomed to looking at society through the eyes of a scientist. Let's therefore discuss some of the ways in which economists apply the logic of science to examine how an economy works.

The Scientific Method: Observation, Theory, and More Observation

Isaac Newton, the famous seventeenth-century scientist and mathematician, allegedly became intrigued one day when he saw an apple fall from an apple tree. This observation motivated Newton to develop a theory of gravity that applies not only to an apple falling to the earth but to any two objects in the universe. Subsequent testing of Newton's theory has shown that it works well in many circumstances (although, as Einstein would later emphasize, not in all circumstances). Because Newton's theory has been so successful at explaining observation, it is still taught today in undergraduate physics courses around the world.

This interplay between theory and observation also occurs in the field of economics. An economist might live in a country experiencing rapid increases in prices and be moved by this observation to develop a theory of inflation. The theory might assert that high inflation arises when the government prints too much money. (As you may recall, this was one of the ten principles of economics in Chapter 1.) To test this theory, the economist could collect and analyze data on prices and money from many different countries. If growth in the quantity of money were not at all related to the rate at which prices are rising, the economist would start to doubt the validity of his theory of inflation. If money growth and inflation were strongly correlated in international data, as in fact they are, the economist would become more confident in his theory.

Although economists use theory and observation like other scientists, they do face an obstacle that makes their task especially challenging: Experiments are often difficult in economics. Physicists studying gravity can drop many objects in their laboratories to generate data to test their theories. By contrast, economists studying inflation are not allowed to manipulate a nation's monetary policy simply to generate useful data. Economists, like astronomers and evolutionary biologists, usually have to make do with whatever data the world happens to give them.

To find a substitute for laboratory experiments, economists pay close attention to the natural experiments offered by history. When a war in the Middle East interrupts the flow of crude oil, for instance, oil prices skyrocket around the world. For consumers of oil and oil products, such an event depresses living standards. For economic policymakers, it poses a difficult choice about how best to respond. But for economic scientists, it provides an opportunity to study the effects of a key natural resource on the world's economies, and this opportunity persists long after the wartime increase in oil prices is over. Throughout this book, therefore, we consider many historical episodes. These episodes are valuable to study because they give us insight into the economy of the past and, more important, because they allow us to illustrate and evaluate economic theories of the present.

The Role of Assumptions

If you ask a physicist how long it would take for a marble to fall from the top of a ten-storey building, she will answer the question by assuming that the marble falls in a vacuum. Of course, this assumption is false. In fact, the building is surrounded by air, which exerts friction on the falling marble and slows it down. Yet the physicist will correctly point out that friction on the marble is so small that its effect is negligible. Assuming that the marble falls in a vacuum greatly simplifies the problem without substantially affecting the answer.

Economists make assumptions for the same reason: Assumptions can simplify the complex world and make it easier to understand. To study the effects of international trade, for example, we may assume that the world consists of only two countries and that each country produces only two goods. Of course, the real world consists of dozens of countries, each of which produces thousands of different types of goods. But by assuming two countries and two goods, we can focus our thinking. Once we understand international trade in an imaginary world with two countries and two goods, we are in a better position to understand international trade in the more complex world in which we live.

→ Economists must sometimes isolate variables to see their true implications

The art in scientific thinking—whether in physics, biology, or economics—is deciding which assumptions to make. Suppose, for instance, that we were dropping a beach ball rather than a marble from the top of the building. Our physicist would realize that the assumption of no friction is far less accurate in this case: Friction exerts a greater force on a beach ball than on a marble because a beach ball is much larger. The assumption that gravity works in a vacuum is reasonable for studying a falling marble but not for studying a falling beach ball.

Similarly, economists use different assumptions to answer different questions. Suppose that we want to study what happens to the economy when the government changes the number of dollars in circulation. An important piece of this analysis, it turns out, is how prices respond. Many prices in the economy change infrequently; the newsstand prices of magazines, for instance, are changed only every few years. Knowing this fact may lead us to make different assumptions when studying the effects of the policy change over different time horizons. For studying the short-run effects of the policy, we may assume that prices do not change much. We may even make the extreme and artificial assumption that all prices completely fixed. For studying the long-run effects of the policy, however, we may assume that all prices are completely flexible. Just as a physicist uses different assumptions when studying falling marbles and falling beach balls, economists use different assumptions when studying the short-run and long-run effects of a change in the quantity of money.

Economic Models

High-school biology teachers teach basic anatomy with plastic replicas of the human body. These models have all the major organs—the heart, the liver, the kidneys, and so on. The models allow teachers to show their students in a simple way how the important parts of the body fit together. Because these plastic models are stylized and omit many details, no one could mistake them for real people. Despite this lack of realism—indeed, because of this lack of realism—studying these models is useful for learning how the human body works.

Economists also use models to learn about the world, but instead of being made of plastic, they are most often composed of diagrams and equations. Like a biology teacher's plastic model, economic models omit many details to allow us to see what is truly important. Just as the biology teacher's model does not include all of the body's muscles and capillaries, an economist's model does not include every feature of the economy.

As we use models to examine various economic issues throughout this book, you will see that all the models are built with assumptions. Just as a physicist begins the analysis of a falling marble by assuming away the existence of friction, economists assume away many of the details of the economy that are irrelevant for studying the question at hand. All models—in physics, biology, or economics—simplify reality in order to improve our understanding of it.

Our First Model: The Circular-Flow Diagram

The economy consists of millions of people engaged in many activities—buying, selling, working, hiring, manufacturing, and so on. To understand how the economy works, we must find some way to simplify our thinking about all these activities. In other words, we need a model that explains, in general terms, how the economy is organized and how participants in the economy interact with one another.

circular-flow diagram
a visual model of the economy that shows how dollars flow through markets among households and firms

Figure 2.1 presents a visual model of the economy, called a **circular-flow diagram**. In this model, the economy is simplified to include only two types of decision makers—households and firms. Firms produce goods and services using inputs, such as labour, land (natural resources), and capital (buildings and machines). These inputs are called the *factors of production*. Households own the factors of production and consume all the goods and services that the firms produce.

Households and firms interact in two types of markets. In the *markets for goods and services*, households are buyers and firms are sellers. In particular, households buy the output of goods and services that firms produce. In the *markets for the factors of production*, households are sellers and firms are buyers. In these markets, households provide the inputs that the firms use to produce goods and services. The circular-flow diagram offers a simple way of organizing all the economic transactions that occur between households and firms in the economy.

FIGURE 2.1

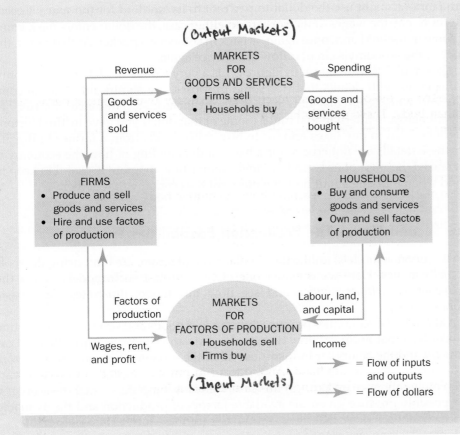

(Output Markets)

MARKETS
FOR
GOODS AND SERVICES
• Firms sell
• Households buy

Revenue

Spending

Goods
and services
sold

Goods and
services
bought

FIRMS
• Produce and sell
  goods and services
• Hire and use factors
  of production

HOUSEHOLDS
• Buy and consume
  goods and services
• Own and sell factors
  of production

Factors of
production

Labour, land,
and capital

MARKETS
FOR
FACTORS OF PRODUCTION
• Households sell
• Firms buy

Wages, rent,
and profit

Income

(Input Markets)

⟶ = Flow of inputs
      and outputs
⟶ = Flow of dollars

The Circular Flow

This diagram is a schematic representation of the organization of the economy. Decisions are made by households and firms. Households and firms interact in the markets for goods and services (where households are buyers and firms are sellers) and in the markets for the factors of production (where firms are buyers and households are sellers). The outer set of arrows shows the flow of dollars, and the inner set of arrows shows the corresponding flow of inputs and outputs.

The two loops of the circular-flow diagram are distinct but related. The inner loop of the circular-flow diagram represents the flows of inputs and outputs. The households sell the use of their labour, land, and capital to the firms in the markets for the factors of production. The firms then use these factors to produce goods and services, which in turn are sold to households in the markets for goods and services. The outer loop of the diagram represents the corresponding flow of dollars. The households spend money to buy goods and services from the firms. The firms use some of the revenue from these sales to pay for the factors of production, such as the wages of their workers. What's left is the profit of the firm owners, who themselves are members of households.

Let's take a tour of the circular flow by following a dollar coin as it makes its way from person to person through the economy. Imagine that the dollar begins at a household, sitting in, say, your pocket. If you want to buy a cup of coffee, you take the dollar to one of the economy's markets for goods and services, such as your local Tim Hortons coffee shop. There you spend it on your favourite drink. When the dollar moves into the Tim Hortons cash register, it becomes revenue for the firm. The dollar doesn't stay at Tim Hortons for long, however, because the firm uses it to buy inputs in the markets for the factors of production. For instance, Tim Hortons might use the dollar to pay rent to its landlord for the space it occupies or to pay the wages of its workers. In either case, the dollar enters the income of some household and, once again, is back in someone's pocket. At that point, the story of the economy's circular flow starts once again.

The circular-flow diagram in Figure 2.1 is a very simple model of the economy. It dispenses with details that, for some purposes, are significant. A more complex and realistic circular-flow model would include, for instance, the roles of government and international trade. (Some of that dollar you gave to Tim Hortons might be used to pay taxes and/or to buy coffee beans from a farmer in Brazil.) Yet these details are not crucial for a basic understanding of how the economy is organized. Because of its simplicity, this circular-flow diagram is useful to keep in mind when thinking about how the pieces of the economy fit together.

Our Second Model: The Production Possibilities Frontier

Most economic models, unlike the circular-flow diagram, are built using the tools of mathematics. Here we consider one of the simplest such models, called the *production possibilities frontier,* and see how this model illustrates some basic economic ideas.

Although real economies produce thousands of goods and services, let's imagine an economy that produces only two goods—cars and computers. Together the car industry and the computer industry use all of the economy's resources, or factors of production. The **production possibilities frontier** is a graph that shows the various combinations of output—in this case, cars and computers—that the economy can possibly produce given the available factors of production and the available production technology that firms can use to turn these factors into output.

Figure 2.2 is an example of a production possibilities frontier. In this economy, if all resources were used in the car industry, the economy would produce 1000 cars per year and no computers. If all resources were used in the computer industry, the economy would produce 3000 computers per year and no cars. The two endpoints of the production possibilities frontier represent these extreme possibilities. More likely, the economy divides its resources between the two industries, producing some cars and some computers. For example, it can produce 600 cars and 2200 computers, shown in the figure by point A. Or by moving some of the factors of production to the car industry from the computer industry, the economy can produce 700 cars and 2000 computers, represented by point B.

Because resources are scarce, not every conceivable outcome is feasible. For example, no matter how resources are allocated between the two industries, the economy cannot produce the number of cars and computers represented by point C. Given the technology available for manufacturing cars and computers, the economy simply does not have enough of the factors of production to support that level of output. With the resources it has, the economy can produce at any point on or inside the production possibilities frontier, but it cannot produce at points outside the frontier.

An outcome is said to be *efficient* if the economy is getting all it can from the scarce resources it has available. Points on (rather than inside) the production possibilities frontier represent efficient levels of production. When the economy is producing at such a point, say point A, there is no way to produce more of one

production possibilities frontier
a graph that shows the combinations of output that the economy can possibly produce given the available factors of production and the available production technology

FIGURE 2.2

**The Production
Possibilities Frontier**

The production possibilities frontier shows the combinations of output—in this case, cars and computers—that the economy can possibly produce. The economy can produce any combination on or inside the frontier. Points outside the frontier are not feasible given the economy's resources.

(handwritten annotations on graph) Inefficiant ; Efficiant ; Impossible

(handwritten note below figure) When it is at maximum efficiancy

good without producing less of the other. Point D represents an *inefficient* outcome. For some reason, perhaps widespread unemployment, the economy is producing less than it could from the resources it has available: It is producing only 300 cars and 1000 computers. If the source of the inefficiency is eliminated, the economy can increase its production of both goods. For example, if the economy moves from point D to point A, its production of cars increases from 300 to 600, and its production of computers increases from 1000 to 2200.

One of the ten principles of economics discussed in Chapter 1 is that people face tradeoffs. The production possibilities frontier shows one tradeoff that society faces. Once we have reached the efficient points on the frontier, the only way of producing more of one good is to produce less of the other. When the economy moves from point A to point B, for instance, society produces 100 more cars, but at the expense of producing 200 fewer computers.

This tradeoff helps us understand another of the ten principles of economics: The cost of something is what you give up to get it. As we learned in Chapter 1, this is called the *opportunity cost*. The production possibilities frontier shows the opportunity cost of one good as measured in terms of the other good. When society moves from point A to point B, it gives up 200 computers to get 100 additional cars. That is, at point A, the opportunity cost of 100 cars is 200 computers. Put another way, the opportunity cost of each car is two computers. Notice that the opportunity cost of a car equals the slope of the production possibilities frontier. (If you don't recall what slope is, you can refresh your memory with the graphing appendix to this chapter.)

(handwritten note in right margin) → Oppurtunity cost isn't constant. Graph is bowed.

The opportunity cost of a car in terms of the number of computers is not a constant in this economy, but rather depends on how many cars and computers that the economy is producing. This is reflected in the shape of the production possibilities frontier. Because the production possibilities frontier in Figure 2.2 is bowed outward, the opportunity cost of a car is highest when the economy is producing many cars and fewer computers, such as at point E, where the frontier is steep. When the economy is producing few cars and many computers, such as at point F, the frontier is flatter, and the opportunity cost of a car is lower.

Economists believe that production possibilities frontiers often have this bowed shape. When the economy is using most of its resources to make computers, such as at point F, the resources best suited to car production, such as skilled autoworkers, are being used in the computer industry. Because these workers probably aren't very good at making computers, the economy won't have to lose much computer production to increase car production by one unit. The opportunity cost of a car in terms of computers is small, and the frontier is relatively flat. By contrast, when the economy is using most of its resources to make cars, such as at point E, the resources best suited to making cars are already being used in the car industry. Producing an additional car means moving some of the best computer technicians out of the computer industry and making them autoworkers. As a result, producing an additional car will mean a substantial loss of computer output. The opportunity cost of a car is high, and the frontier is steep.

The production possibilities frontier shows the tradeoff between the outputs of different goods at a given time, but the tradeoff can change over time. For example, suppose a technological advance in the computer industry raises the number of computers that a worker can produce per week. This advance expands society's set of opportunities. For any given number of cars, the economy can make more computers. If the economy does not produce any computers, it can still produce 1000 cars, so one endpoint of the frontier stays the same. But the rest of the production possibilities frontier shifts outward, as in Figure 2.3.

→ The opportunity cost of producing an entity is highest when the economy is producing more of it + vice versa

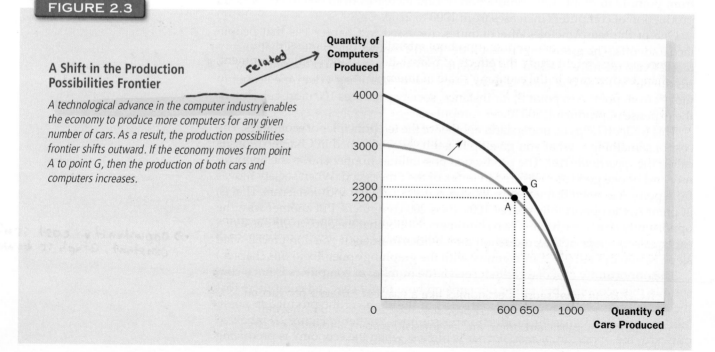

FIGURE 2.3

A Shift in the Production Possibilities Frontier

related →

A technological advance in the computer industry enables the economy to produce more computers for any given number of cars. As a result, the production possibilities frontier shifts outward. If the economy moves from point A to point G, then the production of both cars and computers increases.

This figure illustrates economic growth. Society can move production from a point on the old frontier to a point on the new frontier. Which point it chooses depends on its preferences for the two goods. In this example, society moves from point A to point G, enjoying more computers (2300 instead of 2200) and more cars (650 instead of 600).

The production possibilities frontier simplifies a complex economy to highlight and clarify some basic but powerful ideas. We have used it to illustrate some of the concepts mentioned briefly in Chapter 1: scarcity, efficiency, tradeoffs, opportunity cost, and economic growth. As you study economics, these ideas will recur in various forms. The production possibilities frontier offers one simple way of thinking about them.

Microeconomics and Macroeconomics

Many subjects are studied on various levels. Consider biology, for example. Molecular biologists study the chemical compounds that make up living things. Cellular biologists study cells, which are made up of many chemical compounds and, at the same time, are themselves the building blocks of living organisms. Evolutionary biologists study the many varieties of animals and plants and how species change gradually over the centuries.

Economics is also studied on various levels. We can study the decisions of individual households and firms. Or we can study the interaction of households and firms in markets for specific goods and services. Or we can study the operation of the economy as a whole, which is just the sum of the activities of all these decision makers in all these markets.

The field of economics is traditionally divided into two broad subfields. **Microeconomics** is the study of how households and firms make decisions and how they interact in specific markets. **Macroeconomics** is the study of economy-wide phenomena. A microeconomist might study the effects of rent control on housing in Toronto, the impact of foreign competition on the Canadian auto industry, or the effects of compulsory school attendance on workers' earnings. A macroeconomist might study the effects of borrowing by the federal government, the changes over time in the economy's rate of unemployment, or alternative policies to raise growth in national living standards.

Microeconomics and macroeconomics are closely intertwined. Because changes in the overall economy arise from the decisions of millions of individuals, it is impossible to understand macroeconomic developments without considering the associated microeconomic decisions. For example, a macroeconomist might study the effect of a cut in the federal income tax on the overall production of goods and services. But to analyze this issue, he or she must consider how the tax cut affects the decisions of households about how much to spend on goods and services.

Despite the inherent link between microeconomics and macroeconomics, the two fields are distinct. However, because they address different questions, each field has its own set of models, which are often taught in separate courses.

microeconomics
the study of how households and firms make decisions and how they interact in markets
→ Consumer/household based

macroeconomics
the study of economy-wide phenomena, including inflation, unemployment, and economic growth
→ Broad policy based

QuickQuiz   In what sense is economics like a science? • Draw a production possibilities frontier for a society that produces food and clothing. Show an efficient point, an inefficient point, and an infeasible point. Show the effects of a drought. • Define *microeconomics* and *macroeconomics*.

THE ECONOMIST AS POLICY ADVISER

Often economists are asked to explain the causes of economic events. Why, for example, is unemployment higher for teenagers than for older workers? Sometimes economists are asked to recommend policies to improve economic outcomes. What, for instance, should the government do to improve the economic well-being of teenagers? When economists are trying to explain the world, they are scientists. When they are trying to help improve it, they are policy advisers.

Positive versus Normative Analysis

To help clarify the two roles that economists play, we begin by examining the use of language. Because scientists and policy advisers have different goals, they use language in different ways.

For example, suppose that two people are discussing minimum-wage laws. Here are two statements you might hear:

POLLY: Minimum-wage laws cause unemployment.

NORMA: The government should raise the minimum wage.

Ignoring for now whether you agree with these statements, notice that Polly and Norma differ in what they are trying to do. Polly is speaking like a scientist: She is making a claim about how the world works. Norma is speaking like a policy adviser: She is making a claim about how she would like to change the world.

In general, statements about the world are of two types. One type, such as Polly's, is positive. **Positive statements** are descriptive. They make a claim about how the world *is*. A second type of statement, such as Norma's, is normative. **Normative statements** are prescriptive. They make a claim about how the world *ought to be.*

positive statements → Scientist
claims that attempt to describe the world as it is

normative statements → Policy
claims that attempt to prescribe how the world should be

A key difference between positive and normative statements is how we judge their validity. We can, in principle, confirm or refute positive statements by examining evidence. An economist might evaluate Polly's statement by analyzing data on changes in minimum wages and changes in unemployment over time. By contrast, evaluating normative statements involves values as well as facts. Norma's statement cannot be judged using data alone. Deciding what is good or bad policy is not merely a matter of science. It also involves our views on ethics, religion, and political philosophy.

Positive and normative statements are fundamentally different, but they are often intertwined in a person's set of beliefs. In particular, positive views about how the world works affect normative views about what policies are desirable. Polly's claim that the minimum-wage laws cause unemployment, if true, might lead us to reject Norma's conclusion that the government should raise the minimum wage. Yet our normative conclusions cannot come from positive analysis alone; they involve value judgments as well.

As you study economics, keep in mind the distinction between positive and normative statements because it will help you stay focused on the task at hand. Much of economics is positive. It just tries to explain how the economy works. Yet those who use economics often have goals that are normative. They want to learn how to improve the economy. When you hear economists making normative statements, you know they have crossed the line from scientist to policy adviser.

Economists in Ottawa

U.S. President Harry Truman once said that he wanted to find a one-armed economist. When he asked his economists for advice, they always answered, "On the one hand, . . . On the other hand, ..."

Truman was right in realizing that economists' advice is not always straightforward. This tendency is rooted in one of the ten principles of economics in Chapter 1: People face tradeoffs. Economists are aware that tradeoffs are involved in most policy decisions. A policy might increase efficiency at the cost of equity. It might help future generations but hurt current generations. An economist who says that all policy decisions are easy is an economist not to be trusted.

The Government of Canada, like other governments, relies on the advice of economists. Economists at Finance Canada help design tax policy. Economists at Industry Canada help design and enforce Canada's competition laws. Economists at the Department of Foreign Affairs and International Trade Canada help negotiate trade agreements with other countries. Economists at Human Resources and Skill Development Canada analyze data on workers and on those looking for work to help formulate labour-market policies. Economists at Environment Canada help design environmental regulations. The Canadian International Development Agency employs economists, both on staff and as consultants, to give advice on overseas development projects. Statistics Canada employs economists to collect the data analyzed by other economists and then give policy advice. The Bank of Canada, the quasi-independent institution that sets Canada's monetary policy, employs more than 200 economists to analyze financial markets and macroeconomic developments.

Economists outside the government also give policy advice. The C. D. Howe Institute, the Fraser Institute, the Institute for Research on Public Policy, the Canadian Centre for Policy Alternatives, and other independent organizations publish reports by economists that analyze current issues such as poverty, unemployment, and the deficit. These reports try to influence public opinion and give advice on government policies. Table 2.1 provides the URLs for the websites of some of these organizations; the URLs for all of them can be found in the Internet Resources section of our website at www.nelson.com/mankiwmicro6e.

TABLE 2.1

Websites of Some Major Economic Organizations

Here are the websites for two key government agencies that are responsible for collecting economic data and making economic policy. They are followed by the websites for just a few of the better-known organizations that employ economists and that are often thought to have an influence on government policy.

Department of Finance Canada	www.fin.gc.ca
Bank of Canada	www.bankofcanada.ca
C. D. Howe Institute	www.cdhowe.org
Institute for Research on Public Policy	www.irpp.org
Canadian Centre for Policy Alternatives	www.policyalternatives.ca

The influence of economists on policy goes beyond their role as advisers: Their research and writings often affect policy indirectly. Economist John Maynard Keynes offered this observation:

> The ideas of economists and political philosophers, both when they are right and when they are wrong, are more powerful than is commonly understood. Indeed, the world is ruled by little else. Practical men, who believe themselves to be quite exempt from intellectual influences, are usually the slaves of some defunct economist. Madmen in authority, who hear voices in the air, are distilling their frenzy from some academic scribbler of a few years back.

Although these words were written in 1935, they remain true today. Indeed, the "academic scribbler" now influencing public policy is often Keynes himself.

Why Economists' Advice Is Not Always Followed

Any economist who advises government knows that his or her recommendations are not always heeded. Frustrating as this can be, it is easy to understand. The process by which economic policy is actually made differs in many ways from the idealized policy process assumed in economics textbooks.

Throughout this text, whenever we discuss economic policy, we often focus on one question: What is the best policy for the government to pursue? We act as if policy were set by a benevolent king. Once the king figures out the right policy, he has no trouble putting his ideas into action.

In the real world, figuring out the right policy is only part of the job for the government—sometimes the easiest part. For example, consider a political party that forms the government receiving advice from its economic advisers about what policy is best from their perspective. This is just the beginning of the process. Communication advisers will then assess how best to explain the proposed policy to the public, and they will try to anticipate any misunderstandings that might make the challenge more difficult. Press advisers will anticipate how the news media will report on the proposal and what opinions will likely be expressed on the nation's editorial pages. Political advisers will weigh in to discuss which groups will organize to support or oppose the proposed policy, how this proposal will affect party standing among different groups in the electorate, and whether it will affect support for other policy initiatives. After hearing and weighing all of this advice, a decision will be made on how to proceed.

Making economic policy in a representative democracy is a messy affair—and there are often good reasons why politicians do not advance the policies that economists advocate. Economists offer crucial input into the policy process, but their advice is only one ingredient of a complex recipe.

QuickQuiz Give an example of a positive statement and an example of a normative statement. • Name three parts of government that regularly rely on advice from economists.

→ The success of a policy can often be very political

WHY ECONOMISTS DISAGREE

"If all economists were laid end to end, they would not reach to a conclusion." This quip by George Bernard Shaw is revealing. Economists as a group are often criticized for giving conflicting advice to policymakers.

Why do economists so often appear to give conflicting advice to policymakers? There are two basic reasons:

- Economists may disagree about the validity of alternative positive theories about how the world works.
- Economists may have different values and, therefore, different normative views about what a policy should try to accomplish.

Let's discuss each of these reasons.

Differences in Scientific Judgments

Several centuries ago, astronomers debated whether the earth or the sun was at the centre of the solar system. More recently, meteorologists have debated whether the earth is experiencing global warming and, if so, why. Science is a search for understanding about the world around us. It is not surprising that as the search continues, scientists can disagree about the direction in which truth lies.

Economists often disagree for the same reason. Economics is a young science, and there is still much to be learned. Economists sometimes disagree because they have different hunches about the validity of alternative theories or about the size of important parameters that measure how economic variables are related.

For example, economists disagree about whether the government should levy taxes based on a household's income or its consumption (spending). Advocates of a switch from the current income tax to a consumption tax believe that the change would encourage households to save more because income that is saved would not be taxed. Higher saving, in turn, would free resources for capital accumulation, leading to more rapid growth in productivity and living standards. Advocates of the current income tax system believe that household saving would not respond much to a change in the tax laws. These two groups of economists hold different normative views about the tax system because they have different positive views about the responsiveness of saving to tax incentives.

→ Values, consumption tax harms the poor because they consume a great portion of their income and save less

Differences in Values

Suppose that Peter and Paula both take the same amount of water from the town well. To pay for maintaining the well, the town taxes its residents. Peter has income of $50 000 and is taxed $5000, or 10 percent of his income. Paula has income of $10 000 and is taxed $2000, or 20 percent of her income.

Is this policy fair? If not, who pays too much and who pays too little? Does it matter whether Paula's low income is due to a medical disability or to her decision to pursue a career in acting? Does it matter whether Peter's high income is due to a large inheritance or to his willingness to work long hours at a dreary job?

These are difficult questions on which people are likely to disagree. If the town hired two experts to study how the town should tax its residents to pay for the well, we would not be surprised if they offered conflicting advice.

This simple example shows why economists sometimes disagree about public policy. As we learned earlier in our discussion of normative and positive analysis, policies cannot be judged on scientific grounds alone. Economists give conflicting advice sometimes because they have different values. Perfecting the science of economics will not tell us whether it is Peter or Paula who pays too much.

→ Like politics, there's not always a right answer. Grey area.

Perception versus Reality

Because of differences in scientific judgments and differences in values, some disagreement among economists is inevitable. Yet one should not overstate the amount of disagreement. In many cases, economists do offer a united view.

Table 2.2 contains 17 propositions about economic policy. In a survey of economists in business, government, and academia, these propositions were endorsed

---

TABLE 2.2

Propositions about Which Most Economists Agree

Source: Richard M. Alston, J. R. Kearl, and Michael B. Vaughn, "Is There Consensus among Economists in the 1990s?," *American Economic Review* (May 1992): 203–209; Dan Fuller and Doris Geide-Stevenson, "Consensus among Economists Revisited," *Journal of Economics Education* (Fall 2003): 369–387; Robert Whaples, "Do Economists Agree on Anything? Yes!" *Economists' Voice* (November 2006): 1-6; Robert Whaples, "The Policy Views of American Economic Association Members: The Results of a New Survey," *Econ Journal Watch* (September 2009): 337–348.

Proposition (and percentage of economists who agree)

1. A ceiling on rents reduces the quantity and quality of housing available. (93%)
2. Tariffs and import quotas usually reduce general economic welfare. (93%)
3. Flexible and floating exchange rates offer an effective international monetary arrangement. (90%)
4. Fiscal policy (e.g., tax cut and/or government expenditure increase) has a significant stimulative impact on a less than fully employed economy. (90%)
5. The government should not restrict employers from outsourcing work to foreign countries. (90%)
6. Economic growth in developed countries like Canada leads to greater levels of well-being. (88%)
7. Agricultural subsidies should be eliminated. (85%)
8. An appropriately designed fiscal policy can increase the long-run rate of capital formation. (85%)
9. Local and state governments should eliminate subsidies to professional sports franchises. (85%)
10. If the federal budget is to be balanced, it should be done over the business cycle rather than yearly. (85%)
11. Cash payments increase the welfare of recipients to a greater degree than do transfers-in-kind of equal cash value. (84%)
12. A large federal budget deficit has an adverse effect on the economy. (83%)
13. The redistribution of income is a legitimate role for the government. (83%)
14. Inflation is caused primarily by too much growth in the money supply. (83%)
15. A minimum wage increases unemployment among young and unskilled workers. (79%)
16. The government should restructure the welfare system along the lines of a "negative income tax." (79%)
17. Effluent taxes and marketable pollution permits represent a better approach to pollution control than imposition of pollution ceilings. (78%)

by an overwhelming majority of respondents. Most of these propositions would fail to command a similar consensus among the general public.

The first proposition in the table is about rent control. For reasons we will discuss later, almost all economists believe that rent control adversely affects the availability and quality of housing and is a very costly way of helping the most needy members of society. Nonetheless, some provincial governments choose to ignore the advice of economists and place ceilings on the rents that landlords may charge their tenants.

The second proposition in the table concerns tariffs and import quotas, two policies that restrict trade among nations. For reasons we will discuss more details in later chapters, almost all economists oppose such barriers to free trade. Nonetheless, over the years, Parliament has often chosen to restrict the import of certain goods.

Why do policies such as rent control and trade barriers persist if the experts are united in their opposition? It may be that the realities of the political process stand as immovable obstacles. But it also may be that economists have not yet convinced the general public that these policies are undesirable. One purpose of this book is to make you understand the economist's view of these and other subjects and, perhaps, to persuade you that it is the right one.

QuickQuiz   Why might economic advisers to the Prime Minister disagree about a question of policy?

IN THE NEWS

ENVIRONMENTAL ECONOMISTS

Saving the planet with economics

Green Groups See Potent Tool in Economics

By Jessica E. Vascellaro

Many economists dream of getting high-paying jobs on Wall Street, at prestigious think tanks and universities or at powerful government agencies like the Federal Reserve.

But a growing number are choosing to use their skills not to track inflation or interest rates but to rescue rivers and trees. These are the "green economists," more formally known as environmental economists, who use economic arguments and systems to persuade companies to clean up pollution and to help conserve natural areas.

Working at dozens of advocacy groups and a myriad of state and federal environmental agencies, they are helping to formulate the intellectual framework behind approaches to protecting endangered species, reducing pollution and preventing climate change. They also are becoming a link between left-leaning advocacy groups and the public and private sectors.

"In the past, many advocacy groups interpreted economics as how to make a profit or maximize income," says Lawrence Goulden, a professor of environmental and resource economics at Stanford University in Stanford, Calif. "More economists are realizing that it offers a framework for resource allocation where resources are not only labor and capital but natural resources as well."...

The field of environmental economics began to take form in the 1960s when academics started to apply the tools of economics to the nascent green movement. The discipline grew more popular throughout the 1980s when the Environmental Protection Agency adopted a system of tradable permits for phasing out leaded gasoline. It wasn't until the 1990 amendment to the Clean Air Act, however, that most environmentalists started to take economics seriously.

The amendment implemented a system of tradable allowances for acid rain, a program pushed by Environmental Defense. Under the law, plants that can reduce their emissions more cost-effectively may sell their allowances to more heavy polluters. Today, the program has exceeded its goal of reducing the amount of acid rain to half its 1980 level and is celebrated as evidence that markets can help achieve environmental goals.

Its success has convinced its former critics, who at the time contended that environmental regulation was a matter of ethics, not economics, and favored installing expensive acid rain removal technology in all power plants instead.

Greenpeace, the international environmental giant, was one of the leading opponents of the 1990 amendment. But Kart Davies, research director for Greenpeace USA, said its success and the lack of any significant action on climate policy throughout [the] early 1990s brought the organization around to the concept. "We now believe that [tradable permits] are the most straightforward system of reducing emissions and creating the incentives necessary for massive reductions." . . .

Source: Jessica E. Vascellaro, "Green Groups See Potent Tool In Economics," *The Wall Street Journal,* August 23, 2005, B1. Reprinted by permission of *The Wall Street Journal,* Copyright © 2005 Dow Jones & Company, Inc. All Rights Reserved Worldwide. License number 3102650304938.

LET'S GET GOING

The first two chapters of this book have introduced you to the ideas and methods of economics. We are now ready to get to work. In the next chapter we start learning in more detail about the principles of economic behaviour and economic policy.

As you proceed through this book, you will be asked to draw on many of your intellectual skills. You might find it helpful to keep in mind some advice from the great economist John Maynard Keynes in *Essays in Biography* (1933):

> The study of economics does not seem to require any specialized gifts of an unusually high order. Is it not . . . a very easy subject compared with the higher branches of philosophy or pure science? An easy subject, at which very few excel! The paradox finds its explanation, perhaps, in that the master-economist must possess a rare *combination* of gifts. He must be mathematician, historian, statesman, or philosopher—in some degree. He must understand symbols and speak in words. He must contemplate the particular in terms of the general, and touch abstract and concrete in the same flight of thought. He must study the present in the light of the past for the purposes of the future. No part of man's nature or his institutions must lie entirely outside his regard. He must be purposeful and disinterested in a simultaneous mood; as aloof and incorruptible as an artist, yet sometimes as near the earth as a politician.

It is a tall order. But with practice, you will become more and more accustomed to thinking like an economist.

SUMMARY

- Economists try to address their subject with a scientist's objectivity. Like all scientists, they make appropriate assumptions and build simplified models in order to understand the world around them. Two simple economic models are the circular-flow diagram and the production possibilities frontier.

- The field of economics is divided into two subfields: microeconomics and macroeconomics. Microeconomists study decision making by households and firms and the interaction among households and firms in the marketplace. Macroeconomists study the forces and trends that affect the economy as a whole.

- A positive statement is an assertion about how the world *is*. A normative statement is an assertion about how the world *ought to be*. When economists make normative statements, they are acting more as policy advisers than scientists.

- Economists who advise policymakers offer conflicting advice either because of differences in scientific judgments or because of differences in values. At other times, economists are united in the advice they offer, but policymakers may choose to ignore it.

KEY CONCEPTS

circular-flow diagram, p. 24
production possibilities frontier, p. 26

microeconomics, p. 29
macroeconomics, p. 29

positive statements, p. 30
normative statements, p. 30

QUESTIONS FOR REVIEW

1. How is economics like a science?

2. Why do economists make assumptions?

3. Should an economic model describe reality exactly?

4. Draw and explain a production possibilities frontier for an economy that produces milk and cookies. What happens to this frontier if disease kills half of the economy's cow population?

5. Use a production possibilities frontier to describe the idea of "efficiency."

6. What are the two subfields into which economics is divided? Explain what each subfield studies.

7. What is the difference between a positive and a normative statement? Give an example of each.

8. What is the Bank of Canada?

9. Why do economists sometimes offer conflicting advice to policymakers?

PROBLEMS AND APPLICATIONS

1. Draw a circular-flow diagram. Identify the parts of the model that correspond to the flow of goods and services and the flow of dollars for each of the following activities.

   a. Sam pays a storekeeper $1 for a litre of milk.

   b. Sally earns $7 per hour working at a fast-food restaurant.

   c. Serena spends $10 to see a movie.

   d. Stuart earns $10 000 from his 10 percent ownership of Acme Industrial.

2. Imagine a society that produces military goods and consumer goods, which we'll call "guns" and "butter."
   a. Draw a production possibilities frontier for guns and butter. Explain why it most likely has a bowed-out shape.
   b. Show a point that is impossible for the economy to achieve. Show a point that is feasible but inefficient.
   c. Imagine that the society has two political parties, called the Hawks (who want a strong military) and the Doves (who want a smaller military). Show a point on your production possibilities frontier that the Hawks might choose and a point the Doves might choose.
   d. Imagine that an aggressive neighbouring country reduces the size of its military. As a result, both the Hawks and the Doves reduce their desired production of guns by the same amount. Which party would get the bigger "peace dividend," measured by the increase in butter production? Explain.

3. The first principle of economics discussed in Chapter 1 is that people face tradeoffs. Use a production possibilities frontier to illustrate society's tradeoff between a clean environment and the quantity of industrial output. What do you suppose determines the shape and position of the frontier? Show what happens to the frontier if engineers develop an automobile engine with almost no emissions.

4. Classify the following topics as relating to microeconomics or macroeconomics.
   a. a family's decision about how much income to save
   b. the effect of government regulations on auto emissions
   c. the impact of higher national saving on economic growth
   d. a firm's decision about how many workers to hire
   e. the relationship between the inflation rate and changes in the quantity of money

5. Classify each of the following statements as positive or normative. Explain.
   a. Society faces a short-run tradeoff between inflation and unemployment.
   b. A reduction in the rate of growth of money will reduce the rate of inflation.
   c. The Bank of Canada should reduce the rate of growth of money.
   d. Society ought to require welfare recipients to look for jobs.
   e. Lower tax rates encourage more work and more saving.

6. If you were Prime Minister, would you be more interested in your economic advisers' positive views or their normative views? Why?

7. An economy consists of three workers: Larry, Moe, and Curly. Each works for ten hours per day and can produce two services: mowing lawns and washing cars. In an hour, Larry can either mow one lawn or wash one car, Moe can either mow one lawn or wash two cars, and Curly can either mow two lawns or wash one car.
   a. Calculate how much of each service is produced under the following circumstances, which we label A, B, C, and D:
      • All three spend all their time mowing lawns. (A)
      • All three spend all their time washing cars. (B)
      • All three spend half their time on each activity. (C)
      • Larry spends half his time on each activity, while Moe only washes cars and Curly only mows lawns. (D)
   b. Graph the production possibilities frontier for this economy. Using your answers to part (a), identify points A, B, C, and D on your graph.
   c. Explain why the production possibilities frontier has the shape it does.
   d. Are any of the allocations calculated in part (a) inefficient? Explain.

For more study tools, please visit www.nelson.com/mankiwmicro6e.

APPENDIX

Graphing: A Brief Review

Many of the concepts that economists study can be expressed with numbers—the price of bananas, the quantity of bananas sold, the cost of growing bananas, and so on. Often these economic variables are related to one another; for example, when the price of bananas rises, people buy fewer bananas. One way of expressing the relationships among variables is with graphs.

Graphs serve two purposes. First, when developing economic theories, graphs offer a way to visually express ideas that might be less clear if described with equations or words. Second, when analyzing economic data, graphs provide a way of finding how variables are, in fact, related in the world. Whether we are working with theory or with data, graphs provide a lens through which a recognizable forest emerges from a multitude of trees.

Numerical information can be expressed graphically in many ways, just as a thought can be expressed in words in many ways. A good writer chooses words that will make an argument clear, a description pleasing, or a scene dramatic. An effective economist chooses the type of graph that best suits the purpose.

In this appendix we discuss how economists use graphs to study the mathematical relationships among variables. We also discuss some of the pitfalls that can arise in the use of graphical methods.

Graphs of a Single Variable

Three common types of graphs are shown in Figure 2A.1. The *pie chart* in panel (a) shows how total income in Canada is divided among the sources of income, including wages and salaries, corporation profits, and so on. A slice of the pie represents each source's share of the total. The *bar graph* in panel (b) compares income for three countries. The height of each bar represents the average income in each country. The *time-series graph* in panel (c) traces the Canadian unemployment rate over time. The height of the line shows the unemployment rate in each month. You have probably seen similar graphs in newspapers and magazines.

Graphs of Two Variables: The Coordinate System

The three graphs in Figure 2A.1 are useful in showing how a variable changes over time or across individuals, but they are limited in how much they can tell us. These graphs display information only on a single variable. Economists are often concerned with the relationships between variables. Thus, they need to be able to display two variables on a single graph. The *coordinate system* makes this possible.

Suppose you want to examine the relationship between study time and grade point average. For each student in your class, you could record a pair of numbers: hours per week spent studying and grade point average. These numbers could then be placed in parentheses as an *ordered pair* and appear as a single point on the graph. Albert E., for instance, is represented by the ordered pair

FIGURE 2A.1

Types of Graphs

The pie chart in panel (a) shows how national income is derived from various sources. The bar graph in panel (b) compares the average income in three countries. The time-series graph in panel (c) shows the unemployment rate in Canada from January 2000 to December 2012.

(25 hours/week, 3.5 GPA), while his "what-me-worry?" classmate Alfred E. is represented by the ordered pair (5 hours/week, 2.0 GPA).

We can graph these ordered pairs on a two-dimensional grid. The first number in each ordered pair, called the *x-coordinate,* tells us the horizontal location of the point. The second number, called the *y-coordinate,* tells us the vertical location of the point. The point with both an *x*-coordinate and a *y*-coordinate of zero is known as the *origin.* The two coordinates in the ordered pair tell us where the point is located in relation to the origin: *x* units to the right of the origin and *y* units above it.

Figure 2A.2 graphs grade point average against study time for Albert E., Alfred E., and their classmates. This type of graph is called a *scatterplot* because it plots scattered points. Looking at this graph, we immediately notice that points farther to the right (indicating more study time) also tend to be higher (indicating a better grade point average). Because study time and grade point average typically move in the same direction, we say that these two variables have a *positive correlation.* By contrast, if we were to graph party time and grades, we would likely find that higher party time is associated with lower grades; because these variables typically move in opposite directions, we would call this a *negative correlation.* In either case, the coordinate system makes the correlation between the two variables easy to see.

Curves in the Coordinate System

Students who study more do tend to get higher grades, but other factors also influence a student's grade. Previous preparation is an important factor, for instance, as are talent, attention from teachers, and even eating a good breakfast.

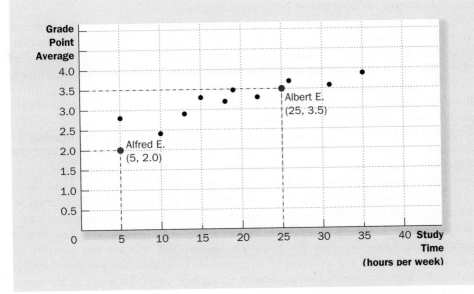

Using the Coordinate System

Grade point average is measured on the vertical axis and study time on the horizontal axis. Albert E., Alfred E., and their classmates are represented by various points. We can see from the graph that students who study more tend to get higher grades.

A scatterplot like Figure 2A.2 does not attempt to isolate the effect that studying has on grades from the effects of other variables. Often, however, economists prefer looking at how one variable affects another, holding everything else constant.

To see how this is done, let's consider one of the most important graphs in economics—the *demand curve*. The demand curve traces the effect of a good's price on the quantity of the good consumers want to buy. Before showing a demand curve, however, consider Table 2A.1, which shows how the number of novels that Emma buys depends on her income and on the price of novels. When novels are cheap, Emma buys them in large quantities. As they become more expensive, she borrows books from the library instead of buying them or chooses to go to the movies instead of reading. Similarly, at any given price, Emma buys more novels when

TABLE 2A.1

Price	Income		
	$20 000	$30 000	$40 000
$10	2 novels	5 novels	8 novels
9	6	9	12
8	10	13	16
7	14	17	20
6	18	21	24
5	22	25	28
	Demand curve, D_3	Demand curve, D_1	Demand curve, D_2

Novels Purchased by Emma

This table shows the number of novels Emma buys at various incomes and prices. For any given level of income, the data on price and quantity demanded can be graphed to produce Emma's demand curve for novels, as shown in Figures 2A.3 and 2A.4.

she has a higher income. That is, when her income increases, she spends part of the additional income on novels and part on other goods.

We now have three variables—the price of novels, income, and the number of novels purchased—which is more than we can represent in two dimensions. To put the information from Table 2A.1 in graphical form, we need to hold one of the three variables constant and trace the relationship between the other two. Because the demand curve represents the relationship between price and quantity demanded, we hold Emma's income constant and show how the number of novels she buys varies with the price of novels.

Suppose that Emma's income is $30 000 per year. If we place the number of novels Emma purchases on the x-axis and the price of novels on the y-axis, we can graphically represent the middle column of Table 2A.1. When the points that represent these entries from the table—5 novels, $10; 9 novels, $9; and so on— are connected, they form a line. This line, pictured in Figure 2A.3, is known as Emma's demand curve for novels; it tells us how many novels Emma purchases at any given price. The demand curve is downward sloping, indicating that a higher price reduces the quantity of novels demanded. Because the quantity of novels demanded and the price move in opposite directions, we say that the two variables are *negatively related*. (Conversely, when two variables move in the same direction, the curve relating them is upward sloping, and we say the variables are *positively related*.)

FIGURE 2A.3

Demand Curve

The line D_1 shows how Emma's purchases of novels depend on the price of novels when her income is held constant. Because the price and the quantity demanded are negatively related, the demand curve slopes downward.

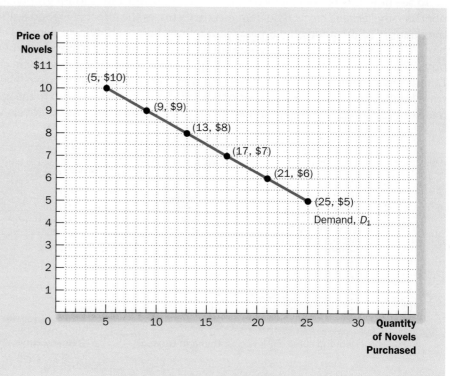

Now suppose that Emma's income rises to $40 000 per year. At any given price, Emma will purchase more novels than she did at her previous level of income. Just as earlier we drew Emma's demand curve for novels using the entries from the middle column of Table 2A.1, we now draw a new demand curve using the entries from the right-hand column of the table. This new demand curve (curve D_2) is pictured alongside the old one (curve D_1) in Figure 2A.4; the new curve is a similar line drawn farther to the right. We, therefore, say that Emma's demand curve for novels *shifts* to the right when her income increases. Likewise, if Emma's income was to fall to $20 000 per year, she would buy fewer novels at any given price and her demand curve would shift to the left (to curve D_3).

In economics, it is important to distinguish between *movements along a curve* and *shifts of a curve*. As we can see from Figure 2A.3, if Emma earns $30 000 per year and novels cost $8 apiece, she will purchase 13 novels per year. If the price of novels falls to $7, Emma will increase her purchases of novels to 17 per year. The demand curve, however, stays fixed in the same place. Emma still buys the same number of novels *at each price*, but as the price falls she moves along her demand curve from left to right. By contrast, if the price of novels remains fixed at $8 but her income rises to $40 000, Emma increases her purchases of novels from 13 to 16 per year. Because Emma buys more novels *at each price*, her demand curve shifts out, as shown in Figure 2A.4.

There is a simple way to tell when it is necessary to shift a curve. When a variable that is not named on either axis changes, the curve shifts. Income is on neither the x-axis nor the y-axis of the graph, so when Emma's income changes, her demand curve must shift. Any change that affects Emma's purchasing habits besides a change

→ Outside influence: income change ∴ curve shifts right

→ Movement along the curve due to a change in price of the product in question. Movement of the curve due to outside influence.

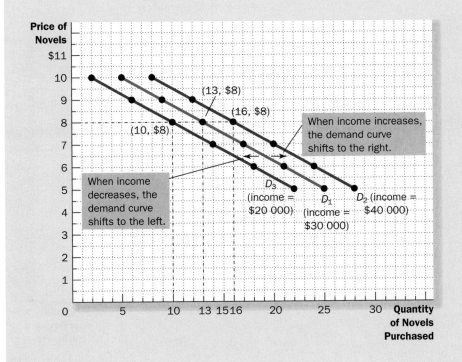

FIGURE 2A.4

Shifting Demand Curves

The location of Emma's demand curve for novels depends on how much income she earns. The more she earns, the more novels she will purchase at any given price, and the farther to the right her demand curve will lie. Curve D_1 represents Emma's original demand curve when her income is $30 000 per year. If her income rises to $40 000 per year, her demand curve shifts to D_2. If her income falls to $20 000 per year, her demand curve shifts to D_3.

Outside Influence
↑

in the price of novels will result in a shift in her demand curve. If, for instance, the public library closes and Emma must buy all the books she wants to read, she will demand more novels at each price, and her demand curve will shift to the right. Or, if the price of movies falls and Emma spends more time at the movies and less time reading, she will demand fewer novels at each price, and her demand curve will shift to the left. By contrast, when a variable on an axis of the graph changes, the curve does not shift. We read the change as a movement along the curve.

Slope

One question we might want to ask about Emma is how much her purchasing habits respond to price. Look at the demand curve pictured in Figure 2A.5. If this curve is very steep, Emma purchases nearly the same number of novels regardless of whether they are cheap or expensive. If this curve is much flatter, Emma purchases many fewer novels when the price rises. To answer questions about how much one variable responds to changes in another variable, we can use the concept of *slope*.

The slope of a line is the ratio of the vertical distance covered to the horizontal distance covered as we move along the line. This definition is usually written out in mathematical symbols as follows:

$$\text{Slope} = \frac{\Delta y}{\Delta x}$$

FIGURE 2A.5

Calculating the Slope of a Line

To calculate the slope of the demand curve, we can look at the changes in the x- and y-coordinates as we move from the point (21 novels, $6) to the point (13 novels, $8). The slope of the line is the ratio of the change in the y-coordinate (−2) to the change in the x-coordinate (+8), which equals −1/4.

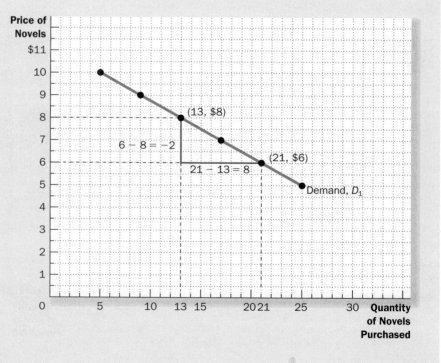

where the Greek letter Δ (delta) stands for the change in a variable. In other words, the slope of a line is equal to the "rise" (change in y) divided by the "run" (change in x). The slope will be a small positive number for a fairly flat upward-sloping line, a large positive number for a steep upward-sloping line, and a negative number for a downward-sloping line. A horizontal line has a slope of zero because in this case the y-variable never changes; a vertical line is said to have an infinite slope because the y-variable can take any value without the x-variable changing at all.

What is the slope of Emma's demand curve for novels? First of all, because the curve slopes down, we know the slope will be negative. To calculate a numerical value for the slope, we must choose two points on the line. With Emma's income at $30 000, she will purchase 21 novels at a price of $6 or 13 novels at a price of $8. When we apply the slope formula, we are concerned with the change between these two points; in other words, we are concerned with the difference between them, which lets us know that we will have to subtract one set of values from the other, as follows:

$$\text{Slope} = \frac{\Delta y}{\Delta x} = \frac{\text{First } y\text{-coordinate} - \text{Second } y\text{-coordinate}}{\text{First } x\text{-coordinate} - \text{Second } x\text{-coordinate}} = \frac{6 - 8}{21 - 13} = -\frac{2}{8} = -\frac{1}{4}$$

Figure 2A.5 shows graphically how this calculation works. Try computing the slope of Emma's demand curve using two different points. You should get exactly the same result, $-\frac{1}{4}$. One of the properties of a straight line is that it has the same slope everywhere. This is not true of other types of curves, which are steeper in → Bowed curves
some places than in others.

The slope of Emma's demand curve tells us something about how responsive her purchases are to changes in the price. A small slope (a number close to zero) means that Emma's demand curve is relatively flat; in this case, she adjusts the number of novels she buys substantially in response to a price change. A larger slope (a number farther from zero) means that Emma's demand curve is relatively steep; in this case, she adjusts the number of novels she buys only slightly in response to a price change.

More detail about how economists use graphs is provided in the appendix to Chapter 4.

Cause and Effect

Economists often use graphs to advance an argument about how the economy works. In other words, they use graphs to argue about how one set of events *causes* another set of events. With a graph like the demand curve, there is no doubt about cause and effect. Because we are varying price and holding all other variables constant, we know that changes in the price of novels cause changes in the quantity Emma demands. Remember, however, that our demand curve came from a hypothetical example. When graphing data from the real world, it is often more difficult to establish how one variable affects another.

The first problem is that it is difficult to hold everything else constant when measuring how one variable affects another. If we are not able to hold variables constant, we might decide that one variable on our graph is causing changes in the other variable, when actually those changes are caused by a third *omitted variable* not pictured on the graph. Even if we have identified the correct two variables to look at, we might run into a second problem—*reverse causality*. In other words, we might decide that A causes B when, in fact, B causes A. The omitted-variable and reverse-causality traps require us to proceed with caution when using graphs to draw conclusions about causes and effects.

Omitted Variables   To see how omitting a variable can lead to a deceptive graph, let's consider an example. Imagine that the government, spurred by public concern about the large number of deaths from cancer, commissions an exhaustive study from Big Brother Statistical Services. Big Brother examines many of the items found in people's homes to see which of them are associated with the risk of cancer. Big Brother reports a strong relationship between two variables: the number of cigarette lighters that a household owns and the probability that someone in the household will develop cancer. Figure 2A.6 shows this relationship.

What should we make of this result? Big Brother advises a quick policy response. It recommends that the government discourage the ownership of cigarette lighters by taxing their sale. It also recommends that the government requires warning labels: "Big Brother has determined that this lighter is dangerous to your health."

In judging the validity of Big Brother's analysis, one question is paramount: Has Big Brother held constant every relevant variable except the one under consideration? If the answer is no, the results are suspect. An easy explanation for Figure 2A.6 is that people who own more cigarette lighters are more likely to smoke cigarettes and that cigarettes, not lighters, cause cancer. If Figure 2A.6 does not hold constant the amount of smoking, it does not tell us the true effect of owning a cigarette lighter.

This story illustrates an important principle: When you see a graph being used to support an argument about cause and effect, it is important to ask whether the movements of an omitted variable could explain the results you see.

Reverse Causality   Economists can also make mistakes about causality by misreading its direction. To see how this is possible, suppose the Association of Canadian Anarchists commissions a study of crime in Canada and arrives at Figure 2A.7, which plots the number of violent crimes per thousand people in

---

FIGURE 2A.6

Graph with an Omitted Variable

The upward-sloping curve shows that members of households with more cigarette lighters are more likely to develop cancer. Yet we should not conclude that ownership of lighters causes cancer, because the graph does not take into account the number of cigarettes smoked.

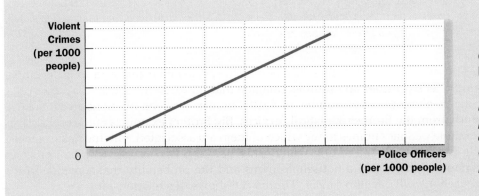

Graph Suggesting Reverse Causality

The upward-sloping curve shows that cities with a higher concentration of police are more dangerous. Yet the graph does not tell us whether police cause crime or crime-plagued cities hire more police.

major cities against the number of police officers per thousand people. The anarchists note the curve's upward slope and argue that because police increase rather than decrease the amount of urban violence, law enforcement should be abolished.

If we could run a controlled experiment, we would avoid the danger of reverse causality. To run an experiment, we would set the number of police officers in different cities randomly and then examine the correlation between police and crime. Figure 2A.7, however, is not based on such an experiment. We simply observe that more dangerous cities have more police officers. The explanation for this may be that more dangerous cities hire more police. In other words, rather than police causing crime, crime may cause an increase in police hiring. Nothing in the graph itself allows us to establish the direction of causality.

It might seem that an easy way to determine the direction of causality is to examine which variable moves first. If we see crime increase and then the police force expand, we reach one conclusion. If we see the police force expand and then crime increase, we reach the other. Yet there is also a flaw with this approach: Often people change their behaviour not in response to a change in their present conditions but in response to a change in their *expectations* of future conditions. A city that expects a major crime wave in the future, for instance, might well hire more police now. This problem is even easier to see in the case of babies and minivans. Couples often buy a minivan in anticipation of the birth of a child. The minivan comes before the baby, but we wouldn't want to conclude that the sale of minivans causes the population to grow!

There is no complete set of rules that says when it is appropriate to draw causal conclusions from graphs. Yet just keeping in mind that cigarette lighters don't cause cancer (omitted variable) and minivans don't cause larger families (reverse causality) will keep you from falling for many faulty economic arguments.

INTERDEPENDENCE AND THE GAINS FROM TRADE

Learning Objectives

In this chapter, you will ...

- Consider how everyone can benefit when people trade with one another
- Learn the meaning of *absolute advantage* and *comparative advantage*
- See how comparative advantage explains the gains from trade
- Apply the theory of comparative advantage to everyday life and national policy

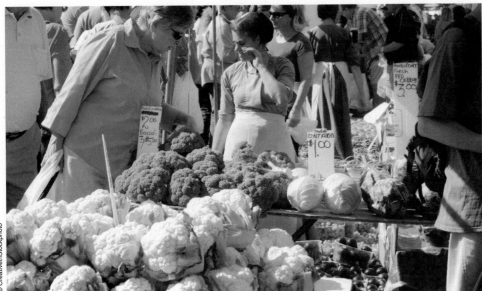

© Creativel/iStockphoto

Consider your typical day. You wake up in the morning, and you pour yourself juice from oranges grown in Florida and coffee from beans grown in Brazil. Over breakfast, you watch a news program broadcast from Toronto on your television set made in China. You get dressed in clothes made of cotton grown in Georgia and sewn in factories in Thailand. You drive to class in a car made of parts manufactured in more than a dozen countries around the world. Then you open up your economics textbook written by authors living in Massachusetts and Alberta, published by a company located in Ontario, and printed on paper made from trees grown in New Brunswick.

Every day you rely on many people from around the world, most of whom you do not know, to provide you with the goods and services that you enjoy. Such interdependence is possible because people trade with one another. Those people who provide you with goods and services are not acting out of generosity or concern for your welfare. Nor is some government agency directing them to make what you want and to give it to you. Instead, people provide you and other consumers with the goods and services they produce because they get something in return.

In subsequent chapters we will examine how our economy coordinates the activities of millions of people with varying tastes and abilities. As a starting point for this analysis, here we consider the reasons for economic interdependence. One of the ten principles of economics highlighted in Chapter 1 is that trade can make everyone better off. This principle explains why people trade with their neighbours and why nations trade with other nations. In this chapter we examine this principle more closely. What exactly do people gain when they trade with one another? Why do people choose to become interdependent?

The answers to these questions are key to understanding the modern global economy. In most countries today, many goods and services consumed are imported from abroad, and many goods and services produced are exported to foreign customers. The analysis in this chapter explains interdependence not only among individuals but also among nations. As we will see, the gains from trade are much the same whether you are buying a haircut from your local barber or a T-shirt made by a worker on the other side of the globe.

A PARABLE FOR THE MODERN ECONOMY

To understand why people choose to depend on others for goods and services and how this choice improves their lives, let's look at a simple economy. Imagine that there are two goods in the world—meat and potatoes. And there are two people in the world—a cattle rancher and a potato farmer—each of whom would like to eat both meat and potatoes.

The gains from trade are most obvious if the rancher can produce only meat and the farmer can produce only potatoes. In one scenario, the rancher and the farmer could choose to have nothing to do with each other. But after several months of eating beef roasted, boiled, broiled, and grilled, the rancher might decide that self-sufficiency is not all it's cracked up to be. The farmer, who has been eating potatoes mashed, fried, baked, and scalloped, would likely agree. It is easy to see that trade would allow them to enjoy greater variety: Each could then have a steak with a baked potato or a burger with fries.

Although this scenario illustrates most simply how everyone can benefit from trade, the gains would be similar if the rancher and the farmer were each capable of producing the other good, but only at great cost. Suppose, for example, that the potato farmer is able to raise cattle and produce meat, but that he is not very good at it. Similarly, suppose that the cattle rancher is able to grow potatoes, but that her land is not very well suited for it. In this case, it would be easy to show that the farmer and the rancher can each benefit by specializing in what he or she does best and then trading with the other.

The gains from trade are less obvious, however, when one person is better at producing *every* good. For example, suppose that the rancher is better at raising cattle *and* better at growing potatoes than the farmer. In this case, should the rancher or farmer choose to remain self-sufficient? Or is there still reason for them to trade with each other? To answer this question, we need to look more closely at the factors that affect such a decision.

Production Possibilities

Suppose that the farmer and the rancher each work 8 hours a day and can devote this time to growing potatoes, raising cattle, or a combination of the two. Panel (a) of Figure 3.1 shows the amount of time each person requires to produce 1 kg of each good. The farmer can produce a kilogram of potatoes in 15 minutes and a kilogram of meat in 60 minutes. The rancher, who is more productive in both activities, can produce a kilogram of potatoes in 10 minutes and a kilogram of meat in 20 minutes. The last two columns in panel (a) in Figure 3.1 show the amounts of meat or potatoes the farmer and rancher can produce if they work an 8-hour day, producing only that good.

FIGURE 3.1

(a) The Production Opportunities

	Minutes Needed to Produce 1 kg of:		Amount of Meat or Potatoes Produced in 8 Hours	
	Meat	Potatoes	Meat	Potatoes
Farmer	60 min/kg	15 min/kg	8 kg	32 kg
Rancher	20 min/kg	10 min/kg	24 kg	48 kg

The Production Possibilities Frontier

Panel (b) shows the combinations of meat and potatoes that the farmer can produce. Panel (c) shows the combinations of meat and potatoes that the rancher can produce. Both production possibilities frontiers are derived from panel (a) and the assumption that the farmer and rancher each work 8 hours a day.

(b) The Farmer's Production Possibilities Frontier

If there is no trade, the farmer chooses this production and consumption.

(c) The Rancher's Production Possibilities Frontier

If there is no trade, the rancher chooses this production and consumption.

Panel (b) of Figure 3.1 illustrates the amounts of meat and potatoes that the farmer can produce. If the farmer devotes all 8 hours of his time to potatoes, he produces 32 kg of potatoes (measured on the horizontal axis) and no meat. If he devotes all his time to meat, he produces 8 kg of meat (measured on the vertical axis) and no potatoes. If the farmer divides his time equally between the two activities, spending 4 hours on each, he produces 16 kg of potatoes and 4 kg of meat. The figure shows these three possible outcomes and all others in between.

This graph is the farmer's production possibilities frontier. As we discussed in Chapter 2, a production possibilities frontier shows the various mixes of output that an economy can produce. It illustrates one of the ten principles of economics in Chapter 1: People face tradeoffs. Here the farmer faces a tradeoff between producing meat and producing potatoes. You may recall that the production possibilities frontier in Chapter 2 was drawn bowed out; in that case, the tradeoff between the two goods depended on the amounts being produced. Here, however, the farmer's technology for producing meat and potatoes (as summarized in panel (a) of Figure 3.1) allows him to switch between one good and the other at a constant rate. Whenever the farmer spends 1 hour less producing meat and 1 hour more producing potatoes, he reduces his output of meat by 1 kg and raises his output of potatoes by 4 kg—and this is true regardless of how much he is already producing. As a result, the production possibilities frontier is a straight line.

Panel (c) of Figure 3.1 shows the production possibilities frontier for the rancher. If the rancher devotes all 8 hours of her time to potatoes, she produces 48 kg of potatoes and no meat. If she devotes all her time to meat, she produces 24 kg of meat and no potatoes. If the rancher divides her time equally, spending 4 hours on each activity, she produces 24 kg of potatoes and 12 kg of meat. Once again, the production possibilities frontier shows all the possible outcomes.

If the farmer and rancher choose to be self-sufficient, rather than trade with each other, then each consumes exactly what he or she produces. In this case, the production possibilities frontier is also the consumption possibilities frontier. That is, without trade, Figure 3.1 shows the possible combinations of meat and potatoes that the farmer and rancher can each consume.

These production possibilities frontiers are useful in showing the tradeoffs that the farmer and rancher face, but they do not tell us what the farmer and rancher will actually choose to do. To determine their choices, we need to know the tastes of the farmer and the rancher. Let's suppose they choose the combinations identified by points A and B in Figure 3.1: The farmer produces and consumes 16 kg of potatoes and 4 kg of meat, while the rancher produces and consumes 24 kg of potatoes and 12 kg of meat.

Specialization and Trade

After several years of eating combination B, the rancher gets an idea and goes to talk to the farmer:

RANCHER: Farmer, my friend, have I got a deal for you! I know how to improve life for both of us. I think you should stop producing meat altogether and devote all your time to growing potatoes. According to my calculations, if you work 8 hours a day growing potatoes, you'll produce 32 kg of potatoes. If you give me 15 of those 32 kg, I'll give you 5 kg of meat in return. In the end, you'll get to eat 17 kg of potatoes and 5 kg of meat, instead of the 16 kg of potatoes and 4 kg of meat you now get. If you go along with my plan, you'll have more of *both* foods. [To illustrate her point, the rancher shows the farmer panel (a) of Figure 3.2.]

FARMER: (*sounding skeptical*) That seems like a good deal for me. But I don't understand why you are offering it. If the deal is so good for me, it can't be good for you too.

RANCHER: Oh, but it is! Suppose I spend 6 hours a day raising cattle and 2 hours growing potatoes. Then I can produce 18 kg of meat and 12 kg of potatoes. After I give you 5 kg of my meat in exchange for 15 kg of your potatoes, I'll end up with 13 kg of meat and 27 kg of potatoes. So I'll also consume more of both foods than I do now. [She points out panel (b) of Figure 3.2.]

FARMER: I don't know. . . . This sounds too good to be true.

RANCHER: It's really not as complicated as it seems at first. Here—I've summarized my proposal for you in a simple table. [The rancher indicates panel (c) of Figure 3.2.]

FARMER: (*after pausing to study panel* [c]) These calculations seem correct, but I'm puzzled. How can this deal make us both better off?

RANCHER: We can both benefit because trade allows each of us to specialize in doing what we do best. You will spend more time growing potatoes and less time raising cattle. I will spend more time raising cattle and less time growing potatoes. As a result of specialization and trade, each of us can consume more meat and more potatoes without working any more hours.

QuickQuiz Draw an example of a production possibilities frontier for Robinson Crusoe, a shipwrecked sailor who spends his time gathering coconuts and catching fish. Does this frontier limit Crusoe's consumption of coconuts and fish if he lives by himself? Does he face the same limits if he can trade with natives on the island?

COMPARATIVE ADVANTAGE: THE DRIVING FORCE OF SPECIALIZATION

The rancher's explanation of the gains from trade, although correct, poses a puzzle: If the rancher is better at both raising cattle and growing potatoes, how can the farmer ever specialize in doing what he does best? The farmer doesn't seem to do anything best. To solve this puzzle, we need to look at the principle of *comparative advantage.*

As a first step in developing this principle, consider the following question: In our example, who can produce potatoes at lower cost—the farmer or the rancher? There are two possible answers, and in these two answers lie the solution to our puzzle and the key to understanding the gains from trade.

FIGURE 3.2

How Trade Expands the Set of Consumption Opportunities

The proposed trade between the farmer and the rancher offers each of them a combination of meat and potatoes that would be impossible in the absence of trade. In panel (a), the farmer gets to consume at point A* rather than point A. In panel (b), the rancher gets to consume at point B* rather than point B. Trade allows each to consume more meat and more potatoes.

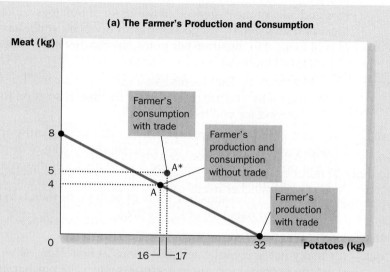

(a) The Farmer's Production and Consumption

Farmer's consumption with trade

Farmer's production and consumption without trade

Farmer's production with trade

(b) The Rancher's Production and Consumption

Rancher's production with trade

Rancher's consumption with trade

Rancher's production and consumption without trade

(c) The Gains from Trade: A Summary

	Farmer		Rancher	
	Meat	Potatoes	Meat	Potatoes
Without Trade:				
Production and Consumption	4 kg	16 kg	12 kg	24 kg
With Trade:				
Production	0 kg	32 kg	18 kg	12 kg
Trade	Gets 5 kg	Gives 15 kg	Gives 5 kg	Gets 15 kg
Consumption	5 kg	17 kg	13 kg	27 kg
Gains from Trade:				
Increase in Consumption	+1 kg	+1 kg	+1 kg	+3 kg

Absolute Advantage

One way to answer the question about the cost of producing potatoes is to compare the inputs required by the two producers. Economists use the term **absolute advantage** when comparing the productivity of one person, firm, or nation to that of another. The producer that requires a smaller quantity of inputs to produce a good is said to have an absolute advantage in producing that good.

In our example, time is the only input, so we can determine absolute advantage by looking at how much time each type of production takes. The rancher has an absolute advantage both in producing meat and in producing potatoes because she requires less time than the farmer to produce a unit of either good. The rancher needs to input only 20 minutes to produce a kilogram of meat, whereas the farmer needs 60 minutes. Similarly, the rancher needs only 10 minutes to produce a kilogram of potatoes, whereas the farmer needs 15 minutes. Based on this information, we can conclude that the rancher has the lower cost of producing potatoes, if we measure cost in terms of the quantity of inputs.

absolute advantage
the comparison among producers of a good according to their productivity

Opportunity Cost and Comparative Advantage

There is another way to look at the cost of producing potatoes. Rather than comparing inputs required, we can compare the opportunity costs. Recall from Chapter 1 that the **opportunity cost** of some item is what we give up to get that item. In our example, we assumed that the farmer and the rancher each spend 8 hours a day working. Time spent producing potatoes, therefore, takes away from time available for producing meat. As the rancher and farmer reallocate time between producing the two goods, they move along their production possibility frontiers; they give up units of one good to produce units of the other. The opportunity cost measures the tradeoff between the two goods that each producer faces.

Let's first consider the rancher's opportunity cost. According to the table in panel (a) of Figure 3.1, producing 1 kg of potatoes takes her 10 minutes of work. When the rancher spends that 10 minutes producing potatoes, she spends 10 minutes less producing meat. Because the rancher needs 20 minutes to produce 1 kg of meat, 10 minutes of work would yield 0.5 kg of meat. Hence, the rancher's opportunity cost of producing 1 kg of potatoes is 0.5 kg of meat.

Now consider the farmer's opportunity cost. Producing 1 kg of potatoes takes him 15 minutes. Because he needs 60 minutes to produce 1 kg of meat, 15 minutes of work would yield 0.25 kg of meat. Hence, the farmer's opportunity cost of 1 kg of potatoes is 0.25 kg of meat.

Table 3.1 shows the opportunity costs of meat and potatoes for the two producers. Notice that the opportunity cost of meat is the inverse of the opportunity cost of potatoes. Because 1 kg of potatoes costs the rancher 0.5 kg of meat, 1 kg of meat costs the rancher 2 kg of potatoes. Similarly, because 1 kg of potatoes costs the farmer 0.25 kg of meat, 1 kg of meat costs the farmer 4 kg of potatoes.

Economists use the term **comparative advantage** when describing the opportunity cost of two producers. The producer who gives up less of other goods to produce good X has the smaller opportunity cost of producing good X and is said to have a comparative advantage in producing it. In our example, the farmer has a lower opportunity cost of producing potatoes than does the rancher: A kilogram of potatoes costs the farmer only 0.25 kg of meat, while it costs the rancher 0.50 kg of meat.

opportunity cost
whatever must be given up to obtain some item

→ Farmer: lower OC
Rancher: Higher OC
∴ Trade makes sense

comparative advantage
the comparison among producers of a good according to their opportunity cost

→ Farmer has the comparative advantage in potatoes

TABLE 3.1

The Opportunity Cost of Meat and Potatoes	Opportunity Cost of:	
	1 kg of Meat	1 kg of Potatoes
Farmer	4 kg potatoes	0.25 kg meat
Rancher	2 kg potatoes	0.50 kg meat

Conversely, the rancher has a lower opportunity cost of producing meat than does the farmer: A kilogram of meat costs the rancher 2 kg of potatoes, while it costs the farmer 4 kg of potatoes. Thus, the farmer has a comparative advantage in growing potatoes, and the rancher has a comparative advantage in producing meat.

Although it is possible for one person to have an absolute advantage in both goods (as the rancher does in our example), it is impossible for one person to have a comparative advantage in both goods. Because the opportunity cost of one good is the inverse of the opportunity cost of the other, if a person's opportunity cost of one good is relatively high, his opportunity cost of the other good must be relatively low. Comparative advantage reflects the relative opportunity cost. Unless two persons have exactly the same opportunity cost, one person will have a comparative advantage in one good, and the other person will have a comparative advantage in the other good.

Comparative Advantage and Trade

The gains from specialization and trade are based not on absolute advantage but rather on comparative advantage. When each person specializes in producing the good for which he or she has a comparative advantage, total production in the economy rises. This increase in the size of the economic pie can be used to make everyone better off.

In our example, the farmer spends more time growing potatoes, and the rancher spends more time producing meat. As a result, the total production of potatoes rises from 40 to 44 kg, and the total production of meat rises from 16 to 18 kg. The farmer and the rancher share the benefits of this increased production.

We can also look at the gains from trade in terms of the price that each party pays the other. Because the farmer and the rancher have different opportunity costs, they can each think they are getting a bargain. That is, each benefits from trade by obtaining a good at a price that is lower than his or her opportunity cost of that good.

Consider the proposed deal from the viewpoint of the farmer. The farmer gets 5 kg of meat in exchange for 15 kg of potatoes. In other words, the farmer buys each kilogram of meat for a price of 3 kg of potatoes. This price of meat is lower than his opportunity cost for 1 kg of meat, which is 4 kg of potatoes. Thus, the farmer benefits from the deal because he gets to buy meat at a good price.

Now consider the deal from the rancher's viewpoint. The rancher buys 15 kg of potatoes for a price of 5 kg of meat. That is, the price of potatoes is one-third of a kilogram of meat. This price of potatoes is lower than her opportunity cost of 1 kg of potatoes, which is 0.5 kg of meat. The rancher benefits because she can buy potatoes at a good price.

THE LEGACY OF ADAM SMITH AND DAVID RICARDO

Economists have long understood the principle of comparative advantage. Here is how the great economist Adam Smith put the argument:

It is a maxim of every prudent master of a family, never to attempt to make at home what it will cost him more to make than to buy. The tailor does not attempt to make his own shoes, but buys them of the shoemaker. The shoemaker does not attempt to make his own clothes but employs a tailor. The farmer attempts to make neither the one nor the other, but employs those different artificers. All of them find it for their interest to employ their whole industry in a way in which they have some advantage over their neighbors, and to purchase with a part of its produce, or what is the same thing, with the price of part of it, whatever else they have occasion for.

David Ricardo

This quotation is from Smith's 1776 book *An Inquiry into the Nature and Causes of the Wealth of Nations*, which was a landmark in the analysis of trade and economic interdependence.

Smith's book inspired David Ricardo, a millionaire stockbroker, to become an economist. In his 1817 book *Principles of Political Economy and Taxation*, Ricardo developed the principle of comparative advantage as we know it today. His defence of free trade was not a mere academic exercise. Ricardo put his economic beliefs to work as a member of the British Parliament, where he opposed the Corn Laws, which restricted the import of grain.

The conclusions of Adam Smith and David Ricardo on the gains from trade have held up well over time. Although economists often disagree on questions of policy, they are united in their support of free trade. Moreover, the central argument for free trade has not changed much in the past two centuries. Even though the field of economics has broadened its scope and refined its theories since the time of Smith and Ricardo, economists' opposition to trade restrictions is still based largely on the principle of comparative advantage.

The moral of the story of the farmer and the rancher should now be clear: *Trade can benefit everyone in society because it allows people to specialize in activities in which they have a comparative advantage.*

The Price of Trade

The principle of comparative advantage establishes that there are gains from specialization and trade, but it leaves open a couple of related questions: What determines the price at which trade takes place? How are the gains from trade shared between the trading parties? The precise answer to these questions is beyond the scope of this chapter, but we can state one general rule: *For both parties to gain from trade, the price at which they trade must lie between the two opportunity costs.*

In our example, the farmer and rancher agreed to trade at a rate of 3 kg of potatoes for each 1 kg of meat. This price is between the rancher's opportunity cost (2 kg of potatoes per 1 kg of meat) and the farmer's opportunity cost (4 kg of potatoes per 1 kg of meat). The price need not be exactly in the middle for both parties to gain, but it must be somewhere between 2 and 4.

To see why the price has to be in this range, consider what would happen if it was not. If the price of 1 kg of meat was below 2 kg of potatoes, both the farmer and the rancher would want to buy meat because the price would be below their opportunity costs. Similarly, if the price of meat was above 4 kg of potatoes, both would want to sell meat, because the price would be above their opportunity costs. But there are only two members of this economy. They cannot both be buyers of meat, nor can they both be sellers. Someone has to take the other side of the deal.

A mutually advantageous trade can be struck at a price between 2 and 4. In this price range, the rancher wants to sell meat to buy potatoes, and the farmer wants to sell potatoes to buy meat. Each party can buy a good at a price that is lower than his or her opportunity cost. In the end, both of them specialize in the good for which he or she has a comparative advantage and are, as a result, better off.

QuickQuiz Robinson Crusoe can gather 10 coconuts or catch 1 fish per hour. His friend Friday can gather 30 coconuts or catch 2 fish per hour. What is Crusoe's opportunity cost of catching one fish? What is Friday's? Who has an absolute advantage in catching fish? Who has a comparative advantage in catching fish?

IN THE NEWS

DOES FREE TRADE CREATE JOBS?

Canada has been involved in many free trade agreements over the years—the most important are with our NAFTA partners, the United States and Mexico—and we are currently involved in talks that may lead to new agreements. While politicians talk about the benefits of these agreements in terms of jobs, columnist William Watson (who teaches economics at McGill University) points out that comparative advantage isn't necessarily about more jobs but about better jobs.

Free-Trade Deals Don't Create Jobs, But They're Still Good for Canada

By William Watson

How many Canadians are currently unemployed because we don't have a free-trade deal with Japan? Not many, I bet. I also bet that if we do get such a deal, and I hope we do, the new Japanese demand for our goods does very little for overall employment. It's therefore unfortunate that in announcing free-

trade talks with the Japanese the prime minister focused on jobs. "This is a truly historic step," the prime minister said in announcing the beginning of negotiations, "that will help create jobs and growth for both countries."

Politicians always say trade deals are about jobs. Brian Mulroney said Canada–U.S. free trade was about "Jobs, jobs, jobs." It wasn't about jobs. Free-trade deals generally aren't about jobs.

Think about it. Suppose we stopped trading altogether. Would the unemploy-

ment rate therefore be 32 per cent (exports equalling 32 per cent of our GDP)?

If we did outlaw trade tomorrow, there would be a huge spike in unemployment. We couldn't possibly eat all the wheat prairie farmers produce. They'd have to find something else to do. But of course outlawing trade also means outlawing imports. So there would be lots of new jobs producing goods and services we had been importing.

Nothing against wheat farmers but, to begin with at least, they might not

APPLICATIONS OF COMPARATIVE ADVANTAGE

The principle of comparative advantage explains interdependence and the gains from trade. Because interdependence is so prevalent in the modern world, the principle of comparative advantage has many applications. Here are two examples, one fanciful and one of great practical importance.

Should Sidney Crosby Shovel His Own Sidewalk?

Sidney Crosby spends a lot of time on the ice. One of the most talented hockey players in the world, he can shoot a puck with a speed and accuracy that most recreational hockey players can only dream of doing. Most likely, he is talented at other physical activities as well. For example, let's imagine that Crosby can shovel his sidewalk faster than anyone else. But just because he *can* shovel his walk quickly, does this mean he *should*?

be so good at producing iPods. The new CanPods we'd all have to get used to might not function very well, not to mention they'd weigh three pounds and cost $2,000 apiece. But, assuming we'd want to keep consuming in the manner to which international trade had accustomed us, with imports illegal there would be lots of jobs in this kind of "import substitution."

Though most of us would therefore be employed, we'd also be poorer. Instead of doing what we're good at, we'd be trying to do what foreigners are good at. With trade we specialize in activities where we have a "comparative advantage." We are more productive in them than in alternative activities.

We don't get more jobs by trading. We get better jobs—jobs that pay more because we're better at them. Most politicians aren't economists so they can be forgiven for saying trade deals create jobs. The prime minister is an economist and must know this. Maybe he believes jobs talk is the only language voters will understand.

Although economists have a professional predisposition toward free trade,

it doesn't automatically follow that binational or regional free-trade deals are a good idea. While they create trade, which is good, they also divert trade, which is bad.

Suppose we do get a free-trade deal with Japan. Japanese cars that currently face a six-percent tariff will come in tariff free. That will create trade because some of us will decide to buy a now-cheaper Japanese car (imported from Japan) rather than a Canadian-made car, whether made here by a North American car company or by Honda, Toyota or Suzuki. That's good. If we Canadian consumers decide that under equal tax treatment the pure imports are what we prefer, more power to us. Canadian car manufacturers will have to either up their game or find something else to do.

But Canada–Japan free trade may also cause "trade diversion." Suppose Korea makes the best cars of all. After our deal with Japan, made-in-Japan cars won't face a tariff coming into Canada. But Korean cars will (unless we also finally get a free-trade deal with Korea after 17 years of negotiation but

never mind that for the moment). Some Canadian car-buyers will respond by switching from made-in-Korea cars to made-in-Japan cars and that's not good: we end up diverting some of our trade away from the world's best producer, Korea, to our new best friend, Japan.

To figure out whether a given free-trade deal is good or bad, you have to look across all industries and calculate whether the deal creates more trade than it diverts, which is not actually an easy calculation to do.

The obvious solution is to go for the truly level playing field and try to get a free-trade deal with everybody—which is exactly what the WTO is for. Seen as a steppingstone to global free trade, free trade with special friends does make sense, even if that's a hard message to get across in Question Period.

Source: "Free-trade deals don't create jobs, but they're still good for Canada" by William Watson, *Ottawa Citizen*, March 27, 2012. Material reprinted with the express permission of: *The Ottawa Citizen*, a division of Postmedia Network Inc.

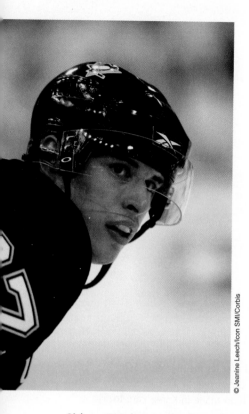

Sidney Crosby

imports
goods and services produced abroad
and sold domestically

exports
goods and services produced
domestically and sold abroad

© Jeanine Leech/Icon SMI/Corbis

To answer this question, we can use the concepts of opportunity cost and comparative advantage. Let's say that Crosby can shovel his walk in one hour. In that same hour, he could film a television commercial and earn $20 000. By contrast, Forrest Gump, the boy next door, can shovel Crosby's walk in two hours. In that same two hours, he could work at McDonald's and earn $20.

In this example, Crosby has an absolute advantage in shovelling sidewalks because he can do the work with a lower input of time. Yet because Crosby's opportunity cost of shovelling the sidewalk is $20 000 and Gump's opportunity cost is only $20, Gump has a comparative advantage in shovelling sidewalks.

The gains from trade in this example are tremendous. Rather than shovelling his own sidewalk, Crosby should make the commercial and hire Gump to shovel the walk. As long as Crosby pays Gump more than $20 and less than $20 000, both of them are better off.

Should Canada Trade with Other Countries?

Just as individuals can benefit from specialization and trade with one another, as the farmer and rancher did, so can populations of people in different countries. Many of the goods and services that Canadians enjoy are produced abroad, and many of the goods and services produced in Canada are sold abroad. Goods and services produced abroad and sold domestically are called **imports**. Goods and services produced domestically and sold abroad are called **exports**.

An interesting question concerns the sources of comparative advantage. For individuals, some of their comparative advantage is "natural"—Sidney Crosby clearly has an innate talent for hockey that most of us do not. This is also true at the country level. Canada has a clear comparative advantage in the provision of natural resources. We are a leading provider of oil, forest products, and agriculture goods to the world market because of our natural geographic, geological, and topological advantages. For example, Canada is a large exporter of pulp and paper products to the United States. This is due both to our large forest areas and to our access to cheap hydroelectricity, which provides the power required to process pulp.

However, hard work, training, education, and experience can create, or enhance, comparative advantage. Raw talent is only part of the reason that some individuals rise to the top of their professions. This is also true at the country level. The Canadian workforce is highly educated, healthy, and productive relative to many countries. This gives Canada a comparative advantage in the production of high-value-added goods that require a skilled labour force.

To see how countries can benefit from trade, suppose there are two countries, Canada and Japan, and two goods, food and cars. Imagine that the two countries produce cars equally well: A Canadian worker and a Japanese worker can each produce 1 car per month. By contrast, because Canada has more and better land, it is better at producing food: A Canadian worker can produce 2 tonnes of food per month, whereas a Japanese worker can produce only 1 tonne of food per month.

The principle of comparative advantage states that each good should be produced by the country that has the smaller opportunity cost of producing that good. Because the opportunity cost of a car is 2 tonnes of food in Canada but only 1 tonne of food in Japan, Japan has a comparative advantage in producing cars. Japan should produce more cars than it wants for its own use and export some of them to Canada. Similarly, because the opportunity cost of a tonne of food is 1 car in Japan but only $\frac{1}{2}$ car in

Canada, Canada has a comparative advantage in producing food. Canada should produce more food than it wants to consume and export some of it to Japan. Through specialization and trade, both countries can have more food and more cars.

In reality, of course, the issues involved in trade among nations are more complex than this example suggests. The most important among these issues is that each country has many citizens with different interests. International trade can make some individuals worse off, even as it makes the country as a whole better off. When Canada exports food and imports cars, the impact on a Canadian farmer is not the same as the impact on a Canadian autoworker. Yet, contrary to the opinions sometimes voiced by politicians and political commentators, international trade is not like war, in which some countries win and others lose. Trade allows all countries to achieve greater prosperity.

QuickQuiz   Suppose that a skilled brain surgeon also happens to be the world's fastest typist. Should he do his own typing or hire a secretary? Explain.

CONCLUSION

You should now understand more fully the benefits of living in an interdependent economy. When Canadians buy tube socks from China, when residents of Manitoba drink apple juice from British Columbia, and when a homeowner hires the kid next door to shovel the sidewalk, the same economics forces are at work. The principle of comparative advantage shows that trade can make everyone better off.

Having seen why interdependence is desirable, you might naturally ask how it is possible. How do free societies coordinate the diverse activities of all the people involved in their economies? What ensures that goods and services will get from those who should be producing them to those who should be consuming them? In a world with only two people, such as the rancher and the farmer, the answer is simple: These two people can directly bargain and allocate resources between themselves. In the real world with billions of people, the answer is less obvious. We take up this issue in the next chapter, where we see that free societies allocate resources through the market forces of supply and demand.

SUMMARY

- Each person consumes goods and services produced by many other people, both in our country and around the world. Interdependence and trade are desirable because they allow everyone to enjoy a greater quantity and variety of goods and services.

- There are two ways to compare the ability of two people in producing a good. The person who can produce the good with the smaller quantity of inputs is said to have an *absolute advantage* in producing the good. The person who has the smaller opportunity

cost of producing the good is said to have a *comparative advantage*. The gains from trade are based on comparative advantage, not absolute advantage.

- Trade makes everyone better off because it allows people to specialize in those activities in which they have a comparative advantage.

- The principle of comparative advantage applies to countries as well as to people. Economists use the principle of comparative advantage to advocate free trade among countries.

KEY CONCEPTS

absolute advantage, p. 55

comparative advantage, p. 55

exports, p. 60

opportunity cost, p. 55

imports, p. 60

QUESTIONS FOR REVIEW

1. Under what conditions is the production possibilities frontier linear rather than bowed out?

2. Explain how absolute advantage and comparative advantage differ.

3. Give an example in which one person has an absolute advantage in doing something but another person has a comparative advantage.

4. Is absolute advantage or comparative advantage more important for trade? Explain your reasoning using the example in your answer to question 3.

5. When two parties trade based on comparative advantage, in what range must the price of the trade lie for both to gain?

6. Will a nation tend to export or import goods for which it has a comparative advantage? Explain.

7. Why do economists oppose policies that restrict trade among nations?

PROBLEMS AND APPLICATIONS

1. Maria can read 20 pages of economics in an hour. She can also read 50 pages of sociology in an hour. She spends 5 hours per day studying.
   a. Draw Maria's production possibilities frontier for reading economics and sociology.
   b. What is Maria's opportunity cost of reading 100 pages of sociology?

2. Canadian and Japanese workers can each produce 4 cars per year. A Canadian worker can produce 10 tonnes of grain per year, whereas a Japanese worker can produce 5 tonnes of grain per year. To keep things simple, assume that each country has 100 million workers.
   a. For this situation, construct a table analogous to panel (a) in Figure 3.1.
   b. Graph the production possibilities frontier of the Canadian and Japanese economies.
   c. For Canada, what is the opportunity cost of a car? Of grain? For Japan, what is the opportunity cost of a car? Of grain? Put this information in a table analogous to Table 3.1.
   d. Which country has an absolute advantage in producing cars? In producing grain?
   e. Which country has a comparative advantage in producing cars? In producing grain?

   f. Without trade, half of each country's workers produce cars and half produce grain. What quantities of cars and grain does each country produce?
   g. Starting from a position without trade, give an example in which trade makes each country better off.

3. Pat and Kris are roommates. They spend most of their time studying (of course), but they leave some time for their favourite activities: making pizza and brewing root beer. Pat takes 4 hours to brew 5 L of root beer and 2 hours to make a pizza. Kris takes 6 hours to brew 5 L of root beer and 4 hours to make a pizza.
   a. What is each roommate's opportunity cost of making a pizza? Who has the absolute advantage in making pizza? Who has the comparative advantage in making pizza?
   b. If Pat and Kris trade products with each other, who will trade away pizza in exchange for root beer?
   c. The price of pizza can be expressed in terms of litres of root beer. What is the highest price at which pizza can be traded that would make both roommates better off? What is the lowest price? Explain.

4. Suppose that there are 10 million workers in Canada, and that each of these workers can produce either 2 cars or 30 tonnes of wheat in a year.
    a. What is the opportunity cost of producing a car in Canada? What is the opportunity cost of producing a tonne of wheat in Canada? Explain the relationship between the opportunity costs of the two goods.
    b. Draw Canada's production possibilities frontier. If Canada chooses to consume 10 million cars, how much wheat can it consume without trade? Label this point on the production possibilities frontier.
    c. Now suppose that the United States offers to buy 10 million cars from Canada in exchange for 20 tonnes of wheat per car. If Canada continues to consume 10 million cars, how much wheat does this deal allow Canada to consume? Label this point on your diagram. Should Canada accept the deal?

5. England and Scotland both produce scones and sweaters. Suppose that an English worker can produce 50 scones per hour or 1 sweater per hour. Suppose that a Scottish worker can produce 40 scones per hour or 2 sweaters per hour.
    a. Which country has the absolute advantage in the production of each good? Which country has the comparative advantage?
    b. If England and Scotland decide to trade, which commodity will Scotland trade to England? Explain.
    c. If a Scottish worker could produce only 1 sweater per hour, would Scotland still gain from trade? Would England still gain from trade? Explain.

6. The following table describes the production possibilities of two cities:

	Red Sweaters per Worker per Hour	Blue Sweaters per Worker per Hour
Montreal	3	3
Toronto	2	1

    a. Without trade, what is the price of blue sweaters (in terms of red sweaters) in Montreal? What is the price in Toronto?
    b. Which city has an absolute advantage in the production of each colour of sweater? Which city has a comparative advantage in the production of each colour of sweater?
    c. If the cities trade with each other, which colour of sweater will each export?
    d. What is the range of prices at which trade can occur?

7. Are the following statements true or false? Explain in each case.
    a. "Two countries can achieve gains from trade even if one of the countries has an absolute advantage in the production of all goods."
    b. "Certain very talented people have a comparative advantage in everything they do."
    c. "If a certain trade is good for one person, it can't be good for the other one."
    d. "If a certain trade is good for one person, it is always good for the other one."
    e. "If trade is good for a country, it must be good for everyone in the country."

8. Canada exports oil and pulp and paper to the rest of the world, and it imports computers and clothing from the rest of the world. Do you think this pattern of trade is consistent with the principle of comparative advantage? Why or why not?

9. Conrad and Barbara produce food and clothing. In an hour, Conrad can produce 1 unit of food or 1 unit of clothing, while Barbara can produce 2 units of food or 3 units of clothing. They each work 10 hours a day.
    a. Who has an absolute advantage in producing food? Who has an absolute advantage in producing clothing? Explain.
    b. Who has a comparative advantage in producing food? Who has a comparative advantage in producing clothing? Explain.
    c. Draw the production possibilities frontier for the household (that is, Conrad and Barbara together) assuming that each spends the same number of hours each day as the other producing food and clothing.
    d. Barbara suggests that, instead, she specialize in making clothing. That is, she will do all of the clothing production, unless her time is fully devoted to clothing, and then Conrad will chip in. What does the household production possibilities frontier look like now?
    e. Conrad suggests that Barbara specialize in producing food. That is, Barbara will do all the food production, unless her time is fully devoted to

food, and then Conrad will chip in. What does the household production possibilities frontier look like under Conrad's proposal?

f. Comparing your answers to parts (c), (d), and (e), which allocation of time makes the most sense? Relate your answer to the theory of comparative advantage.

10. Suppose that in a year a Canadian worker can produce 100 shirts or 20 computers, while a Chinese worker can produce 100 shirts or 10 computers.

a. Graph the production possibilities curve for the two countries. Suppose that without trade the workers in each country spend half their time producing each good. Identify this point in your graph.

b. If these countries were open to trade, which country would export shirts? Give a specific numerical example and show it on your graph. Which country would benefit from trade? Explain.

c. Explain at what price of computers (in terms of shirts) the two countries might trade.

d. Suppose that China catches up with Canadian productivity so that a Chinese worker can produce 100 shirts or 20 computers. What pattern of trade would you predict now? How does this advance in Chinese productivity affect the economic well-being of the citizens of the two countries?

11. An average worker in Brazil can produce 30 mL of soy milk in 20 minutes and 30 mL of coffee in 60 minutes, while an average worker in Peru can produce 30 mL of soy milk in 50 minutes and 30 mL of coffee in 75 minutes.

a. Who has the absolute advantage in coffee? Explain.

b. Who has the comparative advantage in coffee? Explain.

c. If the two countries specialize and trade with each other, who will import coffee? Explain.

d. Assume that the two countries trade and that the country importing coffee trades 60 mL of soy milk for 30 mL of coffee. Explain why both countries will benefit from this trade.

http://   For more study tools, please visit www.nelson.com/mankiwmicro6e.

THE MARKET FORCES OF SUPPLY AND DEMAND

4

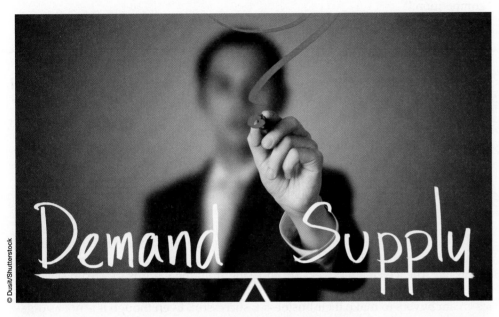

Learning Objectives

In this chapter, you will ...

- Learn the nature of a competitive market

- Examine what determines the demand for a good in a competitive market

- Examine what determines the supply of a good in a competitive market

- See how supply and demand together set the price of a good and the quantity sold

- Consider the key role of prices in allocating scarce resources in market economies

When a cold snap hits Florida, the price of orange juice rises in supermarkets throughout Canada. When the weather turns warm in Quebec every summer, the price of hotel rooms in the Caribbean plummets. When a war breaks out in the Middle East, the price of gasoline in Canada rises and the price of a used SUV falls. What do these events have in common? They all show the workings of supply and demand.

Supply and *demand* are the two words that economists use most often—and for good reason. Supply and demand are the forces that make market economies work. They determine the quantity of each good produced and the price at which it is sold. If you want to know how any event or policy will affect the economy, you must think first about how it will affect supply and demand.

This chapter introduces the theory of supply and demand. It considers how buyers and sellers behave and how they interact with one another. It shows how supply and demand determine prices in a market economy and how prices, in turn, allocate the economy's scarce resources.

MARKETS AND COMPETITION

The terms *supply* and *demand* refer to the behaviour of people as they interact with one another in competitive markets. Before discussing how buyers and sellers behave, let's first consider more fully what we mean by a "market" and "competition."

What Is a Market?

market
a group of buyers and sellers of a particular good or service

→ Markets don't have to be organized in one location.

A **market** is a group of buyers and sellers of a particular good or service. The buyers as a group determine the demand for the product, and the sellers as a group determine the supply of the product.

Markets take many forms. Some markets are highly organized, such as the markets for many agricultural commodities. In these markets, buyers and sellers meet at a specific time and place, where an auctioneer helps set prices and arrange sales.

More often, markets are less organized. For example, consider the market for ice cream in a particular town. Buyers of ice cream do not meet together at any one time. The sellers of ice cream are in different locations and offer somewhat different products. There is no auctioneer calling out the price of ice cream. Each seller posts a price for an ice-cream cone, and each buyer decides how much ice cream to buy at each store. Nonetheless, these consumers and producers of ice cream are closely connected. The ice-cream buyers are choosing from the various ice-cream sellers to satisfy their craving, and the ice-cream sellers are all trying to appeal to the same ice-cream buyers to make their businesses successful. Even though it is not as organized, the group of ice-cream buyers and ice-cream sellers forms a market.

What Is Competition?

competitive market
a market in which there are many buyers and many sellers so that each has a negligible impact on the market price

The market for ice cream, like most markets in the economy, is highly competitive. Each buyer knows that there are several sellers from which to choose, and each seller is aware that his product is similar to that offered by other sellers. As a result, the price of ice cream and the quantity of ice cream sold are not determined by any single buyer or seller. Rather, price and quantity are determined by all buyers and sellers as they interact in the marketplace.

Economists use the term **competitive market** to describe a market in which there are so many buyers and so many sellers that each has a negligible impact on the market price. Each seller of ice cream has limited control over the price because other sellers are offering similar products. A seller has little reason to charge less than the going price, and if he charges more, buyers will make their purchases elsewhere. Similarly, no single buyer of ice cream can influence the price of ice cream because each buyer purchases only a small amount.

In this chapter, we assume that markets are *perfectly competitive*. To reach this highest form of competition, a market must have two characteristics: (1) the goods offered for sale are all exactly the same, and (2) the buyers and sellers are so numerous that no single buyer or seller has any influence over the market price. Because buyers and sellers in perfectly competitive markets must accept the price the market determines, they are said to be *price takers*. At the market price, buyers can buy all they want, and sellers can sell all they want.

There are some markets in which the assumption of perfect competition applies perfectly. In the wheat market, for example, there are thousands of farmers who sell wheat and millions of consumers who use wheat and wheat products. Because no single buyer or seller can influence the price of wheat, each takes the price as given.

Not all goods and services, however, are sold in perfectly competitive markets. Some markets have only one seller, and this seller sets the price. Such a seller is called a *monopoly*. Your local cable television company, for instance, may be a monopoly. Residents of your small town probably have only one cable company from which to buy this service. Still other markets fall between the extremes of perfect competition and monopoly.

Despite the diversity of market types we find in the world, assuming perfect competition is a useful simplification and, therefore, a natural place to start. Perfectly competitive markets are the easiest to analyze because everyone participating in the market takes the price as given by market conditions. Moreover, because some degree of competition is present in most markets, many of the lessons that we learn by studying supply and demand under perfect competition apply in more complicated markets as well.

QuickQuiz   What is a market? • What are the characteristics of a competitive market?

DEMAND

We begin our study of markets by examining the behaviour of buyers. To focus our thinking, let's keep in mind a particular good—ice cream.

The Demand Curve: The Relationship between Price and Quantity Demanded

The **quantity demanded** of any good is the amount of the good that buyers are willing and able to purchase. As we will see, many things determine the quantity demanded of any good, but in our analysis of how markets work, one determinant plays a central role—the price of the good. If the price of ice cream rose to $20 per scoop, you would buy less ice cream. You might buy frozen yogurt instead. If the price of ice cream fell to $0.20 per scoop, you would buy more. Because the quantity demanded falls as the price rises and rises as the price falls, we say that the quantity demanded is *negatively related* to the price. This relationship between price and quantity demanded is true for most goods in the economy and, in fact, is so pervasive that economists call it the **law of demand:** Other things equal, when the price of a good rises, the quantity demanded of the good falls, and when the price falls, the quantity demanded rises.

The table in Figure 4.1 shows how many ice-cream cones Catherine buys each month at different prices of ice cream. If ice cream is free, Catherine eats 12 cones. At $0.50 per cone, Catherine buys 10 cones. As the price rises further, she buys fewer and fewer cones. When the price reaches $3.00, Catherine doesn't buy any ice cream at all. This table is a **demand schedule,** a table that shows the relationship between the price of a good and the quantity demanded, holding constant everything else that influences how much of the good consumers want to buy.

quantity demanded
the amount of a good that buyers are willing and able to purchase

law of demand
the claim that, other things equal, the quantity demanded of a good falls when the price of the good rises

demand schedule
a table that shows the relationship between the price of a good and the quantity demanded

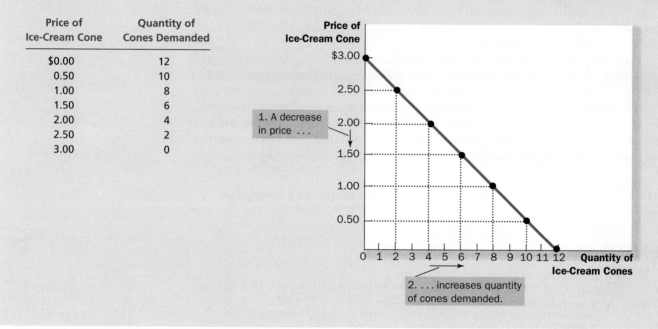

FIGURE 4.1

Catherine's Demand Schedule and Demand Curve

The demand schedule shows the quantity demanded at each price. The demand curve, which graphs the demand schedule, shows how the quantity demanded of the good changes as its price varies. Because a lower price increases the quantity demanded, the demand curve slopes downward.

Price of Ice-Cream Cone	Quantity of Cones Demanded
$0.00	12
0.50	10
1.00	8
1.50	6
2.00	4
2.50	2
3.00	0

1. A decrease in price ...

2. ... increases quantity of cones demanded.

The graph in Figure 4.1 uses the numbers from the table to illustrate the law of demand. By convention, the price of ice cream is on the vertical axis, and the quantity of ice cream demanded is on the horizontal axis. The downward-sloping line relating price and quantity demanded is called the **demand curve.**

demand curve
a graph of the relationship between the price of a good and the quantity demanded

Market Demand versus Individual Demand

The demand curve in Figure 4.1 shows an individual's demand for a product. To analyze how markets work, we need to determine the *market demand,* which is the sum of all the individual demands for a particular good or service.

The table in Figure 4.2 shows the demand schedules for ice cream of two individuals—Catherine and Nicholas. At any price, Catherine's demand schedule tells us how much ice cream she buys, and Nicholas's demand schedule tells us how much ice cream he buys. The market demand at each price is the sum of the two individual demands.

The graph in Figure 4.2 shows the demand curves that correspond to these demand schedules. Notice that we sum the individual demand curves *horizontally* to obtain the market demand curve. That is, to find the total quantity demanded at any price, we add the individual quantities found on the horizontal axis of the individual demand curves. Because we are interested in analyzing how markets work,

FIGURE 4.2

Market Demand as the Sum of Individual Demands

The quantity demanded in a market is the sum of the quantities demanded by all the buyers at each price. Thus, the market demand curve is found by adding horizontally the individual demand curves. At a price of $2, Catherine demands 4 ice-cream cones, and Nicholas demands 3 ice-cream cones. The quantity demanded in the market at this price is 7 cones.

Price of Ice-Cream Cone	Catherine		Nicholas		Market
$0.00	12	+	7	=	19
0.50	10		6		16
1.00	8		5		13
1.50	6		4		10
2.00	4		3		7
2.50	2		2		4
3.00	0		1		1

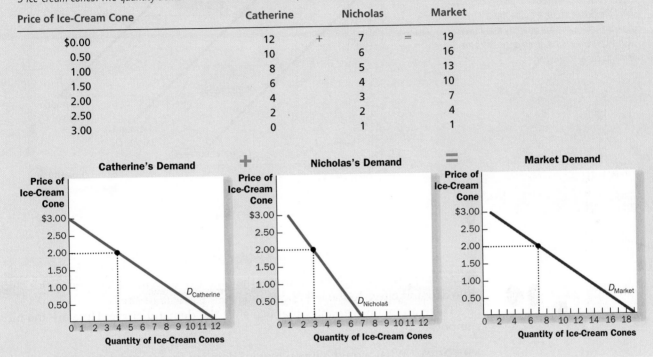

we will work most often with the market demand curve. The market demand curve shows how the total quantity demanded of a good varies as the price of the good varies, while all the other factors that affect how much consumers want to buy are held constant.

Shifts in the Demand Curve

The demand curve for ice cream shows how much ice cream people buy at any given price, holding constant the many other factors beyond price that influence consumers' buying decisions. As a result, this demand curve need not be stable over time. If something happens to alter the quantity demanded at any given price, the demand curve shifts. For example, suppose the Canadian Medical Association discovered that people who regularly eat ice cream live longer, healthier lives. The discovery would raise the demand for ice cream. At any given price, buyers would now want to purchase a larger quantity of ice cream, and the demand curve for ice cream would shift.

Figure 4.3 illustrates shifts in demand. Any change that increases the quantity demanded at every price, such as our imaginary discovery by the Canadian Medical Association, shifts the demand curve to the right and is called *an increase*

→ Outside influence creates a demand curve shift

FIGURE 4.3

Shifts in the Demand Curve

Any change that raises the quantity that buyers wish to purchase at a given price shifts the demand curve to the right. Any change that lowers the quantity that buyers wish to purchase at a given price shifts the demand curve to the left.

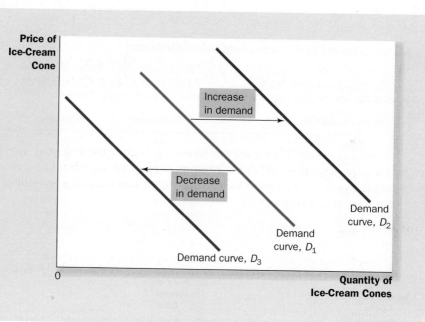

in demand. Any change that reduces the quantity demanded at every price shifts the demand curve to the left and is called *a decrease in demand.*

There are many variables that can shift the demand curve. Here are the most important:

Income   What would happen to your demand for ice cream if you lost your job one summer? Most likely, it would fall. A lower income means that you have less to spend in total, so you would have to spend less on some—and probably most—goods. If the demand for a good falls when income falls, the good is called a **normal good.**

Not all goods are normal goods. If the demand for a good rises when income falls, the good is called an **inferior good.** An example of an inferior good might be bus rides. As your income falls, you are less likely to buy a car or take a cab, and more likely to ride the bus.

Prices of Related Goods   Suppose that the price of frozen yogurt falls. The law of demand says that you will buy more frozen yogurt. At the same time, you will probably buy less ice cream. Because ice cream and frozen yogurt are both cold, sweet, creamy desserts, they satisfy similar desires. When a fall in the price of one good reduces the demand for another good, the two goods are called **substitutes.** Substitutes are often pairs of goods that are used in place of each other, such as hot dogs and hamburgers, sweaters and sweatshirts, and movie tickets and DVD rentals.

Now suppose that the price of hot fudge falls. According to the law of demand, you will buy more hot fudge. Yet, in this case, you will buy more ice cream as well because ice cream and hot fudge are often used together. When a fall in the price of one good raises the demand for another good, the two goods are called

normal good
a good for which, other things equal, an increase in income leads to an increase in demand

inferior good
a good for which, other things equal, an increase in income leads to a decrease in demand

substitutes
two goods for which an increase in the price of one leads to an increase in the demand for the other

complements. Complements are often pairs of goods that are used together, such as gasoline and automobiles, computers and software, and peanut butter and jelly.

Tastes The most obvious determinant of your demand is your tastes. If you like ice cream, you buy more of it. Economists normally do not try to explain people's tastes because tastes are based on historical and psychological forces that are beyond the realm of economics. Economists do, however, examine what happens when tastes change.

Expectations Your expectations about the future may affect your demand for a good or service today. If you expect to earn a higher income next month, you may be more willing to spend some of your current savings buying ice cream. If you expect the price of ice cream to fall tomorrow, you may be less willing to buy an ice-cream cone at today's price.

Number of Buyers In addition to the preceding factors, which influence the behaviour of individual buyers, market demand depends on the number of these buyers. If Peter, another consumer of ice cream, were to join Catherine and Nicholas, the quantity demanded in the market would be higher at every price and the demand curve would shift to the right.

Summary The demand curve shows what happens to the quantity demanded of a good when its price varies, holding constant all the other variables that influence buyers. When one of these other variables changes, the demand curve shifts. Table 4.1 lists all the variables that influence how much consumers choose to buy of a good.

If you have trouble remembering whether you need to shift or move along the demand curve, it helps to recall a lesson from the appendix to Chapter 2. A curve shifts when there is a change in a relevant variable that is not measured on either axis. Because the price is on the vertical axis, a change in price represents a movement along the demand curve. By contrast, income, the prices of related goods, tastes, expectations, and the number of buyers are not measured on either axis, so a change in one of these variables shifts the demand curve.

complements
two goods for which an increase in the price of one leads to a decrease in the demand for the other

→ IPTEN

TABLE 4.1

Variables That Influence Buyers

This table lists the variables that affect how much consumers choose to buy of any good. Notice the special role that the price of the good plays: A change in the good's price represents a movement along the demand curve, whereas a change in one of the other variables shifts the demand curve.

Variable	A Change in This Variable . . .
Price of the good itself	Represents a movement along the demand curve
Income	Shifts the demand curve
Prices of related goods	Shifts the demand curve
Tastes	Shifts the demand curve
Expectations	Shifts the demand curve
Number of buyers	Shifts the demand curve

What is the best way to stop this?

Case Study

TWO WAYS TO REDUCE THE QUANTITY OF SMOKING DEMANDED

Public policymakers often want to reduce the amount that people smoke because of smoking's adverse health effects. There are two ways that policy can attempt to achieve this goal.

One way to reduce smoking is to shift the demand curve for cigarettes and other tobacco products. Public service announcements, mandatory health warnings on cigarette packages, and the prohibition of cigarette advertising on television are all policies aimed at reducing the quantity of cigarettes demanded at any given price. If successful, these policies shift the demand curve for cigarettes to the left, as in panel (a) of Figure 4.4.

Alternatively, policymakers can try to raise the price of cigarettes. If the government taxes the manufacture of cigarettes, for example, cigarette companies pass much of this tax on to consumers in the form of higher prices. A higher price encourages smokers to reduce the number of cigarettes they smoke. In this case, the reduced amount of smoking does not represent a shift in the demand curve. Instead, it represents a movement along the same demand curve to a point with a higher price and lower quantity, as in panel (b) of Figure 4.4.

FIGURE 4.4

Shifts in the Demand Curve versus Movements along the Demand Curve

If warnings on cigarette packages convince smokers to smoke less, the demand curve for cigarettes shifts to the left. In panel (a), the demand curve shifts from D_1 to D_2. At a price of $10.00 per pack, the quantity demanded falls from 20 to 10 cigarettes per day, as reflected by the shift from point A to point B. By contrast, if a tax raises the price of cigarettes, the demand curve does not shift. Instead, we observe a movement to a different point on the demand curve. In panel (b), when the price rises from $10.00 to $20.00, the quantity demanded falls from 20 to 12 cigarettes per day, as reflected by the movement from point A to point C.

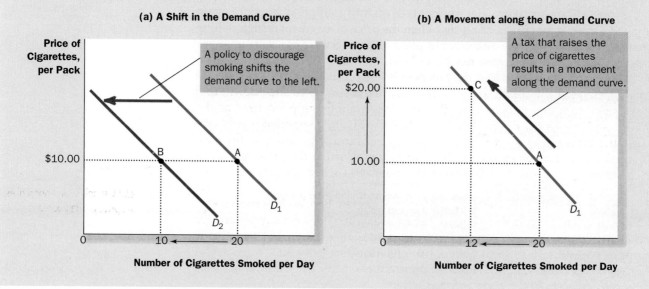

How much does the amount of smoking respond to changes in the price of cigarettes? Economists have attempted to answer this question by studying what happens when the tax on cigarettes changes. They have found that a 10-percent increase in the price causes a 4-percent reduction in the quantity demanded. Teenagers are found to be especially sensitive to the price of cigarettes: A 10-percent increase in the price causes a 12-percent drop in teenage smoking.

A related question is how the price of cigarettes affects the demand for illicit drugs, such as marijuana. Opponents of cigarette taxes often argue that tobacco and marijuana are substitutes, so that high cigarette prices encourage marijuana use. By contrast, many experts on substance abuse view tobacco as a "gateway drug" leading the young to experiment with other harmful substances. Most studies of the data are consistent with this view: They find that lower cigarette prices are associated with greater use of marijuana. In other words, tobacco and marijuana appear to be complements rather than substitutes. ●

QuickQuiz   Make up an example of a monthly demand schedule for pizza, and graph the implied demand curve. • Give an example of something that would shift this demand curve. • Would a change in the price of pizza shift this demand curve?

SUPPLY

We now turn to the other side of the market and examine the behaviour of sellers. Once again, to focus our thinking, let's consider the market for ice cream.

The Supply Curve: The Relationship between Price and Quantity Supplied

The **quantity supplied** of any good or service is the amount that sellers are willing and able to sell. There are many determinants of quantity supplied, but once again price plays a special role in our analysis. When the price of ice cream is high, selling ice cream is profitable, so the quantity supplied is large. Sellers of ice cream work long hours, buy many ice-cream machines, and hire many workers. By contrast, when the price of ice cream is low, the business is less profitable, so sellers produce less ice cream. At a low price, some sellers may even choose to shut down, and their quantity supplied falls to zero. Because the quantity supplied rises as the price rises and falls as the price falls, we say that the quantity supplied is *positively related* to the price of the good. This relationship between price and quantity supplied is called the **law of supply:** Other things equal, when the price of a good rises, the quantity supplied of the good also rises, and when the price falls, the quantity supplied falls as well.

The table in Figure 4.5 shows the quantity supplied by Ben, an ice-cream seller, at various prices of ice cream. At a price below $1.00, Ben does not supply any ice cream at all. As the price rises, he supplies a greater and greater quantity. This is the **supply schedule,** a table that shows the relationship between the price of a good and the quantity supplied, holding constant everything else that influences how much producers of the good want to sell.

quantity supplied
the amount of a good that sellers are willing and able to sell

law of supply
the claim that, other things equal, the quantity supplied of a good rises when the price of the good rises

supply schedule
a table that shows the relationship between the price of a good and the quantity supplied

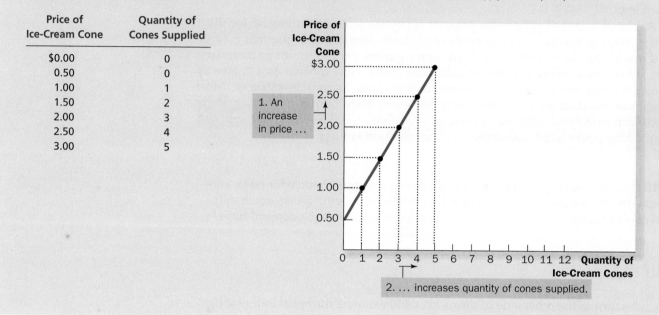

FIGURE 4.5

Ben's Supply Schedule and Supply Curve

The supply schedule shows the quantity supplied at each price. This supply curve, which graphs the supply schedule, shows how the quantity supplied of the good changes as its price varies. Because a higher price increases the quantity supplied, the supply curve slopes upward.

Price of Ice-Cream Cone	Quantity of Cones Supplied
$0.00	0
0.50	0
1.00	1
1.50	2
2.00	3
2.50	4
3.00	5

1. An increase in price …

2. … increases quantity of cones supplied.

supply curve
a graph of the relationship between the price of a good and the quantity supplied

The graph in Figure 4.5 uses the numbers from the table to illustrate the law of supply. The curve relating price and quantity supplied is called the **supply curve.** The supply curve slopes upward because, other things equal, a higher price means a greater quantity supplied.

Market Supply versus Individual Supply

Just as market demand is the sum of the demands of all buyers, market supply is the sum of the supplies of all sellers. The table in Figure 4.6 shows the supply schedules for two ice-cream producers—Ben and Jerry. At any price, Ben's supply schedule tells us the quantity of ice cream Ben supplies, and Jerry's supply schedule tells us the quantity of ice cream Jerry supplies. The market supply is the sum of the two individual supplies.

The graph in Figure 4.6 shows the supply curves that correspond to the supply schedules. As with demand curves, we sum the individual supply curves *horizontally* to obtain the market supply curve. That is, to find the total quantity supplied at any price, we add the individual quantities found on the horizontal axis of the individual supply curves. The market supply curve shows how the total quantity supplied varies as the price of the good varies, holding constant all of the other factors beyond price that influence producers' decisions about how much to sell.

FIGURE 4.6

Market Supply as the Sum of Individual Supplies

The quantity supplied in a market is the sum of the quantities supplied by all the sellers at each price. Thus, the market supply curve is found by adding horizontally the individual supply curves. At a price of $2, Ben supplies 3 ice-cream cones, and Jerry supplies 4 ice-cream cones. The quantity supplied in the market at this price is 7 cones.

Price of Ice-Cream Cone	Ben		Jerry		Market
$0.00	0	+	0	=	0
0.50	0		0		0
1.00	1		0		1
1.50	2		2		4
2.00	3		4		7
2.50	4		6		10
3.00	5		8		13

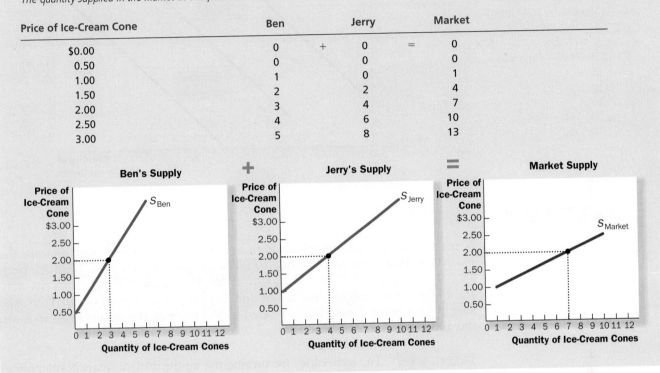

Shifts in the Supply Curve

Because the market supply curve holds other things constant, the curve shifts when one of these factors changes. For example, suppose the price of sugar falls. Sugar is an input into producing ice cream, so the fall in the price of sugar makes selling ice cream more profitable. This raises the supply of ice cream: At any given price, sellers are now willing to produce a larger quantity. Thus, the supply curve for ice cream shifts to the right.

Figure 4.7 illustrates shifts in supply. Any change that raises quantity supplied at every price, such as a fall in the price of sugar, shifts the supply curve to the right and is called *an increase in supply*. Similarly, any change that reduces the quantity supplied at every price shifts the supply curve to the left and is called *a decrease in supply*.

There are many variables that can shift the supply curve. Here are some of the most important variables:

Input Prices   To produce their output of ice cream, sellers use various inputs: cream, sugar, flavouring, ice-cream machines, the buildings in which the ice cream

→Outside influences create a supply curve shift.

FIGURE 4.7

Shifts in the Supply Curve

Any change that raises the quantity that sellers wish to produce at a given price shifts the supply curve to the right. Any change that lowers the quantity that sellers wish to produce at a given price shifts the supply curve to the left.

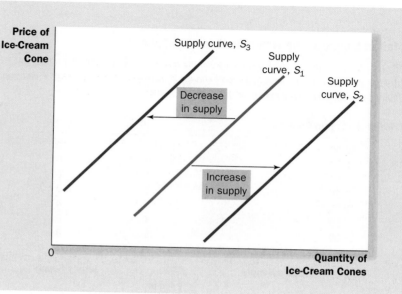

is made, and the labour of workers to mix the ingredients and operate the machines. When the price of one or more of these inputs rises, producing ice cream is less profitable, and firms supply less ice cream. If input prices rise substantially, a firm might shut down and supply no ice cream at all. Thus, the supply of a good is negatively related to the price of the inputs used to make the good.

Technology   The technology for turning the inputs into ice cream is yet another determinant of supply. The invention of the mechanized ice-cream machine, for example, reduced the amount of labour necessary to make ice cream. By reducing firms' costs, the advance in technology raised the supply of ice cream.

Expectations   The amount of ice cream a firm supplies today may depend on its expectations of the future. For example, if it expects the price of ice cream to rise in the future, it will put some of its current production into storage and supply less to the market today.

Number of Sellers   In addition to the preceding factors, which influence the behaviour of individual sellers, market supply depends on the number of sellers. If Ben or Jerry were to retire from the ice-cream business, the supply in the market would fall.

Summary   The supply curve shows what happens to the quantity supplied of a good when its price varies, holding constant all the other variables that influence sellers. When one of these other variables changes, the supply curve shifts. Table 4.2 lists all the variables that influence how much producers choose to sell of a good.

Once again, to help you remember whether you need to shift or move along the supply curve, keep in mind that a curve shifts only when there is a change

TABLE 4.2

Variables That Influence Sellers

This table lists the variables that affect how much producers choose to sell of any good. Notice the special role that the price of the good plays: A change in the good's price represents a movement along the supply curve, whereas a change in one of the other variables shifts the supply curve.

Variable	A Change in This Variable . . .
Price of the good itself	Represents a movement along the supply curve
Input prices	Shifts the supply curve
Technology	Shifts the supply curve
Expectations	Shifts the supply curve
Number of sellers	Shifts the supply curve

in a relevant variable that is not named on either axis. The price is on the vertical axis, so a change in price represents a movement along the supply curve. By contrast, because input prices, technology, expectations, and the number of sellers are not measured on either axis, a change in one of these variables shifts the supply curve.

QuickQuiz   Make up an example of a monthly supply schedule for pizza, and graph the implied supply curve. • Give an example of something that would shift this supply curve. • Would a change in the price of pizza shift this supply curve?

SUPPLY AND DEMAND TOGETHER

Having analyzed supply and demand separately, we now combine them to see how they determine the price and quantity of a good sold in the market.

Equilibrium

Figure 4.8 shows the market supply curve and market demand curve together. Notice that there is one point at which the supply and demand curves intersect. This point is called the market's **equilibrium**. The price at this intersection is called the **equilibrium price**, and the quantity is called the **equilibrium quantity**. Here the equilibrium price is $2.00 per cone, and the equilibrium quantity is 7 ice-cream cones.

The dictionary defines the word *equilibrium* as a situation in which various forces are in balance—and this also describes a market's equilibrium. *At the equilibrium price, the quantity of the good that buyers are willing to buy exactly balances the quantity that sellers are willing to sell.* The equilibrium price is sometimes called the *market-clearing price* because, at this price, everyone in the market has been satisfied: Buyers can buy all they want to buy, and sellers can sell all they want to sell.

The actions of buyers and sellers naturally move markets toward the equilibrium of supply and demand. To see why, consider what happens when the market price is not equal to the equilibrium price.

equilibrium
a situation in which the price has reached the level where quantity supplied equals quantity demanded

equilibrium price
the price that balances quantity supplied and quantity demanded

equilibrium quantity
the quantity supplied and the quantity demanded at the equilibrium price

FIGURE 4.8

The Equilibrium of Supply and Demand

The equilibrium is found where the supply and demand curves intersect. At the equilibrium price, the quantity supplied equals the quantity demanded. Here the equilibrium price is $2: At this price, 7 ice-cream cones are supplied, and 7 ice-cream cones are demanded.

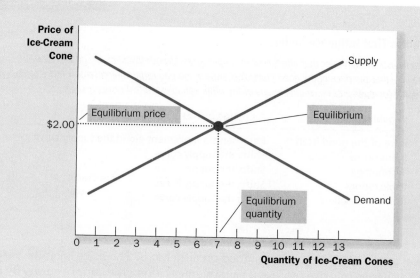

surplus

a situation in which quantity supplied is greater than quantity demanded

shortage

a situation in which quantity demanded is greater than quantity supplied

Suppose first that the market price is above the equilibrium price, as in panel (a) of Figure 4.9. At a price of $2.50 per cone, the quantity of the good supplied (10 cones) exceeds the quantity demanded (4 cones). There is a **surplus** of the good: Suppliers are unable to sell all they want at the going price. A surplus is sometimes called a situation of *excess supply.* When there is a surplus in the ice-cream market, sellers of ice cream find their freezers increasingly full of ice cream they would like to sell but cannot. They respond to the surplus by cutting their prices. Falling prices, in turn, increase the quantity demanded and decrease the quantity supplied. These changes represent movement along the supply and demand curves (not shifts in the curves). Prices continue to fall until the market reaches the equilibrium.

Suppose now that the market price is below the equilibrium price, as in panel (b) of Figure 4.9. In this case, the price is $1.50 per cone, and the quantity of the good demanded exceeds the quantity supplied. There is a **shortage** of the good: Demanders are unable to buy all they want at the going price. A shortage is sometimes called a situation of *excess demand.* When a shortage occurs in the ice-cream market, buyers have to wait in long lines for a chance to buy one of the few cones that are available. With too many buyers chasing too few goods, sellers can respond to the shortage by raising their prices without losing sales. These price increases cause the quantity demanded to fall and the quantity supplied to rise. Once again, these changes represent movements *along* the supply and demand curves, and they move the market toward the equilibrium.

Thus, regardless of whether the price starts off too high or too low, the activities of the many buyers and sellers automatically push the market price toward the equilibrium price. Once the market reaches its equilibrium, all buyers and sellers are satisfied, and there is no upward or downward pressure on the price.

FIGURE 4.9

Markets Not in Equilibrium

In panel (a), there is a surplus. Because the market price of $2.50 is above the equilibrium price, the quantity supplied (10 cones) exceeds the quantity demanded (4 cones). Suppliers try to increase sales by cutting the price of a cone, and this moves the price toward its equilibrium level. In panel (b), there is a shortage. Because the market price of $1.50 is below the equilibrium price, the quantity demanded (10 cones) exceeds the quantity supplied (4 cones). With too many buyers chasing too few goods, suppliers can take advantage of the shortage by raising the price. Hence, in both cases, the price adjustment moves the market toward the equilibrium of supply and demand.

How quickly equilibrium is reached varies from market to market, depending on how quickly prices adjust. In most free markets, surpluses and shortages are only temporary because prices eventually move toward their equilibrium levels. Indeed, this phenomenon is so pervasive that it is called the **law of supply and demand:** The price of any good adjusts to bring the quantity supplied and quantity demanded for that good into balance.

law of supply and demand
the claim that the price of any good adjusts to bring the quantity supplied and the quantity demanded for that good into balance

Three Steps to Analyzing Changes in Equilibrium

So far we have seen how supply and demand together determine a market's equilibrium, which in turn determines the price of the good and the quantity of the good that buyers buy and sellers sell. The equilibrium price and quantity depend on the position of the supply and demand curves. When some event shifts one of these curves, the equilibrium in the market changes, resulting in a new price and a new quantity exchanged between buyers and sellers.

When analyzing how some event affects a market, we proceed in three steps. First, we decide whether the event shifts the supply curve, the demand curve, or in some cases, both curves. Second, we decide whether the curve shifts to the right or to the left. Third, we use the supply-and-demand diagram to compare

TABLE 4.3

A Three-Step Program for Analyzing Changes in Equilibrium

1. Decide whether the event shifts the supply or demand curve (or perhaps both).
2. Decide in which direction the curve shifts.
3. Use the supply-and-demand diagram to see how the shift changes the equilibrium price and quantity.

the initial equilibrium and the new equilibrium, which shows how the shift affects the equilibrium price and quantity. Table 4.3 summarizes these three steps. To see how this recipe is used, let's consider various events that might affect the market for ice cream.

Example: A Change in Market Equilibrium Due to a Shift in Demand

Suppose that one summer the weather is very hot. How does this event affect the market for ice cream? To answer this question, let's follow our three steps.

1. The hot weather affects the demand curve by changing people's taste for ice cream. That is, the weather changes the amount of ice cream that people want to buy at any given price. The supply curve is unchanged because the weather does not directly affect the firms that sell ice cream.
2. Because hot weather makes people want to eat more ice cream, the demand curve shifts to the right. Figure 4.10 shows this increase in demand as the shift in the demand curve from D_1 to D_2. This shift indicates that the quantity of ice cream demanded is higher at every price.
3. At the old price of $2, there is now an excess demand for ice cream, and this shortage induces firms to raise the price. As Figure 4.10 shows, the increase in demand raises the equilibrium price from $2.00 to $2.50 and the equilibrium quantity from 7 to 10 cones. In other words, the hot weather increases the price of ice cream and the quantity of ice cream sold.

Shifts in Curves versus Movements along Curves

Notice that when hot weather drives up the price of ice cream, the quantity of ice cream that firms supply rises, even though the supply curve remains the same. In this case, economists say there has been an increase in "quantity supplied" but no change in "supply."

"Supply" refers to the position of the supply curve, whereas the "quantity supplied" refers to the amount suppliers wish to sell. In this example, supply does not change because the weather does not alter firms' desire to sell at any given price. Instead, the hot weather alters consumers' desire to buy at any given price and thereby shifts the demand curve. The increase in demand causes the equilibrium price to rise. When the price rises, the quantity supplied rises. This increase in quantity supplied is represented by the movement along the supply curve.

FIGURE 4.10

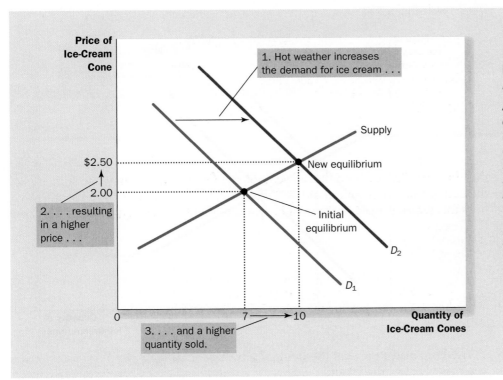

Price of Ice-Cream Cone

1. Hot weather increases the demand for ice cream . . .

Supply

$2.50 .... New equilibrium

2.00

2. . . . resulting in a higher price . . .

Initial equilibrium

D_2

D_1

0   7 →10   **Quantity of Ice-Cream Cones**

3. . . . and a higher quantity sold.

How an Increase in Demand Affects the Equilibrium

An event that raises quantity demanded at any given price shifts the demand curve to the right. The equilibrium price and the equilibrium quantity both rise. Here, an abnormally hot summer causes buyers to demand more ice cream. The demand curve shifts from D_1 to D_2, which causes the equilibrium price to rise from $2.00 to $2.50 and the equilibrium quantity to rise from 7 to 10 cones.

To summarize, a shift *in* the supply curve is called a "change in supply," and a shift *in* the demand curve is called a "change in demand." A movement *along* a fixed supply curve is called a "change in the quantity supplied," and a movement *along* a fixed demand curve is called a "change in the quantity demanded."

Example: A Change in Market Equilibrium Due to a Shift in Supply

Suppose that, during another summer, a hurricane destroys part of the sugar cane crop and drives up the price of sugar. How does this event affect the market for ice cream? Once again, to answer this question, we follow our three steps.

1. The change in the price of sugar, an input into making ice cream, affects the supply curve. By raising the costs of production, it reduces the amount of ice cream that firms want to produce and sell at any given price. The demand curve does not change because the higher cost of inputs does not directly affect the amount of ice cream households wish to buy.
2. The supply curve shifts to the left because, at every price, the total amount that firms are willing to sell is reduced. Figure 4.11 illustrates this decrease in supply as a shift in the supply curve from S_1 to S_2.
3. At the old price of $2, there is now an excess demand for ice cream, and this shortage causes firms to raise the price. As Figure 4.11 shows, the shift in the supply curve raises the equilibrium price from $2.00 to $2.50 and lowers the equilibrium quantity from 7 to 4 cones. As a result of the sugar price increase, the price of ice cream rises, and the quantity of ice cream sold falls.

FIGURE 4.11

How a Decrease in Supply Affects the Equilibrium

An event that reduces quantity supplied at any given price shifts the supply curve to the left. The equilibrium price rises, and the equilibrium quantity falls. Here, an increase in the price of sugar (an input) causes sellers to supply less ice cream. The supply curve shifts from S_1 to S_2, which causes the equilibrium price of ice cream to rise from $2.00 to $2.50 and the equilibrium quantity to fall from 7 to 4 cones.

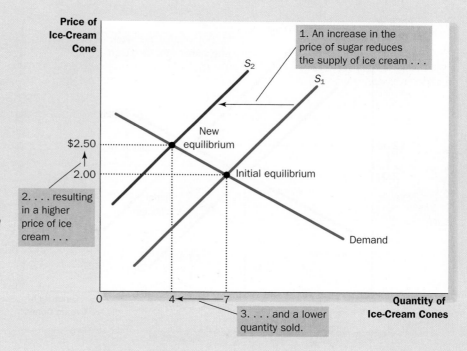

1. An increase in the price of sugar reduces the supply of ice cream . . .

2. . . . resulting in a higher price of ice cream . . .

3. . . . and a lower quantity sold.

Price of Ice-Cream Cone

Quantity of Ice-Cream Cones

Example: Shifts in Both Supply and Demand   Now suppose that the heat wave and the hurricane occur during the same summer. To analyze this combination of events, we again follow our three steps.

1. We determine that both curves must shift. The hot weather affects the demand curve because it alters the amount of ice cream that households want to buy at any given price. At the same time, when the hurricane drives up sugar prices, it alters the supply curve for ice cream because it changes the amount of ice cream that firms want to sell at any given price.
2. The curves shift in the same directions as they did in our previous analysis: The demand curve shifts to the right, and the supply curve shifts to the left. Figure 4.12 illustrates these shifts.
3. As Figure 4.12 shows, there are three possible outcomes that might result, depending on the relative size of the demand and supply shifts. In all cases, the equilibrium price rises. In panel (a), where demand increases substantially while supply falls just a little, the equilibrium quantity also rises. By contrast, in panel (b), where supply falls substantially while demand rises just a little, the equilibrium quantity falls. In panel (c) supply and demand both change by the same magnitude such that the equilibrium quantity stays the same but the price rises. Thus, these events certainly raise the price of ice cream, but their impact on the amount of ice cream sold is ambiguous (that is, it could go lower, higher, or remain the same).

FIGURE 4.12

A Shift in Both Supply and Demand

Here we observe a simultaneous increase in demand and decrease in supply. Three outcomes are possible. In panel (a), the equilibrium price rises from P_1 to P_2, and the equilibrium quantity rises from Q_1 to Q_2. In panel (b), the equilibrium price again rises from P_1 to P_2, but the equilibrium quantity falls from Q_1 to Q_2. Finally, in panel (c), the equilibrium price rises from P_1 to P_2, but the equilibrium quantity remains unchanged at Q_1.

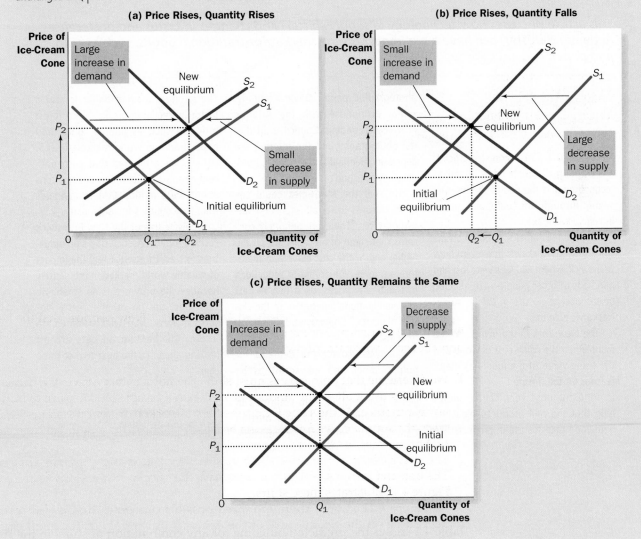

(a) Price Rises, Quantity Rises

(b) Price Rises, Quantity Falls

(c) Price Rises, Quantity Remains the Same

Summary   We have just seen three examples of how to use supply and demand curves to analyze a change in equilibrium. Whenever an event shifts the supply curve, the demand curve, or perhaps both curves, you can use these tools to predict how the event will alter the price and quantity sold in equilibrium.

IN THE NEWS

SUPPLY, DEMAND, AND TECHNOLOGY

This article discusses how technology (a supply shifter) and changes in tastes and preferences (a demand shifter) can have a big impact on the market for traditional goods, such as pulp and paper.

Analysts Say Pulp Mill Closure Signals Tougher Times Ahead

FREDERICTON (CP) – Forestry officials are warning of tough times ahead as technology and the rise of the Internet swing through the pulp and paper industry like an axe.

The axe fell earlier this month on the small town of Nackawic in western New Brunswick, where 400 jobs were lost and hundreds of other people were affected by the abrupt closure of the St. Anne-Nackawic pulp mill.

The New York-based owners of the mill blamed the rising cost of wood and the rising value of the loonie as major reasons for the closure.

Industry observers say it didn't help that the mill produced bleached hardwood pulp for use in products like photographic paper. David Chaundy, senior economist with the Atlantic Provinces Economic Council, said digital photography and the Internet are depressing demand for items like photographic paper and newsprint.

He said the Maritimes could see more closures in its all-important forestry sector. "There are definitely concerns that some of our mills are on the higher end of the cost curve and therefore are more vulnerable to reductions in commodity prices, or, if they're part of a multinational operation, to the closure of plants," Chaundy said. "That risk remains."

Analysts expect the demand for pulp, lumber and newsprint to be weaker over the next two to three years. Competition from countries in the southern hemisphere is hurting Canadian pulp and paper production.

The strong Canadian dollar is also a factor in declining profits, since forest products such as lumber, pulp, and paper trade on world markets in U.S. dollars. It's estimated that each one-cent rise in the Canadian dollar drains about $500 million Cdn in revenues from the country's forest industry.

Yvon Poitras of the New Brunswick Forest Products Association said industries in New Brunswick feel the impact of volatile world markets more acutely because the province is so small. He said there are no other forestry closures in New Brunswick's immediate future. But he said all bets are off looking ahead to the next two or three years.

Source: Canadian Press, "Tough times seen for forestry industry," September 27, 2004. Copyright by The Canadian Press.

Table 4.4 shows the predicted outcome for any combination of shifts in the two curves. To make sure you understand how to use the tools of supply and demand, pick a few entries in this table and make sure you can explain to yourself why the table contains the prediction it does.

QuickQuiz   On the appropriate diagram, show what happens to the market for pizza if the price of tomatoes rises. • On a separate diagram, show what happens to the market for pizza if the price of hamburgers falls.

TABLE 4.4

What Happens to Price and Quantity When Supply or Demand Shifts?

As a quick quiz, make sure you can explain each of the entries in this table using a supply-and-demand diagram.

	No Change in Supply	An Increase in Supply	A Decrease in Supply
No Change in Demand	*P* same *Q* same	*P* down *Q* up	*P* up *Q* down
An Increase in Demand	*P* up *Q* up	*P* ambiguous *Q* up	*P* up *Q* ambiguous
A Decrease in Demand	*P* down *Q* down	*P* down *Q* ambiguous	*P* ambiguous *Q* down

CONCLUSION: HOW PRICES ALLOCATE RESOURCES

This chapter has analyzed supply and demand in a single market. Although our discussion has centred around the market for ice cream, the lessons learned here apply in most other markets as well. Whenever you go to a store to buy something, you are contributing to the demand for that item. Whenever you look for a job, you are contributing to the supply of labour services. Because supply and demand are such pervasive economic phenomena, the model of supply and demand is a powerful tool for analysis. We will be using this model repeatedly in the following chapters.

One of the ten principles of economics discussed in Chapter 1 is that markets are usually a good way to organize economic activity. Although it is still too early to judge whether market outcomes are good or bad, in this chapter we have begun to see how markets work. In any economic system, scarce resources have to be allocated among competing uses. Market economies harness the forces of supply and demand to serve that end. Supply and demand together determine the prices of the economy's many different goods and services; prices in turn are the signals that guide the allocation of resources.

For example, consider the allocation of beachfront land. Because the amount of this land is limited, not everyone can enjoy the luxury of living by the beach. Who gets this resource? The answer is: Whoever is willing to pay the price. The price of beachfront land adjusts until the quantity of land demanded exactly balances the quantity supplied. Thus, in market economies, prices are the mechanism for rationing scarce resources.

Similarly, prices determine who produces each good and how much is produced. For instance, consider farming. Because we need food to survive, it is crucial that some people work on farms. What determines who is a farmer and who is not? In a free society, there is no government planning agency making this decision and ensuring an adequate supply of food. Instead, the allocation of workers to farms is based on the job decisions of millions of workers. This decentralized system works well because these decisions depend on prices. The prices of food and the wages of farm workers (the price of their labour) adjust to ensure that enough people choose to be farmers.

If a person had never seen a market economy in action, the whole idea might seem preposterous. Economies are large groups of people engaged in many interdependent activities. What prevents decentralized decision making from degenerating into chaos? What coordinates the actions of the millions of people with their varying abilities and desires? What ensures that what needs to be done does, in fact, get done? The answer, in a word, is *prices*. If market economies are guided by an invisible hand, as Adam Smith famously suggested, then the price system is the baton that the invisible hand uses to conduct the economic orchestra.

SUMMARY

- Economists use the model of supply and demand to analyze competitive markets. In a competitive market, there are many buyers and sellers, each of whom has little or no influence on the market price.

- The demand curve shows how the quantity of a good demanded depends on the price. According to the law of demand, as the price of a good falls, the quantity demanded rises. Therefore, the demand curve slopes downward.

- In addition to price, other determinants of how much consumers want to buy include income, the prices of substitutes and complements, tastes, expectations, and the number of buyers. If one of these factors changes, the demand curve shifts.

- The supply curve shows how the quantity of a good supplied depends on the price. According to the law of supply, as the price of a good rises, the quantity supplied rises. Therefore, the supply curve slopes upward.

- In addition to price, other determinants of how much producers want to sell include input prices, technology, expectations, and the number of sellers. If one of these factors changes, the supply curve shifts.

- The intersection of the supply and demand curves determines the market equilibrium. At the equilibrium price, the quantity demanded equals the quantity supplied.

- The behaviour of buyers and sellers naturally drives markets toward their equilibrium. When the market price is above the equilibrium price, there is a surplus of the good, which causes the market price to fall. When the market price is below the equilibrium price, there is a shortage, which causes the market price to rise.

- To analyze how any event influences a market, we use the supply-and-demand diagram to examine how the event affects the equilibrium price and quantity. To do this we follow three steps. First, we decide whether the event shifts the supply curve or the demand curve (or both). Second, we decide which direction the curve shifts. Third, we compare the new equilibrium with the initial equilibrium.

- In market economies, prices are the signals that guide economic decisions and thereby allocate scarce resources. For every good in the economy, the price ensures that supply and demand are in balance. The equilibrium price then determines how much of the good buyers choose to purchase and how much sellers choose to produce.

KEY CONCEPTS

market, p. 68
competitive market, p. 68
quantity demanded, p. 69
law of demand, p. 69
demand schedule, p. 69
demand curve, p. 70
normal good, p. 72

inferior good, p. 72
substitutes, p. 72
complements, p. 73
quantity supplied, p. 75
law of supply, p. 75
supply schedule, p. 75
supply curve, p. 76

equilibrium, p. 79
equilibrium price, p. 79
equilibrium quantity, p. 79
surplus, p. 80
shortage, p. 80
law of supply and demand, p. 81

QUESTIONS FOR REVIEW

1. What is a competitive market? Briefly describe the types of markets other than perfectly competitive markets.

2. What are the demand schedule and the demand curve, and how are they related? Why does the demand curve slope downward?

3. Does a change in consumers' tastes lead to a movement along the demand curve or a shift in the demand curve? Does a change in price lead to a movement along the demand curve or a shift in the demand curve?

4. Popeye's income declines and, as a result, he buys more spinach. Is spinach an inferior or a normal good? What happens to Popeye's demand curve for spinach?

5. What are the supply schedule and the supply curve, and how are they related? Why does the supply curve slope upward?

6. Does a change in producers' technology lead to a movement along the supply curve or a shift in the supply curve? Does a change in price lead to a movement along the supply curve or a shift in the supply curve?

7. Define the equilibrium of a market. Describe the forces that move a market toward its equilibrium.

8. Beer and pizza are complements because they are often enjoyed together. When the price of beer rises, what happens to the supply, demand, quantity supplied, quantity demanded, and the price in the market for pizza?

9. Describe the role of prices in market economies.

PROBLEMS AND APPLICATIONS

1. Explain each of the following statements using supply-and-demand diagrams.
    a. When a cold snap hits Florida, the price of orange juice rises in supermarkets throughout Canada.
    b. When the weather turns warm in Quebec every summer, the prices of hotel rooms in Caribbean resorts plummet.
    c. When a war breaks out in the Middle East, the price of gasoline rises, while the price of a used SUV falls.

2. "An increase in the demand for notebooks raises the quantity of notebooks demanded, but not the quantity supplied." Is this statement true or false? Explain.

3. Consider the market for minivans. For each of the events listed below, identify which of the determinants of demand or supply are affected. Also indicate whether demand or supply is increased or decreased. Then show the effect on the price and quantity of minivans.
    a. People decide to have more children.
    b. A strike by steelworkers raises steel prices.
    c. Engineers develop new automated machinery for the production of minivans.
    d. The price of SUVs rises.
    e. A stock market crash lowers people's wealth.

4. Over the past 20 years, technological advances have reduced the cost of computer chips. How do you think this has affected the market for computers? For computer software? For typewriters?

5. Using supply-and-demand diagrams, show the effect of the following events on the market for sweatshirts.
    a. A hurricane in South Carolina damages the cotton crop.
    b. The price of leather jackets falls.
    c. All universities require morning calisthenics in appropriate attire.
    d. New knitting machines are invented.

6. Suppose that in the year 2010, the number of births was temporarily high. How will this baby boom affect the price of baby-sitting services in 2015 and 2025? (Hint: Five-year-olds need baby-sitters, whereas fifteen-year-olds can be baby-sitters.)

7. Ketchup is a complement (as well as a condiment) for hot dogs. If the price of hot dogs rises, what happens to the market for ketchup? For tomatoes? For tomato juice? For orange juice?

8. The market for pizza has the following demand and supply schedules:

Price	Quantity Demanded	Quantity Supplied
$4	135	26
5	104	53
6	81	81
7	68	98
8	53	110
9	39	121

Graph the demand and supply curves. What is the equilibrium price and quantity in this market? If the actual price in this market was *above* the equilibrium price, what would drive the market toward the equilibrium? If the actual price in this market was *below* the equilibrium price, what would drive the market toward the equilibrium?

9. Because bagels and cream cheese are often eaten together, they are complements.
   a. We observe that both the equilibrium price of cream cheese and the equilibrium quantity of bagels have risen. What could be responsible for this pattern—a fall in the price of flour or a fall in the price of milk? Illustrate and explain your answer.
   b. Suppose instead that the equilibrium price of cream cheese has risen but the equilibrium quantity of bagels has fallen. What could be responsible for this pattern—a rise in the price of flour or a rise in the price of milk? Illustrate and explain your answer.

10. Suppose that the price of hockey tickets at your school is determined by market forces. Currently, the demand and supply schedules are as follows:

Price	Quantity Demanded	Quantity Supplied
$4	10 000	8000
8	8 000	8000
12	6 000	8000
16	4 000	8000
20	2 000	8000

a. Draw the demand and supply curves. What is unusual about this supply curve? Why might this be true?
b. What are the equilibrium price and quantity of tickets?
c. Your school plans to increase total enrollment next year by 5000 students. The additional students will have the following demand schedule:

Price	Quantity Demanded
$4	4000
8	3000
12	2000
16	1000
20	0

Now add the old demand schedule and the demand schedule for the new students to calculate the new demand schedule for the entire school. What will be the new equilibrium price and quantity?

11. Consider the markets for DVD movies, TV screens, and tickets to movie theatres.
   a. For each pair, identify whether they are complements or substitutes:
      —DVDs and TV screens
      —DVDs and movie tickets
      —TV screens and movie tickets
   b. Suppose a technological advance reduces the cost of manufacturing TV screens. Draw a diagram to show what happens to the market for TV screens.
   c. Draw two more diagrams to show how the change in the market for TV screens affects the markets for DVDs and movie tickets

12. Market research has revealed the following information about the market for chocolate bars: The demand schedule can be represented by the equation $Q^D = 1600 - 300P$, where Q^D is the quantity demanded and P is the price. The supply schedule can be represented by the equation $Q^S = 1400 + 700P$, where Q^S is the quantity supplied.
   a. Calculate the equilibrium price and quantity in the market for chocolate bars.
   b. Say that in response to a major industry ad campaign, the demand schedule for chocolate bars shifted to the right, as

represented by the equation $Q^D = 1800 - 300P$. What happens to the equilibrium price and quantity of chocolate bars in this case?

c. Returning to the original demand schedule, say that the price of cocoa beans, a major ingredient in the production of chocolate bars, increased because of a drought in sub-Saharan Africa, a major producer of cocoa, changing the supply schedule to $Q^S = 1100 + 700P$. What happens to the equilibrium price and quantity in this case?

13. A survey shows an increase in drug use by young people. In the ensuing debate, two hypotheses are proposed:
   —Reduced police efforts have increased the availability of drugs on the street.
   —Cutbacks in educational efforts have decreased awareness of the dangers of drug addiction.
   a. Use supply-and-demand diagrams to show how each of these hypotheses could lead to an increase in the quantity of drugs consumed.
   b. How could information on what has happened to the price of drugs help us to distinguish between these explanations?

14. Consider the following events: Scientists reveal that consumption of oranges decreases the risk of diabetes and, at the same time, farmers use a new fertilizer that makes orange trees more productive. Illustrate and explain what effect these changes have on the equilibrium price and quantity of oranges.

15. Suppose that the demand curve for concert tickets is linear. When the price of a ticket is $5.00, the number of tickets purchased is 1000; when the price of a ticket is $15.00, the number of tickets purchased is 200. Find the slope of the demand curve.

16. At a price of $320 per tonne, the supply of wheat in Canada is 25 million tonnes and the demand is 26 million tonnes. When the price increases to $340 per tonne, the supply increases to 27 million tonnes and the demand decreases to 22 million tonnes. Assume that both the demand and supply curves are linear.
   a. What is the equation for the demand curve for wheat?
   b. What is the equation of the supply curve for wheat?
   c. Using these equations, what is the equilibrium price and quantity of wheat?

17. The demand and supply functions for hockey sticks are given by

$$Q^D = 286 - 20P$$
$$Q^S = 88 + 40P$$

   a. Graph the supply and the demand curves, clearly showing the intercepts and indicating the slopes of the two curves.
   b. Determine the equilibrium price and quantity of hockey sticks.
   c. Suppose that both the men's and the women's teams win Olympic gold medals, causing an increase in the demand for hockey sticks across the country to $Q^D = 328 - 20P$. What impact does this have on the price of hockey sticks and the quantity sold?

http://   For more study tools, please visit www.nelson.com/mankiwmicro6e.

APPENDIX: THE MATHEMATICS OF MARKET EQUILIBRIUM

The appendix to Chapter 2 presented a review of how economists use graphs to help explain mathematical relationships among variables. We have already seen that these are very valuable tools to help us understand economic relationships.

Sometimes, however, it is useful to be more precise about the nature of these relationships, which requires the explicit use of mathematics. In this appendix, we illustrate how simple mathematical methods can help us solve algebraically for a market's equilibrium price and quantity using supply and demand curves.

In Figure 4.8, we saw how the equilibrium price and quantity for a good are determined by the intersection of the supply and demand curves. Although they don't have to be, for simplicity, we often draw these curves as linear (so our "curves" are actually straight lines!).

The general equation for a linear demand curve is as follows:

$$Q^D = a - bP$$

where Q^D is the quantity demanded and P is the price of the good. The letters a and b are referred to as *demand parameters*. They represent positive numbers that capture the various things that affect demand. Sometimes economists like to use letters or symbols rather than numbers in order to keep the analysis general.

→ a : outside influences

The parameter a can be viewed as incorporating all of the things other than the own price of the good that affect demand (income, prices of other goods, number of buyers, etc.). As these are held constant along the demand curve, we can incorporate them all into the parameter a, which is constant. A change in the parameter a can then be used to represent a shift in the demand curve due to changes in things other than the own price of the good.

The parameter b reflects the sensitivity of demand to changes in its own price. Since b is a positive number and there is a minus sign in front of bP, as the price of the good increases, the quantity demanded falls. Of course, this is because demand curves are downward sloping.

As we have seen, we plot demand curves by putting the price on the vertical axis (the y-axis) and the quantity demanded on the horizontal axis (the x-axis). For a linear demand curve we can determine its intercept with the price axis (the y-intercept) by setting $Q^D = 0$ and solving the demand equation for P. The y-intercept is therefore determined by $0 = a - bP$; solving for P gives $P = a/b$. Similarly, the intercept with the quantity axis (the x-intercept) is determined by setting $P = 0$ and solving for Q^D, which gives $Q^D = a$. Figure 4A.1 plots the demand curve for a general linear demand curve given by the equation $Q^D = a - bP$, identifying the x- and y-intercepts determined above.

We saw in the appendix to Chapter 2 that the slope of a linear demand curve is equal to the "rise over the run" as we move along the line. The "rise" is the change in price measured along the y-axis ($\triangle y$, where you'll recall that Δ is the Greek letter delta, which stands for "change in") as we move from one point on the demand curve to another; the "run" is the change in quantity demanded measured along the x-axis ($\triangle x$). So the slope of the demand curve is measured as $\triangle y / \triangle x$, as we move from one point on the demand curve to another.

Linear Demand and Supply Curves

This diagram illustrates a general linear demand curve given by $Q^D = a - bP$, where a and b are demand parameters, both of which are positive. It also illustrates a general linear supply curve given by $Q^S = c + dP$, where c and d are supply parameters, with d being positive while c is negative. The x-intercept for the demand curve is given by $Q^D = a$ and the y-intercept by $P = a/b$. The slope of the demand curve is $\triangle y/\triangle x = -1/b$. The x-intercept for the supply curve is given by $Q^S = c$, which is negative in this case, and the y-intercept is positive at $P = -c/d$. The slope of the supply curve is $\triangle y/\triangle x = 1/d$. The equilibrium price is determined by setting $Q^D = Q^S$ and solving for $P = (a - c)/(b + d)$. The equilibrium quantity is determined by substituting the equilibrium price into either the demand or supply curve and solving for $Q = (ad + bc)/(b + d)$.

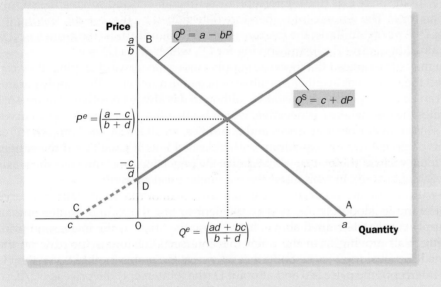

Since the slope of a line is constant all along the line (that is what makes it a line!), we can use any two points on the demand curve to determine its slope. Two particularly useful points on the demand curve are the *x*- and *y*-intercepts determined above. We can use these points to determine the "rise over the run" from moving from the point on the demand curve that intersects the *x*-axis (point A in Figure 4A.1) to the point on the demand curve that intersects the *y*-axis (point B). In this case, the "rise" is the increase in price resulting from moving from point A to point B. At point A (the *x*-intercept), the price is zero and at point B (the *y*-intercept) the price is a/b, therefore the "rise" in moving from point A to point B is $\triangle y = a/b$. Similarly, the "run" is the decrease in quantity demanded resulting from moving from point A to point B. At point A (the *x*-intercept), the quantity demanded is *a*, and at point B (the *y*-intercept), the quantity demanded is 0, therefore the "run" in moving from point A to point B is $\triangle x = -a$. So the slope of the demand curve, the "rise over the run" in moving from point A to point B, is $\triangle y/\triangle x = -(a/b)/a = -1/b$.

The general equation for a linear supply curve is

$$Q^S = c + dP$$

→ C: Outside influences

where Q^S is quantity supplied and P is again the price of the good. The letters c and d are referred to as the *supply parameters*. The parameter c can be viewed as incorporating all of the factors other than the own price of the good that affect supply (technology, input prices, number of sellers, etc.). As these things are held constant along the supply curve, we can incorporate them all into the parameter c, which is constant. A change in the parameter c can thus be used to represent a shift in the supply curve. As will be discussed below, c may be either a positive or a negative number.

The parameter d, which is positive, reflects the sensitivity of supply to changes in its own price. Because d is a positive number and there is a plus sign in front of dP, as the price of the good increases, the quantity supplied increases because supply curves are upward sloping.

As with the demand curve, we can determine the intercept of the linear supply curve with the price axis (the y-intercept) by setting $Q^S = 0$ and solving the supply equation for P. The y-intercept is therefore determined by $0 = c + dP$; solving for P gives $P = -c/d$. Similarly, the intercept with the quantity axis (the x-intercept) is determined by setting $P = 0$ and solving for Q^S, which gives $Q^S = c$.

You may have noticed that because supply curves are upward sloping, they can intersect the x- or y-axis at either a positive or negative number, so the supply parameter c can be either positive or negative (although d is always positive). Figure 4A.1 illustrates the case where c is negative, which is often the case. Since supply curves make sense only for positive prices and quantities, we illustrate the "projection" of the curve into the negative quadrant with a dashed line. We see that if the supply curve intersects the y-axis at a positive price, the projection must intersect the x-axis at a negative quantity in which case the parameter c is negative.

As with the demand curve we can use any two points on the supply curve to determine its slope. Again, it is convenient to use the x- and y-intercepts of the supply curve determined above. In this case the "rise" is the increase in price resulting from moving from the point that intersects the x-axis (point C on the projected supply curve) to the point that intersects the y-axis (point D). At point C (the x-intercept), the price is 0 and at point D (the y-intercept) the price is $-c/d$, so the "rise" in moving from point C to point D on the supply curve is $\triangle y = -c/d$ (which is positive because c is a negative number in this case). Similarly, the "run" is the increase in quantity supplied resulting from moving from point C to point D. At point C (the x-intercept), the quantity supplied is c, and at point D (the y-intercept) the quantity supplied is 0, therefore the "run" is $\triangle x = -c$. So the slope of the supply curve, the "rise over the run", in moving from point C to point D, is $\triangle y / \triangle x = (-c/d)/-c = 1/d$.

We have seen that the market equilibrium price and quantity are determined by the intersection of the demand and supply curves. The equilibrium price is such that the quantity demanded exactly equals the quantity supplied. Using our equations for linear demand and supply curves, we can therefore determine the equilibrium price by setting quantity demanded equal to quantity supplied ($Q^D = Q^S$) and solving for the price P:

$$a - bP = c + dP$$

Using simple algebra to gather terms with P on the left-hand side and the other terms on the right-hand side gives

$$P(b + d) = a - c$$

Dividing both sides by $(b + d)$ to solve for P gives an equilibrium price of

$$P^e = \frac{(a - c)}{(b + d)}$$

You will notice that in order for the equilibrium price to be positive, the demand parameter a must be greater than the supply parameter c. Since a is positive, in the case where c is negative (as in the case illustrated in Figure 4A.1), this is no problem. But if c is a positive number it must be less than a.

To determine the equilibrium quantity in the market, substitute the equilibrium price into the equation for quantity demanded and do some simple algebra to get:

$$Q^D = a - bP^e = a - b\frac{(a - c)}{(b + d)} = \frac{(ad + bc)}{(b + d)}$$

Alternatively, we could substitute the equilibrium price into the equation for the quantity supplied and do some simple algebra to get

$$Q^S = c + dP^e = c + d\frac{(a - c)}{(b + d)} = \frac{(ad + bc)}{(b + d)}$$

As we would expect, at the equilibrium price, quantity demanded equals quantity supplied (denoted Q^e).

The equilibrium for the general linear demand and supply curves is illustrated in Figure 4A.1.

This discussion has taken place using letters (a, b, c, d) for the demand and supply parameters. As mentioned earlier, economists often do this in models in order to keep things general. Of course, demand and supply schedules for particular goods may be represented by particular numerical values for these demand parameters.

For example, let's say that the demand schedule for a good is given by $Q^D = 20 - 2P$ and the supply schedule is given by $Q^S = -10 + 4P$. In this case, $a = 20$, $b = 2$, $c = -10$, and $d = 4$. Using the above general expressions for the x- and y-intercepts and the slopes of the demand and supply curves, we see that for the demand curve, the x-intercept occurs at $Q^D = a = 20$, the y-intercept occurs at $P = a/b = 10$, and the slope of the demand curve is $\triangle y/\triangle x = -1/b = -1/2$. For the supply curve, the x-intercept occurs at $Q^S = c = -10$, the y-intercept occurs at $P = -c/d = 2.5$, and the slope is $\triangle y/\triangle x = 1/d = 1/4$.

We can also substitute the values for the demand and supply parameters into the general equations for the equilibrium prices and quantities for linear demand and supply curves that we derived above to determine an equilibrium price and quantity. The equilibrium price is therefore

$$P^e = \frac{(a - c)}{(b + d)} = \frac{(20 + 10)}{(2 + 4)} = \frac{30}{6} = 5$$

→ Consu :ss sometimes
take t xes to respond
to change...

and the equilibrium quantity is

$$Q^e = \frac{(ad + bc)}{(b + d)} = \frac{(80 - 20)}{(2 + 4)} = \frac{60}{6} = 10$$

Alternatively, we could simply follow the general steps discussed above for these particular demand and supply schedules, as follows:

$$Q^D = 20 - 2P$$
$$Q^S = -10 + 4P$$

Set $Q^D = Q^S$:

$$20 - 2P = -10 + 4P$$

Solve for P:

$$P = \frac{30}{6} = 5$$

Now use the demand curve to get

$$Q^D = 20 - 2(5) = 10$$

which we can confirm by using the supply curve to get

$$Q^S = -10 + 4(5) = 10$$

ELASTICITY AND ITS APPLICATION

Learning Objectives

In this chapter, you will …

- Learn the meaning of the elasticity of demand

- Examine what determines the elasticity of demand

- Learn the meaning of the elasticity of supply

- Examine what determines the elasticity of supply

- Apply the concept of elasticity in three very different markets

Imagine that some event drives up the price of gasoline in Canada. It could be a war in the Middle East that disrupts the world supply of oil, a booming Chinese economy that boosts the world demand for oil, or a new tax on gasoline passed by Parliament. How do you think Canadian consumers would respond to the higher price?

It is easy to answer this question in a broad fashion: Consumers would buy less. That is simply the law of demand that we learned in the previous chapter. But you might want a precise answer: By how much did the consumption of gasoline fall? The answer to this question can be answered by using the concept of *elasticity*, which we develop in this chapter.

Elasticity is a measure of how much buyers and sellers respond to changes in market conditions. When studying how some event or policy affects a market, we can discuss not only the direction of the effects but their magnitude as well. Elasticity is useful in many applications, as we see toward the end of the chapter.

Before proceeding, however, you might be curious about the answer to the gasoline consumption question. Many studies have examined consumers' response to

→ Consumers sometimes take longer to respond to changes.

gasoline prices, and they typically find that the quantity demanded responds more in the long run than it does in the short run. A 10 percent increase in the price of gasoline reduces gasoline consumption by about 2.5 percent after one year and about 6 percent after five years. About half of the long-run reduction in quantity demanded arises because people drive less and half arises because they switch to more fuel-efficient cars. Both responses are reflected in the demand curve and its elasticity.

THE ELASTICITY OF DEMAND

When we introduced demand in Chapter 4, we noted that consumers usually buy more of a good when its price is lower, when their incomes are higher, when the prices of substitutes for the good are higher, or when the prices of complements of the good are lower. Our discussion of demand was qualitative, not quantitative. That is, we discussed the direction in which quantity demanded moves, but not the size of the change. To measure how much consumers respond to changes in these variables, economists use the concept of **elasticity**.

elasticity
a measure of the responsiveness of quantity demanded or quantity supplied to one of its determinants

The Price Elasticity of Demand and Its Determinants

The law of demand states that a fall in the price of a good raises the quantity demanded. The **price elasticity of demand** measures how much the quantity demanded responds to a change in price. Demand for a good is said to be *elastic* if the quantity demanded responds substantially to changes in the price. Demand is said to be *inelastic* if the quantity demanded responds only slightly to changes in the price.

price elasticity of demand
a measure of how much the quantity demanded of a good responds to a change in the price of that good, computed as the percentage change in quantity demanded divided by the percentage change in price

The price elasticity of demand for any good measures how willing consumers are to buy less of the good as its price rises. Because the demand curve reflects the many economic, social, and psychological forces that shape consumer preferences, there is no simple, universal rule for what determines the demand curve's elasticity. Based on experience, however, we can state some rules of thumb about what influences the price elasticity of demand.

→ Elastic: QD change % is greater than price change % (value > 1)
→ Inelastic: QD % change is less than price % change (value between 0 and 1)

Availability of Close Substitutes   Goods with close substitutes tend to have more elastic demand because it is easier for consumers to switch from that good to others. For example, butter and margarine are easily substitutable. A small increase in the price of butter, assuming the price of margarine is held fixed, causes the quantity of butter sold to fall by a large amount. By contrast, because eggs are a food without a close substitute, the demand for eggs is less elastic than the demand for butter.

Necessities versus Luxuries   Necessities tend to have inelastic demands, whereas luxuries have elastic demands. When the price of a visit to the dentist rises, people will not dramatically alter the number of times they go to the dentist, although they might go somewhat less often. By contrast, when the price of sailboats rises, the quantity of sailboats demanded falls substantially. The reason is that most people view dentist visits as a necessity and sailboats as a luxury. Whether a good is a necessity or a luxury depends not on the intrinsic properties of the good but on the preferences of the buyer. For an avid sailor with little concern about his teeth, sailboats might be a necessity with inelastic demand and dentist visits a luxury with elastic demand.

Definition of the Market   The elasticity of demand in any market depends on how we draw the boundaries of the market. Narrowly defined markets tend to have more elastic demand than broadly defined markets because it is easier to find close substitutes for narrowly defined goods. For example, food, a broad category, has a fairly inelastic demand because there are no good substitutes for food. Ice cream, a more narrow category, has a more elastic demand because it is easy to substitute other desserts for ice cream. Vanilla ice cream, a very narrow category, has a very elastic demand because other flavours of ice cream are almost perfect substitutes for vanilla.

→ Shoes vs Nike running shoes

Time Horizon   Goods tend to have more elastic demand over longer time horizons. As we saw in the introduction to this chapter, when the price of gasoline rises, the quantity of gasoline demanded falls only slightly in the first few months. Over time, however, people buy more fuel-efficient cars, switch to public transportation, or move closer to where they work. Within several years, the quantity of gasoline demanded falls substantially.

Computing the Price Elasticity of Demand

Now that we have discussed the price elasticity of demand in general terms, let's be more precise about how it is measured. Economists compute the price elasticity of demand as the percentage change in the quantity demanded divided by the percentage change in the price. That is,

$$\text{Price elasticity of demand} = \frac{\text{Percentage change in quantity demanded}}{\text{Percentage change in price}}$$

For example, suppose that a 10 percent increase in the price of an ice-cream cone causes the amount of ice cream you buy to fall by 20 percent. We calculate your elasticity of demand as

$$\text{Price elasticity of demand} = \frac{20 \text{ percent}}{10 \text{ percent}} = 2$$

In this example, the elasticity is 2, reflecting that the change in the quantity demanded is proportionately twice as large as the change in the price.

Because the quantity demanded of a good is negatively related to its price, the percentage change in quantity will always have the opposite sign as the percentage change in price. In this example, the percentage change in price is a *positive* 10 percent (reflecting an increase), and the percentage change in quantity demanded is a *negative* 20 percent (reflecting a decrease). For this reason, price elasticities of demand are sometimes reported as negative numbers. In this book we follow the common practice of dropping the minus sign and reporting all price elasticities as positive numbers. (Mathematicians call this the *absolute value*.) With this convention, a larger price elasticity implies a greater responsiveness of quantity demanded to changes in price.

The Midpoint Method: A Better Way to Calculate Percentage Changes and Elasticities

If you try calculating the price elasticity of demand between two points on a demand curve, you will quickly notice an annoying problem: The elasticity from point A to point B seems different from the elasticity from point B to point A. For example, consider these numbers:

Point A:	Price = $4	Quantity = 120
Point B:	Price = $6	Quantity = 80

Going from point A to point B, the price rises by 50 percent, and the quantity falls by 33 percent, indicating that the price elasticity of demand is 33/50, or 0.66. By contrast, going from point B to point A, the price falls by 33 percent, and the quantity rises by 50 percent, indicating that the price elasticity of demand is 50/33, or 1.5. This difference arises because the percentage changes are calculated from a different base.

One way to avoid this problem is to use the *midpoint method* for calculating elasticities. The standard way to compute a percentage change is to divide the change by the initial level. By contrast, the midpoint method computes a percentage change by dividing the change by the midpoint (or average) of the initial and final levels. For instance, $5 is the midpoint of $4 and $6. Therefore, according to the midpoint method, a change from $4 to $6 is considered a 40 percent rise because $(6 - 4)/5 \times 100 = 40$. Similarly, a change from $6 to $4 is considered a 40 percent fall.

Because the midpoint method gives the same answer regardless of the direction of change, it is often used when calculating the price elasticity of demand between two points. In our example, the midpoint between point A and point B is

Midpoint: Price = $5   Quantity = 100

According to the midpoint method, when going from point A to point B, the price rises by 40 percent and the quantity falls by 40 percent. Similarly, when going from point B to point A, the price falls by 40 percent and the quantity rises by 40 percent. In both directions, the price elasticity of demand equals 1.

We can express the midpoint method with the following formula for the price elasticity of demand between two points, denoted (Q_1, P_1) and (Q_2, P_2):

$$\text{Price elasticity of demand} = \frac{(Q_2 - Q_1)/[(Q_2 + Q_1)/2]}{(P_2 - P_1)/[(P_2 + P_1)/2]}$$

The numerator is the percentage change in quantity computed using the midpoint method, and the denominator is the percentage change in price computed using the midpoint method. If you ever need to calculate elasticities, you should use this formula.

In this book, however, we rarely perform such calculations. For most of our purposes, what elasticity represents—the responsiveness of quantity demanded to price—is more important than how it is calculated.

The Variety of Demand Curves

Economists classify demand curves according to their elasticity. Demand is *elastic* when the elasticity is greater than 1, so that quantity moves proportionately more than the price. Demand is *inelastic* when the elasticity is less than 1, so that quantity moves proportionately less than the price. If the elasticity is exactly 1, so that quantity moves the same amount proportionately as price, demand is said to have *unit elasticity.*

Because the price elasticity of demand measures how much quantity demanded responds to changes in the price, it is closely related to the slope of the demand curve. The following rule of thumb is a useful guide: The flatter the demand curve that passes through a given point, the greater the price elasticity of demand. The steeper the demand curve that passes through a given point, the smaller the price elasticity of demand.

Figure 5.1 shows five cases. In the extreme case of a zero elasticity shown in panel (a), demand is *perfectly inelastic*, and the demand curve is vertical. In this case, regardless of the price, the quantity demanded stays the same. As the elasticity rises, the demand curve gets flatter and flatter, as shown in panels (b), (c), and (d). At the opposite extreme shown in panel (e), demand is *perfectly elastic*. This occurs as the price elasticity of demand approaches infinity and the demand curve becomes horizontal, reflecting the fact that very small changes in the price lead to huge changes in the quantity demanded.

Finally, if you have trouble keeping straight the terms *elastic* and *inelastic*, here's a memory trick for you: *I*nelastic curves, such as in panel (a) of Figure 5.1, look like the letter *I*. *E*lastic curves, as in panel (e), look like the letter *E*. This is not a deep insight, but it might help on your next exam.

[handwritten margin notes:]

→ Unit Elastic: % change in price = % change in demand

→ Perfectly inelastic: vertical demand curve. Absolute necessities EX: Insulin

→ Perfectly elastic: horizontal demand curve. High priced luxuries

→ Elastic: Flat
   Inelastic: steep

Total Revenue and the Price Elasticity of Demand

When studying changes in supply or demand in a market, one variable we often want to study is **total revenue**, the amount paid by buyers and received by sellers of the good. In any market, total revenue is $P \times Q$, the price of the good times the quantity of the good sold. We can show total revenue graphically, as in Figure 5.2. The height of the box under the demand curve is P, and the width is Q. The area of this box, $P \times Q$, equals the total revenue in this market. In Figure 5.2, where $P = \$4$ and $Q = 100$, total revenue is $\$4 \times 100$, or $\$400$.

How does total revenue change as one moves along the demand curve? The answer depends on the price elasticity of demand. If demand is inelastic, as in panel (a) of Figure 5.3, then an increase in the price causes an increase in total revenue. Here an increase in price from $4 to $5 causes the quantity demanded to fall only from 100 to 90, and so total revenue rises from $400 to $450. An increase in price raises $P \times Q$ because the fall in Q is proportionately smaller than the rise in P. In other words, the extra revenue from selling units at a higher price (represented by area A in the figure) more than offsets the decline in revenue from selling fewer units (represented by area B).

We obtain the opposite result if demand is elastic: An increase in the price causes a decrease in total revenue. In panel (b) of Figure 5.3, for instance, when the price rises from $4 to $5, the quantity demanded falls from 100 to 70, and so total revenue falls from $400 to $350. Because demand is elastic, the reduction in the quantity demanded is so great that it more than offsets the increase

total revenue (in a market)
the amount paid by buyers and received by sellers of a good, computed as the price of the good times the quantity sold

[handwritten table:]

	Price	Revenue
Elastic	↑	↓
Inelastic	↑	↑
Unit	↕	—

FIGURE 5.1

The Price Elasticity of Demand

The price elasticity of demand determines whether the demand curve is steep or flat. Note that all percentage changes are calculated using the midpoint method.

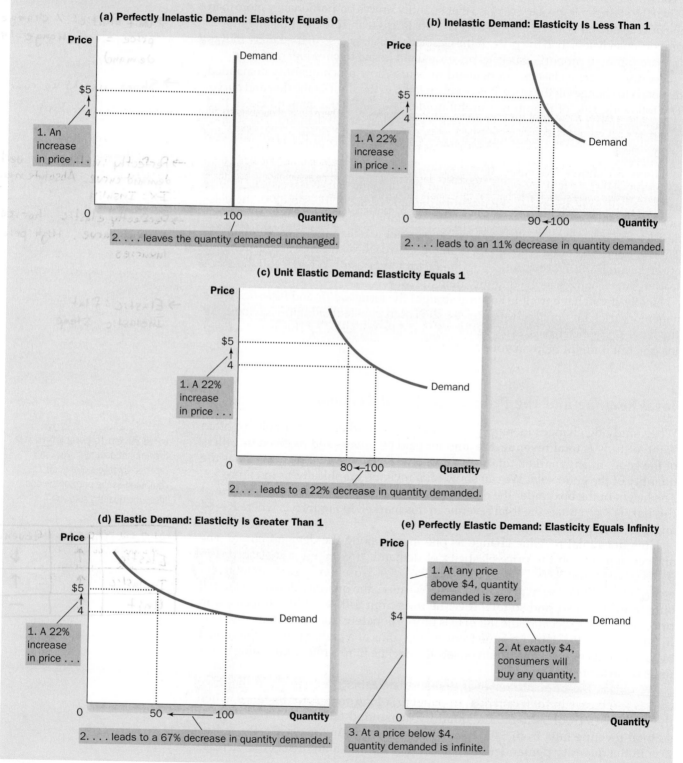

(a) Perfectly Inelastic Demand: Elasticity Equals 0

Price

Demand

$5
4

1. An increase in price . . .

0   100   Quantity

2. . . . leaves the quantity demanded unchanged.

(b) Inelastic Demand: Elasticity Is Less Than 1

Price

$5
4

1. A 22% increase in price . . .

Demand

0   90 ← 100   Quantity

2. . . . leads to an 11% decrease in quantity demanded.

(c) Unit Elastic Demand: Elasticity Equals 1

Price

$5
4

1. A 22% increase in price . . .

Demand

0   80 ← 100   Quantity

2. . . . leads to a 22% decrease in quantity demanded.

(d) Elastic Demand: Elasticity Is Greater Than 1

Price

$5
4

1. A 22% increase in price . . .

Demand

0   50 ← 100   Quantity

2. . . . leads to a 67% decrease in quantity demanded.

(e) Perfectly Elastic Demand: Elasticity Equals Infinity

Price

1. At any price above $4, quantity demanded is zero.

$4   Demand

2. At exactly $4, consumers will buy any quantity.

0   Quantity

3. At a price below $4, quantity demanded is infinite.

A FEW REAL-WORLD ELASTICITIES

We have talked about what elasticity means, what determines it, and how it is calculated. Beyond these general ideas, you might ask for a specific number. How much, precisely, does the price of a particular good influence the quantity demanded?

To answer such a question, economists collect data from market outcomes and apply statistical techniques to estimate the price elasticity of demand. The following are some price elasticities of demand, obtained from various studies, for a range of goods:

Eggs	0.1
Health care	0.2
Rice	0.5
Housing	0.7
Beef	1.6
Restaurant meals	2.3
Mountain Dew	4.4

Luxuries / close substitutes (handwritten, bracketing Beef, Restaurant meals, Mountain Dew)

These kinds of numbers are fun to think about, and they can be useful when comparing markets.

We should take these estimates with a grain of salt, however. One reason is that the statistical techniques used to obtain them require some assumptions about the world, and these assumptions might not be true in practice. (The details of these techniques are beyond the scope of this book, but you will encounter them if you take a course in econometrics.) Another reason is that the price elasticity of demand does not need to be the same at all points on a demand curve, as we will see shortly in the case of a linear demand curve. For both reasons, you should not be surprised if different studies report different price elasticities of demand for the same good.

FIGURE 5.2

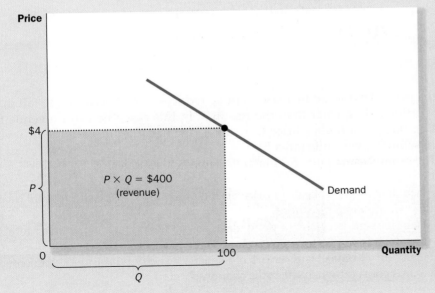

Total Revenue

The total amount paid by buyers, and received as revenue by sellers, equals the area of the box under the demand curve, P × Q. Here, at a price of $4, the quantity demanded is 100, and total revenue is $400.

FIGURE 5.3

How Total Revenue Changes When Price Changes

The impact of a price change on total revenue (the product of price and quantity) depends on the elasticity of demand. In panel (a), the demand curve is inelastic. In this case, an increase in the price leads to a decrease in quantity demanded that is proportionately smaller, so total revenue increases. Here an increase in the price from $4 to $5 causes the quantity demanded to fall from 100 to 90. Total revenue rises from $400 to $450. Area A is the extra revenue from selling units at a higher price; it is equal to ($5 − $4) × 90 = $90. Area B is the decline in revenue from selling fewer units; it is equal to $4 × (100 − 90) = $40. Area A is larger than area B by $50, which is the increase in revenue from an increase in the price from $4 to $5. In panel (b), the demand curve is elastic. In this case, an increase in the price leads to a decrease in quantity demanded that is proportionately larger, so total revenue decreases. Here an increase in the price from $4 to $5 causes the quantity demanded to fall from 100 to 70. Total revenue falls from $400 to $350. In this case the extra revenue from selling units at a higher price (area A) is equal to $70, and the decline in revenue from selling fewer units (area B) is $120. In this case, area A is smaller than area B by $50, which is the decrease in revenue from an increase in the price from $4 to $5.

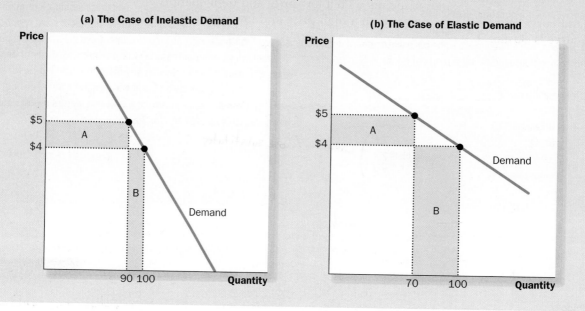

(a) The Case of Inelastic Demand

(b) The Case of Elastic Demand

in the price. That is, an increase in price reduces $P \times Q$ because the fall in Q is proportionately greater than the rise in P. In this case, the extra revenue from selling units at a higher price (area A) is smaller than the decline in revenue from selling fewer units (area B).

The examples in Figure 5.3 illustrate some general rules:

- When demand is inelastic (a price elasticity less than 1), price and total revenue move in the same direction.
- When demand is elastic (a price elasticity greater than 1), price and total revenue move in opposite directions.
- If demand is unit elastic (a price elasticity exactly equal to 1), total revenue remains constant when the price changes.

Elasticity and Total Revenue along a Linear Demand Curve

Let's examine how elasticity varies along a linear demand curve, as shown in Figure 5.4. We know that a straight line has a constant slope. Slope is defined as "rise over run," which here is the ratio of the change in price ("rise") to the change in quantity ("run"). This particular demand curve's slope is constant because each $1 increase in price causes the same two-unit decrease in the quantity demanded.

Even though the slope of a linear demand curve is constant, the elasticity is not. The reason is that the slope is the ratio of *changes* in the two variables, whereas the elasticity is the ratio of *percentage changes* in the two variables. You can see this by looking at the table in Figure 5.4, which shows the demand schedule for the linear demand curve in the graph. The table uses the midpoint method to calculate the price elasticity of demand. At points with a low price and high quantity, the demand curve is inelastic. At points with a high price and low quantity, the demand curve is elastic.

FIGURE 5.4

Elasticity of a Linear Demand Curve

The slope of a linear demand curve is constant, but its elasticity is not. The demand schedule in the table was used to calculate the price elasticity of demand by the midpoint method. At points with a low price and high quantity, the demand curve is inelastic. At points with a high price and low quantity, the demand curve is elastic.

Price	Quantity	Total Revenue (Price × Quantity)	Percentage Change in Price	Percentage Change in Quantity	Elasticity	Description
$7	0	$ 0				
			15	200	13.3	Elastic
6	2	12				
			18	67	3.7	Elastic
5	4	20				
			22	40	1.8	Elastic
4	6	24				
			29	29	1.0	Unit elastic
3	8	24				
			40	22	0.6	Inelastic
2	10	20				
			67	18	0.3	Inelastic
1	12	12				
			200	15	0.1	Inelastic
0	14	0				

IN THE NEWS

THE ELASTICITY OF CAFFEINE

This article describes an increase in the price of Tim Hortons and Starbucks coffee in Canada. According to both chains, prices went up more in Alberta than in the rest of the country because of higher wage costs. Can you think of other reasons? How elastic do you think the demand for coffee is to price changes?

Getting Your Caffeine Fix in Alberta Just Got a Little More Costly

Two major coffee-house chains hiked the price of a cuppa joe this week—the apparent result of the high cost of hiring and retaining staff.

Coffee and food items at Tim Hortons locations across the province cost about a dime more on Monday than they did the day before. On Tuesday, Starbucks outlets throughout Alberta increased their brewed coffee and tea prices by 10 cents a cup and their espresso and blended beverages by 15 cents.

The rise in the price of caffeinated black-gold seems to be yet another response to the province's oil boom: the Alberta price hikes are the highest in North America.

The only other province to see a Tim Hortons price increase on Monday was Quebec, while Starbucks announced a five-cent hike for all of the United States and Canada.

A medium double-double from Tim Hortons in Edmonton is now more expensive than in other major Canadian cities.

But Michael Percy, dean of the School of Business at the University of Alberta, doesn't think the extra dime will get between patrons and their caffeine fix. "Those types of (routine) purchases tend to be insensitive to those kinds of price increases," he said.

Moreover, he said, people are building expectations of higher prices because they're also making more money, creating an upward spiral of costs. Still, Percy said, retail businesses such as Tim Hortons and Starbucks have to strike a precarious balance in Alberta. They must pay their employees more to retain them, which forces them to hike up prices, he said. But they can't raise prices so high they'll lose patrons. "These businesses are put between a rock and a hard place," Percy said.

A TD Economics report released Tuesday showed fears that lower-income workers in non-resource jobs would suffer in Alberta's high-inflation environment were unfounded.

"In fact," the report said, "the greatest wage gains have occurred in the non-resources sector, which has led to a narrowing of the wage gap between the higher-paying and lower-paying industries."

A spokeswoman for Tim Hortons said she's confident customers will keep lining up. "As far as Tim Hortons is concerned, we still feel we provide a very good quality product at a very good price," Diane Slopek-Weber said.

She said Tim Hortons regularly reviews prices on a regional basis, focusing on factors such as the cost of energy, labour, garbage collection and gas. Based on those factors and others, Slopek-Weber said, price increases were specific to Alberta and Quebec.

A release from Starbucks suggests a similar logic, saying the larger Alberta price increase is due to regional factors, particularly rising costs within the business. Generally, prices went up across the board at Starbucks due to "our current environment of rising energy, fuel and supply chain costs," the release said.

BEAN COUNTER: What customers are paying for . . .

Tim Hortons (medium coffee in downtown location):

Vancouver:	$1.19
Edmonton:	$1.35
Toronto:	$1.24
Montreal:	$1.34
Halifax:	$1.24

Starbucks (tall coffee in downtown location):

Vancouver:	$1.75
Edmonton:	$1.80
Toronto:	$1.75
Montreal:	$1.88
Halifax:	$1.88

Source: Dominique Blain, "Our Java Prices Don't Jive with the Rest of Canada," *The Edmonton Journal*, October 4, 2006. Material reprinted with the express permission of: The Edmonton Journal, a division of Postmedia Network Inc.

The table also presents total revenue at each point on the demand curve. These numbers illustrate the relationship between total revenue and elasticity. When the price is $1, for instance, demand is inelastic, and a price increase to $2 raises total revenue. When the price is $5, demand is elastic, and a price increase to $6 reduces total revenue. Between $3 and $4, demand is exactly unit elastic, and total revenue is the same at these two prices.

The linear demand curve illustrates that the price elasticity of demand need not be the same at all points on a demand curve. A constant elasticity is possible (in which case the demand curve will not be linear), but it is not always the case.

Other Demand Elasticities

In addition to the price elasticity of demand, economists also use other elasticities to describe the behaviour of buyers in a market.

The Income Elasticity of Demand
The **income elasticity of demand** measures how the quantity demanded changes as consumer income changes. It is calculated as the percentage change in quantity demanded divided by the percentage change in income. That is,

$$\text{Income elasticity of demand} = \frac{\text{Percentage change in quantity demanded}}{\text{Percentage change in income}}$$

income elasticity of demand
a measure of how much the quantity demanded of a good responds to a change in consumers' income, computed as the percentage change in quantity demanded divided by the percentage change in income

→ Deal with certain types of goods + purchasing habits.

As we discussed in Chapter 4, most goods are *normal goods:* Higher income raises quantity demanded. Because quantity demanded and income move in the same direction, normal goods have positive income elasticities. A few goods, such as bus rides, are *inferior goods:* Higher income lowers the quantity demanded. Because quantity demanded and income move in opposite directions, inferior goods have negative income elasticities.

Even among normal goods, income elasticities vary substantially in size. Necessities, such as food and clothing, tend to have small income elasticities because consumers, regardless of how low their incomes, choose to buy some of these goods. Luxuries, such as caviar and diamonds, tend to have large income elasticities because consumers feel that they can do without these goods altogether if their income is too low.

The Cross-Price Elasticity of Demand
The **cross-price elasticity of demand** measures how the quantity demanded of one good changes as the price of another good changes. It is calculated as the percentage change in quantity demanded of good 1 divided by the percentage change in the price of good 2. That is,

$$\text{Cross-price elasticity of demand} = \frac{\text{Percentage change in quantity demanded of good 1}}{\text{Percentage change in price of good 2}}$$

cross-price elasticity of demand
a measure of how much the quantity demanded of one good responds to a change in the price of another good, computed as the percentage change in quantity demanded of the first good divided by the percentage change in the price of the second good

Whether the cross-price elasticity is a positive or negative number depends on whether the two goods are substitutes or complements. As we discussed in Chapter 4, substitutes are goods that are typically used in place of one another, such as hamburgers and hot dogs. An increase in hot dog prices induces people

→ Substitutes: positive CPE
→ Complements: negative CPE

to grill hamburgers instead. Because the price of hot dogs and the quantity of hamburgers demanded move in the same direction, the cross-price elasticity is positive. Conversely, complements are goods that are typically used together, such as computers and software. In this case, the cross-price elasticity is negative, indicating that an increase in the price of computers reduces the quantity of software demanded.

QuickQuiz   Define the price elasticity of demand. • Explain the relationship between total revenue and the price elasticity of demand.

THE ELASTICITY OF SUPPLY

When we introduced supply in Chapter 4, we noted that producers of a good offer to sell more of it when the price of the good rises, when their input prices fall, or when their technology improves. To turn from qualitative to quantitative statements about quantity supplied, we once again use the concept of elasticity.

The Price Elasticity of Supply and Its Determinants

price elasticity of supply
a measure of how much the quantity supplied of a good responds to a change in the price of that good, computed as the percentage change in quantity supplied divided by the percentage change in price

The law of supply states that higher prices raise the quantity supplied. The **price elasticity of supply** measures how much the quantity supplied responds to changes in the price. Supply of a good is said to be *elastic* if the quantity supplied responds substantially to changes in the price. Supply is said to be *inelastic* if the quantity supplied responds only slightly to changes in the price.

The price elasticity of supply depends on the flexibility of sellers to change the amount of the good they produce. For example, beachfront land has an inelastic supply because it is almost impossible to produce more of it. By contrast, manufactured goods, such as books, cars, and televisions, have elastic supplies because the firms that produce them can run their factories longer in response to a higher price.

In most markets, a key determinant of the price elasticity of supply is the time period being considered. Supply is usually more elastic in the long run than in the short run. Over short periods of time, firms cannot easily change the size of their factories to make more or less of a good. Thus, in the short run, the quantity supplied is not very responsive to the price. By contrast, over longer periods, firms can build new factories or close old ones. In addition, new firms can enter a market, and old firms can shut down. Thus, in the long run, the quantity supplied can respond substantially to price changes.

→ Long Run: Elastic, as sellers have more time to respond to price changes

→ Short Run: Inelastic, as sellers don't have enough time to react to price changes

Computing the Price Elasticity of Supply

Now that we have some idea about what the price elasticity of supply is, let's be more precise. Economists compute the price elasticity of supply as the percentage change in the quantity supplied divided by the percentage change in the price. That is,

$$\text{Price elasticity of supply} = \frac{\text{Percentage change in quantity supplied}}{\text{Percentage change in price}}$$

(Same as Price Elasticity of Demand)

For example, suppose that an increase in the price of milk from $2.85 to $3.15 per four-litre container raises the amount that dairy farmers produce from 9000 to 11 000 L per month. Using the midpoint method, we calculate the percentage change in price as

$$\text{Percentage change in price} = (3.15 - 2.85)/3.00 \times 100 = 10 \text{ percent}$$

Similarly, we calculate the percentage change in quantity supplied as

$$\text{Percentage change in quantity supplied} = (11\ 000 - 9000)/10\ 000 \times 100 = 20 \text{ percent}$$

In this case, the price elasticity of supply is

$$\text{Price elasticity of supply} = \frac{20 \text{ percent}}{10 \text{ percent}} = 2.0$$

In this example, the elasticity of 2 reflects the fact that the quantity supplied moves proportionately twice as much as the price.

The Variety of Supply Curves

Because the price elasticity of supply measures the responsiveness of quantity supplied to the price, it is reflected in the appearance of the supply curve. Figure 5.5 shows five cases. In the extreme case of a zero elasticity, as shown in panel (a), supply is *perfectly inelastic* and the supply curve is vertical. In this case, the quantity supplied is the same regardless of the price. As the elasticity rises, the supply curve gets flatter, which shows that the quantity supplied responds more to changes in the price. At the opposite extreme shown in panel (e), supply is *perfectly elastic*. This occurs as the price elasticity of supply approaches infinity and the supply curve becomes horizontal, meaning that very small changes in the price lead to very large changes in the quantity supplied.

→ Perfectly Inelastic : limited production goods

In some markets, the elasticity of supply is not constant but varies over the supply curve. Figure 5.6 shows a typical case for an industry in which firms have factories with a limited capacity for production. For low levels of quantity supplied, the elasticity of supply is high, indicating that firms respond substantially to changes in the price. In this region, firms have capacity for production that is not being used, such as plants and equipment sitting idle for all or part of the day. Small increases in price make it profitable for firms to begin using this idle capacity. As the quantity supplied rises, firms begin to reach capacity. Once capacity is fully used, increasing production further requires the construction of new plants. To induce firms to incur this extra expense, the price must rise substantially, so supply becomes less elastic.

Figure 5.6 presents a numerical example of this phenomenon. When the price rises from $3 to $4 (a 29 percent increase, according to the midpoint method), the quantity supplied rises from 100 to 200 (a 67 percent increase). Because quantity supplied moves proportionately more than the price, the supply curve has elasticity greater than 1. By contrast, when the price rises from $12 to $15 (a 22 percent increase), the quantity supplied rises from 500 to 525 (a 5 percent increase). In this case, quantity supplied moves proportionately less than the price, so the elasticity is less than 1.

FIGURE 5.5

The Price Elasticity of Supply

The price elasticity of supply determines whether the supply curve is steep or flat. Note that all percentage changes are calculated using the midpoint method.

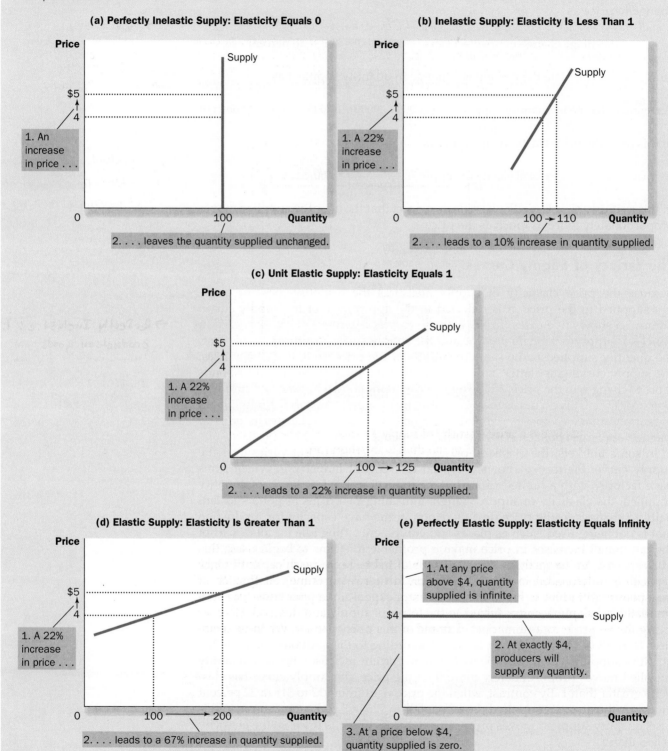

(a) Perfectly Inelastic Supply: Elasticity Equals 0

Price

Supply

$5
4

1. An increase in price . . .

0   100   Quantity

2. . . . leaves the quantity supplied unchanged.

(b) Inelastic Supply: Elasticity Is Less Than 1

Price

Supply

$5
4

1. A 22% increase in price . . .

0   100 → 110   Quantity

2. . . . leads to a 10% increase in quantity supplied.

(c) Unit Elastic Supply: Elasticity Equals 1

Price

Supply

$5
4

1. A 22% increase in price . . .

0   100 → 125   Quantity

2. . . . leads to a 22% increase in quantity supplied.

(d) Elastic Supply: Elasticity Is Greater Than 1

Price

Supply

$5
4

1. A 22% increase in price . . .

0   100 ——→ 200   Quantity

2. . . . leads to a 67% increase in quantity supplied.

(e) Perfectly Elastic Supply: Elasticity Equals Infinity

Price

1. At any price above $4, quantity supplied is infinite.

$4   Supply

2. At exactly $4, producers will supply any quantity.

0   Quantity

3. At a price below $4, quantity supplied is zero.

FIGURE 5.6

How the Price Elasticity of Supply Can Vary

Because firms often have a maximum capacity for production, the elasticity of supply may be very high at low levels of quantity supplied and very low at high levels of quantity supplied. Here, an increase in price from $3 to $4 increases the quantity supplied from 100 to 200. Because the increase in quantity supplied of 67 percent (computed using the midpoint method) is larger than the increase in price of 29 percent, the supply curve is elastic in this range. By contrast, when the price rises from $12 to $15, the quantity supplied rises only from 500 to 525. Because the increase in quantity supplied of 5 percent is smaller than the increase in price of 22 percent, the supply curve is inelastic in this range.

QuickQuiz   Define the price elasticity of supply. • Explain why the price elasticity of supply might be different in the long run than in the short run.

THREE APPLICATIONS OF SUPPLY, DEMAND, AND ELASTICITY

Can good news for farming be bad news for farmers? Why did the Organization of the Petroleum Exporting Countries (OPEC) fail to keep the price of oil high? Does drug interdiction increase or decrease drug-related crime? At first, these questions might seem to have little in common. Yet all three questions are about markets, and all markets are subject to the forces of supply and demand. Here we apply the versatile tools of supply, demand, and elasticity to answer these seemingly complex questions.

Can Good News for Farming Be Bad News for Farmers?

Imagine yourself as a Saskatchewan wheat farmer. Because you earn all of your income from selling wheat, you devote much effort to making your land as productive as possible. You monitor weather and soil conditions, check your fields for pests and disease, and study the latest advances in farm technology. You know that the more wheat you grow, the more you will have to sell after the harvest, and the higher your income and your standard of living will be.

One day, the University of Saskatchewan announces a major discovery. Researchers in its College of Agriculture and Bioresources have devised a new hybrid of wheat that raises by 20 percent the amount that farmers can produce from each hectare of land. How should you react to the news? Does this discovery make you better or worse off than you were before?

Recall from Chapter 4 that we answer such questions in three steps. First, we examine whether the supply or demand curve shifts. Second, we consider in which direction the curve shifts. Third, we use the supply-and-demand diagram to see how the market equilibrium changes.

In this case, the discovery of the new hybrid affects the supply curve. Because the hybrid increases the amount of wheat that can be produced on each hectare of land, farmers are now willing to supply more wheat at any given price. In other words, the supply curve shifts to the right. The demand curve remains the same because consumers' desire to buy wheat products at any given price is not affected by the introduction of a new hybrid. Figure 5.7 shows an example of such a change. When the supply curve shifts from S_1 to S_2, the quantity of wheat sold increases from 100 to 110, and the price of wheat falls from $3 to $2.

Does this discovery make farmers better off? As a first cut at answering this question, consider what happens to the total revenue received by farmers. Farmers' total revenue is $P \times Q$, the price of the wheat times the quantity sold. The discovery affects farmers in two conflicting ways: The hybrid allows farmers to produce more wheat (Q rises), but now each tonne of wheat sells for less (P falls).

→ Advancement in technology leads to lower input costs, shift in supply curve to the right

---

FIGURE 5.7

An Increase in Supply in the Market for Wheat

When an advance in farm technology increases the supply of wheat from S_1 to S_2, the price of wheat falls. Because the demand for wheat is inelastic, the increase in the quantity sold from 100 to 110 is proportionately smaller than the decrease in the price from $3 to $2. As a result, farmers' total revenue falls from $300 ($3 × 100) to $220 ($2 × 110).

Price of Wheat

2. . . . leads to a large fall in price . . .

$3

2

1. When demand is inelastic, an increase in supply . . .

S_1 S_2

Demand

0   100 →110   Quantity of Wheat

3. . . . and a proportionately smaller increase in quantity sold. As a result, revenue falls from $300 to $220.

Whether total revenue rises or falls depends on the elasticity of demand. In practice, the demand for basic foodstuffs such as wheat is usually inelastic, for these items are relatively inexpensive and have few good substitutes. When the demand curve is inelastic, as it is in Figure 5.7, a decrease in price causes total revenue to fall. You can see this in the figure: The price of wheat falls substantially, whereas the quantity of wheat sold rises only slightly. Total revenue falls from $300 to $220. Thus, the discovery of the new hybrid lowers the total revenue that farmers receive for the sale of their crops.

If farmers are made worse off by the discovery of this new hybrid, why do they adopt it? The answer to this question goes to the heart of how competitive markets work. Because each farmer is a small part of the market for wheat, he or she takes the price of wheat as given. For any given price of wheat, it is better to use the new hybrid in order to produce and sell more wheat. Yet when all farmers do this, the supply of wheat rises, the price falls, and farmers are worse off.

Although this example may at first seem only hypothetical, in fact it helps to explain a major change in the Canadian economy over the past century. Two hundred years ago, most Canadians lived on farms. Knowledge about farm methods was sufficiently primitive that most people had to be farmers to produce enough food. Yet, over time, advances in farm technology increased the amount of food that each farmer could produce. This increase in food supply, together with inelastic food demand, caused farm revenues to fall, which in turn encouraged people to leave farming.

A few numbers show the magnitude of this historic change. As recently as 1950, about 25 percent of the Canadian labour force worked on farms. Today, less than 3 percent of the labour force of employed Canadians work on farms. This change coincides with tremendous advances in farm productivity: Despite the huge percentage drop in the number of farmers, Canadian farms now produce more than twice the output of crops and livestock that they did in 1950.

This analysis of the market for farm products also helps to explain a seeming paradox of public policy: Certain farm programs try to help farmers by restricting the amount of milk and eggs that farmers are allowed to produce. The purpose of these programs is to reduce the supply of milk and eggs and thereby raise prices. Because demand is inelastic, farmers as a group receive greater total revenue if they supply a smaller amount of milk and eggs to the market. No single farmer would choose to restrict supply on his or her own, since each takes the market price as given. But if all farmers do so together, each of them can be better off.

When analyzing the effects of farm technology or farm policy, it is important to keep in mind that what is good for farmers is not necessarily good for society as a whole. Improvement in farm technology can be bad for farmers who become increasingly unnecessary, but it is surely good for consumers who pay less for food. Similarly, a policy aimed at reducing the supply of farm products may raise the incomes of farmers, but it does so at the expense of consumers.

Why Did OPEC Fail to Keep the Price of Oil High?

Many of the most disruptive events for the world's economies over the past several decades have originated in the world market for oil. In the 1970s, members of OPEC decided to raise the world price of oil in order to increase their incomes.

These countries accomplished this goal by jointly reducing the amount of oil they supplied. From 1973 to 1974, the price of oil (adjusted for overall inflation) rose more than 50 percent. Then, a few years later, OPEC did the same thing again: From 1979 to 1981, the price of oil approximately doubled.

Yet OPEC found it difficult to maintain a high price. From 1982 to 1985, the price of oil steadily declined about 10 percent per year. Dissatisfaction and disarray soon prevailed among the OPEC countries. In 1986, cooperation among OPEC members completely broke down, and the price of oil plunged 45 percent. In 1990, the price of oil (adjusted for overall inflation) was back to where it began in 1970, and it stayed at that low level throughout most of the 1990s.

In the first decade of the twenty-first century, the price of oil fluctuated substantially once again, but the main driving force was changes in world demand rather than OPEC supply restrictions. Early in the decade, oil demand and prices spiked up, in part because of a large and rapidly growing Chinese economy. They plunged in 2008–09 as the world economy fell into a deep recession and then started rising once again as the world economy started to recover. In 2012, prices started to weaken again as the recovery started to weaken.

The OPEC episode of the 1970s and 1980s shows how supply and demand can behave differently in the short run and in the long run. In the short run, both the supply and demand for oil are relatively inelastic. Supply is inelastic because the quantity of known oil reserves and the capacity for oil extraction cannot be changed quickly. Demand is inelastic because buying habits do not respond immediately to changes in price. Many drivers with old gas-guzzling cars, for instance, will just pay the higher price. Thus, as panel (a) of Figure 5.8 shows, the short-run supply-and-demand curves are steep. When the supply of oil shifts from S_1 to S_2, the price increase from P_1 to P_2 is large.

The situation is very different in the long run. Over long periods of time, producers of oil outside of OPEC respond to high prices by increasing oil exploration and by building new extraction capacity. Consumers respond with greater conservation, for instance by replacing old inefficient cars with newer efficient ones. Thus, as panel (b) of Figure 5.8 shows, the long-run supply-and-demand curves are more elastic. In the long run, the shift in the supply curve from S_1 to S_2 causes a much smaller increase in the price.

This analysis shows why OPEC succeeded in maintaining a high price for oil only in the short run. When OPEC countries agreed to reduce their production of oil, they shifted the supply curve to the left. Even though each OPEC member sold less oil, the price rose by so much in the short run that OPEC incomes rose. By contrast, in the long run when supply and demand are more elastic, the same reduction in supply, measured by the horizontal shift in the supply curve, caused a smaller increase in the price. Thus, OPEC's coordinated reduction in supply proved less profitable in the long run. The cartel learned that raising prices is easier in the short run than in the long run.

Does Drug Interdiction Increase or Decrease Drug-Related Crime?

A persistent problem facing our society is the use of illegal drugs, such as heroin, cocaine, Ecstasy, and crack. Drug use has several adverse effects. One is that drug dependence can ruin the lives of drug users and their families. Another is that drug addicts often turn to robbery and other violent crimes to obtain the money

FIGURE 5.8

A Reduction in Supply in the World Market for Oil

When the supply of oil falls, the response depends on the time horizon. In the short run, supply and demand are relatively inelastic, as in panel (a). Thus, when the supply curve shifts from S_1 to S_2, the price rises substantially. By contrast, in the long run, supply and demand are relatively elastic, as in panel (b). In this case, the same size shift in the supply curve (S_1 to S_2) causes a smaller increase in the price.

needed to support their habit. To discourage the use of illegal drugs, Canadian governments devote millions of dollars each year to reducing the flow of drugs into the country. Let's use the tools of supply and demand to examine this policy of drug interdiction.

Suppose the government increases the number of officers devoted to the war on drugs. What happens in the market for illegal drugs? As usual, we answer this question in three steps. First, we consider whether the supply or demand curve shifts. Second, we consider the direction of the shift. Third, we see how the shift affects the equilibrium price and quantity.

Although the purpose of drug interdiction is to reduce drug use, its direct impact is on the sellers of drugs rather than on the buyers. When the government stops some drugs from entering the country and arrests more smugglers, it raises the cost of selling drugs and, therefore, reduces the quantity of drugs supplied at any given price. The demand for drugs—the amount buyers want at any given price—is not changed. As panel (a) of Figure 5.9 shows, interdiction shifts the supply curve to the left from S_1 to S_2 and leaves the demand curve the same. The equilibrium price of drugs rises from P_1 to P_2, and the equilibrium quantity falls from Q_1 to Q_2. The fall in the equilibrium quantity shows that drug interdiction does reduce drug use.

But what about the amount of drug-related crime? To answer this question, consider the total amount that drug users pay for the drugs they buy. Because few drug addicts are likely to break their destructive habits in response to a higher price, it is likely that the demand for drugs is inelastic, as it is drawn in the figure.

FIGURE 5.9

Policies to Reduce the Use of Illegal Drugs

Drug interdiction reduces the supply of drugs from S_1 to S_2, as shown in panel (a). If the demand for drugs is inelastic, then the total amount paid by drug users rises, even as the amount of drug use falls. By contrast, drug education reduces the demand for drugs from D_1 to D_2, as shown in panel (b). Because both price and quantity fall, the amount paid by drug users falls.

1. Drug interdiction reduces the supply of drugs . . .

1. Drug education reduces the demand for drugs . . .

(a) Drug Interdiction

(b) Drug Education

2. . . . which raises the price . . .

3. . . . and reduces the quantity sold.

2. . . . which lowers the price . . .

3. . . . and reduces the quantity sold.

If demand is inelastic, then an increase in price raises total revenue in the drug market. That is, because drug interdiction raises the price of drugs proportionately more than it reduces drug use, it raises the total amount of money that drug users pay for drugs. Addicts who already had to steal to support their habits would have an even greater need for quick cash. Thus, drug interdiction could increase drug-related crime. → By adding more $ into the system

Because of this adverse effect of drug interdiction, some analysts argue for alternative approaches to the drug problem. Rather than trying to reduce the supply of drugs, policymakers might try to reduce the demand by pursuing a policy of drug education. Successful drug education has the effects shown in panel (b) of Figure 5.9. The demand curve shifts to the left from D_1 to D_2. As a result, the equilibrium quantity falls from Q_1 to Q_2, and the equilibrium price falls from P_1 to P_2. Total revenue, which is price times quantity, also falls. Thus, in contrast to drug interdiction, drug education can reduce both drug use and drug-related crime.

Advocates of drug interdiction might argue that the effects of this policy are different in the long run than in the short run because the elasticity of demand may depend on the time horizon. The demand for drugs is probably inelastic over short periods of time because higher prices do not substantially affect drug use by established addicts. But demand may be more elastic over longer periods of time because higher prices would discourage experimentation with drugs among the young and, over time, lead to fewer drug addicts. In this case, drug interdiction would increase drug-related crime in the short run while decreasing it in the long run.

QuickQuiz   How might a drought that destroys half of all farm crops be good for farmers? If such a drought is good for farmers, why don't farmers destroy their own crops in the absence of a drought?

CONCLUSION

According to an old quip, even a parrot can become an economist simply by learning to say "supply and demand." These last two chapters should have convinced you that there is much truth in this statement. The tools of supply and demand allow you to analyze many of the most important events and policies that shape the economy. You are now well on your way to becoming an economist.

SUMMARY

- The price elasticity of demand measures how much the quantity demanded responds to changes in the price. Demand tends to be more elastic if close substitutes are available, if the good is a luxury rather than a necessity, if the market is narrowly defined, or if buyers have substantial time to react to a price change.

- The price elasticity of demand is calculated as the percentage change in quantity demanded divided by the percentage change in price. If the elasticity is less than 1, so that quantity demanded moves proportionately less than the price, demand is said to be inelastic. If the elasticity is greater than 1, so that quantity demanded moves proportionately more than the price, demand is said to be elastic.

- Total revenue, the total amount paid for a good, equals the price of the good times the quantity sold. For inelastic demand curves, total revenue moves in the same direction as the price. For elastic demand curves, total revenue moves in the opposite direction as the price.

- The income elasticity of demand measures how much the quantity demanded responds to changes in consumers' income. The cross-price elasticity of demand measures how much the quantity demanded of one good responds to changes in the price of another good.

- The price elasticity of supply measures how much the quantity supplied responds to changes in the price. This elasticity often depends on the time horizon under consideration. In most markets, supply is more elastic in the long run than in the short run.

- The price elasticity of supply is calculated as the percentage change in quantity supplied divided by the percentage change in price. If the elasticity is less than 1, so that quantity supplied moves proportionately less than the price, supply is said to be inelastic. If the elasticity is greater than 1, so that quantity supplied moves proportionately more than the price, supply is said to be elastic.

- The tools of supply and demand can be applied in many different kinds of markets. This chapter uses them to analyze the market for wheat, the market for oil, and the relationship of drug interdiction and the amount of drug-related crime.

KEY CONCEPTS

elasticity, p. 98
price elasticity of
 demand, p. 98

total revenue (in a market), p. 101
income elasticity of
 demand, p. 107

cross-price elasticity of
 demand, p. 107
price elasticity of supply, p. 108

QUESTIONS FOR REVIEW

1. Define the price elasticity of demand and the income elasticity of demand.

2. List and explain the four determinants of the price elasticity of demand discussed in the chapter.

3. What is the main advantage of using the midpoint method for calculating elasticity?

4. If the elasticity is greater than 1, is demand elastic or inelastic? If the elasticity equals 0, is demand perfectly elastic or perfectly inelastic?

5. On a supply-and-demand diagram, show equilibrium price, equilibrium quantity, and the total revenue received by producers.

6. If demand is elastic, how will an increase in price change total revenue? Explain.

7. What do we call a good whose income elasticity is less than 0?

8. How is the price elasticity of supply calculated? Explain what this measures.

9. What is the price elasticity of supply of Picasso paintings?

10. Is the price elasticity of supply usually larger in the short run or in the long run? Why?

11. How can elasticity help explain why drug interdiction could reduce the supply of drugs, yet possibly increase drug-related crime?

PROBLEMS AND APPLICATIONS

1. For each of the following pairs of goods, which good would you expect to have more elastic demand and why?
   a. required textbooks or mystery novels
   b. Beethoven recordings or classical music recordings in general
   c. heating oil during the next six months or heating oil during the next five years
   d. root beer or water

2. Suppose that business travellers and vacationers have the following demand for airline tickets from Toronto to Montreal:

Price	Quantity Demanded (business travellers)	Quantity Demanded (vacationers)
$150	2100 tickets	1000 tickets
200	2000	800
250	1900	600
300	1800	400

   a. As the price of tickets rises from $200 to $250, what is the price elasticity of demand for (i) business travellers and (ii) vacationers?

   (Use the midpoint method in your calculations.)
   b. Why might vacationers have a different elasticity than business travellers?

3. Suppose that your demand schedule for DVDs is as follows:

Price	Quantity Demanded (income = $10 000)	Quantity Demanded (income = $12 000)
$ 8	40	50
10	32	45
12	24	30
14	16	20
16	8	12

   a. Use the midpoint method to calculate your price elasticity of demand as the price of DVDs increases from $8 to $10 if (i) your income is $10 000, and (ii) your income is $12 000.
   b. Calculate your income elasticity of demand as your income increases from $10 000 to $12 000 if (i) the price is $12, and (ii) the price is $16.

4. Emily has decided always to spend one-third of her income on clothing.
   a. What is her income elasticity of clothing demand?
   b. What is her price elasticity of clothing demand?
   c. If Emily's tastes change and she decides to spend only one-fourth of her income on clothing, how does her demand curve change? What are her income elasticity and price elasticity now?

5. *The Globe and Mail* (December 16, 1997) reported that milk consumption declined following price increases: "Since the early 1980s, the price of milk in Canada has increased 22 per cent. As prices rose, the demand for milk fell off. Total [consumption] of milk on a per capita basis dropped . . . to 2.62 hectolitres in 1995 from 2.92 hectolitres in 1986."
   a. Use these data to estimate the price elasticity of demand for milk.
   b. According to your estimate, what happens to milk producers' revenue when the price of milk rises?
   c. Why might your estimate of the elasticity be unreliable? (Hint: Notice that *The Globe and Mail* is careless about the distinction between demand and quantity demanded.)

6. Two drivers—Tom and Jerry—each drive up to a gas station. Before looking at the price, each places an order. Tom says, "I'd like 40 litres of gas." Jerry says, "I'd like $40 worth of gas." What is each driver's price elasticity of demand?

7. You are the curator of a museum. The museum is running short of funds, so you decide to increase revenue. Should you increase or decrease the price of admission? Explain.

8. Consider public policy aimed at smoking.
   a. Studies indicate that the price elasticity of demand for cigarettes is about 0.4. If a pack of cigarettes currently costs $10 and the government wants to reduce smoking by 20 percent, by how much should it increase the price?
   b. If the government permanently increases the price of cigarettes, will the policy have a greater effect on smoking one year from now or five years from now?

c. Studies also find that teenagers have a higher price elasticity than do adults. Why might this be true?

9. Suppose that the price elasticity of demand for heating oil is 0.2 in the short run and 0.7 in the long run.
   a. If the price of heating oil rises from $0.45 to $0.55 per litre, what happens to the quantity of heating oil demanded in the short run? In the long run? (Use the midpoint method in your calculations.)
   b. Why might this elasticity depend on the time horizon?

10. Pharmaceutical drugs have an inelastic demand, and computers have an elastic demand. Suppose that technological advance doubles the supply of both products (that is, the quantity supplied at each price is twice what it was).
    a. What happens to the equilibrium price and quantity in each market?
    b. Which product experiences a greater change in price?
    c. Which product experiences a greater change in quantity?
    d. What happens to total consumer spending on each product?

11. Some years ago, flooding along the Red River in Manitoba destroyed thousands of hectares of wheat.
    a. Farmers whose crops were destroyed by the floods were much worse off, but farmers whose crops were not destroyed benefited from the floods. Why?
    b. What information would you need about the market for wheat to assess whether farmers as a group were hurt or helped by the floods?

12. Explain why the following might be true: A drought around the world raises the total revenue that farmers receive from the sale of grain, but a drought only in Alberta reduces the total revenue that Alberta farmers receive.

13. A price change causes the quantity demanded of a good to decrease by 30 percent, while the total revenue of that good increases by 15 percent. Is the demand curve elastic or inelastic? Explain.

14. The equilibrium price of coffee mugs rose sharply last month, but the equilibrium quantity was the same as ever. Three people tried to explain the situation. Which explanations could be right? Explain your logic.

   BILLY: Demand increased, but supply was totally inelastic.

   MARIAN: Supply increased, but so did demand.

   VALERIE: Supply decreased, but demand was totally inelastic.

15. You have the following information about good X and good Y:

   • Income elasticity of demand for good X: -3

   • Cross-price elasticity of demand for good X with respect to the price of good Y: 2

Would an increase in income and a decrease in the price of good Y unambiguously decrease the demand for good X? Why or why not?

16. Consider two demand curves. The first is linear, with the demand curve given by $Q^D = 100 - 20P$. The second is nonlinear, with the demand curve given by $Q^D = 60/P$. For each of these demand curves, compute the quantity demanded at prices of $1, $2, $3, $4, $5, and $6. Graph each of the demand curves. Use the midpoint method to calculate the price elasticity of demand between $1 and $2, and between $4 and $5 for each demand curve. Compare the price elasticities in these cases. In particular, how does the elasticity of the nonlinear demand curve for the two price movements differ from the elasticity of the linear demand curve for the same price movements?

http://

For more study tools, please visit www.nelson.com/mankiwmicro6e.

SUPPLY, DEMAND, AND GOVERNMENT POLICIES

6

Dusit/Shutterstock

Learning Objectives

In this chapter, you will ...

- Examine the effects of government policies that place a ceiling on prices

- Examine the effects of government policies that put a floor under prices

- Consider how a tax on a good affects the price of the good and the quantity sold

- Learn that taxes levied on buyers and taxes levied on sellers are equivalent

- See how the burden of a tax is split between buyers and sellers

Economists have two roles. As scientists, they develop and test theories to explain the world around them. As policy advisers, they use their theories to help change the world for the better. The focus of the preceding two chapters has been scientific. We have seen how supply and demand determine the price of a good and the quantity of the good sold. We have also seen how various events shift supply and demand and thereby change the equilibrium price and quantity.

This chapter offers our first look at policy. Here we analyze various types of government policy using only the tools of supply and demand. As you will see, the analysis yields some surprising insights. Policies often have effects that their architects did not intend or anticipate.

We begin by considering policies that directly control prices. For example, rent-control laws dictate a maximum rent that landlords may charge tenants. Minimum-wage laws dictate the lowest wage that firms may pay workers. Price controls are usually enacted when policymakers believe that the market price of a good or service is unfair to buyers or sellers. Yet, as we will see, these policies can generate inequities of their own.

Taxes: the price we pay for a civilised society (services)

After our discussion of price controls, we will consider the impact of taxes. Policymakers use taxes both to influence market outcomes and to raise revenue for public purposes. Although the prevalence of taxes in our economy is obvious, their effects are not. For example, when the government levies a tax on the amount that firms pay their workers, do the firms or the workers bear the burden of the tax? The answer is not at all clear—until we apply the powerful tools of supply and demand.

CONTROLS ON PRICES

To see how price controls affect market outcomes, let's look once again at the market for ice cream. As we saw in Chapter 4, if ice cream is sold in a competitive market free of government regulation, the price of ice cream adjusts to balance supply and demand: At the equilibrium price, the quantity of ice cream that buyers want to buy exactly equals the quantity that sellers want to sell. To be concrete, suppose the equilibrium price is $3 per cone.

Not everyone may be happy with the outcome of this free-market process. Let's say the Canadian Association of Ice-Cream Eaters complains that the $3 price is too high for everyone to enjoy a cone a day (their recommended daily allowance). Meanwhile, the Canadian Organization of Ice-Cream Makers complains that the $3 price—the result of "cutthroat competition"—is too low and is depressing the incomes of its members. Each of these groups lobbies the government to pass laws that alter the market outcome by directly controlling the price of an ice-cream cone.

Because buyers of any good always want a lower price while sellers want a higher price, the interests of the two groups conflict. If the Ice-Cream Eaters are successful in their lobbying, the government imposes a legal maximum on the price at which ice cream can be sold. Because the price is not allowed to rise above this level, the legislated maximum is called a **price ceiling**. By contrast, if the Ice-Cream Makers are successful, the government imposes a legal minimum on the price. Because the price cannot fall below this level, the legislated minimum is called a **price floor**. Let us consider the effects of these policies in turn.

price ceiling
a legal maximum on the price at which a good can be sold

price floor
a legal minimum on the price at which a good can be sold

How Price Ceilings Affect Market Outcomes

When the government, moved by the complaints and campaign contributions of the Ice-Cream Eaters, imposes a price ceiling on the market for ice cream, two outcomes are possible. In panel (a) of Figure 6.1, the government imposes a price ceiling of $4 per cone. In this case, because the price that balances supply and demand ($3) is below the ceiling, the price ceiling is *not binding*. Market forces naturally move the economy to the equilibrium, and the price ceiling has no effect on the price or the quantity sold.

→ *If a price ceiling is above the equilibrium price, it is non-binding and has no effects.* ↓

Panel (b) of Figure 6.1 shows the other, more interesting, possibility. In this case, the government imposes a price ceiling of $2 per cone. Because the equilibrium price of $3 is above the price ceiling, the ceiling is a *binding constraint* on the market. The forces of supply and demand tend to move the price toward the equilibrium price, but when the market price hits the ceiling, it can rise no further. Thus, the market price equals the price ceiling. At this price, the quantity of ice cream demanded (125 cones in the figure) exceeds the quantity supplied

FIGURE 6.1

A Market with a Price Ceiling

In panel (a), the government imposes a price ceiling of $4. Because the price ceiling is above the equilibrium price of $3, the price ceiling has no effect, and the market can reach the equilibrium of supply and demand. In this equilibrium, quantity supplied and quantity demanded both equal 100 cones. In panel (b), the government imposes a price ceiling of $2. Because the price ceiling is below the equilibrium price of $3, the market price equals $2. At this price, 125 cones are demanded and only 75 are supplied, so there is a shortage of 50 cones.

(a) A Price Ceiling That Is Not Binding

(b) A Price Ceiling That Is Binding

(75 cones). There is a shortage of ice cream; 50 people who want to buy ice cream at the going price are unable to.

When a shortage of ice cream develops because of this price ceiling, some mechanism for rationing ice cream will naturally develop. The mechanism could be long lines: Buyers who are willing to arrive early and wait in line get a cone, while those unwilling to wait do not. Alternatively, sellers could ration ice cream according to their own personal biases, selling it only to friends, relatives, or members of their own racial or ethnic group. Notice that even though the price ceiling was motivated by a desire to help buyers of ice cream, not all buyers benefit from the policy. Some buyers do get to pay a lower price, although they may have to wait in line to do so, but other buyers cannot get any ice cream at all.

This example in the market for ice cream shows a general result: *When the government imposes a binding price ceiling on a competitive market, a shortage of the good arises, and sellers must ration the scarce goods among the large number of potential buyers.* The rationing mechanisms that develop under price ceilings are rarely desirable. Long lines are inefficient, because they waste buyers' time. Discrimination according to seller bias is both inefficient (because the good does not necessarily go to the buyer who values it most highly) and potentially unfair. By contrast, the rationing mechanism in a free, competitive market is both efficient and impersonal. When the market for ice cream reaches its equilibrium, anyone who wants to pay the market price can get a cone. Free markets ration goods with prices.

Case Study

LINES AT THE GAS PUMP

As we discussed in the preceding chapter, in 1973 the Organization of the Petroleum Exporting Countries (OPEC) raised the price of crude oil in world oil markets. Because crude oil is the major input used to make gasoline, the higher oil prices reduced the supply of gasoline. In Canada the price of gas increased, but there were very few shortages. In the United States, it was very different. Long lines at gas stations became commonplace, and American motorists often had to wait for hours to buy only a few litres of gas.

What was responsible for the long gas lines? Most people blame OPEC. Surely, if OPEC had not raised the price of crude oil, the shortage of gasoline would not have occurred. Yet economists blame U.S. government regulations that limited the price that oil companies could charge for gasoline.

Figure 6.2 shows what happened. As shown in panel (a), before OPEC raised the price of crude oil, the equilibrium price of gasoline, P_1, was below the price ceiling. The price regulation, therefore, had no effect. When the price of crude oil

---

FIGURE 6.2

The Market for Gasoline with a Price Ceiling

Panel (a) shows the gasoline market when the price ceiling is not binding because the equilibrium price, P_1, is below the ceiling. Panel (b) shows the gasoline market after an increase in the price of crude oil (an input into making gasoline) shifts the supply curve to the left from S_1 to S_2. In an unregulated market, the price would have risen from P_1 to P_2. The price ceiling, however, prevents this from happening. At the binding price ceiling, consumers are willing to buy Q_D, but producers of gasoline are willing to sell only Q_S. The difference between quantity demanded and quantity supplied, $Q_D - Q_S$, measures the gasoline shortage.

rose, however, the situation changed. The increase in the price of crude oil raised the cost of producing gasoline, and this reduced the supply of gasoline. As panel (b) shows, the supply curve shifted to the left, from S_1 to S_2. In an unregulated market, this shift in supply would have raised the equilibrium price of gasoline from P_1 to P_2, and no shortage would have resulted. Instead, the price ceiling prevented the price from rising to the equilibrium level. At the price ceiling, producers were willing to sell Q_S, and consumers were willing to buy Q_D. Thus, the shift in supply caused a severe shortage at the regulated price.

Eventually, the laws regulating the price of gasoline were repealed. Lawmakers came to understand that they were partly responsible for the many hours Americans lost waiting in line to buy gasoline. Today, when the price of crude oil changes, the price of gasoline can adjust to bring supply and demand into equilibrium. In Canada there were no price controls on gasoline in 1973, and so no long gas lines either. ●

Case Study

RENT CONTROL IN THE SHORT RUN AND LONG RUN

One common example of a price ceiling is rent control. In some provinces, the provincial government places a ceiling on rents that landlords may charge their tenants. For example, in Canada, some form of rent control exists in the provinces of Ontario, Quebec, British Columbia, Manitoba, and Prince Edward Island. The goal of this policy is to help the poor by making housing more affordable. Economists often criticize rent control, arguing that it is a highly inefficient way to help the poor raise their standard of living. One economist has called rent control "the best way to destroy a city, other than bombing."

The adverse effects of rent control are less apparent to the general population because these effects occur over many years. In the short run, landlords have a fixed number of apartments to rent, and they cannot adjust this number quickly as market conditions change. Moreover, the number of people searching for housing in a city may not be highly responsive to rents in the short run because people take time to adjust their housing arrangements. Therefore, the short-run supply and demand for housing are relatively inelastic.

Panel (a) of Figure 6.3 shows the short-run effects of rent control on the housing market. As with any binding price ceiling, rent control causes a shortage. Yet because supply and demand are inelastic in the short run, the initial shortage caused by rent control is small. The primary effect in the short run is to reduce rents.

The long-run story is very different because the buyers and sellers of rental housing respond more to market conditions as time passes. On the supply side, landlords respond to low rents by not building new apartments and by failing to maintain existing ones. On the demand side, low rents encourage people to find their own apartments (rather than living with their parents or sharing apartments

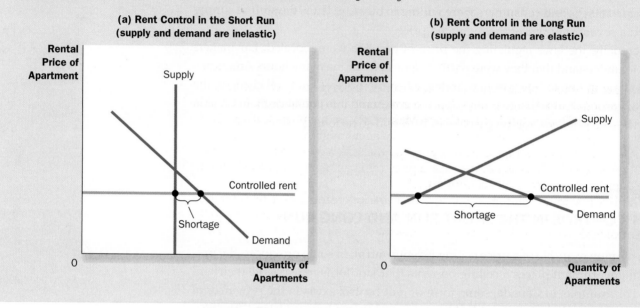

FIGURE 6.3

Rent Control in the Short Run and in the Long Run

Panel (a) shows the short-run effects of rent control: Because the supply and demand for apartments are relatively inelastic, the price ceiling imposed by a rent-control law causes only a small shortage of housing. Panel (b) shows the long-run effects of rent control: Because the supply and demand for apartments are more elastic, rent control causes a large shortage.

with roommates) and induce more people to move into a city. Therefore, both supply and demand are more elastic in the long run.

Panel (b) of Figure 6.3 illustrates the housing market in the long run. When rent control depresses rents below the equilibrium level, the quantity of apartments supplied falls substantially, and the quantity of apartments demanded rises substantially. The result is a large shortage of housing.

In provinces with rent control, landlords use various mechanisms to ration housing. Some landlords keep long waiting lists. Others give a preference to tenants without children. Still others discriminate on the basis of race. Sometimes, apartments are allocated to those willing to offer under-the-table payments to building superintendents. In essence, these bribes bring the total price of an apartment (including the bribe) closer to the equilibrium price.

To understand fully the effects of rent control, we have to remember one of the ten principles of economics from Chapter 1: People respond to incentives. In free markets, landlords try to keep their buildings clean and safe because desirable apartments command higher prices. By contrast, when rent control creates shortages and waiting lists, landlords lose their incentive to respond to tenants' concerns. Why should a landlord spend his money to maintain and improve his property when people are waiting to get in as it is? In the end, tenants get lower rents, but they also get lower-quality housing.

Policymakers often react to the effects of rent control by imposing additional regulations. For example, there are laws that make racial discrimination in housing illegal and require landlords to provide minimally adequate living conditions. These laws, however, are difficult and costly to enforce. By contrast, when rent control is eliminated and a market for housing is regulated by the forces of competition, such laws are less necessary. In a free market, the price of housing adjusts to eliminate the shortages that give rise to undesirable landlord behaviour. ●

How Price Floors Affect Market Outcomes

To examine the effects of another kind of government price control, let's return to the market for ice cream. Imagine now that the government is persuaded by the pleas of the Canadian Organization of Ice-Cream Makers, whose members feel that the $3 equilibrium price is too low. In this case, the government might institute a price floor. Price floors, like price ceilings, are an attempt by the government to maintain prices at other than equilibrium levels. Whereas a price ceiling places a legal maximum on prices, a price floor places a legal minimum.

When the government imposes a price floor on the ice-cream market, two outcomes are possible. If the government imposes a price floor of $2 per cone when the equilibrium price is $3, we obtain the outcome in panel (a) of Figure 6.4. In this case, because

FIGURE 6.4

A Market with a Price Floor

In panel (a), the government imposes a price floor of $2. Because this is below the equilibrium price of $3, the price floor has no effect. The market price adjusts to balance supply and demand. At the equilibrium, quantity supplied and quantity demanded both equal 100 cones. In panel (b), the government imposes a price floor of $4, which is above the equilibrium price of $3. Therefore, the market price equals $4. Because 120 cones are supplied at this price and only 80 are demanded, there is a surplus of 40 cones.

(a) A Price Floor That Is Not Binding

(b) A Price Floor That Is Binding

the equilibrium price is above the floor, the price floor is not binding. Market forces naturally move the economy to the equilibrium, and the price floor has no effect.

Panel (b) of Figure 6.4 shows what happens when the government imposes a price floor of $4 per cone. In this case, because the equilibrium price of $3 is below the floor, the price floor is a binding constraint on the market. The forces of supply and demand tend to move the price toward the equilibrium price, but when the market price hits the floor, it can fall no further. The market price equals the price floor. At this floor, the quantity of ice cream supplied (120 cones) exceeds the quantity demanded (80 cones). Some people who want to sell ice cream at the going price are unable to. *Thus, a binding price floor causes a surplus.*

Just as price ceilings and shortages can lead to undesirable rationing mechanisms, so can price floors and surpluses. In the case of a price floor, some sellers are unable to sell all they want at the market price. The sellers who appeal to the personal biases of the buyers, perhaps due to racial or familial ties, are better able to sell their goods than those who do not. By contrast, in a free market, the price serves as the rationing mechanism, and sellers can sell all they want at the equilibrium price.

Case Study

THE MINIMUM WAGE

An important example of a price floor is the minimum wage. Minimum-wage laws dictate the lowest price for labour that any employer may pay. Minimum-wage rates differ by province and territory, as shown in Table 6.1. In 2012, minimum wages ranged from a low of $9.75 per hour in Alberta to a high of $11.00 in Nunavut. In some provinces, lower rates apply for inexperienced workers and for restaurant and bar staff, who can earn tips to supplement their wages. Many

TABLE 6.1

Alberta	$ 9.75
Quebec	9.90
New Brunswick	10.00
Newfoundland and Labrador	10.00
Northwest Territories	10.00
Prince Edward Island	10.00
Saskatchewan	10.00
British Columbia	10.25
Manitoba	10.25
Ontario	10.25
Nova Scotia	10.30
Yukon	10.30
Nunavut	11.00

Source: Human Resources and Skills Development Canada, March 1, 2013, Current and Forthcoming Minimum Hourly Wage Rates for Experienced Adult Workers in Canada.

FIGURE 6.5

How the Minimum Wage Affects the Labour Market

Panel (a) shows a labour market in which the wage adjusts to balance labour supply and labour demand. Panel (b) shows the impact of a binding minimum wage. Because the minimum wage is a price floor, it causes a surplus: The quantity of labour supplied exceeds the quantity demanded. The result is unemployment.

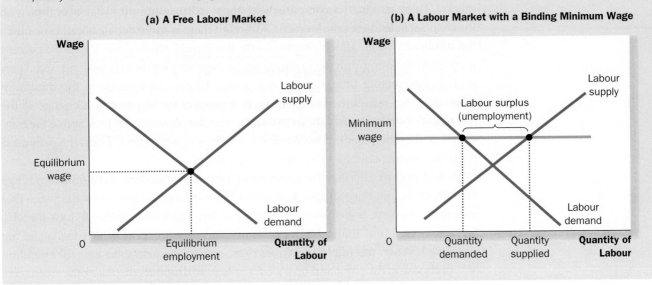

(a) A Free Labour Market

(b) A Labour Market with a Binding Minimum Wage

other countries have minimum-wage laws as well. In the United States the federally mandated minimum wage is $7.25 (although some states mandate higher minimum wages, the highest being Washington state at $9.19).

To examine the effects of a minimum wage, we must consider the market for labour. Panel (a) of Figure 6.5 shows the labour market, which, like all markets, is subject to the forces of supply and demand. Workers determine the supply of labour, and firms determine the demand. If the government doesn't intervene, the wage normally adjusts to balance labour supply and labour demand.

Panel (b) of Figure 6.5 shows the labour market with a minimum wage. If the minimum wage is above the equilibrium level, as it is here, the quantity of labour supplied exceeds the quantity demanded. The result is unemployment. Thus, the minimum wage raises the incomes of those workers who have jobs, but it lowers the incomes of those workers who cannot find jobs.

To fully understand the minimum wage, keep in mind that the economy contains not a single labour market, but many labour markets for different types of workers. The impact of the minimum wage depends on the skill and experience of the worker. Highly skilled and experienced workers are not affected, because their equilibrium wages are well above the minimum. For these workers, the minimum wage is not binding.

The minimum wage has its greatest impact on the market for teenage labour. The equilibrium wages of teenagers are low because teenagers are among the least skilled and least experienced members of the labour force. In addition, teenagers are often willing to accept a lower wage in exchange for on-the-job training. (Some teenagers are willing to work as "interns" for no pay at all. Because internships pay nothing, however, the minimum wage does not apply to them. If it did, these jobs might not exist.) As a result, the minimum wage is more often binding for teenagers than for other members of the labour force.

Many economists have studied how minimum-wage laws affect the teenage labour market. These researchers compare the changes in the minimum wage over time with the changes in teenage employment. Although there is some debate about how much the minimum wage affects employment, the typical study finds that a 10 percent increase in the minimum wage depresses teenage employment between 1 and 3 percent. In interpreting this estimate, note that a 10 percent increase in the minimum wage does not raise the average wage of teenagers by 10 percent. A change in the law does not directly affect those teenagers who are already paid well above the minimum, and enforcement of minimum-wage laws is not perfect. Thus, the estimated drop in employment of 1 to 3 percent is significant.

In addition to altering the quantity of labour demanded, the minimum wage also alters the quantity supplied. Because the minimum wage raises the wage that teenagers can earn, it increases the number of teenagers who choose to look for jobs. Studies have found that a higher minimum wage influences which teenagers are employed. When the minimum wage rises, some teenagers who are still attending school choose to drop out and take jobs. These new dropouts displace other teenagers who had already dropped out of school and who now become unemployed.

The minimum wage is a frequent topic of debate. Economists are about evenly divided on the issue. In a 2006 survey of Ph.D. economists, 47 percent favoured eliminating the minimum wage, while 14 percent would maintain it at its current level and 38 percent would increase it. Advocates of the minimum wage view the policy as one way to raise the income of the working poor. They correctly point out that workers who earn the minimum wage can afford only a meagre standard of living. For example, at a minimum wage of $10.00 per hour, two adults working 40 hours a week for every week of the year at minimum-wage jobs had a total annual income of only $41 600, which was about 60 percent of median family income in 2012. Many advocates of the minimum wage admit that it has some adverse effects, including unemployment, but they believe that these effects are small and that, all things considered, a higher minimum wage makes the poor better off.

Opponents of the minimum wage contend that it is not the best way to combat poverty. They note that a high minimum wage causes unemployment, encourages teenagers to drop out of school, and prevents some unskilled workers from getting the on-the-job training they need. Moreover, opponents of the minimum wage point out that the minimum wage is a poorly targeted policy. Not all minimum-wage workers are heads of households trying to help their families escape poverty. In fact, fewer than a third of minimum-wage earners are in families with incomes below the poverty line. Many are teenagers from middle-class homes working at part-time jobs for extra spending money. ●

Evaluating Price Controls

One of the ten principles of economics discussed in Chapter 1 is that markets are usually a good way to organize economic activity. This principle explains why economists usually oppose price ceilings and price floors. To economists, prices are not the outcome of some haphazard process. Prices, they contend, are the result of the millions of business and consumer decisions that lie behind the supply and demand curves. Prices have the crucial job of balancing supply and demand and, thereby, coordinating economic activity. When policymakers set prices by legal decree, they obscure the signals that normally guide the allocation of society's resources.

Another of the ten principles of economics is that governments can sometimes improve market outcomes. Indeed, policymakers are led to control prices because they view the market's outcome as unfair. Price controls are often aimed at helping the poor. For instance, rent-control laws try to make housing affordable for everyone, and minimum-wage laws try to help people escape poverty.

Yet price controls often hurt those they are trying to help. Rent control may keep rents low, but it also discourages landlords from maintaining their buildings and

IN THE NEWS

PRICE CONTROLS ON BEER (AND MILK)?

In their quest to improve market outcomes, governments sometimes impose policies with the intention of achieving one outcome, but end up achieving another. Moreover, they sometimes impose policies that end up pursuing completely contradictory objectives. A good example in Canada is price controls on beer and dairy products.

Controlling Beverage Prices Is Nothing More Than Corporate Welfare

By Jesse Kline

A few years ago, I visited China and found that, in many places, it was actually cheaper to drink beer than bottled water. The same is true in the UK. In Canada, however, one might think the sky was falling at the mere mention of the possibility that beer could become less expensive than milk.

The Quebec Brewers Association— which represents Molson and Labatt,

Canada's largest beer producers that control around 90% of the market—is lobbying the provincial government to change the way it calculates the floor price of beer, which would, in effect, raise the minimum price in Quebec.

The obvious benefit of raising the minimum is that it gives producers an excuse to charge more for their product, thereby increasing their profit margins. There are, however, many other advantages for the big producers that come from having a government-mandated floor price.

First, it prevents Molson and Labatt from getting involved in a price war. In

most cases, if two companies colluded on price, it would be illegal. But if the government does it for them, the companies are free and clear.

The minimum price also acts as a barrier to entry into the marketplace. Since the two companies already have the brand recognition and sell their product at the lowest price possible under the law, it is difficult for a new company to enter the market and compete based on the price point. The regulation helps these companies maintain their market share against would-be competitors.

→ In Canada these price controls essentially creates monopoly

The brewers, however, claim a more altruistic reason for wanting to increase the price. They say the price should be more closely tied to the cost of other items at Quebec grocery stores. "The reason why we have a minimum price at all is for social reasons," said Molson spokesperson Marie-Hélène Lagacé in an interview with the *Financial Post*. "And we fear that if the price of beer as an industry rises lower than the price of milk or butter, we have a social issue."

Similar arguments have been made about other products. Many processed foods are cheaper than fresh fruit and vegetables, so perhaps the government should tax unhealthy foods and subsidize the stuff that's good for your health. Except I don't think we're in any danger of having people substitute beer for milk in their Lucky Charms.

Moreover, there is no deep social meaning embedded in the price of a product. It is merely the point where supply and demand intersect. At least in theory. The big problem with the argument put forward by the brewers is that the price of milk and butter is also determined by the government and, like beer, it is set way above market value.

You may be surprised to find out that, according to the federal government, Canadian dairy products are "world-renowned for their excellence" and this is all thanks to strict government regulation of the industry.

Where would we be without the government setting quotas on dairy production or centrally planned support prices for butter and skim milk powder? Or imposing import tariffs as high as 300%? Or provincial dairy boards establishing targets for the retail price of milk?

Well, for one thing, we wouldn't have some of the highest dairy prices in the world; costs probably wouldn't increase at almost double the rate of inflation; and people in lower income brackets would be able to afford more of a product that's good for their health.

But don't expect government policies to actually help the average hardworking Canadian who is trying to provide their children with a hearty breakfast and unwind with a cold one at the end of the day. As long as we continue to allow governments to set the price of our beverages, the policies will have the effect of lining the pockets of dairy farmers and big alcohol producers, at the expense of everyone else.

makes housing hard to find. Minimum-wage laws may raise the incomes of some workers, but they also cause other workers to be unemployed.

Helping those in need can be accomplished in ways other than controlling prices. For instance, the government can make housing more affordable by paying a fraction of the rent for poor families. Unlike rent control, such rent subsidies do not reduce the quantity of housing supplied and, therefore, do not lead to housing shortages. Similarly, wage subsidies raise the living standards of the working poor without discouraging firms from hiring them.

Although these alternative policies are often better than price controls, they are not perfect. Rent and wage subsidies cost the government money and, therefore, require higher taxes. As we see in the next section, taxation has costs of its own.

QuickQuiz   Define *price ceiling* and *price floor,* and give an example of each. Which leads to a shortage? Which leads to a surplus? Why?

TAXES

All governments—from the federal government in Ottawa to the local governments in small towns—use taxes to raise revenue for public projects, such as roads, schools, and national defence. Because taxes are such an important policy instrument, and because they affect our lives in many ways, the study of taxes is a topic to which we return several times throughout this book. In this section we begin our study of how taxes affect the economy.

To set the stage for our analysis, imagine that a local government decides to hold an annual ice-cream celebration—with a parade, fireworks, and speeches by town officials. To raise revenue to pay for the event, it decides to place a $0.50 tax on the sale of ice-cream cones. When the plan is announced, our two lobbying groups swing into action. The Canadian Organization of Ice-Cream Makers claims that its members are struggling to survive in a competitive market, and it argues that *buyers* of ice cream should have to pay the tax. The Canadian Association of Ice-Cream Eaters claims that consumers of ice cream are having trouble making ends meet, and it argues that *sellers* of ice cream should pay the tax. The town mayor, hoping to reach a compromise, suggests that half the tax be paid by the buyers and half be paid by the sellers.

To analyze these proposals, we need to address a simple but subtle question: When the government levies a tax on a good, who bears the burden of the tax? The people buying the good? The people selling the good? Or, if buyers and sellers share the tax burden, what determines how the burden is divided? Can the government simply legislate the division of the burden, as the mayor is suggesting, or is the division determined by more fundamental forces in the economy? Economists use the term **tax incidence** to refer to the distribution of a tax burden. As we will see, some surprising lessons about tax incidence arise just by applying the tools of supply and demand.

tax incidence
the manner in which the burden of a tax is shared among participants in a market

How Taxes on Buyers Affect Market Outcomes

We begin by considering a tax levied on buyers of a good. Suppose, for instance, that our local government passes a law requiring buyers of ice-cream cones to send $0.50 to the government for each ice-cream cone they buy. How does this law affect the buyers and sellers of ice cream? To answer this question, we can follow the three steps in Chapter 4 for analyzing supply and demand: (1) We decide whether the law affects the supply curve or demand curve. (2) We decide which way the curve shifts. (3) We examine how the shift affects the equilibrium.

Step One   The immediate impact of the tax is on the demand for ice cream. The supply curve is not affected because, for any given price of ice cream, sellers have the same incentive to provide ice cream to the market. By contrast, buyers now have to pay a tax to the government (as well as the price to the sellers) whenever they buy ice cream. Thus, the tax shifts the demand curve for ice cream.

→ Outside influence causes the shift

Step Two   We next determine the direction of the shift. Because the tax on buyers makes buying ice cream less attractive, buyers demand a smaller quantity of ice cream at every price. As a result, the demand curve shifts to the left (or, equivalently, downward), as shown in Figure 6.6.

We can, in this case, be precise about how much the curve shifts. Because of the $0.50 tax levied on buyers, the effective price to buyers is now $0.50 higher than the market price (whatever the market price happens to be). For example, if the market price of a cone happened to be $2.00, the effective price to buyers would be $2.50. Because buyers look at their total cost including the tax, they demand a quantity

FIGURE 6.6

A Tax on Buyers

When a tax of $0.50 is levied on buyers, the demand curve shifts down by $0.50 from D_1 to D_2. The equilibrium quantity falls from 100 to 90 cones. The price that sellers receive falls from $3.00 to $2.80. The price that buyers pay (including the tax) rises from $3.00 to $3.30. Even though the tax is levied on buyers, buyers and sellers share the burden of the tax.

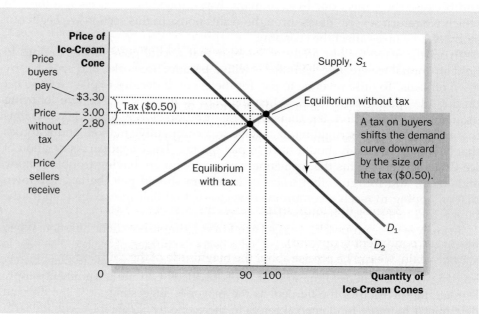

of ice cream as if the market price were $0.50 higher than it actually is. In other words, to induce buyers to demand any given quantity, the market price must now be $0.50 lower to make up for the effect of the tax. Thus, the tax shifts the demand curve *downward* from D_1 to D_2 by exactly the size of the tax ($0.50).

Step Three   Having determined how the demand curve shifts, we can now see the effect of the tax by comparing the initial equilibrium and the new equilibrium. You can see in Figure 6.6 that the equilibrium price of ice cream falls from $3.00 to $2.80 and the equilibrium quantity falls from 100 to 90 cones. Because sellers sell less and buyers buy less in the new equilibrium, the tax on ice cream reduces the size of the ice-cream market.

Implications   We can now return to the question of tax incidence: Who pays the tax? Although buyers send the entire tax to the government, buyers and sellers share the burden. Because the market price falls from $3.00 to $2.80 when the tax is introduced, sellers receive $0.20 less for each ice-cream cone than they did without the tax. Thus, the tax makes sellers worse off. Buyers pay sellers a lower price ($2.80), but the effective price including the tax rises from $3.00 before the tax to $3.30 with the tax ($2.80 + $0.50 = $3.30). Thus, the tax also makes buyers worse off.

To sum up, the analysis yields two lessons:

- Taxes discourage market activity. When a good is taxed, the quantity of the good sold is smaller in the new equilibrium.
- Buyers and sellers share the burden of taxes. In the new equilibrium, buyers pay more for the good, and sellers receive less.

→Buyers now pay a higher price, with some going to the gov't and less going to the seller

How Taxes on Sellers Affect Market Outcomes

Now consider a tax levied on sellers of a good. Suppose the local government passes a law requiring sellers of ice-cream cones to send $0.50 to the government for each cone they sell. What are the effects of this law? Again, we apply our three steps.

Step One   In this case, the immediate impact of the tax is on the sellers of ice cream. Because the tax is not levied on buyers, the quantity of ice cream demanded at any given price is the same; thus, the demand curve does not change. By contrast, the tax on sellers makes the ice-cream business less profitable at any given price, so it shifts the supply curve.

Step Two   Because the tax on sellers raises the cost of producing and selling ice cream, it reduces the quantity supplied at every price. The supply curve shifts to the left (or, equivalently, upward).

Once again, we can be precise about the magnitude of the shift. For any market price of ice cream, the effective price to sellers—the amount they get to keep after paying the tax—is $0.50 lower. For example, if the market price of a cone happened to be $2.00, the effective price received by sellers would be $1.50. Whatever the market price, sellers will supply a quantity of ice cream as if the price were $0.50 lower than it is. Put differently, to induce sellers to supply any given quantity, the market price must now be $0.50 higher to compensate for the effect of the tax. Thus, as shown in Figure 6.7, the supply curve shifts *upward* from S_1 to S_2 by exactly the size of the tax ($0.50).

Step Three   Having determined how the supply curve shifts, we can now compare the initial and the new equilibrium. The figure shows that the equilibrium

FIGURE 6.7

A Tax on Sellers

When a tax of $0.50 is levied on sellers, the supply curve shifts up by $0.50 from S_1 to S_2. The equilibrium quantity falls from 100 to 90 cones. The price that buyers pay rises from $3.00 to $3.30. The price that sellers receive (after paying the tax) falls from $3.00 to $2.80. Even though the tax is levied on sellers, buyers and sellers share the burden of the tax.

price of ice cream rises from $3.00 to $3.30, and the equilibrium quantity falls from 100 to 90 cones. Once again, the tax reduces the size of the ice-cream market. And once again, buyers and sellers share the burden of the tax. Because the market price rises, buyers pay $0.30 more for each cone than they did before the tax was enacted. Sellers receive a higher price than they did without the tax, but the effective price (after paying the tax) falls from $3.00 to $2.80.

Implications   If you compare Figures 6.6 and 6.7, you will notice a surprising conclusion: *Taxes on buyers and taxes on sellers are equivalent.* In both cases, the tax places a wedge between the price that buyers pay and the price that sellers receive. The wedge between the buyers' price and the sellers' price is the same, regardless of whether the tax is levied on buyers or sellers. In either case, the wedge shifts the relative position of the supply and demand curves. In the new equilibrium, buyers and sellers share the burden of the tax. The only difference between taxes on buyers and taxes on sellers is who sends the money to the government.

The equivalence of these two taxes is easy to understand if we imagine that the government collects the $0.50 ice-cream tax in a bowl on the counter of each ice-cream store. When the government levies the tax on buyers, the buyer is required to place $0.50 in the bowl every time a cone is bought. When the government levies the tax on sellers, the seller is required to place $0.50 in the bowl after the sale of each cone. Whether the $0.50 goes directly from the buyer's pocket into the bowl, or indirectly from the buyer's pocket into the seller's hand and then into the bowl, does not matter. Once the market reaches its new equilibrium, buyers and sellers share the burden, regardless of how the tax is levied.

Case Study

CAN PARLIAMENT DISTRIBUTE THE BURDEN OF A PAYROLL TAX?

If you have ever received a paycheque, you probably noticed that taxes were deducted from the amount you earned. One of these taxes is called Employment Insurance (EI). The federal government uses the revenue from the EI tax to pay for benefits to unemployed workers, as well as for training programs and other policies. EI is an example of a payroll tax, which is a tax on the wages that firms pay their workers. In 2010, the total EI tax for the typical worker was about 4 percent of earnings.

Who do you think bears the burden of this payroll tax—firms or workers? When Parliament passed this legislation, it tried to mandate a division of the tax burden. According to the law, 58 percent of the tax is paid by firms, and 42 percent is paid by workers. That is, 58 percent of the tax is paid out of firm revenue, and 42 percent is deducted from workers' paycheques. The amount that shows up as a deduction on your pay stub is the worker contribution.

FIGURE 6.8

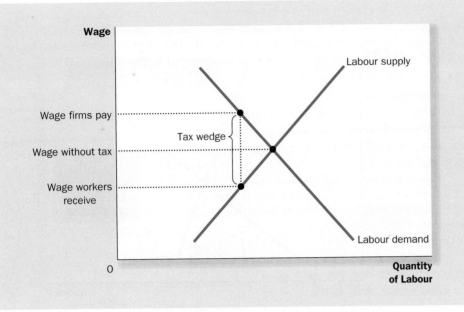

A Payroll Tax

A payroll tax places a wedge between the wage that workers receive and the wage that firms pay. Comparing wages with and without the tax, you can see that workers and firms share the tax burden. This division of the tax burden between workers and firms does not depend on whether the government levies the tax on workers, levies the tax on firms, or divides the tax equally between the two groups.

Our analysis of tax incidence, however, shows that lawmakers cannot so easily dictate the distribution of a tax burden. To illustrate, we can analyze a payroll tax as merely a tax on a good, where the good is labour and the price is the wage. The key feature of the payroll tax is that it places a wedge between the wage that firms pay and the wage that workers receive. Figure 6.8 shows the outcome. When a payroll tax is enacted, the wage received by workers falls, and the wage paid by firms rises. In the end, workers and firms share the burden of the tax, much as the legislation requires. Yet this division of the tax burden between workers and firms has nothing to do with the legislated division: The division of the burden in Figure 6.8 is not necessarily 58–42 percent, and the same outcome would prevail if the law levied the entire tax on workers or if it levied the entire tax on firms.

This example shows that the most basic lesson of tax incidence is often overlooked in public debate. Lawmakers can decide whether a tax comes from the buyer's pocket or from the seller's, but they cannot legislate the true burden of a tax. Rather, tax incidence depends on the forces of supply and demand. ●

Elasticity and Tax Incidence

When a good is taxed, buyers and sellers of the good share the burden of the tax. But how exactly is the tax burden divided? Only rarely will it be shared equally. To see how the burden is divided, consider the impact of taxation in the two markets

FIGURE 6.9

How the Burden of a Tax Is Divided

In panel (a), the supply curve is elastic, and the demand curve is inelastic. In this case, the price received by sellers falls only slightly, while the price paid by buyers rises substantially. Thus, buyers bear most of the burden of the tax. In panel (b), the supply curve is inelastic, and the demand curve is elastic. In this case, the price received by sellers falls substantially, while the price paid by buyers rises only slightly. Thus, sellers bear most of the burden of the tax.

(a) Elastic Supply, Inelastic Demand

1. When supply is more elastic than demand . . .
2. . . . the incidence of the tax falls more heavily on consumers . . .
3. . . . than on producers.

(b) Inelastic Supply, Elastic Demand

1. When demand is more elastic than supply . . .
2. . . . the incidence of the tax falls more heavily on producers . . .
3. . . . than on consumers.

in Figure 6.9. In both cases, the figure shows the initial demand curve, the initial supply curve, and a tax that drives a wedge between the amount paid by buyers and the amount received by sellers. (Not drawn in either panel of the figure is the new supply or demand curve. Which curve shifts depends on whether the tax is levied on buyers or sellers. As we have seen, this is irrelevant for the incidence of the tax.) The difference in the two panels is the relative elasticity of supply and demand.

Panel (a) of Figure 6.9 shows a tax in a market with very elastic supply and relatively inelastic demand. That is, sellers are very responsive to changes in the price of the good (so the supply curve is relatively flat), whereas buyers are not very responsive (so the demand curve is relatively steep). When a tax is imposed on a market with these elasticities, the price received by sellers does not fall much, so sellers bear only a small burden. By contrast, the price paid by buyers rises substantially, indicating that buyers bear most of the burden of the tax.

Panel (b) of Figure 6.9 shows a tax in a market with relatively inelastic supply and very elastic demand. In this case, sellers are not very responsive to changes in the price (so the supply curve is steeper), while buyers are very responsive (so the demand curve is flatter). The figure shows that when a tax is imposed, the price paid by buyers does not rise much, while the price received by sellers falls substantially. Thus, sellers bear most of the burden of the tax.

The two panels of Figure 6.9 show a general lesson about how the burden of a tax is divided: *A tax burden falls more heavily on the side of the market that is less elastic.* Why is this true? In essence, the elasticity measures the willingness of buyers or sellers to leave the market when conditions become unfavourable. A small elasticity of demand means that buyers do not have good alternatives to consuming this particular good. A small elasticity of supply means that sellers do not have good alternatives to producing this particular good. When the good is taxed, the side of the market with fewer good alternatives cannot easily leave the market and must, therefore, bear more of the burden of the tax.

We can apply this logic to the payroll tax discussed in the previous case study. Most labour economists believe that the supply of labour is much less elastic than the demand. This means that workers, rather than firms, bear most of the burden of the payroll tax. In other words, the distribution of the tax burden is not at all close to the 58–42 split that lawmakers intended.

QuickQuiz   In a supply-and-demand diagram, show how a tax on car buyers of $1000 per car affects the quantity of cars sold and the price of cars. In another diagram, show how a tax on car sellers of $1000 per car affects the quantity of cars sold and the price of cars. In both of your diagrams, show the change in the price paid by car buyers and the change in price received by car sellers.

CONCLUSION

The economy is governed by two kinds of laws: the laws of supply and demand and the laws enacted by governments. In this chapter we have begun to see how these laws interact. Price controls and taxes are common in various markets in the economy, and their effects are frequently debated in the press and among policymakers. Even a little bit of economic knowledge can go a long way toward understanding and evaluating these policies.

In subsequent chapters we analyze many government policies in greater detail. We examine the effects of taxation more fully, and consider a broader range of policies than we considered here. Yet the basic lessons of this chapter will not change: When analyzing government policies, supply and demand are the first and most useful tools of analysis.

SUMMARY

- A price ceiling is a legal maximum on the price of a good or service. An example is rent control. If the price ceiling is below the equilibrium price, so the price ceiling is binding, the quantity demanded exceeds the quantity supplied. Because of the resulting shortage, sellers must in some way ration the good or service among buyers.

- A price floor is a legal minimum on the price of a good or service. An example is the minimum wage. If the price floor is above the equilibrium price, so the price floor is binding, the quantity supplied exceeds the quantity demanded. Because of the resulting surplus, buyers' demands for the good or service must in some way be rationed among sellers.

- When the government levies a tax on a good, the equilibrium quantity of the good falls. That is, a tax on a market shrinks the size of the market.

- A tax on a good places a wedge between the price paid by buyers and the price received by sellers. When the market moves to the new equilibrium, buyers pay more for the good and sellers receive less for it. In this sense, buyers and sellers share the tax burden. The incidence of a tax (that is, the division of the tax burden) does not depend on whether the tax is levied on buyers or sellers.

- The incidence of a tax depends on the price elasticities of supply and demand. The burden tends to fall on the side of the market that is less elastic because that side of the market can respond less easily to the tax by changing the quantity bought or sold.

KEY CONCEPTS

price ceiling, p. 122

price floor, p. 122

tax incidence, p. 133

QUESTIONS FOR REVIEW

1. Give an example of a price ceiling and an example of a price floor.

2. Which causes a shortage of a good—a price ceiling or a price floor? Which causes a surplus?

3. What mechanisms allocate resources when the price of a good is not allowed to bring supply and demand into equilibrium?

4. Explain why economists usually oppose controls on prices.

5. What is the difference between a tax paid by buyers and a tax paid by sellers?

6. How does a tax on a good affect the price paid by buyers, the price received by sellers, and the quantity sold?

7. What determines how the burden of a tax is divided between buyers and sellers? Why?

PROBLEMS AND APPLICATIONS

1. Lovers of classical music persuade Parliament to impose a price ceiling of $40 per concert ticket. Does this policy get more or fewer people to attend classical music concerts?

2. The government has decided that the free-market price of cheese is too low.
   a. Suppose the government imposes a binding price floor in the cheese market. Use a supply-and-demand diagram to show the effect of this policy on the price of cheese and the quantity of cheese sold. Is there a shortage or surplus of cheese?
   b. Farmers complain that the price floor has reduced their total revenue. Is this possible? Explain.

c. In response to farmers' complaints, the government agrees to purchase all of the surplus cheese at the price floor. Compared to the basic price floor, who benefits from this new policy? Who loses?

3. A recent study found that the demand and supply schedules for Frisbees are as follows:

Price per Frisbee	Quantity Demanded	Quantity Supplied
$11	1 million	15 million
10	2	12
9	4	9
8	6	6
7	8	3
6	10	1

a. What are the equilibrium price and quantity of Frisbees?

b. Frisbee manufacturers persuade the government that Frisbee production improves scientists' understanding of aerodynamics and thus is important for national security. A concerned Parliament votes to impose a price floor $2 above the equilibrium price. What is the new market price? How many Frisbees are sold?

c. Irate students march on Ottawa and demand a reduction in the price of Frisbees. An even more concerned Parliament votes to repeal the price floor and impose a price ceiling $1 below the former price floor. What is the new market price? How many Frisbees are sold?

4. Suppose the provincial government requires beer drinkers to pay a $2 tax on each case of beer purchased.

a. Draw a supply-and-demand diagram of the market for beer without the tax. Show the price paid by consumers, the price received by producers, and the quantity of beer sold. What is the difference between the price paid by consumers and the price received by producers?

b. Now draw a supply-and-demand diagram for the beer market with the tax. Show the price paid by consumers, the price received by producers, and the quantity of beer sold. What is the difference between the price paid by consumers and the price received by producers? Has the quantity of beer sold increased or decreased?

5. An MP wants to raise tax revenue and make workers better off. A staff member proposes raising the payroll tax paid by firms and using part of the extra revenue to reduce the payroll tax paid by workers. Would this accomplish the MP's goal?

6. If the government places a $500 tax on luxury cars, will the price paid by consumers rise by more than $500, less than $500, or exactly $500? Explain.

7. Parliament decides that Canada should reduce air pollution by reducing its use of gasoline. It imposes a $0.50 tax for each litre of gasoline sold.

a. Should it impose this tax on producers or consumers? Explain carefully, using a supply-and-demand diagram.

b. If the demand for gasoline were more elastic, would this tax be more effective or less effective in reducing the quantity of gasoline consumed? Explain with both words and a diagram.

c. Are consumers of gasoline helped or hurt by this tax? Why?

d. Are workers in the oil industry helped or hurt by this tax? Why?

8. A case study in this chapter discusses the minimum-wage law.

a. Suppose the minimum wage is above the equilibrium wage in the market for unskilled labour. Using a supply-and-demand diagram of the market for unskilled labour, show the market wage, the number of workers who are employed, and the number of workers who are unemployed. Also show the total wage payments to unskilled workers.

b. Now suppose the provincial government proposes an increase in the minimum wage. What effect would this increase have on employment? Does the change in employment depend on the elasticity of demand, the elasticity of supply, both elasticities, or neither?

c. What effect would this increase in the minimum wage have on unemployment? Does the change in unemployment depend on the elasticity of demand, the elasticity of supply, both elasticities, or neither?

d. If the demand for unskilled labour were inelastic, would the proposed increase in the minimum wage raise or lower total wage payments to unskilled workers? Would your answer change if the demand for unskilled labour were elastic?

9. The Canadian government administers two programs that affect the market for cigarettes. Health Canada media campaigns and labelling requirements are aimed at making the public aware of the dangers of cigarette smoking. At the same time, Agriculture and Agri-Food Canada imposes production quotas on tobacco farmers, which raise the price of tobacco above the equilibrium price.

   a. How do these two programs affect cigarette consumption? Use a graph of the cigarette market in your answer.

   b. What is the combined effect of these two programs on the price of cigarettes?

   c. Cigarettes are also heavily taxed. What effect does this tax have on cigarette consumption?

10. A subsidy is the opposite of a tax. With a $0.50 tax on the buyers of ice-cream cones, the government collects $0.50 for each cone purchased; with a $0.50 subsidy for the buyers of ice-cream cones, the government pays buyers $0.50 for each cone purchased.

   a. Show the effect of a $0.50 per cone subsidy on the demand curve for ice-cream cones, the effective price paid by consumers, the effective price received by sellers, and the quantity of cones sold.

   b. Do consumers gain or lose from this policy? Do producers gain or lose? Does the government gain or lose?

11. At the Pengrowth Saddledome, home of the Calgary Flames, seating is limited to about 17 000. Hence, the number of tickets issued is fixed at that figure. (Assume that all seats are equally desirable and are sold at the same price.) Seeing a golden opportunity to raise revenue, the City of Calgary levies a per-ticket tax of $5 to be paid by the hockey ticket buyer. Calgary sports fans, a famously civic-minded lot, dutifully send in the $5 per ticket. Draw a well-labelled graph showing the impact of the tax. On whom does the tax burden fall—the team's owners, the fans, or both? Why?

12. Say the demand schedule for ice-cream cones can be represented by the equation $Q^D = 160 - 3P$, where Q^D is the quantity demanded and P is the price. The supply schedule can be represented by $Q^S = 140 + 7P$, where Q^S is the quantity supplied.

   a. Calculate the equilibrium price and quantity in the market for ice-cream cones.

   b. Say the Canadian Association of Ice-Cream Eaters complains that the equilibrium price calculated in part (a) is too high, and their members cannot eat enough ice-cream cones at this price. They lobby the government to impose a price ceiling on ice-cream cones of $1. What is the quantity demanded at this price? The quantity supplied? Is there a shortage or surplus of ice cream? How big is it? What if a $2.50 price ceiling was imposed instead?

   c. Say instead that the Canadian Association of Ice-Cream Makers lobbies the government, arguing that the equilibrium price is too low for their members to make a decent living. They want a price floor of $3 per cone. What is the quantity demanded at this price? The quantity supplied? Is there a shortage or a surplus of ice cream? What is it? What if a price floor of $1.50 was imposed instead?

13. The demand and supply functions for hockey sticks are given by

   $$Q^D = 286 - 20P$$

   $$Q^S = 88 + 40P$$

   In order to raise revenue to finance minor hockey so that Canada can continue its gold medal streak at the Olympics, the federal government decides to impose a tax of $2 per hockey stick sold, to be paid by the buyers of hockey sticks.

   a. Determine the equilibrium price and quantity of hockey sticks both before and after the tax. How is the burden of the tax shared between buyers and seller?

   b. How many hockey sticks would be sold before the tax is imposed? After the tax?

   c. Graph the supply and the demand curves for hockey both before and after the tax, clearly showing the intercepts and equilibrium outcomes.

   d. What would happen if the tax was paid by the sellers of hockey sticks instead of the buyers?

http:// For more study tools, please visit www.nelson.com/mankiwmicro6e.

APPENDIX: THE MATHEMATICS OF MARKET EQUILIBRIUM WITH TAXES

In the appendix to Chapter 4, we showed you how to solve algebraically for the equilibrium price in a competitive market characterized by linear demand and supply curves. We saw in this chapter that when a tax is imposed on a good, there are, in effect, two types of prices in equilibrium because the tax places a wedge between the price that buyers pay and the price that sellers receive. In this appendix, we show you how to adapt the approach explained in the appendix to Chapter 4 to account for taxes.

We again start by using a general approach, using letters to represent the demand and supply parameters. Begin by considering the equations for linear demand and supply curves without any taxes:

$$Q^D = a - bP$$

$$Q^S = c + dP$$

Now consider a tax imposed on the buyers of the good. Say the tax is equal to \$T per unit of the good purchased. As discussed earlier in this chapter, the effective price of the good to the buyers is now $P + T$, since it is the price of the good including the tax that determines demand. This means that the demand curve in the presence of a tax paid by the buyers should be written as

$$Q^D = a - b(P + T)$$

Recall from the appendix to Chapter 4 that a change in the demand parameter a represents a shift in the demand curve. Rewriting the demand equation as $Q^D = (a - bT) - bP$, we see that the tax acts just like a downward shift in the demand curve. This is illustrated in Figure 6A.1, where we see that the x-intercept of the new demand curve occurs at $Q^D = a - bT$, and the y-intercept at $P = (a/b) - T$. Thus, the tax results in a downward shift of the demand curve by the amount of the tax. The supply curve remains the same, because P is the price received by sellers.

We can then proceed exactly as in the appendix to Chapter 4 and set the quantity demanded equal to quantity supplied to determine the equilibrium prices in the presence of the tax:

$$(a - bT) - bP = c + dP$$

Using simple algebra to gather terms with P on the left-hand side and the other terms on the right-hand side gives

$$P(b + d) = a - c - bT$$

FIGURE 6A.1

Market Equilibrium with Linear Demand and Supply Curves and a Tax on Buyers

This figure illustrates the market equilibrium for linear demand and supply curves given by the equations $Q^D = a - bP$ and $Q^S = c + dP$. In the absence of the tax, the equilibrium price is determined by setting $Q^D = Q^S$ and solving for $P_0 = \frac{(a-c)}{(b+d)}$. When a tax of \$T per unit is imposed on buyers of the good, the demand curve becomes $Q^D = a - b(P + T)$. Again setting $Q^D = Q^S$ and solving for $P_S = P_0 - \frac{Tb}{(b+d)}$ gives the "seller's price" of the good. The "buyer's price" is $P_B = P_S + T = P_0 + \frac{Td}{(b+d)}$.

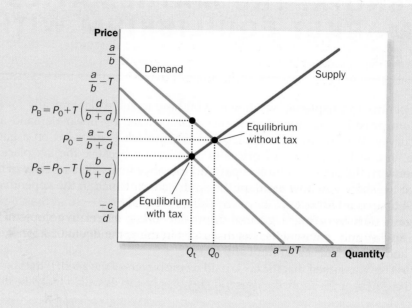

Dividing both sides by $(b + d)$ to solve for P gives the equilibrium price received by sellers of

$$P = \frac{(a - c)}{(b + d)} - \frac{Tb}{(b + d)}$$

which we write as

$$P_S = P_0 - \frac{Tb}{(b + d)}$$

where P_S is the equilibrium "seller's price" and P_0 is the equilibrium price without the tax (just set $T = 0$ to get $P_0 = \frac{(a-c)}{(b+d)}$. We thus see that the price received by sellers is lower in the presence of the tax by the amount $\frac{Tb}{(b+d)}$. As discussed in the main body of the chapter, the seller shares in the burden of the tax imposed on buyers by receiving a lower price.

To determine the effective price paid by buyers, we note that it is simply the price received by sellers plus the tax, or $P_S + T$. Using the equilibrium price received by sellers determined above, we add T to both sides to get

$$P_B = P_S + T = P_0 - \frac{Tb}{(b + d)} + T$$

where P_B is the equilibrium "buyer's price." Gathering terms on the right-hand side in T gives the equilibrium price paid by buyers of

$$P_B = P_S + T = P_0 + \frac{Td}{(b + d)}$$

and we see that the tax increases the price paid by buyers by the amount $\frac{Td}{(b+d)}$; buyers also share in the burden of the tax by having to pay a higher price. This is all illustrated in Figure 6A.1.

Notice that the amount that the seller's price P_S goes down due to the tax is $\frac{Tb}{(b+d)}$, while the amount that the buyer's price P_B goes up is $\frac{Td}{(b+d)}$. The amount that the seller's price goes down plus the amount that the buyer's price goes up is therefore

$$\frac{Tb}{(b+d)} + \frac{Td}{(b+d)} = \frac{T(b+d)}{(b+d)} = T$$

which is equal to the amount of the tax. This reflects the simple fact that the tax imposes a wedge equal to T between the seller's and the buyer's price. It also means that the share of the tax T borne by sellers is equal to $\frac{b}{(b+d)}$ and the share of the tax borne by buyers is $\frac{d}{(b+d)}$. These shares depend on the relative slopes of the supply and demand curves, which as discussed in the appendix to Chapter 4, are equal to $\frac{1}{d}$ and $\frac{-1}{b}$, respectively.

So far we have assumed that the tax is paid by the buyers of the good. If the tax was paid by the sellers of the good, the demand and supply curves would look like this:

$$Q^D = a - bP$$

$$Q^S = c + d(P - T)$$

where P is now the price paid by buyers and $P - T$ is the effective price received by sellers. Proceeding exactly as above, we would find that the price paid by buyers and the price received by sellers are exactly the same, which confirms that taxes on buyers and taxes on sellers are equivalent.

By way of example, let's use the same demand and supply schedules used in the appendix to Chapter 4 and impose a $1 tax on the buyers of the good. This gives

$$Q^D = 20 - 2(P + 1)$$

$$Q^S = -10 + 4P$$

Setting $Q^D = Q^S$,

$$20 - 2(P + 1) = -10 + 4P$$

Solve for P:

$$P = \frac{28}{6} = 4\frac{2}{3}$$

which is the price received by sellers. The price paid by buyers is then $P + T = 4\frac{2}{3} + 1 = 5\frac{2}{3}$. In the absence of the tax, the equilibrium price is $5. So we see that both buyers and sellers share in the burden of the tax: buyers pay $\frac{2}{3}$ of a dollar more than they did in the absence of the tax, and sellers receive $\frac{1}{3}$ of a dollar less.

SUPPLY AND DEMAND II: MARKETS AND WELFARE

CHAPTER 7

CONSUMERS, PRODUCERS, AND THE EFFICIENCY OF MARKETS

Learning Objectives

In this chapter, you will…

- Examine the link between buyers' willingness to pay for a good and the demand curve
- Learn how to define and measure consumer surplus
- Examine the link between sellers' cost of producing a good and the supply curve
- Learn how to define and measure producer surplus
- See that the equilibrium of supply and demand maximizes total surplus in a market

When consumers go to grocery stores to buy their turkeys for a holiday dinner, they may be disappointed that the price of turkey is as high as it is. At the same time, when farmers bring to market the turkeys they have raised, they wish the price of turkey was even higher. These views are not surprising: Buyers always want to pay less, and sellers always want to be paid more. But is there a "right price" for turkey from the standpoint of society as a whole?

In previous chapters we saw how, in market economies, the forces of supply and demand determine the prices of goods and services and the quantities sold. So far, however, we have described the way markets allocate scarce resources without directly addressing the question of whether these market allocations are desirable. In other words, our analysis has been *positive* (what is) rather than *normative* (what should be). We know that the price of turkey adjusts to ensure that the quantity of turkey supplied equals the quantity of turkey demanded. But, at this equilibrium, is the quantity of turkey produced and consumed too small, too large, or just right?

In this chapter we discuss **welfare economics**, the study of how the allocation of resources affects economic well-being. We begin by examining the benefits that buyers and sellers receive from taking part in a market. We then examine how society can make these benefits as large as possible. This analysis leads to a profound conclusion: The equilibrium of supply and demand in a market maximizes the total benefits received by buyers and sellers.

As you may recall from Chapter 1, one of the ten principles of economics is that markets are usually a good way to organize economic activity. The study of welfare economics explains this principle more fully. It also answers our question

welfare economics
the study of how the allocation of resources affects economic well-being

about the right price of turkey: The price that balances the supply and demand for turkey is, in a particular sense, the best one because it maximizes the total welfare of turkey consumers and turkey producers. No consumer or producer of turkeys aims to achieve this goal, but their joint action directed by market prices moves them toward a welfare-maximizing outcome, as if led by an invisible hand.

CONSUMER SURPLUS

We begin our study of welfare economics by looking at the benefits buyers receive from participating in a market.

Willingness to Pay

willingness to pay
the maximum amount that a buyer will pay for a good

Imagine that you own a mint-condition recording of Elvis Presley's first album. Because you are not an Elvis Presley fan, you decide to sell it. One way to do so is to hold an auction.

Four Elvis fans show up for your auction: John, Paul, George, and Ringo. Each of them would like to own the album, but there is a limit to the amount that each is willing to pay for it. Table 7.1 shows the maximum price that each of the four possible buyers would pay. Each buyer's maximum is called his **willingness to pay**, and it measures how much that buyer values the good. Each buyer would be eager to buy the album at a price less than his willingness to pay, would refuse to buy the album at a price more than his willingness to pay, and would be indifferent about buying the album at a price exactly equal to his willingness to pay.

To sell your album, you begin the bidding at a low price, say $10. Because all four buyers are willing to pay much more, the price rises quickly. The bidding stops when John bids $80 (or slightly more). At this point, Paul, George, and Ringo have dropped out of the bidding because they are unwilling to bid any more than $80. John pays you $80 and gets the album. Note that the album has gone to the buyer who values the album most highly.

consumer surplus
a buyer's willingness to pay minus the amount the buyer actually pays

What benefit does John receive from buying the Elvis Presley album? In a sense, John has found a real bargain: He is willing to pay $100 for the album but pays only $80 for it. We say that John receives *consumer surplus* of $20. **Consumer surplus** is the amount a buyer is willing to pay for a good minus the amount the buyer actually pays for it.

Consumer surplus measures the benefit to buyers of participating in a market. In this example, John receives a $20 benefit from participating in the auction

TABLE 7.1

Four Possible Buyers' Willingness to Pay

Buyer	Willingness to Pay
John	$100
Paul	80
George	70
Ringo	50

because he pays only $80 for a good he values at $100. Paul, George, and Ringo get no consumer surplus from participating in the auction because they left without the album and without paying anything.

Now consider a somewhat different example. Suppose that you had two identical Elvis Presley albums to sell. Again, you auction them off to the four possible buyers. To keep things simple, we assume that both albums are to be sold for the same price and that no buyer is interested in buying more than one album. Therefore, the price rises until two buyers are left.

In this case, the bidding stops when John and Paul bid $70 (or slightly higher). At this price, John and Paul are each happy to buy an album, and George and Ringo are not willing to bid any higher. John and Paul each receive consumer surplus equal to his willingness to pay minus the price. John's consumer surplus is $30, and Paul's is $10. John's consumer surplus is higher now than it was previously because he gets the same album but pays less for it. The total consumer surplus in the market is $40.

Using the Demand Curve to Measure Consumer Surplus

Consumer surplus is closely related to the demand curve for a product. To see how they are related, let's continue our example and consider the demand curve for this rare Elvis Presley album.

We begin by using the willingness to pay of the four possible buyers to find the demand schedule for the album. The table in Figure 7.1 shows the demand schedule that corresponds to Table 7.1. If the price is above $100, the quantity

FIGURE 7.1

The Demand Schedule and the Demand Curve

The table shows the demand schedule for the buyers in Table 7.1. The graph shows the corresponding demand curve. Note that the height of the demand curve reflects buyers' willingness to pay.

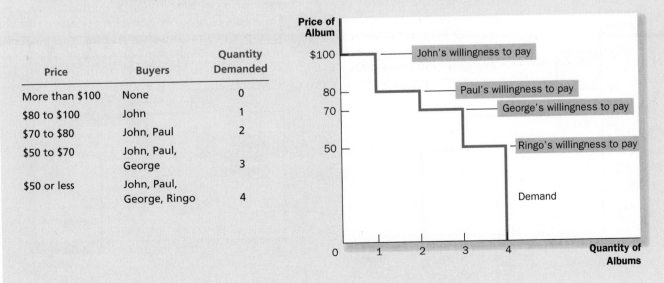

Price	Buyers	Quantity Demanded
More than $100	None	0
$80 to $100	John	1
$70 to $80	John, Paul	2
$50 to $70	John, Paul, George	3
$50 or less	John, Paul, George, Ringo	4

demanded in the market is 0 because no buyer is willing to pay that much. If the price is between $80 and $100, the quantity demanded is 1 because only John is willing to pay such a high price. If the price is between $70 and $80, the quantity demanded is 2 because both John and Paul are willing to pay the price. We can continue this analysis for other prices as well. In this way, the demand schedule is derived from the willingness to pay of the four possible buyers.

The graph in Figure 7.1 shows the demand curve that corresponds to this demand schedule. Note the relationship between the height of the demand curve and the buyers' willingness to pay. At any quantity, the price given by the demand curve shows the willingness to pay of the *marginal buyer*, the buyer who would leave the market first if the price was any higher. At a quantity of 4 albums, for instance, the demand curve has a height of $50, the price that Ringo (the marginal buyer) is willing to pay for an album. At a quantity of 3 albums, the demand curve has a height of $70, the price that George (who is now the marginal buyer) is willing to pay.

Because the demand curve reflects buyers' willingness to pay, we can also use it to measure consumer surplus. Figure 7.2 uses the demand curve to compute consumer surplus in our example. In panel (a), the price is $80 (or slightly above), and the quantity demanded is 1. Note that the area above the price and below the demand curve equals $20. This amount is exactly the consumer surplus we computed earlier when only 1 album is sold.

Panel (b) of Figure 7.2 shows consumer surplus when the price is $70 (or slightly above). In this case, the area above the price and below the demand curve equals

FIGURE 7.2

Measuring Consumer Surplus with the Demand Curve

In panel (a), the price of the good is $80, and the consumer surplus is $20. In panel (b), the price of the good is $70, and the consumer surplus is $40.

the total area of the two rectangles: John's consumer surplus at this price is $30 and Paul's is $10. This area equals a total of $40. Once again, this amount is the consumer surplus we computed earlier.

The lesson from this example holds for all demand curves: *The area below the demand curve and above the price measures the consumer surplus in a market.* The reason is that the height of the demand curve measures the value buyers place on the good, as measured by their willingness to pay for it. The difference between this willingness to pay and the market price is each buyer's consumer surplus. Thus, the total area below the demand curve and above the price is the sum of the consumer surplus of all buyers in the market for a good or service.

How a Lower Price Raises Consumer Surplus

Because buyers always want to pay less for the goods they buy, a lower price makes buyers of a good better off. But how much does buyers' well-being rise in response to a lower price? We can use the concept of consumer surplus to answer this question precisely.

Figure 7.3 shows a typical downward-sloping demand curve. Although this demand curve appears somewhat different in shape from the steplike demand curves in our previous two figures, the ideas we have just developed apply

FIGURE 7.3

How the Price Affects Consumer Surplus

In panel (a), the price is P_1, the quantity demanded is Q_1, and consumer surplus equals the area of the triangle ABC. When the price falls from P_1 to P_2, as in panel (b), the quantity demanded rises from Q_1 to Q_2, and the consumer surplus rises to the area of the triangle ADF. The increase in consumer surplus (area BCFD) occurs in part because existing consumers now pay less (area BCED) and in part because new consumers enter the market at the lower price (area CEF).

nonetheless: Consumer surplus is the area above the price and below the demand curve. In panel (a), consumer surplus at a price of P_1 is the area of triangle ABC.

Now suppose that the price falls from P_1 to P_2, as shown in panel (b). The consumer surplus now equals area ADF. The increase in consumer surplus attributable to the lower price is the area BCFD.

This increase in consumer surplus is composed of two parts. First, those buyers who were already buying Q_1 of the good at the higher price P_1 are better off because they now pay less. The increase in consumer surplus of existing buyers is the reduction in the amount they pay; it equals the area of the rectangle BCED. Second, some new buyers enter the market because they are now willing to buy the good at the lower price. As a result, the quantity demanded in the market increases from Q_1 to Q_2. The consumer surplus these newcomers receive is the area of the triangle CEF.

What Does Consumer Surplus Measure?

Our goal in developing the concept of consumer surplus is to make normative judgments about the desirability of market outcomes. Now that you have seen what consumer surplus is, let's consider whether it is a good measure of economic well-being.

Imagine that you are a policymaker trying to design a good economic system. Would you care about the amount of consumer surplus? Consumer surplus, the amount that buyers are willing to pay for a good minus the amount they actually pay for it, measures the benefit that buyers receive from a good *as the buyers themselves perceive it*. Thus, consumer surplus is a good measure of economic well-being if policymakers want to respect the preferences of buyers.

In some circumstances, policymakers might choose not to care about consumer surplus because they do not respect the preferences that drive buyer behaviour. For example, drug addicts are willing to pay a high price for heroin. Yet we would not say that addicts get a large benefit from being able to buy heroin at a low price (even though addicts might say they do). From the standpoint of society, willingness to pay in this instance is not a good measure of the buyers' benefit, and consumer surplus is not a good measure of economic well-being, because addicts are not looking after their own best interests.

In most markets, however, consumer surplus does reflect economic well-being. Economists normally presume that buyers are rational when they make decisions and that their preferences should be respected. In this case, consumers are the best judges of how much benefit they receive from the goods they buy.

QuickQuiz   Draw a demand curve for turkey. In your diagram, show a price of turkey and the consumer surplus that results from that price. Explain in words what this consumer surplus measures.

PRODUCER SURPLUS

We now turn to the other side of the market and consider the benefits sellers receive from participating in a market. As you will see, our analysis of sellers' welfare is similar to our analysis of buyers' welfare.

Cost and the Willingness to Sell

Imagine now that you are a homeowner, and you need to get your house painted. You turn to four sellers of painting services: Mary, Frida, Georgia, and Grandma. Each painter is willing to do the work for you if the price is right. You decide to take bids from the four painters and auction off the job to the painter who will do the work for the lowest price.

Each painter is willing to take the job if the price she would receive exceeds her cost of doing the work. Here the term **cost** should be interpreted as the painters' opportunity cost: It includes the painters' out-of-pocket expenses (for paint, brushes, and so on) as well as the value that the painters place on their own time. Table 7.2 shows each painter's cost. Because a painter's cost is the lowest price she would accept for her work, cost is a measure of her willingness to sell her services. Each painter would be eager to sell her services at a price greater than her cost, and she would refuse to sell her services at a price less than her cost. At a price exactly equal to her cost, she would be indifferent about selling her services: She would be equally happy getting the job or walking away without incurring the cost.

When you take bids from the painters, the price might start off high, but it quickly falls as the painters compete for the job. Once Grandma has bid $600 (or slightly less), she is the sole remaining bidder. Grandma is happy to do the job for this price because her cost is only $500. Mary, Frida, and Georgia are unwilling to do the job for less than $600. Note that the job goes to the painter who can do the work at the lowest cost.

What benefit does Grandma receive from getting the job? Because she is willing to do the work for $500 but gets $600 for doing it, we say that she receives *producer surplus* of $100. **Producer surplus** is the amount a seller is paid minus the cost of production. Producer surplus measures the benefit to sellers of participating in a market.

Now consider a somewhat different example. Suppose that you have two identical houses that need painting. Again, you auction off the jobs to the four painters. To keep things simple, let's assume that no painter is able to paint both houses and that you will pay the same amount to paint each house. Therefore, the price falls until two painters are left.

In this case, the bidding stops when Georgia and Grandma each offer to do the job for a price of $800 (or slightly less). At this price, Georgia and Grandma are willing to do the work, and Mary and Frida are not willing to bid a lower price. At

– Game of opportunity costs

cost
the value of everything a seller must give up to produce a good

producer surplus
the amount a seller is paid for a good minus the seller's cost

TABLE 7.2

The Costs of Four Possible Sellers

Seller	Cost
Mary	$900
Frida	800
Georgia	600
Grandma	500

a price of $800, Grandma receives producer surplus of $300, and Georgia receives producer surplus of $200. The total producer surplus in the market is $500.

Using the Supply Curve to Measure Producer Surplus

Just as consumer surplus is closely related to the demand curve, producer surplus is closely related to the supply curve. To see how, let's continue our example.

We begin by using the costs of the four painters to find the supply schedule for painting services. The table in Figure 7.4 shows the supply schedule that corresponds to the costs in Table 7.2. If the price is below $500, none of the four painters is willing to do the job, so the quantity supplied is zero. If the price is between $500 and $600, only Grandma is willing to do the job, so the quantity supplied is 1. If the price is between $600 and $800, Grandma and Georgia are willing to do the job, so the quantity supplied is 2, and so on. Thus, the supply schedule is derived from the costs of the four painters.

The graph in Figure 7.4 shows the supply curve that corresponds to this supply schedule. Note that the height of the supply curve is related to the sellers' costs. At any quantity, the price given by the supply curve shows the cost of the *marginal seller*, the seller who would leave the market first if the price was any lower. At a quantity of 4 houses, for instance, the supply curve has a height of $900, the cost that Mary (the marginal seller) incurs to provide her painting services. At a quantity of 3 houses, the supply curve has a height of $800, the cost that Frida (who is now the marginal seller) incurs.

FIGURE 7.4

The Supply Schedule and the Supply Curve

The table shows the supply schedule for the sellers in Table 7.2. The graph shows the corresponding supply curve. Note that the height of the supply curve reflects sellers' costs.

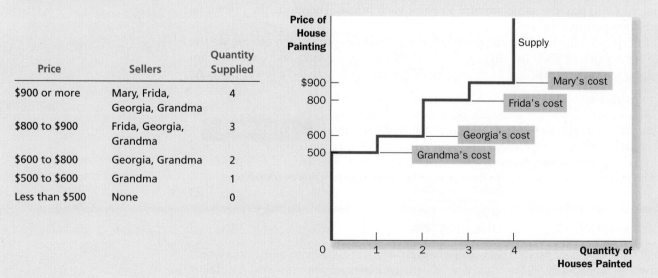

Price	Sellers	Quantity Supplied
$900 or more	Mary, Frida, Georgia, Grandma	4
$800 to $900	Frida, Georgia, Grandma	3
$600 to $800	Georgia, Grandma	2
$500 to $600	Grandma	1
Less than $500	None	0

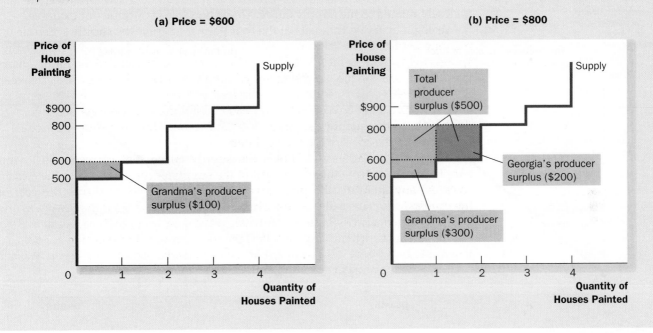

FIGURE 7.5

Measuring Producer Surplus with the Supply Curve

In panel (a), the price of the good is $600, and the producer surplus is $100. In panel (b), the price of the good is $800, and the producer surplus is $500.

Because the supply curve reflects sellers' costs, we can use it to measure producer surplus. Figure 7.5 uses the supply curve to compute producer surplus in our example. In panel (a), we assume that the price is $600. In this case, the quantity supplied is 1. Note that the area below the price and above the supply curve equals $100. This amount is exactly the producer surplus we computed earlier for Grandma.

Panel (b) of Figure 7.5 shows producer surplus at a price of $800. In this case, the area below the price and above the supply curve equals the total area of the two rectangles. This area equals $500, the producer surplus we computed earlier for Georgia and Grandma when two houses needed painting.

The lesson from this example applies to all supply curves: *The area below the price and above the supply curve measures the producer surplus in a market.* The logic is straightforward: The height of the supply curve measures sellers' costs, and the difference between the price and the cost of production is each seller's producer surplus. Thus, the total area is the sum of the producer surplus of all sellers.

How a Higher Price Raises Producer Surplus

You will not be surprised to hear that sellers always want to receive a higher price for the goods they sell. But how much does sellers' well-being rise in response to a higher price? The concept of producer surplus offers a precise answer to this question.

How the Price Affects Producer Surplus

In panel (a), the price is P_1, the quantity supplied is Q_1, and producer surplus equals the area of the triangle ABC. When the price rises from P_1 to P_2, as in panel (b), the quantity supplied rises from Q_1 to Q_2, and the producer surplus rises to the area of the triangle ADF. The increase in producer surplus (area BCFD) occurs in part because existing producers now receive more (area BCED) and in part because new producers enter the market at the higher price (area CEF).

(a) Producer Surplus at Price P_1

(b) Producer Surplus at Price P_2

Figure 7.6 shows a typical upward-sloping supply curve. Even though this supply curve differs in shape from the steplike supply curves in the previous figure, we measure producer surplus in the same way: Producer surplus is the area below the price and above the supply curve. In panel (a), the price is P_1, and producer surplus is the area of triangle ABC.

Panel (b) shows what happens when the price rises from P_1 to P_2. Producer surplus now equals area ADF. This increase in producer surplus has two parts. First, those sellers who were already selling Q_1 of the good at the lower price P_1 are better off because they now get more for what they sell. The increase in producer surplus for existing sellers equals the area of the rectangle BCED. Second, some new sellers enter the market because they are now willing to produce the good at the higher price, resulting in an increase in the quantity supplied from Q_1 to Q_2. The producer surplus of these newcomers is the area of the triangle CEF.

As this analysis shows, we use producer surplus to measure the well-being of sellers in much the same way as we use consumer surplus to measure the well-being of buyers. Because these two measures of economic welfare are so similar, it is natural to use them together. And, indeed, that is exactly what we do in the next section.

QuickQuiz   Draw a supply curve for turkey. In your diagram, show a price of turkey and the producer surplus that results from that price. Explain in words what this producer surplus measures.

MARKET EFFICIENCY

Consumer surplus and producer surplus are the basic tools that economists use to study the welfare of buyers and sellers in a market. These tools can help us address a fundamental economic question: Is the allocation of resources determined by free markets in any way desirable?

The Benevolent Social Planner

To evaluate market outcomes, we introduce into our analysis a new, hypothetical character, called the *benevolent social planner*. The benevolent social planner is an all-knowing, all-powerful, well-intentioned dictator. This planner wants to maximize the economic well-being of everyone in society. What do you suppose this planner should do? Should he just leave buyers and sellers at the equilibrium that they reach naturally on their own? Or can he increase economic well-being by altering the market outcome in some way?

To answer this question, the benevolent social planner must first decide how to measure the economic well-being of a society. One possible measure is the sum of consumer and producer surplus, which we call *total surplus*. Consumer surplus is the benefit that buyers receive from participating in a market, and producer surplus is the benefit that sellers receive. It is therefore natural to use total surplus as a measure of society's economic well-being.

To better understand this measure of economic well-being, recall how we measure consumer and producer surplus. We define consumer surplus as

Consumer surplus = Value to buyers − Amount paid by buyers

Similarly, we define producer surplus as

Producer surplus = Amount received by sellers − Cost to sellers

When we add consumer and producer surplus together, we obtain

Total surplus = Value to buyers − Amount paid by buyers
+ Amount received by sellers − Cost to sellers

The amount paid by buyers equals the amount received by sellers, so the middle two terms in this expression cancel each other. As a result, we can write total surplus as

Total surplus = Value to buyers − Cost to sellers

Total surplus in a market is the total value to buyers of the goods, as measured by their willingness to pay, minus the total cost to sellers of providing those goods.

efficiency

the property of a resource allocation of maximizing the total surplus received by all members of society

If an allocation of resources maximizes total surplus, we say that the allocation exhibits **efficiency**. If an allocation is not efficient, then some of the gains from trade among buyers and sellers are not being realized. For example, an allocation is inefficient if a good is not being produced by the sellers with lowest cost. In this case, moving production from a high-cost producer to a low-cost producer will lower the total cost to sellers and raise total surplus. Similarly, an allocation is inefficient if a good is not being consumed by the buyers who value it most highly. In this case, moving consumption of the good from a buyer with a low valuation to a buyer with a high valuation will raise total surplus.

equity

the fairness of the distribution of well-being among the members of society

In addition to efficiency, the social planner might also care about **equity**—the fairness of the distribution of well-being among the various buyers and sellers. In essence, the gains from trade in a market are like a pie to be distributed among the market participants. The question of efficiency is whether the pie is as big as possible. The question of equality concerns how the pie is sliced and how the portions are distributed among members of society.

In this chapter we concentrate on efficiency as the social planner's goal. Keep in mind, however, that real policymakers often care about equity as well. That is, they care about both the size of the economic pie and how the pie gets sliced and distributed among members of society.

Evaluating the Market Equilibrium

Figure 7.7 shows consumer and producer surplus when a market reaches the equilibrium of supply and demand. Recall that consumer surplus equals the area above the price and under the demand curve, and producer surplus equals the area below the

FIGURE 7.7

Consumer and Producer Surplus in the Market Equilibrium

Total surplus—the sum of consumer and producer surplus—is the area between the supply and demand curves up to the equilibrium quantity.

price and above the supply curve. Thus, the total area between the supply and demand curves up to the point of equilibrium represents the total surplus in this market.

Is this equilibrium allocation of resources efficient? Does it maximize total surplus? To answer these questions, keep in mind that when a market is in equilibrium, the price determines which buyers and sellers participate in the market. Those buyers who value the good more than the price (represented by the segment AE on the demand curve) choose to buy the good; those buyers who value it less than the price (represented by the segment EB) do not. Similarly, those sellers whose costs are less than the price (represented by the segment CE on the supply curve) choose to produce and sell the good; those sellers whose costs are greater than the price (represented by the segment ED) do not.

These observations lead to two insights about market outcomes:

1. Free markets allocate the supply of goods to the buyers who value them most highly, as measured by their willingness to pay.
2. Free markets allocate the demand for goods to the sellers who can produce them at the lowest cost.

Thus, given the quantity produced and sold in a market equilibrium, the social planner cannot increase economic well-being by changing the allocation of consumption among buyers or the allocation of production among sellers.

But can the social planner raise total economic well-being by increasing or decreasing the quantity of the good? The answer is no, as stated in this third insight about market outcomes:

3. Free markets produce the quantity of goods that maximizes the sum of consumer and producer surplus.

Figure 7.8 illustrates why this is true. To interpret this figure, keep in mind that the demand curve reflects the value to buyers and the supply curve reflects the cost to sellers. At any quantity below the equilibrium level, such as Q_1, the value to the marginal buyer exceeds the cost to the marginal seller. As a result, increasing the quantity produced and consumed raises total surplus. This continues to be true until the quantity reaches the equilibrium level. Similarly, at any quantity beyond the equilibrium level, such as Q_2, the value to the marginal buyer is less than the cost to the marginal seller. In this case, decreasing the quantity raises total surplus, and this continues to be true until quantity falls to the equilibrium level. To maximize total surplus, the social planner would choose the quantity where the supply and demand curves intersect.

Together, these three insights tell us that the market outcome makes the sum of consumer and producer surplus as large as it can be. In other words, the equilibrium outcome is an efficient allocation of resources. The benevolent social planner can, therefore, leave the market outcome just as he finds it. This policy of leaving well enough alone goes by the French expression *laissez faire,* which literally translates to "allow them to do."

Society is lucky that the social planner doesn't need to intervene. Although it has been a useful exercise imagining what an all-knowing, all-powerful, well-intentioned dictator would do, let's face it: Such characters are hard to come by. Dictators are rarely benevolent, and even if we found someone so virtuous, he would lack crucial information.

FIGURE 7.8

The Efficiency of the Equilibrium Quantity

At quantities less than the equilibrium quantity, such as Q_1, the value to buyers exceeds the cost to sellers. At quantities greater than the equilibrium quantity, such as Q_2, the cost to sellers exceeds the value to buyers. Therefore, the market equilibrium maximizes the sum of producer and consumer surplus.

Suppose our social planner tried to choose an efficient allocation of resources on his own, instead of relying on market forces. To do so, he would need to know the value of a particular good to every potential consumer in the market and the cost of every potential producer. And he would need this information not only for this market but for every one of the many thousands of markets in the economy. The task is practically impossible, which explains why centrally planned economies never work very well.

The planner's job becomes easy, however, once he takes on a partner: Adam Smith's invisible hand of the marketplace. The invisible hand takes all the information about buyers and sellers into account and guides everyone in the market to the best outcome as judged by the standard of economic efficiency. It is truly a remarkable feat. That is why economists so often advocate free markets as the best way to organize economic activity.

Case Study

SHOULD TICKET SCALPING BE ILLEGAL?

"Psssst . . . need a ticket?" We've all seen them at major sporting events, concerts, and even museum and art exhibit openings. Sometimes they lurk in the shadows, sometimes they market their wares blatantly. Perhaps you've even engaged in a business transaction with one of them.

"They," of course, are ticket scalpers. Whether or not ticket scalping is illegal depends on where you live. Twenty-two states and dozens of major cities in the United States have strict laws against ticket scalping, but in Canada, ticket scalping is illegal only in Ontario and Manitoba.

Why is ticket scalping illegal? Some invoke equity arguments, claiming that it is fairer to let everyone stand in line than to let tickets go to the highest bidder. But this begs the question of why event tickets are different from other goods in this regard. Moreover, why is discriminating in favour of people who have more free (or less valuable) time fairer than discriminating in favour of people with more money? And why is it fairer to force everyone to stand in line and engage in unproductive activity? While there are some concerns about counterfeit tickets, scalping would seem to be the prototypical example of the victimless crime.

For the most part, economists argue that restrictions on scalping inconvenience the public, reduce the audience for cultural and sports events, waste police time, deprive the government of tax revenue, and actually drive up the cost of many tickets. Moreover, we have learned that one of the characteristics of market outcomes is that free markets allocate goods to the buyers who value them most highly. By restricting ticket scalping, some governments effectively introduce inefficiencies into the market for tickets.

Ticket brokers such as Canada's Ticketmaster are catching on. In 2009, Ticketmaster introduced a system that it calls "dynamic pricing." This involves reserving a batch of prime seats for each event that it then auctions off on its website. In this way, these tickets will go to those who value them most. And Ticketmaster and the artist get the money, rather than the scalper. ●

QuickQuiz   Draw the supply and demand for turkey. In the equilibrium, show producer and consumer surplus. Explain why producing more turkey would lower total surplus.

CONCLUSION: MARKET EFFICIENCY AND MARKET FAILURE

This chapter introduced the basic tools of welfare economics—consumer and producer surplus—and used them to evaluate the efficiency of free markets. We showed that the forces of supply and demand allocate resources efficiently. That is, even though each buyer and seller in a market is concerned only about his or her own welfare, they are together led by an invisible hand to an equilibrium that maximizes the total benefits to buyers and sellers.

A word of warning is in order. To conclude that markets are efficient, we made several assumptions about how markets work. When these assumptions do not hold, our conclusion that the market equilibrium is efficient may no longer be true. As we close this chapter, let's consider briefly two of the most important of these assumptions.

First, our analysis assumed that markets are perfectly competitive. In the world, however, competition is sometimes far from perfect. In some markets, a single

IN THE NEWS

ROCKON-OMICS

As the following article shows, everyone can profit by thinking a little like an economist. In this case, rocker Jack White shows how to grab a little producer surplus.

What Jack White Can Teach Us about Economics

By Adam Ozimek

You don't think of rock stars as the bearers of economics lessons. But Jack White recently demonstrated an admirable understanding of basic economics. White's record label, Third Man Records, puts out limited prints of records in order to meet customer demand "to be involved in collecting rare and interesting vinyl." There is a problem with this though. If you make something rare and valuable, the market price will be high. So when White set the prices low, people would show up at the Third Man store and buy up dozens of copies then sell them on eBay for hundreds of dollars.

Here's where the economic insight comes in. Many artists in this position would complain about the greedy resellers and that would be the end of it. But White realized that 1) if customers want rare and valuable albums they will be expensive, 2) the market price will be reached no matter what they sell them for initially, and 3) if someone is going to profit it might as well be the creators. So instead of selling them cheap, he auctioned them off at eBay, and as one would expect from the high prices in resale markets some albums sold for $300. As one also might expect, due to people's general lack of economic

knowledge and the demands of consumers to get valuable things without paying for them, fans were upset and complained about the "exploitative" auctions. But rather than backing down, White defended the economic wisdom of decision:

> We sell a Wanda Jackson split record for 10 bucks, the eBay flipper turns around and sells it for 300. . . . If 300 is what it's worth, then why doesn't Third Man Records sell it for 300? If we sell them for more, the artist gets more, the flipper gets nothing. We're not in the business of making flippers a living. We're in the business of giving fans what they want.

He went on to explain that if rarity and value is what you want, then a high price is what you'll get:

> Make no mistake, we could make twenty thousand split color whatevers for you, and they'll be worth 20 bucks, and you'll pay 20 bucks for them, and you'll never talk about them, desire them, hunt to find them, etc. Why should eBay flippers, who are not real fans, dictate the price, make all the profit (taken from the artist and the label) and take the records out of the hands of real fans. There's a guy who waits in a black

SUV down the block from Third Man who hires homeless people to go buy him tri colors when they are on sale. Doesn't even get out of his car. Should he be charged ten bucks or two hundred? Don't be spoiled, don't insult people who are trying to give you what you want.

Ok, so let's forgive White the error saying that the resellers, or flippers, "dictate the price." Sure they may set a price, but it is the supply, set by Third Man and Jack White, and the demand of the customers that actually dictate the price. Nevertheless, Jack White is clearly a man who thinks like an economist. By giving the profit to the creators instead of the resellers, this gives White, Third Man, and their artists more incentive to create more albums. Fans should be happy about this, but instead they're indignant. They should take White's advice:

> Don't get mad at Third Man for giving you exactly what you've asked for. And seriously stop all of the whining, because what you communicate to us is that all of the trouble we go to isn't worth it because nothing we do will make you happy.

Source: "What Jack White Can Teach Us About Economics" by Adam Ozimek. From *Forbes Magazine*, May 25, 2012.

buyer or seller (or a small group of them) may be able to control market prices. This ability to influence prices is called *market power*. Market power can cause markets to be inefficient because it keeps the price and quantity away from the equilibrium of supply and demand.

Second, our analysis assumed that the outcome in a market matters only to the buyers and sellers in that market. Yet, in the world, the decisions of buyers and sellers sometimes affect people who are not participants in the market at all. Pollution is the classic example of a market outcome that affects people not in the market. The use of agricultural pesticides, for instance, affects not only the manufacturers who make them and the farmers who use them, but many others who breathe air or drink water that has been polluted with these pesticides. Such side effects, called *externalities*, cause welfare in a market to depend on more than just the value to the buyers and the cost to the sellers. Because buyers and sellers do not take these side effects into account when deciding how much to consume and produce, the equilibrium in a market can be inefficient from the standpoint of society as a whole.

Market power and externalities are examples of a general phenomenon called *market failure*—the inability of some unregulated markets to allocate resources efficiently. When markets fail, public policy can potentially remedy the problem and increase economic efficiency. Microeconomists devote much effort to studying when market failure is likely and what sorts of policies are best at correcting market failures. As you continue your study of economics, you will see that the tools of welfare economics developed here are readily adapted to that endeavour.

Despite the possibility of market failure, the invisible hand of the marketplace is extraordinarily important. In many markets, the assumptions we made in this chapter work well, and the conclusion of market efficiency applies directly. Moreover, our analysis of welfare economics and market efficiency can be used to shed light on the effects of various government policies. In the next two chapters we apply the tools we have just developed to study two important policy issues—the welfare effects of taxation and of international trade.

SUMMARY

- Consumer surplus equals buyers' willingness to pay for a good minus the amount they actually pay for it, and it measures the benefit that buyers receive from participating in a market. Consumer surplus can be computed by finding the area below the demand curve and above the price.

- Producer surplus equals the amount that sellers receive for their goods minus their costs of production, and it measures the benefit that sellers receive from participating in a market. Producer surplus can be computed by finding the area below the price and above the supply curve.

- An allocation of resources that maximizes the sum of consumer and producer surplus is said to be efficient. Policymakers are often concerned with the efficiency, as well as the equity, of economic outcomes.

- The equilibrium of supply and demand maximizes the sum of consumer and producer surplus. That is, the invisible hand of the marketplace leads buyers and sellers to allocate resources efficiently.

- Markets do not allocate resources efficiently in the presence of market failures such as market power or externalities.

KEY CONCEPTS

welfare economics, p. 149
willingness to pay, p. 150
consumer surplus, p. 150

cost, p. 155
producer surplus, p. 155
efficiency, p. 160

equity, p. 160

QUESTIONS FOR REVIEW

1. Explain how buyers' willingness to pay, consumer surplus, and the demand curve are related.

2. Explain how sellers' costs, producer surplus, and the supply curve are related.

3. In a supply-and-demand diagram, show producer and consumer surplus in the market equilibrium.

4. What is efficiency? Is it the only goal of economic policymakers?

5. What does the invisible hand do?

6. Name two types of market failure. Explain why each may cause market outcomes to be inefficient.

PROBLEMS AND APPLICATIONS

1. A drought in Nova Scotia reduces the apple harvest. What happens to consumer surplus in the market for apples? What happens to consumer surplus in the market for apple juice? Illustrate your answers with diagrams.

2. Suppose the demand for French bread rises. What happens to producer surplus in the market for French bread? What happens to producer surplus in the market for flour? Illustrate your answer with diagrams.

3. It is a hot day, and Bert is thirsty. Here is the value he places on a bottle of water:

Value of first bottle	$7
Value of second bottle	5
Value of third bottle	3
Value of fourth bottle	1

   a. From this information, derive Bert's demand schedule. Graph his demand curve for bottled water.

   b. If the price of a bottle of water is $4, how many bottles does Bert buy? How much consumer surplus does Bert get from his purchases? Show Bert's consumer surplus in your graph.

   c. If the price falls to $2, how does quantity demanded change? How does Bert's consumer surplus change? Show these changes in your graph.

4. Ernie owns a water pump. Because pumping large amounts of water is harder than pumping small amounts, the cost of producing a bottle of water rises as he pumps more. Here is the cost he incurs to produce each bottle of water:

Cost of first bottle	$1
Cost of second bottle	3
Cost of third bottle	5
Cost of fourth bottle	7

   a. From this information, derive Ernie's supply schedule. Graph his supply curve for bottled water.

   b. If the price of a bottle of water is $4, how many bottles does Ernie produce and sell? How much producer surplus does Ernie get from these sales? Show Ernie's producer surplus in your graph.

   c. If the price rises to $6, how does quantity supplied change? How does Ernie's producer surplus change? Show these changes in your graph.

5. Consider a market in which Bert from problem 3 is the buyer and Ernie from problem 4 is the seller.

a. Use Ernie's supply schedule and Bert's demand schedule to find the quantity supplied and quantity demanded at prices of $2, $4, and $6. Which of these prices brings supply and demand into equilibrium?

b. What are consumer surplus, producer surplus, and total surplus in this equilibrium?

c. If Ernie produced and Bert consumed one fewer bottle of water, what would happen to total surplus?

d. If Ernie produced and Bert consumed one additional bottle of water, what would happen to total surplus?

6. The cost of producing flat-screen TVs has fallen over the past decade. Let's consider some implications of this fact.

a. Use a supply-and-demand diagram to show the effect of falling production costs on the price and quantity of flat-screen TVs sold.

b. In your diagram, show what happens to consumer surplus and producer surplus.

c. Suppose the supply of flat-screen TVs is very elastic. Who benefits most from falling production costs—consumers or producers of these TVs?

7. Four consumers are willing to pay the following amounts for haircuts:

Jerry: $7   Oprah: $2   Ricki: $8   Montel: $5

Four haircutting businesses have the following costs:

Firm A: $3   Firm B: $6   Firm C: $4   Firm D: $2

Each firm has the capacity to produce only one haircut. For efficiency, how many haircuts should be given? Which businesses should cut hair, and which consumers should have their hair cut? How large is the maximum possible total surplus?

8. Suppose a technological advance reduces the cost of making computers.

a. Use a supply-and-demand diagram to show what happens to price, quantity, consumer surplus, and producer surplus in the market for computers.

b. Computers and adding machines are substitutes. Use a supply-and-demand diagram to show what happens to price,

quantity, consumer surplus, and producer surplus in the market for adding machines. Should adding machine producers be happy or sad about the technological advance in computers?

c. Computers and software are complements. Use a supply-and-demand diagram to show what happens to price, quantity, consumer surplus, and producer surplus in the market for software. Should software producers be happy or sad about the technological advance in computers?

d. Does this analysis help explain why software producer Bill Gates is one of the world's richest men?

9. Melissa buys an iPod for $120 and gets consumer surplus of $80.

a. What is her willingness to pay?

b. If she had bought the iPod on sale for $90, what would her consumer surplus have been?

c. If the price of an iPod was $250, what would her consumer surplus have been?

10. The supply and demand for broccoli are described by the following equations:

$$\text{Supply: } Q^S = 4P - 80$$
$$\text{Demand: } Q^D = 100 - 2P$$

Q is in tonnes, and P is in dollars per bushel.

a. Graph the supply curve and the demand curve. What is the equilibrium price and quantity?

b. Calculate consumer surplus, producer surplus, and total surplus at the equilibrium.

c. If a dictator who hated broccoli was to ban the vegetable, who would bear the larger burden—the buyers or sellers of broccoli?

11. A friend of yours is considering two providers of cellphone services. Provider A charges $120 per month for the service, regardless of the number of phone calls made. Provider B does not have a fixed service fee but instead charges $1 per minute for calls. Your friend's monthly demand for minutes of calling is given by the equation $Q^D = 150 - 50P$, where P is the price of a minute.

a. With each provider, what is the cost to your friend of an extra minute on the phone?

b. In light of your answer to (a), how many minutes would your friend spend on the phone with each provider?

c. How much would he end up paying each provider every month?

d. How much consumer surplus would he obtain with each provider? (Hint: Graph the demand curve and recall the formula for the area of a triangle.)

e. Which provider would you recommend that your friend choose? Why?

12. The demand for broccoli in the Kingdom of Vegan is described by a linear demand curve: $Q^D = 100 - 2P$. Say the price of broccoli is set by the ruler of the kingdom, Mr. Potato Head. Say initially that the price is $5 per bunch of broccoli.

a. What is the equilibrium quantity demanded at this price and the consumer surplus?

b. Now say that in order to encourage people to consume more broccoli, Mr. Potato Head decrees that the price of broccoli will decline to $4. What is the new equilibrium quantity? The change in consumer surplus?

http:// For more study tools, please visit www.nelson.com/mankiwmicro6e.

APPENDIX: THE MATHEMATICS OF CONSUMER AND PRODUCER SURPLUS

In the appendix to Chapter 4, we showed you how to use simple mathematics to determine equilibrium prices and quantities for linear supply and demand curves. Here we show you how to calculate consumer and producer surplus for linear supply and demand curves. We actually concentrate on *changes* in consumer and producer surplus associated with price changes, because this is what economists tend to focus on. It is straightforward to extend the approach to calculate total amount of consumer and producer surplus associated with an equilibrium outcome.

Figure 7.3 in this chapter identifies the change in consumer surplus associated with a decrease in the price of a good from P_1 to P_2 as the sum of two areas: the area of the rectangle BCED, which is the additional consumer surplus to initial consumers, and the area of the triangle CEF, which is the consumer surplus to new consumers.

The area of the rectangle BCED is equal to its height times its width. The height is simply the change in price, $P_1 - P_2$, and the width is the quantity demanded at the original price, Q_1. Thus the area of the rectangle is

$$\text{Area BCED} = Q_1(P_1 - P_2)$$

The area of a triangle CEF is equal to one-half of its height times its width (or base). The height is again the change in price, $P_1 - P_2$, and the base is the change in the quantity demanded due to the reduction in the price, $Q_2 - Q_1$. Thus, the area of the triangle is

$$\text{Area CEF} = \left(\frac{1}{2}\right)(P_1 - P_2)(Q_2 - Q_1)$$

Adding these two areas together gives you the change in consumer surplus associated with a decrease in the price from P_1 to P_2.

A similar approach can be used to calculate the change in producer surplus associated with a price increase, as shown in Figure 7.6. This diagram illustrates that the change in producer surplus associated with an increase in the price of a good from P_1 to P_2 is the sum of two areas: the area of the rectangle BCED, which is the additional producer surplus to the initial producers, and area of the triangle CEF, which is the producer surplus accruing to new producers.

Using a similar approach as we did for the change in consumer surplus, we can see that:

$$\text{Area BCED} = Q_1(P_1 - P_2)$$

$$\text{Area CEF} = \left(\frac{1}{2}\right)(P_1 - P_2)(Q_2 - Q_1)$$

Adding these two areas together gives you the change in producer surplus associated with an increase in the price from P_1 to P_2.

→ Taxes often help
  increase equity

APPLICATION: THE COSTS OF TAXATION

Learning Objectives

In this chapter, you will...

- Examine how taxes reduce consumer and producer surplus
- Learn the meaning and causes of the deadweight loss of a tax
- Consider why some taxes have larger deadweight losses than others
- Examine how tax revenue and deadweight loss vary with the size of a tax

Taxes are often the source of heated debate. Political parties in Canada often debate the proper size and shape of the tax system, yet no one would deny that some level of taxation is necessary.

Because taxation has such a major impact on the modern economy, we return to the topic several times throughout this book as we expand the set of tools we have at our disposal. We began our study of taxes in Chapter 6. There we saw how a tax on a good affects its price and the quantity sold and how the forces of supply and demand divide the burden of a tax between buyers and sellers. In this chapter we extend this analysis and look at how taxes affect welfare, the economic well-being of participants in a market.

The effects of taxes on welfare might at first seem obvious. The government enacts taxes to raise revenue, and that revenue must come out of someone's pocket. As we saw in Chapter 6, both buyers and sellers are worse off when a good is taxed: A tax raises the price buyers pay and lowers the price sellers receive. Yet to understand fully how taxes affect economic well-being, we must compare the reduced welfare of buyers and sellers to the amount of revenue the government raises. The tools of consumer and producer surplus allow us to make this comparison. The analysis will show that the costs of taxes to buyers and sellers exceeds the revenue raised by the government.

While this chapter is devoted to discussing the costs of taxation, it is important to remember that taxes give rise to important benefits as well. One of the ten principles of economics in Chapter 1 is that governments can sometimes improve market outcomes. Taxes are one of the ways that governments can do this.

For example, governments must often provide goods and services such as roads, parks, police, and national defence, which are not well provided by the market; they need revenue to do this. We will discuss this in detail in Chapter 11. Also, sometimes governments can impose taxes to achieve a more efficient outcome when markets don't function properly, as in the case of so-called "corrective taxes," which will be discussed in Chapter 10. Finally, governments are also concerned with the distribution of income in society, and the tax system can play an important role in achieving equity objectives; we will pay some attention to this in Chapter 20.

→ Taxes often help increase equity

The tax system thus plays an important and beneficial role in the economy. As Oliver Wendell Holmes, Jr., a member of the U.S. Supreme Court during the early 1900s, once said, "Taxes are what we pay for a civilized society." (These words are engraved on the U.S. Internal Revenue Service building in Washington, DC.) However, it is important to understand the nature of the costs associated with taxes.

THE DEADWEIGHT LOSS OF TAXATION

We begin by recalling one of the surprising lessons from Chapter 6: It does not matter whether a tax on a good is levied on buyers or sellers of the good. When a tax is levied on buyers, the demand curve shifts downward by the size of the tax; when it is levied on sellers, the supply curve shifts upward by that amount. In either case, when the tax is enacted, the price paid by buyers rises, and the price received by sellers falls. In the end, buyers and sellers share the burden of the tax, regardless of how it is levied.

Figure 8.1 shows these effects. To simplify our discussion, this figure does not show a shift in either the supply or demand curve, although one curve must shift. Which curve shifts depends on whether the tax is levied on sellers (the supply

FIGURE 8.1

The Effects of a Tax

A tax on a good places a wedge between the price that buyers pay and the price that sellers receive. The quantity of the good sold falls.

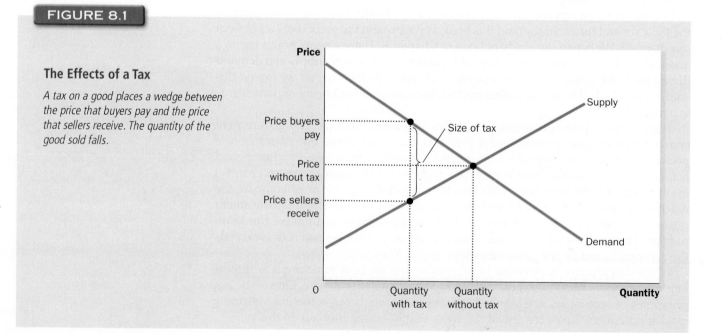

curve shifts) or buyers (the demand curve shifts). In this chapter, we can simplify the graphs by not bothering to show the shift. The key result for our purposes here is that the tax places a wedge between the price buyers pay and the price sellers receive. Because of this tax wedge, the quantity sold falls below the level that would be sold without a tax. In other words, a tax on a good causes the size of the market for the good to shrink. These results should be familiar from Chapter 6.

How a Tax Affects Market Participants

Let's use the tools of welfare economics to measure the gains and losses from a tax on a good. To do this, we must take into account how the tax affects buyers, sellers, and the government. The benefit received by buyers in a market is measured by consumer surplus—the amount buyers are willing to pay for the good minus the amount they actually pay for it. The benefit received by sellers in a market is measured by producer surplus—the amount sellers receive for the good minus their costs. These are precisely the measures of economic welfare we used in Chapter 7.

What about the third interested party, the government? If T is the size of the tax and Q is the quantity of the good sold, then the government gets total tax revenue of $T \times Q$. It can use this tax revenue to provide services, such as roads, police, and public education, or to help the needy. Therefore, to analyze how taxes affect economic well-being, we use tax revenue to measure the government's benefit from the tax. Keep in mind, however, that this benefit actually accrues not to government but to those on whom the revenue is spent.

Figure 8.2 shows that the government's tax revenue is represented by the rectangle between the supply and demand curves. The height of this rectangle is the

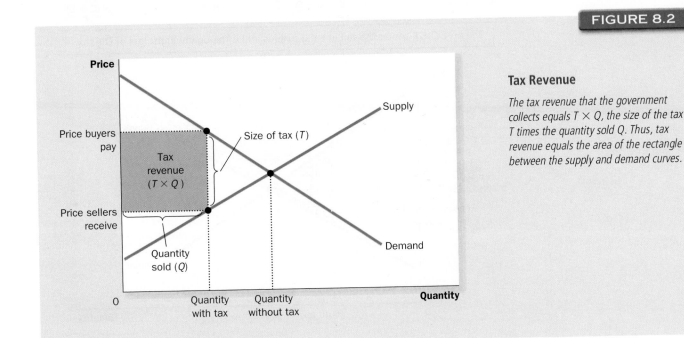

FIGURE 8.2

Tax Revenue

The tax revenue that the government collects equals $T \times Q$, the size of the tax T times the quantity sold Q. Thus, tax revenue equals the area of the rectangle between the supply and demand curves.

size of the tax, T, and the width of the rectangle is the quantity of the good sold, Q. Because a rectangle's area is its height times its width, this rectangle's area is $T \times Q$, which equals the tax revenue.

Welfare without a Tax   To see how a tax affects welfare, we begin by considering welfare before the government has imposed a tax. Figure 8.3 shows the supply-and-demand diagram and marks the key areas with the letters A through F.

Without a tax, the price and quantity are found at the intersection of the supply and demand curves. The price is P_1, and the quantity sold is Q_1. Because the demand curve reflects buyers' willingness to pay, consumer surplus is the area between the demand curve and the price, A + B + C. Similarly, because the supply curve reflects sellers' costs, producer surplus is the area between the supply curve and the price, D + E + F. In this case, because there is no tax, tax revenue equals zero.

FIGURE 8.3

How a Tax Affects Welfare

A tax on a good reduces consumer surplus (by the area B + C) and producer surplus (by the area D + E). Because the fall in producer and consumer surplus exceeds tax revenue (area B + D), the tax is said to impose a deadweight loss (area C + E).

	Without Tax	With Tax	Change
Consumer Surplus	A + B + C	A	−(B + C)
Producer Surplus	D + E + F	F	−(D + E)
Tax Revenue	None	B + D	+(B + D)
Total Surplus	A + B + C + D + E + F	A + B + D + F	−(C + E)

The area C + E shows the fall in total surplus and is the deadweight loss of the tax.

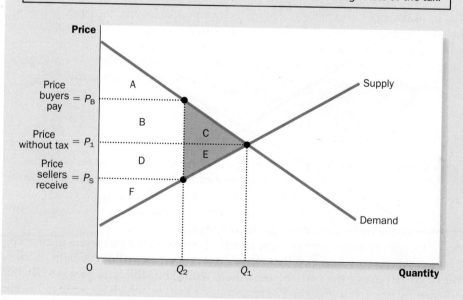

Total surplus—the sum of consumer and producer surplus—equals the area A + B + C + D + E + F. In other words, as we saw in Chapter 7, total surplus is the area between the supply and demand curves up to the equilibrium quantity. The "Without Tax" column of the table in Figure 8.3 summarizes these conclusions.

Welfare with a Tax   Now consider welfare after the tax is enacted. The price paid by buyers rises from P_1 to P_B, so consumer surplus now equals only area A (the area below the demand curve and above the buyer's price). The price received by sellers falls from P_1 to P_S, so producer surplus now equals only area F (the area above the supply curve and below the seller's price). The quantity sold falls from Q_1 to Q_2, and the government collects tax revenue equal to the area B + D.

To compute total surplus with the tax, we add consumer surplus, producer surplus, and tax revenue. Thus, we find that total surplus is area A + B + D + F. The "With Tax" column of the table provides a summary of these results.

Changes in Welfare   We can now see the effects of the tax by comparing welfare before and after the tax is enacted. The last column in the table in Figure 8.3 shows the changes. The tax causes consumer surplus to fall by the area B + C and producer surplus to fall by the area D + E. Tax revenue rises by the area B + D. Not surprisingly, the tax makes buyers and sellers worse off and the government better off.

The change in total welfare includes the change in consumer surplus (which is negative), the change in producer surplus (which is also negative), and the change in tax revenue (which is positive). When we add these three pieces together, we find that total surplus in the market falls by the area C + E. *Thus, the losses to buyers and sellers from a tax exceed the revenue raised by the government.* The fall in total surplus that results when a tax (or some other policy) distorts a market outcome is called the **deadweight loss**. The area C + E measures the size of the deadweight loss.

To understand why taxes impose deadweight losses, recall one of the ten principles of economics in Chapter 1: People respond to incentives. In Chapter 7 we saw that markets normally allocate scarce resources efficiently. That is, the equilibrium of supply and demand maximizes the total surplus of buyers and sellers in a market. When a tax raises the price to buyers and lowers the price to sellers, however, it gives buyers an incentive to consume less and sellers an incentive to produce less than they otherwise would. As buyers and sellers respond to these incentives, the size of the market shrinks below its optimum. Thus, because taxes distort incentives, they cause markets to allocate resources inefficiently.

deadweight loss
the fall in total surplus that results from a market distortion, such as a tax

Deadweight Losses and the Gains from Trade

To gain some intuition for why taxes result in deadweight losses, consider an example. Imagine that Joe cleans Jane's house each week for $100. The opportunity cost of Joe's time is $80, and the value of a clean house to Jane is $120. Thus, Joe and Jane each receive a $20 benefit from their deal. The total surplus of $40 measures the gains from trade in this particular transaction.

Now suppose that the government levies a $50 tax on the providers of cleaning services. There is now no price that Jane can pay Joe that will leave both of them better off after paying the tax. The most Jane would be willing to pay is $120, but then Joe would be left with only $70 after paying the tax, which is less than his $80 opportunity cost. Conversely, for Joe to receive his opportunity cost of $80, Jane would need to pay $130, which is above the $120 value she places on a clean house. As a result, Jane and Joe cancel their arrangement. Joe goes without the income, and Jane lives in a dirtier house.

The tax has made Joe and Jane worse off by a total of $40 because they have lost this amount of surplus. At the same time, the government collects no revenue from Joe and Jane because they decide to cancel their arrangement. The $40 is pure deadweight loss: It is a loss to buyers and sellers in a market not offset by an increase in government revenue. From this example, we can see the ultimate source of deadweight losses: *Taxes cause deadweight losses because they prevent buyers and sellers from realizing some of the gains from trade.*

The area of the triangle between the supply and demand curves (area C + E in Figure 8.3) measures these losses. This loss can be seen most easily in Figure 8.4 by recalling that the demand curve reflects the value of the good to consumers and that the supply curve reflects the costs of producers. When the tax raises the price to buyers to P_B and lowers the price to sellers to P_S, the marginal buyers and sellers leave the market, so the quantity sold falls from Q_1 to Q_2. Yet, as the figure shows, the value of the good to these buyers still exceeds the cost to these sellers. As in our example with Joe and Jane, the gains from trade—the difference between buyers' value and sellers' cost—is less than the tax. Thus, these trades do not get made once the tax is imposed. The deadweight loss is the surplus lost because the tax discourages these mutually advantageous trades.

QuickQuiz Draw the supply and demand curves for cookies. If the government imposes a tax on cookies, show what happens to the quantity sold, the price paid by buyers, and the price paid by sellers. In your diagram, show the deadweight loss from the tax. Explain the meaning of the deadweight loss.

> → Individuals won't do something because of a tax, which creates deadweight loss

FIGURE 8.4

The Deadweight Loss

When the government imposes a tax on a good, the quantity sold falls from Q_1 to Q_2. As a result, some of the potential gains from trade among buyers and sellers do not get realized. These lost gains from trade create the deadweight loss.

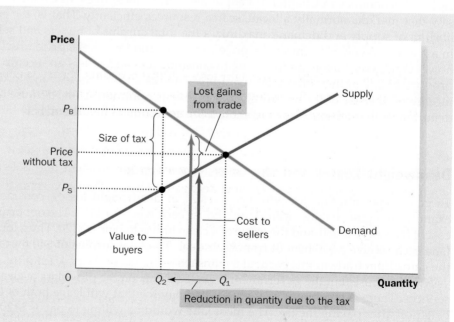

THE DETERMINANTS OF THE DEADWEIGHT LOSS

What determines whether the deadweight loss from a tax is large or small? The answer is the price elasticities of supply and demand, which measure how much the quantity supplied and quantity demanded respond to changes in the price.

Let's consider first how the elasticity of supply affects the size of the deadweight loss. In the top two panels of Figure 8.5, the demand curve and the size of the tax are the same. The only difference in these figures is the elasticity of the supply curve. In panel (a), the supply curve is relatively inelastic: Quantity supplied responds only slightly to changes in the price. In panel (b), the supply curve is relatively elastic: Quantity supplied responds substantially to changes in the price. Notice that the deadweight loss, the area of the triangle between the supply and demand curves, is larger when the supply curve is more elastic.

Similarly, the bottom two panels of Figure 8.5 show how the elasticity of demand affects the size of the deadweight loss. Here the supply curve and the size of the tax are held constant. In panel (c) the demand curve is relatively inelastic, and the deadweight loss is small. In panel (d) the demand curve is more elastic, and the deadweight loss from the tax is larger.

The lesson from this figure is easy to explain. A tax has a deadweight loss because it induces buyers and sellers to change their behaviour. The tax raises the price paid by buyers, so they consume less. At the same time, the tax lowers the price received by sellers, so they produce less. Because of these changes in behaviour, the size of the market shrinks below the optimum. The elasticities of supply and demand measure how much sellers and buyers respond to the changes in the price and, therefore, determine how much the tax distorts the market outcome. Hence, *the greater the elasticities of supply and demand, the greater the deadweight loss of a tax.*

Case Study

THE DEADWEIGHT LOSS DEBATE

Supply, demand, elasticity, deadweight loss—all this economic theory is enough to make your head spin. But believe it or not, these ideas go to the heart of a profound political question: How big should the government be? The debate hinges on these concepts because the larger the deadweight loss of taxation, the larger the cost of any government program. If taxation entails large deadweight losses, then these losses are a strong argument for a leaner government that does less and taxes less. But if taxes impose small deadweight losses, then government programs are less costly than they otherwise might be.

So how big are the deadweight losses of taxation? This is a question about which economists disagree. To see the nature of the disagreement, consider the most important tax in the Canadian economy—the tax on labour. Employment Insurance contributions are a tax on labour. Both the federal and provincial income taxes are, to a large extent, labour taxes, because the source of most income is labour earnings. A labour tax places a wedge between the wage that

FIGURE 8.5

Tax Distortions and Elasticities

In panels (a) and (b), the demand curve and the size of the tax are the same, but the price elasticity of supply is different. Notice that the more elastic the supply curve, the larger the deadweight loss of the tax. In panels (c) and (d), the supply curve and the size of the tax are the same, but the price elasticity of demand is different. Notice that the more elastic the demand curve, the larger the deadweight loss of the tax.

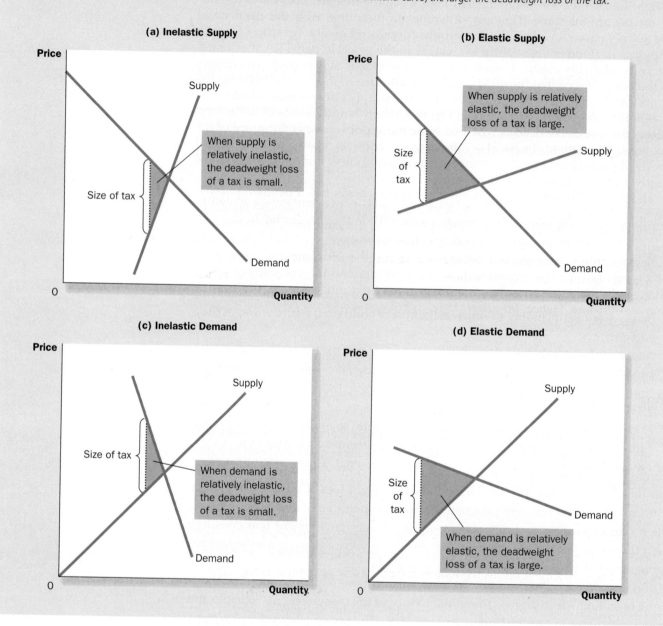

(a) Inelastic Supply

Price

Supply

When supply is relatively inelastic, the deadweight loss of a tax is small.

Size of tax

Demand

0 — Quantity

(b) Elastic Supply

Price

When supply is relatively elastic, the deadweight loss of a tax is large.

Size of tax

Supply

Demand

0 — Quantity

(c) Inelastic Demand

Price

Supply

Size of tax

When demand is relatively inelastic, the deadweight loss of a tax is small.

Demand

0 — Quantity

(d) Elastic Demand

Price

Supply

Size of tax

Demand

When demand is relatively elastic, the deadweight loss of a tax is large.

0 — Quantity

firms pay and the wage that workers receive. If we add all forms of labour taxes together, the marginal tax rate on labour income—the tax on the last dollar of earnings—is over 50 percent for many workers.

Although the size of the labour tax is easy to determine, the deadweight loss of this tax is less straightforward. Economists disagree about whether this 50 percent labour tax has a small or a large deadweight loss. This disagreement arises because economists hold different views about the elasticity of labour supply.

Economists who argue that labour taxes are not very distorting believe that labour supply is fairly inelastic. Most people, they claim, would work full-time regardless of the wage. If so, the labour supply curve is almost vertical, and a tax on labour has a small deadweight loss.

Economists who argue that labour taxes are highly distorting believe that labour supply is more elastic. They admit that some groups of workers may supply their labour inelastically but claim that many other groups respond more to incentives. Here are some examples:

- Many workers can adjust the number of hours they work—for instance, by working overtime or by choosing jobs with longer or shorter hours. The higher the wage, the more hours they choose to work.
- Some families have second earners—a spouse—with some discretion over whether to do unpaid work at home or paid work in the marketplace. When deciding whether to take a job, these second earners compare the benefits of being at home (including savings on the cost of child care) with the wages they could earn.
- Many of the elderly can choose when to retire, and their decisions are partly based on the wage. Once they are retired, the wage determines their incentive to work part-time.
- Some people consider engaging in illegal economic activity, such as the drug trade, or working at jobs that pay "under the table" to evade taxes. Economists call this the *underground economy*. In deciding whether to work in the underground economy or at a legitimate job, these potential criminals compare what they can earn by breaking the law with the wage they can earn legally.

In each of these cases, the quantity of labour supplied responds to the wage (the price of labour). Thus, the decisions of these workers are distorted when their labour earnings are taxed. Labour taxes encourage workers to work fewer hours, second earners to stay at home, the elderly to retire early, and the unscrupulous to enter the underground economy.   *If the assumption is that labour is elastic*

These two views of labour taxation persist to this day. Indeed, whenever you see two political candidates debating whether the government should provide more services or reduce the tax burden, keep in mind that part of the disagreement may rest on different views about the elasticity of labour supply and the deadweight loss of taxation. ●

IN THE NEWS

WEIGHT LOSS VS. DEADWEIGHT LOSS

More and more countries around the world are implementing so-called "fat taxes" on unhealthy food. This is an example of governments using the tax system to affect consumer behaviour, in this case with the objective of encouraging a more healthy lifestyle. But in pursing the laudable objective of reducing obesity and encouraging weight loss, are governments ignoring other types of losses associated with these taxes?

Fat Tax Would Need to Be Fat Alright

By Chantaie Allick

Researchers in the United Kingdom have found a way to effectively implement a "fat tax" on unhealthy food. The key is to make it large enough—a minimum of 20 per cent is needed to improve public health.

A hefty food tax has the potential to improve overall health, its proponents say. It also has the potential to draw a lot of controversy.

Mark Bittman, the New York Times food writer and author, has spoken out against unhealthy "non-foods" like pop and says he would support taxing them. He blames soda companies and others that produce sugary drinks for the global obesity pandemic.

Bittman has argued that we should subsidize healthy foods to encourage people to eat them and discourage them from buying unhealthy foods by making their costs less appealing. The researchers from Oxford University would seem to agree. They have reviewed recent literature on efforts to determine a rate that reduces consumption and have written about their findings in the British Medical Journal.

A growing number of countries are introducing taxes on sugary food and drinks: Denmark has a "fat tax," Hungary a "junk food tax" and France a tax on sweetened drinks.

One study predicted that a 20 per cent tax on sugary drinks in the United States would reduce the prevalence of obesity by 3.5 per cent.

"The people that will benefit the most will be the poorer people in society," study lead Oliver Mytton said in a phone interview.

He warns that this type of tax should be introduced as part of a larger tax strategy that includes subsidies for healthy foods.

Policy-makers have to look beyond single taxes in isolation and not rely on it as the only solution to the global obesity pandemic, he said.

"Nobody likes taxes, but people do appreciate the benefit of when it's done well," said Mytton.

The food industry, which in many countries receives significant government subsidies, has argued that the taxes would be ineffective, unfair and lead to job losses.

The Oxford researchers say similar arguments were used by the tobacco industry in the fight against cigarette taxes.

In Toronto, a number of restaurants have begun making their own drinks as an alternative to popular sodas that are high in sugar. For instance, a 355 mL can of Coke contains 39 grams of sugar. There are 41 grams of sugar in a can of Pepsi and 46 grams in Mountain Dew.

Alistair Cameron, the chef at Cheeswerks on Bathurst St., said their homemade drinks—made from fresh and local fruits—are a healthier alternative to ordinary pop even though they contain two tablespoons (25 grams) of sugar per glass.

"Coke and Pepsi have their secret recipes; no one really knows what goes into them. This way, we tell them. It's basically sugar and fruit," he said.

Cameron said some customers are disappointed they can't order the familiar pops there, but most are excited to try the restaurant's artisan alternatives.

He said he supports the idea of taxing sugary drinks like soda and other unhealthy foods.

Source: Reprinted with permission—Torstar Syndication Services.

QuickQuiz   The demand for beer is more elastic than the demand for milk. Would a tax on beer or a tax on milk have a larger deadweight loss? Why?

DEADWEIGHT LOSS AND TAX REVENUE AS TAXES VARY

Taxes rarely stay the same for long periods of time. Policymakers in local, provincial, territorial, and federal governments are always considering raising one tax or lowering another. Here we consider what happens to the deadweight loss and tax revenue when the size of a tax changes.

Figure 8.6 shows the effects of a small, medium, and large tax, holding constant the market's supply and demand curves. The deadweight loss—the reduction in total surplus that results when the tax reduces the size of a market below the optimum—equals the area of the triangle between the supply and demand curves. For the small tax in panel (a), the area of the deadweight loss triangle is quite small. But as the size of a tax rises in panels (b) and (c), the deadweight loss grows larger and larger.

Indeed, the deadweight loss of a tax rises even more rapidly than the size of the tax. The reason is that the deadweight loss is an area of a triangle, and an area of a triangle depends on the *square* of its size. If we double the size of a tax, for instance, the base and height of the triangle double, so the deadweight loss rises by a factor of 4. If we triple the size of a tax, the base and height triple, so the deadweight loss rises by a factor of 9.

The government's tax revenue is the size of the tax times the amount of the good sold. As Figure 8.6 shows, tax revenue equals the area of the rectangle between the supply and demand curves. For the small tax in panel (a), tax revenue is small. As the size of a tax rises from panel (a) to panel (b), tax revenue grows. But as the size of the tax rises further from panel (b) to panel (c), tax revenue falls because the higher tax drastically reduces the size of the market. For a very large tax, no revenue would be raised, because people would stop buying and selling the good altogether.

The last two panels of Figure 8.6 summarize these results. In panel (d) we see that as the size of a tax increases, its deadweight loss quickly gets larger. By contrast, panel (e) shows that tax revenue first rises with the size of the tax, but then, as the tax gets larger, the market shrinks so much that tax revenue starts to fall.

Case Study

THE LAFFER CURVE AND SUPPLY-SIDE ECONOMICS

One day in 1974, economist Arthur Laffer sat in a Washington restaurant with some prominent journalists and politicians. He took out a napkin and drew a figure on it to show how tax rates affect tax revenue. It looked much like panel (e) of our Figure 8.6. Laffer then suggested that the United States was on the downward-sloping side of this curve. Tax rates were so high, he argued, that reducing them would actually raise tax revenue.

FIGURE 8.6

Deadweight Loss and Tax Revenue from Three Taxes of Different Sizes

The deadweight loss is the reduction in total surplus due to the tax. Tax revenue is the amount of the tax times the amount of the good sold. In panel (a), a small tax has a small deadweight loss and raises a small amount of revenue. In panel (b), a somewhat larger tax has a larger deadweight loss and raises a larger amount of revenue. In panel (c), a very large tax has a very large deadweight loss, but because it has reduced the size of the market so much, the tax raises only a small amount of revenue. Panels (d) and (e) summarize these conclusions. Panel (d) shows that as the size of the tax grows larger, the deadweight loss grows larger. Panel (e) shows that tax revenue first rises then falls. This relationship is sometimes called the Laffer curve.

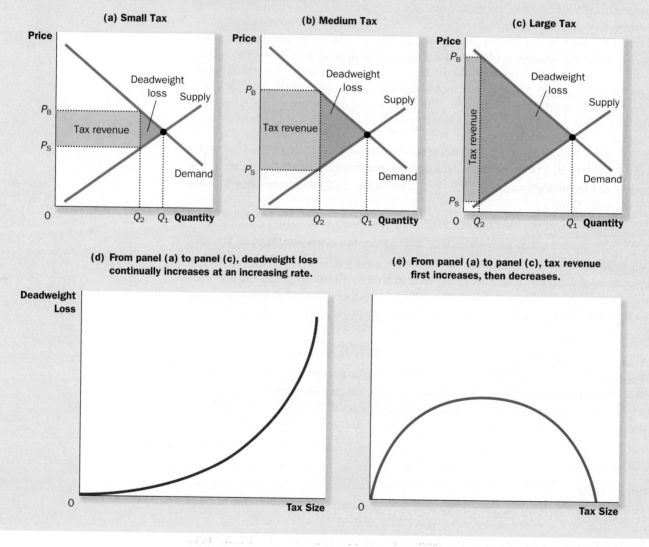

(a) Small Tax

(b) Medium Tax

(c) Large Tax

(d) From panel (a) to panel (c), deadweight loss continually increases at an increasing rate.

(e) From panel (a) to panel (c), tax revenue first increases, then decreases.

Most economists were skeptical of Laffer's suggestion. The idea that a cut in tax rates could raise tax revenue was correct as a matter of economic theory, but there was more doubt about whether it would do so in practice. There was little evidence for Laffer's view that U.S. tax rates had in fact reached such extreme levels.

Nonetheless, the *Laffer curve* (as it became known) captured the imagination of Ronald Reagan. David Stockman, budget director in the first Reagan administration, offers the following story:

> [Reagan] had once been on the Laffer curve himself. "I came into the Big Money making pictures during World War II," he would always say. At that time the wartime income surtax hit 90 percent. "You could only make four pictures and then you were in the top bracket," he would continue. "So we all quit working after four pictures and went off to the country." High tax rates caused less work. Low tax rates caused more. His experience proved it.

When Reagan ran for president in 1980, he made cutting taxes part of his platform. Reagan argued that taxes were so high that they were discouraging hard work. He argued that lower taxes would give people the proper incentive to work, which would raise economic well-being and perhaps even tax revenue. Because the cut in tax rates was intended to encourage people to increase the quantity of labour they supplied, the views of Laffer and Reagan became known as *supply-side economics*.

Economists continue to debate Laffer's argument. Many believe that subsequent history refuted Laffer's conjecture that lower tax rates would raise tax revenue. Yet, because history is open to alternative interpretations, other economists view the events of the 1980s as more favourable to the supply-siders. To evaluate Laffer's hypothesis definitively, we would need to rerun history without the Reagan tax cuts and see if tax revenues were higher or lower. Unfortunately, that experiment is impossible.

Some economists take an intermediate position on this issue. They believe that while an overall cut in tax rates normally reduces revenue, some taxpayers at some times may find themselves on the wrong side of the Laffer curve. Other things equal, a tax cut is more likely to raise tax revenue if the cut applies to those taxpayers facing the highest tax rates. In addition, Laffer's argument may be more compelling when considering countries with much higher tax rates than the United States. In Sweden in the early 1980s, for instance, the typical worker faced a marginal tax rate of about 80 percent. Such a high tax rate provides a substantial disincentive to work. Studies have suggested that Sweden would indeed have raised more tax revenue if it had lowered its tax rates.

Economists disagree about these issues in part because there is no consensus about the size of the relevant elasticities. The more elastic supply and demand are in any market, the more taxes in the market distort behaviour, and the more likely it is that a tax cut will raise tax revenue. There is no debate, however, about the general lesson: How much revenue the government gains or loses from a tax change cannot be computed just by looking at tax rates. It also depends on how the tax change affects people's behaviour. •

QuickQuiz   If the government doubles the tax on gasoline, can you be sure that revenue from the gasoline tax will rise? Can you be sure that the deadweight loss from the gasoline tax will rise? Explain.

CONCLUSION

In this chapter, we have used the tools developed in the previous chapter to further our understanding of taxes. One of the ten principles of economics discussed in Chapter 1 is that markets are usually a good way to organize economic activity. In Chapter 7, we used the concepts of producer and consumer surplus to make this principle more precise. Here, we have seen that when the government imposes taxes on buyers or sellers of a good, society loses some of the benefits of market efficiency. Taxes are costly to market participants, not only because taxes transfer resources from those participants to the government, but also because they alter incentives and distort market outcomes.

The analysis presented here and in Chapter 6 should give you a good basis for understanding the economic impact of taxes, but this is not the end of the story. Taxes play an important role in modern economies. Microeconomists study how best to design a tax system, including how to strike the right balance between equality and efficiency. Macroeconomists study how taxes influence the overall economy and how policymakers can use the tax system to stabilize economic activity and to achieve more rapid economic growth. So don't be surprised that, as you continue your study of economics, the subject of taxation comes up yet again.

SUMMARY

- A tax on a good reduces the welfare of buyers and sellers of the good, and the reduction in consumer and producer surplus usually exceeds the revenue raised by the government. The fall in total surplus—the sum of consumer surplus, producer surplus, and tax revenue—is called the *deadweight loss of the tax.*

- Taxes have deadweight losses because they cause buyers to consume less and sellers to produce less, and this change in behaviour shrinks the size

of the market below the level that maximizes total surplus. Because the elasticities of supply and demand measure how much market participants respond to market conditions, larger elasticities imply larger deadweight losses.

- As a tax grows larger, it distorts incentives more, and its deadweight loss grows larger. Tax revenue first rises with the size of a tax. Eventually, however, a larger tax reduces tax revenue because it reduces the size of the market.

KEY CONCEPTS

deadweight loss, p. 175

QUESTIONS FOR REVIEW

1. What happens to consumer and producer surplus when the sale of a good is taxed? How does the change in consumer and producer surplus compare to the tax revenue? Explain.

2. Draw a supply-and-demand diagram with a tax on the sale of the good. Show the deadweight loss. Show the tax revenue.

3. How do the elasticities of supply and demand affect the deadweight loss of a tax? Why do they have this effect?

4. Why do experts disagree about whether labour taxes have small or large deadweight losses?

5. What happens to the deadweight loss and tax revenue when a tax is increased?

PROBLEMS AND APPLICATIONS

1. The market for pizza is characterized by a downward-sloping demand curve and an upward-sloping supply curve.
   a. Draw the competitive market equilibrium. Label the price, quantity, consumer surplus, and producer surplus. Is there any deadweight loss? Explain.
   b. Suppose that the government forces each pizzeria to pay a $1 tax on each pizza sold. Illustrate the effect of this tax on the pizza market, being sure to label the consumer surplus, producer surplus, government revenue, and deadweight loss. How does each area compare to the pre-tax case?
   c. If the tax was removed, pizza eaters and sellers would be better off, but the government would lose tax revenue. Suppose that consumers and producers voluntarily transferred some of their gains to the government. Could all parties (including the government) be better off than they were with a tax? Explain using the labelled areas in your graph.

2. Evaluate the following two statements. Do you agree? Why or why not?
   a. "A tax that has no deadweight loss cannot raise any revenue for the government."
   b. "A tax that raises no revenue for the government cannot have any deadweight loss."

3. Consider the market for rubber bands.
   a. If this market has very elastic supply and very inelastic demand, how would the burden of a tax on rubber bands be shared between consumers and producers? Use the tools of consumer surplus and producer surplus in your answer.
   b. If this market has very inelastic supply and very elastic demand, how would the burden of a tax on rubber bands be shared between consumers and producers? Contrast your answer with your answer to part (a).

4. Suppose that the government imposes a tax on heating oil.
   a. Would the deadweight loss from this tax likely be greater in the first year after it is imposed or in the fifth year? Explain.
   b. Would the revenue collected from this tax likely be greater in the first year after it is imposed or in the fifth year? Explain.

5. After economics class one day, your friend suggests that taxing food would be a good way to raise revenue because the demand for food is quite inelastic. In what sense is taxing food a "good" way to raise revenue? In what sense is it not a "good" way to raise revenue?

6. U.S. Senator Daniel Patrick Moynihan once introduced a bill that would levy a 10 000 percent tax on certain hollow-tipped bullets.
   a. Do you expect that this tax would raise much revenue? Why or why not?
   b. Even if the tax would raise no revenue, what might be Senator Moynihan's reason for proposing it?

7. The government places a tax on the purchase of socks.
   a. Illustrate the effect of this tax on equilibrium price and quantity in the sock market. Identify the following areas both before and after the imposition of the tax: total spending by consumers, total revenue for producers, and government tax revenue.

b. Does the price received by producers rise or fall? Can you tell whether total receipts for producers rise or fall? Explain.

c. Does the price paid by consumers rise or fall? Can you tell whether total spending by consumers rises or falls? Explain carefully. (Hint: Think about elasticity.) If total consumer spending falls, does consumer surplus rise? Explain.

8. Suppose the government currently raises $100 million through a $0.01 tax on widgets, and another $100 million through a $0.10 tax on gadgets. If the government doubled the tax rate on widgets and eliminated the tax on gadgets, would it raise more tax revenue than it does today, less tax revenue, or the same amount? Explain.

9. Suppose the Canadian government decides that it needs to raise an additional $100 million in tax revenues. One Cabinet minister argues for a tax on all soft drinks. A second Cabinet minister argues for a tax on cola only, since this would give consumers a choice of paying the tax (by drinking cola) or avoiding it (by switching to another soft drink).

a. Which market has the more elastic supply and demand curves: the market for cola, or the market for all soft drinks?

b. To raise the same $100 million in revenue, which would require a higher rate: a tax on cola, or a tax on all soft drinks?

c. Which would cause a larger deadweight loss: a tax on cola, or a tax on all soft drinks?

d. Which would be the better tax? Explain.

10. Hotel rooms in Smalltown go for $100, and 1000 rooms are rented on a typical day.

a. To raise revenue, the mayor decides to charge hotels a tax of $10 per rented room. After the tax is imposed, the going rate for hotel rooms rises to $108, and the number of rooms rented falls to 900. Calculate the amount of revenue this tax raises for Smalltown and the deadweight loss of the tax. (Hint: The area of a triangle is $\frac{1}{2} \times$ base $\times$ height.)

b. The mayor now doubles the tax to $20. The price rises to $116, and the number of rooms rented falls to 800. Calculate tax revenue and deadweight loss with this larger tax. Do they double, more than double, or less than double? Explain.

11. This chapter analyzed the welfare effects of a tax on a good. Consider now the opposite policy. Suppose that the government *subsidizes* a good: For each unit of the good sold, the government pays $2 to the buyer. How does the subsidy affect consumer surplus, producer surplus, tax revenue, and total surplus? Does a subsidy lead to a deadweight loss? Explain.

12. Suppose that a market is described by the following supply and demand equations:

$$Q^S = 2P$$
$$Q^D = 300 - P$$

a. Solve for the equilibrium price and the equilibrium quantity.

b. Suppose that a tax of T is placed on buyers, so the new demand equation is

$$Q^D = 300 - (P + T)$$

Solve for the new equilibrium. What happens to the price received by sellers, the price paid by buyers, and the quantity sold?

c. Tax revenue is $T \times Q$. Use your answer to part (b) to solve for tax revenue as a function of T. Graph this relationship for T between 0 and 300.

d. The deadweight loss of a tax is the area of the triangle between the supply and demand curves. Recalling that the area of a triangle is $\frac{1}{2} \times$ base $\times$ height, solve for deadweight loss as a function of T. Graph this relationship for T between 0 and 300.
(Hint: Looking sideways, the base of the deadweight loss triangle is T, and the height is the difference between the quantity sold with the tax and the quantity sold without the tax.)

e. The government now levies a tax on this good of $200 per unit. Is this a good policy? Why or why not? Can you propose a better policy?

http:// For more study tools, please visit www.nelson.com/mankiwmicro6e.

APPENDIX: THE MATHEMATICS OF DEADWEIGHT LOSS

In previous appendixes, we have used mathematics and linear demand and supply curves to allow us to be more precise about some important economic relationships. We use a similar approach here to be more precise about the concept of deadweight loss.

Figure 8.3 in this chapter shows how the various areas between the supply and demand curves can be used to determine how taxes affect welfare. In this diagram, and in the subsequent discussion about Figure 8.4, it was shown that the area $C + D$ in Figure 8.3 is the deadweight loss of the tax. In the case of linear supply and demand curves, this is the area of a triangle that, using a similar technique to that used in the appendix to Chapter 7, can be calculated as one-half of the height times the base. The height of the triangle in this case is the amount of the tax, T per unit, and the base is the change in quantity demanded due to the increase in the price that buyers pay because of the tax, $Q_1 - Q_2$. Thus, the deadweight loss of a tax imposed at T per unit is simply

$$\text{Deadweight loss} = \left(\frac{1}{2}\right) T(Q_1 - Q_2)$$

APPLICATION: INTERNATIONAL TRADE

Thinkstock

If you check the labels on the clothes you are now wearing, you will probably find that some of your clothes were made in another country. A century ago the textiles and clothing industry was a major part of the Canadian economy, but that is no longer the case. Faced with foreign competitors that could produce quality goods at low cost, many Canadian firms found it increasingly difficult to produce and sell textiles and clothing at a profit. As a result, they laid off their workers and shut down their factories. Today, much of the textiles and clothing that Canadians consume are imported from abroad.

The story of the textiles industry raises important questions for economic policy: How does international trade affect economic well-being? Who gains and who loses from free trade among countries, and how do the gains compare to the losses?

Chapter 3 introduced the study of international trade by applying the principle of comparative advantage. According to this principle, all countries can benefit from trading with one another because trade allows each country to specialize in doing what it does best. But the analysis in Chapter 3 was incomplete. It did not explain how the international marketplace achieves these gains from trade or how the gains are distributed among various economic participants.

We now return to the study of international trade and take up these questions. Over the past several chapters, we have developed many tools for analyzing how markets work: supply, demand, equilibrium, consumer surplus, producer surplus, and so on. With these tools we can learn more about the effects of international trade on economic well-being.

THE DETERMINANTS OF TRADE

Consider the market for textiles. The textile market is well suited to examining the gains and losses from international trade: Textiles are made in many countries around the world, and there is much world trade in textiles. Moreover, the textile market is one in which policymakers often consider (and sometimes implement) trade restrictions to protect domestic producers from foreign competitors. We examine here the textile market in the imaginary country of Isoland.

The Equilibrium without Trade

As our story begins, the Isolandian textile market is isolated from the rest of the world. By government decree, no one in Isoland is allowed to import or export textiles, and the penalty for violating the decree is so large that no one dares try.

Because there is no international trade, the market for textiles in Isoland consists solely of Isolandian buyers and sellers. As Figure 9.1 shows, the domestic price adjusts to balance the quantity supplied by domestic sellers and the quantity demanded by domestic buyers. The figure shows the consumer and producer surplus in the

FIGURE 9.1

The Equilibrium without International Trade

When an economy cannot trade in world markets, the price adjusts to balance domestic supply and demand. This figure shows consumer and producer surplus in an equilibrium without international trade for the textile market in the imaginary country of Isoland.

equilibrium without trade. The sum of consumer and producer surplus measures the total benefits that buyers and sellers receive from participating in the textile market.

Now suppose that, in an election upset, Isoland elects a new president. The president campaigned on a platform of "change" and promised the voters bold new ideas. Her first act is to assemble a team of economists to evaluate Isolandian trade policy. She asks them to report back on three questions:

1. If the government allowed Isolandians to import and export textiles, what would happen to the price of textiles and the quantity of textiles sold in the domestic textile market?
2. Who would gain from free trade in textiles and who would lose, and would the gains exceed the losses?
3. Should a tariff (a tax on textile imports) or an import quota (a limit on textile imports) be part of the new trade policy?

After reviewing supply and demand in their favourite textbook (this one, of course), the Isolandian economics team begins its analysis.

The World Price and Comparative Advantage

The first issue our economists take up is whether Isoland is likely to become a textile importer or a textile exporter. In other words, if free trade was allowed, would Isolandians end up buying or selling textiles in world markets?

To answer this question, the economists compare the current Isolandian price of textiles to the price of textiles in other countries. We call the price prevailing in world markets the **world price**. If the world price of textiles is higher than the domestic price, then Isoland would become an exporter of textiles once trade is permitted. Isolandian textile producers would be eager to receive the higher prices available abroad and would start selling their textiles to buyers in other countries. Conversely, if the world price of textiles is lower than the domestic price, then Isoland would become an importer of textiles. Because foreign sellers offer a better price, Isolandian textile consumers would quickly start buying textiles from other countries.

In essence, comparing the world price and the domestic price before trade indicates whether Isoland has a comparative advantage in producing textiles. The domestic price reflects the opportunity cost of textiles: It tells us how much an Isolandian must give up to get one unit of textiles. If the domestic price is low, the cost of producing textiles in Isoland is low, suggesting that Isoland has a comparative advantage in producing textiles relative to the rest of the world. If the domestic price is high, then the cost of producing textiles in Isoland is high, suggesting that foreign countries have a comparative advantage in producing textiles.

As we saw in Chapter 3, trade among nations is ultimately based on comparative advantage. That is, trade is beneficial because it allows each nation to specialize in doing what it does best. By comparing the world price and the domestic price before trade, we can determine whether Isoland is better or worse at producing textiles than the rest of the world.

world price
the price of a good that prevails in the world market for that good

> *[handwritten notes in right margin:]*
> — Will a country be a buyer or seller under the right conditions?
>
> — If a country can make a profit (world > domestic) they will export. They have the comparative advantage

QuickQuiz The country Autarka does not allow international trade. In Autarka, you can buy a wool suit for 100 grams of gold. Meanwhile, in neighbouring countries, you can buy the same suit for 60 grams of gold. If Autarka was to allow free trade, would it import or export suits?

THE WINNERS AND LOSERS FROM TRADE

To analyze the welfare effects of free trade, the Isolandian economists begin with the assumption that Isoland is a small economy compared to the rest of the world. This small-economy assumption means that Isoland's actions have little effect on world markets. Specifically, any change in Isoland's trade policy will not affect the world price of textiles. The Isolandians are said to be *price takers* in the world economy. That is, they take the world price of textiles as given. They can sell textiles at this price and be exporters or buy textiles at this price and be importers.

The small-economy assumption is not necessary to analyze the gains and losses from international trade. But the Isolandian economists know from experience (and from reading Chapter 2 of this book) that making simplifying assumptions is a key part of building a useful economic model. The assumption that Isoland is a small economy simplifies the analysis, and the basic lessons do not change in the more complicated case of a large economy. Nonetheless, it turns out to be a pretty accurate characterization of the Canadian economy, which accounts for under 2 percent of world GDP.

The Gains and Losses of an Exporting Country

Figure 9.2 shows the Isolandian textile market when the domestic equilibrium price before trade is below the world price. Once free trade is allowed, the domestic price rises to equal the world price. No seller of textiles would accept less than the world price, and no buyer would pay more than the world price.

After the domestic price has risen to equal to the world price, the domestic quantity supplied differs from the domestic quantity demanded. The supply curve shows the quantity of textiles supplied by Isolandian sellers. The demand curve shows the quantity of textiles demanded by Isolandian buyers. Because the domestic quantity supplied is greater than the domestic quantity demanded, Isoland sells textiles to other countries. Thus, Isoland becomes a textile exporter.

Although domestic quantity supplied and domestic quantity demanded differ, the textile market is still in equilibrium because there is now another participant in the market: the rest of the world. One can view the horizontal line at the world price as representing the demand for textiles from the rest of the world. This demand curve is perfectly elastic because Isoland, as a small economy, can sell as many textiles as it wants at the world price.

Now consider the gains and losses from opening up trade. Clearly, not everyone benefits. Trade forces the domestic price to rise to the world price. Domestic producers of textiles are better off because they can now sell textiles at a higher price, but domestic consumers of textiles are worse off because they have to buy textiles at a higher price.

To measure these gains and losses, we look at the changes in consumer and producer surplus. Before trade is allowed, the price of textiles adjusts to balance domestic supply and domestic demand. Consumer surplus, the area between the demand curve and the before-trade price, is area A + B. Producer surplus, the area between the supply curve and the before-trade price, is area C. Total surplus before trade, the sum of consumer and producer surplus, is area A + B + C.

After trade is allowed, the domestic price rises to the world price. Consumer surplus is area A (the area between the demand curve and the world price).

[handwritten margin note: -Surpluses/Shortages determine whether a country will buy or sell in the world market.]

FIGURE 9.2

International Trade in an Exporting Country

Once trade is allowed, the domestic price rises to equal the world price. The supply curve shows the quantity of textiles produced domestically, and the demand curve shows the quantity consumed domestically. Exports from Isoland equal the difference between the domestic quantity supplied and the domestic quantity demanded at the world price. Sellers are better off (producer surplus rises from C to B + C + D), and buyers are worse off (consumer surplus falls from A + B to A). Total surplus rises by an amount equal to area D, indicating that trade raises the economic well-being of the country as a whole.

	Before Trade	After Trade	Change
Consumer Surplus	A + B	A	−B
Producer Surplus	C	B + C + D	+(B + D)
Total Surplus	A + B + C	A + B + C + D	+D

The area D shows the increase in total surplus and represents the gains from trade.

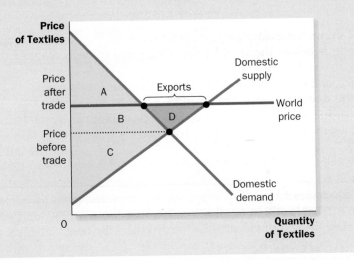

- Exporter: Demand Curve

Producer surplus is area B + C + D (the area between the supply curve and the world price). Thus, total surplus with trade is area A + B + C + D.

These welfare calculations show who wins and who loses from trade in an exporting country. Sellers benefit because producer surplus increases by the area B + D. Buyers are worse off because consumer surplus decreases by the area B. Because the gains of sellers exceed the losses of buyers by the area D, total surplus in Isoland increases.

This analysis of an exporting country yields two conclusions:

1. When a country allows trade and becomes an exporter of a good, domestic producers of the good are better off and domestic consumers of the good are worse off.

- Exporter if domestic price was lower

2. Trade raises the economic well-being of a nation in the sense that the gains of the winners exceed the losses of the losers.

The Gains and Losses of an Importing Country

Now suppose that the domestic price before trade is above the world price. Once again, after free trade is allowed, the domestic price must equal the world price. As Figure 9.3 shows, the domestic quantity supplied is less than the domestic quantity demanded. The difference between the domestic quantity demanded and the domestic quantity supplied is bought from other countries, and Isoland becomes a textile importer.

FIGURE 9.3

International Trade in an Importing Country

Once trade is allowed, the domestic price falls to equal the world price. The supply curve shows the amount produced domestically, and the demand curve shows the amount consumed domestically. Imports equal the difference between the domestic quantity demanded and the domestic quantity supplied at the world price. Buyers are better off (consumer surplus rises from A to A + B + D), and sellers are worse off (producer surplus falls from B + C to C). Total surplus rises by an amount equal to area D, indicating that trade raises the economic well-being of the country as a whole.

	Before Trade	After Trade	Change
Consumer Surplus	A	A + B + D	+(B + D)
Producer Surplus	B + C	C	−B
Total Surplus	A + B + C	A + B + C + D	+D

The area D shows the increase in total surplus and represents the gains from trade.

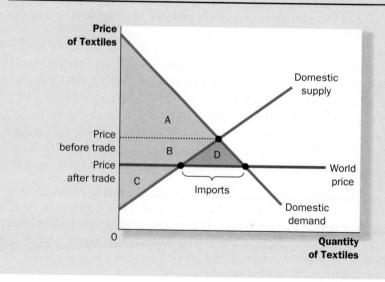

−Importer: Supply Curve

In this case, the horizontal line at the world price represents the supply of the rest of the world. This supply curve is perfectly elastic because Isoland is a small economy and, therefore, can buy as many textiles as it wants at the world price.

Now consider the gains and losses from trade. Once again, not everyone benefits. When trade forces the domestic price to fall, domestic consumers are better off (they can now buy textiles at a lower price), and domestic producers are worse off (they now have to sell textiles at a lower price). Changes in consumer and producer surplus measure the size of the gains and losses, as shown in the graph and table in Figure 9.3. Before trade, consumer surplus is area A, producer surplus is area B + C, and total surplus is area A + B + C. After trade is allowed, consumer surplus is area A + B + D, producer surplus is area C, and total surplus is area A + B + C + D.

— 3rd world economies exporting cheap goods to N.A.

These welfare calculations show who wins and who loses from trade in an importing country. Buyers benefit because consumer surplus increases by the area B + D. Sellers are worse off because producer surplus falls by the area B. The gains of buyers exceed the losses of sellers, and total surplus increases by the area D.

This analysis of an importing country yields two conclusions parallel to those for an exporting country:

1. When a country allows trade and becomes an importer of a good, domestic consumers of the good are better off, and domestic producers of the good are worse off.
2. Trade raises the economic well-being of a nation in the sense that the gains of the winners exceed the losses of the losers.

— Importer :D domestic price is higher

Having completed our analysis of trade, we can better understand one of the ten principles of economics in Chapter 1: Trade can make everyone better off. If Isoland opens up its textile market to international trade, that change will create winners and losers, regardless of whether Isoland ends up exporting or importing textiles. In either case, however, the gains of the winners exceed the losses of the losers, so the winners could compensate the losers and still be better off. In this sense, trade *can* make everyone better off. But *will* trade make everyone better off? Probably not. In practice, compensation for the losers from international trade is rare. Without such compensation, opening up to international trade is a policy that expands the size of the economic pie, while perhaps leaving some participants in the economy with a smaller slice.

We can now see why the debate over trade policy is so often contentious. Whenever a policy creates winners and losers, the stage is set for a political battle. Nations sometimes fail to enjoy the gains from trade simply because the losers from free trade have more political clout than the winners. The losers lobby for trade restrictions, such as tariffs and import quotas.

The Effects of a Tariff

The Isolandian economists next consider the effects of a **tariff**—a tax on imported goods. The economists quickly realize that a tariff on textiles will have no effect if Isoland becomes a textile exporter. If no one in Isoland is interested in importing textiles, a tax on textile imports is irrelevant. The tariff matters only if Isoland becomes a textile importer. Concentrating their attention on this case, the economists compare welfare with and without the tariff.

tariff
a tax on goods produced abroad and sold domestically

Figure 9.4 shows the Isolandian market for textiles. Under free trade, the domestic price equals the world price. A tariff raises the price of imported textiles above the world price by the amount of the tariff. Domestic suppliers of textiles, who compete with suppliers of imported textiles, can now sell their textiles for the world price plus the amount of the tariff. Thus, the price of textiles—both imported and domestic—rises by the amount of the tariff and is, therefore, closer to the price that would prevail without trade.

FIGURE 9.4

The Effects of a Tariff

A tariff reduces the quantity of imports and moves a market closer to the equilibrium that would exist without trade. Total surplus falls by an amount equal to area D + F. These two triangles represent the deadweight loss from the tariff.

	Before Tariff	After Tariff	Change
Consumer Surplus	A + B + C + D + E + F	A + B	−(C + D + E + F)
Producer Surplus	G	C + G	+C
Government Revenue	None	E	+E
Total Surplus	A + B + C + D + E + F + G	A + B + C + E + G	−(D + F)

> The area D + F shows the fall in total surplus and represents the deadweight loss of the tariff.

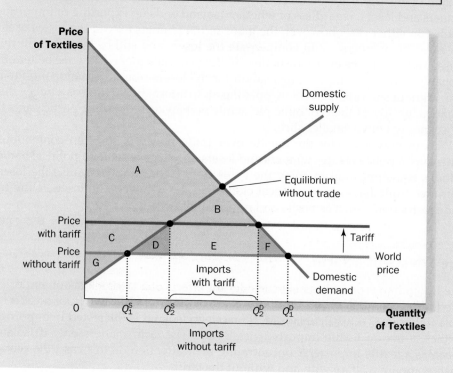

The change in price affects the behaviour of domestic buyers and sellers. Because the tariff raises the price of textiles, it reduces the domestic quantity demanded from Q_1^D to Q_2^D and raises the domestic quantity supplied from Q_1^S to Q_2^S. *Thus, the tariff reduces the quantity of imports and moves the domestic market closer to its equilibrium without trade.*

Now consider the gains and losses from the tariff. Because the tariff raises the domestic price, domestic sellers are better off and domestic buyers are worse off. In addition, the government raises revenue. To measure these gains and losses, we look at the changes in consumer surplus, producer surplus, and government revenue. These changes are summarized in the table in Figure 9.4.

Before the tariff, the domestic price equals the world price. Consumer surplus, the area between the demand curve and the world price, is area A + B + C + D + E + F. Producer surplus, the area between the supply curve and the world price, is area G. Government revenue equals zero. Total surplus—the sum of consumer surplus, producer surplus, and government revenue—is area A + B + C + D + E + F + G.

Once the government imposes a tariff, the domestic price exceeds the world price by the amount of the tariff. Consumer surplus is now area A + B. Producer surplus is area C + G. Government revenue, which is the quantity of after-tariff imports times the size of the tariff, is area E. Thus, total surplus with the tariff is area A + B + C + E + G.

To determine the total welfare effects of the tariff, we add the change in consumer surplus (which is negative), the change in producer surplus (positive), and the change in government revenue (positive). We find that total surplus in the market decreases by the area D + F. This fall in total surplus is called the *deadweight loss* of the tariff.

IMPORT QUOTAS: ANOTHER WAY TO RESTRICT TRADE

Beyond tariffs, another way that nations sometimes restrict international trade is by putting limits on how much of a good can be imported. In this book, we will not analyze such a policy, other than to point out the conclusion: Import quotas are much like tariffs. Both tariffs and import quotas reduce the quantity of imports, raise the domestic price of the good, decrease the welfare of domestic consumers, increase the welfare of domestic producers, and cause deadweight losses.

There is only one difference between these two types of trade restriction: A tariff raises revenue for the government, whereas an import quota creates surplus for those who get the licences to import.

The profit for the holder of an import licence is the difference between the domestic price (at which the licence holder sells the imported good) and the world price (at which the licence holder buys it).

Tariffs and import quotas are even more similar if the government charges a fee for the import licences. Suppose the government sets the licence fee equal to the difference between the domestic price and the world price. In this case, all of the profit of licence holders is paid to the government in licence fees, and the import quota works exactly like a tariff. Consumer surplus, producer surplus, and government revenue are precisely the same under the two policies.

A tariff causes a deadweight loss because a tariff is a type of tax. Like most taxes, it distorts incentives and pushes the allocation of scarce resources away from the optimum. In this case, we can identify two effects. First, when the tariff raises the domestic price of textiles above the world price, it encourages domestic producers to increase production from Q_1^S to Q_2^S. Even though the cost of making these incremental units exceeds the cost of buying them at the world price, the tariff makes it profitable for domestic producers to manufacture them nonetheless. Second, when the tariff raises the price that domestic textile consumers have to pay, it encourages them to reduce consumption of textiles from Q_1^D to Q_2^D. Even though domestic consumers value these incremental units at more than the world price, the tariff induces them to cut back their purchases. Area D represents the deadweight loss from the overproduction of textiles, and area F represents the deadweight loss from the underconsumption of textiles. The total deadweight loss of the tariff is the sum of these two triangles.

The Lessons for Trade Policy

The team of Isolandian economists can now write to the new president:

Dear Madam President,

You asked us three questions about opening up trade. After much hard work, we have the answers.

Question: If the government allowed Isolandians to import and export textiles, what would happen to the price of textiles and the quantity of textiles sold in the domestic textile market?

Answer: Once trade is allowed, the Isolandian price of textiles would be driven to equal the price prevailing around the world.

If the world price is now higher than the Isolandian price, our price would rise. The higher price would reduce the amount of textiles Isolandians consume and raise the amount of textiles that Isolandians produce. Isoland would, therefore, become a textile exporter. This occurs because, in this case, Isoland would have a comparative advantage in producing textiles.

Conversely, if the world price is now lower than the Isolandian price, our price would fall. The lower price would raise the amount of textiles that Isolandians consume and lower the amount of textiles that Isolandians produce. Isoland would, therefore, become a textile importer. This occurs because, in this case, other countries would have a comparative advantage in producing textiles.

Question: Who would gain from free trade in textiles and who would lose, and would the gains exceed the losses?

Answer: The answer depends on whether the price rises or falls when trade is allowed. If the price rises, producers of textiles gain, and consumers of textiles lose. If the price falls, consumers gain, and producers lose. In both cases, the gains are larger than the losses. Thus, free trade raises the total welfare of Isolandians.

Question: Should a tariff or an import quota be part of the new trade policy?

Answer: A tariff, like most taxes, has deadweight losses: The revenue raised would be smaller than the losses to the buyers and sellers. In this case,

Free Trade Effects

Price ↑ = producers gain
       consumers lose

Price ↓ = producers lose
       consumers gain

the deadweight losses occur because the tariff would move the economy closer to our current no-trade equilibrium. An import quota works much like a tariff and would cause similar deadweight losses. The best policy, from the standpoint of economic efficiency, would be to allow trade without a tariff or an import quota.

We hope you find these answers helpful as you decide on your new policy.

Your faithful servants,
Isolandian Economics Team

QuickQuiz Draw the supply and demand curves for wool suits in the country of Autarka. When trade is allowed, the price of a suit falls from 100 to 60 grams of gold. In your diagram, what is the change in consumer surplus, the change in producer surplus, and the change in total surplus? How would a tariff on suit imports alter these effects?

Other Benefits of International Trade

The conclusions of the Isolandian economics team are based on the standard analysis of international trade. The team's analysis uses the most fundamental tools in the economist's toolbox: supply, demand, and producer and consumer surplus. It shows that there are winners and losers when a nation opens itself up to trade, but the gains to the winners exceed the losses of the losers.

The case for free trade can be made even stronger, however, because there are several other economic benefits of trade beyond those emphasized in the standard analysis. Here, in a nutshell, are some of these other benefits:

- **Increased variety of goods.** Goods produced in different countries are not exactly the same. German beer, for instance, is not the same as Canadian beer. Free trade gives consumers in all countries greater variety from which to choose.
- **Lower costs through economies of scale.** Some goods can be produced at low cost only if they are produced in large quantities—a phenomenon called *economies of scale*. A firm in a small country cannot take full advantage of economies of scale if it can sell only in a small domestic market. Free trade gives firms access to larger world markets and allows them to realize economies of scale more fully.
- **Increased competition.** A company shielded from foreign competitors is more likely to have market power, which in turn gives it the ability to raise prices above competitive levels. This is a type of market failure. Opening up trade fosters competition and gives the invisible hand a better chance to work its magic.
- **Enhanced flow of ideas.** The transfer of technological advances around the world is often thought to be linked to the trading of the goods that embody those advances. The best way for a poor agricultural nation to learn about the computer revolution, for instance, is to buy some computers from abroad rather than trying to make them domestically.

Thus, free international trade increases variety for consumers, allows firms to take advantage of economies of scale, makes markets more competitive, and facilitates the spread of technology. If the Isolandian economists also took these effects into account, their advice to their president would be even more forceful.

THE ARGUMENTS FOR RESTRICTING TRADE

The letter from the economics team persuades the new president of Isoland to consider opening up trade in textiles. She notes that the domestic price is now high compared to the world price. Free trade would, therefore, cause the price of textiles to fall and hurt domestic textile producers. Before implementing the new policy, she asks Isolandian textile companies to comment on the economists' advice.

Not surprisingly, the textile companies are opposed to free trade in textiles. They believe that the government should protect the domestic textile industry from foreign competition. Let's consider some of the arguments they might give to support their position and how the economics team would respond.

The Jobs Argument

Opponents of free trade often argue that trade with other countries destroys domestic jobs. In our example, free trade in textiles would cause the price of textiles to fall, reducing the quantity of textiles produced in Isoland and thus reducing employment in the Isolandian textile industry. Some Isolandian textile workers would lose their jobs.

Yet free trade creates jobs at the same time that it destroys them. When Isolandians buy textiles from other countries, those countries obtain the resources to buy other goods from Isoland. Isolandian workers would move from the textile industry to those industries in which Isoland has a comparative advantage. Although the transition may impose hardship on some workers in the short run, it allows Isolandians as a whole to enjoy a higher standard of living.

Opponents of trade are often skeptical that trade creates jobs. They might respond that *everything* can be produced more cheaply abroad. Under free trade, they might argue, Isolandians could not be profitably employed in any industry. As Chapter 3 explains, however, the gains from trade are based on comparative advantage, not absolute advantage. Even if one country is better than another country at producing everything, each country can still gain from trading with the other. Workers in each country will eventually find jobs in the industry in which that country has a comparative advantage.

The National-Security Argument

When an industry is threatened with competition from other countries, opponents of free trade often argue that the industry is vital for national security. For example, if Isoland was considering free trade in steel, domestic steel companies might point out that steel is used to make guns and tanks. Free trade would allow Isoland to become dependent on foreign countries to supply steel. If a war later broke out, Isoland might be unable to produce enough steel and weapons to defend itself.

Economists acknowledge that protecting key industries may be appropriate when there are legitimate concerns over national security. Yet they fear that this argument may be used too quickly by producers eager to gain at consumers' expense.

One should be wary of the national-security argument when it is made by representatives of industry rather than the defence establishment. Companies have an incentive to exaggerate their role in national defence to obtain protection from foreign competition. A nation's generals may see things very differently. Indeed, when the military is a consumer of an industry's output, it would benefit from imports. Cheaper steel in Isoland, for example, would allow the Isolandian military to accumulate a stockpile of weapons at lower cost.

The Infant-Industry Argument

New industries sometimes argue for temporary trade restrictions to help them get started. After a period of protection, the argument goes, these industries will mature and be able to compete with foreign firms. Similarly, older industries sometimes argue that they need temporary protection to help them adjust to new conditions. Canada's "National Policy," started by Sir John A. Macdonald in 1878, could be seen as an attempt to protect the infant Canadian manufacturing sector from foreign (especially U.S.) competition. This protection from foreign competition lasted for 110 years, until the Canada–U.S. Free Trade Agreement of 1989.

Economists are often skeptical about such claims. The primary reason is that the infant-industry argument is difficult to implement in practice. To apply protection successfully, the government would need to decide which industries will eventually be profitable and decide whether the benefits of establishing these industries exceed the costs to consumers of protection. Yet "picking winners" is extraordinarily difficult. It is made even more difficult by the political process, which often awards protection to those industries that are politically powerful. And once a powerful industry is protected from foreign competition, the "temporary" policy is hard to remove.

In addition, many economists are skeptical about the infant-industry argument even in principle. Suppose, for instance, that the Isolandian textile industry is young and unable to compete profitably against foreign rivals. Yet there is reason to believe that the industry can be profitable in the long run. In this case, the owners of the firms should be willing to incur temporary losses to obtain the eventual profits. Protection is not necessary for an industry to grow. Firms in various industries—such as many Internet firms today—incur temporary losses in the hope of growing and becoming profitable in the future. And many of them succeed, even without protection from foreign competition.

The Unfair-Competition Argument

A common argument is that free trade is desirable only if all countries play by the same rules. If firms in different countries are subject to different laws and regulations, then it is unfair (the argument goes) to expect the firms to compete in the international marketplace. For instance, suppose that the government of Neighbourland subsidizes its textile industry by giving textile companies large tax breaks. The Isolandian textile industry might argue that it should be protected from this foreign competition because Neighbourland is not competing fairly.

Would it, in fact, hurt Isoland to buy textiles from another country at a subsidized price? Certainly, Isolandian textile producers would suffer, but Isolandian textile consumers would benefit from the low price. The case for free trade is no different: The gains of the consumers from buying at the low price would exceed the losses of the producers. Neighbourland's subsidy to its textile industry may be a bad policy, but it is the taxpayers of Neighbourland who bear the burden. Isoland can benefit from the opportunity to buy textiles at a subsidized price.

The Protection-as-a-Bargaining-Chip Argument

Another argument for trade restrictions concerns the strategy of bargaining. Many policymakers claim to support free trade but, at the same time, argue that trade restrictions can be useful when we bargain with our trading partners. They claim that the threat of a trade restriction can help remove a trade restriction already imposed by a foreign government. For example, Isoland might threaten to impose a tariff on textiles unless Neighbourland removes its tariff on wheat. If Neighbourland responds to this threat by removing its tariff, the result can be freer trade.

The problem with this bargaining strategy is that the threat may not work. If it doesn't work, the country has a difficult choice. It can carry out its threat and implement the trade restriction, which would reduce its own economic welfare. Or it can back down from its threat, which would cause it to lose prestige in international affairs. Faced with this choice, the country would probably wish that it had never made the threat in the first place.

Case Study

TRADE AGREEMENTS AND THE WORLD TRADE ORGANIZATION

A country can take one of two approaches to achieving free trade. It can take a *unilateral* approach and remove its trade restrictions on its own. This is the approach that Great Britain took in the nineteenth century and that Chile and South Korea have taken in more recent years. Alternatively, a country can take a *multilateral* approach and reduce its trade restrictions while other countries do the same. In other words, it can bargain with its trading partners in an attempt to reduce trade restrictions around the world.

One important example of the multilateral approach is the North American Free Trade Agreement (NAFTA), which in 1993 lowered trade barriers among the United States, Mexico, and Canada. Another is the General Agreement on Tariffs and Trade (GATT), which is a continuing series of negotiations among many of the world's countries with the goal of promoting free trade. Canada helped to found GATT after World War II in response to the high tariffs imposed during the Great Depression of the 1930s. Many economists believe that the high tariffs contributed to the economic hardship during that period. GATT has successfully reduced the average tariff among member countries from about 40 percent after World War II to about 5 percent today.

The rules established under GATT are now enforced by an international institution called the World Trade Organization (WTO). The WTO was established in 1995 and has its headquarters in Geneva, Switzerland. As of March 2013, 159 countries had joined the organization, accounting for 97 percent of world trade. The functions of the WTO are to administer trade agreements, provide a forum for negotiations, and handle disputes that arise among member countries.

What are the pros and cons of the multilateral approach to free trade? One advantage is that the multilateral approach has the potential to result in freer trade

IN THE NEWS

A RETHINK OF CANADA'S TRADE FOCUS

Canada is, and always has been, a trading country closely linked to the United States. This article argues for a different approach.

Look Beyond the U.S.

America's pre-eminence is in decline. If Canada is to prosper, we must seek new foreign trade partners.

By Jack M. Mintz

At the beginning of this decade, elite opinion held that our priority for trade should be to deepen our relationship with the United States, our most important trading partner. Having ended this decade, it is far from clear that this is the best approach for Canada. The U.S. is a waning star. We need to branch out to other countries where growth will be more pronounced as well as to strengthen our bargaining position with an increasingly protectionist partner.

Our past trade strategy focused on the United States, especially after the terrorist attacks that resulted in 3,000 deaths in New York and Washington, D.C. Canadians debated whether we should pursue a "Big Idea," a term coined by U of T's Wendy Dobson, such as a common market, a custom union or just some new trade partnership to reduce regulatory, tax and other barriers with the United States. Sure, we looked at some new trade deals with Chile and Israel but most attention was paid to our relationship with the United States, and secondarily to Mexico, our other NAFTA partner.

We are now in a different world. The United States is on the precipice of decline as it struggles with a sick housing market, excessive public and private debt loads, an antiquated tax system, anti-growth regulatory policies, falling productivity with an aging population and increasing isolationism. It is hard to see the U.S. growing at its historical 3% over the coming decade. With high unemployment and distrust of the benefits from globalization, U.S. trade policy is becoming more inward with trade agreement initiatives being replaced by "Buy American" provisions.

The U.S. share of world GDP (about a fifth) will continue to fall this coming decade as emerging and developing countries almost double their size. By 2030, China will be the second largest economy in the world, rivaling the U.S. for economic domination. Other emerging economies, including Brazil, India and Indonesia with growth rates double that of the U.S., could be major markets for Canadian exporters. It would be a mistake for Canada to ignore markets beyond North America.

The Australians have been particularly adept at growing international markets for their products and services, heavily dominated by mining. In 2008, Australian exports to Japan were $51-billion, followed by China

($33-billion), Korea ($18.5-billion), India ($15.4-billion) and the United States ($11.4-billion). Which country will grow faster in the future—Canada or Australia? Not a hard question to answer.

In our relations with the U.S. elephant, we have little leverage to negotiate trade improvements since we have no credible threat to turn elsewhere. A good example is energy exports to the U.S. market. If the U.S. wishes to penalize consumption of our oil sand production, we have little room to manoeuvre. But if we export to Asia and other markets, we improve our negotiating position significantly.

The same could be argued for lumber, minerals, manufactured products and services. Trade with the U.S. is economical because of lower transport costs and cultural similarity. However, as the U.S. increases its protectionism, Canada may simply turn to other markets where tariffs, regulations, and other costs are eased relative to the United States.

So what would a new trade strategy look like? First principle: Don't throw out the baby with the bath water. Given our good trading relationship with the U.S., we should try to negotiate better terms that would reduce trade barriers by pursuing policies that harmonize regulations, reduce cross-border withholding taxes and ease congestion at the border. We should also seek exemptions from

U.S. protectionist legislation—it has worked before and may again.

Second principle: Develop new markets for Canadian exporters, especially with growing parts of the world. In some countries, Canadians are highly respected (the Chinese still talk about Norman Bethune). And we can leverage our multicultural business communities who have good contacts elsewhere. Our goal should be to establish new free trade agreements with large countries such as Brazil, China, Europe, Korea, India and Japan so that we can develop new markets elsewhere.

Third principle: Continue pursuing competitiveness and innovation so that we can benefit from greater world-wide trade. This is the policy framework of the federal government in recent years and, despite the recession, there is no need to change course. Competition, taxation, regulation and innovation policies should be reformed to encourage a more dynamic economy with successful businesses competing abroad. If we have a successful economy, our exchange rate will rise but this only means that Canadians are becoming richer as we more easily buy goods and services imported from abroad.

There is a big world out there beyond the U.S. and it is getting even bigger.

Source: Jack Mintz, "Look Beyond the U.S.," *National Post,* January 14, 2010. Material reprinted with the express permission of: The National Post, a division of Postmedia Network, Inc.

than a unilateral approach because it can reduce trade restrictions abroad as well as at home. If international negotiations fail, however, the result could be more restricted trade than under a unilateral approach.

In addition, the multilateral approach may have a political advantage. In most markets, producers are fewer and better organized than consumers—and thus wield greater political influence. Reducing the Isolandian tariff on textiles, for example, may be politically difficult if considered by itself. The textile companies would oppose free trade, and the users of textiles who would benefit are so numerous that organizing their support would be difficult. Yet suppose that Neighbourland promises to reduce its tariff on wheat at the same time that Isoland reduces its tariff on textiles. In this case, the Isolandian wheat farmers, who are also politically powerful, would back the agreement. Thus, the multilateral approach to free trade can sometimes win political support when a unilateral reduction cannot. ●

QuickQuiz   The textile industry of Autarka advocates a ban on the import of wool suits. Describe five arguments its lobbyists might make. Give a response to each of these arguments.

CONCLUSION

Economists and the general public often disagree about free trade. In 1988, for example, Canada faced the question of whether to sign the Canada–U.S. Free Trade Agreement, which reduced trade restrictions between Canada and the United States. Opinion polls showed the general public in Canada to be about evenly split on the issue. Prime Minister Brian Mulroney campaigned for the free trade agreement and won re-election, but with a minority of the popular vote. Opponents viewed free trade as a threat to job security and the Canadian standard of living. By contrast, economists overwhelmingly supported the agreement. They viewed free trade as a way of allocating production efficiently and raising living standards in both countries.

Economists see the benefits of trade between countries in the same way that they see the benefits of trade between provinces, or between cities, or between people. Individuals would have a much lower standard of living if they had to produce all their own food, clothing, and housing. So would a city. So would a province. The United States has always had unrestricted trade among the states, and the country as a whole has benefited from the specialization that trade allows in such a large market. With a few exceptions, Canada, too, has free trade among the provinces: Ontario builds cars, Alberta pumps oil, British Columbia saws lumber, and so on. The world could similarly benefit from free trade among countries.

To better understand economists' view of trade, let's continue our parable. Suppose that the country of Isoland ignores the advice of its economics team and decides not to allow free trade in textiles. The country remains in the equilibrium without international trade.

Then, one day, some Isolandian inventor discovers a new way to make textiles at very low cost. The process is quite mysterious, however, and the inventor insists on keeping it a secret. What is odd is that the inventor doesn't need traditional inputs such as cotton or wool. The only material input he needs is wheat. And even more oddly, to manufacture textiles from wheat, he hardly needs any labour input at all.

The inventor is hailed as a genius. Because everyone buys clothing, the lower cost of textiles allows all Isolandians to enjoy a higher standard of living. Workers who had previously produced textiles do suffer when their factories close, but eventually they find work in other industries. Some become farmers and grow the wheat that the inventor turns into textiles. Others enter new industries that emerge as a result of higher Isolandian living standards. Everyone understands that the displacement of these workers is an inevitable part of progress and economic growth.

After several years, a newspaper reporter decides to investigate this mysterious new textile process. She sneaks into the inventor's factory and learns that the inventor is a fraud. The inventor has not been making textiles at all. Instead, he has been smuggling wheat abroad in exchange for textiles from other countries. The only thing that the inventor had discovered was the gains from international trade.

When the truth is revealed, the government shuts down the inventor's operation. The price of textiles rises, and workers return to jobs in textile factories. Living standards in Isoland fall back to their former levels. The inventor is jailed and held up to public ridicule. After all, he was no inventor. He was just an economist.

SUMMARY

- The effects of free trade can be determined by comparing the domestic price without trade to the world price. A low domestic price indicates that the country has a comparative advantage in producing the good and that the country will become an exporter. A high domestic price indicates that the rest of the world has a comparative advantage in producing the good and that the country will become an importer.

- When a country allows trade and becomes an exporter of a good, producers of the good are better off, and consumers of the good are worse off. When a country allows trade and becomes an importer of a good, consumers are better off, and producers are worse off. In both cases, the gains from trade exceed the losses.

- A tariff—a tax on imports—moves a market closer to the equilibrium that would exist without trade and, therefore, reduces the gains from trade. Although domestic producers are better off and the government raises revenue, the losses to consumers exceed these gains.

- There are various arguments for restricting trade: protecting jobs, defending national security, helping infant industries, preventing unfair competition, and responding to foreign trade restrictions. Although some of these arguments have some merit in some cases, economists believe that free trade is usually the better policy.

KEY CONCEPTS

world price, p. 191   tariff, p. 195

QUESTIONS FOR REVIEW

1. What does the domestic price that prevails without international trade tell us about a nation's comparative advantage?

2. When does a country become an exporter of a good? An importer?

3. Draw the supply-and-demand diagram for an importing country. What is consumer surplus and producer surplus before trade is allowed? What is consumer surplus and producer surplus with free trade? What is the change in total surplus?

4. Describe what a tariff is, and describe its economic effects.

5. List five arguments often given to support trade restrictions. How do economists respond to these arguments?

6. What is the difference between the unilateral and multilateral approaches to achieving free trade? Give an example of each.

PROBLEMS AND APPLICATIONS

1. Canada represents a small part of the world apple market.
   a. Draw a diagram depicting the equilibrium in the Canadian apple market without international trade. Identify the equilibrium price, equilibrium quantity, consumer surplus, and producer surplus.
   b. Suppose that the world apple price is below the Canadian price before trade, and that the Canadian apple market is now opened to trade. Identify the new equilibrium price, quantity consumed, quantity produced domestically, and quantity imported. Also show the change in the surplus of domestic consumers and producers. Has domestic total surplus increased or decreased?

2. The world price of wine is below the price that would prevail in Canada in the absence of trade.

   a. Assuming that Canadian imports of wine are a small part of total world wine production, draw a graph for the Canadian market for wine under free trade. Identify consumer surplus, producer surplus, and total surplus in an appropriate table.
   b. Now suppose that an unusual shift of the Gulf Stream leads to an unseasonably cold summer in Europe, destroying much of the grape harvest there. What effect does this shock have on the world price of wine? Using your graph and table from part (a), show the effect on consumer surplus, producer surplus, and total surplus in Canada. Who are the winners and losers? Is Canada as a whole better off or worse off?

3. Suppose that Parliament imposes a tariff on imported clothes to protect the Canadian clothing industry from foreign competition.

Assuming that Canada is a price taker in the world clothing market, show the following on a diagram: (a) the change in the quantity of imports, (b) the loss to Canadian consumers, (c) the gain to Canadian manufacturers, (d) government revenue, and (e) the deadweight loss associated with the tariff. The loss to consumers can be decomposed into three pieces: a transfer to domestic producers, a transfer to the government, and a deadweight loss. Use your diagram to identify these three pieces.

4. Most Canadian dairy farmers oppose free trade, and most Canadian lumber producers support it. For simplicity, assume that Canada is a small country in the markets for both milk and lumber, and that without free trade, Canada would not trade these goods internationally. (Both of these assumptions are false, but they do not affect the qualitative responses to the following questions.)

   a. Based on who opposes and who supports free trade, do you think the world milk price is above or below the Canadian no-trade milk price? Do you think the world lumber price is above or below the Canadian no-trade lumber price? Now analyze the welfare consequences of free trade for both markets.

   b. Considering both markets together, would free trade make Canadian producers as a group better off or worse off? Would it make Canadian consumers as a group better off or worse off? Does it make Canada as a whole better off or worse off?

5. Imagine that winemakers in British Columbia petitioned the provincial government to tax wines imported from Ontario. They argue that this tax would both raise tax revenue for the provincial government and raise employment in the BC wine industry. Do you agree with these claims? Is it a good policy?

6. The nation of Textilia does not allow imports of clothing. In its equilibrium without trade, a T-shirt costs $20 and the equilibrium quantity is 3 million T-shirts. One day, after reading Adam Smith's *The Wealth of Nations* while on vacation, the president decides to open the Textilian market to international trade. The market price of a T-shirt falls to the world price of $16. The number of T-shirts consumed in Textilia

rises to 4 million, while the number of T-shirts produced declines to 1 million.

   a. Illustrate in a graph the situation just described. Your graph should show all of the numbers.

   b. Calculate the change in consumer surplus, producer surplus, and total surplus that results from opening up trade. (Hint: Recall that the area of a triangle is $\frac{1}{2} \times$ base $\times$ height.)

7. Assume that Canada is an importer of televisions and that there are no trade restrictions. Canadian consumers buy 1 million televisions per year, of which 400 000 are produced domestically and 600 000 are imported.

   a. Suppose that a technological advance among Japanese television manufacturers causes the world price of televisions to fall by $100. Draw a graph to show how this change affects the welfare of Canadian consumers and Canadian producers and how it affects total surplus in Canada.

   b. After the fall in price, consumers buy 1.2 million televisions, of which 200 000 are produced domestically and 1 million are imported. Calculate the change in consumer surplus, producer surplus, and total surplus from the price reduction.

   c. If the government responded by putting a $100 tariff on imported televisions, what would this do? Calculate the revenue that would be raised and the deadweight loss. Would it be a good policy from the standpoint of Canadian welfare? Who might support the policy?

   d. Suppose that the fall in price is attributable not to technological advance but to a $100 per television subsidy from the Japanese government to Japanese industry. How would this affect your analysis?

8. Consider a small country that exports steel. Suppose that a "pro-trade" government decides to subsidize the export of steel by paying a certain amount for each tonne sold abroad. How does this export subsidy affect the domestic price of steel, the quantity of steel produced, the quantity of steel consumed, and the quantity of steel exported? How does it affect consumer surplus, producer surplus, government revenue, and total surplus? (Hint: The analysis of an export subsidy is similar to the analysis of a tariff.)

9. Consider the arguments for restricting trade.
   a. Assume you are a lobbyist for timber, an established industry suffering from low-priced foreign competition. Which two or three of the five arguments do you think would be most persuasive to the average member of Parliament as to why he or she should support trade restrictions? Explain your reasoning.
   b. Now assume you are an astute student of economics (hopefully not a hard assumption). Although all the arguments for restricting trade have their shortcomings, name the two or three arguments that seem to make the most economic sense to you. For each, describe the economic rationale for and against these arguments for trade restrictions.

10. China is a major producer of grains, such as wheat, corn, and rice. In 2008, the Chinese government, concerned that grain exports were driving up food prices for domestic consumers, imposed a tax on grain exports. Draw the graph that describes the market for grain in an exporting country. Use this graph as the starting point to answer the following questions.
    a. How does an export tax affect domestic grain prices?
    b. How does it affect the welfare of domestic consumers, the welfare of domestic producers, and government revenue?
    c. What happens to total welfare in China, as measured by the sum of consumer surplus, producer surplus, and tax revenue?

11. Consider a country that imports a good from abroad. For each of the following statements, say whether it is true or false. Explain your answer.
    a. "The greater the elasticity of demand, the greater the gains from trade."
    b. "If demand is perfectly inelastic, there are no gains from trade."
    c. "If demand is perfectly inelastic, consumers do not benefit from trade."

12. Kawmin is a small country that produces and consumes jelly beans. The world price of jelly beans is $1 per bag, and Kawmin's domestic demand and supply for jelly beans are governed by the following equations:

Demand: $Q^D = 8 - P$
Supply: $Q^S = P$

where P is in dollars per bag and Q is in bags of jelly beans.
    a. Draw a well-labelled graph of the situation in Kawmin if the nation does not allow trade. Calculate the following (recalling that the area of a triangle is $\frac{1}{2} \times$ base $\times$ height): the equilibrium price and quantity, consumer surplus, producer surplus, and total surplus.
    b. Kawmin then opens the market to trade. Draw another graph to describe the new situation in the jelly bean market. Calculate the equilibrium price, quantities of consumption and production, imports, consumer surplus, producer surplus, and total surplus.
    c. After awhile, the czar of Kawmin responds to the pleas of jelly bean producers by placing a $1 per bag tariff on jelly bean imports. On a graph, show the effects of this tariff. Calculate the equilibrium price, quantities of consumption and production, imports, consumer surplus, producer surplus, government revenue, and total surplus.
    d. What are the gains from opening up trade? What are the deadweight losses from restricting trade with the tariff? Give numerical answers.

13. Having rejected a tariff on textiles (a tax on imports), the president of Isoland is now considering the same-sized tax on textile consumption (including both imported and domestically produced textiles).
    a. Using Figure 9.4, identify the quantity consumed and the quantity produced in Isoland under a textile consumption tax.
    b. Construct a table similar to that in Figure 9.4 for the textile consumption tax.
    c. Which raises more revenue for the government—the consumption tax or the tariff? Which has a smaller deadweight loss? Explain.

THE ECONOMICS OF THE PUBLIC SECTOR

4

EXTERNALITIES 10

Firms that make and sell paper also create, as a by-product of the manufacturing process, a chemical called *dioxin*. Scientists believe that once dioxin enters the environment, it raises the population's risk of cancer, birth defects, and other health problems.

Is the production and release of dioxin a problem for society? In Chapters 4 through 9 we examined how markets allocate scarce resources with the forces of supply and demand, and we saw that the equilibrium of supply and demand is typically an efficient allocation of resources. To use Adam Smith's famous metaphor, the invisible hand of the marketplace leads self-interested buyers and sellers in a market to maximize the total benefit that society derives from that market. This insight is the basis for one of the ten principles of economics in Chapter 1: Markets are usually a good way to organize economic activity. Should we conclude, therefore, that the invisible hand prevents firms in the paper market from emitting too much dioxin?

Markets do many things well, but they do not do everything well. In this chapter we begin our study of another of the ten principles of economics: Governments can sometimes improve market outcomes. We examine why markets sometimes fail to allocate resources efficiently, how government policies can potentially improve the market's allocation, and what kinds of policies are likely to work best.

externality

the uncompensated impact of one person's actions on the well-being of a bystander

The market failures examined in this chapter fall under a general category called *externalities*. An **externality** arises when a person engages in an activity that influences the well-being of a bystander but neither pays nor receives any compensation for that effect. If the impact on the bystander is adverse, it is called a *negative externality*; if it is beneficial, it is called a *positive externality*. In the presence of externalities, society's interest in a market outcome extends beyond the well-being of buyers and sellers who participate in the market; it also includes the well-being of bystanders who are affected indirectly. Because buyers and sellers neglect the external effects of their actions when deciding how much to demand or supply, the market equilibrium is not efficient when there are externalities. That is, the equilibrium fails to maximize the total benefit to society as a whole. The release of dioxin into the environment, for instance, is a negative externality. Self-interested paper firms will not consider the full cost of the pollution they create and, therefore, will emit too much pollution unless the government prevents or discourages them from doing so.

Externalities come in many varieties, as do the policy responses that try to deal with the market failure. Here are some examples:

- The exhaust from automobiles is a negative externality because it creates smog that other people have to breathe. As a result of this externality, drivers tend to pollute too much. The federal government attempts to solve this problem by setting emission standards for cars. It also taxes gasoline to reduce the amount that people drive.
- Restored historic buildings convey a positive externality because people who walk or ride by them can enjoy their beauty and the sense of history that these buildings provide. Building owners do not get the full benefit of restoration and, therefore, tend to discard older buildings too quickly. Many local governments respond to this problem by regulating the destruction of historic buildings and by providing tax breaks to owners who restore them.
- Barking dogs create a negative externality because neighbours are disturbed by the noise. Dog owners do not bear the full cost of the noise and, therefore, tend to take too few precautions to prevent their dogs from barking. Local governments address this problem by making it illegal to "disturb the peace."
- Research into new technologies provides a positive externality because it creates knowledge that other people can use. Because inventors cannot capture the full benefits of their inventions, they tend to devote too few resources to research. The federal government addresses this problem partially through the patent system, which gives inventors exclusive rights to their inventions for a period of time.
- A large body of scientific research suggests that carbon dioxide and other greenhouse gas emissions associated with the use of fossil fuels contributes to global warming. This in turn is thought to be associated with changes in ocean levels, weather patterns, and other climate-related changes. Individuals do not take full account of these externalities when consuming energy and therefore tend to consume too much. Governments around the world have addressed this by imposing taxes on carbon emissions as well as by implementing cap-and-trade systems with tradable permits.

In each of these cases, some decision maker fails to take account of the external effects of his or her behaviour. The government responds by trying to influence this behaviour to protect the interests of bystanders.

EXTERNALITIES AND MARKET INEFFICIENCY

In this section we use the tools from Chapter 7 to examine how externalities affect economic well-being. The analysis shows precisely why externalities cause markets to allocate resources inefficiently. Later in the chapter we examine various ways in which private actors and public policymakers may remedy this type of market failure.

Welfare Economics: A Recap

We begin by recalling the key lessons of welfare economics from Chapter 7. To make our analysis concrete, we will consider a specific market—the market for aluminum. Figure 10.1 shows the supply and demand curves in the market for aluminum.

As you should recall from Chapter 7, the supply and demand curves contain important information about costs and benefits. The demand curve for aluminum reflects the value of aluminum to consumers, as measured by the prices they are willing to pay. At any given quantity, the height of the demand curve shows the willingness to pay of the marginal buyer. In other words, it shows the value to the consumer of the last unit of aluminum bought. Similarly, the supply curve reflects the costs of producing aluminum. At any given quantity, the height of the supply curve shows the cost to the marginal seller. In other words, it shows the cost to the producer of the last unit of aluminum sold.

In the absence of government intervention, the price adjusts to balance the supply and demand for aluminum. The quantity produced and consumed in the market equilibrium, shown as Q_{MARKET} in Figure 10.1, is efficient in the sense that it maximizes the sum of producer and consumer surplus. That is, the market allocates resources in a way that maximizes the total value to the consumers who buy and use aluminum minus the total costs to the producers who make and sell aluminum.

FIGURE 10.1

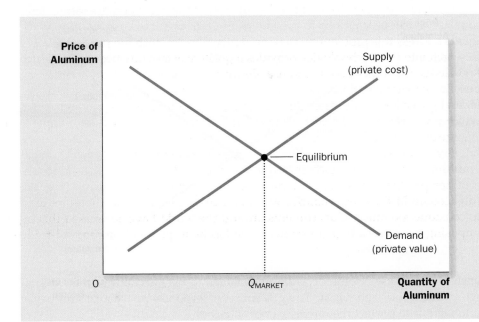

The Market for Aluminum

The demand curve reflects the value to buyers, and the supply curve reflects the costs of sellers. The equilibrium quantity, Q_{MARKET}, maximizes the total value to buyers minus the total costs of sellers. In the absence of externalities, therefore, the market equilibrium is efficient.

Negative Externalities

Now let's suppose that aluminum factories emit pollution: For each unit of aluminum produced, a certain amount of smoke enters the atmosphere. Because this smoke creates a health risk for those who breathe the air, it is a negative externality. How does this externality affect the efficiency of the market outcome?

Because of the externality, the cost to *society* of producing aluminum is larger than the cost to the aluminum producers. For each unit of aluminum produced, the *social cost* includes the private costs of the aluminum producers plus the costs to those bystanders affected adversely by the pollution. Figure 10.2 shows the social cost of producing aluminum. The social-cost curve is above the supply curve because it takes into account the external costs imposed on society by aluminum production. The difference between these two curves reflects the cost of the pollution emitted.

What quantity of aluminum should be produced? To answer this question, we once again consider what a benevolent social planner would do. The planner wants to maximize the total surplus derived from the market—the value to consumers of aluminum minus the cost of producing aluminum. The planner understands, however, that the cost of producing aluminum includes the external costs of the pollution.

The planner would choose the level of aluminum production at which the demand curve crosses the social-cost curve. This intersection determines the optimal amount of aluminum from the standpoint of society as a whole. Below this level of production, the value of the aluminum to consumers (as measured by the height of the demand curve) exceeds the social cost of producing it (as measured by the height of the social-cost curve). The planner does not produce more than

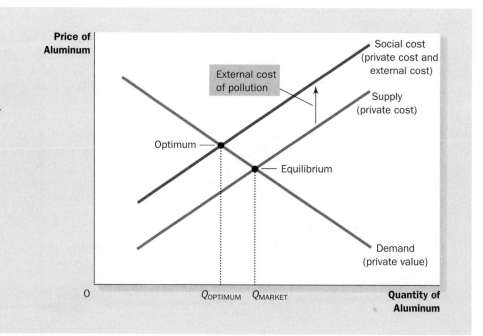

FIGURE 10.2

Pollution and the Social Optimum

In the presence of a negative externality, such as pollution, the social cost of the good exceeds the private cost. The optimal quantity, $Q_{OPTIMUM}$, is therefore smaller than the equilibrium quantity, Q_{MARKET}.

this level because the social cost of producing additional aluminum exceeds the value to consumers.

Note that the equilibrium quantity of aluminum, Q_{MARKET}, is larger than the socially optimal quantity, $Q_{OPTIMUM}$. This inefficiency occurs because the market equilibrium reflects only the private costs of production. In the market equilibrium, the marginal consumer values aluminum at less than the social cost of producing it. That is, at Q_{MARKET} the demand curve lies below the social-cost curve. Thus, reducing aluminum production and consumption below the market equilibrium level raises total economic well-being.

We can measure the value of this increase in economic well-being using the concept of *deadweight loss* introduced in Chapters 8 and 9. In those chapters the deadweight loss was the reduction in total surplus that resulted from the imposition of a tax or tariff. The same approach can be used to measure the reduction in total surplus associated with the inefficient allocation of resources due to the presence of an externality.

Figure 10.3 shows how we use the concepts of consumer and producer surplus to determine the deadweight loss of the externality caused by the aluminum factory emitting pollution. The equilibrium is determined by the intersection of the supply curve, which reflects the private cost of producing aluminum, and the demand curve. The equilibrium quantity is Q_{MARKET} and the price is P_{MARKET}.

At the equilibrium level of aluminum production, Q_{MARKET}, and the corresponding market price, P_{MARKET}, consumer surplus is measured in the usual way as the area between the demand curve and the equilibrium price, A + B + C + D. The measure of producer surplus is slightly more complicated but follows the same logic used in Chapters 8 and 9. We showed in Chapter 7 that in the absence of a market failure, producer surplus is simply the amount received by sellers less the cost to those sellers. In the presence of an externality, the basic idea is the same. However, rather than using the private cost to sellers of producing aluminum, as

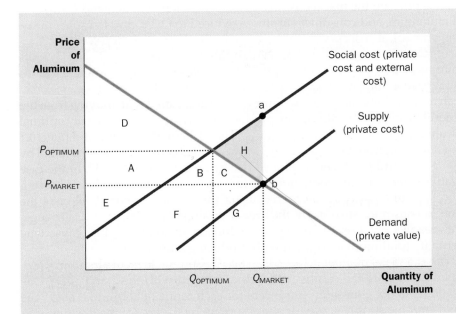

FIGURE 10.3

Deadweight Loss of a Negative Externality

A negative externality means that the social-cost curve lies above the demand curve at the market equilibrium quantity, Q_{MARKET}. Compared with the social optimum, $Q_{OPTIMUM}$, consumer surplus at the market equilibrium is higher by area A + B + C, and producer surplus measured using the social-cost curve is lower by A + B + C + H. The net effect is a reduction in total surplus, shown by deadweight loss triangle H.

TABLE 10.1

Deadweight Loss of a Negative Production Externality

This table refers to the areas marked in Figure 10.3 to show how a negative externality generates a deadweight loss in the economy.

	At Q_{MARKET}	At $Q_{OPTIMUM}$	Change
Consumer surplus	A + B + C + D	D	−(A + B + C)
Producer surplus	E − (B + C + H)	A + E	A + B + C + H
Total surplus	D + A + E − H	D + A + E	H

measured by the height of the supply or private-cost curve, we use the *social cost* of producing aluminum, as measured by the height of the social-cost curve.

The social-cost curve includes both the private costs of the aluminum producers and the external costs imposed on bystanders affected by the pollution. In Figure 10.3, the cost to society of producing the quantity of aluminum sold is the area between the social-cost curve and the market quantity, Q_{MARKET}, area F + G + B + C + H. The amount received by the sellers is simply the quantity of aluminum sold, Q_{MARKET}, times the market price of aluminum, P_{MARKET}, which is given by area E + F + G. So, producer surplus measured using the social cost of producing aluminum is the amount received by sellers less the social cost to society, or (E + F + G) − (F + G + B + C + H), which simplifies to E − (B + C + H).

Total surplus at the market equilibrium level of aluminum production then consists of consumer surplus (A + B + C + D) plus producer surplus [E − (B + C + H)]. The "At Q_{MARKET}" column of Table 10.1 summarizes these conclusions.

Now consider economic welfare measured at the socially optimal level of aluminum production, $Q_{OPTIMUM}$. The price of aluminum that would generate this socially optimal level of production is $P_{OPTIMUM}$. We will discuss below ways in which this price might be achieved. For now, let's say that the social planner simply imposes this price on the market. At this price, consumers will demand $Q_{OPTIMUM}$ units of aluminum, and consumer surplus is reduced to D. Producer surplus measured using the social-cost curve is the amount received by sellers at price $P_{OPTIMUM}$, the area of rectangle A + E + F + B, less the social cost of producing $Q_{OPTIMUM}$ units of aluminum, area F + B. This gives a producer surplus of A + E. These conclusions are summarized in the "At $Q_{OPTIMUM}$" column of Table 10.1.

We can now see the change in economic welfare associated with moving from the market equilibrium level of aluminum production, Q_{MARKET}, to the socially optimal level of aluminum production, $Q_{OPTIMUM}$. The "Change" column of Table 10.1 shows that moving from Q_{MARKET} to $Q_{OPTIMUM}$ causes consumer surplus to fall by area A + B + C, and producer surplus to rise by area A + B + C + H. In the case of a negative externality in production, the increase in producer surplus of moving from Q_{MARKET} to $Q_{OPTIMUM}$, measured using the social-cost curve, exceeds the reduction in consumer surplus by the area of triangle H in Figure 10.3. Triangle H is the deadweight loss to society, or reduction in total surplus, caused by the externality (pollution) associated with producing aluminum.

How can the social planner achieve the socially optimal level of aluminum production and eliminate the deadweight loss associated with the externality? One way would be to tax aluminum producers for each tonne of aluminum sold. The tax would shift the supply curve for aluminum up by the size of the tax. If the tax accurately reflects the external cost of pollutants, the new supply curve coincides with the social-cost curve. In the new market equilibrium, aluminum producers would produce the socially optimum quantity of aluminum.

The use of such a tax is called **internalizing the externality** because it gives buyers and sellers in the market an incentive to take into account the external effects of their actions. Aluminum producers would, in essence, take the costs of pollution into account when deciding how much aluminum to supply because the tax would make them pay for these external costs. And, because the market price would reflect the tax on producers, consumers of aluminum would have an incentive to use a smaller quantity. The policy is based on one of the ten principles of economics: People respond to incentives. Later in this chapter, we consider in more detail how policymakers can deal with externalities.

internalizing the externality
alter incentives so that people take account of the external effects of their actions

Positive Externalities

Although some activities impose costs on third parties, others yield benefits. For example, consider education. To a large extent, the benefit of education is private: The consumer of education becomes a more productive worker and thus reaps much of the benefit in the form of higher wages. Beyond these private benefits, however, education also yields positive externalities. One externality is that a more educated population leads to more informed voters, which means better government for everyone. Another externality is that a more educated population tends to mean lower crime rates. A third externality is that a more educated population may encourage the development and dissemination of technological advances, leading to higher productivity and wages for everyone. Because of these three positive externalities, a person may prefer to have neighbours who are well educated.

The analysis of positive externalities is similar to the analysis of negative externalities. As Figure 10.4 shows, the demand curve does not reflect the value to

FIGURE 10.4

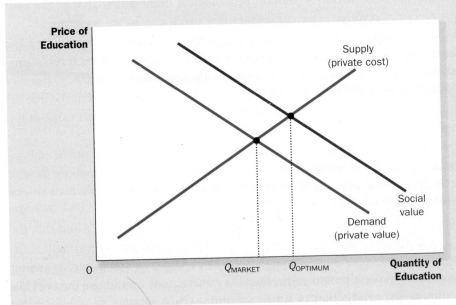

Education and the Social Optimum

In the presence of a positive externality, the social value of the good exceeds the private value. The optimal quantity, $Q_{OPTIMUM}$, is therefore larger than the equilibrium quantity, Q_{MARKET}.

society of the good. Because the social value is greater than the private value, the social-value curve lies above the demand curve. The optimal quantity is found where the social-value curve and the supply curve (which represents costs) intersect. Hence, the socially optimal quantity is greater than the quantity determined by the private market.

Once again, the government can correct the market failure by inducing market participants to internalize the externality. The appropriate response in the case of positive externalities is exactly the opposite to the case of negative externalities. To move the market equilibrium closer to the social optimum, a positive externality requires a subsidy. In fact, that is exactly the policy the government follows: Education is heavily subsidized through public schools and government scholarships.

To summarize: *Negative externalities lead markets to produce a larger quantity than is socially desirable. Positive externalities lead markets to produce a smaller quantity than is socially desirable. To remedy the problem, the government can internalize the externality by taxing goods that have negative externalities and subsidizing goods that have positive externalities.*

Case Study

TECHNOLOGY SPILLOVERS AND GOVERNMENT POLICY

A potentially important type of positive externality is called a *technology spillover*—the impact of one firm's research and production efforts on other firms' access to technological advance. For example, consider the market for industrial robots. Robots are at the frontier of a rapidly changing technology. Whenever a firm builds a robot, there is some chance that the firm will discover a new and better design. This new design will benefit not only this firm but society as a whole because the design will enter society's pool of technological knowledge. That is, the new design may have positive externalities for other producers in the economy.

In this case, the government can internalize the externality by subsidizing the production of robots. If the government paid firms a subsidy for each robot produced, the supply curve would shift down by the amount of the subsidy, and this shift would increase the equilibrium quantity of robots. To ensure that the market equilibrium equals the social optimum, the subsidy should equal the value of the technology spillover.

How large are technology spillovers, and what do they imply for public policy? This is an important question, because technological progress is the key to why living standards rise over time. Yet it is also a difficult question on which economists often disagree.

Some economists believe that technology spillovers are pervasive and that the government should encourage those industries that yield the largest spillovers. For instance, these economists argue that if making computer chips yields greater spillovers than making potato chips, then the government should use the tax laws to encourage the production of more computer chips relative to potato chips.

The Canadian tax laws do this by offering special tax breaks for expenditures on research and development. Some other nations go further by subsidizing specific industries that supposedly offer large technology spillovers. Government intervention in the economy that aims to promote technology-enhancing industries is sometimes called *industrial policy.*

Other economists are skeptical about industrial policy. Even if technology spillovers are common, the success of an industrial policy requires that the government be able to measure the size of the spillovers from different markets. This measurement problem is difficult at best. Moreover, without precise measurements, the political system may end up subsidizing those industries with the most political clout, rather than those that yield the largest positive externalities.

Governments also conduct research directly. An example in Canada is the federal government's National Research Council, which comprises research institutes and programs in various disciplines. Governments also provide direct funding for government research through various granting programs. An example is the Industrial Research Assistance Program (IRAP), which provides direct funding to research undertaken by small and medium-sized businesses. Of course, government support of postsecondary education, trains researchers, and funds research in universities.

Another way to deal with technology spillovers is patent protection. The patent laws protect inventors by giving them exclusive rights to their inventions for a period of time. When a firm makes a technological breakthrough, it can patent the idea and capture much of the economic benefit for itself. The patent is said to internalize the externality by giving the firm a *property right* over its invention. If other firms want to use the new technology, they have to obtain permission from the inventing firm and pay it a royalty. Thus, the patent system gives firms a greater incentive to engage in research and other activities that advance technology. ●

QuickQuiz   Give an example of a negative externality and a positive externality.
● Explain why market outcomes are inefficient in the presence of externalities.

PUBLIC POLICIES TOWARD EXTERNALITIES

We have discussed why externalities lead markets to allocate resources inefficiently but have mentioned only briefly how this inefficiency can be remedied. In practice, both public policymakers and private individuals respond to externalities in various ways. All of the remedies share the goal of moving the allocation of resources closer to the social optimum.

This section considers governmental solutions. As a general matter, the government can respond to externalities in one of two ways. *Command-and-control policies* regulate behaviour directly. *Market-based policies* provide incentives so that private decision makers will choose to solve the problem on their own.

Command-and-Control Policies: Regulation

The government can remedy an externality by making certain behaviours either required or forbidden. For example, it is a crime to dump poisonous chemicals into the water supply. In this case, the external costs to society far exceed the benefits to the polluter. The government therefore institutes a command-and-control policy that prohibits this act altogether.

In most cases of pollution, however, the situation is not this simple. It would be impossible to prohibit all polluting activity. For example, virtually all forms of transportation—even the horse—produce some undesirable polluting by-products. But it would not be sensible for the government to ban all transportation. Thus, instead of trying to eradicate pollution altogether, society has to weigh the costs and benefits to decide the kinds and quantities of pollution it will allow. In Canada, environmental policy is shared among all three levels of government—federal, provincial and territorial, and municipal. At the federal level, Environment Canada is the department responsible for developing and enforcing regulations aimed at protecting the environment.

Environmental regulations can take many forms. Sometimes Environment Canada dictates a maximum level of pollution that a factory may emit. Other times Environment Canada requires that firms adopt a particular technology to reduce emissions. For example, in 2011, the federal government announced regulations that will require all new coal-fired power generation plants commissioned after 2015 to match to the lower greenhouse gas emissions associated with natural gas generation. In all cases, to design good rules, the government regulators need to know the details about specific industries and about the alternative technologies that those industries could adopt. This information is often difficult for government regulators to obtain.

Market-Based Policy 1: Corrective Taxes and Subsidies

Instead of regulating behaviour in response to an externality, the government can use market-based policies to align private incentives with social efficiency. For instance, as we saw earlier, the government can internalize the externality by imposing taxes on activities that have negative externalities and subsidizing activities that have positive externalities. Taxes enacted to deal with the effects of negative externalities are called **corrective taxes**. They are also called *Pigovian taxes* after economist Arthur Pigou (1877–1959), an early advocate of their use. Pigou's writings in the 1920s predated by some 40 years the publication of Rachael Carson's book *Silent Spring*, which is widely credited with helping launch the environmental movement. So environmental concerns are hardly new subjects for economists.

An ideal corrective tax would equal the external cost from an activity with negative externalities, and an ideal corrective subsidy would equal the external benefit from an activity with positive externalities. For example, consider again Figure 10.3 (p. 215), which considered an externality in the aluminum market. In Figure 10.3, the corrective tax is the difference between the social-cost curve and the private-supply curve. In the diagram, this is equal to the distance between a and b, which is the difference between the social and private cost of producing an additional unit of aluminum.

corrective taxes
taxes enacted to correct the effects of negative externalities

Economists usually prefer corrective taxes over regulations as a way to deal with pollution because such taxes can reduce pollution at a lower cost to society. To see why, let us consider an example.

Suppose that two factories—a paper mill and a steel mill—are each dumping 500 tonnes of glop into a river every year. Environment Canada decides that it wants to reduce the amount of pollution. It considers two solutions:

1. Regulation: Environment Canada could tell each factory to reduce its pollution to 300 tonnes of glop per year.
2. Corrective tax: Environment Canada could levy a tax on each factory of $50 000 for each tonne of glop it emits.

The regulation would dictate a level of pollution, whereas the tax would give factory owners an economic incentive to reduce pollution. Which solution do you think is better?

Most economists would prefer the tax. They would first point out that a tax is just as effective as a regulation in reducing the overall level of pollution. Environment Canada can achieve whatever level of pollution it wants by setting the tax at the appropriate level. The higher the tax, the larger the reduction in pollution. Indeed, if the tax is high enough, the factories will close down altogether, reducing pollution to zero.

Although regulation and corrective taxes are both capable of reducing pollution, the tax accomplishes this goal more efficiently. The regulation requires each factory to reduce pollution by the same amount, but an equal reduction is not necessarily the least expensive way to clean up the water. It is possible that the paper mill can reduce pollution at lower cost than the steel mill. If so, the paper mill would respond to the tax by reducing pollution substantially to avoid the tax, whereas the steel mill would respond by reducing pollution less and paying the tax.

In essence, the corrective tax places a price on the right to pollute. Just as markets allocate goods to those buyers who value them most highly, a corrective tax allocates pollution to those factories that face the highest cost of reducing it. Whatever the level of pollution Environment Canada chooses, it can achieve this goal at the lowest total cost using a tax.

Economists also argue that corrective taxes are better for the environment. Under the command-and-control policy of regulation, the factories have no reason to reduce emission further once they have reached the target of 300 tonnes of glop. By contrast, the tax gives the factories an incentive to develop cleaner technologies, because a cleaner technology would reduce the amount of tax the factory has to pay.

Corrective taxes are unlike most other taxes. As we discussed in Chapter 8, most taxes distort incentives and move the allocation of resources away from the social optimum. The reduction in economic well-being—that is, in consumer and producer surplus—exceeds the amount of revenue the government raises, resulting in a deadweight loss. By contrast, when externalities are present, society also cares about the well-being of the bystanders who are affected. Corrective taxes alter incentives to account for the presence of externalities and thereby move the allocation of resources closer to the social optimum. Thus, while corrective taxes raise revenue for the government, they also enhance economic efficiency.

"If the gas tax was any larger, I'd take the bus."

Case Study

WHY IS GASOLINE TAXED SO HEAVILY?

In many nations, gasoline is among the most heavily taxed goods. The gas tax can be viewed as a corrective tax aimed at three negative externalities associated with driving:

1. *Congestion:* If you have ever been stuck in bumper-to-bumper traffic, you have probably wished that there were fewer cars on the road. A gasoline tax keeps congestion down by encouraging people to take public transportation, carpool more often, and live closer to work.
2. *Accidents:* Whenever a person buys a large car or a sport utility vehicle, he makes himself safer, but he puts his neighbours at risk. A person driving a typical car is much more likely to die if hit by a sport utility vehicle than if hit

IN THE NEWS

BRITISH COLUMBIA CARBON TAX

British Columbia has one of the most comprehensive carbon taxes in Canada. While businesses express great concern about "competitiveness," most economists support the imposition of such tax.

Carbon Tax Bumps Up B.C. Fuels Prices

Tax puts province's businesses at a disadvantage, says Business Council

B.C. residents face another across-the-board increase in fuel taxes in what's become a Canada Day convention.

The province's carbon tax on gasoline, diesel and all oil-based fuels, as well as natural gas and coal, has jumped every July 1 since 2008.

Friday's increase adds another 1.11 cents per litre to gasoline prices and another 1.15 cents per cubic metre on natural gas.

The gasoline carbon tax now totals 5.56 cents on every litre. It will rise another 1.11 cents to 6.67 cents per litre July 1, 2012—the last year of the increases in the current legislation.

The purpose of the tax is to encourage energy conservation in order to fight global warming.

Some consider a penny or so more per litre every year a small price—perhaps too small—in the war against climate change, while others suggest B.C. has been fighting alone and it's time to consider a retreat.

Only Escalating Carbon Tax Jurisdiction

"The problem for British Columbia is that we are dancing alone: we are the only jurisdiction in North America to levy a broadly based carbon tax that rises over time," said Jock Finlayson, spokesman for the Business Council of B.C.

"An ever-increasing made-in-B.C. carbon tax isn't sustainable if other provinces and states decline to follow the same path."

Quebec has been charging petroleum companies a carbon tax of just under one cent per litre since 2007 and Alberta forces most petroleum companies to contribute to a government technology fund, but B.C. has North America's only escalating carbon tax.

B.C. introduced its carbon tax as part of former premier Gordon Campbell's by another car. The gas tax is an indirect way of making people pay when their large, gas-guzzling vehicles impose risk on others. It would induce them to take this risk into account when choosing what vehicle to purchase.

3. *Pollution:* The burning of fossil fuels such as gasoline is widely believed to be the cause of global warming. Experts disagree about how dangerous this threat is, but there is no doubt that the gas tax reduces the risk by reducing the use of gasoline.

So the gas tax, rather than causing deadweight losses like most taxes, could actually make the economy work better. It means less traffic congestion, safer roads, and a cleaner environment.

How high should the tax on gasoline be? Taxes on gasoline vary throughout the world. Most European countries impose gasoline taxes that are much higher than those in Canada, while the United States imposes much lower taxes. A 2007 study published in the *Journal of Economic Literature* summarized the research on the size of the various externalities associated with driving. It concluded that the optimal corrective

plan to legislate cuts to greenhouse gas emissions by more than 33 per cent by 2020.

The most recent statistics provided in the government's Greenhouse Gas Inventory Report indicate the province has a long way to go to meet its reduction targets.

In 2007, B.C.'s total greenhouse gas emissions were 68 megatonnes. In 2008, greenhouse gas emissions increased to 68.7 megatonnes.

Provincial legislation on greenhouse gas emissions reduction sets interim reduction targets of six per cent by 2012 and 18 per cent by 2016.

Prof. Andrew Weaver, a climate expert at the University of Victoria, said B.C. earned worldwide credibility for introducing its visionary carbon tax.

He said he still favours a go-slow approach to the tax, maintaining the current annual increases, to allow business and residents to continue getting used to paying a price for carbon emissions.

Businesses Balk

But the business council, one of the largest business organizations in the province, says the tax hurts B.C. businesses.

Finlayson said the carbon tax is unfair because B.C. businesses pay the carbon tax while their competitors outside of the province do not. Although the levy is "revenue neutral," meaning carbon tax revenues are returned to businesses and taxpayers in the form of tax breaks, most businesses still balk.

"The expectations, I think, B.C. had a few years ago was that other jurisdictions, including in North America, would be following suit quite quickly, and so far that hasn't been happening," he said.

But Matt Horne, a climate expert at the Pembina Institute, said some businesses are starting to use the carbon tax to their advantage. He said the University of British Columbia, University of Northern B.C. and

the resort community of Whistler have all embarked on energy efficiency projects that have cut their energy costs.

"There are a bunch of projects around the province where the business case is definitely made better because of the carbon tax," he said. "It's an important driver on those projects happening."

He said recent polling indicated British Columbians are supportive of the carbon tax, and there is disappointment among environmentalists that no other North American jurisdictions have followed B.C.'s lead and instituted their own.

There are no scheduled carbon tax increases after 2012. The current government budget forecasts $740 million in carbon tax revenues this year and $950 million next year.

Source: "The years in, B.C. still on its own with carbon tax to fight climate change" by Dirk Meissner, June 30, 2011 © The Canadian Press.

tax on gasoline was about 55 cents per litre. Gasoline taxes vary across Canada, but on average are about 35 percent of the price. At a price of $1.10 per litre, taxes are thus about 39 cents. This is lower than the optimal corrective tax of 55 cents.

The tax revenue from a higher gasoline tax could be used to lower other taxes that distort incentives and cause deadweight losses. This type of "environmental tax shift" has been advocated by many economists. In addition, some of the burdensome government regulations that require automakers to produce more fuel-efficient cars would prove unnecessary. This idea, however, has never proven politically popular. ●

Market-Based Policy 2: Tradable Pollution Permits

Returning to our example of the paper mill and the steel mill, let us suppose that, despite the advice of its economists, Environment Canada adopts the regulation and requires each factory to reduce its pollution to 300 tonnes of glop per year. Then one day, after the regulation is in place and both mills have complied, the two firms go to Environment Canada with a proposal. The steel mill wants to increase its emission of glop by 100 tonnes. The paper mill has agreed to reduce its emission by the same amount if the steel mill pays it $5 million. Should Environment Canada allow the two factories to make this deal?

From the standpoint of economic efficiency, allowing the deal is good policy. The deal must make the owners of the two factories better off because they are voluntarily agreeing to it. Moreover, the deal does not have any external effects because the total amount of pollution remains the same. Thus, social welfare is enhanced by allowing the paper mill to sell its right to pollute to the steel mill.

The same logic applies to any voluntary transfer of the right to pollute from one firm to another. If Environment Canada allows firms to make these deals, it will, in essence, have created a new scarce resource: pollution permits. A market to trade these permits will eventually develop, and that market will be governed by the forces of supply and demand. The invisible hand will ensure that this new market efficiently allocates the right to pollute. That is, the permits will end up in the hands of those firms that value them most highly, as judged by their willingness to pay. A firm's willingness to pay for the right to pollute, in turn, will depend on its cost of reducing pollution: The more costly it is for a firm to cut back on pollution, the more it will be willing to pay for a permit.

An advantage of allowing a market for pollution permits is that the initial allocation of pollution permits among firms does not matter from the standpoint of economic efficiency. Those firms that can reduce pollution most easily would be willing to sell whatever permits they get, and those firms that can reduce pollution only at high cost would be willing to buy whatever permits they need. As long as there is a free market for the pollution rights, the final allocation will be efficient whatever the initial allocation.

Reducing pollution using pollution permits may seem very different from using corrective taxes, but the two policies have much in common. In both cases, firms pay for their pollution. With corrective taxes, polluting firms must pay a tax to the government. With pollution permits, polluting firms must pay to buy the permit. (Even firms that already own permits must pay to pollute: The opportunity cost of polluting is what they could have received by selling their permits on the open market.) Both corrective taxes and pollution permits internalize the externality of pollution by making it costly for firms to pollute.

The similarity of the two policies can be seen by considering the market for pollution. Both panels in Figure 10.5 show the demand curve for the right to pollute. This curve shows that the lower the price of polluting, the more firms will choose to pollute. In panel (a), Environment Canada uses a corrective tax to set a price for pollution. In this case, the supply curve for pollution rights is perfectly elastic (because firms can pollute as much as they want by paying the tax), and the position of the demand curve determines the quantity of pollution. In panel (b), Environment Canada sets a quantity of pollution by issuing pollution permits. In this case, the supply curve for pollution rights is perfectly inelastic (because the quantity of pollution is fixed by the number of permits), and the position of the demand curve determines the price of pollution. Hence, for any given demand curve for pollution, Environment Canada can achieve any point on the demand curve either by setting a price with a corrective tax or by setting a quantity with pollution permits.

In some circumstances, however, selling pollution permits may be better than levying a corrective tax. Suppose Environment Canada wants no more than 600 tonnes of glop to be dumped into the river. But, because Environment Canada does not know the demand curve for pollution, it is not sure what size tax would achieve that goal. In this case, it can simply auction off 600 pollution permits. The auction price would yield the appropriate size of the corrective tax.

The idea of the government auctioning off the right to pollute may at first sound like a figment of some economist's imagination and, in fact, that is how the idea began. But increasingly pollution permits, like corrective taxes, are now widely viewed as a cost-effective way to keep the environment clean.

FIGURE 10.5

The Equivalence of Corrective Taxes and Pollution Permits

In panel (a), Environment Canada sets a price on pollution by levying a corrective tax, and the demand curve determines the quantity of pollution. In panel (b), Environment Canada limits the quantity of pollution by limiting the number of pollution permits, and the demand curve determines the price of pollution. The price and quantity of pollution are the same in the two cases.

(a) Corrective Tax

Price of Pollution

1. A corrective tax sets the price of pollution . . .

Corrective tax

Demand for pollution rights

2. . . . which, together with the demand curve, determines the quantity of pollution.

Quantity of Pollution

(b) Pollution Permits

Price of Pollution

Supply of pollution permits

1. Pollution permits set the quantity of pollution . . .

Demand for pollution rights

2. . . . which, together with the demand curve, determines the price of pollution.

Quantity of Pollution

Emission permit trading systems (also known as *cap and trade*) are common throughout the world. For example, the European Union Emission Trading Scheme for greenhouse gas emissions is the largest emissions trading scheme in the world. Policy discussions on climate change policy in Canada have focused on developing a North American permit trading system.

Objections to the Economic Analysis of Pollution

Some people object to the use of pollution permits and other market-based solutions to pollution on the grounds that it is simply not right to allow someone to pollute for a fee. Clean air and clean water, they argue, are fundamental human rights that should not be debased by considering them in economic terms. How can you put a price on clean air and clean water? The environment is so important, they claim, that we should protect it as much as possible, regardless of the cost.

IN THE NEWS

BRITISH COLUMBIA LEADS THE WAY

British Columbia has one of the most comprehensive carbon taxes in the world. Most economists, throughout the political spectrum, support the imposition of such tax. This article argues that the United States should follow British Columbia's lead.

The Most Sensible Tax of All

By Yoram Bauman and Shi-Ling Hsu

On Sunday, the best climate policy in the world got even better: British Columbia's carbon tax—a tax on the carbon content of all fossil fuels burned in the province—increased from $25 to $30 per metric ton of carbon dioxide, making it more expensive to pollute.

This was good news not only for the environment but for nearly everyone who pays taxes in British Columbia, because the carbon tax is used to reduce taxes for individuals and businesses. Thanks to this tax swap, British Columbia has lowered its corporate income tax rate to 10 percent from 12 percent, a rate that is among the lowest in the Group of 8 wealthy nations. Personal income taxes for people earning less than $119,000 per year are now the lowest in Canada, and there are targeted rebates for low-income and rural households.

The only bad news is that this is the last increase scheduled in British Columbia. In our view, the reason is simple: the province is waiting for the rest of North America to catch up so that its tax system will not become unbalanced or put energy-intensive industries at a competitive disadvantage.

The United States should jump at the chance to adopt a similar revenue-neutral tax swap. It's an opportunity to reduce existing taxes, clean up the environment and increase personal freedom and energy security.

Let's start with the economics. Substituting a carbon tax for some of our current taxes—on payroll, on investment, on businesses and on workers—is a no-brainer. Why tax good things when you can tax bad things, like emissions? The idea has support from economists across the political spectrum, from Arthur B. Laffer and N. Gregory Mankiw on the right to Peter Orszag and

Economists have little sympathy with this type of argument. To economists, good environmental policy begins by acknowledging the first of the ten principles of economics in Chapter 1: People face tradeoffs. Certainly, clean air and clean water have value. But their value must be compared to their opportunity cost—that is, to what one must give up to obtain them. Eliminating all pollution is impossible. Trying to eliminate all pollution would reverse many of the technological advances that allow us to enjoy a high standard of living. Few people would be willing to accept poor nutrition, inadequate medical care, or shoddy housing to make the environment as clean as possible.

Economists argue that a clean environment can be viewed as simply another good. Like all normal goods, it has a positive income elasticity: Rich countries can afford a cleaner environment than poor ones and, therefore, usually have more rigorous environmental protection. In addition, like most other goods, clean air and water obey the law of demand: The lower the price of environmental protection, the more the public will want. The economic approach of using pollution permits and corrective taxes reduces the cost of environmental protection and should, therefore, increase the public's demand for a clean environment.

Joseph E. Stiglitz on the left. That's because economists know that a carbon tax swap can reduce the economic drag created by our current tax system and increase long-run growth by nudging the economy away from consumption and borrowing and toward saving and investment.

Of course, carbon taxes also lower carbon emissions. Economic theory suggests that putting a price on pollution reduces emissions more affordably and more effectively than any other measure. This conclusion is supported by empirical evidence from previous market-based policies, like those in the 1990 amendments to the Clean Air Act that targeted sulfur dioxide emissions. British Columbia's carbon tax is only four years old, but preliminary data show that greenhouse gas emissions are down 4.5 percent even as population and gross domestic product have been growing. Sales of motor gasoline have fallen by 2 percent since 2007, compared with a 5 percent increase for Canada as a whole.

What would a British Columbia-style carbon tax look like in the United States? According to our cal-culations, a British Columbia-style $30 carbon tax would generate about $145 billion a year in the United States. That could be used to reduce individual and corporate income taxes by 10 percent, and afterward there would still be $35 billion left over. If recent budget deals are any guide, Congress might choose to set aside half of that remainder to reduce estate taxes (to please Republicans) and the other half to offset the impacts of higher fuel and electricity prices resulting from the carbon tax on low-income households through refundable tax credits or a targeted reduction in payroll taxes (to please Democrats).

Revenue from a carbon tax would most likely decline over time as Americans reduce their carbon emissions, but for many years to come it could pay for big reductions in existing taxes. It would also promote energy conservation and steer investment into clean technology and other productive economic activities.

Lastly, the carbon tax would actually give Americans more control over how much they pay in taxes. Households and businesses could reduce their carbon tax payments simply by reducing their use of fossil fuels. Americans would trim their carbon footprints—and their tax burdens—by investing in energy efficiency at home and at work, switching to less-polluting vehicles and pursuing countless other innovations. All of this would be driven not by government mandates but by Adam Smith's invisible hand.

A carbon tax makes sense whether you are a Republican or a Democrat, a climate change skeptic or a believer, a conservative or a conservationist (or both). We can move past the partisan fireworks over global warming by turning British Columbia's carbon tax into a made-in-America solution.

QuickQuiz A glue factory and a steel mill emit smoke containing a chemical that is harmful if inhaled in large amounts. Describe three ways the town government might respond to this externality. What are the pros and cons of each of your solutions?

PRIVATE SOLUTIONS TO EXTERNALITIES

Although externalities tend to cause markets to be inefficient, government action is not always needed to solve the problem. In some circumstances, people can develop private solutions.

The Types of Private Solutions

Sometimes, the problem of externalities is solved with moral codes and social sanctions. Consider, for instance, why most people do not litter. Although there are laws against littering, these laws are not vigorously enforced. Most people do not litter just because it is the wrong thing to do. The Golden Rule taught to most children is "Do unto others as you would have them do unto you." This moral injunction tells us to take account of how our actions affect other people. In economic terms, it tells us to internalize externalities.

Another private solution to externalities is charities, many of which are established to deal with externalities. For example, Greenpeace, whose goal is to protect the environment, is a nonprofit organization funded with private donations. As another example, colleges and universities receive gifts from alumni, corporations, and foundations in part because education has positive externalities for society. The government encourages this private solution to externalities through the tax system by allowing an income tax deduction for charitable donations.

The private market can often solve the problem of externalities by relying on the self-interest of the relevant parties. Sometimes the solution takes the form of integrating different types of businesses. For example, consider an apple grower and a beekeeper who are located next to each other. Each business confers a positive externality on the other: By pollinating the flowers on the trees, the bees help the orchard produce apples. At the same time, the bees use the nectar they get from the apple trees to produce honey. Nonetheless, when the apple grower is deciding how many trees to plant and the beekeeper is deciding how many bees to keep, they neglect the positive externality. As a result, the apple grower plants too few trees and the beekeeper keeps too few bees. These externalities could be internalized if the beekeeper bought the apple orchard or if the apple grower bought the beehives: Both activities would then take place within the same firm, and this single firm could choose the optimal number of trees and bees. Internalizing externalities is one reason that some firms are involved in more than one type of business.

Another way for the private market to deal with external effects is for the interested parties to enter into a contract. In the forgoing example, a contract between the apple grower and the beekeeper can solve the problem of too few trees and too few bees. The contract can specify the number of trees, the number of bees, and perhaps a payment from one party to the other. By setting the right number of trees and bees, the contract can solve the inefficiency that normally arises from these externalities and make both parties better off.

The Coase Theorem

How effective is the private market in dealing with externalities? A famous result, called the **Coase theorem** after economist Ronald Coase, suggests that it can be very effective in some circumstances. According to the Coase theorem, if private parties can bargain without cost over the allocation of resources, then the private market will always solve the problem of externalities and allocate resources efficiently.

Coase theorem
the proposition that if private parties can bargain without cost over the allocation of resources, they can solve the problem of externalities on their own

To see how the Coase theorem works, consider an example. Suppose that Dick owns a dog named Spot. Spot barks and disturbs Jane, Dick's neighbour. Dick gets a benefit from owning the dog, but the dog confers a negative externality on Jane. Should Dick be forced to send Spot to the pound, or should Jane have to suffer sleepless nights because of Spot's barking?

Consider first what outcome is socially efficient. A social planner, considering the two alternatives, would compare the benefit that Dick gets from the dog to the cost that Jane bears from the barking. If the benefit exceeds the cost, it is efficient for Dick to keep the dog and for Jane to live with the barking. Yet if the cost exceeds the benefit, then Dick should get rid of the dog.

According to the Coase theorem, the private market will reach the efficient outcome on its own. How? Jane can simply offer to pay Dick to get rid of the dog. Dick will accept the deal if the amount of money Jane offers is greater than the benefit of keeping the dog.

By bargaining over the price, Dick and Jane can always reach the efficient outcome. For instance, suppose that Dick gets a $500 benefit from the dog and Jane bears an $800 cost from the barking. In this case, Jane can offer Dick $600 to get rid of the dog, and Dick will gladly accept. Both parties are better off than they were before, and the efficient outcome is reached.

It is possible, of course, that Jane would not be willing to offer any price that Dick would accept. For instance, suppose that Dick gets a $1000 benefit from the dog and Jane bears an $800 cost from the barking. In this case, Dick would turn down any offer below $1000, while Jane would not offer any amount above $800. Therefore, Dick ends up keeping the dog. Given these costs and benefits, however, this outcome is efficient.

So far, we have assumed that Dick has the legal right to keep a barking dog. In other words, we have assumed that Dick can keep Spot unless Jane pays him enough to induce him to give up the dog voluntarily. How different would the outcome be, on the other hand, if Jane had the legal right to peace and quiet?

According to the Coase theorem, the initial distribution of rights does not matter for the market's ability to reach the efficient outcome. For instance, suppose that Jane can legally compel Dick to get rid of the dog. Although having this right works to Jane's advantage, it probably will not change the outcome. In this case, Dick can offer to pay Jane to allow him to keep the dog. If the benefit of the dog to Dick exceeds the cost of the barking to Jane, then Dick and Jane will strike a bargain in which Dick keeps the dog.

Although Dick and Jane can reach the efficient outcome regardless of how rights are initially distributed, the distribution of rights is not irrelevant: It determines the distribution of economic well-being. Whether Dick has the right to a barking dog or Jane the right to peace and quiet determines who pays whom in the final bargain. But, in either case, the two parties can bargain with each other and solve the externality problem. Dick will end up keeping the dog only if the benefit exceeds the cost.

To sum up: *The Coase theorem says that private economic actors can potentially solve the problem of externalities among themselves. Whatever the initial distribution of rights, the interested parties can reach a bargain in which everyone is better off and the outcome is efficient.*

Why Private Solutions Do Not Always Work

Despite the appealing logic of the Coase theorem, private actors on their own often fail to resolve the problems caused by externalities. The Coase theorem applies only when the interested parties have no trouble reaching and enforcing an agreement. In the real world, however, bargaining does not always work, even when a mutually beneficial agreement is possible.

transaction costs
the costs that parties incur in the process of agreeing to and following through on a bargain

Sometimes the interested parties fail to solve an externality problem because of **transaction costs**, the costs that parties incur in the process of agreeing to and following through on a bargain. In our example, imagine that Dick and Jane speak different languages so that, to reach an agreement, they will need to hire a translator. If the benefit of solving the barking problem is less than the cost of the translator, Dick and Jane might choose to leave the problem unsolved. In more realistic examples, the transaction costs are the expenses not of translators but of the lawyers required to draft and enforce contracts.

At other times, bargaining simply breaks down. The recurrence of wars and labour strikes shows that reaching agreement can be difficult and that failing to reach agreement can be costly. The problem is often that each party tries to hold out for a better deal. For example, suppose that Dick gets a $500 benefit from the dog, and Jane bears an $800 cost from the barking. Although it is efficient for Jane to pay Dick to get rid of the dog, there are many prices that could lead to this outcome. Dick might demand $750, and Jane might offer only $550. As they haggle over the price, the inefficient outcome with the barking dog persists.

Reaching an efficient bargain is especially difficult when the number of interested parties is large because coordinating everyone is costly. For example, consider a factory that pollutes the water of a nearby lake. The pollution confers a negative externality on the local fishermen. According to the Coase theorem, if the pollution is inefficient, then the factory and the fishermen could reach a bargain in which the fishermen pay the factory not to pollute. If there are many fishermen, however, trying to coordinate them all to bargain with the factory may be almost impossible.

When private bargaining does not work, the government can sometimes play a role. The government is an institution designed for collective action. In this example, the government can act on behalf of the fishermen, even when it is impractical for the fishermen to act for themselves. We saw, in previous sections, several ways in which the government can deal with the problem of externalities.

QuickQuiz   Give an example of a private solution to an externality. • What is the Coase theorem? • Why are private economic actors sometimes unable to solve the problems caused by an externality?

CONCLUSION

The invisible hand is powerful but not omnipotent. A market's equilibrium maximizes the sum of producer and consumer surplus. When the buyers and sellers in the market are the only interested parties, this outcome is efficient from the standpoint of society as a whole. But when there are external effects, such as pollution, evaluating a market outcome requires taking into account the well-being of third parties as well. In this case, the invisible hand of the marketplace may fail to allocate resources efficiently.

In some cases, people can solve the problem of externalities on their own. The Coase theorem suggests that the interested parties can bargain among themselves and agree on an efficient solution. Sometimes, however, an efficient outcome cannot be reached, perhaps because the large number of interested parties makes bargaining difficult.

When people cannot solve the problem of externalities privately, the government often steps in. Yet, even now, society should not abandon market forces entirely. Rather, the government can address the problem by requiring decision makers to bear the full costs of their actions. Corrective taxes on emissions and pollution permits, for instance, are designed to internalize the externality of pollution. More and more, they are the policy of choice for those interested in protecting the environment. Market forces, properly redirected, are often the best remedy for market failure.

SUMMARY

- When a transaction between a buyer and seller directly affects a third party, the effect is called an *externality*. Negative externalities, such as pollution, cause the socially optimal quantity in a market to be less than the equilibrium quantity. Positive externalities, such as technology spillovers, cause the socially optimal quantity to be greater than the equilibrium quantity.

- Governments pursue various policies to remedy the inefficiencies caused by externalities. Sometimes the government prevents socially inefficient activity by regulating behaviour. Other times it internalizes an externality using corrective taxes. Another public policy is to issue permits. For instance, the government could protect the environment by issuing a limited number of

pollution permits. The end result of this policy is largely the same as imposing corrective taxes on polluters.

- Those affected by externalities can sometimes solve the problem privately. For instance, when one business confers an externality on another business, the two businesses can internalize the externality by merging. Alternatively, the interested parties can solve the problem by negotiating a contract. According to the Coase theorem, if people can bargain without cost, then they can always reach an agreement in which resources are allocated efficiently. In many cases, however, reaching a bargain among the many interested parties is difficult, so the Coase theorem does not apply.

KEY CONCEPTS

externality, p. 212
internalizing the externality,
  p. 217

corrective taxes, p. 220
Coase theorem, p. 229

transaction costs, p. 230

QUESTIONS FOR REVIEW

1. Give an example of a negative externality and an example of a positive externality.

2. Draw a supply-and-demand diagram to explain the effect of a negative externality in production.

3. In what way does the patent system help society solve an externality problem?

4. List some of the ways that the problems caused by externalities can be solved without government intervention.

5. Imagine that you are a nonsmoker sharing a room with a smoker. According to the Coase theorem, what determines whether your roommate smokes in the room? Is this outcome efficient? How do you and your roommate reach this solution?

6. What are corrective taxes? Why do economists prefer them over regulations as a way to protect the environment from pollution?

PROBLEMS AND APPLICATIONS

1. Consider two ways to protect your car from theft. The Club (a car steering wheel lock) makes it difficult for a car thief to take your car. LoJack (a car tracking and recovery system) makes it easier for the police to catch a car thief. Which of these types of protection conveys a negative externality on other car owners? Which conveys a positive externality? Do you think there are any policy implications of your analysis?

2. Do you agree with the following statements? Why or why not?
   a. "The benefits of corrective taxes as a way to reduce pollution have to be weighed against the deadweight losses that these taxes cause."
   b. "When deciding whether to levy a corrective tax on consumers or producers, the government should be careful to levy the tax on the side of the market generating the externality."

3. Consider the market for fire extinguishers.
   a. Why might fire extinguishers exhibit positive externalities?
   b. Draw a graph of the market for fire extinguishers, labelling the demand curve, the social-value curve, the supply curve, and the social-cost curve.
   c. Indicate the market equilibrium level of output and the efficient level of output. Give an intuitive explanation for why these quantities differ.
   d. If the external benefit is $10 per extinguisher, describe a government policy that would result in the efficient outcome.

4. Ringo loves playing rock-and-roll music at high volume. Luciano loves opera and hates rock and roll. Unfortunately, they are next-door neighbours in an apartment building with paper-thin walls.
   a. What is the externality here?
   b. What command-and-control policy might the landlord impose? Could such a policy lead to an inefficient outcome?
   c. Suppose the landlord lets the tenants do whatever they want. According to the Coase theorem, how might Ringo and Luciano reach an efficient outcome on their own? What might prevent them from reaching an efficient outcome?

5. Greater consumption of alcohol leads to more motor vehicle accidents and, thus, imposes costs on people who do not drink and drive.
   a. Illustrate the market for alcohol, labelling the demand curve, the social-value curve, the supply curve, the social-cost curve, the market equilibrium level of output, and the efficient level of output.
   b. On your graph, shade the area corresponding to the deadweight loss of the market equilibrium. (Hint: The deadweight loss occurs because some units of alcohol are consumed for which the social cost exceeds the social value.) Explain.

6. Many observers believe that the levels of pollution in our society are too high.
   a. If society wishes to reduce overall pollution by a certain amount, why is it efficient to have different amounts of reduction at different firms?

b. Command-and-control approaches often rely on uniform reductions among firms. Why are these approaches generally unable to target the firms that should undertake larger reductions?

c. Economists argue that appropriate corrective taxes or tradable pollution rights will result in efficient pollution reduction. How do these approaches target the firms that should undertake larger reductions?

7. The many identical residents of Whoville love drinking Zlurp. Each resident has the following willingness to pay for the tasty refreshment:

First bottle	$5	Fourth bottle	2
Second bottle	4	Fifth bottle	1
Third bottle	3	Further bottles	0

a. The cost of producing Zlurp is $1.50, and the competitive suppliers sell it at this price. (The supply curve is horizontal.) How many bottles will each Whovillian consume? What is each person's consumer surplus?

b. Producing Zlurp creates pollution. Each bottle has an external cost of $1. Taking this additional cost into account, what is total surplus per person in the allocation you described in part (a)?

c. Cindy Lou Who, one of the residents of Whoville, decides on her own to reduce her consumption of Zlurp by one bottle. What happens to Cindy's welfare (her consumer surplus minus the cost of pollution she experiences)? How does Cindy's decision affect total surplus in Whoville?

d. Mayor Grinch imposes a $1 tax on Zlurp. What is consumption per person now? Calculate consumer surplus, the external cost, government revenue, and total surplus per person.

e. Based on your calculations, would you support the mayor's policy? Why or why not?

8. Figure 10.5 (p. 225) shows that for any given demand curve for the right to pollute, the government can achieve the same outcome either by setting a price with a corrective tax or by setting a quantity with pollution permits. Suppose there is a sharp improvement in the technology for controlling pollution.

a. Using graphs similar to those in Figure 10.5, illustrate the effect of this development on the demand for pollution rights.

b. What is the effect on the price and quantity of pollution under each regulatory system? Explain.

9. Suppose that the government decides to issue tradable permits for a certain form of pollution.

a. Does it matter for economic efficiency whether the government distributes or auctions the permits? Why or why not?

b. If the government chooses to distribute the permits, does the allocation of permits among firms matter for efficiency? Explain.

10. A local drama company proposes a new neighbourhood theatre in Vancouver. Before approving the building permit, the city planner completes a study of the theatre's impact on the surrounding community.

a. One finding of the study is that theatres attract traffic, which adversely affects the community. The city planner estimates that the cost to the community from the extra traffic is $5 per ticket. What kind of an externality is this? Why?

b. Graph the market for theatre tickets, labelling the demand curve, the social-value curve, the supply curve, the social-cost curve, the market equilibrium level of output, and the efficient level of output. Also show the per-unit amount of the externality.

c. On further review, the city planner uncovers a second externality. Rehearsals for the plays tend to run until late at night, with actors, stagehands, and other theatre members coming and going at various hours. The planner has found that the increased foot traffic improves the safety of the surrounding streets, an estimated benefit to the community of $2 per ticket. What kind of externality is this? Why?

d. On a new graph, illustrate the market for theatre tickets in the case of these two externalities. Again, label the demand curve, the social-value curve, the supply curve, the social-cost curve, the market equilibrium level of output, the efficient level of output, and the per-unit amount of both externalities.

e. Describe a government policy that would result in an efficient outcome.

11. There are three industrial firms in Happy Valley.

Firm	Initial Pollution Level	Cost of Reducing Pollution by 1 Unit
A	70 units	$20
B	80	25
C	50	10

The government wants to reduce pollution to 120 units, so it gives each firm 40 tradable pollution permits.

a. Who sells permits and how many do they sell? Who buys permits and how many do they buy? Briefly explain why the sellers and buyers are each willing to do so. What is the total cost of pollution reduction in this situation?

b. How much higher would the costs of pollution reduction be if the permits could not be traded?

12. The market for a particular chemical, called Negext, is described by the following equations. Demand is given by

$$Q^D = 100 - 5P$$

Supply is given by

$$Q^S = 5P$$

where Q is measured as units of Negext and P is price in dollars per unit.

a. Find the equilibrium price and quantity. Compute consumer surplus, producer surplus, and total surplus in the market equilibrium.

b. For each unit of Negext produced, 4 units of pollution are emitted, and each unit of pollution imposes a cost on society of $1. Compute the total cost of pollution when the market for Negext is in equilibrium. What is total surplus from this market after taking into account the cost of pollution?

c. Would banning Negext increase or decrease welfare? Why?

d. Suppose that the government restricts emissions to 100 units of pollution. Graph the Negext market under this constraint. Find the new equilibrium price and quantity and show them on your graph. Compute how this policy affects consumer surplus, producer surplus, and the cost of pollution. Would you recommend this policy? Why?

e. Suppose that instead of restricting pollution, the government imposes a tax on producers equal to $4 for each unit of chemical produced. Calculate the new equilibrium price and quantity, as well as consumer surplus, producer surplus, tax revenue, and the cost of pollution. What is total surplus now? Would you recommend this policy? Why?

f. New research finds the social cost of pollution is actually higher than $1. How would that change the optimal policy response? Is there some cost of pollution that would make it sensible to ban Negext? If so, what is it?

http:// For more study tools, please visit www.nelson.com/mankiwmicro6e.

PUBLIC GOODS AND COMMON RESOURCES

Learning Objectives

In this chapter, you will...

- Learn the defining characteristics of public goods and common resources

- Examine why private markets fail to provide public goods

- Consider some of the important public goods in our economy

- See why the cost–benefit analysis of public goods is both necessary and difficult

- Examine why people tend to use common resources too much

- Consider some of the important common resources in our economy

An old song lyric maintains that "the best things in life are free." A moment's thought reveals a long list of goods that the songwriter could have had in mind. Nature provides some of them, such as rivers, mountains, beaches, lakes, and oceans. The government provides others, such as playgrounds, parks, and parades. In each case, people do not pay a fee when they choose to enjoy the benefit of the good.

Goods without prices provide a special challenge for economic analysis. Most goods in our economy are allocated in markets, in which buyers pay for what they receive and sellers are paid for what they provide. For these goods, prices are the signals that guide the decisions of buyers and sellers. When goods are available free of charge, however, the market forces that normally allocate resources in our economy are absent.

In this chapter we examine the problems that arise for goods without market prices. Our analysis will shed light on one of the ten principles of economics in Chapter 1: Governments can sometimes improve market outcomes. When a good does not have a price attached to it, private markets cannot ensure that the good is produced and consumed in the proper amounts. In such cases, government policy can potentially remedy the market failure and raise economic well-being.

THE DIFFERENT KINDS OF GOODS

How well do markets work in providing the goods that people want? The answer to this question depends on the good being considered. As we discussed in Chapter 6, we can rely on the market to provide the efficient number of ice-cream cones: The price of ice-cream cones adjusts to balance supply and demand, and this equilibrium maximizes the sum of producer and consumer surplus. Yet, as we discussed in Chapter 10, we cannot rely on the market to prevent aluminum manufacturers from polluting the air we breathe: Buyers and sellers in a market typically do not take account of the external effects of their decisions. Thus, markets work well when the good is ice cream, but they work badly when the good is clean air.

In thinking about the various goods in the economy, it is useful to group them according to two characteristics:

1. Is the good **excludable**? Can people be prevented from using the good?
2. Is the good **rival in consumption**? Does one person's use of the good diminish another person's ability to use it?

Using these two characteristics, Figure 11.1 divides goods into four categories:

1. **Private goods** are both excludable and rival in consumption. Consider an ice-cream cone, for example. An ice-cream cone is excludable because it is possible to prevent someone from eating an ice-cream cone—you just don't give it to him. An ice-cream cone is rival in consumption because if one person eats an ice-cream cone, another person cannot eat the same cone. Most goods in the economy are private goods like ice-cream cones: You don't get one unless you pay for it, and once you have it, you are the only person who benefits. When we analyzed supply and demand in Chapters 4, 5, and 6 and the efficiency of markets in Chapters 7, 8, and 9, we implicitly assumed that goods were both excludable and rival in consumption.

2. **Public goods** are neither excludable nor rival in consumption. That is, people cannot be prevented from using a public good, and one person's use of a public

excludability
the property of a good whereby a person can be prevented from using it

rival in consumption
the property of a good whereby one person's use diminishes other people's use

private goods
goods that are both excludable and rival

public goods
goods that are neither excludable nor rival

FIGURE 11.1

Four Types of Goods

Goods can be grouped into four categories according to two characteristics: (1) A good is excludable *if people can be prevented from using it; (2) a good is* rival *in consumption if one person's use of the good diminishes other people's use of it. This diagram gives examples of goods in each category.*

| | | Rival in Consumption? | |
		Yes	No
Excludable?	**Yes**	Private Goods • Ice-cream cones • Clothing • Congested toll roads	Club Goods • Fire protection • Cable TV • Uncongested toll roads
	No	Common Resources • Fish in the ocean • The environment • Congested nontoll roads	Public Goods • Tornado siren • National defence • Uncongested nontoll roads

good does not reduce another person's ability to use it. For example, national defence is a public good. Once the country is defended from foreign aggressors, it is impossible to prevent any single person from enjoying the benefit of this defence. Moreover, when one person enjoys the benefit of national defence, he or she does not reduce the benefit to anyone else.

3. **Common resources** are rival in consumption but not excludable. For example, fish in the ocean are a rival good: When one person catches fish, there are fewer fish for the next person to catch. Yet these fish are not an excludable good because, given the vast size of an ocean, it is difficult to stop fishermen from taking fish out of it.

4. **Club goods** are excludable but not rival in consumption. For instance, consider fire protection in a small town. It is easy to exclude someone from using this good: The fire department can just let that person's house burn down. But fire protection is not rival in consumption: Once a town has paid for the fire department, the additional cost of protecting one more house is small. (We discuss club goods again in Chapter 15, where we see that they are one type of a *natural monopoly*.)

common resources
goods that are rival but not excludable

club goods
goods that are excludable but not rival

Although Figure 11.1 offers a clean separation of goods into four categories, the boundaries between the categories are sometimes fuzzy. Whether goods are excludable or rival in consumption is often a matter of degree. Fish in an ocean may not be excludable because monitoring fishing is so difficult, but a large enough Coast Guard could make fish at least partly excludable. Similarly, although fish are generally rival in consumption, this would be less true if the population of fishermen was small relative to the population of fish. (Think of North American fishing waters before the arrival of European settlers.) For purposes of our analysis, however, it will be helpful to group goods into these four categories.

In this chapter, we examine goods that are not excludable: public goods and common resources. Because people cannot be prevented from using these goods, they are available to everyone free of charge. The study of public goods and common resources is closely related to the study of externalities. For both of these types of goods, externalities arise because something of value has no price attached to it. If one person was to provide a public good, other people would be better off. They would receive a benefit without paying for it—a positive externality. Similarly, when one person uses a common resource such as the fish in the ocean, other people are worse off because there are fewer fish to catch. They suffer a loss but are not compensated for it—a negative externality. Because of these external effects, private decisions about consumption and production can lead to an inefficient allocation of resources, and government intervention can potentially raise economic well-being.

QuickQuiz   Define *public goods* and *common resources,* and give an example of each.

PUBLIC GOODS

To understand how public goods differ from other goods and why they present problems for society, let's consider an example: a fireworks display. This good is not excludable because it is impossible to prevent someone from seeing fireworks, and it is not rival in consumption because one person's enjoyment of fireworks does not reduce anyone else's enjoyment of them.

The Free-Rider Problem

The citizens of Smalltown, Canada, like seeing fireworks on Canada Day. Each of the town's 500 residents places a $10 value on the experience. The cost of putting on a fireworks display is $1000. Because the $5000 of benefits exceed the $1000 of costs, it is efficient for Smalltown residents to have a fireworks display on Canada Day.

Would the private market produce the efficient outcome? Probably not. Imagine that Ellen, a Smalltown entrepreneur, decided to put on a fireworks display. Ellen would surely have trouble selling tickets to the event because her potential customers would quickly figure out that they could see the fireworks even without a ticket. Because fireworks are not excludable, people have an incentive to be free riders. A **free rider** is a person who receives the benefit of a good but avoids paying for it. Because people would have an incentive to be free riders rather than ticket buyers, the market would fail to produce an efficient outcome.

One way to view this market failure is that it arises because of an externality. If Ellen did put on the fireworks display, she would confer an external benefit on those who saw the display without paying for it. When deciding whether to put on the display, Ellen ignores these external benefits. Even though a fireworks display is socially desirable, it is not privately profitable. As a result, Ellen makes the socially inefficient decision not to put on the display.

Although the private market fails to supply the fireworks display demanded by Smalltown residents, the solution to Smalltown's problem is obvious: The local government can sponsor a Canada Day celebration. The town council can raise everyone's taxes by $2 and use the revenue to hire Ellen to produce the fireworks. Everyone in Smalltown is better off by $8—the $10 at which residents value the fireworks minus the $2 tax bill. Ellen can help Smalltown reach the efficient outcome as a public employee even though she could not do so as a private entrepreneur.

The story of Smalltown is simplified, but it is also realistic. In fact, many local governments in Canada do pay for fireworks on Canada Day. Moreover, the story shows a general lesson about public goods: Because public goods are not excludable, the free-rider problem prevents the private market from supplying them. The government, however, can potentially remedy the problem. If the government decides that the total benefits exceed the costs, it can provide the public good and pay for it with tax revenue, making everyone better off.

Some Important Public Goods

There are many examples of public goods. Here we consider three of the most important.

National Defence   The defence of the country from foreign aggressors is a classic example of a public good. Once the country is defended, it is impossible to prevent any single person from enjoying the benefit of this defence, which makes it nonexcludable. Moreover, when one person enjoys the benefit of national defence, he does not reduce the benefit of anyone else. Thus, national defence is neither excludable nor rival in consumption.

National defence in Canada falls under the control of the federal government. In 2009 the federal government spent about $19 billion on national defence, or

free rider
a person who receives the benefit of a good but avoids paying for it

around $560 per person. While this is a lot of money, other countries spend even more. In 2009 the U.S. federal government spent a total of US$661 billion, or about US$2150 per person, on national defence. People disagree about whether this amount is too small or too large, but almost no one doubts that some government spending for national defence is necessary. Even economists who advocate for small government agree that national defence is a public good that government should provide.

Basic Research   Knowledge is created through research. In evaluating the appropriate public policy toward knowledge creation, it is important to distinguish general knowledge from specific technological knowledge. Specific technological knowledge, such as the invention of a longer-lasting battery, a smaller microchip, or a better digital music player, can be patented. The patent gives the inventor the exclusive right to the knowledge he or she has created for a period of time. Anyone else who wants to use the patented information must pay the inventor for the right to do so. In other words, the patent makes the knowledge created by the inventor excludable.

By contrast, general knowledge is a public good. For example, a mathematician cannot patent a theorem. Once a theorem is proved, the knowledge is not excludable: The theorem enters society's general pool of knowledge that anyone can use without charge. The theorem is also not rival in consumption: One person's use of the theorem does not prevent any other person from using the theorem.

Profit-seeking firms spend a lot on research trying to develop new products that they can patent and sell, but they do not spend much on basic research. Their incentive, instead, is to free-ride on the general knowledge created by others. As a result, in the absence of any public policy, society would devote too few resources to creating new knowledge.

The government tries to provide the public good of general knowledge in various ways. Federal government agencies, such as the Natural Sciences and Engineering Research Council of Canada and the Social Sciences and Humanities Research Council of Canada, subsidize basic research in medicine, mathematics, physics, chemistry, biology, and even economics. Determining the appropriate level of governmental support for basic research is difficult because the benefits are hard to measure. Morover, members of Parliament who determine the funding for these sorts of programs have little expertise in science and, therefore, are not in the best position to judge what lines of research will produce the largest benefits. So, while basic research is surely a public good, we should not be surprised if the public sector fails to pay for the right amount and the right kinds.

Fighting Poverty   Many government programs are aimed at helping poor people. The welfare programs administered by the provinces and territories provide some income for low-income individuals. Many municipalities provide subsidized housing for low-income families. Other benefits to low-income individuals are delivered through the tax system by means of refundable tax credits, the value of which declines as a person's income increases.

Economists disagree among themselves about what role the government should play in fighting poverty. Although we discuss this debate more fully in Chapter 20, here we note one important argument: Advocates of antipoverty programs claim that fighting poverty is a public good. Even if everyone prefers living in a society without poverty, fighting poverty is not a "good" that private actions will adequately provide.

To see why, suppose someone tried to organize a group of wealthy individuals to try to eliminate poverty. They would be providing a public good. This good would not be rival in consumption: One person's enjoyment of living in a society without poverty would not reduce anyone else's enjoyment of it. The good would not be excludable: Once poverty is eliminated, no one can be prevented from taking pleasure in this fact. As a result, there would be a tendency for people to free-ride on the generosity of others, enjoying the benefits of poverty elimination without contributing to the cause.

Because of the free-rider problem, eliminating poverty through private charity will probably not work. Yet government action can solve this problem. Taxing the wealthy to raise the living standards of the poor can potentially make everyone better off. The poor are better off because they now enjoy a higher standard of living, and those paying the taxes are better off because they enjoy living in a society with less poverty.

Case Study

ARE LIGHTHOUSES PUBLIC GOODS?

Some goods can switch between being public goods and being private goods depending on the circumstances. For example, a fireworks display is a public good if performed in a town with many residents. Yet if performed at a private amusement park such as Canada's Wonderland, a fireworks display is more like a private good because visitors to the park pay for admission.

Another example is a lighthouse. Economists have long used lighthouses as an example of a public good. Lighthouses mark specific locations along the coast so that passing ships can avoid treacherous waters. The benefit that the lighthouse provides to the ship captain is neither excludable nor rival in consumption, so each captain has an incentive to free-ride by using the lighthouse to navigate without paying for the service. Because of this free-rider problem, private markets usually fail to provide the lighthouses that ship captains need. As a result, most lighthouses today are operated by the government.

In some cases, however, lighthouses may be closer to private goods. On the coast of England in the nineteenth century, some lighthouses were privately owned and operated. Instead of trying to charge ship captains for the service, however, the owner of the lighthouse charged the owner of the nearby port. If the port owner did not pay, the lighthouse owner turned off the light, and ships avoided that port.

In deciding whether something is a public good, one must determine the number of beneficiaries and whether these beneficiaries can be excluded from using the good. A free-rider problem arises when the number of beneficiaries is large and exclusion of any one of them is impossible. If a lighthouse benefits many ship captains, it is a public good. Yet if it primarily benefits a single port owner, it is more like a private good. ●

What kind of good?

Robert Vautour/iStockphoto

The Difficult Job of Cost–Benefit Analysis

So far we have seen that the government provides public goods because the private market on its own will not produce an efficient quantity. Yet deciding that the government must play a role is only the first step. The government must then determine what kinds of public goods to provide and in what quantities.

Suppose that the government is considering a public project, such as building a new highway. To judge whether to build the highway, it must compare the total benefits of all those who would use it to the costs of building and maintaining it. To make this decision, the government might hire a team of economists and engineers to conduct a study, called a **cost–benefit analysis**, the goal of which is to estimate the total costs and benefits of the project to society as a whole.

Cost–benefit analysts have a tough job. Because the highway will be available to everyone free of charge, there is no price with which to judge the value of the highway. Simply asking people how much they would value the highway is not reliable: Quantifying benefits is difficult using the results from a questionnaire, and respondents have little incentive to tell the truth. Those who would use the highway have an incentive to exaggerate the benefit they receive to get the highway built. Those who would be harmed by the highway have an incentive to exaggerate the costs to them to prevent the highway from being built.

The efficient provision of public goods is, therefore, intrinsically more difficult than the efficient provision of private goods. Private goods are provided in the market. Buyers of a private good reveal the value they place on it by the prices they are willing to pay. Sellers reveal their costs by the prices they are willing to accept. By contrast, cost–benefit analysts do not observe any price signals when evaluating whether the government should provide a public good. Their findings on the costs and benefits of public projects are, therefore, rough approximations at best.

cost–benefit analysis
a study that compares the costs and benefits to society of providing a public good

→ How much public goods will be used by consumers instead of how much a consumer will pay.

Case Study

HOW MUCH IS A LIFE WORTH?

Imagine that you have been elected to serve as a member of your local town council. The town engineer comes to you with a proposal: The town can spend $10 000 to build and operate a traffic light at a town intersection that now has only a stop sign. The benefit of the traffic light is increased safety. The engineer estimates, based on data from similar intersections, that the traffic light would reduce the risk of a fatal traffic accident over the lifetime of the traffic light from 1.6 to 1.1 percent. Should you spend the money for the new light?

To answer this question, you turn to cost–benefit analysis. But you quickly run into an obstacle: The costs and benefits must be measured in the same units if you are to compare them meaningfully. The cost is measured in dollars, but the benefit—the possibility of saving a person's life—is not directly monetary. To make your decision, you have to put a dollar value on a human life.

At first, you may be tempted to conclude that a human life is priceless. After all, there is probably no amount of money that you could be paid to voluntarily give up your life or that of a loved one. This suggests that a human life has an infinite dollar value.

For the purposes of cost–benefit analysis, however, this answer leads to non-sensical results. If we truly placed an infinite value on human life, we should be placing traffic lights on every street corner. Similarly, we should all be driving large cars with all the latest safety features, instead of smaller ones with fewer safety features. Yet traffic lights are not at every corner, and people sometimes choose to buy small cars without side-impact air bags or antilock brakes. In both our public and private decisions, we are at times willing to risk our lives to save some money.

Once we have accepted the idea that a person's life does have an implicit dollar value, how can we determine what that value is? One approach, sometimes used by courts to award damages in wrongful-death suits, is to look at the total amount of money a person would have earned if he or she had lived. Economists are often critical of this approach. It has the bizarre implication that the life of a retired or disabled person has no value.

A better way to value human life is to look at the risks that people are voluntarily willing to take and how much they must be paid for taking them. Mortality risk varies across jobs, for example. Construction workers in high-rise buildings face greater risk of death on the job than office workers do. By comparing wages in risky and less risky occupations, controlling for education, experience, and other determinants of wages, economists can get some sense about what value people put on their own lives.

Health economists have made estimates of the "value of a statistical life" (VSL) in Canada. Understanding that these values are very uncertain, Health Canada presents a range of estimates based on research in this area: a low of $3.5 million, a mid-level estimate of $5.8 million, and a high of $11.7 million (all measured in 2002 Canadian dollars).

Using these figures we can return to our original example and respond to the town engineer. The traffic light reduces the risk of fatality by 0.5 percentage points. So the expected benefit from having the traffic light ranges from $17 500 (0.005 × $3.5 million) using the low VSL estimate to a high of $58 500 using the high VSL estimate. Even the lower estimate of the benefit exceeds the cost of $10 000, so you should approve the project. ●

QuickQuiz   What is the *free-rider problem*? • Why does the free-rider problem induce the government to provide public goods? • How should the government decide whether to provide a public good?

COMMON RESOURCES

Common resources, like public goods, are not excludable: They are available free of charge to anyone who wants to use them. Common resources are, however, rival in consumption: One person's use of the common resource reduces other people's ability to use it. Thus, common resources give rise to a new problem. Once the good is provided, policymakers need to be concerned about how much it is used. This problem is best understood from the classic parable called the **Tragedy of the Commons**.

Tragedy of the Commons
a parable that illustrates why common resources get used more than is desirable from the standpoint of society as a whole

The Tragedy of the Commons

Consider life in a small medieval town. Of the many economic activities that take place in the town, one of the most important is raising sheep. Many of the town's families own flocks of sheep and support themselves by selling the sheep's wool, which is used to make clothing.

As our story begins, the sheep spend much of their time grazing on the land surrounding the town, called the Town Common. No family owns the land. Instead, the town residents own the land collectively, and all the residents are allowed to graze their sheep on it. Collective ownership works well because land is plentiful. As long as everyone can get all the good grazing land they want, the Town Common is not a rival good, and allowing residents' sheep to graze for free causes no problems. Everyone in the town is happy.

As the years pass, the population of the town grows, and so does the number of sheep grazing on the Town Common. With a growing number of sheep and a fixed amount of land, the land starts to lose its ability to replenish itself. Eventually, the land is grazed so heavily that it becomes barren. With no grass left on the Town Common, raising sheep is impossible, and the town's once prosperous wool industry disappears. Many families lose their source of livelihood.

What causes the tragedy? Why do the shepherds allow the sheep population to grow so large that it destroys the Town Common? The reason is that social and private incentives differ. Avoiding the destruction of the grazing land depends on the collective action of the shepherds. If the shepherds acted together, they could reduce the sheep population to a size that the Town Common can support. Yet no single family has an incentive to reduce the size of its own flock because each flock represents only a small part of the problem.

In essence, the Tragedy of the Commons arises because of an externality. When one family's flock grazes on the common land, it reduces the quality of the land available for other families. Because people neglect this negative externality when deciding how many sheep to own, the result is an excessive number of sheep.

If the tragedy had been foreseen, the town could have solved the problem in various ways. It could have regulated the number of sheep in each family's flock, internalized the externality by taxing sheep, or auctioned off a limited number of sheep-grazing permits. That is, the medieval town could have dealt with the problem of overgrazing in the way that modern society deals with the problem of pollution.

In the case of land, however, there is a simpler solution. The town can divide up the land among town families. Each family can enclose its parcel of land with a fence and then protect it from excessive grazing. In this way, the land becomes a private good rather than a common resource. This outcome in fact occurred during the enclosure movement in England in the seventeenth century.

→ Privatization

The Tragedy of the Commons is a story with a general lesson: When one person uses a common resource, that person diminishes other people's enjoyment of it. Because of this negative externality, common resources tend to be used excessively. The government can solve the problem by reducing use of the common resource through regulation or taxes. Alternatively, the government can sometimes turn the common resource into a private good.

This lesson has been known for thousands of years. The ancient Greek philosopher Aristotle pointed out the problem with common resources: "What is common to many is taken least care of, for all men have greater regard for what is their own than for what they possess in common with others."

Some Important Common Resources

There are many examples of common resources. In almost all cases, the same problem arises as in the Tragedy of the Commons: Private decision makers use the common resource too much. Governments often regulate behaviour or impose fees to mitigate the problem of overuse.

IN THE NEWS

ARE ECONOMICS STUDENTS GRINCHES?

This article describes some research that examines the extent to which students contribute to a public good. It finds that economics students tend to contribute less to public goods than other students. The author concludes that "we" could do a better job of providing "balance" in economics education. An alternative conclusion is that students who choose to major in economics better understand the underlying incentives.

The Dismal Education
By Yoram Bauman

The stereotypes about economists are well known: that we're selfish Grinches; that we don't read human interest stories because they don't interest us; that the only reason we don't sell our children is that we think they'll be worth more later.

But are the stereotypes true? And if so is the cause nature or nurture? In other words, are selfish people disproportionately likely to become economists? Or is there something about being an economist (or being on the receiving end of economics education) that *makes* people selfish?

Academic research suggests that there's a good deal of truth to the stereotype. Many studies have looked at how economists behave in what are called public goods situations. A key feature of these situations is that you can benefit from public goods even if you don't contribute to them. You can watch PBS without making a donation; you can enjoy clean air even if you drive a car that pollutes. Such goods, however, give rise to the so-called free-rider problem: acting selfishly makes sense for each individual (why sacrifice if you

don't have to?) but as more and more people choose to act selfishly, the good disappears and everyone loses.

Public goods run counter to Adam Smith's "invisible hand" theory in that self-interested behavior by individuals does not, as the theory would have it, lead to good outcomes for society as a whole. These situations flummox just about everybody—look at all the trouble that nations and individuals are having in dealing with climate change—but economists and economics students appear to be especially likely to free-ride and act in ways that are "anti-social" rather than "pro-social."

Clean Air and Water As we discussed in Chapter 10, markets do not adequately protect the environment. Pollution is a negative externality that can be remedied with regulations or with corrective taxes on polluting activities. One can view this market failure as an example of a common-resource problem. Clean air and clean water are common resources like open grazing land, and excessive pollution is like excessive grazing. Environmental degradation is a modern Tragedy of the Commons.

Congested Roads Roads can be either public goods or common resources. If a road is not congested, then one person's use does not affect anyone else. In this case, use is not rival in consumption, and the road is a public good. Yet if a road is congested, then use of that road yields a negative externality. When one additional person drives on the road, it becomes more crowded, and other people must drive more slowly. In this case, the road is a common resource.

My research with the economist Elaina Rose, published in August in the Journal of Economic Behavior and Organization, has looked at a real-life public goods situation faced by students at the University of Washington. During our study period (1999 to 2002), when students went online to register for classes each quarter, they were asked if they wanted to donate $3 to support Wash PIRG, a left-leaning activist group. Students were also asked if they wanted to donate $3 to Affordable Tuition Now (ATN), a group that lobbied for "sensible tuition rates, quality financial aid and adequate funding."

You may question whether these groups actually serve the common good, but that's mostly beside the point. Regardless of the groups' actual social value, a purely self-interested individual would choose to free-ride rather than contribute; after all, a single $3 donation is not going to make a noticeable difference in tuition rates.

Our data showed that each group received donations from about 10 percent of the students each quarter.

Although students remained anonymous, we could look at all of the 8,743 members of our data set and determine what their majors were, when they took economics classes (if at all) and whether or not they donated to ATN or Wash PIRG during each quarter of our study period.

In line with previous research, what we found supported the Grinch stereotype. About 5 percent of economics majors donated to Wash PIRG in a given quarter, compared with 8 percent for other arts and sciences majors. A similar divide—10 percent versus almost 15 percent—occurred with respect to donations to ATN.

We also found evidence that the giving behavior of students who became economics majors was driven by nature, not nurture: taking economics classes did not have a significant negative effect on later giving by economics majors.

But taking economics classes *did* have a significant negative effect on later giving by students who *did not* become economics majors. One interpretation of these results is that students who were not economics majors suffered a "loss of innocence" after taking an economics class, presumably because of exposure to certain ideas (like the invisible hand) or certain people (like economics teachers).

In contrast, students who became economics majors did not suffer a loss of innocence. This may be because they lost their innocence in high school—other research suggests that pre-university exposure to economics reduces giving—or perhaps even because economics majors were "born guilty."

Our research suggests that economics education could do a better job of providing balance. Learning about the shortcomings as well as the successes of free markets is at the heart of any good economics education, and students—especially those who are not destined to major in the field—deserve to hear both sides of the story.

One way for the government to address the problem of road congestion is to charge drivers a toll. A toll is, in essence, a corrective tax on the externality of congestion. Sometimes, as in the case of local roads, tolls are not a practical solution because the cost of collecting them is too high. However, technological innovations have lowered the cost of collecting tolls. For example, the 407 Express Toll Route is a privately operated highway just north of Toronto. It uses a system of cameras and transponders to toll vehicles automatically; there are no toll booths.

Sometimes congestion is a problem only at certain times of day. If a bridge is heavily travelled only during rush hour, for instance, the congestion externality is larger during this time than during other times of day. The efficient way to deal with these externalities is to charge higher tolls during rush hour. This toll would provide an incentive for drivers to alter their schedules and would reduce traffic when congestion is greatest.

Another policy that responds to the problem of road congestion, discussed in a case study in the previous chapter, is the tax on gasoline. Gasoline is a complementary good to driving: An increase in the price of gasoline tends to reduce the quantity of driving demanded. Therefore, a gasoline tax reduces road congestion. A gasoline tax, however, is an imperfect solution to road congestion. The problem is that the gasoline tax affects other decisions besides the amount of driving on congested roads. For example, the gasoline tax discourages driving on noncongested roads, even though there is no congestion externality for these roads.

Fish, Whales, and Other Wildlife   Many species of animals are common resources. Fish and whales, for instance, have commercial value, and anyone can go to the ocean and catch whatever is available. Each person has little incentive to maintain the species for the next year. Just as excessive grazing can destroy the Town Common, excessive fishing and whaling can destroy commercially valuable marine populations.

Oceans remain one of the least regulated common resources. Two problems prevent an easy solution. First, many countries have access to the oceans, so any solution would require international cooperation among countries that hold different values. Second, because the oceans are so vast, enforcing any agreement is difficult. As a result, fishing rights have been a frequent source of international tension among normally friendly countries.

In Canada, various laws aim to protect fish and other wildlife. For example, the government charges for fishing and hunting licences, and it restricts the lengths of the fishing and hunting seasons. Fishermen are often required to throw back small fish, and hunters can kill only a limited number of animals. All these laws reduce the use of a common resource and help maintain animal populations.

Case Study

THE COLLAPSE OF THE ATLANTIC COD FISHERY

The Atlantic Ocean off the shores of Newfoundland was once so full of cod that in 1497 explorer John Cabot marvelled that they actually blocked his ship. In the centuries to follow, boats from fishing nations around the world flocked to Canada's east coast to exploit the abundance of northern cod. Five hundred years later, the cod are virtually gone. What happened?

The population of northern cod had yielded an overall annual catch of about 250 000 tonnes for more than a century prior to the mid-1950s. Until then, most of the fishing took place mainly in small craft in waters relatively close to shore, using traditional techniques that involved fishing from dories or small trawlers.

In the mid-1950s, Newfoundland's dories were displaced by a new breed of factory fishing vessel. These new "factory trawlers," or "draggers," came from Germany, Great Britain, Spain, Portugal, Poland, the Soviet Union, Cuba, and even East Asia, and legally fished to within 20 kilometres of the eastern Canadian coast. They set and hauled enormous baglike nets that plowed and scraped the ocean bottom, quickly processing and deep-freezing the fish on board. Catches of northern cod increased substantially throughout the late 1950s and early 1960s as fishing vessels from around the world enjoyed essentially unencumbered access to the north Atlantic fishery off Canada's east coast. With no meaningful regulation of the resource, the catch peaked at just over 800 000 tonnes in the late 1960s.

The distant-water fleet, new technology, and virtually unlimited access to the common property resource subjected the northern cod to intense pressure, and by 1975 the declining northern cod population was yielding just 300 000 tonnes annually. Concerned that stocks were being reduced to almost nothing, Canada passed legislation in 1976 to extend their national jurisdictions over marine resources to 370 kilometres, prohibiting foreign boats from fishing within this limit.

In recognition of the overfishing that resulted from unregulated access to the fish stocks, Canada also initiated a quota system for fishing the northern cod, by implementing total allowable catch (TAC) limits based on the concept of maximum sustainable yield (MSY)—the maximum amount of fish that could be taken from a stock without depleting it. Unfortunately, when setting TAC limits the government considered short-term economic and political factors as well as biological ones in establishing its quota, which meant that TACs figures were set too high.

Although the 370-kilometre limit and a new regulatory regime were intended to conserve and restore fish stocks, they actually resulted in a larger Canadian fishing fleet to replace foreign fishers, as throughout the 1980s the Canadian government promoted more and more investment in the Atlantic fishery. In the mid-1980s, scientists began warning that the stock was declining and recommended the TAC limits be cut in half. Instead of acting immediately and reducing catch quotas at the first signs of overfishing, the federal government delayed conservation action and implemented only moderate reductions in the TAC limits, fearing the massive unemployment that would have resulted from shutting down the industry.

In 1992, the biomass estimate for northern cod was the lowest ever measured and the Canadian minister of Fisheries and Oceans had no choice but to declare a ban on fishing northern cod. Over 40 000 people lost their jobs, and the marine ecosystem is still in a state of collapse.

The collapse of the cod fishery is a prototypical example of what can go wrong with a common property resource, even in the presence of the government's attempt to manage the resource. While Canada finally introduced measures that in principle could have preserved the fish stocks and protected them from the Tragedy of the Commons, the government acted too slowly and based quotas on short-term political and economic considerations. This provides an example of how ill-conceived government intervention might not ultimately address market failures and improve market outcomes. ●

QuickQuiz Why do governments try to limit the use of common resources?

CONCLUSION: THE IMPORTANCE OF PROPERTY RIGHTS

In this and the previous chapter, we have seen there are some "goods" that the market does not provide adequately. Markets do not ensure that the air we breathe is clean or that our country is defended from foreign aggressors. Instead, societies rely on the government to protect the environment and to provide for national defence.

The problems we considered in these chapters arise in many different markets, but they share a common theme. In all cases, the market fails to allocate resources efficiently because *property rights* are not well established. That is, some item of value does not have an owner with the legal authority to control it. For example, although no one doubts that the "good" of clean air or national defence is valuable, no one has the right to attach a price to it and profit from its use. A factory pollutes too much because no one charges the factory for the pollution it emits. The market does not provide for national defence because no one can charge those who are defended for the benefit they receive.

When the absence of property rights causes a market failure, the government can potentially solve the problem. Sometimes, as in the sale of pollution permits, the solution is for the government to help define property rights and thereby unleash market forces. Other times, as in the restriction on hunting seasons, the solution is for the government to regulate private behaviour. Still other times, as in the provision of national defence, the solution is for the government to supply a good that the market fails to supply. In all cases, if the policy is well planned and well run, it can make the allocation of resources more efficient and thus raise economic well-being.

SUMMARY

- Goods differ in whether they are excludable and whether they are rival in consumption. A good is excludable if it is possible to prevent someone from using it. A good is rival in consumption if one person's use of the good reduces other people's ability to use the same unit of the good. Markets work best for private goods, which are both excludable and rival in consumption. Markets do not work as well for other types of goods.

- Public goods are neither rival in consumption nor excludable. Examples of public goods include fireworks displays, national defence, and the creation of fundamental knowledge. Because

people are not charged for their use of the public good, they have an incentive to free-ride when the good is provided privately. Therefore, governments provide public goods, making their decision about the quantity based on cost–benefit analysis.

- Common resources are rival in consumption but not excludable. Examples include common grazing land, clean air, and congested roads. Because people are not charged for their use of common resources, they tend to use them excessively. Therefore, governments try to limit the use of common resources.

KEY CONCEPTS

excludability, p. 236
rival in consumption, p. 236
private goods, p. 236

public goods, p. 236
common resources, p. 237
club goods, p. 237

free rider, p. 238
cost–benefit analysis, p. 241
Tragedy of the Commons, p. 243

QUESTIONS FOR REVIEW

1. Explain what is meant by a good being "excludable." Explain what is meant by a good being "rival in consumption." Is a pizza excludable? Is it rival in consumption?

2. Define and give an example of a public good. Can the private market provide this good on its own? Explain.

3. What is cost–benefit analysis of public goods? Why is it important? Why is it hard?

4. Define and give an example of a common resource. Without government intervention, will people use this good too much or too little? Why?

PROBLEMS AND APPLICATIONS

1. Both public goods and common resources involve externalities.
   a. Are the externalities associated with public goods generally positive or negative? Use examples in your answer. Is the free-market quantity of public goods generally greater or less than the efficient quantity?
   b. Are the externalities associated with common resources generally positive or negative? Use examples in your answer. Is the free-market use of common resources generally greater or less than the efficient use?

2. Think about the goods and services provided by your local government.
   a. Using the classification in Figure 11.1 (p. 236), explain into which category each of the following goods falls:
      • police protection
      • snowplowing
      • education
      • rural roads
      • city streets
   b. Why do you think the government provides items that are not public goods?

3. Charlie loves watching *Teletubbies* on his local public TV station, but he never sends any money to support the station during its fundraising drives.

   a. What name do economists have for people like Charlie?
   b. How can the government solve the problem caused by people like Charlie?
   c. Can you think of ways the private market can solve this problem? How does the existence of cable TV alter the situation?

4. Some economists argue that private firms will not undertake the efficient amount of basic scientific research.
   a. Explain why this is so. In your answer, classify basic research in one of the categories shown in Figure 11.1.
   b. What sort of policy has Canada adopted in response to this problem?
   c. It is often argued that this policy increases the technological capability of Canadian producers relative to that of foreign firms. Is this argument consistent with your classification of basic research in part (a)? (Hint: Can excludability apply to some potential beneficiaries of a public good and not others?)

5. Why is there litter along most highways but rarely in people's yards?

6. High-income people are willing to pay more than lower-income people to avoid the risk of death. For example, they are more likely to

pay for safety features on cars. Do you think cost–benefit analysts should take this fact into account when evaluating public projects? Consider, for instance, a rich town and a poor town, both of which are considering the installation of a traffic light. Should the rich town use a higher dollar value for a human life in making this decision? Why or why not?

7. Four roommates are planning to spend the weekend in their dorm room watching old movies, and they are debating how many to watch. The following table shows their willingness to pay for each film.

	Orson	Alfred	Woody	Ingmar
First film	$7	$5	$3	$2
Second film	6	4	2	1
Third film	5	3	1	0
Fourth film	4	2	0	0
Fifth film	3	1	0	0

a. Within the dorm room, is the showing of a movie a public good? Why or why not?
b. If it costs $8 to rent a movie, how many movies should the roommates rent to maximize total surplus?
c. If they choose the optimal number from part (b) and then split the cost of renting the movies equally, how much surplus does each person obtain from watching the movies?
d. Is there any way to split the cost to ensure that everyone benefits? What practical problems does this solution raise?
e. Suppose they agree in advance to choose the efficient number and to split the cost of the movies equally. When Orson is asked his willingness to pay, will he have an incentive to tell the truth? If so, why? If not, what will he be tempted to say?
f. What does this example teach you about the optimal provision of public goods?

8. Wireless, high-speed Internet is provided for free in the airport of the city of Communityville.
a. At first, only a few people use the service. What type of a good is this and why?
b. Eventually, as more people find out about the service and start using it, the speed of the connection begins to fall. Now what type of a good is the wireless Internet service?
c. What problem might result and why? What is one possible way to correct this problem?

9. The town of Wiknam has five residents, whose only activity is producing and consuming fish. They produce fish in two ways. Each person who works on a fish farm raises two fish per day. Each person who goes fishing in the town lake catches X fish per day. X depends on N, the number of residents fishing in the lake. In particular,

$$X = 6 - N$$

Each resident is attracted to the job that pays more fish.
a. Why do you suppose that X, the productivity of each fisherman, falls as N, the number of fishermen, rises? What economic term would you use to describe the fish in the town lake? Would the same description apply to the fish from the farms? Explain.
b. The town's Freedom Party thinks every individual should have the right to choose between fishing in the lake and farming without government interference. Under its policy, how many of the residents would fish in the lake and how many would work on fish farms? How many fish are produced?
c. The town's Efficiency Party thinks Wiknam should produce as many fish as it can. To achieve this goal, how many of the residents should fish in the lake and how many should work on the farms? (Hint: Create a table that shows the number of fish produced—on farms, from the lake, and in total—for each N from 0 to 5.)
d. The Efficiency Party proposes achieving its goal by taxing each person fishing in the lake by an amount equal to T fish per day. It will then distribute the proceeds equally among all Wiknam residents. (Fish are assumed to be divisible, so these rebates need not be whole numbers.) Calculate the value of T that would yield the outcome you derived in part (c). Compared with the Freedom Party's hands-off policy, who benefits and who loses from the imposition of the Efficiency Party's fishing tax?

http://
For more study tools, please visit www.nelson.com/mankiwmicro6e.

THE DESIGN OF THE TAX SYSTEM

Thinkstock

As Benjamin Franklin said, "In this world nothing is certain but death and taxes." Taxes are inevitable because we as citizens expect the government to provide us with various goods and services. The previous two chapters have started to shed light on one of the ten principles of economics from Chapter 1: The government can sometimes improve market outcomes. When the government remedies an externality (such as air pollution), provides a public good (such as national defence), or regulates the use of a common resource (such as fish in a public lake), it can raise economic well-being. Yet the benefits of government come with costs. For the government to perform these and its many other functions, it needs to raise revenue through taxation.

We began our study of taxation in earlier chapters, where we saw how a tax on a good affects supply and demand for that good. In Chapter 6 we saw that a tax reduces the quantity sold in a market, and we examined how the burden of a tax is shared by buyers and sellers, depending on the elasticities of supply and demand. In Chapter 8 we examined how taxes affect economic well-being. We learned that taxes cause *deadweight losses:* The reduction in consumer and producer surplus resulting from a tax exceeds the revenue raised by the government.

In this chapter we build on these lessons to discuss the design of a tax system. We begin with a financial overview of Canadian governments. When thinking about the tax system, it is useful to know some basic facts about how Canadian governments raise and spend money. We then consider the fundamental principles of taxation. Most people agree that taxes should impose as small a cost on society as possible and that the burden of taxes should be distributed fairly. That is, the tax system should be both *efficient* and *equitable*. As we will see, however, stating these goals is easier than achieving them.

A FINANCIAL OVERVIEW OF CANADIAN GOVERNMENTS

How much of the nation's income do governments take as taxes? Figure 12.1 shows government revenue, including federal, provincial and territorial, and local governments, as a percentage of total income for the Canadian economy. It shows that, over time, governments have taken a larger and larger share of total income. In 1961, governments collected 28 percent of total income; in 2011, they collected about 38 percent. In other words, as the economy's income has grown, governments have grown even more.

The overall size of government tells only part of the story. Behind the total dollar figures lie thousands of individual decisions about taxes and spending. To understand the governments' finances more fully, let's look at how the total breaks down into some broad categories.

Table 12.1 compares the tax burden for the G7 countries, which consist of seven of the world's major developed economies, as measured by total government

FIGURE 12.1

Government Revenue as a Percentage of GDP

This figure shows the revenue of the federal government and of provincial, territorial, and local governments as a percentage of gross domestic product (GDP), which measures the total income of the economy. It shows that government plays a large role in the Canadian economy and that its role has grown over time.

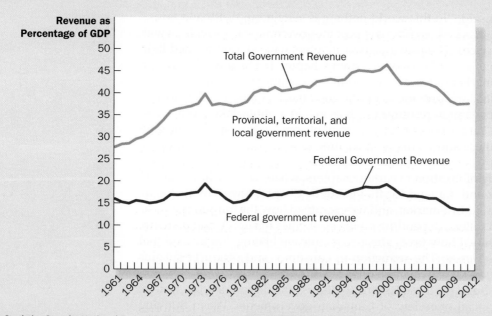

Source: Statistics Canada, National Economic Financial Accounts (Table 380-0007). Includes Canada Pension and Quebec Pension Plan. Excludes intergovernmental transfers. Reproduced and distributed on an "as is" basis with the permission of Statistics Canada.

TABLE 12.1

Total Government Tax Revenue as a Percentage of GDP: G7 Countries

Country	Tax Revenue as % of GDP
France	42.9%
Italy	43.0
Germany	36.3
United Kingdom	35.0
Canada	31.0
United States	24.8
Japan	26.9
G7 Average	34.3

Source: OECD (2012), "Total tax revenue," Taxation: Key Tables from OECD, No. 2. http://dx.doi .org/10.1787/taxrev-table-2012-1-en.

tax revenue (federal, provincial and territorial, and local) as a percentage of the nation's total income. Canada's tax burden is slightly below the G7 average, but it is quite a bit higher than the United States. Before examining government revenue in more detail, it is useful to know a few things about the structure of the government sector in Canada.

Canada has a *federalist* structure, which means political power is divided between the federal government and the provincial and territorial governments, with greater power going to the federal government. The third level of government, local or municipal, is granted powers by the provincial and territorial governments. The British North America (BNA) Act of 1867, Canada's Constitution, sets out the responsibilities of the federal and provincial and territorial governments. The BNA Act has been amended several times, most recently in 1982; however, the federalist structure has remained intact. In fact, it is one of the defining features of our country.

The federal government is responsible for matters of national interest, including national defence and foreign policy, international trade, competition policy, criminal law, and money and banking. The federal government is also responsible for delivering some of Canada's national social programs, such as Employment Insurance and the Canada Pension Plan. This level of government has essentially unlimited taxing powers.

The provinces and territories are responsible for the areas of health care, education, welfare, natural resources within their boundaries, and civil law. The provinces and territories have extensive taxing powers, although they are less extensive than the federal government's. Compared with provincial/territorial and state governments in most other federations, including the United States, Canadian provinces and territories have a great deal of power, accounting for more than half of the activities undertaken by the public sector in Canada. Local governments—cities, towns, and municipalities—are creatures of the provinces and territories, from which they receive their spending and taxing authority. Figure 12.1 reveals that most of the growth in the size of the Canadian government sector over the past 40 years has taken place at the provincial/territorial and local levels.

An important aspect of our federalist government structure is the role of *transfers* from the federal government to the provinces and territories. Although the federal government is not directly responsible for programs related to health, education, and welfare, it has been able to exercise substantial influence in these areas through the "power of the purse." The most important transfer programs in Canada are the Canada Social Transfer (CST) and the Canada Health Transfer (CHT). The CST is funding for programs in postsecondary education, social services (welfare), and early childhood development, while the CHT is intended to finance health programs. However, both the CST and the CHT are largely unconditional per capita grants that simply enter general provincial and territorial government revenues and may be used as these governments see fit.

Another important feature of the Canadian federation is the role of *equalization payments.* Under this system, the federal government provides general-purpose transfers to the "have-not" provinces so that they can provide services that are roughly comparable in quality to those provided by the "have" provinces. At the time of writing, the "have" provinces—the ones that do not receive equalization payments—are Alberta, British Columbia, Saskatchewan, and Newfoundland and Labrador. The remaining provinces receive various amounts of equalization payments, depending on their need. Yukon, Northwest Territories, and Nunavut receive similar payments under a separate system.

The Federal Government

The federal government collects just under 40 percent of the taxes in our economy. It raises this money in a number of ways, and it finds even more ways to spend it.

Receipts Table 12.2 shows total federal government revenue in the 2010–11 fiscal year ended March 31. Total revenue in this year was $237 billion. To bring this huge number down to earth, we can divide it by the Canadian population. We then find that the average Canadian paid about $6900 to the federal government in 2010.

TABLE 12.2

Federal Government Revenue, 2010–11

Revenue Source	Amount (in billons)	Amount per Person	% of Revenue
Personal income taxes	$113.5	$3291	48
Corporate income taxes	30	870	13
Goods and Services Tax	28	812	12
Excise taxes and duties	14.5	420	6
Employment Insurance payroll taxes	17.5	507	7
Other	33.5	971	14
Total	$ 237	$6871	100

Source: Adapted from Department of Finance Canada, Fiscal Reference Tables—2011.
Note: Numbers may not add up due to rounding.

The biggest source of revenue for the federal government is the personal income tax, which accounts for almost half of total federal revenue. In 2010, over 14 million Canadian taxpayers filled out tax returns to determine how much income tax they owed. Taxpayers are required to report their income from all sources: employment income, interest on savings, dividends from corporations in which they own shares, and so on. An individual's *tax liability* (how much the person owes in taxes) is then based on that person's total income.

A person's tax liability is not simply proportional to the person's income. Instead, the law requires a more complicated calculation. Taxable income is computed by subtracting from total income various deductions for things such as contributions to registered pension plans and registered retirement savings plans—both of which will be discussed later—child-care expenses, and so on. The person's basic tax liability is then calculated from taxable income using the schedule shown in Table 12.3.

Table 12.3 presents the *marginal tax rate*—the rate of tax applied to each additional dollar of income. There are four federal *tax brackets* in Canada (five if you count people who don't pay taxes at all because they don't earn enough income). Because the marginal tax rate rises as people enter higher tax brackets, higher-income individuals pay a larger percentage of their income in taxes than do lower-income individuals. (We will discuss the concept of the marginal tax rate more fully later in this chapter.) Note that the tax rates in Table 12.3 are federal tax rates only; provinces and territories also levy personal income taxes, as will be discussed later in the chapter. From this basic tax liability are deducted various tax credits in order to determine the individual's final tax liability. There are many credits, including a basic individual credit that everyone receives, a spousal credit, a child tax credit for dependent children, a credit for charitable donations, and other credits for low-income individuals.

Another important source of federal revenue is the Goods and Services Tax (GST), which accounts for about 12 percent of federal government revenue. The GST is levied at a 5 percent rate on the sales of most goods in Canada, with some notable exceptions such as most food. The average Canadian paid $812 in GST in 2010. Excise and customs duties brought in an additional $420 per person, or 6 percent of federal revenue. Excise taxes are sales taxes on specific goods, such as gasoline, cigarettes, and alcohol. Customs duties are taxes applied to goods imported into the country. Total taxes on the sale of goods and

TABLE 12.3

Federal Personal Income Tax Rates, 2011

On taxable income . . .	The tax rate is
Up to $41 544	15%
From $41 544–$83 088	22
From $83 088–$128 800	26
Over $128 800	29

Source: Canada Revenue Agency.

services, consisting of the GST plus excise taxes and customs duties, account for 18 percent of federal revenue, or $1232 per person.

The corporate income tax accounts for 13 percent of federal revenue, or about $870 per person. A corporation is a business that is set up as a separate legal entity. The government taxes each corporation on the basis of its profits—the amount the corporation receives for its goods or services minus the cost of producing them.

Another important revenue source for the federal government is payroll taxes used to finance the Employment Insurance (EI) program. A *payroll tax* is a tax on the wages that a firm pays its workers. In Canada, EI payroll taxes are paid by both employees and employers. Table 12.2 shows that the average Canadian paid about $500 in EI payroll taxes in 2010. Another program that is financed by payroll taxes is the Canada Pension Plan (CPP), which provides pensions to all retired Canadians. CPP payroll taxes are not included in Table 12.2 because the program operates under a separate budget.

Spending   Table 12.4 shows federal government spending in 2010–11. Total spending was $270 billion, or about $7830 per person. Approximately 11 percent of this went to pay the interest on the federal government's debt. The remaining 89 percent, or $6931 per person, was devoted to *program spending*—that is, all government expenditures that are not debt payments.

One of the largest categories of federal government expenditures, aside from debt payments, is payments to elderly people under the Old Age Security program, which in 2010 accounted for 13 percent of total spending. Payments to senior citizens are likely to grow in importance as increases in life expectancy and decreases in birthrates cause this population to grow more rapidly than the total population. Another important source of government-provided income for seniors is the CPP. As mentioned above, payments made under the CPP are accounted for separately.

TABLE 12.4

Federal Government Spending 2010–11

Category	Amount (in billions)	Amount per Person	% of Spending
Old Age Security	$ 36	$1044	13
Canada Health and Social Transfer	37	1073	14
Equalization	29	841	11
Employment Insurance	19	551	7
National defence	21	609	8
Other	97	2813	36
Total program spending	239	6931	89
Debt service	31	899	11
Total spending	$270	$7830	100

Source: Adapted from Department of Finance Canada, Fiscal Reference Tables—2011.

Transfers to the provinces under the CHT and CST account for 14 percent of program expenditures; equalization payments account for an additional 11 percent. Total transfers to the provinces and territories thus make up 25 percent of federal government expenditures.

Payments under the EI program in 2010 amounted to $19 billion, or about 7 percent of total federal spending. It is interesting to note that the federal government collected $17.5 billion in EI payroll taxes in the same year (see Table 12.2). That is, EI spending exceeded EI revenue by $1.5 billion. This was largely due to the lingering effects of the 2008 recession and the ensuing slowdown in economic growth over the past couple of years.

In 2010, spending on national defence accounted for 8 percent of total federal expenditures. Canada spends substantially less in this area than the United States, which devotes roughly 20 percent of federal government expenditures to national defence.

You may have noticed that total federal revenue, shown in Table 12.2, falls short of total spending in Table 12.4. This excess of spending over revenue is called a **budget deficit** (if revenue exceeds spending, a **budget surplus** results). In 2010–11, the budget deficit was $33 billion.

budget deficit
an excess of government spending over government receipts

budget surplus
an excess of government receipts over government spending

Provincial/Territorial and Local Governments

Provincial/territorial and local governments collect about 60 percent of taxes in the economy. Let's look at how they obtain tax revenue and how they spend it.

Receipts   Table 12.5 shows the total revenue of provincial/territorial governments in 2008: $342 billion, or $10 118 per person. However, $64 billion of total provincial/territorial revenue (19 percent) came from transfers from the federal government. Provincial/territorial own-source revenues therefore amounted to $278 billion, or $8225 per person.

TABLE 12.5

Provincial/Territorial Government Revenue, 2008–2009

Category	Amount (in billions)	Amount per Person	% of Revenue
Personal income taxes	$ 75	$ 2 219	22%
Corporate income taxes	19	562	6
Provincial sales taxes	38	1 124	11
Excise taxes	30	888	9
Property taxes	9	266	3
Payroll taxes	10	296	3
Health premiums	3	89	1
Federal government transfers	64	1 893	19
Other	94	2 781	27
Total	342	10 118	100

Source: Adapted from Statistics Canada, CANSIM database www.cansim.statcan.gc.ca, 385-0001.

The single most important source of revenue for the provinces and territories, as for the federal government, is personal income taxes. In 2008, personal income taxes accounted for 22 percent of total provincial/territorial revenue, or about $2219 per person. The provinces and territories levy personal taxes on the same taxable income base as the federal government, but determine their own tax rates and brackets on top of the federal taxes. All provinces and territories except Alberta have several tax brackets. For example, Quebec has three tax brackets, with marginal tax rates ranging from 16 percent up to 24 percent. Alberta, on the other hand, imposes a flat 10 percent rate on all income. Provincial/territorial personal taxes are added to federal taxes. Thus, for a resident of Alberta, the top marginal tax rate is 39 percent, consisting of the 29 percent top federal rate and the 10 percent flat Alberta rate.

The next-largest revenue source for the provinces is provincial sales taxes (PST), which account for 11 percent of total provincial revenue. All of the provinces except Alberta levy sales taxes collected at the retail level. None of the territories levy this tax. Newfoundland and Labrador, Prince Edward Island, Nova Scotia, New Brunswick, and Ontario have all harmonized their PST with the federal GST. As seen in Table 12.6, the rates range from 5 percent to 10 percent. Excise taxes on goods such as gasoline, cigarettes, and alcohol comprise another 9 percent of total provincial revenue. Thus, total taxes on consumption (general sales taxes plus excise taxes) account for 20 percent of provincial revenue.

The provinces also levy their own taxes on corporations. The most important of these is the corporate income tax, which accounts for 6 percent of provincial revenues.

TABLE 12.6

Provincial Sales Tax (PST) Rates, as of April 1, 2013

Province/Territory	PST Rate
British Columbia	Varies from 7% to 12%
Alberta	No PST
Saskatchewan	5%
Manitoba	7%
Ontario	*HST: 13% (8% PST)
Quebec	9.975%
Newfoundland and Labrador	HST: 13% (8% PST)
Nova Scotia	HST: 15% (10% PST)
New Brunswick	HST: 13% (8% PST)
Prince Edward Island	HST: 14% (9% PST)
Northwest Territories	No PST
Nunavut	No PST
Yukon	No PST

*HST stands for *harmonized sales tax*, which is the combination of the provincial sales tax with the federal Goods and Services Tax (5% GST in all cases above).
Source: Canada Revenue Agency, GST/HST Rates, January 3, 2013.

TABLE 12.7

Provincial/Territorial Government Spending, 2008–2009

Category	Amount (in billions)	Amount per Person	% of Spending
Health	$ 115	$3 402	33%
Education	82	2 426	23
Social services	62	1 834	18
Transportation and communication	17	503	5
Resource conservation and industrial development	12	355	3
Police and protection	12	355	3
Debt service	24	710	7
Other	26	769	7
Total	350	10 355	100

Source: Adapted from the Statistics Canada CANSIM database http://cansim.statcan.gc.ca, 385-0001.
Note: Numbers may not add up due to rounding.

Provincial health premiums and payroll taxes together make up 4 percent of provincial revenues. Most provinces levy a payroll tax, paid by employers, to help fund health programs. Saskatchewan levies no such tax, and Alberta and British Columbia impose lump-sum health care premiums on a yearly basis that are paid by employees.

Spending   Table 12.7 shows total provincial/territorial government spending in 2008 and how it breaks down. Spending on health, education, and social services ("the big three") account for the lion's share of provincial spending—74 percent of total spending in 2008, or $7662 per person. Health is the biggest single component, followed by education and social services. Education includes spending on primary, secondary, and postsecondary schools. Health includes expenditures on hospital care, medical care, and preventive care. Social services primarily consist of welfare programs for low-income people.

Provincial/territorial government spending on police and protection, transportation and communication, and resource conservation and industrial development accounted for 11 percent of provincial spending. Debt service charges accounted for 7 percent.

Notice that total provincial/territorial government spending exceeds total provincial/territorial government revenue in Table 12.5—the aggregate provincial/territorial budget in 2008 was in a slight deficit situation.

QuickQuiz   What are the two most important sources of tax revenue for the federal government? • What are the two most important sources of tax revenue for provincial, territorial, and local governments?

TAXES AND EFFICIENCY

Now that we have seen how Canadian governments at various levels raise and spend money, let's consider how one might evaluate their tax policy. The primary aim of a tax system is to raise revenue for the governments. But there are many ways to raise any given amount of money. In designing a tax system, policymakers have two objectives: efficiency and equity.

One tax system is more efficient than another if it raises the same amount of revenue at a smaller cost to taxpayers. What are the costs of taxes to taxpayers? The most obvious cost is the tax payment itself. This transfer of money from the taxpayer to the government is an inevitable feature of any tax system. Yet taxes also impose two other costs, which well-designed tax policy tries to avoid or, at least, minimize:

1. The deadweight losses that result when taxes distort the decisions that people make
2. The administrative burdens that taxpayers bear as they comply with the tax laws

An efficient tax system is one that imposes small deadweight losses and small administrative burdens.

Deadweight Losses

One of the ten principles of economics is that people respond to incentives, and this includes incentives provided by the tax system. If the government taxes ice cream, people eat less ice cream and more frozen yogurt. If the government taxes housing, people live in smaller houses and spend more of their income on other things. If the government taxes labour earnings, people work less and enjoy more leisure.

Because taxes distort incentives, they entail deadweight losses. As we first discussed in Chapter 8, the deadweight loss of a tax is the reduction in economic well-being of taxpayers in excess of the amount of revenue raised by the government. The deadweight loss is the inefficiency that a tax creates as people allocate resources according to the tax incentive rather than the true costs and benefits of the goods and services that they buy and sell.

To recall how taxes cause deadweight losses, consider an example. Suppose that Joe places an $8 value on a pizza, and Jane places a $6 value on it. If there is no tax on pizza, the price of pizza will reflect the cost of making it. Let's suppose that the price of pizza is $5, so both Joe and Jane choose to buy one. Both consumers get some surplus of value over the amount paid. Joe gets consumer surplus of $3, and Jane gets consumer surplus of $1. Total surplus is $4.

Now suppose that the government levies a $2 tax on pizza and the price of pizza rises to $7. Joe still buys a pizza, but now he has consumer surplus of only $1. Jane now decides not to buy a pizza because its price is higher than its value to her. The government collects tax revenue of $2 on Joe's pizza. Total consumer surplus has fallen by $3 (from $4 to $1). Because total surplus has fallen by more than the tax revenue, the tax has a deadweight loss. In this case, the deadweight loss is $1.

Notice that the deadweight loss comes not from Joe, the person who pays the tax, but from Jane, the person who doesn't. The reduction of $2 in Joe's surplus exactly offsets the amount of revenue the government collects. The deadweight loss arises because the tax causes Jane to alter her behaviour. When the tax raises the price of pizza, Jane is worse off, and yet there is no offsetting revenue to the government. This reduction in Jane's welfare is the deadweight loss of the tax.

Case Study

SHOULD INCOME OR CONSUMPTION BE TAXED?

When taxes induce people to change their behaviour—such as inducing Jane to buy less pizza—the taxes cause deadweight losses and make the allocation of resources less efficient. As we have already seen, much government revenue comes from the individual income tax. In a case study in Chapter 8, we discussed how this tax discourages people from working as hard as they otherwise might. Another inefficiency caused by this tax is that it discourages people from saving.

Consider a person 25 years old who is considering saving $100. If he puts this money into a savings account that earns 8 percent and leaves it there, he would have $2172 when he retires at age 65. Yet if the government taxes one-fourth of his interest income each year, the effective interest rate is only 6 percent. After 40 years of earning 6 percent, the $100 grows to only $1029, less than half of what it would have been without taxation. Thus, because interest income is taxed, saving is much less attractive.

Some economists advocate eliminating the current tax system's disincentive toward saving by changing the basis of taxation. Rather than taxing the amount of income that people *earn,* the government could tax the amount that people *spend.* Under this proposal, all income that is saved would not be taxed until the saving is later spent. This alternative system, called a *consumption tax,* would not distort people's saving decisions.

A tax on consumption can be implemented in several ways. The approach that most people are familiar with is a sales tax on goods and services purchased by consumers. Examples include provincial sales taxes and the federal government's GST.

Some economists have suggested another approach to taxing consumption. People can do two basic things with their income: They can spend (consume) it, or they can save it. This gives rise to the model: Income = Consumption + Savings (or $I = C + S$). Rearranging this model, an individual's consumption can be defined simply as income minus savings (or $C = I - S$). This suggests that the tax system could be used to tax consumption in the following way. The individual's total income (I) could be determined and savings (S) could be allowed as a deduction. The interest (or dividends or capital gains) earned on the amount saved would then accumulate tax-free. When, some time later, the individual withdraws the savings in order to consume, the amount withdrawn would be fully taxable.

In fact, Canada's personal income tax system works in a very similar way. All contributions to registered retirement savings plans (RRSPs) and registered pension plans (RPPs), up to a maximum of $23 820 per year, are fully deductible from income. Moreover, interest earned in these plans accumulates tax-free, and withdrawals may be made at any time, at which point they are fully taxable. RRSPs and RPPs are vehicles intended to encourage people to save for their retirement. For people who do most of their saving through RRSPs and RPPs—and figures show that very few Canadians contribute up to the allowed limits—Canada's personal income tax functions like a tax on consumption.

Combined with provincial sales taxes and the GST, the tax treatment of RPPs and RRSPs suggests that Canada's tax system as a whole raises most of its revenue by taxing consumption rather than income. ●

Administrative Burden

If you ask the typical person on April 30 for an opinion about the tax system, you might hear about the headache of filling out tax forms. The administrative burden of any tax system is part of the inefficiency it creates. This burden includes not only the time spent in April filling out forms but also the time spent throughout the year keeping records for tax purposes and the resources the government has to use to enforce the tax laws.

Many taxpayers—especially those in higher tax brackets—hire tax lawyers and accountants to help them with their taxes. These experts in the complex tax laws fill out the tax forms for their clients and help clients arrange their affairs in a way that reduces the amount of taxes owed. This behaviour is legal tax avoidance, which is different from illegal tax evasion.

Critics of our tax system say that these advisers help their clients avoid taxes by abusing some of the detailed provisions of the tax laws, often dubbed "loopholes." In some cases, loopholes are government mistakes: They arise from ambiguities or omissions in the tax laws. More often, they arise because the government has chosen to give special treatment to specific types of behaviour. An example of this is the special provision for contributions to RRSPs and RPPs discussed earlier.

The resources devoted to complying with the tax laws are a type of deadweight loss. The government gets only the amount of taxes paid. By contrast, the taxpayer loses not only this amount but also the time and money spent documenting, computing, and avoiding taxes.

The administrative burden of the tax system could be reduced by simplifying the tax laws. Yet simplification is often politically difficult. Most people are ready to simplify the tax laws by eliminating the loopholes that benefit others, yet few are eager to give up the loopholes that they use. In the end, the complexity of the tax laws results from the political process as various taxpayers with their own special interests lobby for their causes.

Average Tax Rates versus Marginal Tax Rates

When discussing the efficiency and equity of income taxes, economists distinguish between two notions of the tax rate: the average and the marginal. The **average tax rate** is total taxes paid divided by total income. The **marginal tax rate** is the extra taxes paid on an additional dollar of income.

For example, suppose that the government taxes 20 percent of the first $50 000 of income and 50 percent of all income above $50 000. Under this tax, a person who makes $60 000 pays a tax of $15 000: 20 percent of the first $50 000 (0.20 × $50 000 = $10 000) plus 50 percent of the next $10 000 (0.50 × $10 000 = $5000). For this person, the average tax rate is $15 000/$60 000, or 25 percent. But the marginal tax rate is 50 percent. If the taxpayer earned an additional dollar of income, that dollar would be subject to the 50 percent tax rate, so the amount the taxpayer would owe to the government would rise by $0.50.

The marginal and average tax rates each contain a useful piece of information. If we are trying to gauge the sacrifice made by a taxpayer, the average tax rate is more appropriate because it measures the fraction of income paid in taxes. By contrast, if we are trying to gauge how much the tax system distorts incentives, the marginal tax rate is more meaningful. One of the ten principles of economics in Chapter 1 is that rational people think at the margin. A corollary to this principle is that the marginal tax rate measures how much the tax system discourages people from working. If you are thinking of working an extra few hours, the marginal tax rate determines how much the government takes of your additional earnings. It is the marginal tax rate, therefore, that determines the deadweight loss of an income tax.

average tax rate
total taxes paid divided by total income

marginal tax rate
the extra taxes paid on an additional dollar of income

Lump-Sum Taxes

Suppose the government imposes a tax of $4000 on everyone. That is, everyone owes the same amount, regardless of earnings or any actions that a person might take. Such a tax is called a **lump-sum tax**.

A lump-sum tax shows clearly the difference between average and marginal tax rates. For a taxpayer with income of $20 000, the average tax rate of a $4000 lump-sum tax is 20 percent; for a taxpayer with income of $40 000, the average tax rate is 10 percent. For both taxpayers, the marginal tax rate is zero because no tax is owed on an additional dollar of income.

A lump-sum tax is the most efficient tax possible. Because a person's decisions do not alter the amount owed, the tax does not distort incentives and, therefore, does not cause deadweight losses. Because everyone can easily compute the amount owed and because there is no benefit to hiring tax lawyers and accountants, the lump-sum tax imposes a minimal administrative burden on taxpayers.

If lump-sum taxes are so efficient, why do we rarely observe them in the real world? The reason is that efficiency is only one goal of the tax system. A lump-sum tax would take the same amount from the poor and the rich, an outcome most people would view as unfair. To understand the tax systems that we observe, in the next section, we consider the other major goal of tax policy: equity.

lump-sum tax
a tax that is the same amount for every person

QuickQuiz   What is meant by the *efficiency* of a tax system? • What can make a tax system inefficient?

TAXES AND EQUITY

Although economists tend to focus on the efficiency aspects of the tax system, Canadian policy debates about taxes tend to be dominated by discussions about the fairness of the tax system—in particular, whether its burden is distributed fairly. Of course, if we are to rely on the government to provide some of the goods and services we want, taxes must fall on someone. In this section we consider the equity of a tax system. How should the burden of taxes be divided among the population? How do we evaluate whether a tax system is fair? Everyone agrees that the tax system should be equitable, but there is much disagreement about what equity means and how the equity of a tax system can be judged.

The Benefits Principle

benefits principle
the idea that people should pay taxes based on the benefits they receive from government services

One principle of taxation, called the **benefits principle**, states that people should pay taxes based on the benefits they receive from government services. This principle tries to make public goods similar to private goods. It seems fair that a person who often goes to the movies pays more in total for movie tickets than a person who rarely goes. Similarly, a person who gets great benefit from a public good should pay more for it than a person who gets little benefit.

The gasoline tax, for instance, is sometimes justified using the benefits principle. In some provinces and territories, revenues from the gasoline tax are used to build and maintain roads. Because those who buy gasoline are the same people who use the roads, the gasoline tax might be viewed as a fair way to pay for this government service.

The benefits principle can also be used to argue that wealthy citizens should pay higher taxes than poorer ones. Why? Simply because the wealthy benefit more from public services. Consider, for example, the benefits of police protection from theft. Citizens with much to protect get greater benefit from police services than do those with less to protect. Therefore, according to the benefits principle, the wealthy should contribute more than the poor to the cost of maintaining the police force. The same argument can be used for many other public services, such as fire protection, national defence, and the court system.

It is even possible to use the benefits principle to argue for antipoverty programs funded by taxes on the wealthy. As we discussed in Chapter 11, people prefer living in a society without poverty, suggesting that antipoverty programs are a public good. If the wealthy place a greater dollar value on this public good than members of the middle class do, perhaps just because the wealthy have more to spend, then, according to the benefits principle, they should be taxed more heavily to pay for these programs.

The Ability-to-Pay Principle

ability-to-pay principle
the idea that taxes should be levied on a person according to how well that person can shoulder the burden

Another way to evaluate the equity of a tax system is called the **ability-to-pay principle**, which states that taxes should be levied on a person according to how well that person can shoulder the burden. This principle is sometimes justified by the claim that all citizens should make an "equal sacrifice" to support the government. The magnitude of a person's sacrifice, however, depends not only on the size of the person's tax payment but also on that person's income and other

TABLE 12.8

Three Tax Systems

	Proportional Tax		Regressive Tax		Progressive Tax	
Income	Amount of Tax	Percent of Income	Amount of Tax	Percent of Income	Amount of Tax	Percent of Income
$ 50 000	$12 500	25%	$15 000	30%	$10 000	20%
100 000	25 000	25	25 000	25	25 000	25
200 000	50 000	25	40 000	20	60 000	30

circumstances. A $1000 tax paid by a poor person may require a larger sacrifice than a $10 000 tax paid by a rich one.

The ability-to-pay principle leads to two corollary notions of equity: vertical equity and horizontal equity. **Vertical equity** states that taxpayers with a greater ability to pay taxes should contribute a larger amount. **Horizontal equity** states that taxpayers with similar abilities to pay should contribute the same amount. Although these notions of equity are widely accepted, applying them to evaluate a tax system is rarely straightforward.

Vertical Equity   If taxes are based on ability to pay, then richer taxpayers should pay more than poorer taxpayers. But how much more should the rich pay? Much of the debate over tax policy concerns this question.

Consider the three tax systems in Table 12.8. In each case, taxpayers with higher incomes pay more. Yet the systems differ in how quickly taxes rise with income. The first system is called **proportional** because all taxpayers pay the same fraction of income. The second system is called **regressive** because high-income taxpayers pay a smaller fraction of their income, even though they pay a larger amount. The third system is called **progressive** because high-income taxpayers pay a larger fraction of their income.

Which of these three tax systems is most fair? There is no obvious answer, and economic theory does not offer any help in trying to find one. Equity, like beauty, is in the eye of the beholder.

vertical equity
the idea that taxpayers with a greater ability to pay taxes should pay larger amounts

horizontal equity
the idea that taxpayers with similar abilities to pay taxes should pay the same amount

proportional tax
a tax for which high-income and low-income taxpayers pay the same fraction of income

regressive tax
a tax for which high-income taxpayers pay a smaller fraction of their income than do low-income taxpayers

progressive tax
a tax for which high-income taxpayers pay a larger fraction of their income than do low-income taxpayers

Case Study

HOW THE TAX BURDEN IS DISTRIBUTED

Much of the debate over tax policy relates to whether the wealthy pay their fair share of taxes. There is no objective way to make this judgment. However, when evaluating this issue for yourself, it is useful to know how the burden of the current tax system is distributed among families with different incomes. To do this properly, we must take account of the fact that those who bear the burden of a tax may not be those who actually pay the tax.

TABLE 12.9

The Burden of Income Taxes and Transfers, 2010

Group	Average Family Market Income	Income Taxes as a % of Income	% of All Income	% of Income Taxes	Transfers as a % of Income	% of Transfers
Bottom fifth	$ 6 700	13%	2.0%	2.0%	133%	19%
Second fifth	23 100	10	7.0	4.0	52	26
Third fifth	45 400	14	14.0	12.0	23	22
Fourth fifth	77 000	16	24.0	22.0	12	19
Top fifth	164 900	22	52.0	62.0	4	14

Source: Adapted from Statistics Canada publication, "Income in Canada," Catalogue 75-202-X, June 2009. Numbers may not add up due to rounding.

Table 12.9 presents some data on how federal income taxes are distributed among income classes. To construct this table, families are ranked according to their income and placed into five groups of equal size, called *quintiles*.

The second column of the table shows the average income of each group. The poorest one-fifth of families had average income of $6700, and the richest one-fifth had average income of $164 900.

The next column of the table shows total income taxes paid as a percentage of income. As you can see, the Canadian income tax system is progressive. The poorest fifth of families paid 13 percent of their income in taxes, and the richest fifth paid 22 percent.

The fourth and fifth columns compare the distribution of income and the distribution of taxes. The poorest quintile earns 2.0 percent of all income and pays 2.0 percent of all taxes. The richest quintile earns 52.0 percent of all income and pays 62.0 percent of all taxes.

The fifth and sixth columns show that the transfer system is even more progressive. The poorest fifth of families receive well over 100 percent of their market income in transfers; the richest fifth just 4 percent. Indeed, the lowest three quintiles all receive more in transfers than they pay in income taxes.

The analysis here looks at just income taxes. A more complete study would incorporate other taxes, including the GST, provincial sales taxes, excise taxes, corporate taxes, and property taxes. ●

Horizontal Equity   If taxes are based on ability to pay, then similar taxpayers should pay similar amounts of taxes. But what determines if two taxpayers are similar? Families differ in many ways. To evaluate whether tax laws are horizontally equitable, one must determine which differences are relevant for a family's ability to pay and which differences are not.

Suppose the Smith and Jones families each have income of $50 000. The Smiths have no children, but Mr. Smith has an illness that causes medical expenses of $20 000. The Joneses are in good health, but they have four children. Two of the Jones children are in university, generating tuition bills of $30 000. Would it be fair for these two families to pay the same tax because they have the same income? Would it be more fair to give the Smiths a tax break to help them offset their high medical expenses? Would it be more fair to give the Joneses a tax break to help them with their tuition expenses?

There are no easy answers to these questions. In practice, the Canadian income tax is filled with special provisions that alter a family's tax based on its specific circumstances.

Tax Incidence and Tax Equity

Tax incidence—the study of who bears the burden of taxes—is central to evaluating tax equity. As we first saw in Chapter 6, the person who bears the burden of a tax is not always the person who gets the tax bill from the government. Because taxes alter supply and demand, they alter equilibrium prices. As a result, they affect people beyond those who, according to statute, actually pay the tax. When evaluating the vertical and horizontal equity of any tax, it is important to take account of these indirect effects.

Many discussions of tax equity ignore the indirect effects of taxes and are based on what economists mockingly call the *flypaper theory* of tax incidence. According to this theory, the burden of a tax, like a fly on flypaper, sticks wherever it first lands. This assumption, however, is rarely valid.

For example, a person not trained in economics might argue that a tax on expensive fur coats is vertically equitable because most buyers of furs are wealthy. Yet if these buyers can easily substitute other luxuries for furs, then a tax on furs might only reduce the sale of furs. In the end, the burden of the tax will fall more on those who make and sell furs than on those who buy them. Because most workers who make furs are not wealthy, the equity of a fur tax could be quite different from what the flypaper theory indicates.

Case Study

WHO PAYS THE CORPORATE INCOME TAX?

The corporate income tax provides a good example of the importance of tax incidence for tax policy. The corporate tax is popular among voters. After all, corporations are not people. Voters are always eager to have their taxes reduced and have some impersonal corporation pick up the tab.

But before deciding that the corporate income tax is a good way for the government to raise revenue, we should consider who bears the burden of the corporate tax. This is a difficult question on which economists disagree, but one thing is certain: *People pay all taxes*. When the government levies a tax on a corporation, the corporation is more like a tax collector than a taxpayer. The burden of the tax ultimately falls on people—the owners, customers, or workers of the corporation.

This worker pays part of the corporate income tax.

IN THE NEWS

CORPORATE TAXES AND WAGES

This article from The Economist *magazine argues that workers end up bearing the burden of corporate taxes.*

A Toll on the Common Man: Why Taxes on Companies Are Bad for Workers

Cutting taxes, as Germany's coalition government is learning, can be harder than raising them. On June 16th the country's parliament approved a big increase in value-added tax, to take effect in 2007. Trimming Germany's heavy corporate taxes is proving harder. German firms face tax rates of nearly 40%, the highest in Europe (see chart). The government wants to push them below 30%, to boost investment and discourage firms from moving to lower-tax countries, especially in central and eastern Europe. But the idea faces stiff opposition. "They're reaching into the wallets of the little people to give corporations tax relief," says Renate Künast, parliamentary leader of the left-of-centre Green party.

Ms Künast's views are echoed by many politicians in many countries. There are few taxes politicians like more—and economists like less—than today's levies on companies' profits. Politicians much prefer to tax impersonal firms, which cannot vote, than workers, who can. America, for instance, has the second-

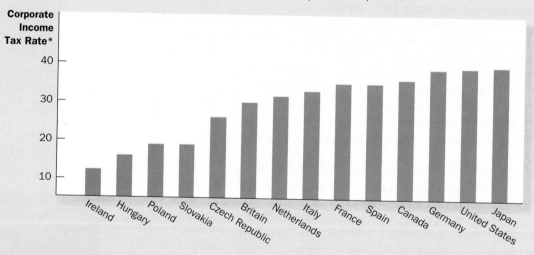

Taxing Business: Top Rates of Corporate Tax,* 2005

*Combined national and local taxes
Source: Organisation for Economic Co-operation and Development.

Many economists believe that workers and customers bear much of the burden of the corporate income tax. To see why, consider an example. Suppose that the government decides to raise the tax on the income earned by car companies. At first, this tax hurts the owners of the car companies, who receive less profit. But, over highest rate of corporate-income tax in the OECD (behind Japan). Yet even George Bush's tax-cutting administration has not sought to lower it. To economists, in contrast, the notion that firms pay tax makes little sense: in fact, people do.

But which people, exactly? If corporate taxes are borne mainly by shareholders, left-wing politicians can plausibly claim that cutting them is a boon to the rich, because richer people own more shares (even though the far-from-rich own lots too, through their pension funds). But if the taxes are shifted to consumers through higher prices or to workers through lower wages, reducing them would benefit Ms Künast's "little people."

Economists have been debating who pays corporate taxes for decades. In a classic paper in 1962, Arnold Harberger, an American economist, argued that if neither capital nor goods can cross national borders, the burden of corporate taxation falls squarely on the owners of capital. Neither workers nor consumers bear any of it. But nor does the burden fall solely on affluent shareholders. Mr Harberger pointed out that capital would shift between firms and non-corporate investments, such as partnerships or property. The tax's burden would be shared by all owners of capital, including farmers and homeowners.

This analysis has since been refined by many researchers (including Mr Harberger himself). Most now agree that workers do, in effect, pay some of the tax formally levied on companies. One route is through lower saving. Corporate-income taxes, like all taxes on capital, make saving and investment less attractive.

Lower investment means a smaller capital stock, less capital per worker and hence lower wages. Several studies have found a negative link between corporate-tax rates and investment.

Globalisation sharpens this effect. Capital can now move easily from high-tax to low-tax countries. That implies less investment and lower real wages in high-tax countries, but gains for workers in low-tax countries. The effect ought to be bigger in small, open economies, where an infusion of foreign capital can quickly boost productivity, than in large, less open ones.

Around the world, corporate-tax rates have been falling. Twenty years ago, most rich countries had a top rate of over 40%. Today, none does. Small economies with low corporate-tax rates, from Ireland to Slovakia, have boomed thanks to huge foreign investment. Anecdotal evidence suggests that workers have gained as corporate taxes have fallen.

Oddly, there has been little empirical analysis of the size of this effect. In a new paper,[†] Kevin Hassett and Aparna Mathur of the American Enterprise Institute, a free-market think-tank, try to fill the gap. They examine the relationship between corporate taxes and wages for manufacturing workers in 72 countries over 22 years. Their goal is to tease out whether differences in corporate-tax rates affect wages once other influences on pay, such as productivity and the power of unions, are taken into account.

The results are striking. On average, a 1% increase in the corporate-tax rate is associated with a 0.8% drop in wages over the next five years. And, just as theory would predict, the effect is bigger in smaller economies than in larger ones. The economists find that international tax competition matters too: their work suggests that a 1% cut in a neighbouring country's corporate-income tax pushes down wages at home by 0.5%. This suggests that corporate taxes have a huge effect on wages. At face value, it implies that if Germany cut its corporate-tax burden by 25%, as its government intends, wages ought eventually to rise by a fifth.

That is staggering—but almost certainly overstated. For one thing, the effect appears implausibly fast. In theory, the burden of corporate taxes shifts gradually from capital to workers as firms invest in low-tax countries. It is hard to believe that enough changes within five years to affect wages as much as Mr Hassett and Ms Mathur report. More likely, the strong negative link between corporate taxes and wages reflects the omission, or mismeasurement, of other things that affect pay.

But even if their precise figures look questionable, Mr Hassett and Ms Mathur make a point that politicians in Germany and elsewhere ought to heed. In today's world, high taxes on companies hurt the "little people" they are supposed to please.

[†]"Taxes and Wages": American Enterprise Institute for Public Policy Research, July 6, 2006: www.aei.org/paper/24629.

time, these owners will respond to the tax. Because producing cars is less profitable, they invest less in building new car factories. Instead, they invest their wealth in other ways—for example, by buying larger houses or by building factories in other industries or other countries. With fewer car factories, the supply of cars declines, as does the demand for autoworkers. Thus, a tax on corporations making cars causes the price of cars to rise and the wages of autoworkers to fall.

The corporate income tax shows how dangerous the flypaper theory of tax incidence can be. The corporate income tax is popular in part because it appears to be paid by rich corporations. Yet those who bear the ultimate burden of the tax—the customers and workers of corporations—are often not rich. If the true incidence of the corporate tax was more widely known, this tax might be less popular among voters. ●

QuickQuiz Explain the *benefits principle* and the *ability-to-pay principle*. ● What are *vertical equity* and *horizontal equity*? ● Why is studying tax incidence important for determining the equity of a tax system?

CONCLUSION: THE TRADEOFF BETWEEN EQUITY AND EFFICIENCY

Almost everyone agrees that equity and efficiency are the two most important goals of the tax system. But often these two goals conflict. Many proposed changes in the tax laws increase efficiency while reducing equity, or increase equity while reducing efficiency. People disagree about tax policy often because they attach different weights to these two goals. As a result, tax policy is often the subject of heated political debate. Indeed, elections may be won and lost on the basis of the weights the political parties attach to the conflicting goals of efficiency and equity.

Economics alone cannot determine the best way to balance the goals of efficiency and equity. This issue involves political philosophy as well as economics. But economists do have an important role in the political debate over tax policy: They can shed light on the tradeoffs that society faces and can help us avoid policies that sacrifice efficiency without any benefit in terms of equity.

SUMMARY

- Canadian governments raise revenue using various taxes. The most important tax for the federal and the provincial/territorial governments is the personal income tax.

- The efficiency of a tax system refers to the costs it imposes on taxpayers. There are two costs of taxes beyond the transfer of resources from the taxpayer to the government. The first is the distortion in the allocation of resources that arises as taxes alter incentives and behaviour. The second is the administrative burden of complying with the tax laws.

- The equity of a tax system concerns whether the tax burden is distributed fairly among the population. According to the benefits principle, it is fair for people to pay taxes based on the benefits they receive from the government. According to the ability-to-pay principle, it is fair for people to pay taxes based on their capability to handle the financial burden. When evaluating the equity of a tax system, it is important to remember a lesson from the study of tax incidence: The distribution of tax burdens is not the same as the distribution of tax bills.

- When considering changes in the tax laws, policymakers often face a tradeoff between efficiency and equity. Much of the debate over tax policy arises because people give different weights to these two goals.

KEY CONCEPTS

budget deficit, p. 257
budget surplus, p. 257
average tax rate, p. 263
marginal tax rate, p. 263

lump-sum tax, p. 263
benefits principle, p. 264
ability-to-pay principle, p. 264
vertical equity, p. 265

horizontal equity, p. 265
proportional tax, p. 265
regressive tax, p. 265
progressive tax, p. 265

QUESTIONS FOR REVIEW

1. Over the past several decades, has government grown more or less slowly than the rest of the economy?

2. What are the two most important sources of revenue for the federal government?

3. Why is the burden of a tax to taxpayers greater than the revenue received by the government?

4. Why do some economists advocate taxing consumption rather than income?

5. Give two arguments why wealthy taxpayers should pay more taxes than poor taxpayers.

6. What is the concept of horizontal equity, and why is it hard to apply?

PROBLEMS AND APPLICATIONS

1. Government spending in Canada has grown as a share of national income over time. What changes in our economy and our society might explain this trend? Do you expect the trend to continue?

2. In a published source or on the Internet, find out whether the Canadian federal government had a budget deficit or surplus last year. What do policymakers expect to happen over the next few years?

3. Many of the tables in this chapter use data from Statistics Canada. To answer the following questions, use any Statistics Canada data source that is available to you, such as CANSIM (Statistics Canada's online database) or Statistics Canada catalogues. Provide some numbers to support your answers.
   a. Figure 12.1 (p. 252) shows that government revenue as a percentage of total income has increased over time. Is this increase primarily attributable to changes in federal government revenue or in provincial/territorial and local government revenue?
   b. Looking at the combined revenue of the federal government and provincial/territorial and local governments, how has the composition of total revenue changed

over time? Are personal income taxes more or less important? Sales taxes? Corporate profits taxes?
   c. Looking at federal government transfers to the provinces and territories, have these transfers increased or decreased over time as a share of total provincial/territorial revenue?

4. Explain how individuals' behaviour is affected by the following features of the federal tax laws.
   a. Contributions to charity are tax deductible.
   b. Sales of beer are taxed.
   c. Realized capital gains are taxed, but accrued gains are not. (When someone owns a share of stock that rises in value, she has an "accrued" capital gain. If she sells the share, she has a "realized" gain.)

5. Suppose that your province raises its sales tax from 5 percent to 6 percent. The government forecasts a 20 percent increase in sales tax revenue. Is this plausible? Explain.

6. Categorize each of the following funding schemes as examples of the benefits principle or the ability-to-pay principle.
   a. Visitors to many national parks pay an entrance fee.

b. Local property taxes support elementary and secondary schools.

c. An airport trust fund collects a tax on each plane ticket sold and uses the money to improve airports and the air traffic control system.

7. Any income tax schedule embodies two types of tax rates—average tax rates and marginal tax rates.

a. The average tax rate is defined as total taxes paid divided by income. For the proportional tax system presented in Table 12.8 (p. 265), what are the average tax rates for people earning $50 000, $100 000, and $200 000? What are the corresponding average tax rates in the regressive and progressive tax systems?

b. The marginal tax rate is defined as the extra taxes paid on additional income divided by the increase in income. Calculate the marginal tax rate for the proportional tax system as income rises from $50 000 to $100 000. Calculate the marginal tax rate as income rises from $100 000 to $200 000. Calculate the corresponding marginal tax rates for the regressive and progressive tax systems.

c. Describe the relationship between average tax rates and marginal tax rates for each of these three systems. In general, which rate is relevant for someone deciding whether to accept a job that pays slightly more than her current job? Which rate is relevant for judging the vertical equity of a tax system?

8. If a salesman takes a client to lunch, part of the cost of the lunch is a deductible business expense for his company. Some MPs have argued that this feature of the tax laws benefits relatively wealthy businesspeople and should

be eliminated. Yet their arguments have been met with greater opposition from eating and drinking establishments than from companies themselves. Explain.

9. Provincial/territorial welfare programs have very high "clawback" rates. For example, when a person receiving welfare earns money from employment, that person's welfare benefits decline by as much as 75 cents for each dollar earned. What do you think is the effect of this feature of welfare programs on the labour supply of low-income individuals? Explain.

10. Federal payroll taxes to fund the EI program are levied at a combined rate of 4.51 percent up to an income ceiling of $47 400.

a. If there was no limit on the income level at which these taxes apply, would they be proportional, progressive, or regressive? With the limit, are the taxes proportional, progressive, or regressive?

b. The amount of EI benefits that people receive depends on the amount of payroll taxes they paid. Relative to people who had low earnings, people who had higher earnings and paid more in taxes receive more benefits, but not proportionally more. Does this feature of the EI system make EI a progressive or a regressive payroll tax?

11. What is the efficiency justification for taxing consumption rather than income? Suppose that Ottawa reduced personal tax rates and, to raise the same amount of revenue, increased the GST rate. Would this make the Canadian tax system more or less progressive? Explain.

12. Payroll taxes to fund the EI system are paid by both employees and employers. Does this legal division of responsibility indicate the true incidence of these taxes? Explain.

http:// For more study tools, please visit www.nelson.com/mankiwmicro6e.

FIRM BEHAVIOUR AND THE ORGANIZATION OF INDUSTRY

5

THE COSTS OF PRODUCTION

13

Learning Objectives

In this chapter, you will...

- Examine what items are included in a firm's costs of production

- Analyze the link between a firm's production process and its total costs

- Learn the meaning of average total cost and marginal cost and how they are related

- Consider the shape of a typical firm's cost curves

- Examine the relationship between short-run and long-run costs

Chad Mcdermott/Dreamstime.com

The economy is made up of thousands of firms that produce the goods and services you enjoy every day: General Motors produces automobiles, General Electric produces light bulbs, and General Mills produces breakfast cereals. Some firms, such as these three, are large; they employ thousands of workers and have thousands of shareholders who share in the firms' profits. Other firms, such as the local barbershop or candy store, are small; they employ only a few workers and are owned by a single person or family.

In previous chapters we used the supply curve to summarize firms' production decisions. According to the law of supply, firms are willing to produce and sell a greater quantity of a good when the price of the good is higher, and this response leads to a supply curve that slopes upward. For analyzing many questions, the law of supply is all you need to know about firm behaviour.

In this chapter and the ones that follow, we examine firm behaviour in more detail. This topic will give you a better understanding of what decisions lie behind the supply curve in a market. In addition, it will introduce you to a part of economics called *industrial organization*—the study of how firms' decisions regarding prices and quantities depend on the market conditions they face. The town in which you live, for instance, may have several pizzerias but only one cable television company. How does this difference in the number of firms affect the prices in these markets and the efficiency of the market outcomes? The field of industrial organization addresses exactly this question.

Before we turn to these issues, however, we need to discuss the costs of production. All firms, from Bell Canada Enterprises to your local deli, incur costs as they produce the goods and carry out the services that they sell. As we will see in the coming chapters, a firm's costs are a key determinant of its production and pricing decisions. In this chapter, we define some of the variables that economists use to measure a firm's costs, and we consider the relationships among them.

A word of warning: This topic can seem dry and technical. To be honest, some might even call it boring. But it provides a crucial foundation for the fascinating topics that follow.

WHAT ARE COSTS?

We begin our discussion of costs at Hungry Helen's Cookie Factory. Helen, the owner of the firm, buys flour, sugar, chocolate chips, and other cookie ingredients. She also buys the mixers and ovens, and hires workers to run this equipment. She then sells the resulting cookies to consumers. By examining some of the issues that Helen faces in her business, we can learn some lessons about costs that apply to all firms in the economy.

Total Revenue, Total Cost, and Profit

We begin with the firm's objective. To understand what decisions a firm makes, we must understand what it is trying to do. It is conceivable that Helen started her firm because of an altruistic desire to provide the world with cookies or, perhaps, out of love for the cookie business. More likely, Helen started her business to make money. Economists normally assume that the goal of a firm is to maximize profit, and they find that this assumption works well in most cases.

total revenue (for a firm)
the amount a firm receives for the sale of its output

total cost
the market value of the inputs a firm uses in production

profit
total revenue minus total cost

What is a firm's profit? The amount that the firm receives for the sale of its output (cookies) is called its **total revenue**. The amount that the firm pays to buy inputs (flour, sugar, workers, ovens, etc.) is called its **total cost**. Helen gets to keep any revenue that is not needed to cover costs. **Profit** is a firm's total revenue minus its total cost. That is,

$$\text{Profit} = \text{Total revenue} - \text{Total cost}$$

Helen's objective is to make her firm's profit as large as possible.

To see how a firm goes about maximizing profit, we must consider fully how to measure its total revenue and its total cost. Total revenue is the easy part: It equals the quantity of output the firm produces times the price at which it sells its output. If Helen produces 10 000 cookies and sells them at $2 a cookie, her total revenue is $20 000. By contrast, the measurement of a firm's total cost is more subtle.

Costs as Opportunity Costs

When measuring costs at Hungry Helen's Cookie Factory or any other firm, it is important to keep in mind one of the ten principles of economics from Chapter 1: The cost of something is what you give up to get it. Recall that the *opportunity cost* of an item refers to all those things that must be forgone to acquire that item. When economists speak of a firm's cost of production, they include all the opportunity costs of making its output of goods and services.

— Opportunity Cost including in total cost

While some of a firm's opportunity costs of production are obvious, others are less so. When Helen pays $1000 for flour, that $1000 is an opportunity cost because Helen can no longer use that $1000 to buy something else. Similarly, when Helen hires workers to make the cookies, the wages she pays are part of the firm's costs. Because these costs require the firm to pay out some money, they are called **explicit costs**. By contrast, some of a firm's opportunity costs, called **implicit costs**, do not require a cash outlay. Imagine that Helen is skilled with computers and could earn $100 per hour working as a programmer. For every hour that Helen works at her cookie factory, she gives up $100 in income, and this forgone income is also part of her costs.

This distinction between explicit and implicit costs highlights an important difference between how economists and accountants analyze a business. Economists are interested in studying how firms make production and pricing decisions. Because these decisions are based on both explicit and implicit costs, economists include both when measuring a firm's costs. By contrast, accountants have the job of keeping track of the money that flows into and out of firms. As a result, they measure the explicit costs but often ignore the implicit costs.

The difference between economists and accountants is easy to see in the case of Hungry Helen's Cookie Factory. When Helen gives up the opportunity to earn money as a computer programmer, her accountant will not count this as a cost of her cookie business. Because no money flows out of the business to pay for this cost, it never shows up on the accountant's financial statements. An economist, however, will count the forgone income as a cost because it will affect the decisions that Helen makes in her cookie business. For example, if Helen's wage as a computer programmer rises from $100 to $500 per hour, she might decide that running her cookie business is too costly and choose to shut down the factory to become a full-time computer programmer.

explicit costs
input costs that require an outlay of money by the firm

implicit costs
input costs that do not require an outlay of money by the firm

The Cost of Capital as an Opportunity Cost

An important implicit cost of almost every business is the opportunity cost of the financial capital that has been invested in the business. Suppose, for instance, that Helen used $300 000 of her savings to buy her cookie factory from the previous owner. If Helen had instead left this money deposited in a savings account that pays an interest rate of 5 percent, she would have earned $15 000 per year. To own her cookie factory, therefore, Helen has given up $15 000 per year in interest income. This forgone $15 000 is one of the implicit opportunity costs of Helen's business.

As we have already noted, economists and accountants treat costs differently, and this is especially true in their treatment of the cost of capital. An economist views the $15 000 in interest income that Helen gives up every year as a cost of her business, even though it is an implicit cost. Helen's accountant, however, will not show this $15 000 as a cost because no money flows out of the business to pay for it.

To further explore the difference between economists and accountants, let's change the example slightly. Suppose now that Helen did not have the entire $300 000 to buy the factory but, instead, used $100 000 of her own savings and borrowed $200 000 from a bank at an interest rate of 5 percent. Helen's accountant, who measures only explicit costs, will now count the $10 000 interest paid on the bank loan every year as a cost because this amount of money now flows out of the firm. By contrast, according to an economist, the opportunity cost of owning the business is still $15 000. The opportunity cost equals the interest on the bank loan (an explicit cost of $10 000) plus the forgone interest on savings (an implicit cost of $5000).

Economic Profit versus Accounting Profit

economic profit
total revenue minus total cost, including both explicit and implicit costs

accounting profit
total revenue minus total explicit cost

Now let's return to the firm's objective—profit. Because economists and accountants measure costs differently, they also measure profit differently. An economist measures a firm's **economic profit** as the firm's total revenue minus all the opportunity costs (explicit and implicit) of producing the goods and services sold. An accountant measures the firm's **accounting profit** as the firm's total revenue minus only the firm's explicit costs.

Figure 13.1 summarizes this difference. Notice that because the accountant ignores the implicit costs, accounting profit is usually larger than economic profit. For a business to be profitable from an economist's standpoint, total revenue must cover all the opportunity costs, both explicit and implicit.

Economic profit is an important concept because it is what motivates the firms that supply goods and services. As we will see, a firm making positive economic profit will stay in business. It is covering all its opportunity costs and has some revenue left to reward the firm owners. When a firm is making economic losses (that is, when economic profits are negative), the business owners are failing to make enough to cover all the costs of production. Unless conditions change, the firm owners will eventually close the business down and exit the industry. To understand how industries evolve, we need to keep an eye on economic profit.

QuickQuiz   Farmer McDonald gives banjo lessons for $20 an hour. One day, he spends 10 hours planting $100 worth of seeds on his farm. What opportunity cost has he incurred? What cost would his accountant measure? If these seeds will yield $200 worth of crops, does McDonald earn an accounting profit? Does he earn an economic profit?

FIGURE 13.1

Economists versus Accountants

Economists include all opportunity costs when analyzing a firm, whereas accountants measure only explicit costs. Therefore, economic profit is smaller than accounting profit.

PRODUCTION AND COSTS

Firms incur costs when they buy inputs to produce the goods and services that they plan to sell. In this section we examine the link between a firm's production process and its total cost. Once again, we consider Hungry Helen's Cookie Factory.

In the analysis that follows, we make an important simplifying assumption: We assume that the size of Helen's factory is fixed and that Helen can vary the quantity of cookies produced only by changing the number of workers. This assumption is realistic in the short run, but not in the long run. That is, Helen cannot build a larger factory overnight, but she can do so within a year or so. This analysis, therefore, should be viewed as describing the production decisions that Helen faces in the short run. We examine the relationship between costs and time horizon more fully later in the chapter.

The Production Function

Table 13.1 shows how the quantity of cookies Helen's factory produces per hour depends on the number of workers. As you see in the first two columns, if there are no workers in the factory, Helen produces no cookies. When there is 1 worker, she produces 50 cookies. When there are 2 workers, she produces 90 cookies, and so on. Panel (a) of Figure 13.2 presents a graph of these two columns of numbers. The number of workers is on the horizontal axis, and the number of cookies produced is on the vertical axis. This relationship between the quantity of inputs (workers) and quantity of output (cookies) is called the **production function**.

One of the ten principles of economics introduced in Chapter 1 is that rational people think at the margin. As we will see in future chapters, this idea is the key to understanding the decision a firm makes about how many workers to hire and how much output to produce. To take a step toward understanding these decisions, the third column in the table gives the marginal product of a worker.

production function
the relationship between quantity of inputs used to make a good and the quantity of output of that good

TABLE 13.1

A Production Function and Total Cost: Hungry Helen's Cookie Factory

Number of Workers	Output (quantity of cookies produced per hour)	Marginal Product of Labour	Cost of Factory	Cost of Workers	Total Cost of Inputs (cost of factory + cost of workers)
0	0		$30	$ 0	$30
		50			
1	50		30	10	40
		40			
2	90		30	20	50
		30			
3	120		30	30	60
		20			
4	140		30	40	70
		10			
5	150		30	50	80

FIGURE 13.2

(a) Hungry Helen's Production Function

A production function shows the relationship between the number of workers hired and the quantity of output produced. Here the number of workers hired (on the horizontal axis) is from the first column in Table 13.1, and the quantity of output produced (on the vertical axis) is from the second column. The production function gets flatter as the number of workers increases, which reflects diminishing marginal product.

(b) Hungry Helen's Total-Cost Curve

A total-cost curve shows the relationship between the quantity of output produced and total cost of production. Here the quantity of output produced (on the horizontal axis) is from the second column in Table 13.1, and the total cost (on the vertical axis) is from the sixth column. The total-cost curve gets steeper as the quantity of output increases because of diminishing marginal product.

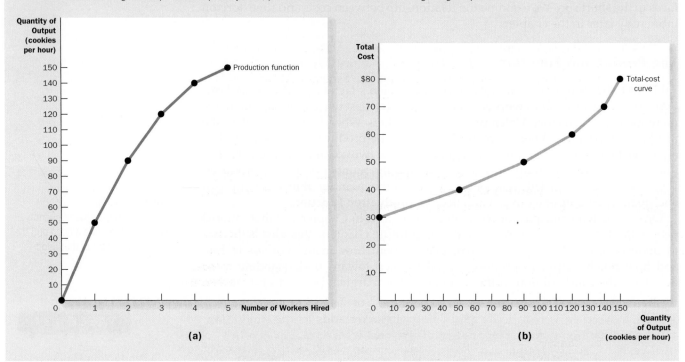

(a)

(b)

marginal product
the increase in output that arises from an additional unit of input

diminishing marginal product
the property whereby the marginal product of an input declines as the quantity of the input increases

The **marginal product** of any input in the production process is the increase in the quantity of output obtained from one additional unit of that input, holding all other inputs constant. When the number of workers goes from 1 to 2, cookie production increases from 50 to 90, so the marginal product of the second worker is 40 cookies. And when the number of workers goes from 2 to 3, cookie production increases from 90 to 120, so the marginal product of the third worker is 30 cookies. In the table, the marginal product is shown halfway between two rows because it represents the change in output as the number of workers increases from one level to another.

Notice that as the number of workers increases, the marginal product declines. The second worker has a marginal product of 40 cookies, the third worker has a marginal product of 30 cookies, and the fourth worker has a marginal product of 20 cookies. This property is called **diminishing marginal product**. At first, when only a few workers are hired, they have easy access to Helen's kitchen equipment.

As the number of workers increases, additional workers have to share equipment and work in more crowded conditions. Eventually, the kitchen is so crowded that the workers start getting in each other's way. Hence, as more and more workers are hired, each additional worker contributes fewer additional cookies to total production.

Diminishing marginal product is also apparent in Figure 13.2. The production function's slope (rise over run) tells us the change in Helen's output of cookies (rise) for each additional input of labour (run). That is, the slope of the production function measures the marginal product of a worker. As the number of workers increases, the marginal product declines, and the production function becomes flatter.

From the Production Function to the Total-Cost Curve

The last three columns of Table 13.1 show Helen's cost of producing cookies. In this example, the cost of Helen's factory is $30 per hour, and the cost of a worker is $10 per hour. If she hires 1 worker, her total cost is $40. If she hires 2 workers, her total cost is $50, and so on. With this information, the table now shows how the number of workers Helen hires is related to the quantity of cookies she produces and to her total cost of production.

Our goal in the next several chapters is to study firms' production and pricing decisions. For this purpose, the most important relationship in Table 13.1 is between quantity produced (in the second column) and total costs (in the sixth column). Panel (b) of Figure 13.2 graphs these two columns of data with the quantity produced on the horizontal axis and total cost on the vertical axis. This graph is called the *total-cost curve.*

Now compare the total-cost curve in panel (b) with the production function in panel (a). These two curves are opposite sides of the same coin. The total-cost curve gets steeper as the amount produced rises, whereas the production function gets flatter as production rises. These changes in slope occur for the same reason. High production of cookies means that Helen's kitchen is crowded with many workers. Because the kitchen is crowded, each additional worker adds less to production, reflecting diminishing marginal product. Therefore, the production function is relatively flat. But now turn this logic around: When the kitchen is crowded, producing an additional cookie requires a lot of additional labour and is thus very costly. Therefore, when the quantity produced is large, the total-cost curve is relatively steep.

QuickQuiz   If Farmer Jones plants no seeds on his farm, he gets no harvest. If he plants 1 bag of seeds, he gets 3 bushels of wheat. If he plants 2 bags, he gets 5 bushels. If he plants 3 bags, he gets 6 bushels. A bag of seeds costs $100, and seeds are his only cost. Use these data to graph the farmer's production function and total-cost curve. Explain their shapes.

THE VARIOUS MEASURES OF COST

Our analysis of Hungry Helen's Cookie Factory demonstrated how a firm's total cost reflects its production function. From data on a firm's total cost, we can derive several related measures of cost, which will turn out to be useful when we

TABLE 13.2

The Various Measures of Cost: Thirsty Thelma's Lemonade Stand

Quantity of Lemonade (glasses per hour)	Total Cost	Fixed Cost	Variable Cost	Average Fixed Cost	Average Variable Cost	Average Total Cost	Marginal Cost
0	$3.00	$3.00	$0.00	—	—	—	
							$0.30
1	3.30	3.00	0.30	$3.00	$0.30	$3.30	
							0.50
2	3.80	3.00	0.80	1.50	0.40	1.90	
							0.70
3	4.50	3.00	1.50	1.00	0.50	1.50	
							0.90
4	5.40	3.00	2.40	0.75	0.60	1.35	
							1.10
5	6.50	3.00	3.50	0.60	0.70	1.30	
							1.30
6	7.80	3.00	4.80	0.50	0.80	1.30	
							1.50
7	9.30	3.00	6.30	0.43	0.90	1.33	
							1.70
8	11.00	3.00	8.00	0.38	1.00	1.38	
							1.90
9	12.90	3.00	9.90	0.33	1.10	1.43	
							2.10
10	15.00	3.00	12.00	0.30	1.20	1.50	

analyze production and pricing decisions in future chapters. To see how these related measures are derived, we consider the example in Table 13.2. This table presents cost data on Helen's neighbour: Thirsty Thelma's Lemonade Stand.

The first column of the table shows the number of glasses of lemonade that Thelma might produce, ranging from 0 to 10 glasses per hour. The second column shows Thelma's total cost of producing lemonade. Figure 13.3 plots Thelma's total-cost curve. The quantity of lemonade (from the first column) is on the horizontal axis, and total cost (from the second column) is on the vertical axis. Thirsty Thelma's total-cost curve has a shape similar to Hungry Helen's. In particular, it becomes steeper as the quantity produced rises, which (as we have discussed) reflects diminishing marginal product.

Fixed and Variable Costs

fixed costs
costs that do not vary with the quantity of output produced

Thelma's total cost can be divided into two types. Some costs, called **fixed costs**, do not vary with the quantity of output produced. They are incurred even if the firm produces nothing at all. Thelma's fixed costs include any rent she pays because this cost is the same regardless of how much lemonade Thelma produces. Similarly, if

FIGURE 13.3

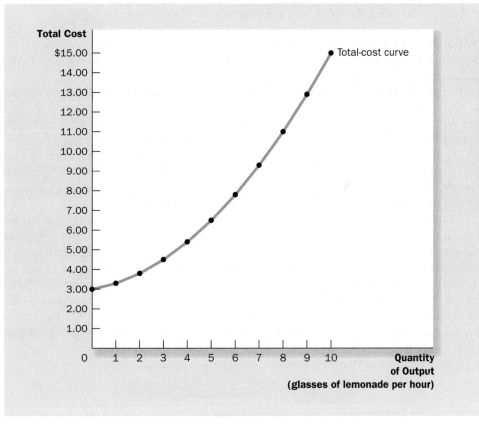

Thirsty Thelma's Total-Cost Curve

Here the quantity of output produced (on the horizontal axis) is from the first column in Table 13.2, and the total cost (on the vertical axis) is from the second column. As in panel (b) of Figure 13.2, the total-cost curve gets steeper as the quantity of output increases because of diminishing marginal product.

Thelma needs to hire a full-time bookkeeper to pay bills, regardless of the quantity of lemonade produced, the bookkeeper's salary is a fixed cost. The third column in Table 13.2 shows Thelma's fixed cost, which in this example is $3.00.

Some of the firm's costs, called **variable costs**, change as the firm alters the quantity of output produced. Thelma's variable costs include the cost of lemons, sugar, paper cups, and straws: The more lemonade Thelma makes, the more of these items she needs to buy. Similarly, if Thelma has to hire more workers to make more lemonade, the salaries of these workers are variable costs. The fourth column of the table shows Thelma's variable cost. The variable cost is 0 if she produces nothing, $0.30 if she produces 1 glass of lemonade, $0.80 if she produces 2 glasses, and so on.

A firm's total cost is the sum of fixed and variable costs. In Table 13.2, total cost in the second column equals fixed cost in the third column plus variable cost in the fourth column.

variable costs
costs that do vary with the quantity of output produced

Average and Marginal Costs

As the owner of her firm, Thelma has to decide how much to produce. A key part of this decision is how her costs will vary as she changes the level of production. In making this decision, Thelma might ask her production supervisor the following two questions about the cost of producing lemonade:

- How much does it cost to make the typical glass of lemonade?
- How much does it cost to increase production of lemonade by 1 glass?

Although at first these two questions might seem to have the same answer, they do not. Both answers will turn out to be important for understanding how firms make production decisions.

To find the cost of the typical unit produced, we would divide the firm's costs by the quantity of output it produces. For example, if the firm produces 2 glasses per hour, its total cost is $3.80, and the cost of the typical glass is $3.80/2, or $1.90. Total cost divided by the quantity of output is called **average total cost**. Because total cost is just the sum of fixed and variable costs, average total cost can be expressed as the sum of average fixed cost and average variable cost. **Average fixed cost** is the fixed cost divided by the quantity of output, and **average variable cost** is the variable cost divided by the quantity of output.

Average total cost tells us the cost of the typical unit, but it does not tell us how much total cost will change as the firm alters its level of production. The last column in Table 13.2 shows the amount that total cost rises when the firm increases production by 1 unit of output. This number is called **marginal cost**. For example, if Thelma increases production from 2 to 3 glasses, total cost rises from $3.80 to $4.50, so the marginal cost of the third glass of lemonade is $4.50 minus $3.80, or $0.70. In the table, the marginal cost appears halfway between the two rows because it represents a change in total cost as quantity of output increases from one level to another.

It may be helpful to express these definitions mathematically:

$$\text{Average total cost} = \text{Total cost/Quantity}$$

$$ATC = TC/Q$$

and

$$\text{Marginal cost} = \text{Change in total cost/Change in quantity}$$

$$MC = \Delta TC/\Delta Q$$

Here Δ, the Greek letter *delta*, represents the change in a variable. These equations show how average total cost and marginal cost are derived from total cost. *Average total cost tells us the cost of a typical unit of output if total cost is divided evenly over all the units produced. Marginal cost tells us the increase in total cost that arises from producing an additional unit of output.* As we will see more fully in the next chapter, Thelma, our lemonade entrepreneur, will find the concepts of average total cost and marginal cost useful when deciding how much lemonade to produce.

Cost Curves and Their Shapes

Just as in previous chapters we found graphs of supply and demand useful when analyzing the behaviour of markets, we will find graphs of average and marginal cost useful when analyzing the behaviour of firms. Figure 13.4 graphs Thelma's costs using the data from Table 13.2. The horizontal axis measures the quantity the firm produces, and the vertical axis measures marginal and average costs.

average total cost
total cost divided by the quantity of output

average fixed cost
fixed costs divided by the quantity of output

average variable cost
variable costs divided by the quantity of output

marginal cost
the increase in total cost that arises from an extra unit of production

Costs

Thirsty Thelma's Average-Cost and Marginal-Cost Curves

This figure shows the average total cost (ATC), average fixed cost (AFC), average variable cost (AVC), and marginal cost (MC) for Thirsty Thelma's Lemonade Stand. All of these curves are obtained by graphing the data in Table 13.2. These cost curves show three features that are typical of many firms: (1) Marginal cost rises with the quantity of output. (2) The average-total-cost curve is U-shaped. (3) The marginal-cost curve crosses the average-total-cost curve at the minimum of average total cost.

The graph shows four curves: average total cost (*ATC*), average fixed cost (*AFC*), average variable cost (*AVC*), and marginal cost (*MC*).

The cost curves shown here for Thirsty Thelma's Lemonade Stand have some features that are common to the cost curves of many firms in the economy. Let's examine three features in particular: the shape of marginal cost, the shape of average total cost, and the relationship between marginal and average total cost.

Rising Marginal Cost   Thirsty Thelma's marginal cost rises with the quantity of output produced. This reflects the property of diminishing marginal product. When Thelma is producing a small quantity of lemonade, she has few workers and much of her equipment is not being used. Because she can easily put these idle resources to use, the marginal product of an extra worker is large, and the marginal cost of an extra glass of lemonade is small. By contrast, when Thelma is producing a large quantity of lemonade, her stand is crowded with workers and most of her equipment is fully utilized. Thelma can produce more lemonade by adding workers, but these new workers have to work in crowded conditions and may have to wait to use the equipment. Therefore, when the quantity of lemonade being produced is already high, the marginal product of an extra worker is low, and the marginal cost of an extra glass of lemonade is large.

U-Shaped Average Total Cost   Thirsty Thelma's average-total-cost curve is U-shaped. To understand why this is so, remember that average total cost is the sum of average fixed cost and average variable cost. Average fixed cost always declines as output rises because the fixed cost is spread over a larger number of units. Average variable cost typically rises as output increases because of diminishing marginal product.

Average total cost reflects the shapes of both average fixed cost and average variable cost. As shown in Figure 13.4, at very low levels of output, such as 1 or 2 glasses of lemonade per hour, average total cost is very high. Even though average variable cost is low, average fixed cost is high because the fixed cost is spread over only a few units. As output increases, the fixed cost is spread more widely. Average fixed cost declines, rapidly at first and then more slowly. As a result, average total cost also declines until Thirsty Thelma's output reaches 5 glasses of lemonade per hour, when average total cost is $1.30 per glass. When the firm produces more than 6 glasses of lemonade per hour, however, the increase in average variable cost becomes the dominant force, and average total cost starts rising. The tug of war between average fixed cost and average variable cost generates the U-shape in average total cost.

The bottom of the U-shape occurs at the quantity that minimizes average total cost. This quantity is sometimes called the **efficient scale** of the firm. For Thirsty Thelma, the efficient scale is 5 or 6 glasses of lemonade per hour. If she produces more or less than this amount, her average total cost rises above the minimum of $1.30. At lower levels of output, average total cost is higher than $1.30 because the fixed cost is spread over so few units. At higher levels of output, average total cost is higher than $1.30 because the marginal product of inputs has diminished significantly. At the efficient scale, these two forces are balanced to yield the lowest average total cost.

efficient scale
the quantity of output that minimizes average total cost

The Relationship between Marginal Cost and Average Total Cost

If you look at Figure 13.4 (or back at Table 13.2), you will see something that may be surprising at first. *Whenever marginal cost is less than average total cost, average total cost is falling. Whenever marginal cost is greater than average total cost, average total cost is rising.* This feature of Thirsty Thelma's cost curves is not a coincidence from the particular numbers used in the example: It is true for all firms.

To see why, consider an analogy. Average total cost is like your cumulative grade point average. Marginal cost is like the grade in the next course you will take. If your grade in your next course is less than your grade point average, your grade point average will fall. If your grade in your next course is higher than your grade point average, your grade point average will rise. The mathematics of average and marginal costs is exactly the same as the mathematics of average and marginal grades.

This relationship between average total cost and marginal cost has an important corollary: *The marginal-cost curve crosses the average-total-cost curve at its minimum.* Why? At low levels of output, marginal cost is below average total cost, so average total cost is falling. But after the two curves cross, marginal cost rises above average total cost. For the reason we have just discussed, average total cost must start to rise at this level of output. Hence, this point of intersection is the minimum of average total cost. As you will see in the next chapter,

FIGURE 13.5

Typical Cost Curves

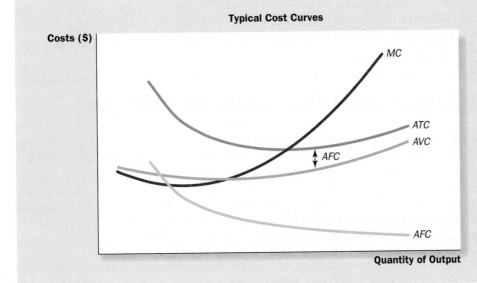

Costs ($)

MC

ATC

AVC

AFC

AFC

Quantity of Output

Cost Curves for a Typical Firm

Many firms experience increasing marginal product before diminishing marginal product. As a result, they have cost curves shaped like those in this figure. Notice that marginal cost and average variable cost fall for a while before starting to rise.

this point of minimum average total cost plays a key role in the analysis of competitive firms.

Typical Cost Curves

In the examples we have studied so far, the firms exhibit diminishing marginal product and, therefore, rising marginal cost at all levels of output. Yet actual firms are often a bit more complicated than this. In many firms, diminishing marginal product does not start to occur immediately after the first worker is hired. Depending on the production process, the second or third worker might have higher marginal product than the first because a team of workers can divide tasks and work more productively than a single worker. Such firms would first experience increasing marginal product for a while before diminishing marginal product sets in.

Figure 13.5 shows the cost curves for such a firm, including average total cost (*ATC*), average fixed cost (*AFC*), average variable cost (*AVC*), and marginal cost (*MC*). At low levels of output, the firm experiences increasing marginal product, and the marginal-cost curve falls. Eventually, the firm starts to experience diminishing marginal product, and the marginal-cost curve starts to rise. This combination of increasing and then diminishing marginal product also makes the average-variable-cost curve U-shaped.

Despite these differences from the Thirsty Thelma example, the cost curves shown here share the three properties that are most important to remember:

1. Marginal cost eventually rises with the quantity of output.
2. The average-total-cost curve is U-shaped.
3. The marginal-cost curve crosses the average-total-cost curve at the minimum of average total cost.

QuickQuiz   Suppose Honda's total cost of producing 4 cars is $225 000 and its total cost of producing 5 cars is $250 000. What is the average total cost of producing 5 cars? What is the marginal cost of the fifth car? • Draw the marginal-cost curve and the average-total-cost curve for a typical firm, and explain why these curves cross where they do.

COSTS IN THE SHORT RUN AND IN THE LONG RUN

We noted earlier in this chapter that a firm's costs might depend on the time horizon being examined. Let's examine more precisely why this might be the case.

The Relationship between Short-Run and Long-Run Average Total Cost

For many firms, the division of total costs between fixed and variable costs depends on the time horizon. Consider, for instance, a car manufacturer, such as Ford Motor Company. Over a period of only a few months, Ford cannot adjust the number or sizes of its car factories. The only way it can produce additional cars is to hire more workers at the factories it already has. The cost of these factories is, therefore, a fixed cost in the short run. By contrast, over a period of several years, Ford can expand the size of its factories, build new factories, or close old ones. Thus, the cost of its factories is a variable cost in the long run.

Because many decisions are fixed in the short run but variable in the long run, a firm's long-run cost curves differ from its short-run cost curves. Figure 13.6 shows

FIGURE 13.6

Average Total Cost in the Short and Long Runs

Because fixed costs are variable in the long run, the average-total-cost curve in the short run differs from the average-total-cost curve in the long run.

an example. The figure presents three short-run average-total-cost curves—for a small, medium, and large factory. It also presents the long-run average-total-cost curve. As the firm moves along the long-run curve, it is adjusting the size of the factory to the quantity of production.

This graph shows how short-run and long-run costs are related. The long-run average-total-cost curve is a much flatter U-shape than the short-run average-total-cost curve. In addition, all the short-run curves lie on or above the long-run curve. These properties arise because firms have greater flexibility in the long run. In essence, in the long run, the firm gets to choose which short-run curve it wants to use. But in the short run, it has to use whatever short-run curve it chose in the past.

The figure shows an example of how a change in production alters costs over different time horizons. When Ford wants to increase production from 1000 to 1200 cars per day, it has no choice in the short run but to hire more workers at its existing medium-sized factory. Because of diminishing marginal product, average total cost rises from $10 000 to $12 000 per car. In the long run, however, Ford can expand both the size of the factory and its workforce, and average total cost returns to $10 000.

How long does it take for a firm to get to the long run? The answer depends on the firm. It can take a year or longer for a major manufacturing firm, such as a car company, to build a larger factory. By contrast, a person running a lemonade stand can go and buy a larger pitcher within an hour or less. There is, therefore, no single answer about how long it takes a firm to adjust its production facilities.

Economies and Diseconomies of Scale

The shape of the long-run average-total-cost curve conveys important information about the technology for producing a good. When long-run average total cost declines as output increases, there are said to be **economies of scale**. When long-run average total cost rises as output increases, there are said to be **diseconomies of scale**. When long-run average total cost does not vary with the level of output, there are said to be **constant returns to scale**. In this example, Ford has economies of scale at low levels of output, constant returns to scale at intermediate levels of output, and diseconomies of scale at high levels of output.

What might cause economies or diseconomies of scale? Economies of scale often arise because higher production levels allow *specialization* among workers, which permits each worker to become better at his or her assigned tasks. For instance, if Ford hires a large number of workers and produces a large number of cars, it can reduce costs with modern assembly-line production. Diseconomies of scale can arise because of *coordination problems* that are inherent in any large organization. The more cars Ford produces, the more stretched the management team becomes, and the less effective the managers become at keeping costs down.

This analysis shows why long-run average-total-cost curves are often U-shaped. At low levels of production, the firm benefits from increased size because it can take advantage of greater specialization. Coordination problems, meanwhile, are not yet acute. By contrast, at high levels of production,

economies of scale
the property whereby long-run average total cost falls as the quantity of output increases

diseconomies of scale
the property whereby long-run average total cost rises as the quantity of output increases

constant returns to scale
the property whereby long-run average total cost stays the same as the quantity of output changes

IN THE NEWS

THE ECONOMICS OF VERY BIG SHIPS

The following article illustrates how increased trade associated with globalization allows shipping companies to realize huge economies of scale moving goods.

Economies of Scale Made Steel

Aboard one of the world's largest container ships, moving almost imperceptibly through the seas off Vietnam, it's easy to appreciate the economies of scale that allow a T-shirt made in China to be sent to the Netherlands for just 2.5 cents.

The *Eleonora Maersk* and the other seven ships in her class are among the biggest ever built: almost 400 m long, or the length of four football pitches, and another half-pitch across. The ship can carry 7,500 or so 40-foot containers, each of which can hold 70,000 T-shirts. On the voyage your correspondent took, the *Eleonora* was carrying Europe's New Year celebrations: 1,850 tonnes of fireworks, including 30 tonnes of gunpowder.

To move all this cargo from China to Europe in just over three weeks, the *Eleonora* boasts the largest internal-combustion engine ever built, as powerful as 1,000 family cars. This engine turns the longest propeller shaft (130 m) ever made, at the end of which is the largest propeller, at 130 tonnes. Yet the ship is so automated that it requires a mere 13 people to crew it. Reassuringly, most captains prefer to take a few more.

Maersk Lines, the world's biggest container-shipping company and owner of the *Eleonora*, is betting that, given the current economics of world trade, the only way to go is yet bigger. In February

it announced an order for 20 even larger ships with a capacity of 18,000 twenty-foot equivalent units (TEUs), the standard measure of container size. (The *Eleonora* can carry a mere 15,000.) The new ships will cost $200 m each. And judging by this year's order books, Maersk's example will be followed by others. Singapore's Neptune Orient Lines has ordered ten vessels of 14,000 TEUs; Orient Overseas Container Line has ordered ten of 13,000 TEUs. This is excellent news for South Korean shipyards.

Most of these vessels will be designed for the Europe–Asia run—now the world's busiest trade route. Given the rising price of fuel, many shippers think they need huge ships to turn a profit. Fears of a renewed slowdown in global trade accelerate the rush to find economies of scale.

Freight rates have plummeted in recent months, thanks to weakening demand and an oversupply of container ships, many of them ordered in the optimistic years before 2008. Freight rates on the Europe–Asia run are now below $700 per TEU, less than half the peak a year ago. At this price, says Janet Lewis, an analyst at Macquarie, a bank, "It's hard for any container company to be making any cash."

Recent financial results bear this out. On November 9th Maersk said its container business had lost $297 m in the latest quarter. Neptune posted a third-quarter loss of $91 m, having made a profit of $282 m a year earlier. Japan's

"K" Line reported a loss of $239 m on its container-shipping unit in the fiscal first half. And things could get a lot worse.

Companies are searching for new strategies to differentiate themselves from rivals, or merely to survive. Maersk has launched what it calls the "Daily Maersk" service on the China–Europe run, deploying 70 vessels to promise daily deliveries to Felixstowe, Bremerhaven and Rotterdam, the three main European container ports. The firm is hoping to deliver 95% of these containers on time, up from 80% for its own service on that route. This would be far higher than the industry average of about 65%. If a container arrives more than a day late, Maersk pledges to compensate the customer. Orient Overseas, by contrast, is focusing on the quality of its cargo-handling. It charges more, for example, to ship perishable items, such as blood plasma.

Given the stormy waters that may well be ahead, it seems likely that shippers will seek economies of scale not only from bigger ships but also from mergers. The industry is too crowded, many analysts believe. Smaller firms may soon be swallowed like containers vanishing into the hold of the *Eleonora Maersk*.

Source: "Economies of Scale Made Steel." November 12, 2011, p. 72. © The Economist Newspaper Limited, London 2011. All rights reserved. Reprinted with permission. Further reproduction prohibited. www.economist.com

the benefits of specialization have already been realized, and coordination problems become more severe as the firm grows larger. Thus, long-run average total cost is falling at low levels of production because of increasing specialization and rising at high levels of production because of increasing coordination problems.

QuickQuiz   If Bombardier produces 9 jets per month, its long-run total cost is $9.0 million per month. If it produces 10 jets per month, its long-run total cost is $9.5 million per month. Does Bombardier exhibit economies or diseconomies of scale?

CONCLUSION

The purpose of this chapter has been to develop some tools that we can use to study how firms make production and pricing decisions. You should now understand what economists mean by the term *costs* and how costs vary with the quantity of output a firm produces. To refresh your memory, Table 13.3 summarizes some of the definitions we have encountered.

By themselves, of course, a firm's cost curves do not tell us what decisions the firm will make. But they are an important component of that decision, as we will begin to see in the next chapter.

TABLE 13.3

The Many Types of Cost: A Summary

Term	Definition	Mathematical Description
Explicit costs	Costs that require an outlay of money by the firm	—
Implicit costs	Costs that do not require an outlay of money by the firm	—
Fixed costs	Costs that do not vary with the quantity of output produced	FC
Variable costs	Costs that do vary with the quantity of output produced	VC
Total cost	The market value of all the inputs that a firm uses in production	$TC = FC + VC$
Average fixed cost	Fixed costs divided by the quantity of output	$AFC = FC/Q$
Average variable cost	Variable costs divided by the quantity of output	$AVC = VC/Q$
Average total cost	Total cost divided by the quantity of output	$ATC = TC/Q$
Marginal cost	The increase in total cost that arises from an extra unit of production	$MC = \Delta TC/\Delta Q$

SUMMARY

- The goal of firms is to maximize profit, which equals total revenue minus total cost.

- When analyzing a firm's behaviour, it is important to include all the opportunity costs of production. Some of the opportunity costs, such as the wages a firm pays its workers, are explicit. Other opportunity costs, such as the wages the firm owner gives up by working in the firm rather than taking another job, are implicit. Economic profit takes both explicit and implicit costs into account, whereas accounting profit considers only explicit costs.

- A firm's costs reflect its production process. A typical firm's production function becomes flatter as the quantity of an input increases, displaying the property of diminishing marginal product. As a result, a firm's total-cost curve becomes steeper as the quantity produced rises.

- A firm's total costs can be divided between fixed costs and variable costs. Fixed costs are costs that do not change when the firm alters the quantity of output produced. Variable costs are costs that do change when the firm alters the quantity of output produced.

- From a firm's total cost, two related measures of cost are derived. Average total cost is total cost divided by the quantity of output. Marginal cost is the amount by which total cost rises if output increases by 1 unit.

- When analyzing firm behaviour, it is often useful to graph average total cost and marginal cost. For a typical firm, marginal cost rises with the quantity of output. Average total cost first falls as output increases and then rises as output increases further. The marginal-cost curve always crosses the average-total-cost curve at the minimum of average total cost.

- A firm's costs often depend on the time horizon being considered. In particular, many costs are fixed in the short run but variable in the long run. As a result, when the firm changes its level of production, average total cost may rise more in the short run than in the long run.

KEY CONCEPTS

total revenue (for a firm), p. 276
total cost, p. 276
profit, p. 276
explicit costs, p. 277
implicit costs, p. 277
economic profit, p. 278
accounting profit, p. 278

production function, p. 279
marginal product, p. 280
diminishing marginal
  product, p. 280
fixed costs, p. 282
variable costs, p. 283
average total cost, p. 284

average fixed cost, p. 284
average variable cost, p. 284
marginal cost, p. 284
efficient scale, p. 286
economies of scale, p. 289
diseconomies of scale, p. 289
constant returns to scale, p. 289

QUESTIONS FOR REVIEW

1. What is the relationship between a firm's total revenue, profit, and total cost?

2. Give an example of an opportunity cost that an accountant might not count as a cost. Why would the accountant ignore this cost?

3. What is marginal product, and what does it mean if it is diminishing?

4. Draw a production function that exhibits diminishing marginal product of labour. Draw the associated total-cost curve. (In both cases, be sure to label the axes.) Explain the shapes of the two curves you have drawn.

5. Define total cost, average total cost, and marginal cost. How are they related?

6. Draw the marginal-cost and average-total-cost curves for a typical firm. Explain why the curves have the shapes that they do and why they cross where they do.

7. How and why does a firm's average-total-cost curve differ in the short run and in the long run?

8. Define *economies of scale* and explain why they might arise. Define *diseconomies of scale* and explain why they might arise.

PROBLEMS AND APPLICATIONS

1. This chapter discusses many types of costs: opportunity cost, total cost, fixed cost, variable cost, average total cost, and marginal cost. Fill in the type of cost that best completes each phrase below:
   a. The true cost of taking some action is its _____.
   b. _____ is falling when marginal cost is below it, and rising when marginal cost is above it.
   c. A cost that does not depend on the quantity produced is a(n) _____.
   d. In the ice-cream industry in the short run, _____ includes the cost of cream and sugar, but not the cost of the factory.
   e. Profits equal total revenue less _____.
   f. The cost of producing an extra unit of output is the _____.

2. Your aunt is thinking about opening a hardware store. She estimates that it would cost $500 000 per year to rent the location and buy the stock. In addition, she would have to quit her $50 000 per year job as an accountant.
   a. Define *opportunity cost*.
   b. What is your aunt's opportunity cost of running a hardware store for a year? If your aunt thought she could sell $510 000 worth of merchandise in a year, should she open the store? Explain.

3. The city government is considering two tax proposals:
   • a lump-sum tax of $300 on each producer of hamburgers
   • a tax of $1 per burger, paid by producers of hamburgers
   a. Which of the following curves—average fixed cost, average variable cost, average total cost, and marginal cost—would shift as a result of the lump-sum tax? Why? Show this in a graph. Label the graph as precisely as possible.
   b. Which of these same four curves would shift as a result of the per-burger tax? Why? Show this in a new graph. Label the graph as precisely as possible.

4. A commercial fisherman notices the following relationship between hours spent fishing and the quantity of fish caught:

Hours	Quantity of Fish (in kilograms)
0	0
1	10
2	18
3	24
4	28
5	30

   a. What is the marginal product of each hour spent fishing?
   b. Use these data to graph the fisherman's production function. Explain its shape.
   c. The fisherman has a fixed cost of $10 (his pole). The opportunity cost of his time is $5 per hour. Graph the fisherman's total-cost curve. Explain its shape.

5. Nimbus Ltd. makes brooms and then sells them door to door. Here is the relationship between the number of workers and Nimbus's output in a given day:

Workers	Output	Marginal Product	Total Cost	Average Total Cost	Marginal Cost
0	0		____	____	
1	20	____	____	____	____
2	50	____	____	____	____
3	90	____	____	____	____
4	120	____	____	____	____
5	140	____	____	____	____
6	150	____	____	____	____
7	155	____	____	____	____

   a. Fill in the column of marginal products. What pattern do you see? How might you explain it?
   b. A worker costs $100 per day, and the firm has fixed costs of $200. Use this information to fill in the column for total cost.
   c. Fill in the column for average total cost. (Recall that $ATC = TC/Q$.) What pattern do you see?

d. Now fill in the column for marginal cost. (Recall that $MC = \Delta TC/\Delta Q$.) What pattern do you see?

e. Compare the column for marginal product and the column for marginal cost. Explain the relationship.

f. Compare the column for average total cost and the column for marginal cost. Explain the relationship.

6. A firm uses two inputs in production: capital and labour. In the short run, the firm cannot adjust the amount of capital it is using, but it can adjust the size of its workforce. What happens to the firm's average total cost curve, the average variable cost curve, and the marginal cost curve when

a. the cost of renting capital increases?

b. the cost of hiring labour increases?

7. Consider the following cost information for a pizzeria:

Q (dozens)	Total Cost	Variable Cost
0	$300	$ 0
1	350	50
2	390	90
3	420	120
4	450	150
5	490	190
6	540	240

a. What is the pizzeria's fixed cost?

b. Construct a table in which you calculate the marginal cost per dozen pizzas using the information on total cost. Also calculate the marginal cost per dozen pizzas using the information on variable cost. What is the relationship between these sets of numbers? Comment.

8. You are thinking about setting up a lemonade stand. The stand itself costs $200. The ingredients for each cup of lemonade cost $0.50.

a. What is your fixed cost of doing business? What is your variable cost per cup?

b. Construct a table showing your total cost, average total cost, and marginal cost for output levels varying from 0 to 40 L. (Hint: There are 4 cups in a litre.) Draw the three cost curves.

9. Your cousin Vinnie owns a painting company with fixed costs of $200 and the following schedule for variable costs:

Quantity of Houses Painted per Month	1	2	3	4	5	6	7
Variable Costs	$10	$20	$40	$80	$160	$320	$640

Calculate average fixed cost, average variable cost, and average total cost for each quantity. What is the efficient scale of the painting company?

10. Healthy Harry's Juice Bar has the following cost schedules:

Q (vats)	Variable Cost	Total Cost
0	$ 0	$ 30
1	10	40
2	25	55
3	45	75
4	70	100
5	100	130
6	135	165

a. Calculate average variable cost, average total cost, and marginal cost for each quantity.

b. Graph all three curves. What is the relationship between the marginal-cost curve and the average-total-cost curve? Between the marginal-cost curve and the average-variable-cost curve? Explain.

11. Consider the following table of long-run total cost for three different firms:

Quantity	1	2	3	4	5	6	7
Firm A	$60	$70	$80	$90	$100	$110	$120
Firm B	11	24	39	56	75	96	119
Firm C	21	34	49	66	85	106	129

Does each of these firms experience economies of scale or diseconomies of scale?

12. You are the chief financial officer for a firm that sells digital music players. Your firm has the following average total cost schedule:

Quantity	Average Total Cost
600 players	$300
601 players	301

Your current level of production is 600 devices, all of which have been sold. Someone calls, desperate to buy one of your music players. The caller offers you $550 for it. Should you accept the offer? Why or why not?

http://

For more study tools, please visit www.nelson.com/mankiwmicro6e.

FIRMS IN COMPETITIVE MARKETS

Learning Objectives

In this chapter, you will...

- Learn what characteristics make a market competitive
- Examine how competitive firms decide how much output to produce
- Examine how competitive firms decide when to shut down production temporarily
- Examine how competitive firms decide whether to exit or enter a market
- See how firm behaviour determines a market's short-run and long-run supply curves

14

If your local gas station raised the price it charges for gasoline by 20 percent, it would see a large drop in the amount of gasoline it sold. Its customers would quickly switch to buying their gasoline at other gas stations. By contrast, if your local water company raised the price of water by 20 percent, it would see only a small decrease in the amount of water it sold. People might water their lawns less often and buy more water-efficient shower heads, but they would be hard-pressed to reduce water consumption greatly and would be unlikely to find another supplier. The difference between the gasoline market and the water market is obvious: Many firms supply gasoline, but only one firm supplies water. As you might expect, this difference in market structure shapes the pricing and production decisions of the firms that operate in these markets.

In this chapter we examine the behaviour of competitive firms, such as your local gas station. You may recall that a market is competitive if each buyer and seller is small compared to the size of the market and, therefore, has little ability to influence market prices. By contrast, if a firm can influence the market price of the good it sells, it is said to have *market power*. Later in the book, we examine the behaviour of firms with market power, such as your local water company.

Our analysis of competitive firms in this chapter will shed light on the decisions that lie behind the supply curve in a competitive market. Not surprisingly, we will find that a market supply curve is tightly linked to firms' costs of production. Less obvious, however, is the question of which among a firm's various costs—fixed, variable, average, and marginal—are most relevant for its decision about the quantity to supply at any given price. We will see that all these measures of cost play important and interrelated roles.

WHAT IS A COMPETITIVE MARKET?

Our goal in this chapter is to examine how firms make production decisions in competitive markets. As a background for this analysis, we begin by considering what a competitive market is.

The Meaning of Competition

competitive market
a market in which there are many buyers and many sellers so that each has a negligible impact on the market price

Buyers and sellers are "price takers"

A **competitive market**, sometimes called a *perfectly competitive market*, has two characteristics:

1. There are many buyers and many sellers in the market.
2. The goods offered by the various sellers are largely the same.

As a result of these conditions, the actions of any single buyer or seller in the market have a negligible impact on the market price. Each buyer and seller takes the market price as given.

An example is the market for milk. No single buyer of milk can influence the price of milk because each buyer purchases a small amount relative to the size of the market. Similarly, each seller of milk has limited control over the price because many other sellers are offering milk that is essentially identical. Because each seller can sell all he wants to at the going price, he has little reason to charge less, and if he charges more, buyers will go elsewhere. Buyers and sellers in competitive markets must accept the price the market determines and, therefore, are said to be *price takers*.

In addition to the forgoing two conditions for competition, there is a third condition sometimes thought to characterize perfectly competitive markets:

3. Firms can freely enter or exit the market.

If, for instance, anyone can decide to start a dairy farm, and if any existing dairy farmer can decide to leave the dairy business, then the dairy industry would satisfy this condition. It should be noted that much of the analysis of competitive firms does not rely on the assumption of free entry and exit because this condition is not necessary for firms to be price takers. Yet, as we will see later in this chapter, if there is free entry and exit in a competitive market, it is a powerful force in shaping the long-run equilibrium.

The Revenue of a Competitive Firm

A firm in a competitive market, like most other firms in the economy, tries to maximize profit, which equals total revenue minus total cost. To see how it does this, we first consider the revenue of a competitive firm. To keep matters concrete, let's consider a specific firm: the Smith Family Dairy Farm.

The Smith farm produces a quantity of milk, Q, and sells each unit at the market price, P. The farm's total revenue is $P \times Q$. For example, if a 4-L jug of milk sells for $6 and the farm sells 1000 jugs, its total revenue is $6000.

Because the Smith farm is small compared to the country's market for milk, it takes the price as given by market conditions. This means, in particular, that the price of milk does not depend on the quantity of output that the Smith farm produces and sells. If the Smiths double the amount of milk they produce, the price of milk remains the same, and their total revenue doubles. As a result, total revenue is proportional to the amount of output.

Table 14.1 shows the revenue for the Smith Family Dairy Farm. The first two columns show the amount of output the farm produces and the price at which it sells its output. The third column is the farm's total revenue. The table assumes that the price of milk is $6 per jug, so total revenue is simply $6 times the number of jugs.

Just as the concepts of average and marginal were useful in the preceding chapter when analyzing costs, they are also useful when analyzing revenue. To see what these concepts tell us, consider these two questions:

1. How much revenue does the farm receive for the typical jug of milk?
2. How much additional revenue does the farm receive if it increases production of milk by 1 jug?

The last two columns in Table 14.1 answer these questions.

The fourth column in the table shows **average revenue**, which is total revenue (from the third column) divided by the amount of output (from the first column). Average revenue tells us how much revenue a firm receives for the typical unit sold. In Table 14.1, you can see that average revenue equals $6, the price of a jug of milk. This illustrates a general lesson that applies not only to competitive firms but to other firms as well. Total revenue is the price times the quantity $(P \times Q)$, and average revenue is total revenue $(P \times Q)$ divided by the quantity (Q). Therefore, *for all firms, average revenue equals the price of the good.*

average revenue
total revenue divided by the quantity sold

TABLE 14.1

Total, Average, and Marginal Revenue for a Competitive Firm

Quantity (Q)	Price (P)	Total Revenue $(TR = P \times Q)$	Average Revenue $(AR = TR/Q)$	Marginal Revenue $(MR = \Delta TR/\Delta Q)$
1 jug	$6	$ 6	$6	
				$6
2	6	12	6	
				6
3	6	18	6	
				6
4	6	24	6	
				6
5	6	30	6	
				6
6	6	36	6	
				6
7	6	42	6	
				6
8	6	48	6	

marginal revenue
the change in total revenue from
an additional unit sold

The fifth column shows **marginal revenue**, which is the change in total revenue from the sale of each additional unit of output. In Table 14.1, marginal revenue equals $6, the price of a jug of milk. This result illustrates a lesson that applies only to competitive firms. Total revenue is $P \times Q$, and P is fixed for a competitive firm. Therefore, when Q rises by 1 unit, total revenue rises by P dollars. *For competitive firms, marginal revenue equals the price of the good.*

QuickQuiz   When a competitive firm doubles the amount it sells, what happens to the price of its output and its total revenue?

PROFIT MAXIMIZATION AND THE COMPETITIVE FIRM'S SUPPLY CURVE

The goal of a competitive firm is to maximize profit, which equals total revenue minus total cost. We have just discussed the firm's revenue, and in the last chapter we discussed the firm's costs. We are now ready to examine how the firm maximizes profit and how that decision leads to its supply curve.

A Simple Example of Profit Maximization

Let's begin our analysis of the firm's supply decision with the example in Table 14.2. In the first column of the table is the number of 4-L jugs of milk the Smith Family

TABLE 14.2

Profit Maximization: A Numerical Example

Quantity	Total Revenue	Total Cost	Profit	Marginal Revenue	Marginal Cost	Change in Profit
(Q)	(TR)	(TC)	(TR − TC)	(MR = ΔTR/ΔQ)	(MC = ΔTC/ΔQ)	(MR − MC)
0 jugs	$ 0	$ 3	−$3			
				$6	$2	$4
1	6	5	1			
				6	3	3
2	12	8	4			
				6	4	2
3	18	12	6			
				6	5	1
4	24	17	7			
				6	6	0
5	30	23	7			
				6	7	−1
6	36	30	6			
				6	8	−2
7	42	38	4			
				6	9	−3
8	48	47	1			

Dairy Farm produces. The second column shows the farm's total revenue, which is $6 times the number of jugs. The third column shows the farm's total cost. Total cost includes fixed costs, which are $3 in this example, and variable costs, which depend on the quantity produced.

The fourth column shows the farm's profit, which is computed by subtracting total cost from total revenue. If the farm produces nothing, it has a loss of $3. If it produces 1 jug, it has a profit of $1. If it produces 2 jugs, it has a profit of $4, and so on. To maximize profit, the Smith farm chooses the quantity that makes profit as large as possible. In this example, profit is maximized when the farm produces 4 or 5 jugs of milk, when the profit is $7.

There is another way to look at the Smith farm's decision: The Smiths can find the profit-maximizing quantity by comparing the marginal revenue and marginal cost from each unit produced. The fifth and sixth columns in Table 14.2 compute marginal revenue and marginal cost from the changes in total revenue and total cost, and the last column shows the change in profit for each additional 4-L jug of milk produced. The first jug of milk the farm produces has a marginal revenue of $6 and a marginal cost of $2; hence, producing that jug increases profit by $4 (from –$3 to $1). The second jug produced has a marginal revenue of $6 and a marginal cost of $3, so that jug increases profit by $3 (from $1 to $4). As long as marginal revenue exceeds marginal cost, increasing the quantity produced raises profit.

Once the Smith farm has reached 5 4-L jugs of milk, however, the situation changes. The sixth jug would have marginal revenue of $6 and marginal cost of $7, so producing it would reduce profit by $1 (from $7 to $6). As a result, the Smiths would not produce beyond 5 jugs of milk.

One of the ten principles of economics in Chapter 1 is that rational people think at the margin. We now see how the Smith Family Dairy Farm can apply this principle. If marginal revenue is greater than marginal cost—as it is at 1, 2, or 3 jugs—the Smiths should increase the production of milk because it will put more money in their pockets (marginal revenue) than it takes out (marginal cost). If marginal revenue is less than marginal cost—as it is at 6, 7, or 8 jugs—the Smiths should decrease production. If the Smiths think at the margin and make incremental adjustments to the level of production, they are naturally led to produce the profit-maximizing quantity.

The Marginal-Cost Curve and the Firm's Supply Decision

To extend this analysis of profit maximization, consider the cost curves in Figure 14.1. These cost curves have the three features that, as we discussed in the previous chapter, are thought to describe most firms: The marginal-cost curve (MC) is upward sloping. The average-total-cost curve (ATC) is U-shaped. And the marginal-cost curve crosses the average-total-cost curve at the minimum of average total cost. The figure also shows a horizontal line at the market price (P). The price line is horizontal because the firm is a price taker: The price of the firm's output is the same regardless of the quantity that the firm decides to produce. Keep in mind that, for a competitive firm, the firm's price equals both its average revenue (AR) and its marginal revenue (MR).

We can use Figure 14.1 to find the quantity of output that maximizes profit. Imagine that the firm is producing at Q_1. At this level of output, marginal revenue

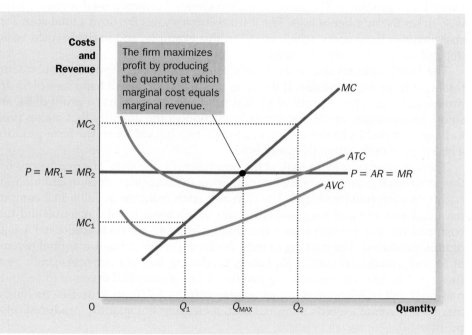

FIGURE 14.1

Profit Maximization for a Competitive Firm

This figure shows the marginal-cost curve (MC), the average-total-cost curve (ATC), and the average-variable-cost curve (AVC). It also shows the market price (P), which equals marginal revenue (MR) and average revenue (AR). At the quantity Q_1, marginal revenue MR_1 exceeds marginal cost MC_1, so raising production increases profit. At the quantity Q_2, marginal cost MC_2 is above marginal revenue MR_2, so reducing production increases profit. The profit-maximizing quantity Q_{MAX} is found where the horizontal price line intersects the marginal-cost curve.

is greater than marginal cost. That is, if the firm raised its level of production and sales by 1 unit, the additional revenue (MR_1) would exceed the additional costs (MC_1). Profit, which equals total revenue minus total cost, would increase. Hence, if marginal revenue is greater than marginal cost, as it is at Q_1, the firm can increase profit by increasing production.

A similar argument applies when output is at Q_2. In this case, marginal cost is greater than marginal revenue. If the firm reduced production by 1 unit, the costs saved (MC_2) would exceed the revenue lost (MR_2). Therefore, if marginal revenue is less than marginal cost, as it is at Q_2, the firm can increase profit by reducing production.

Where do these marginal adjustments to level of production end? Regardless of whether the firm begins with production at a low level (such as Q_1) or at a high level (such as Q_2), the firm will eventually adjust production until the quantity produced reaches Q_{MAX}. This analysis yields three general rules for profit maximization:

1. If marginal revenue is greater than marginal cost, the firm should increase its output.
2. If marginal cost is greater than marginal revenue, the firm should decrease its output.
3. At the profit-maximizing level of output, marginal revenue and marginal cost are exactly equal.

These rules are the key to rational decision making by a profit-maximizing firm. They apply not only to competitive firms but, as we will see in the next chapter, to other types of firms as well.

FIGURE 14.2

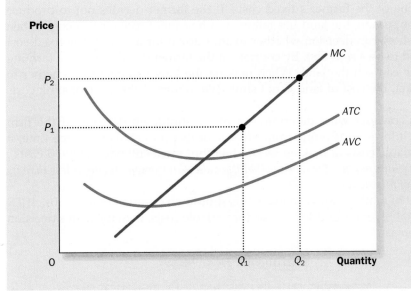

Marginal Cost as the Competitive Firm's Supply Curve

An increase in the price from P_1 to P_2 leads to an increase in the firm's profit-maximizing quantity from Q_1 to Q_2. Because the marginal-cost curve shows the quantity supplied by the firm at any given price, it is the firm's supply curve (see Figure 14.3, page 303).

We can now see how the competitive firm decides the quantity of its good to supply to the market. Because a competitive firm is a price taker, its marginal revenue equals the market price. For any given price, the competitive firm's profit-maximizing quantity of output is found by looking at the intersection of the price with the marginal-cost curve. In Figure 14.1, that quantity of output is Q_{MAX}.

Suppose the price prevailing in this market rises, perhaps because of an increase in market demand. Figure 14.2 shows how a competitive firm responds to an increase in the price. When the price is P_1, the firm produces quantity Q_1, the quantity that equates marginal cost to the price. When the price rises to P_2, the firm finds that marginal revenue is now higher than marginal cost at the previous level of output, so the firm increases production. The new profit-maximizing quantity is Q_2, at which marginal cost equals the new higher price. *In essence, because the firm's marginal-cost curve determines the quantity of the good the firm is willing to supply at any price, it is the competitive firm's supply curve.* There are, however, some caveats to this conclusion, which we examine next.

The Firm's Short-Run Decision to Shut Down

So far we have been analyzing the question of how much a competitive firm will produce. In some circumstances, however, the firm will decide to shut down and not produce anything at all.

Here we need to distinguish between a temporary shutdown of a firm and the permanent exit of a firm from the market. A *shutdown* refers to a short-run decision not to produce anything during a specific period of time because of current market conditions. *Exit* refers to a long-run decision to leave the market. The short-run and long-run decisions differ because most firms cannot avoid their fixed costs in the short run but can do so in the long run. That is, a firm that shuts down temporarily still has to pay its fixed costs, whereas a firm that exits the market saves both its fixed and its variable costs.

For example, consider the production decision that a farmer faces. The cost of the land is one of the farmer's fixed costs. If the farmer decides not to produce any crops one season, the land lies fallow and he cannot recover this cost. When making the short-run decision whether to shut down for a season, the fixed cost of land is said to be a *sunk cost.* By contrast, if the farmer decides to leave farming altogether, he can sell the land. When making the long-run decision whether to exit the market, the cost of land is not sunk. (We return to the issue of sunk costs shortly.)

Now let's consider what determines a firm's shutdown decision. If the firm shuts down, it loses all revenue from the sale of its product. At the same time, it saves the variable costs of making its product (but must still pay the fixed costs). Thus, *the firm shuts down if the revenue that it would earn from producing is less than its variable costs of production.*

A small bit of mathematics can make this shutdown criterion more useful. If TR stands for total revenue, and VC stands for variable costs, then the firm's decision can be written as

$$\text{Shut down if } TR < VC$$

The firm shuts down if total revenue is less than variable cost. By dividing both sides of this inequality by the quantity Q, we can write it as

$$\text{Shut down if } TR/Q < VC/Q$$

Notice that this can be further simplified. TR/Q is total revenue divided by quantity, which is average revenue. As we discussed previously, average revenue for any firm is simply the good's price, P. Similarly, VC/Q is average variable cost AVC. Therefore, the firm's shutdown criterion is

$$\text{Shut down if } P < AVC$$

That is, a firm chooses to shut down if the price of the good is less than the average variable cost of production. This criterion is intuitive: When choosing to produce, the firm compares the price it receives for the typical unit to the average variable cost that it must incur to produce the typical unit. If the price doesn't cover the average variable cost, the firm is better off stopping production altogether. Thus, the price that coincides with the minimum point on the average-*variable*-cost curve is sometimes referred to as the *shutdown price.* If the market price is less than the shutdown price, the firm shuts down and ceases production. If conditions change in the future so that the price exceeds the shutdown price, the firm can reopen. Of course we could just as easily refer to it as the *start-up price.*

We now have a full description of a competitive firm's profit-maximizing strategy. If the firm produces anything, it produces the quantity at which marginal cost equals the price of the good. Yet if the price is less than average variable cost at that quantity, the firm is better off shutting down and not producing anything. These results are illustrated in Figure 14.3.

There are two parts to the competitive firm's short-run supply curve, with a discontinuity at the short-run shutdown price. For prices from zero up to the shutdown price, the firm supplies zero output and the short-run supply curve lies along the vertical axis. For prices above the short-run shutdown price,

FIGURE 14.3

Costs

MC

Firm's short-run
supply curve

ATC

AVC

Shutdown
price

0

Quantity

**The Competitive Firm's Short-Run
Supply Curve**

*In the short run, the competitive firm's
supply curve is its marginal-cost curve (MC)
above average variable cost (AVC). If the
price falls below average variable cost, the
firm is better off shutting down.*

the competitive firm's *short-run* supply curve is the portion of its marginal-cost curve that lies above average *variable* cost.

Spilt Milk and Other Sunk Costs

Sometime in your life you have probably been told, "Don't cry over spilt milk," or "Let bygones be bygones." These adages hold a deep truth about rational decision making. Economists say that a cost is a **sunk cost** when it has already been committed and cannot be recovered. Because nothing can be done about sunk costs, you can ignore them when making decisions about various aspects of life, including business strategy.

Our analysis of the firm's shutdown decision is one example of the irrelevance of sunk costs. We assume that the firm cannot recover its fixed costs by temporarily stopping production. That is, regardless of the quantity of output supplied (even if it is zero), the firm still has to pay its fixed costs. As a result, the firm's fixed costs are sunk in the short run, and the firm can safely ignore these costs when deciding how much to produce. The firm's short-run supply curve is the part of the marginal-cost curve that lies above average variable cost, and the size of the fixed cost does not matter for this supply decision.

The irrelevance of sunk costs is also important for personal decisions. Imagine, for instance, that you place a $15 value on seeing a newly released movie. You buy a ticket for $10, but before entering the theatre, you lose the ticket. Should you buy another ticket? Or should you now go home and refuse to pay a total of $20 to see the movie? The answer is that you should buy another ticket. The benefit of seeing the movie ($15) still exceeds the opportunity cost (the $10 for the second ticket). The $10 you paid for the lost ticket is a sunk cost. As with spilt milk, there is no point in crying about it.

sunk cost
a cost that has already been committed and cannot be recovered

Case Study

NEAR-EMPTY RESTAURANTS AND OFF-SEASON MINIATURE GOLF

Have you ever walked into a restaurant for lunch and found it almost empty? Why, you might have asked, does the restaurant even bother to stay open? It might seem that the revenue from so few customers could not possibly cover the cost of running the restaurant.

In making the decision whether to open for lunch, a restaurant owner must keep in mind the distinction between fixed and variable costs. Many of a restaurant's costs—the rent, kitchen equipment, tables, plates, silverware, and so on—are fixed. Shutting down during lunch would not reduce these costs. In other words, these costs are sunk in the short run. When the owner is deciding whether to serve lunch, only the variable costs—the price of the additional food and the wages of the extra staff—are relevant. The owner shuts down the restaurant at lunchtime only if the revenue from the few lunchtime customers fails to cover the restaurant's variable costs.

An operator of a miniature-golf course in a summer resort community faces a similar decision. Because revenue varies substantially from season to season, the firm must decide when to open and when to close. Once again, the fixed costs—the costs of buying the land and building the course—are irrelevant. The miniature-golf course should be open for business only during those times of year when its revenue exceeds its variable costs. ●

The Firm's Long-Run Decision to Exit or Enter a Market

A firm's long-run decision to exit the market is similar to its shutdown decision. If the firm exits, it again will lose all revenue from the sale of its product, but now it saves on both fixed and variable costs of production. Thus, *the firm exits the market if the revenue it would get from producing is less than its total costs.*

We can again make this criterion more useful by writing it mathematically. If TR stands for total revenue, and TC stands for total cost, then the firm's criterion can be written as

$$\text{Exit if } TR < TC$$

The firm exits if total revenue is less than total cost. By dividing both sides of this inequality by quantity Q, we can write it as

$$\text{Exit if } TR/Q < TC/Q$$

We can simplify this further by noting that TR/Q is average revenue, which equals the price P, and that TC/Q is average total cost ATC. Therefore, the firm's exit criterion is

$$\text{Exit if } P < ATC$$

Staying open can be profitable, even with many tables empty.

Robert Holmes/Corbis

That is, a firm chooses to exit if the price of the good is less than the average total cost of production. Thus, the price that coincides with the minimum point on the average-*total*-cost curve is sometimes referred to as the *exit price*. The exit price is related to the firm's efficient scale, as discussed in Chapter 13. If the market price is less than the exit price, the firm exits the industry.

It is useful to point out the difference between the exit price, a long-run concept, and the shutdown price, a short-run concept. The exit price coincides with the minimum point on the average-total-cost curve, while the shutdown price coincides with the minimum point on the average-variable-cost curve.

A parallel analysis applies to an entrepreneur who is considering starting a firm. The firm will enter the market if such an action would be profitable, which occurs if the price of the good exceeds the average total cost of production. The entry criterion is

$$\text{Enter if } P > ATC$$

The criterion for entry is exactly the opposite of the criterion for exit.

We can now describe a competitive firm's long-run profit-maximizing strategy. If the firm is in the market, it produces the quantity at which marginal cost equals the price of the good. Yet if the price is less than the average total cost at that quantity, the firm chooses to exit (or not enter) the market. These results are illustrated in Figure 14.4.

In this diagram, for simplicity, *ATC* is drawn as U-shaped, without an extended horizontal portion coinciding with a range of production under constant returns to scale. There are two parts to the competitive firm's long-run supply curve, with a discontinuity at the exit price. For prices from zero up to the exit price, the firm exits (or chooses not to enter) the market, and the long-run supply curve lies along the vertical axis. For prices above the exit price, the competitive firm's *long-run* supply curve is the portion of its marginal-cost curve that lies above average *total* cost.

FIGURE 14.4

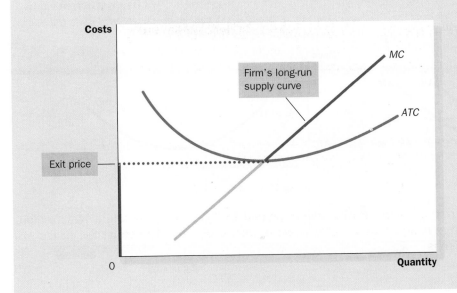

The Competitive Firm's Long-Run Supply Curve

In the long run, the competitive firm's supply curve is its marginal-cost curve (MC) above average total cost (ATC). If the price falls below average total cost, the firm is better off exiting the market.

Measuring Profit in Our Graph for the Competitive Firm

As we study exit and entry, it is useful to analyze the firm's profit in more detail. Recall that profit equals total revenue (*TR*) minus total cost (*TC*):

$$\text{Profit} = TR - TC$$

We can rewrite this definition by multiplying and dividing the right-hand side by *Q*:

$$\text{Profit} = (TR/Q - TC/Q) \times Q$$

But note that TR/Q is average revenue, which is the price *P*, and TC/Q is average total cost *ATC*. Therefore,

$$\text{Profit} = (P - ATC) \times Q$$

This way of expressing the firm's profit allows us to measure profit in our graphs.

Panel (a) of Figure 14.5 shows a firm earning positive profit. As we have already discussed, the firm maximizes profit by producing the quantity at which price equals marginal cost. Now look at the shaded rectangle. The height of the rectangle is $P - ATC$, the difference between price and average total cost. The width of the rectangle is *Q*, the quantity produced. Therefore, the area of the rectangle is $(P - ATC) \times Q$, which is the firm's profit.

FIGURE 14.5

Profit as the Area between Price and Average Total Cost

The area of the shaded box between price and average total cost represents the firm's profit. The height of this box is price minus average total cost (P – ATC), and the width of the box is the quantity of output (Q). In panel (a), price is above average total cost, so the firm has positive profit. In panel (b), price is less than average total cost, so the firm has losses.

Similarly, panel (b) of this figure shows a firm with losses (negative profit). In this case, maximizing profit means minimizing losses, a task accomplished once again by producing the quantity at which price equals marginal cost. Now consider the shaded rectangle. The height of the rectangle is $ATC - P$, and the width is Q. The area is $(ATC - P) \times Q$, which is the firm's loss. Because a firm in this situation is not making enough revenue to cover its average total cost, the firm would choose to exit the market.

QuickQuiz   How does the price faced by a profit-maximizing competitive firm compare to its marginal cost? Explain. • When does a profit-maximizing competitive firm decide to shut down? When does a profit-maximizing competitive firm decide to exit a market?

THE SUPPLY CURVE IN A COMPETITIVE MARKET

Now that we have examined the supply decision of a single firm, we can discuss the supply curve for a market. There are two cases to consider. First, we examine a market with a fixed number of firms. Second, we examine a market in which the number of firms can change as old firms exit the market and new firms enter. Both cases are important, for each applies over a specific time horizon. Over short periods of time, it is often difficult for firms to enter and exit, so the assumption of a fixed number of firms is appropriate. But over long periods of time, the number of firms can adjust to changing market conditions.

The Short Run: Market Supply with a Fixed Number of Firms

Consider first a market with 1000 identical firms. For any given price, each firm supplies a quantity of output so that its marginal cost equals the price, as shown in panel (a) of Figure 14.6. That is, as long as price is above average variable cost, each firm's marginal-cost curve is its supply curve. The quantity of output supplied to the market equals the sum of the quantities supplied by each of the 1000 individual firms. Thus, to derive the market supply curve, we add the quantity supplied by each firm in the market. As panel (b) of Figure 14.6 shows, because the firms are identical, the quantity supplied to the market is 1000 times the quantity supplied by each firm.

The Long Run: Market Supply with Entry and Exit

Now consider what happens if firms are able to enter or exit the market. Let's suppose that everyone has access to the same technology for producing the good and access to the same markets to buy the inputs into production. Therefore, all current and potential firms have the same cost curves.

Decisions about entry and exit in a market of this type depend on the incentives facing the owners of existing firms and the entrepreneurs who could start new firms. If firms already in the market are profitable, then new firms will have an incentive to enter the market. This entry will expand the number of firms, increase the quantity of the good supplied, and drive down prices and profits. Conversely,

FIGURE 14.6

Market Supply with a Fixed Number of Firms

In the short run, the number of firms in the market is fixed. As a result, the market supply curve, shown in panel (b), reflects the individual firms' marginal-cost curves, shown in panel (a). Here, in a market of 1000 firms, the quantity of output supplied to the market is 1000 times the quantity supplied by each firm.

if firms in the market are making losses, then some existing firms will exit the market. Their exit will reduce the number of firms, decrease the quantity of the good supplied, and drive up prices and profits. *At the end of this process of entry and exit, firms that remain in the market must be making zero economic profit.*

Recall that we can write a firm's profits as

$$\text{Profit} = (P - ATC) \times Q$$

This equation shows that an operating firm has zero profit if and only if the price of the good equals the average total cost of producing that good. If price is above average total cost, profit is positive, which encourages new firms to enter. If price is less than average total cost, profit is negative, which encourages some firms to exit. *The process of entry and exit ends only when price and average total cost are driven to equality.*

This analysis has a surprising implication. We noted earlier in the chapter that competitive firms produce so that price equals marginal cost. We just noted that free entry and exit forces price to equal average total cost. But if price is to equal both marginal cost and average total cost, these two measures of cost must equal each other. Marginal cost and average total cost are equal, however, only when the firm is operating at the minimum of average total cost. Recall from the preceding chapter that the level of production with lowest average total cost is called the firm's *efficient scale*. Therefore, *the long-run equilibrium of a competitive market with free entry and exit must have firms operating at their efficient scale.*

FIGURE 14.7

Market Supply with Entry and Exit

Firms will enter or exit the market until profit is driven to zero. Thus, in the long run, price equals the minimum of average total cost, as shown in panel (a). The number of firms adjusts to ensure that all demand is satisfied at this price. The long-run market supply curve is horizontal at this price, as shown in panel (b).

(a) Firm's Zero-Profit Condition

(b) Market Supply

Panel (a) of Figure 14.7 shows a firm in such a long-run equilibrium. In this figure, price P equals marginal cost MC, so the firm is maximizing profits. Price also equals average total cost ATC, so profits are zero. New firms have no incentive to enter the market, and existing firms have no incentive to leave the market.

From this analysis of firm behaviour, we can determine the long-run supply curve for the market. In a market with free entry and exit, there is only one price consistent with zero profit—the minimum of average total cost. As a result, the long-run market supply curve must be horizontal at this price, as in panel (b) of Figure 14.7. Any price above this level would generate profit, leading to entry and an increase in the total quantity supplied. Any price below this level would generate losses, leading to exit and a decrease in the total quantity supplied. Eventually, the number of firms in the market adjusts so that price equals the minimum of average total cost, and there are enough firms to satisfy all the demand at this price.

Why Do Competitive Firms Stay in Business If They Make Zero Profit?

At first, it might seem odd that competitive firms earn zero profit in the long run. After all, people start businesses to make a profit. If entry eventually drives profit to zero, there might seem to be little reason to stay in business.

To understand the zero-profit condition more fully, recall that profit equals total revenue minus total cost, and that total cost includes all the opportunity costs of the firm. In particular, total cost includes the opportunity cost of the time and money that the firm owners devote to the business. In the zero-profit equilibrium, the firm's revenue must compensate the owners for these opportunity costs.

Consider an example. Suppose that a farmer had to invest $1 million to establish his farm, which otherwise he could have deposited in a bank and earned $50 000 a year in interest. In addition, he had to give up another job that would have paid him $30 000 a year. Then the farmer's opportunity cost of farming includes both the interest he could have earned and the forgone wages—a total of $80 000. Even if his profit is driven to zero, his revenue from farming compensates him for these opportunity costs.

Keep in mind that accountants and economists measure costs differently. As we discussed in the previous chapter, accountants keep track of explicit costs but usually miss implicit costs. That is, they measure costs that require an outflow of money from the firm, but they fail to include opportunity costs of production that do not involve an outflow of money. As a result, in the zero-profit equilibrium, economic profit is zero, but accounting profit is positive. Our farmer's accountant, for instance, would conclude that the farmer earned an accounting profit of $80 000, which is enough to keep the farmer in business.

A Shift in Demand in the Short Run and Long Run

Now that we have a more complete understanding of how many firms make supply decisions, we can better explain how markets respond to changes in demand. Because firms can enter and exit a market in the long run but not in the short run, the response of a market to a change in demand depends on the time horizon. To see this, let's trace the effects of a shift in demand.

Suppose the market for milk begins in long-run equilibrium. Firms are earning zero profit, so price equals the minimum of average total cost. Panel (a) of Figure 14.8 shows this situation. The long-run equilibrium is point A, the quantity sold in the market is Q_1, and the price is P_1.

Now suppose scientists discover that milk has miraculous health benefits. As a result, the demand curve for milk shifts outward from D_1 to D_2, as in panel (b). The short-run equilibrium moves from point A to point B; as a result, the quantity rises from Q_1 to Q_2, and the price rises from P_1 to P_2. All of the existing firms respond to the higher price by raising the amount produced. Because each firm's supply curve reflects its marginal-cost curve, how much they each increase production is determined by the marginal-cost curve. In the new short-run equilibrium, the price of milk exceeds average total cost, so the firms are making positive profit.

Over time, the profit generated in this market encourages new firms to enter. Some farmers may switch to milk from other farm products, for example. As the number of firms grows, the short-run supply curve shifts to the right from S_1 to S_2, as in panel (c), and this shift causes the price of milk to fall. Eventually, the price is driven back down to the minimum of average total cost, profits are zero, and firms stop entering. Thus, the market reaches a new long-run equilibrium, point C. The price of milk has returned to P_1, but the quantity produced has risen to Q_3. Each firm is again producing at its efficient scale, but because more firms are in the dairy business, the quantity of milk produced and sold is higher.

FIGURE 14.8

An Increase in Demand in the Short Run and Long Run

The market starts in a long-run equilibrium, shown as point A in panel (a). In this equilibrium, each firm makes zero profit, and the price equals the minimum average total cost. Panel (b) shows what happens in the short run when demand rises from D_1 to D_2. The equilibrium goes from point A to point B, price rises from P_1 to P_2, and the quantity sold in the market rises from Q_1 to Q_2. Because price now exceeds average total cost, firms make profits, which over time encourages new firms to enter the market. This entry shifts the short-run supply curve to the right from S_1 to S_2, as shown in panel (c). In the new long-run equilibrium, point C, price has returned to P_1 but the quantity sold has increased to Q_3. Profits are again zero, price is back to the minimum of average total cost, but the market has more firms to satisfy the greater demand.

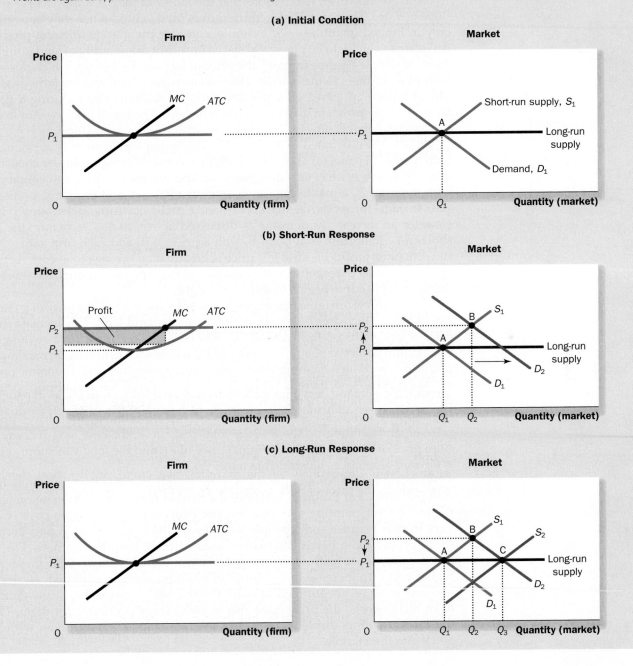

Why the Long-Run Supply Curve Might Slope Upward

So far we have seen that entry and exit can cause the long-run market supply curve to be horizontal (or perfectly elastic). The essence of our analysis is that there are a large number of potential entrants, each of which faces the same costs. As a result, the long-run market supply curve is horizontal at the minimum of average total cost. When the demand for the good increases, the long-run result is an increase in the number of firms and in the total quantity supplied, without any change in the price.

There are, however, two reasons that the long-run market supply curve might slope upward. The first is that some resources used in production may be available only in limited quantities. For example, consider the market for farm products. Anyone can choose to buy land and start a farm, but the quantity of land is limited. As more people become farmers, the price of farmland is bid up, which raises the costs of all farmers in the market. Thus, an increase in demand for farm products cannot induce an increase in quantity supplied without also inducing a rise in farmers' costs, which in turn means a rise in price. The result is a long-run market supply curve that is upward sloping, even with free entry into farming.

This case is illustrated in Figure 14.9. The initial equilibrium is at point A in both panels. In panel (a) at point A, each firm is maximizing profits by choosing a quantity where price equals marginal cost, and we are in a long-run equilibrium with the price P_1 equal to minimum average total cost and economic profits are zero. In panel (b) at point A, market demand equals short-run market supply. Now consider an increase in demand as discussed above, to D_2. As before, the new short-run equilibrium is at point B, with a price of P_2 and each firm earns short-run economic profits because this price is greater than average total cost. As firms enter the market in response to the existence of these positive profits, the short-run market supply curve begins to shift to the right.

Now, however, imagine that as new firms enter the market, the price of an input, say farmland, increases because entering firms demand land. This increase in the price of land shifts up the average total cost curve for all firms. The new long-run equilibrium occurs at point C at a price of P_3, where each firm is again maximizing profits by choosing a quantity where price equals marginal cost. Economic profits are again zero—and there is no further entry—because the equilibrium price is equal to the minimum of the new average-total-cost curve, ATC_2. The new short-run supply curve is S_2. Because the entry of firms into the market drives up the price of land, shifting up the average total cost curve, the new long-run equilibrium price of P_3 is higher than original price of P_1, and the long-run supply curve is upward-sloping, as illustrated in panel (b).

A second reason for an upward-sloping supply curve is that firms may have different costs. For example, consider the market for painters. Anyone can enter the market for painting services, but not everyone has the same costs. Costs vary in part because some people work faster than others and in part because some people have better alternative uses of their time than others. For any given price, those with lower costs are more likely to enter than those with higher costs. To increase the quantity of painting services supplied, additional entrants must be encouraged to enter the market. Because these new entrants have higher costs, the price must rise to make entry profitable for them. Thus, the market supply curve for painting services slopes upward even with free entry into the market.

FIGURE 14.9

An Upward Sloping Long-Run Supply Curve

The market starts in long-run equilibrium at point A in both panels. In panel (a) at point A, each firm is maximizing profits by choosing a quantity where price equals marginal cost, and we are in a long-run equilibrium, with the price P_1 equal to average total cost and economic profits are zero. In panel (b) at point A, market demand equals short-run market supply. Panel (b) shows what happens in the short-run as demand increases from D_1 to D_2. The short-run equilibrium goes from point A to point B, and the price rises from P_1 to P_2. Because the price exceeds average total costs, firms make profits, which over time attract entrants into the market. This entry shifts the short-run supply curve to the right. It also bids up the price of an input to the production of the good, say land, which shifts up the average total cost curve. In the new long-run equilibrium, the price is P_3, which is equal to the minimum of the new long-run average-cost curve, ATC_2. Profits are again zero and there are more firms to satisfy the greater demand, but the new equilibrium price P_3 is higher than the original price P_1 because of the increase in average total costs associated with entry. This generates an upward sloping long-run supply curve as shown in panel (b).

Notice that if firms have different costs, some firms earn profit even in the long run. In this case, the price in the market reflects the average total cost of the *marginal firm*—the firm that would exit the market if the price was any lower. This firm earns zero profit, but firms with lower costs earn positive profit. Entry does not eliminate this profit because would-be entrants have higher costs than firms already in the market. Higher-cost firms will enter only if the price rises, making the market profitable for them.

Thus, for these two reasons, the long-run supply curve in a market may be upward sloping rather than horizontal, indicating that a higher price is necessary to induce a larger quantity supplied. Nonetheless, the basic lesson about entry and exit remains true: *Because firms can enter and exit more easily in the long run than in the short run, the long-run supply curve is typically more elastic than the short-run supply curve.*

QuickQuiz   In the long run with free entry and exit, is the price in a market equal to marginal cost, average total cost, both, or neither? Explain with a diagram.

CONCLUSION: BEHIND THE SUPPLY CURVE

We have been discussing the behaviour of competitive profit-maximizing firms. You may recall from Chapter 1 that one of the ten principles of economics is that rational people think at the margin. This chapter has applied this idea to the competitive firm. Marginal analysis has given us a theory of the supply curve in a competitive market and, as a result, a deeper understanding of market outcomes.

We have learned that when you buy a good from a firm in a competitive market, you can be assured that the price you pay is close to the cost of producing that good. In particular, if firms are competitive and profit-maximizing, the price of a good equals the marginal cost of making that good. In addition, if firms can freely enter and exit the market, the price also equals the lowest possible average total cost of production.

Although we have assumed throughout this chapter that firms are price takers, many of the tools developed here are also useful for studying firms in less competitive markets. In the next chapter we will examine the behaviour of firms with market power. Marginal analysis will again be useful in analyzing these firms, but it will have quite different implications.

SUMMARY

- Because a competitive firm is a price taker, its revenue is proportional to the amount of output it produces. The price of the good equals both the firm's average revenue and its marginal revenue.

- To maximize profit, a firm chooses a quantity of output such that marginal revenue equals marginal cost. Because marginal revenue for a competitive firm equals the market price, the firm chooses quantity so that price equals marginal cost. Thus, the firm's marginal cost curve is its supply curve.

- In the short run when a firm cannot recover its fixed costs, the firm will choose to shut down temporarily if the price of the good is less than average variable cost. In the long run when the firm can recover both fixed and variable costs, it will choose to exit if the price is less than average total cost.

- In a market with free entry and exit, profits are driven to zero in the long run. In this long-run equilibrium, all firms produce at the efficient scale, price equals the minimum of average total cost, and the number of firms adjusts to satisfy the quantity demanded at this price.

- Changes in demand have different effects over different time horizons. In the short run, an increase in demand raises prices and leads to profits, and a decrease in demand lowers prices and leads to losses. But if firms can freely enter and exit the market, then in the long run the number of firms adjusts to drive the market back to the zero-profit equilibrium.

KEY CONCEPTS

competitive market, p. 296
average revenue, p. 297

marginal revenue, p. 298

sunk cost, p. 303

QUESTIONS FOR REVIEW

1. What is meant by a competitive firm?

2. Draw the cost curves for a typical firm. For a given price, explain how the firm chooses the level of output that maximizes profit. At that level of output, show on your graph the firm's total revenue and total costs.

3. Under what conditions will a firm shut down temporarily? Explain.

4. Under what conditions will a firm exit a market? Explain.

5. Does a firm's price equal marginal cost in the short run, in the long run, or both? Explain.

6. Does a firm's price equal the minimum of average total cost in the short run, in the long run, or both? Explain.

7. Are market supply curves typically more elastic in the short run or in the long run? Explain.

PROBLEMS AND APPLICATIONS

1. You go out to the best restaurant in town and order a lobster dinner for $40. After eating half of the lobster, you realize that you are quite full. Your date wants you to finish your dinner, because you can't take it home and because "you've already paid for it." What should you do? Relate your answer to the material in this chapter.

2. Bob's lawn-mowing service is a profit-maximizing, competitive firm. Bob mows lawns for $27 each. His total cost each day is $280, of which $30 is a fixed cost. He mows 10 lawns a day. What can you say about Bob's short-run decision regarding shutdown and his long-run decision regarding exit?

3. Consider total cost and total revenue given in the table below:

Quantity	0	1	2	3	4	5	6	7
Total Cost	$8	$9	$10	$11	$13	$19	$27	$37
Total Revenue	0	8	16	24	32	40	48	56

a. Calculate profit for each quantity. How much should the firm produce to maximize profit?

b. Calculate marginal revenue and marginal cost for each quantity. Graph them. (Hint: Put the points between whole numbers. For example, the marginal cost between 2 and 3 should be graphed at 2.5.) At what quantity do these curves cross? How does this relate to your answer to part (a)?

c. Can you tell whether this firm is in a competitive industry? If so, can you tell whether the industry is in a long-run equilibrium?

4. In 2003, a single case in Alberta of bovine spongiform encephalopathy, also known as mad cow disease, temporarily shut down export markets for Canadian beef.

a. Using firm and industry diagrams, show the short-run effect of declining demand for Canadian beef due to the shutdown of its export markets. Label the diagram carefully and write out in words all of the changes that you can identify.

b. Although export markets eventually began to open up later that same year, the demand for Canadian beef remained low. On a new diagram, show the long-run effect of the declining demand. Explain in words.

5. Suppose the book-printing industry is competitive and begins in a long-run equilibrium.

a. Draw a diagram describing the typical firm in the industry.

b. Hi-Tech Printing Company invents a new process that sharply reduces the cost of printing books. What happens to Hi-Tech's profits and the price of books in the short run when Hi-Tech's patent prevents other firms from using the new technology?

c. What happens in the long run when the patent expires and other firms are free to use the technology?

6. Many small boats are made of fibreglass, which is derived from crude oil. Suppose that the price of oil rises.
   a. Using diagrams, show what happens to the cost curves of an individual boat-making firm and to the market supply curve.
   b. What happens to the profits of boat makers in the short run? What happens to the number of boat makers in the long run?

7. Suppose that the Canadian textile industry is competitive, and there is no international trade in textiles. In long-run equilibrium, the price per unit of cloth is $30.
   a. Describe the equilibrium using graphs for the entire market and for an individual producer.
   Now suppose that textile producers in other countries are willing to sell large quantities of cloth in Canada for only $25 per unit.
   b. Assuming that Canadian textile producers have large fixed costs, what is the short-run effect of these imports on the quantity produced by an individual producer? What is the short-run effect on profits? Illustrate your answer with a graph.
   c. What is the long-run effect on the number of Canadian firms in the industry?

8. Suppose there are 1000 hot-pretzel stands operating in Toronto. Each stand has the usual U-shaped average-total-cost curve. The market demand curve for pretzels slopes downward, and the market for pretzels is in long-run competitive equilibrium.
   a. Draw the current equilibrium, using graphs for the entire market and for an individual pretzel stand.
   b. Now the city decides to restrict the number of pretzel-stand licences, reducing the number of stands to only 800. What effect will this action have on the market and on an individual stand that is still operating? Use graphs to illustrate your answer.
   c. Suppose that the city decides to charge a licence fee for the 800 licences. How will this affect the number of pretzels sold by an individual stand, and the stand's profit? The city wants to raise as much revenue as possible and also wants to ensure that

800 pretzel stands remain in the city. By how much should the city increase the licence fee? Show the answer on your graph.

9. The market for apple pies in the city of Ectenia is competitive and has the following demand schedule:

Price	Quantity Demanded
$ 1	1200 pies
2	1100
3	1000
4	900
5	800
6	700
7	600
8	500
9	400
10	300
11	200
12	100
13	0

Each producer in the market has fixed costs of $9 and the following marginal cost:

Quantity	Marginal cost
1 pie	$ 2
2	4
3	6
4	8
5	10
6	12

a. Compute each producer's total cost and average total cost for 1 to 6 pies.
b. The price of a pie is now $11. How many pies are sold? How many pies does each producer make? How many producers are there? How much profit does each producer earn?
c. Is the situation described in part (b) a long-run equilibrium? Why or why not?
d. Suppose that in the long run there is free entry and exit. How much profit does each producer earn in the long-run equilibrium? What is the market price and number of pies each producer makes? How many pies are sold? How many pie producers are operating?

10. Ball Bearings Inc. faces costs of production as follows:

Quantity	Total Fixed Costs	Total Variable Costs
0	$100	$ 0
1	100	50
2	100	70
3	100	90
4	100	140
5	100	200
6	100	360

a. Calculate the company's average fixed costs, average variable costs, average total costs, and marginal costs.

b. The price of a case of ball bearings is $50. Seeing that she can't make a profit, the chief executive officer (CEO) decides to shut down operations. What are the firm's profits/losses? Was this a wise decision? Explain.

c. Vaguely remembering his introductory economics course, the chief financial officer tells the CEO it is better to produce 1 case of ball bearings because marginal revenue equals marginal cost at that quantity. What are the firm's profits/losses at that level of production? Was this the best decision? Explain.

11. A firm in a competitive market receives $500 in total revenue and has marginal revenue of $10. What is the average revenue, and how many units were sold?

12. A profit-maximizing firm in a competitive market is currently producing 100 units of output. It has average revenue of $10, average total cost of $8, and fixed costs of $200.
   a. What is profit?
   b. What is marginal cost?
   c. What is average variable cost?
   d. Is the efficient scale of the firm more than, less than, or exactly 100 units?

13. The market for fertilizer is perfectly competitive. Firms in the market are producing output, but are currently experiencing economic losses.

a. How does the price of fertilizer compare to the average total cost, the average variable cost, and the marginal cost of producing fertilizer?

b. Draw two graphs, side by side, illustrating the present situation for the typical firm and in the market.

c. Assuming there is no change in demand or in the firms' cost curves, explain what will happen in the long run to the price of fertilizer, marginal cost, average total cost, the quantity supplied by each firm, and the total quantity supplied to the market.

14. Analyze the two following scenarios for firms in competitive markets:
   a. Suppose that $TC = 100 + 15Q$, where TC is total cost and Q is the quantity produced. What is the minimum price necessary for this firm to produce any output in the short run?
   b. Suppose that $MC = 4Q$, where MC is marginal cost. The perfectly competitive firm maximizes profits by producing 10 units of output. At what price does it sell these units?

15. There is a single production technology available to firms that might choose to operate in the market for hammers. Suppose all firms have access to a technology that gives the following total cost (TC) for producing a quantity (Q) of hammers: $TC = 3 + 3Q^2$, for any $Q > 0$, but the costs of production are equal to zero if $Q = 0$. The marginal cost of producing hammers is $MC = 6Q$.
   a. What is the equation for the average variable cost (AVC) and the average total cost (ATC)?
   b. If the price of hammers is P, find the supply curve of a single firm, for all possible prices $P > 0$.
   For the following two parts suppose that there is free entry into the hammer market, and the cost functions of firms don't change. The market demand for hammers is given by $Q^D = 600 - 50P$.
   c. What is the long-run equilibrium price in the market and how much does each firm produce at this price?
   d. How many firms in total are in the market?

MONOPOLY

15

Chad Mcdermott/Dreamstime.com

Learning Objectives

In this chapter, you will...

- Learn why some markets have only one seller
- Analyze how a monopoly determines the quantity to produce and the price to charge
- See how the monopoly's decisions affect economic well-being
- See why monopolies try to charge different prices to different customers
- Consider the various public policies aimed at solving the problem of monopoly

If you own a personal computer, it probably uses some version of Windows, the operating system sold by Microsoft Corporation. When Microsoft first designed Windows many years ago, it applied for and received a copyright from the government. The copyright gives Microsoft the exclusive right to make and sell copies of the Windows operating system. So if a person wants to buy a copy of Windows, he or she has little choice but to give Microsoft the approximately $100 that the firm has decided to charge for its product. Microsoft is said to have a *monopoly* in the market for Windows.

Microsoft's business decisions are not well described by the model of firm behaviour we developed in the previous chapter. In that chapter we analyzed competitive markets, in which there are many firms offering essentially identical products, so each firm has little influence over the price it receives. By contrast, a monopoly such as Microsoft has no close competitors and, therefore, can influence the market price of its product. While a competitive firm is a *price taker*, a monopoly firm is a *price maker*.

In this chapter we examine the implications of this market power. We will see that market power alters the relationship between a firm's costs and the price at which it sells its product to the market. A competitive firm takes the price of its output as given by the market and then chooses the quantity it will supply so that price equals marginal cost. By contrast, the price charged by a monopoly exceeds marginal cost. This result is clearly true in the case of Microsoft's Windows. The marginal cost of Windows—the extra cost that Microsoft would incur by printing one more copy of the program onto a CD—is only a few dollars. The market price of Windows is many times its marginal cost.

It is not surprising that monopolies charge high prices for their products. Customers of monopolies might seem to have little choice but to pay whatever the monopoly charges. But, if so, why does a copy of Windows not cost $1000? Or $10 000? The reason, of course, is that if Microsoft set the price that high, fewer people would buy the product. People would buy fewer computers, switch to other operating systems, or make illegal copies. A monopoly firm can control the price of the good it sells, but because a high price reduces the quantity that its customers buy, the monopoly's profits are not unlimited.

As we examine the production and pricing decisions of monopolies, we also consider the implications of monopoly for society as a whole. Monopoly firms, like competitive firms, aim to maximize profit. But this goal has very different ramifications for competitive and monopoly firms. As we first saw in Chapter 7, self-interested buyers and sellers in competitive markets are unwittingly led by an invisible hand to promote general economic well-being. By contrast, because monopoly firms are unchecked by competition, the outcome in a market with a monopoly is often not in the best interest of society.

One of the ten principles of economics in Chapter 1 is that governments can sometimes improve market outcomes. The analysis in this chapter will shed more light on this principle. As we examine the problems that monopolies raise for society, we will also discuss the various ways in which government policymakers might respond to these problems. The U.S. government, for example, keeps a close eye on Microsoft's business decisions. In 1994, it prevented Microsoft from buying Intuit, a software firm that sells the leading program for personal finance, on the grounds that the combination of Microsoft and Intuit would concentrate too much market power in one firm. Similarly, in 1998 the U.S. Justice Department objected when Microsoft started integrating its Internet browser into its Windows operating system, claiming that this addition would extend the firm's market power into new areas. To this day, Microsoft continues to wrangle with regulators around the world.

WHY MONOPOLIES ARISE

monopoly
a firm that is the sole seller of a product without close substitutes

A firm is a **monopoly** if it is the sole seller of its product and if its product does not have close substitutes. The fundamental cause of monopoly is *barriers to entry:* A monopoly remains the only seller in its market because other firms cannot enter the market and compete with it. Barriers to entry, in turn, have three main sources:

1. *Monopoly resources:* A key resource is owned by a single firm.
2. *Government-created monopolies:* The government gives a single firm the exclusive right to produce some good or service.
3. *Natural monopolies:* A single firm can produce output at a lower cost than can a large number of producers.

Let's briefly discuss each of these.

Monopoly Resources

The simplest way for a monopoly to arise is for a single firm to own a key resource. For example, consider the market for water in an early Canadian small town. If dozens of town residents have working wells, the competitive model discussed in the preceding chapter describes the behaviour of sellers. As a result, the price of a litre of water is driven to equal the marginal cost of pumping an extra litre. But if there is only one well in town and it is impossible to get water from anywhere else, then the owner of the well has a monopoly on water. Not surprisingly, the monopolist has much greater market power than any single firm in a competitive market. In the case of a necessity like water, the monopolist could command quite a high price, even if the marginal cost is low.

The tsunami that hit in Japan in 2011 revealed how important monopoly ownership of key resources can be in the integrated global supply chain network. Just as some financial institutions proved "too big to fail" in the 2008 financial crisis, some Japanese suppliers were shown to be too crucial to do without. Two firms, Mitsubishi Gas Chemical Company and Hitachi Chemical Company, control about 90 percent of the market for a specialty resin used to bond parts of microchips that go into smartphones and other devices. The compact battery in Apple's iPods relies on a polymer made by Kureha Corporation, which holds 70 percent of the market. These firms exhibit substantial market power over key inputs into important consumer devices, which is reflected in their high prices. Moreover, all three suffered significant damage in the tsunami, throwing the worldwide supply chain into disarray.

Although exclusive ownership of a key resource is a potential cause of monopoly, in practice, monopolies rarely arise for this reason. Actual economies are large, and resources are owned by many people. Indeed, because many goods are traded internationally, the natural scope of their markets is often worldwide. There are, therefore, few examples of firms that own a resource for which there are no close substitutes.

Government-Created Monopolies

In many cases, monopolies arise because the government has given one person or firm the exclusive right to sell some good or service. Sometimes the monopoly arises from the sheer political clout of the would-be monopolist. Kings, for example, once granted exclusive business licences to their friends and allies. At other times, the government grants a monopoly because doing so is viewed to be in the public interest.

The patent and copyright laws are two important examples of how the government creates a monopoly to serve the public interest. When a pharmaceutical company discovers a new drug, it can apply to the government for a patent. If the government deems the drug to be truly original, it approves the patent, which gives the company the exclusive right to manufacture and sell the drug for 20 years. Similarly, when a novelist finishes a book, she can copyright it. The copyright is a government guarantee that no one can print and sell the work without the author's permission. The copyright makes the novelist a monopolist in the sale of her novel.

The effects of patent and copyright laws are easy to see. Because these laws give one producer a monopoly, they lead to higher prices than would occur under competition. But by allowing these monopoly producers to charge higher prices and earn higher profits, the laws also encourage some desirable behaviour. Drug companies are allowed to be monopolists in the drugs they discover in order to encourage research. Authors are allowed to be monopolists in the sale of their books to encourage them to write more and better books.

-Gov't patronage in the business world

Thus, the laws governing patents and copyrights have a benefit and costs. The benefit of the patent and copyright laws is the increased incentive for creative activity. This benefit is offset, to some extent, by the costs of monopoly pricing, which we examine fully later in this chapter.

Natural Monopolies

natural monopoly
a monopoly that arises because a single firm can supply a good or service to an entire market at a smaller cost than could two or more firms

— arise through economies oF scale

An industry is a **natural monopoly** when a single firm can supply a good or service to an entire market at a lower cost than could two or more firms. A natural monopoly arises when there are economies of scale over the relevant range of output. Figure 15.1 shows the average total costs of a firm with economies of scale. In this case, a single firm can produce any amount of output at least cost. That is, for any given amount of output, a larger number of firms leads to less output per firm and higher average total cost.

An example of a natural monopoly is the distribution of water. To provide water to residents of a town, a firm must build a network of pipes throughout the town. If two or more firms were to compete in the provision of this service, each firm would have to pay the fixed cost of building a network. Thus, the average total cost of water is lowest if a single firm serves the entire market.

We saw other examples of natural monopolies when we discussed public goods and common resources in Chapter 11. We noted that *club goods* are excludable but not rival in consumption. An example is a bridge used so infrequently that it is never congested. The bridge is excludable because a toll collector can prevent someone from using it. The bridge is not rival in consumption because use of the bridge by one person does not diminish the ability of others to use it. Because there is a fixed cost of building the bridge and a negligible marginal cost of additional users, the

FIGURE 15.1

Economies of Scale as a Cause of Monopoly

When a firm's average-total-cost curve continually declines, the firm has what is called a natural monopoly. In this case, when production is divided among more firms, each firm produces less, and average total cost rises. As a result, a single firm can produce any given amount at the smallest cost.

average total cost of a trip across the bridge (the total cost divided by the number of trips) falls as the number of trips rises. Hence, the bridge is a natural monopoly.

When a firm is a natural monopoly, it is less concerned about new entrants eroding its monopoly power. Normally, a firm has trouble maintaining a monopoly position without ownership of a key resource or government protection. The monopolist's profit attracts entrants into the market, and these entrants make the market more competitive. By contrast, entering a market in which another firm has a natural monopoly is unattractive. Would-be entrants know that they cannot achieve the same low costs that the monopolist enjoys because, after entry, each firm would have a smaller piece of the market.

In some cases, the size of the market is one determinant of whether an industry is a natural monopoly. Again, consider a bridge across a river. When the population is small, the bridge may be a natural monopoly. A single bridge can satisfy the entire demand for trips across the river at lowest cost. Yet as the population grows and the bridge becomes congested, satisfying the entire demand may require two or more bridges across the same river. Thus, as a market expands, a natural monopoly can evolve into a competitive market.

An example of a near-monopoly bridge relevant to Canada is the Ambassador Bridge between Windsor, Ontario, and Detroit, Michigan. It is the busiest international border crossing in North America, accounting for over 20 percent of the trade flow between Canada and the United States, and it is owned and operated by a private U.S. company, Detroit International Bridge Company. While there is some competition for border crossing in the area (for example, the Detroit–Windsor Tunnel, which is jointly owned by the two cities), the high volume of traffic and the relative lack of competition has allowed the owner of the Ambassador Bridge to charge the highest bridge tolls in North America. The near-monopoly of the Ambassador Bridge is currently under threat due to a proposed government-owned second Windsor–Detroit bridge.

→ People need to use the bridge, and since it's a monopoly, owners of the bridge make massive profits.

QuickQuiz   What are the three reasons that a market might have a monopoly?
• Give two examples of monopolies, and explain the reason for each.

HOW MONOPOLIES MAKE PRODUCTION AND PRICING DECISIONS

Now that we know how monopolies arise, we can consider how a monopoly firm decides how much of its product to make and what price to charge for it. The analysis of monopoly behaviour in this section is the starting point for evaluating whether monopolies are desirable and what policies the government might pursue in monopoly markets.

Monopoly versus Competition

The key difference between a competitive firm and a monopoly is the monopoly's ability to influence the price of its output. A competitive firm is small relative to the market in which it operates and, therefore, takes the price of its output as given by market conditions. By contrast, because a monopoly is the sole producer in its market, it can alter the price of its good by adjusting the quantity it supplies to the market.

Price takers vs Price Makers

FIGURE 15.2

Demand Curves for Competitive and Monopoly Firms

Because competitive firms are price takers, they in effect face horizontal demand curves, as in panel (a). Because a monopoly firm is the sole producer in its market, it faces the downward-sloping market demand curve, as in panel (b). As a result, the monopoly has to accept a lower price if it wants to sell more output.

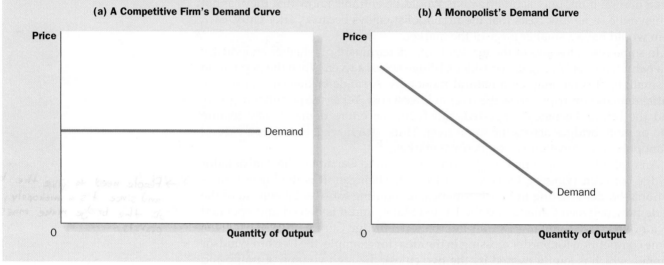

One way to view this difference between a competitive firm and a monopoly is to consider the demand curve that each firm faces. When we analyzed profit maximization by competitive firms in the preceding chapter, we drew the market price as a horizontal line. Because a competitive firm can sell as much or as little as it wants at this price, the competitive firm faces a horizontal demand curve, as in panel (a) of Figure 15.2. In effect, because the competitive firm sells a product with many perfect substitutes (the products of all the other firms in its market), the demand curve that any one firm faces is perfectly elastic.

By contrast, because a monopoly is the sole producer in its market, its demand curve is the market demand curve. Thus, the monopolist's demand curve slopes downward for all the usual reasons, as in panel (b) of Figure 15.2. If the monopolist raises the price of its good, consumers buy less of it. Looked at another way, if the monopolist reduces the quantity of output it sells, the price of its output increases.

The market demand curve provides a constraint on a monopoly's ability to profit from its market power. A monopolist would prefer, if it were possible, to charge a high price and sell a large quantity at that high price. The market demand curve makes that outcome impossible. In particular, the market demand curve describes the combinations of price and quantity that are available to a monopoly firm. By adjusting the quantity produced (or, equivalently, the price charged), the monopolist can choose any point on the demand curve, but it cannot choose a point off the demand curve.

What point on the demand curve will the monopolist choose? As with competitive firms, we assume that the monopolist's goal is to maximize profit. Because the firm's profit is total revenue minus total costs, our next task in explaining monopoly behaviour is to examine a monopolist's revenue.

TABLE 15.1

Quantity of Water (Q)	Price (P)	Total Revenue (TR = P × Q)	Average Revenue (AR = TR/Q)	Marginal Revenue (MR = ΔTR/ΔQ)
0 litres	$11	$ 0	—	
				$10
1	10	10	$10	
				8
2	9	18	9	
				6
3	8	24	8	
				4
4	7	28	7	
				2
5	6	30	6	
				0
6	5	30	5	
				−2
7	4	28	4	
				−4
8	3	24	3	

A Monopoly's Total, Average, and Marginal Revenue

A Monopoly's Revenue

Consider a town with a single producer of water. Table 15.1 shows how the monopoly's revenue might depend on the amount of water produced.

The first two columns show the monopolist's demand schedule. If the monopolist produces 1 L of water, it can sell that litre for $10. If it produces 2 L, it must lower the price to $9 in order to sell both litres. And if it produces 3 L, it must lower the price to $8. And so on. If you graphed these two columns of numbers, you would get a typical downward-sloping demand curve.

The third column of the table presents the monopolist's *total revenue*. It equals the quantity sold (from the first column) times the price (from the second column). The fourth column computes the firm's *average revenue*, the amount of revenue the firm receives per unit sold. We compute average revenue by taking the number for total revenue in the third column and dividing it by the quantity of output in the first column. As we discussed in the previous chapter, average revenue always equals the price of the good. This is true for monopolists as well as for competitive firms.

The last column of Table 15.1 computes the firm's *marginal revenue*, the amount of revenue that the firm receives for each additional unit of output. We compute marginal revenue by taking the change in total revenue when output increases by 1 unit. For example, when the firm is producing 3 L of water, it receives total revenue of $24. Raising production to 4 L increases total revenue to $28. Thus, marginal revenue is $28 minus $24, or $4.

Table 15.1 shows a result that is important for understanding monopoly behaviour: *A monopolist's marginal revenue is always less than the price of its good.* For example, if the firm raises production of water from 3 to 4 L, it will increase total revenue by only $4, even though it will be able to sell each litre for $7. For a monopoly, marginal revenue is lower than price because a monopoly faces a downward-sloping demand curve. To increase the amount sold, a monopoly firm must lower the price of its good. Hence, to sell the fourth litre of water, the monopolist must get $1 less revenue for each of the first three litres. This $3 loss accounts for the difference between the price of the fourth litre ($7) and the marginal revenue of that fourth litre ($4).

Marginal revenue for monopolies is very different from marginal revenue for competitive firms. When a monopoly increases the amount it sells, it has two effects on total revenue ($P \times Q$):

1. *The output effect:* More output is sold, so Q is higher, which tends to increase total revenue.
2. *The price effect:* The price falls, so P is lower, which tends to decrease total revenue.

$MR < Demand / AR / P$

Because a competitive firm can sell all it wants at the market price, there is no price effect. When it increases production by 1 unit, it receives the market price for that unit, and it does not receive any less for the units it was already selling. That is, because the competitive firm is a price taker, its marginal revenue equals the price of its good. By contrast, when a monopoly increases production by 1 unit, it must reduce the price it charges for every unit it sells, and this cut in price reduces revenue on the units it was already selling. As a result, a monopoly's marginal revenue is less than its price.

Figure 15.3 graphs the demand curve and the marginal-revenue curve for a monopoly firm. (Because the firm's price equals its average revenue, the demand curve is also the average-revenue curve.) These two curves always start at the same point on the vertical axis because the marginal revenue of the first unit sold equals the price of the good. But for the reason we just discussed, the monopolist's marginal revenue on all units after the first is less than the price of the good. Thus, a monopoly's marginal-revenue curve lies below its demand curve.

FIGURE 15.3

Demand and Marginal-Revenue Curves for a Monopoly

The demand curve shows how the quantity affects the price of the good. The marginal-revenue curve shows how the firm's revenue changes when the quantity increases by 1 unit. Because the price on all units sold must fall if the monopoly increases production, marginal revenue is always less than the price.

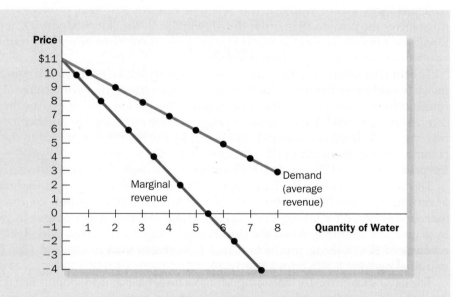

You can see in the figure (as well as in Table 15.1) that marginal revenue can even become negative. Marginal revenue is negative when the price effect on revenue is greater than the output effect. In this case, when the firm produces an extra unit of output, the price falls by enough to cause the firm's total revenue to decline, even though the firm is selling more units.

Profit Maximization

Now that we have considered the revenue of a monopoly firm, we are ready to examine how such a firm maximizes profit. Recall from Chapter 1 that one of the ten principles of economics is that rational people think at the margin. This lesson is as true for monopolists as it is for competitive firms. Here we apply the logic of marginal analysis to the monopolist's decision about how much to produce.

Figure 15.4 graphs the demand curve, the marginal-revenue curve, and the cost curves for a monopoly firm. All these curves should seem familiar: The demand and marginal-revenue curves are like those in Figure 15.3, and the cost curves are like those we encountered in the previous two chapters. These curves contain all the information we need to determine the level of output that a profit-maximizing monopolist will choose.

Suppose, first, that the firm is producing at a low level of output, such as Q_1. In this case, marginal cost is less than marginal revenue. If the firm increased production by 1 unit, the additional revenue would exceed the additional costs, and profit would rise. Thus, when marginal cost is less than marginal revenue, the firm can increase profit by producing more units.

A similar argument applies at high levels of output, such as Q_2. In this case, marginal cost is greater than marginal revenue. If the firm reduced production by 1 unit, the costs saved would exceed the revenue lost. Thus, if marginal cost is greater than marginal revenue, the firm can raise profit by reducing production.

MC < MR ↑ production for more profit

MC > MR ↓ production for more profit.

Max Profit: MR = MC

FIGURE 15.4

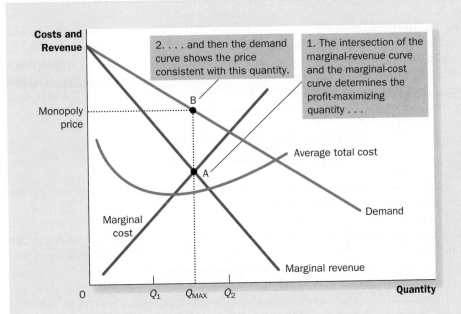

Profit Maximization for a Monopoly

A monopoly maximizes profit by choosing the quantity at which marginal revenue equals marginal cost (point A). It then uses the demand curve to find the price that will induce consumers to buy that quantity (point B).

2. . . . and then the demand curve shows the price consistent with this quantity.

1. The intersection of the marginal-revenue curve and the marginal-cost curve determines the profit-maximizing quantity . . .

Costs and Revenue

Monopoly price

Average total cost

Marginal cost

Demand

Marginal revenue

Quantity

0   Q_1 Q_{MAX} Q_2

WHY A MONOPOLY DOES NOT HAVE A SUPPLY CURVE

You may have noticed that we have analyzed the price in a monopoly market using the market demand curve and the firm's cost curves. We have not made any mention of the market supply curve. By contrast, when we analyzed prices in competitive markets beginning in Chapter 4, the two most important words were always *supply* and *demand*.

What happened to the supply curve? Although monopoly firms make decisions about what quantity to supply (in the way described in this chapter), a monopoly does not have a supply curve. A supply curve tells us the quantity that firms choose to supply at any given price. This concept makes sense when we are analyzing competitive firms, which are price takers. But a monopoly firm is a price maker, not a price taker. It is not meaningful to ask what amount such a firm would produce at any price because the firm sets the price at the same time as it chooses the quantity to supply.

Indeed, the monopolist's decision about how much to supply is impossible to separate from the demand curve it faces. The shape of the demand curve determines the shape of the marginal-revenue curve, which in turn determines the monopolist's profit-maximizing quantity. In a competitive market, supply decisions can be analyzed without knowing the demand curve, but that is not true in a monopoly market. Therefore, we never talk about a monopoly's supply curve.

In the end, the firm adjusts its level of production until the quantity reaches Q_{MAX}, at which marginal revenue equals marginal cost. *Thus, the monopolist's profit-maximizing quantity of output is determined by the intersection of the marginal-revenue curve and the marginal-cost curve.* In Figure 15.4, this intersection occurs at point A.

You might recall from the previous chapter that competitive firms also choose the quantity of output at which marginal revenue equals marginal cost. In following this rule for profit maximization, competitive firms and monopolies are alike. But there is also an important difference between these types of firms: The marginal revenue of a competitive firm equals its price, whereas the marginal revenue of a monopoly is less than its price. That is,

$$\text{For a competitive firm:} \quad P = MR = MC$$
$$\text{For a monopoly firm:} \quad P > MR = MC$$

The equality of marginal revenue and marginal cost determines the profit-maximizing quantity for both types of firms. What differs is how the price is related to marginal revenue and marginal cost.

How does the monopoly find the profit-maximizing price for its product? The demand curve answers this question because the demand curve relates the amount that customers are willing to pay to the quantity sold. Thus, after the monopoly firm chooses the quantity of output that equates marginal revenue and marginal cost, it uses the demand curve to find the highest price it can charge for that quantity. In Figure 15.4, the profit-maximizing price is found at point B.

We can now see a key difference between markets with competitive firms and markets with a monopoly firm: *In competitive markets, price equals marginal cost. In monopolized markets, price exceeds marginal cost.* As we will see in a moment, this finding is crucial to understanding the social cost of monopoly.

A Monopoly's Profit

How much profit does the monopoly make? To see the monopoly's profit, recall that profit equals total revenue (TR) minus total costs (TC):

$$\text{Profit} = TR - TC$$

We can rewrite this as

$$\text{Profit} = (TR/Q - TC/Q) \times Q$$

TR/Q is average revenue, which equals the price P, and TC/Q is average total cost ATC. Therefore,

$$\text{Profit} = (P - ATC) \times Q$$

This equation for profit (which also holds for competitive firms) allows us to measure the monopolist's profit in our graph.

Consider the shaded box in Figure 15.5. The height of the box (the segment BC) is price minus average total cost, $P - ATC$, which is the profit on the typical unit sold. The width of the box (the segment DC) is the quantity sold, Q_{MAX}. Therefore, the area of this box is the monopoly firm's total profit.

FIGURE 15.5

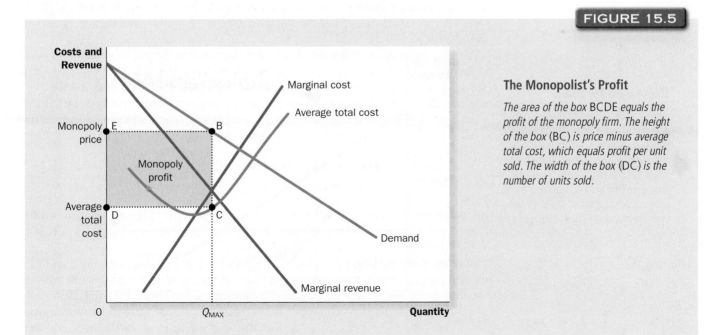

The Monopolist's Profit

The area of the box BCDE equals the profit of the monopoly firm. The height of the box (BC) is price minus average total cost, which equals profit per unit sold. The width of the box (DC) is the number of units sold.

Case Study
MONOPOLY DRUGS VERSUS GENERIC DRUGS

According to our analysis, prices are determined quite differently in monopolized markets from the way they are in competitive markets. A natural place to test this theory is the market for pharmaceutical drugs because this market takes on both market structures. When a firm discovers a new drug, patent laws give the firm a monopoly on the sale of that drug. But eventually the firm's patent runs out, and any company can make and sell the drug. At that time, the market switches from being monopolistic to being competitive.

What should happen to the price of a drug when the patent runs out? Figure 15.6 shows the market for a typical drug. In this figure, the marginal cost of the drug is constant. (This is approximately true for many drugs.)

During the life of the patent, the monopoly firm maximizes profit by producing the quantity at which marginal revenue equals marginal cost and charging a price well above marginal cost. But when the patent runs out, the profit from making the drug should encourage new firms to enter the market. As the market becomes more competitive, the price should fall to equal marginal cost.

Experience is, in fact, consistent with our theory. When the patent on a drug expires, other companies quickly enter and begin selling so-called generic products that are chemically identical to the former monopolist's brand-name product. And just as our analysis predicts, the price of the competitively produced generic drug is well below the price that the monopolist was charging.

FIGURE 15.6

The Market for Drugs

When a patent gives a firm a monopoly over the sale of a drug, the firm charges the monopoly price, which is well above the marginal cost of making the drug. When the patent on a drug runs out, new firms enter the market, making it more competitive. As a result, the price falls from the monopoly price to marginal cost.

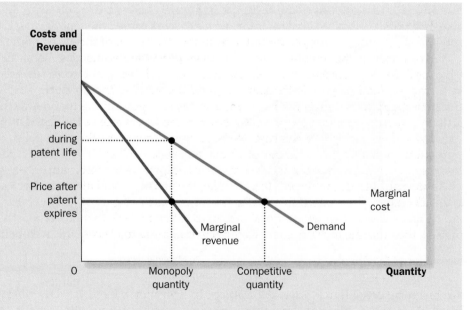

The expiration of a patent, however, does not cause the monopolist to lose all its market power. Some consumers remain loyal to the brand-name drug, perhaps out of fear that the new generic drugs are not actually the same as the drug they have been using for years. As a result, the former monopolist can continue to charge a price above the price charged by its new competitors. For example, one of the top-selling brand-name prescription drugs on the market in Canada is the cholesterol-lowering drug Lipitor. Although the price varies by province, a one-month supply costs about $85. The generic equivalent, Atorvastatin, which is the same medicine, sells for about $46. This price differential can persist because some consumers are not convinced that the two pills are perfect substitutes. While it is clear that the generic equivalent is much cheaper, many analysts have found that generic drug prices in Canada are much higher than they are in other countries. This is because several factors, including some government policies, have restricted the amount of competition between generic drug manufacturers in Canada, where the market is dominated by two large companies, Apotex and Teva (formerly Teva Novopharm).●

QuickQuiz Explain how a monopolist chooses the quantity of output to produce and the price to charge.

THE WELFARE COST OF MONOPOLY

Is monopoly a good way to organize a market? We have seen that a monopoly, in contrast to a competitive firm, charges a price above marginal cost. From the standpoint of consumers, this high price makes monopoly undesirable. At the same time, however, the monopoly is earning profit from charging this high price. From the standpoint of the owners of the firm, the high price makes monopoly very desirable. Is it possible that the benefits to the firm's owners exceed the costs imposed on consumers, making monopoly desirable from the standpoint of society as a whole?

We can answer this question using the tools of welfare economics. Recall from Chapter 7 that total surplus measures the economic well-being of buyers and sellers in a market. Total surplus is the sum of consumer surplus and producer surplus. Consumer surplus is consumers' willingness to pay for a good minus the amount they actually pay for it. Producer surplus is the amount producers receive for a good minus their costs of producing it. In this case, there is a single producer—the monopolist.

You can probably guess the result of this analysis. In Chapter 7, we concluded that the equilibrium of supply and demand in a competitive market is not only a natural outcome but a desirable one. In particular, the invisible hand of the market leads to an allocation of resources that makes total surplus as large as it can be. Because a monopoly leads to an allocation of resources different from that in a competitive market, the outcome must, in some way, fail to maximize total economic well-being.

The Deadweight Loss

We begin by considering what the monopoly firm would do if it were run by a benevolent social planner. The social planner cares not only about the profit

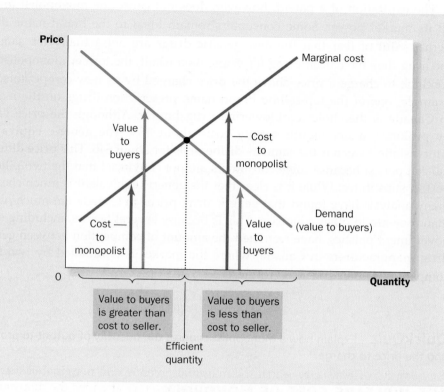

FIGURE 15.7

The Efficient Level of Output

A benevolent social planner who wanted to maximize total surplus in the market would choose the level of output where the demand curve and marginal-cost curve intersect. Below this level, the value of the good to the marginal buyer (as reflected in the demand curve) exceeds the marginal cost of making the good. Above this level, the value to the marginal buyer is less than marginal cost.

earned by the firm's owners but also about the benefits received by the firm's consumers. The planner tries to maximize total surplus, which equals producer surplus (profit) plus consumer surplus. Keep in mind that total surplus equals the value of the good to consumers minus the costs of making the good incurred by the monopoly producer.

Figure 15.7 analyzes what level of output a benevolent social planner would choose. The demand curve reflects the value of the good to consumers, as measured by their willingness to pay for it. The marginal-cost curve reflects the costs of the monopolist. *Thus, the socially efficient quantity is found where the demand curve and the marginal-cost curve intersect.* Below this quantity, the value to consumers exceeds the marginal cost of providing the good, so increasing output would raise total surplus. Above this quantity, the marginal cost exceeds the value to consumers, so decreasing output would raise total surplus. At the optimal quantity, the value of an extra unit to consumers exactly equals the marginal cost of production.

If the social planner were running the monopoly, the firm could achieve this efficient outcome by charging the price found at the intersection of the demand and marginal-cost curves. Thus, like a competitive firm and unlike a profit-maximizing monopoly, a social planner would charge a price equal to marginal cost. Because this price would give consumers an accurate signal about the cost of producing the good, consumers would buy the efficient quantity.

We can evaluate the welfare effects of monopoly by comparing the level of output that the monopolist chooses to the level of output that a social planner would choose. As we have seen, the monopolist chooses to produce and sell

FIGURE 15.8

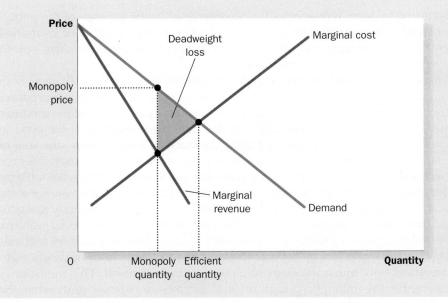

The Inefficiency of Monopoly

Because a monopoly charges a price above marginal cost, not all consumers who value the good at more than its cost buy it. Thus, the quantity produced and sold by a monopoly is below the socially efficient level. The deadweight loss is represented by the area of the triangle between the demand curve (which reflects the value of the good to consumers) and the marginal-cost curve (which reflects the costs of the monopoly producer).

the quantity of output at which the marginal-revenue and marginal-cost curves intersect; the social planner would choose the quantity at which the demand and marginal-cost curves intersect. Figure 15.8 shows the comparison. *The monopolist produces less than the socially efficient quantity of output.*

We can also view the inefficiency of monopoly in terms of the monopolist's price. Because the market demand curve describes a negative relationship between the price and quantity of the good, a quantity that is inefficiently low is equivalent to a price that is inefficiently high. When a monopolist charges a price above marginal cost, some potential consumers value the good at more than its marginal cost but less than the monopolist's price. These consumers do not end up buying the good. Because the value these consumers place on the good is greater than the cost of providing it to them, this result is inefficient. Thus, monopoly pricing prevents some mutually beneficial trades from taking place.

The inefficiency of monopoly can be measured with a deadweight loss triangle, as illustrated in Figure 15.8. Because the demand curve reflects the value to consumers and the marginal-cost curve reflects the costs to the monopoly producer, the area of the deadweight loss triangle between the demand curve and the marginal-cost curve equals the total surplus lost because of monopoly pricing. It is the reduction in economic well-being that results from the monopoly's use of its market power.

The deadweight loss caused by monopoly is similar to the deadweight loss caused by a tax. Indeed, a monopolist is like a private tax collector. As we saw in Chapter 8, a tax on a good places a wedge between consumers' willingness to pay (as reflected by the demand curve) and producers' costs (as reflected by the supply curve). Because a monopoly exerts its market power by charging a price above marginal cost, it creates a similar wedge. In both cases, the wedge causes the quantity sold to fall short of the social optimum. The difference between the two cases is that the government gets the revenue from a tax, whereas a private firm gets the monopoly profit.

–Gov't intervention needed since the monopolist quantity isn't efficient

The Monopoly's Profit: A Social Cost?

It is tempting to decry monopolies for "profiteering" at the expense of the public. And, indeed, a monopoly firm does earn a higher profit by virtue of its market power. According to the economic analysis of monopoly, however, the firm's profit is not in itself necessarily a problem for society.

Welfare in a monopolized market, like all markets, includes the welfare of both consumers and producers. Whenever a consumer pays an extra dollar to a producer because of a monopoly price, the consumer is worse off by a dollar, and the producer is better off by the same amount. This transfer from the consumers of the good to the owners of the monopoly does not affect the market's total surplus—the sum of consumer and producer surplus. In other words, the monopoly profit itself does not represent a shrinkage in the size of the economic pie; it merely represents a bigger slice for producers and a smaller slice for consumers. Unless consumers are for some reason more deserving than producers—a normative judgment about equity that goes beyond the realm of economic efficiency—the monopoly profit is not a social problem.

The problem in a monopolized market arises because the firm produces and sells a quantity of output below the level that maximizes total surplus. The deadweight loss measures how much the economic pie shrinks as a result. This inefficiency is connected to the monopoly's high price: Consumers buy fewer units when the firm raises its price above marginal cost. But keep in mind that the profit earned on the units that continue to be sold is not the problem. The problem stems from the inefficiently low quantity of output. Put differently, if the high monopoly price did not discourage some consumers from buying the good, it would raise producer surplus by exactly the amount it reduced consumer surplus, leaving total surplus the same as could be achieved by a benevolent social planner.

There is, however, a possible exception to this conclusion. Suppose that a monopoly firm has to incur additional costs to maintain its monopoly position. For example, a firm with a government-created monopoly might need to hire lobbyists to convince lawmakers to continue its monopoly. In this case, the monopoly may use up some of its monopoly profits paying for these additional costs. If so, the social loss from monopoly includes both these costs and the deadweight loss resulting from a price above marginal cost.

For example, earlier in the chapter the near monopoly Windsor–Detroit Ambassador Bridge was discussed. In response to a proposed government-owned bridge, the owners of the Ambassador Bridge have spent millions on advertising opposing the second bridge and sponsored a petition calling for a plebiscite. These costs can be viewed as social costs incurred to protect its monopoly position.

QuickQuiz   How does a monopolist's quantity of output compare to the quantity of output that maximizes total surplus?

PRICE DISCRIMINATION

price discrimination
the business practice of selling the same good at different prices to different customers

So far we have been assuming that the monopoly firm charges the same price to all customers. Yet in many cases firms try to sell the same good to different customers for different prices, even though the costs of producing for the two customers are the same. This practice is called **price discrimination**.

Before discussing the behaviour of a price-discriminating monopolist, we should note that price discrimination is not possible when a good is sold in a competitive market. In a competitive market, many firms are selling the same good at the market price. No firm is willing to charge a lower price to any customer because the firm can sell all it wants at the market price. And if any firm tried to charge a higher price to a customer, that customer would buy from another firm. For a firm to price-discriminate, it must have some market power.

A Parable about Pricing

To understand why a monopolist would want to price-discriminate, let's consider a simple example. Imagine that you are the president of Readalot Publishing Company. Readalot's best-selling author has just written her latest novel. To keep things simple, let's imagine that you pay the author a flat $2 million for the exclusive rights to publish the book. Let's also assume that the cost of printing the book is zero. Readalot's profit, therefore, is the revenue it gets from selling the book minus the $2 million it has paid to the author. Given these assumptions, how would you, as Readalot's president, decide the book's price?

Your first step is to estimate the demand for the book. Readalot's marketing department tells you that the book will attract two types of readers. The book will appeal to the author's 100 000 die-hard fans who are willing to pay as much as $30 for the book. In addition, the book will appeal to about 400 000 less enthusiastic readers who will pay up to $5.

If Readalot charges a single price to all consumers, what price maximizes profit? There are two natural prices to consider: $30 is the highest price Readalot can charge and still get the 100 000 die-hard fans, and $5 is the highest price it can charge and still get the entire market of 500 000 potential readers. It is a matter of simple arithmetic to solve Readalot's problem. At a price of $30, Readalot sells 100 000 copies, has revenue of $3 million, and makes profit of $1 million. At a price of $5, it sells 500 000 copies, has revenue of $2.5 million, and makes a profit of $500 000. Thus, Readalot maximizes profit by charging $30 and forgoing the opportunity to sell to the 400 000 less enthusiastic readers.

Notice that Readalot's decision causes a deadweight loss. There are 400 000 readers willing to pay $5 for the book, and the marginal cost of providing it to them is zero. Thus, $2 million of total surplus is lost when Readalot charges the higher price. This deadweight loss is the usual inefficiency that arises whenever a monopolist charges a price above marginal cost.

Now suppose that Readalot's marketing department makes an important discovery: These two groups of readers are in separate markets. All the die-hard fans live in Australia, and all the other readers live in Canada. Moreover, it is difficult for readers in one country to buy books in the other.

In response to this discovery, Readalot can change its marketing strategy and increase profits. To the 100 000 Australian readers, it can charge $30 for the book. To the 400 000 Canadian readers, it can charge $5 for the book. In this case, revenue is $3 million in Australia and $2 million in Canada, for a total of $5 million. Profit is then $3 million, which is substantially greater than the $1 million the company could earn charging the same $30 price to all customers. Not surprisingly, Readalot chooses to follow this strategy of price discrimination.

[handwritten margin notes:]
— Higher price = more revenue, but alienating section of market
— Lower price = Higher demand, lower revenue

— Two types of consumers in two different markets = two different prices to maximize revenue

The story of Readalot Publishing is hypothetical, but it describes accurately the business practice of many publishing companies. Textbooks, for example, are often sold at a lower price in Europe than in Canada. Even more important is the price differential between hardcover books and paperbacks. When a publisher has a new novel, it initially releases an expensive hardcover edition and later releases a cheaper paperback edition. The difference in price between these two editions far exceeds the difference in printing costs. The publisher's goal is just as in our example. By selling the hardcover to die-hard fans and the paperback to less enthusiastic readers, the publisher price-discriminates and raises its profit.

The Moral of the Story

Like any parable, the story of Readalot Publishing is stylized. Yet, also like any parable, it teaches some important and general lessons. In this case, there are three lessons to be learned about price discrimination.

The first and most obvious lesson is that price discrimination is a rational strategy for a profit-maximizing monopolist. In other words, by charging different prices to different customers, a monopolist can increase its profit. In essence, a price-discriminating monopolist charges each customer a price closer to that customer's willingness to pay than is possible with a single price.

The second lesson is that price discrimination requires the ability to separate customers according to their willingness to pay. In our example, customers were separated geographically. But sometimes monopolists choose other differences, such as age or income, to distinguish among customers.

A corollary to this second lesson is that certain market forces can prevent firms from price-discriminating. In particular, one such force is *arbitrage,* the process of buying a good in one market at a low price and selling it in another market at a higher price in order to profit from the price difference. In our example, suppose that Australian bookstores could buy the book in Canada and resell it to Australian readers. This arbitrage would prevent Readalot from price-discriminating because no Australian would buy the book at the higher price.

The third lesson from our parable is perhaps the most surprising: Price discrimination can raise economic welfare. Recall that a deadweight loss arises when Readalot charges a single $30 price, because the 400 000 less enthusiastic readers do not end up with the book, even though they value it at more than its marginal cost of production. By contrast, when Readalot price-discriminates, all readers end up with the book, and the outcome is efficient. Thus, price discrimination can eliminate the inefficiency inherent in monopoly pricing.

Note that the increase in welfare from price discrimination shows up as higher producer surplus rather than higher consumer surplus. In our example, consumers are no better off for having bought the book: The price they pay exactly equals the value they place on the book, so they receive no consumer surplus. The entire increase in total surplus from price discrimination accrues to Readalot Publishing in the form of higher profit.

The Analytics of Price Discrimination

Let's consider a bit more formally how price discrimination affects economic welfare. We begin by assuming that the monopolist can price-discriminate perfectly.

FIGURE 15.9

Welfare with and without Price Discrimination

Panel (a) shows a monopolist that charges the same price to all customers. Total surplus in this market equals the sum of profit (producer surplus) and consumer surplus. Panel (b) shows a monopolist that can perfectly price-discriminate. Because consumer surplus equals zero, total surplus now equals the firm's profit. Comparing these two panels, you can see that perfect price discrimination raises profit, raises total surplus, and lowers consumer surplus.

(a) Monopolist with Single Price

(b) Monopolist with Perfect Price Discrimination

Perfect price discrimination describes a situation in which the monopolist knows exactly the willingness to pay each customer and can charge each customer a different price. In this case, the monopolist charges each customer exactly his willingness to pay, and the monopolist gets the entire surplus in every transaction. Perfect price discrimination is sometimes referred to as first-degree price discrimination.

Figure 15.9 illustrates producer and consumer surplus with and without price discrimination. To keep things simple, this figure is drawn assuming constant per unit costs—that is, marginal and average cost are constant and equal. Without price discrimination, the firm charges a single price above marginal cost, as shown in panel (a). Because some potential customers who value the good at more than marginal cost do not buy it at this high price, the monopoly causes a deadweight loss. Yet when a firm can perfectly price-discriminate, as shown in panel (b), each customer who values the good at more than marginal cost buys the good and is charged his willingness to pay. All mutually beneficial trades take place, there is no deadweight loss, and the entire surplus derived from the market goes to the monopoly producer in the form of profit.

In reality, of course, price discrimination is not perfect. Customers do not walk into stores with signs displaying their willingness to pay. Instead, firms price-discriminate by dividing customers into groups: young versus old, weekday versus weekend shoppers, Canadians versus Australians, and so on. Unlike those in our parable of Readalot Publishing, customers within each group differ in their willingness to pay for the product, making perfect price discrimination impossible.

Imperfect price discrimination comes in two forms, referred to as second- and third-degree price discrimination. Second-degree price discrimination involves charging different prices to the same customer for different units that the customer buys. For example, many firms offer lower prices to customers who buy large quantities. A bakery might charge $0.50 for each donut but $5 for a dozen. This is a form of price discrimination because the customer pays a higher price for the first unit bought than for the twelfth. Quantity discounts are often a successful way of price-discriminating because a customer's willingness to pay for an additional unit declines as the customer buys more units.

Third-degree price discrimination can be achieved when the market can be segmented and when the segments have different elasticities of demand. A good example of third-degree price discrimination is movie tickets. Many movie theatres charge a lower price for children and senior citizens than for other patrons. This fact is hard to explain in a competitive market. In a competitive market, price equals marginal cost, and the marginal cost of providing a seat for a child or senior citizen is the same as the marginal cost of providing a seat for anyone else. Yet this fact is easily explained if movie theatres have some local monopoly power and if children and senior citizens have a lower willingness to pay for a ticket. In this case, movie theatres raise their profit by price-discriminating.

This is illustrated in Figure 15.10 for the case of two market segments—adults and children. The total market demand in panel (a) is the sum of the demand of the two market segments, given in panels (b) and (c). It is assumed that the adult

FIGURE 15.10

Third-Degree Price Discrimination

Panels (b) and (c) show the demand and marginal-revenue curves for the adult and child segment of the market for movie tickets. Panel (a) sums these curves to give the demand and marginal-revenue curves for the total market. The monopolist maximizes profits by setting $MC = MR$ and selling a total quantity of Q_T [panel (a)], but this involves charging different prices in each market: P_A in the adult market [panel (b)] and P_C in the child market [panel (c)], with Q_A tickets sold to adults and Q_C tickets sold to children. The adult price is higher than the child price because the adult demand is less elastic.

demand curve is less elastic than the child demand curve, and that the price at which the demand of children is equal to zero is lower than the equivalent price for adults. This means that there is a kink in the total market-demand curve at the point where the children's demand curve kicks in. This kink is translated into the marginal-revenue curve as well.

The movie theatre decides on the total number of tickets to sell by equating MC with MR in panel (a). However there is not just one price. By drawing a horizontal line through the $MC = MR$ point until it intersects with the MR curves for adults (MR_A) and children (MR_C) and then reading the price off the respective demand curves determines the price in each market segment, P_A and P_C, as well as the number of tickets sold in each market, Q_A and Q_C. Not surprisingly the price in the adult market is higher because the demand curve is less elastic.

How does imperfect price discrimination affect welfare? The analysis of these pricing schemes is quite complicated, and it turns out that there is no general answer to this question. Compared to the monopoly outcome with a single price, imperfect price discrimination can raise, lower, or leave unchanged total surplus in a market. The only certain conclusion is that price discrimination raises the monopoly's profit—otherwise the firm would choose to charge all customers the same price.

[handwritten margin note: MC = MR is profit-max quantity, price is where this meets the demand curve]

Examples of Price Discrimination

Firms in our economy use various business strategies aimed at charging different prices to different customers. We have considered the example of quantity discounts and movie tickets. Now that we understand the economics of price discrimination, let's consider some other examples.

Airline Prices   Seats on airplanes are sold at many different prices. Most airlines charge a lower price for a round-trip ticket between two cities if the traveller stays over a Saturday night. At first this seems odd. Why should it matter to the airline whether a passenger stays over a Saturday night? The reason is that this rule provides a way to separate business travellers and personal travellers. A passenger on a business trip has a high willingness to pay and, most likely, does not want to stay over a Saturday night. By contrast, a passenger travelling for personal reasons has a lower willingness to pay and is more likely to be willing to stay over a Saturday night. Thus, the airlines can successfully price-discriminate by charging a lower price for passengers who stay over a Saturday night.

Discount Coupons   Many companies offer discount coupons to the public in newspapers and magazines. More recently, these coupons are available online via websites such as Groupon. Buyers have to clip coupons, or in Groupon's case, click a daily deal, in order to buy the good at a lower price. Why do companies offer these coupons? Why don't they just cut the price of the product to begin with?

One answer is that coupons allow companies to price-discriminate. Companies know that not all customers are willing to spend time to clip out coupons or sign up for Groupon and check on daily deals. Moreover, the willingness to use coupons is related to the consumer's willingness to pay. A rich and busy executive

Low-income = low willingness to pay = coupon price discrimination to people who wouldn't buy the product otherwise

is unlikely to spend her time clipping discount coupons out of the newspaper, and she is probably willing to pay a higher price for many goods. A person who is unemployed is more likely to clip coupons and to have a lower willingness to pay. Younger people who not only are more tech-savvy but may have a lower willingness to pay are more likely to use sites like Groupon. So, by charging a lower price only to those customers who use coupons, firms can successfully price-discriminate.

Financial Aid   Many colleges and universities give financial aid to needy students. One can view this policy as a type of price discrimination. Wealthy students have greater financial resources and, therefore, a higher willingness to pay than needy students. By charging high tuition and selectively offering financial aid, schools charge prices to customers based on the value they place on going to that school. This behaviour is like that of any price-discriminating monopolist.

QuickQuiz   Give two examples of price discrimination. • How does perfect price discrimination affect consumer surplus, producer surplus, and total surplus?

PUBLIC POLICY TOWARD MONOPOLIES

We have seen that monopolies, in contrast to competitive markets, fail to allocate resources efficiently. Monopolies produce less than the socially desirable quantity of output and, as a result, charge prices above marginal cost. Policymakers in the government can respond to the problem of monopoly in one of four ways:

1. By trying to make monopolized industries more competitive
2. By regulating the behaviour of the monopolies
3. By turning some private monopolies into public enterprises
4. By doing nothing at all

Increasing Competition with Competition Law

One way that the government can respond to the inefficiencies resulting from market power in general, and monopoly in particular, is through legislation designed to encourage competition and discourage the use of monopoly practices. For example, if a merger between two companies would make the industry less competitive and, as a result, reduce the economic well-being of the country as a whole, the government could pass laws that prevent such mergers.

Competition law in Canada is enforced by the Competition Bureau, a unit within the federal government's Industry Canada. Lawyers and economists in the bureau investigate anticompetitive practices that fall within the scope of the act. When appropriate, cases may be referred for criminal prosecution to the attorney general of Canada. In other instances, a case may be referred to the Competition Tribunal for review and adjudication.

The tribunal is a quasi-judicial body that is similar to a court. It consists of judges and lay members who are experts from the business, academic, and civil service communities. In most of the cases it deals with, the tribunal must determine whether a particular practice or action has an adverse effect on competition. If it concludes that there is an anticompetitive effect, the tribunal can issue an order to prohibit the practice or action. For example, the tribunal can block a merger or require that a firm divest itself of assets. In 2005, the Competition Bureau ruled that the merger of two of Canada's largest movie theatre companies, Cineplex Galaxy and Famous Players, would have substantial anticompetitive effects. Although the merger was allowed to proceed, the Bureau ordered Cineplex Galaxy to sell 35 theatres in 17 cities with total annual box-office revenues of about $100 million.

Competition law in Canada prevents other kinds of anticompetitive practices, some of which we will discuss in Chapter 16.

Competition laws have costs as well as benefits. Sometimes companies merge not to reduce competition but to lower costs through more efficient joint production. The benefits of greater efficiency as a result of mergers are called *synergies*. These considerations are particularly important in a global context because some Canadian companies are large and dominant in the domestic market but small in the international market. For example, although the banking market in Canada is dominated by the "Big Five," these banks are small players on the international banking scene. Some bankers have argued that Canadian banks can compete in international markets only by realizing the synergies that would result when operations are combined. Using this argument, four of Canada's largest banks sought permission to merge in 1998: the Royal Bank with the Bank of Montreal, and the Canadian Imperial Bank of Commerce with the Toronto-Dominion Bank. Both merger deals were rejected by the federal government.

If competition laws are to raise social welfare, the government must be able to determine which mergers are desirable and which are not. That is, it must be able to measure and compare the social benefit from synergies with the social cost of reduced competition. However, critics of competition laws are skeptical that the government can perform the necessary cost–benefit analysis with sufficient accuracy.

Regulation

Another way in which the government deals with the problem of monopoly is by regulating the behaviour of monopolists. This solution is common in the case of natural monopolies, such as water and electric companies. These companies are not allowed to charge any price they want. Instead, government agencies regulate their prices.

What price should the government set for a natural monopoly? This question is not as easy as it might at first appear. One might conclude that the price should equal the monopolist's marginal cost. If price equals marginal cost, customers will buy the quantity of the monopolist's output that maximizes total surplus, and the allocation of resources will be efficient.

There are, however, two practical problems with marginal-cost pricing as a regulatory system. The first is illustrated in Figure 15.11. Natural monopolies, by definition, have declining average total cost. As we discussed in Chapter 13, when average total cost is declining, marginal cost is less than average total cost. If regulators are to set price equal to marginal cost, that price will be less than the

- economies of scale

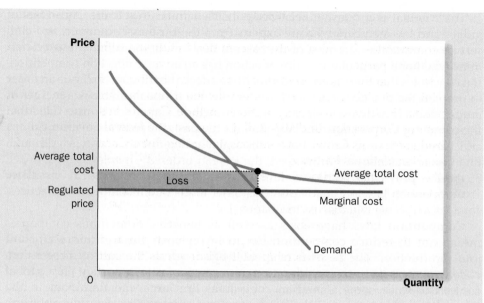

FIGURE 15.11

Marginal-Cost Pricing for a Natural Monopoly

Because a natural monopoly has declining average total cost, marginal cost is less than average total cost. Therefore, if regulators require a natural monopoly to charge a price equal to marginal cost, price will be below average total cost, and the monopoly will lose money.

firm's average total cost, and the firm will lose money. Instead of charging such a low price, the monopoly firm would just exit the industry.

Regulators can respond to this problem in various ways, none of which is perfect. One way is to subsidize the monopolist. In essence, the government picks up the losses inherent in marginal-cost pricing. Yet to pay for the subsidy, the government needs to raise money through taxation, which involves its own deadweight losses. Alternatively, the regulators can allow the monopolist to charge a price higher than marginal cost. If the regulated price equals average total cost, the monopolist earns exactly zero economic profit. Yet average-cost pricing leads to deadweight losses because the monopolist's price no longer reflects the marginal cost of producing the good. In essence, average-cost pricing is like a tax on the good the monopolist is selling.

The second problem with marginal-cost pricing as a regulatory system (and with average-cost pricing as well) is that it gives the monopolist no incentive to reduce costs. Each firm in a competitive market tries to reduce its costs because lower costs mean higher profits. But if a regulated monopolist knows that regulators will reduce prices whenever costs fall, the monopolist will not benefit from lower costs. In practice, regulators deal with this problem by allowing monopolists to keep some of the benefits from lower costs in the form of higher profit, a practice that requires some departure from marginal-cost pricing.

Public Ownership

The third policy used by the government to deal with monopoly is public ownership. That is, rather than regulating a natural monopoly that is run by a private firm, the government can run the monopoly itself. In contrast to the United States, where there is very little public ownership, this solution is common in many European countries. It is also relatively common in Canada, although somewhat less so in recent years.

In Canada, government ownership occurs at both the federal and the provincial/territorial levels. Government-owned firms are known as Crown corporations. Federal Crown corporations include Canada Post, the Canadian Broadcasting Corporation, and VIA Rail. In the past, the federal government has privatized some of its Crown corporations, including Petro-Canada, Air Canada, and Canadian National Railway.

At the provincial/territorial level, Crown corporations exist in insurance (Saskatchewan Government Insurance), hydroelectricity (Manitoba Hydro and Hydro-Québec), and telecommunications (Saskatchewan Tel). Gas and water utilities are also publicly owned in most provinces/territories.

Economists usually prefer private to public ownership of natural monopolies. The key issue is how the ownership of the firm affects the costs of production. Private owners have an incentive to minimize costs as long as they reap part of the benefit in the form of higher profit. If the firm's managers are doing a bad job of keeping costs down, the firm's owners will fire them. By contrast, if the government bureaucrats who run a monopoly do a bad job, the losers are the customers and taxpayers, whose only recourse is the political system. The bureaucrats may become a special-interest group and attempt to block cost-reducing reforms. Put simply, as a way of ensuring that firms are well run, the voting booth is less reliable than the profit motive.

Doing Nothing

Each of the forgoing policies aimed at reducing the problem of monopoly has drawbacks. As a result, some economists argue that it is often best for the government not to try to remedy the inefficiencies of monopoly pricing. Here is the assessment of economist George Stigler, who won the Nobel Prize for his work in industrial organization, writing in the *Fortune Encyclopedia of Economics*:

> A famous theorem in economics states that a competitive enterprise economy will produce the largest possible income from a given stock of resources. No real economy meets the exact conditions of the theorem, and all real economies will fall short of the ideal economy—a difference called "market failure." In my view, however, the degree of "market failure" for the American economy is much smaller than the "political failure" arising from the imperfections of economic policies found in real political systems.

As this quotation makes clear, determining the proper role of the government in the economy requires judgments about politics as well as economics.

QuickQuiz   Describe the ways policymakers can respond to the inefficiencies caused by monopolies. List a potential problem with each of these policy responses.

IN THE NEWS

PRICE DISCRIMINATION: OPPORTUNITIES FOR ARBITRAGE

In order for a firm to price-discriminate it must be difficult, or costly, for buyers to resell the good at a higher price. If this was not the case, an opportunity for arbitrage arises. Arbitrage occurs when an individual purchases a good at a low price and then immediately (or shortly thereafter) sells it for a higher price.

One common form of price discrimination is for firms to sell the same good for different prices in different countries, with demand conditions dictating the price in each country. Businesses hope that arbitrage will be too costly in this case. As the following article shows, if they are determined enough, arbitragers can take advantage of this.

A Different Kind of Package Holiday

The same Louis Vuitton handbag costs about 40% more in Japan than in France. To economists, this is a market imperfection begging for arbitrage. And Hong Kong, that bastion of entrepreneurship, is obliging. Here is how.

Nine Hong Kong Chinese recently spent a fortnight travelling through Europe. They started in Frankfurt and ended in Rome, passing through one city a day. Early every morning, a van picked them up from their hotel and drove them to the first Louis Vuitton store on the day's agenda. It parked around the corner, and the Chinese entered the store in pairs. They each bought as many Louis Vuitton handbags as they could carry and then returned to the van, in order to be transferred to the next store.

It was gruelling work, complains a girl from the van. She, like the rest in the group, went on the trip because it was an all-expenses-paid way to see Europe. (In fact, those who bought more than their quota of handbags even earned a bonus.) But the itinerary did not allow for any sightseeing at all, and for meals the group are given Chinese takeaway in the van.

The sales staff in the stores tended to be rude; the tour's "boss," says the girl, had expressly asked for bags "with a certain monogram pattern" that is all the rage in Japan, and one shop simply refused to sell her the nine bags she brought to the counter.

The boss never introduced himself to the group, but when his troops returned he stood near the arrivals hall at Hong Kong's airport, watching them claim their luggage. His business seems to be going well—another tour group is apparently already on the way. Savvy Hong Kong tourists claim to know of several competing organisers—an industry, in other words. Nor is Louis Vuitton the only target: Gucci tours have also taken place.

Should companies whose prices are being arbitraged in this way mind? Louis Vuitton's sales benefit from such tourism, after all. "We definitely do not think that a sale is a sale," complains an irate spokeswoman in Paris. "It took 150 years to build this brand," she says, and losing part of the retail network to a netherworld of shady Asians damages it.

So Louis Vuitton, along with other owners of luxury brands, is working with the authorities to crack down on such tourism. This is tricky, not only because of arbitrageurs tending to pay cash, but also because Louis Vuitton would hate to confuse them with its genuine customers from Asia, who have also been known to binge on bags.

CONCLUSION: THE PREVALENCE OF MONOPOLY

This chapter has discussed the behaviour of firms that have control over the prices they charge. We have seen that these firms behave very differently from the competitive firms studied in the previous chapter. Table 15.2 summarizes some of the key similarities and differences between competitive and monopoly markets.

From the standpoint of public policy, a crucial result is that monopolists produce less than the socially efficient quantity and charge prices above marginal cost. As a result, they cause deadweight losses. In some cases, these inefficiencies can be mitigated through price discrimination by the monopolist, but other times they call for policymakers to take an active role.

How prevalent are the problems of monopoly? There are two answers to this question.

In one sense, monopolies are common. Most firms have some control over the prices they charge. They are not forced to charge the market price for their goods, because their goods are not exactly the same as those offered by other firms. A Ford Taurus is not the same as a Toyota Camry. Ben & Jerry's ice cream is not the same as Breyers'. Each of these goods has a downward-sloping demand curve, which gives each producer some degree of monopoly power.

Yet firms with substantial monopoly power are quite rare. Few goods are truly unique. Most have substitutes that, even if not exactly the same, are very similar. Ben & Jerry can raise the price of its ice cream a little without losing all its sales, but if the company raises it very much, sales will fall substantially as its customers switch to another brand.

In the end, monopoly power is a matter of degree. It is true that many firms have some monopoly power. It is also true that their monopoly power is usually limited. In these cases, we will not go far wrong assuming that firms operate in competitive markets, even if that is not precisely the case.

TABLE 15.2

	Competition	Monopoly	
Similarities			Competition versus Monopoly: A Summary Comparison
Goal of firms	Maximize profits	Maximize profits	
Rule for maximizing	$MR = MC$	$MR = MC$	
Can earn economic profits in the short run?	Yes	Yes	
Differences			
Number of firms	Many	One	
Marginal revenue	$MR = P$	$MR < P$	
Price	$P = MC$	$P > MC$	
Produces welfare-maximizing level of output?	Yes	No	
Entry in long run?	Yes	No	
Can earn economic profits in long run?	No	Yes	
Price discrimination possible?	No	Yes	

SUMMARY

- A monopoly is a firm that is the sole seller in its market. A monopoly arises when a single firm owns a key resource, when the government gives a firm the exclusive right to produce a good, or when a single firm can supply the entire market at a lower cost than many firms could.

- Because a monopoly is the sole producer in its market, it faces a downward-sloping demand curve for its product. When a monopoly increases production by 1 unit, it causes the price of its good to fall, which reduces the amount of revenue earned on all units produced. As a result, a monopoly's marginal revenue is always below the price of its good.

- Like a competitive firm, a monopoly firm maximizes profit by producing the quantity at which marginal revenue equals marginal cost. The monopoly then chooses the price at which that quantity is demanded. Unlike a competitive firm, a monopoly firm's price exceeds its marginal revenue, so its price exceeds marginal cost.

- A monopolist's profit-maximizing level of output is below the level that maximizes the sum of consumer and producer surplus. That is, when the monopoly charges a price above marginal cost, some consumers who value the good more than its cost of production do not buy it. As a result, monopoly causes deadweight losses similar to those caused by taxes.

- Monopolists often can raise their profits by charging different prices for the same good based on a buyer's willingness to pay. This practice of price discrimination can raise economic welfare by getting the good to some consumers who otherwise would not buy it. In the extreme case of perfect price discrimination, the deadweight losses of monopoly are completely eliminated. More generally, when price discrimination is imperfect, it can either raise or lower welfare compared to the outcome with a single monopoly price.

- Policymakers can respond to the inefficiency of monopoly behaviour in four ways. (1) They can use the antitrust laws to try to make the industry more competitive. (2) They can regulate the prices that the monopoly charges. (3) They can turn the monopolist into a government-run enterprise. (4) Or, if the market failure is deemed small compared to the inevitable imperfections of policies, they can do nothing at all.

KEY CONCEPTS

monopoly, p. 320   natural monopoly, p. 322   price discrimination, p. 334

QUESTIONS FOR REVIEW

1. Give an example of a government-created monopoly. Is creating this monopoly necessarily bad public policy? Explain.

2. Define *natural monopoly*. What does the size of a market have to do with whether an industry is a natural monopoly?

3. Why is a monopolist's marginal revenue less than the price of its good? Can marginal revenue ever be negative? Explain.

4. Draw the demand, marginal-revenue, and marginal-cost curves for a monopolist. Show the profit-maximizing level of output. Show the profit-maximizing price.

5. In your diagram from the previous question, show the level of output that maximizes total surplus. Show the deadweight loss from the monopoly. Explain your answer.

6. What gives the government the power to regulate mergers between firms? From the standpoint of the welfare of society, give a good reason and a bad reason that two firms might want to merge.

7. Describe the two problems that arise when regulators tell a natural monopoly that it must set a price equal to marginal cost.

8. Give two examples of price discrimination. In each case, explain why the monopolist chooses to follow this business strategy.

PROBLEMS AND APPLICATIONS

1. A publisher faces the following demand schedule for the next novel of one of its popular authors:

Price	Quantity Demanded
$100	0
90	100 000
80	200 000
70	300 000
60	400 000
50	500 000
40	600 000
30	700 000
20	800 000
10	900 000
0	1 000 000

The author is paid $2 million to write the book, and the marginal cost of publishing the book is a constant $10 per book.

a. Compute total revenue, total cost, and profit at each quantity. What quantity would a profit-maximizing publisher choose? What price would it charge?

b. Compute marginal revenue. (Recall that $MR = \Delta TR/\Delta Q$.) How does marginal revenue compare to the price? Explain.

c. Graph the marginal-revenue, marginal-cost, and demand curves. At what quantity do the marginal-revenue and marginal-cost curves cross? What does this signify?

d. In your graph, shade in the deadweight loss. Explain in words what this means.

e. If the author was paid $3 million instead of $2 million to write the book, how would this affect the publisher's decision regarding the price to charge? Explain.

f. Suppose the publisher was not profit-maximizing but was concerned with maximizing economic efficiency. What price would it charge for the book? How much profit would it make at this price?

2. A small town is served by many competing supermarkets, which have constant marginal cost.

a. Using a diagram of the market for groceries, show the consumer surplus, producer surplus, and total surplus.

b. Now suppose that the independent supermarkets combine into one chain. Using a new diagram, show the new consumer surplus, producer surplus, and total surplus. Relative to the competitive market, what is the transfer from consumers to producers? What is the deadweight loss?

3. Johnny Rockabilly has just finished recording his latest CD. His record company's marketing department determines that the demand for the CD is as follows:

Price	Number of CDs
$24	10 000
22	20 000
20	30 000
18	40 000
16	50 000
14	60 000

The company can produce the CD with no fixed cost and a variable cost of $5 per CD.

a. Find total revenue for quantity equal to 10 000, 20 000, and so on. What is the marginal revenue for each 10 000 increase in the quantity sold?

b. What quantity of CDs would maximize profit? What would be the price? What would be the profit?

c. If you were Johnny's agent, what recording fee would you advise Johnny to demand from the record company? Why?

4. A company is considering building a bridge across a river. The bridge would cost $2 million to build and nothing to maintain. The following table shows the company's anticipated demand over the lifetime of the bridge.

Price per Crossing	Number of Crossings (in thousands)
$8	0
7	100
6	200
5	300
4	400
3	500
2	600
1	700
0	800

a. If the company was to build the bridge, what would be its profit-maximizing price? Would that be the efficient level of output? Why or why not?

b. If the company is interested in maximizing profit, should it build the bridge? What would be its profit or loss?

c. If the government was to build the bridge, what price should it charge?

d. Should the government build the bridge? Explain.

5. Larry, Curly, and Moe run the only saloon in town. Larry wants to sell as many drinks as possible without losing money. Curly wants the saloon to bring in as much revenue as possible. Moe wants to make the largest possible profits. Using a single diagram of the saloon's demand curve and its cost curves, show the price and quantity combinations favoured by each of the three partners. Explain.

6. For many years, both local and long-distance phone services have been provided by provincially owned or regulated monopolies.

a. Explain why long-distance phone service was originally a natural monopoly.

b. Over the past two decades, technological developments have allowed companies to launch communications satellites that can transmit a limited number of calls. How did the growing role of satellites change the cost structure of long-distance phone service?

c. In response to these technological developments, some provinces/territories have deregulated the long-distance market in Canada. Local phone service has remained regulated. Why might it be efficient to have competition in long-distance phone service and regulated monopolies in local phone service?

7. Many schemes for price-discriminating involve some cost. For example, discount coupons take up the time and resources of both the buyer and the seller. This question considers the implications of costly price discrimination. To keep things simple, let's assume that our monopolist's production costs are simply proportional to output, so that average total cost and marginal cost are constant and equal to each other.

a. Draw the cost, demand, and marginal-revenue curves for the monopolist. Show the price the monopolist would charge without price discrimination.

b. In your diagram, mark the area equal to the monopolist's profit and call it X. Mark the area equal to consumer surplus and call it Y. Mark the area equal to the deadweight loss and call it Z.

c. Now suppose that the monopolist can perfectly price-discriminate. What is the monopolist's profit? (Give your answer in terms of X, Y, and Z.)

d. What is the change in the monopolist's profit from price discrimination? What is the change in total surplus from price discrimination? Which change is larger? Explain. (Give your answers in terms of X, Y, and Z.)

e. Now suppose that there is some cost of price discrimination. To model this cost, let's assume that the monopolist has to pay a fixed cost C in order to price-discriminate. How would a monopolist make the decision whether to pay this fixed cost? (Give your answer in terms of X, Y, Z, and C.)

f. How would a benevolent social planner, who cares about total surplus, decide whether the monopolist should price-discriminate? (Give your answer in terms of X, Y, Z, and C.)

g. Compare your answers to parts (e) and (f). How does the monopolist's incentive to price-discriminate differ from the social planner's? Is it possible that the monopolist will price-discriminate even though it is not socially desirable?

8. Consider the relationship between monopoly pricing and price elasticity of demand.

a. Explain why a monopolist will never produce a quantity at which the demand curve is inelastic. (Hint: If demand is inelastic and the firm raises its price, what happens to total revenue and total costs?)

b. Draw a diagram for a monopolist, precisely labelling the portion of the demand curve that is inelastic. (Hint: The answer is related to the marginal-revenue curve.)

c. On your diagram, show the quantity and price that maximizes total revenue.

9. If the government wanted to encourage a monopoly to produce the socially efficient quantity, should it use a per-unit tax or a per-unit subsidy? Explain how this tax or subsidy would achieve the socially efficient level of output. Among the various interested parties—the monopoly firm, the monopoly's consumers, and other taxpayers—who would support the policy and who would oppose it?

10. You live in a town with 300 adults and 200 children, and you are thinking about putting on a play to entertain your neighbours and make some money. This type of play has a fixed cost of $2000, but selling an extra ticket has zero marginal cost. Here are the demand schedules for your two types of customer:

Price	Adults	Children
$10	0	0
9	100	0
8	200	0
7	300	0
6	300	0
5	300	100
4	300	200
3	300	200
2	300	200
1	300	200
0	300	200

a. To maximize profit, what price would you charge for an adult ticket? For a child's ticket? How much profit do you make?
b. The town council passes a law prohibiting you from charging different prices to different customers. What price do you set for a ticket now? How much profit do you make?
c. Who is worse off because of the law prohibiting price discrimination? Who is better off? (If you can, quantify the changes in welfare.)
d. If the fixed cost of the play was $3000 rather than $2000, how would your answers to parts (a), (b), and (c) change?

11. The residents of the town Ectenia all love economics, and the mayor proposes building an economics museum. The museum has a fixed cost of $2 400 000 and no variable costs. There are 100 000 town residents, and each has the same demand for museum visits: $Q^D = 10 - P$, where P is the price of admission.
a. Graph the museum's average-total-cost curve and its marginal-cost curve. What kind of market would describe the museum?
b. The mayor proposes financing the museum with a lump-sum tax of $24 and then opening the museum free to the public. How many times would each person visit? Calculate the benefit each person would get from the museum, measured as consumer surplus minus the new tax.
c. The mayor's anti-tax opponent says the museum should finance itself by charging an admission fee. What is the lowest price the museum can charge without incurring losses? (Hint: Find the number of visits and museum profits for prices of $2, $3, $4, and $5.)
d. For the break-even price you found in part (c), calculate each resident's consumer surplus. Compared with the mayor's plan, who is better off with this admission fee, and who is worse off? Explain.
e. What real-world considerations absent in the above problem might argue in favour of an admission fee?

12. Only one firm produces and sells soccer balls in the country of Wiknam, and as the story begins, international trade in soccer balls is prohibited. The following equations describe the monopolist's demand, marginal revenue, total cost, and marginal cost:

$$\text{Demand: } P = 10 - Q$$
$$\text{Marginal Revenue: } MR = 10 - 2Q$$
$$\text{Total Cost: } TC = 3 + Q + 0.5Q^2$$
$$\text{Marginal Cost: } MC = 1 + Q$$

where Q is quantity and P is the price measured in Wiknamian dollars.
a. How many soccer balls does the monopolist produce? At what price are they sold? What is the monopolist's profit?
b. One day, the king of Wiknam decrees that henceforth there will be free trade—either imports or exports—of soccer balls at the world price of $6. The firm is now a price taker in a competitive market. What happens to domestic production of soccer balls? To

domestic consumption? Does Wiknam export or import soccer balls?

c. In our analysis of international trade in Chapter 9, a country becomes an exporter when the price without trade is below the world price and an importer when the price without trade is above the world price. Does that conclusion hold in your answers to parts (a) and (b)? Explain.

d. Suppose that the world price was not $6 but, instead, happened to be exactly the same as the domestic price without trade as determined in part (a). Would allowing trade have changed anything in the Wiknamian economy? Explain. How does the result here compare with the analysis in Chapter 9?

13. Based on market research, a film production company obtains the following information about the demand and production costs of its new DVD:

$$\text{Price} = 1000 - 10Q$$
$$\text{Total Revenue} = 1000Q - 10Q^2$$
$$\text{Marginal Revenue} = 1000 - 20Q$$
$$\text{Marginal Cost} = 100 + 10Q$$

where Q indicates the number of copies sold and P is the price in cents.

a. Find the price and quantity that maximizes the company's profit.

b. Find the price and quantity that would maximize social welfare.

c. Calculate the deadweight loss from monopoly.

d. Suppose, in addition to the costs above, the director of the film has to be paid. The company is considering four options:
  i. A flat fee of 2000 cents
  ii. 50 percent of the profits
  iii. 150 cents per unit sold
  iv. 50 percent of the revenue

For each option, calculate the profit-maximizing price and quantity. Which, if any, of these compensation schemes would alter the deadweight loss from monopoly? Explain.

http://

For more study tools, please visit www.nelson.com/mankiwmicro6e.

MONOPOLISTIC COMPETITION

Learning Objectives

In this chapter, you will...

- Analyze competition among firms that sell differentiated products

- Compare the outcome under monopolistic competition and under perfect competition

- Consider the desirability of outcomes in monopolistically competitive markets

- Examine the debate over the effects of advertising

- Review the debate over the role of brand names

You walk into a bookstore to buy a book to read during your vacation. On the store's shelves, you find a Kathy Reichs mystery, novels by Michael Ondaatje and Margaret Atwood, and many other choices. When you pick out a book and buy it, what kind of market are you participating in?

On the one hand, the market for books seems competitive. As you look over the shelves at the bookstore, you find many authors and many publishers vying for your attention. A buyer in this market has thousands of competing products from which to choose. And because anyone can enter the industry by writing and publishing a book, the book business is not very profitable. For every highly paid novelist, there are hundreds of struggling ones.

On the other hand, the market for books seems monopolistic. Because each book is unique, publishers have some latitude in choosing what price to charge. The sellers in this market are price makers rather than price takers. And indeed, the price of books greatly exceeds marginal cost. The price of a typical hardcover novel, for instance, is about $25, whereas the cost of printing one additional copy of the novel is less than $5.

The market for novels fits neither the competitive nor the monopoly model. Instead, it is best described by the model of monopolistic competition, the subject of this chapter. The term *monopolistic competition* might at first seem to be an oxymoron, like *jumbo shrimp*. But as we will see, monopolistically competitive industries are monopolistic in some ways and competitive in others. The model describes not only the publishing industry but also the market for many other goods and services.

BETWEEN MONOPOLY AND PERFECT COMPETITION

The previous two chapters analyzed markets with many competitive firms and markets with a single monopoly firm. In Chapter 14, we saw that the price in a perfectly competitive market always equals the marginal cost of production. We also saw that, in the long run, entry and exit drive economic profit to zero, so the price also equals average total cost. In Chapter 15, we saw how monopoly firms can use their market power to keep prices above marginal cost, leading to a positive economic profit for the firm and a deadweight loss for society. Competition and monopoly are extreme forms of market structure. Competition occurs when there are many firms in a market offering essentially identical products; monopoly occurs when there is only one firm in a market.

Although the cases of perfect competition and monopoly illustrate some important ideas about how markets work, most markets in the economy include elements of both these cases and, therefore, are not completely described by either of them. The typical firm in the economy faces competition, but the competition is not so rigorous as to make the firm a price taker like the firms analyzed in Chapter 14. The typical firm also has some degree of market power, but its market power is not so great that the firm can be described exactly by the monopoly model presented in Chapter 15. In other words, many industries fall somewhere between the polar cases of perfect competition and monopoly. Economists call this situation *imperfect competition*.

oligopoly
a market structure in which only a few sellers offer similar or identical products

One type of imperfectly competitive market is an **oligopoly**, which is a market with only a few sellers, each offering a product that is similar or identical to the products offered by other sellers. Economists measure a market's domination by a small number of firms with a statistic called the *concentration ratio*, which is the percentage of total output in the market supplied by the four largest firms. In the Canadian economy, most industries have a four-firm concentration ratio under 50 percent, but in some industries, the biggest firms play a more dominant role. Highly concentrated industries include breakfast cereal (which has a concentration ratio of 78 percent), aircraft manufacturing (81 percent), electric lamp bulbs (89 percent), household laundry equipment (93 percent), and cigarettes (95 percent). These industries are best described as oligopolies.

monopolistic competition
a market structure in which many firms sell products that are similar but not identical

↓
competitive market
with product differentiation

A second type of imperfectly competitive market is called **monopolistic competition**. This describes a market structure in which there are many firms selling products that are similar but not identical. In a monopolistically competitive market, each firm has a monopoly over the product it makes, but many other firms make similar products that compete for the same customers.

To be more precise, monopolistic competition describes a market with the following attributes:

- *Many sellers:* There are many firms competing for the same group of customers.
- *Product differentiation:* Each firm produces a product that is at least slightly different from those of other firms. Thus, rather than being a price taker, each firm faces a downward-sloping demand curve.
- *Free entry and exit:* Firms can enter or exit the market without restriction. Thus, the number of firms in the market adjusts until economic profits are driven to zero.

A moment's thought reveals a long list of markets with these attributes: books, DVDs, computer games, restaurants, piano lessons, cookies, clothing, and so on.

Monopolistic competition, like oligopoly, is a market structure that lies between the extreme cases of competition and monopoly. But oligopoly and monopolistic competition are quite different. Oligopoly departs from the perfectly competitive ideal of Chapter 14 because there are only a few sellers in the market. The small number of sellers makes rigorous competition less likely and strategic interactions among them vitally important. By contrast, under monopolistic competition, there are many sellers, each of which is small compared to the market. A monopolistically competitive market departs from the perfectly competitive ideal because each of the sellers offers a somewhat different product.

Figure 16.1 summarizes the four types of market structure. The first question to ask about any market is how many firms there are. If there is only one firm, the market is a monopoly. If there are only a few firms, the market is an oligopoly. If there are many firms, we need to ask another question: Do the firms sell identical or differentiated products? If the many firms sell differentiated products, the market is monopolistically competitive. If the many firms sell identical products, the market is perfectly competitive.

Because reality is never as clear-cut as theory, at times you may find it hard to decide what structure best describes a market. There is, for instance, no magic number that separates "few" from "many" when counting the number of firms. (Do the approximately dozen companies that now sell cars in Canada make this market an oligopoly or more competitive? The answer is open to debate.) Similarly, there is no sure way to determine when products are differentiated and when they are identical. (Are different brands of milk really the same? Again, the answer is debatable.) When analyzing actual markets, economists have to keep in mind the lessons learned from studying all types of market structure and then apply each lesson as it seems appropriate.

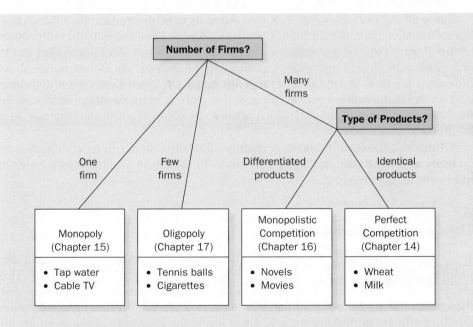

FIGURE 16.1

The Four Types of Market Structure

Economists who study industrial organization divide markets into four types—monopoly, oligopoly, monopolistic competition, and perfect competition.

Source: From MANKIW. *Principles of Economics*, 4E. © 2007 Cengage Learning.

Now that we understand how economists define the various types of market structure, we can continue our analysis of each of them. In the next chapter, we analyze oligopoly. In this chapter we examine monopolistic competition.

QuickQuiz Define *oligopoly* and *monopolistic competition* and give an example of each.

COMPETITION WITH DIFFERENTIATED PRODUCTS

To understand monopolistically competitive markets, we first consider the decisions facing an individual firm. We then examine what happens in the long run as firms enter and exit the industry. Next, we compare the equilibrium under monopolistic competition to the equilibrium under perfect competition that we examined in Chapter 14. Finally, we consider whether the outcome in a monopolistically competitive market is desirable from the standpoint of society as a whole.

The Monopolistically Competitive Firm in the Short Run

Each firm in a monopolistically competitive market is, in many ways, like a monopoly. Because its product is different from those offered by other firms, it faces a downward-sloping demand curve. (By contrast, a perfectly competitive firm faces a horizontal demand curve at the market price.) Thus, the monopolistically competitive firm follows a monopolist's rule for profit maximization: It chooses the quantity at which marginal revenue equals marginal cost and then uses its demand curve to find the price consistent with that quantity.

Figure 16.2 shows the cost, demand, and marginal-revenue curves for two typical firms, each in a different monopolistically competitive industry. In both panels of this figure, the profit-maximizing quantity is found at the intersection of the marginal-revenue and marginal-cost curves. The two panels in this figure show different outcomes for the firm's profit. In panel (a), price exceeds average total cost, so the firm makes a profit. In panel (b), price is below average total cost. In this case, the firm is unable to make a positive profit, so the best the firm can do is to minimize its losses.

All this should seem familiar. A monopolistically competitive firm chooses its quantity and price just as a monopoly does. In the short run, these two types of market structure are similar.

The Long-Run Equilibrium

The situations depicted in Figure 16.2 do not last long. When firms are making profits, as in panel (a), new firms have an incentive to enter the market. This entry increases the number of products from which customers can choose and, therefore, reduces the demand faced by each firm already in the market. In other words, profit encourages entry, and entry shifts the demand curves faced by the

FIGURE 16.2

Monopolistic Competitors in the Short Run

Monopolistic competitors, like monopolists, maximize profit by producing the quantity at which marginal revenue equals marginal cost. The firm in panel (a) makes a profit because, at this quantity, price is above average total cost. The firm in panel (b) experiences losses because, at this quantity, price is less than average total cost.

incumbent firms to the left. As the demand for incumbent firms' products fall, these firms experience declining profit.

Conversely, when firms are experiencing losses, as in panel (b), firms in the market have an incentive to exit. As firms exit, customers have fewer products from which to choose. This decrease in the number of firms expands the demand faced by those firms that stay in the market. In other words, losses encourage exit, and exit shifts the demand curves of the remaining firms to the right. As the demand for the remaining firms' products rises, these firms experience rising profit (that is, declining losses).

This process of entry and exit continues until the firms in the market are making exactly zero economic profit. Figure 16.3 depicts the long-run equilibrium. Once the market reaches this equilibrium, new firms have no incentive to enter, and existing firms have no incentive to exit.

Notice that the demand curve in this figure just barely touches the average-total-cost curve. Mathematically, we say the two curves are *tangent* to each other. These two curves must be tangent once entry and exit have driven profit to zero. Because profit per unit sold is the difference between price (found on the demand curve) and average total cost, the maximum profit is zero only if these two curves touch each other without crossing. Also note that this point of tangency occurs at the same quantity where marginal revenue equals marginal cost. That these two points line up is not a coincidence: It is required because this

FIGURE 16.3

A Monopolistic Competitor in the Long Run

In a monopolistically competitive market, if firms are making profit, new firms enter, and the demand curves for the incumbent firms shift to the left. Similarly, if firms are experiencing losses, old firms exit, and the demand curves of the remaining firms shift to the right. Because of these shifts in demand, a monopolistically competitive firm eventually finds itself in the long-run equilibrium shown here. In this long-run equilibrium, price equals average total cost, and the firm earns zero profit.

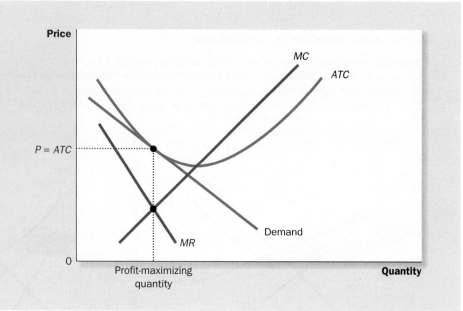

In the long run, the profit-max quantity is where Demand is tanget to ATC

particular quantity maximizes profit and the maximum profit is exactly zero in the long run.

To sum up, two characteristics describe the long-run equilibrium in a monopolistically competitive market:

1. As in a monopoly market, price exceeds marginal cost. This conclusion arises because profit maximization requires marginal revenue to equal marginal cost and because the downward-sloping demand curve makes marginal revenue less than the price.
2. As in a competitive market, price equals average total cost. This conclusion arises because free entry and exit drive economic profit to zero.

The second characteristic shows how monopolistic competition differs from monopoly. Because a monopoly is the sole seller of a product without close substitutes, it can earn positive economic profit, even in the long run. By contrast, because there is free entry into a monopolistically competitive market, the economic profit of a firm in this type of market is driven to zero.

Monopolistic versus Perfect Competition

Figure 16.4 compares the long-run equilibrium under monopolistic competition to the long-run equilibrium under perfect competition. (Chapter 14 discussed the equilibrium with perfect competition.) There are two noteworthy differences between monopolistic and perfect competition—excess capacity and the markup.

FIGURE 16.4

Monopolistic versus Perfect Competition

Panel (a) shows the long-run equilibrium in a monopolistically competitive market, and panel (b) shows the long-run equilibrium in a perfectly competitive market. Two differences are notable: (1) The perfectly competitive firm produces at the efficient scale, where average total cost is minimized. By contrast, the monopolistically competitive firm produces at less than the efficient scale. (2) Price equals marginal cost under perfect competition, but price is above marginal cost under monopolistic competition.

Excess Capacity

As we have just seen, entry and exit drive each firm in a monopolistically competitive market to a point of tangency between its demand and average-total-cost curves. Panel (a) of Figure 16.4 shows that the quantity of output at this point is smaller than the quantity that minimizes average total cost. Thus, under monopolistic competition, firms produce on the downward-sloping portion of their average-total-cost curves. In this way, monopolistic competition contrasts starkly with perfect competition. As panel (b) of Figure 16.4 shows, free entry in competitive markets drives firms to produce at the minimum of average total cost.

The quantity that minimizes average total cost is called the *efficient scale* of the firm. In the long run, perfectly competitive firms produce at the efficient scale, whereas monopolistically competitive firms produce below this level. Firms are said to have *excess capacity* under monopolistic competition. In other words, a monopolistically competitive firm, unlike a perfectly competitive firm, could increase the quantity it produces and lower the average total cost of production. The firm forgoes this opportunity because it would need to cut its price to sell the additional output. It is more profitable for a monopolistic competitor to continue operating with excess capacity.

Excess capacity: ↑ Quantity
↓ ATC

Markup over Marginal Cost   A second difference between perfect competition and monopolistic competition is the relationship between price and marginal cost. For a competitive firm, such as that shown in panel (b) of Figure 16.4, price equals marginal cost. For a monopolistically competitive firm, such as that shown in panel (a), price exceeds marginal cost because the firm always has some market power.

How is this markup over marginal cost consistent with free entry and zero profit? The zero-profit condition ensures only that price equals average total cost. It does *not* ensure that price equals marginal cost. Indeed, in the long-run equilibrium, monopolistically competitive firms operate on the declining portion of their average-total-cost curves, so marginal cost is below average total cost. Thus, for price to equal average total cost, price must be above marginal cost.

In this relationship between price and marginal cost, we see a key behavioural difference between perfect competitors and monopolistic competitors. Imagine that you were to ask a firm the following question: "Would you like to see another customer come through your door ready to buy from you at your current price?" A perfectly competitive firm would answer that it didn't care. Because price exactly equals marginal cost, the profit from an extra unit sold is zero. By contrast, a monopolistically competitive firm is always eager to get another customer. Because its price exceeds marginal cost, an extra unit sold at the posted price means more profit.

According to an old quip, monopolistically competitive markets are those in which sellers send holiday greeting cards to the buyers. Trying to attract more customers makes sense only if price exceeds marginal cost.

Monopolistic Competition and the Welfare of Society

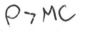

Is the outcome in a monopolistically competitive market desirable from the standpoint of society as a whole? Can policymakers improve on the market outcome? In previous chapters, we evaluated markets from the standpoint of efficiency—that is, whether society is getting the most it can out of its scarce resources. We learned that competitive markets lead to efficient outcomes, unless there are externalities, and that monopoly markets lead to deadweight losses. Monopolistically competitive markets are more complex than either of these polar cases, so evaluating welfare in these markets is a more subtle exercise.

One source of inefficiency is the markup of price over marginal cost. Because of the markup, some consumers who value the good at more than the marginal cost of production (but less than the price) will be deterred from buying it. Thus, a monopolistically competitive market has the normal deadweight loss of monopoly pricing.

Although this outcome is clearly undesirable compared to the first-best outcome of price equal to marginal cost, there is no easy way for policymakers to fix the problem. To enforce marginal-cost pricing, policymakers would need to regulate all firms that produce differentiated products. Because such products are so common in the economy, the administrative burden of such regulation would be overwhelming.

Moreover, regulating monopolistic competitors would entail all the problems of regulating natural monopolies. In particular, because monopolistic competitors are making zero profits already, requiring them to lower their prices to equal marginal cost would cause them to make losses. To keep these firms in business, the government would need to help them cover these losses. Rather than raising taxes to pay for these subsidies, policymakers may decide it is better to live with the inefficiency of monopolistic pricing.

Another way in which monopolistic competition may be socially inefficient is that the number of firms in the market may not be the "ideal" one. That is, there may be too much or too little entry. One way to think about this problem is in terms of the externalities associated with entry. Whenever a new firm considers entering the market with a new product, it takes into account only the profit it would make. Yet its entry would also have two external effects:

1. *The product-variety externality:* Because consumers get some consumer surplus from the introduction of a new product, entry of a new firm conveys a positive externality on consumers.
2. *The business-stealing externality:* Because other firms lose customers and profits from the entry of a new competitor, entry of a new firm imposes a negative externality on existing firms.

Thus, in a monopolistically competitive market, there are both positive and negative externalities associated with the entry of new firms. Depending on which externality is larger, a monopolistically competitive market could have either too few or too many products.

Both of these externalities are closely related to the conditions for monopolistic competition. The product-variety externality arises because a new firm would offer a product different from those of the existing firms. The business-stealing externality arises because firms post a price above marginal cost and, therefore, are always eager to sell additional units. Conversely, because perfectly competitive firms produce identical goods and charge a price equal to marginal cost, neither of these externalities exists under perfect competition.

In the end, we can conclude only that monopolistically competitive markets do not have all the desirable welfare properties of perfectly competitive markets. That is, the invisible hand does not ensure that total surplus is maximized under monopolistic competition. Yet because the inefficiencies are subtle, hard to measure, and hard to fix, there is no easy way for public policy to improve the market outcome.

QuickQuiz List the three key attributes of monopolistic competition. • Draw and explain a diagram to show the long-run equilibrium in a monopolistically competitive market. How does this equilibrium differ from that in a perfectly competitive market?

ADVERTISING

It is nearly impossible to go through a typical day in a modern economy without being bombarded with advertising. Whether you are reading a newspaper, watching television, surfing the Internet, or driving down the highway, some firm will try to convince you to buy its product. Such behaviour is a natural feature of monopolistic competition (as well as some oligopolistic industries). When firms sell differentiated products and charge prices above marginal cost, each firm has an incentive to advertise in order to attract more buyers to its particular product.

The amount of advertising varies substantially across products. Firms that sell highly differentiated consumer goods, such as over-the-counter drugs, perfumes, soft drinks, razor blades, breakfast cereals, and dog food, typically spend between

IN THE NEWS

INSUFFICIENT VARIETY AS A MARKET FAILURE

University of Pennsylvania economist Joel Waldfogel argues that, in the presence of large fixed costs, the market may insufficiently service customers with unusual preferences.

If the Shoe Doesn't Fit, Blame the Tyranny of the Market.

By Joel Waldfogel

Last week, Nike unveiled a shoe designed specifically for American Indians. The sneaker has both a native-theme design and—more importantly—a wider shape to accommodate the distinctly shaped feet of American Indians. With diabetes and related conditions near epidemic levels in some tribes, American Indian leaders were happy to welcome this comfortable product. If anything, what seems odd is that it took so long. After all, free-market economists have told us for decades that we should rely on market decisions, not the government, to meet our needs, because it's the market that satisfies everyone's every desire.

And yet it turns out that it's the Indian's long wait for a good sneaker

that's typical. For small groups with preferences outside the norm, the market often fails to deliver, as I argue in my new book, *The Tyranny of the Market: Why You Can't Always Get What You Want*.

John Stuart Mill pointed out that voting gives rise to a tyranny of the majority. If we vote on what color shirts to make—or whether to make wide or narrow shoes—then the majority gets what it prefers, and the minority does not. The market, on the other hand, is supposed to work differently. As Milton Friedman eloquently put it in 1962, "the characteristic feature of action through political channels is that it tends to require or enforce substantial conformity. The great advantage of the market is that it permits wide diversity. Each man can vote, as it were, for the color of tie he wants and get it; he does not have to see what color the majority wants and then, if he is in the minority, submit." This is a wonderful argument.

Except that for many products and for many people, it's wrong.

Two simple conditions that prevail in many markets mean that individual taste alone doesn't determine individual satisfaction. These conditions are (1) big setup costs and (2) preferences that differ across groups; when they're present, an individual's satisfaction is a function of how many people share his or her tastes. In other words, in these cases, markets share some of the objectionable features of government. They give bigger groups more and better options.

In my research, I've discovered that this phenomenon is widespread. Ten years ago, I started studying radio-station listening patterns. I noticed that people listened to the radio more in metro areas of the United States with relatively large populations. This is not terribly surprising. In larger cities, more stations can attract enough listeners and advertising revenue to cover their

10 and 20 percent of revenue for advertising. Firms that sell industrial products, such as drill presses and communications satellites, typically spend very little on advertising. And firms that sell homogeneous products, such as wheat, peanuts, or crude oil, spend nothing at all.

For the economy as a whole, spending on advertising comprises about 2 percent of total firm revenue. This spending takes many forms, including commercials on television and radio, space in newspapers and magazines, direct mail, the Yellow Pages, billboards, and the Internet.

costs and stay on the air. With more to choose from on the dial, residents tune in more. So, in this situation of high fixed costs (each station needs a following to keep broadcasting), people help one another by making more options viable.

But who benefits whom? When I looked at black and white listeners separately, I noticed something surprising. Blacks listen more in cities with larger black populations, and whites listen more in cities with larger white populations. Black listening does not increase where there's a higher white population, and white listening does not increase with a higher black population. Which means that while overall people help each other by increasing the number of stations on the dial, blacks do not help whites, and whites do not help blacks. Similar patterns arise for Hispanics and non-Hispanics.

A closer look at the data—necessary only because I'm a middle-aged white economist—showed why this was happening. Blacks and whites don't listen to the same radio stations. The black-targeted formats account for about two-thirds of black listening and only 3 percent of white listening. Similarly, the formats that attract the largest white audiences, like country, attract almost no blacks. This means that if you dropped Larry the Cable Guy and a few thousand of his friends from a helicopter (with parachutes) into a metro area, you'd create more demand for country and perhaps album-rock stations, which would be nice for white listeners. But the influx wouldn't help black listeners at all.

In this example, different population groups don't help each other, but they don't hurt each other, either. Sometimes, though, the effect that groups have on each other through the market is actually negative. Industries like daily newspapers offer essentially one product per market. Because the paper can be pitched to appeal to one group or another, the larger one group is, the less the product is tailored to anyone else. This is the tyranny of the majority translated almost literally from politics into markets.

This brings us back to Nike's new shoe. Foot Locker is full of options that fit me and most other Americans. But American Indians make up just 1.5 percent of the U.S. population, and with feet on average three sizes wider, they need different-sized shoes. If we had all voted in a national election on whether the Ministry of Shoes should make wide or typical-width shoes, we surely would have chosen the latter. That's why Friedman condemned government allocation. And yet the market made the same choice. If Nike's announcement looks like a solution to this problem of ignored minority preference, it really isn't. The company took too many years to bring the shoe on line, and according to the Associated Press, the new sneaker "represents less of a financial opportunity than a goodwill and branding effort."

The tyranny of the market arises elsewhere. With drug development costs near $1 billion, if you are going to be sick, hope that your disease is common enough to attract the interest of drug makers. If you want to fly from your town to Chicago, hope that your city is big enough to fill a plane every day.

When you're not so lucky, you benefit when the government steps in on your behalf, with subsidies for research on drugs for rare diseases or for air service to small locales. For a generation, influential economists have argued for letting the market decide a wide array of questions, to protect your freedom to choose whatever you want. This is true—if everyone agrees with you.

Source: Joel Waldfogel, "If the Shoe Doesn't Fit, Blame the Tyranny of the Market." From *Slate* © October 4, 2007 The Slate Group. All Rights Reserved. Used by permission and protected by the Copyright Laws of the United States. The printing, copying, redistribution, or retransmission of this Content without express written permission is prohibited.

The Debate over Advertising

Is society wasting the resources it devotes to advertising? Or does advertising serve a valuable purpose? Assessing the social value of advertising is difficult and often generates heated argument among economists. Let's consider both sides of the debate.

The Critique of Advertising

Critics of advertising argue that firms advertise in order to manipulate people's tastes. Much advertising is psychological rather than informational. Consider, for example, the typical television commercial for some brand of soft drink. The commercial most likely does not tell the viewer about the product's price or quality. Instead, it might show a group of happy people at a party on a beach on a beautiful sunny day. In their hands are cans of the soft drink. The goal of the commercial is to convey a subconscious (if not subtle) message: "You too can have many friends and be happy, if only you drink our product." Critics of advertising argue that such a commercial creates a desire that otherwise might not exist.

Critics also argue that advertising impedes competition. Advertising often tries to convince consumers that products are more different than they truly are. By increasing the perception of product differentiation and fostering brand loyalty, advertising makes buyers less concerned with price differences among similar goods. With a less elastic demand curve, each firm charges a larger markup over marginal cost.

The Defence of Advertising Defenders of advertising argue that firms use advertising to provide information to customers. Advertising conveys the prices of the goods being offered for sale, the existence of new products, and the locations of retail outlets. This information allows customers to make better choices about what to buy and, thus, enhances the ability of markets to allocate resources efficiently.

Defenders also argue that advertising fosters competition. Because advertising allows customers to be more fully informed about all the firms in the market, customers can more easily take advantage of price differences. Thus, each firm has less market power. In addition, advertising allows new firms to enter more easily, because it gives entrants a means to attract customers from existing firms.

Over time, policymakers have come to accept the view that advertising can make markets more competitive. One important example is the regulation of advertising for certain professions, such as lawyers, doctors, and pharmacists. In the past, these groups succeeded in getting governments to prohibit advertising in their fields on the grounds that advertising was "unprofessional." In recent years, however, the courts have concluded that the primary effect of these restrictions on advertising was to curtail competition. They have, therefore, overturned many of the laws that prohibit advertising by members of these professions.

Case Study

CANADA GOOSE FLYING HIGH

Marketing campaigns can help differentiate a product from the competition. An example of such a product is the distinctive Canadian goose down-filled parkas made by Canada Goose, the Canadian maker of outdoor apparel. The likes of Emma Watson, Matt Damon, Hayden Christensen, Maggie Gyllenhaal, and Hilary Duff have all been seen sporting the company's jackets. They've also shown up onscreen: Nicolas Cage wore a Canada Goose parka in *National Treasure* (2004), Jessica Alba appeared in one in *Good Luck Chuck* (2007), and Kate Beckinsale donned one in *Whiteout* (2009).

The parkas were originally designed for hard-core outdoor use—Canada Goose claims they can withstand temperatures as low as –70°C. From the beginning, the company aspired to make its name synonymous with quality, especially the quality of its goose down, which is obtained from Hutterite farmers across Canada. Hutterite farmers keep small flocks of geese and allow them to mature before being plucked. This means the down is larger, creating more pockets in which warm air is trapped. It also means Hutterite down is more expensive, which is what makes Canada Goose jackets so expensive and feeds into their "elite" perception.

While temperatures as low as –70°C are not likely to occur in Hollywood, the company has turned Canada Goose parkas into the latest "must-have" fashion accessory through the use of a savvy marketing campaign designed to emphasize the elite nature of the product. The company's approach has not been to stage a high-cost advertising campaign, but rather to use product placement and so-called "guerrilla marketing" tactics. This involves not only appearances in Hollywood movies, but placing the product with security personnel and ushers at outdoor winter sporting events and bouncers, valets, and doormen at Fairmont hotels—anyone who operates in a cold environment. These "human billboards" have served as effective ambassadors for the product. These advertising tactics are particularly effective and important in the social media age, where a picture of Emma Watson wearing a Canada Goose parka can go viral on the Internet.

The fashion market is notoriously fickle. Whether Canada Goose continues to fly high, or goes the way of other must-have products of the past, remains to be seen. But the recent success of the company shows how important product differentiation supported by innovative marketing geared toward social media can be. ●

Advertising as a Signal of Quality

Many types of advertising contain little apparent information about the product being advertised. Consider a firm introducing a new breakfast cereal. A typical advertisement might have some highly paid actor eating the cereal and exclaiming how wonderful it tastes. How much information does the advertisement really provide?

The answer is: more than you might think. Defenders of advertising argue that even advertising that appears to contain little hard information may in fact tell consumers something about product quality. The willingness of the firm to spend a large amount of money on advertising can itself be a *signal* to consumers about the quality of the product being offered.

Consider the problem facing two firms—Post and Kellogg. Each company has just come up with a recipe for a new cereal that it would sell for $3 a box. To keep things simple, let's assume that the marginal cost of making cereal is zero, so the $3 is all profit. Each company knows that if it spends $10 million on advertising, it will convince 1 million consumers to try its new cereal. And each company knows that if consumers like the cereal, they will buy it not once but many times.

First consider Post's decision. Based on market research, Post knows that its cereal is only mediocre. Although advertising would sell one box to each of 1 million consumers, the consumers would quickly learn that the cereal is not very good and stop buying it. Post decides it is not worth paying $10 million in advertising to get only $3 million in sales. So it does not bother to advertise. It sends its cooks back to the drawing board to find another recipe.

Kellogg, on the other hand, knows that its cereal is great. Each person who tries it will buy a box a month for the next year. Thus, the $10 million in advertising will bring in $36 million in sales. Advertising is profitable here because Kellogg has a good product that consumers will buy repeatedly. Thus, Kellogg chooses to advertise.

Now that we have considered the behaviour of the two firms, let's consider the behaviour of consumers. We began by asserting that consumers are inclined to try a new cereal that they see advertised. But is this behaviour rational? Should a consumer try a new cereal just because the seller has chosen to advertise it?

In fact, it may be completely rational for consumers to try new products that they see advertised. In our story, consumers decide to try Kellogg's new cereal because Kellogg advertises. Kellogg chooses to advertise because it knows that its cereal is quite good, while Post chooses not to advertise because it knows that its cereal is only mediocre. By its willingness to spend money on advertising, Kellogg signals to consumers the quality of its cereal. Each consumer thinks, quite sensibly, "Boy, if Kellogg Company is willing to spend so much money advertising this new cereal, it must be really good."

What is most surprising about this theory of advertising is that the content of the advertisement is irrelevant. Kellogg signals the quality of its product by its willingness to spend money on advertising. What the advertisements say is not as important as the fact that consumers know ads are expensive. By contrast, cheap advertising cannot be effective at signalling quality to consumers. In our example, if an advertising campaign cost less than $3 million, both Post and Kellogg would use it to market their new cereals. Because both good and mediocre cereals would be advertised, consumers could not infer the quality of a new cereal from the fact that it is advertised. Over time, consumers would learn to ignore such cheap advertising.

This theory can explain why firms pay famous actors large amounts of money to make advertisements that, on the surface, appear to convey no information at all. The information is not in the advertisement's content, but simply in its existence and expense.

Brand Names

Advertising is closely related to the existence of brand names. In many markets, there are two types of firms. Some firms sell products with widely recognized brand names, while other firms sell generic substitutes. For example, in a typical drugstore, you can find Bayer aspirin on the shelf next to a generic aspirin. In a typical grocery store, you can find Pepsi next to less familiar colas. Most often, the firm with the brand name spends more on advertising and charges a higher price for its product.

Just as there is disagreement about the economics of advertising, there is disagreement about the economics of brand names. Let's consider both sides of the debate.

Critics of brand names argue that brand names cause consumers to perceive differences that do not really exist. In many cases, the generic good is almost indistinguishable from the brand-name good. Consumers' willingness to pay more for the brand-name good, these critics assert, is a form of irrationality fostered by advertising. Economist Edward Chamberlin, one of the early developers of the theory of monopolistic competition, concluded from this argument that brand names were bad for the economy. He proposed that the government discourage their use by refusing to enforce the exclusive trademarks that companies use to identify their products.

More recently, economists have defended brand names as a useful way for consumers to ensure that the goods they buy are of high quality. There are two related arguments. First, brand names provide consumers with *information* about quality when quality cannot be easily judged in advance of purchase. Second, brand names give firms an *incentive* to maintain high quality, because firms have a financial stake in maintaining the reputation of their brand names.

To see how these arguments work in practice, consider a famous brand name: McDonald's. Imagine that you are driving through an unfamiliar town and want to stop for lunch. You see a McDonald's and a local restaurant next to it. Which do you choose? The local restaurant may in fact offer better food at lower prices, but you have no way of knowing that. By contrast, McDonald's offers a consistent product across many cities. Its brand name is useful to you as a way of judging the quality of what you are about to buy.

The McDonald's brand name also ensures that the company has an incentive to maintain quality. For example, if some customers were to become ill from bad food sold at a McDonald's, the news would be disastrous for the company. McDonald's would lose much of the valuable reputation that it has built up with years of expensive advertising. As a result, it would lose sales and profit not just in the outlet that sold the bad food but in its many outlets throughout the country. By contrast, if

GALBRAITH VERSUS HAYEK

Two of the great economists of the twentieth century were Canadian-born John Kenneth Galbraith and Austrian Friedrich Hayek. They held very different views about advertising, which to a large extent reflected their views about the capitalist system more broadly.

John Kenneth Galbraith's most famous book was *The Affluent Society*, published in 1958. In it, he argued that corporations use advertising to create demand for products that people otherwise do not want or need. The market system should not be applauded, he believed, for satisfying desires that it has itself created. Galbraith was skeptical that economic growth was leading to higher levels of well-being, because people's aspirations were being made to keep pace with their increased material prosperity. He worried that as advertising and salesmanship artificially enhanced the desire for private goods, public spending on such items as better schools and better parks suffered. The end result, according to Galbraith, was "private opulence and public squalor." Galbraith's policy recommendation was clear: Increase the size of government.

Friedrich Hayek's most famous book was *The Road to Serfdom*, published in 1944. It argued that an extensive government role in the economy inevitably means a sacrifice of personal freedoms. Hayek also wrote a well-known critique of Galbraith in 1961, addressing in particular Galbraith's view of advertising. Hayek observed that advertising was merely one example of a broader phenomenon: Many preferences are created by the social environment. Literature, art, and music are all acquired tastes. A person's demand for hearing a Mozart concerto may have been created in a music appreciation class, but this fact does not make the desire less legitimate or the music professor a sinister influence. Hayek concluded, "It is because each individual producer thinks that consumers can be persuaded to like his products that he endeavors to influence them. But though this effort is part of the influences which shape consumers' taste, no producer can in any real sense 'determine' them."

Although these two economists disagreed about the roles of advertising, markets, and government, they did have one thing in common: great acclaim. In 1974, Hayek won the Nobel Prize in Economic Sciences. In 2000, U.S. President Clinton awarded Galbraith (who spent much of his professional life in the United States) the National Medal of Freedom. And even though their most famous works were written decades ago, they are still well worth reading today.

some customers were to become ill from bad food at a local restaurant, that restaurant might have to close down, but the lost profits would be much smaller. Hence, McDonald's has a greater incentive to ensure that its food is safe.

The debate over brand names thus centres on the question of whether consumers are rational in preferring brand names over generic substitutes. Critics of brand names argue that brand names are the result of an irrational consumer response to advertising. Defenders of brand names argue that consumers have good reason to pay more for brand-name products because they can be more confident about the quality of these products.

QuickQuiz   How might advertising make markets less competitive? How might it make markets more competitive? • Give the arguments for and against brand names.

CONCLUSION

Monopolistic competition is true to its name: It is a hybrid of monopoly and competition. Like a monopoly, each monopolistic competitor faces a downward-sloping demand curve and, as a result, charges a price above marginal cost. As in a perfectly competitive market, there are many firms, and entry and exit drive the profit of each monopolistic competitor toward zero in the long run. Table 16.1 summarizes these lessons.

TABLE 16.1

Monopolistic
Competition:
Between Perfect
Competition and
Monopoly

	Market Structure		
	Perfect Competition	Monopolistic Competition	Monopoly
Features that all three market structures share			
Goal of firms	Maximize profits	Maximize profits	Maximize profits
Rule for maximizing	$MR = MC$	$MR = MC$	$MR = MC$
Can earn economic profits in the short run?	Yes	Yes	Yes
Features that monopoly and monopolistic competition share			
Price taker?	Yes	No	No
Price	$P = MC$	$P > MC$	$P > MC$
Produces welfare-maximizing level of output?	Yes	No	No
Features that perfect competition and monopolistic competition share			
Number of firms	Many	Many	One
Entry in long run?	Yes	Yes	No
Can earn economic profits in long run?	No	No	Yes

Because monopolistically competitive firms produce differentiated products, each firm advertises in order to attract customers to its own brand. To some extent, advertising manipulates consumers' tastes, promotes irrational brand loyalty, and impedes competition. To a larger extent, advertising provides information, establishes brand names of reliable quality, and fosters competition.

The theory of monopolistic competition seems to describe many markets in the economy. It is somewhat disappointing, therefore, that the theory does not yield simple and compelling advice for public policy. From the standpoint of the economic theorist, the allocation of resources in monopolistically competitive markets is not perfect. Yet, from the standpoint of a practical policymaker, there may be little that can be done to improve it.

SUMMARY

- A monopolistically competitive market is characterized by three attributes: many firms, differentiated products, and free entry.

- The equilibrium in a monopolistically competitive market differs from that in a perfectly competitive market in two related ways. First, each firm in a monopolistically competitive market has excess capacity. That is, it operates on the downward-sloping portion of the average-total-cost curve. Second, each firm charges a price above marginal cost.

- Monopolistic competition does not have all the desirable properties of perfect competition. There is the standard deadweight loss of monopoly

caused by the markup of price over marginal cost. In addition, the number of firms (and thus the variety of products) can be too large or too small. In practice, the ability of policymakers to correct these inefficiencies is limited.

- The product differentiation inherent in monopolistic competition leads to the use of advertising and brand names. Critics of advertising and brand names argue that firms use them to take advantage of consumer irrationality and to reduce competition. Defenders of advertising and brand names argue that firms use them to inform consumers and to compete more vigorously on price and product quality.

KEY CONCEPTS

oligopoly, p. 352

monopolistic competition, p. 352

QUESTIONS FOR REVIEW

1. Describe the three attributes of monopolistic competition. How is monopolistic competition like monopoly? How is it like perfect competition?

2. Draw a diagram depicting a firm in a monopolistically competitive market that is making profits. Now show what happens to this firm as new firms enter the industry.

3. Draw a diagram of the long-run equilibrium in a monopolistically competitive market. How is price related to average total cost? How is price related to marginal cost?

4. Does a monopolistic competitor produce too much or too little output compared to the most efficient level? What practical considerations

make it difficult for policymakers to solve this problem?

5. How might advertising reduce economic well-being? How might advertising increase economic well-being?

6. How might advertising with no apparent informational content in fact convey information to consumers?

7. Explain two benefits that might arise from the existence of brand names.

PROBLEMS AND APPLICATIONS

1. Classify the following markets as perfectly competitive, monopolistic, or monopolistically competitive, and explain your answers.
   a. wooden #2 pencils
   b. bottled water
   c. copper
   d. local telephone service
   e. peanut butter
   f. lipstick

2. For each of the following characteristics, say whether it describes a perfectly competitive firm, a monopolistically competitive firm, both, or neither.
   a. sells a differentiated product from its competitors
   b. has marginal revenue less than price
   c. earns economic profit in the long run
   d. produces at minimum of average total cost in the long run
   e. equates marginal revenue and marginal cost
   f. charges a price above marginal cost

3. For each of the following characteristics, say whether it describes a monopoly firm, a monopolistically competitive firm, both, or neither.
   a. faces a downward-sloping demand curve
   b. has marginal revenue less than price
   c. faces the entry of new firms selling similar products
   d. earns economic profit in the long run
   e. equates marginal revenue and marginal cost
   f. produces the socially efficient quantity of output

4. Sparkle is one firm of many in the market for toothpaste, which is in long-run equilibrium.
   a. Draw a diagram showing Sparkle's demand curve, marginal-revenue curve, average-total-cost curve, and marginal-cost curve. Label Sparkle's profit-maximizing output and price.
   b. What is Sparkle's profit? Explain.
   c. On your diagram, show the consumer surplus derived from the purchase of Sparkle toothpaste. Also show the deadweight loss relative to the efficient level of output.
   d. If the government forced Sparkle to produce the efficient level of output, what would happen to the firm? What would happen to Sparkle's customers?

5. You are hired as the consultant to a monopolistically competitive firm. The firm reports the following information about its price, marginal cost, and average total cost. Can the firm possibly be maximizing profit? If not, what should it do to increase profit? If the firm is profit-maximizing, is the firm in a long-run equilibrium? If not, what will happen to restore long-run equilibrium?
   a. $P < MC, P < ATC$
   b. $P > MC, P < ATC$
   c. $P = MC, P > ATC$
   d. $P > MC, P = ATC$

6. For each of the following pairs of firms, explain which firm would be more likely to engage in advertising:
   a. a family-owned farm or a family-owned restaurant
   b. a manufacturer of forklifts or a manufacturer of cars
   c. a company that invented a very reliable watch or a company that invented a less reliable watch that costs the same amount to make

7. The makers of Tylenol pain reliever do a lot of advertising and have very loyal customers. In contrast, the makers of generic acetaminophen do no advertising, and their customers shop only for the lowest price. Assume that the marginal costs of Tylenol and generic acetaminophen are the same and constant.

a. Draw a diagram showing Tylenol's demand, marginal-revenue, and marginal-cost curves. Label Tylenol's price and markup over marginal cost.

b. Repeat part (a) for a producer of generic acetaminophen. How do the diagrams differ? Which company has the bigger markup? Explain.

c. Which company has the greater incentive for careful quality control? Why?

8. Sleek Sneakers Co. is one of many firms in the market for shoes.

a. Assume that Sleek is currently earning short-run economic profits. On a correctly labelled diagram, show Sleek's profit-maximizing output and price, as well as the area representing profit.

b. What happens to Sleek's price, output, and profit in the long run? Explain this change in words, and show it on a new diagram.

c. Suppose that over time, consumers become more focused on stylistic differences among shoe brands. How would this change in attitude affect each firm's price elasticity of demand? In the long run, how will this change in demand affect Sleek's price, output, and profits?

d. At the profit-maximizing price you identified in part (c), is Sleek's demand curve elastic or inelastic? Explain.

9. Among monopoly, oligopoly, monopolistic competition, and perfect competition, how would you classify the markets for each of the following drinks?

a. tap water
b. bottled water
c. cola
d. beer

10. The market for peanut butter in Nutville is monopolistically competitive and in long-run equilibrium. One day, consumer advocate Skippy Jif discovers that all brands of peanut butter in Nutville are identical. Thereafter, the market becomes perfectly competitive and again reaches its long-run equilibrium. Using an appropriate diagram, explain whether each of the following variables increases, decreases, or stays the same for the typical firm in the market:

a. price
b. quantity
c. average total cost
d. marginal cost
e. profit

11. Consider a monopolistically competitive market with N firms. Each firm's business opportunities are described by the following equations:

Demand:	$Q = 100/N - P$
Marginal Revenue:	$MR = 100/N - 2Q$
Total Cost:	$TC = 50 + Q^2$
Marginal Cost:	$MC = 2Q$

a. How does N, the number of firms in the market, affect each firm's demand curve? Why?

b. How many units does each firm produce? (The answer to this question and the next two depend on N.)

c. What price does each firm charge?

d. How much profit does each firm make?

e. In the long run, how many firms will exist in this market?

http://   For more study tools, please visit www.nelson.com/mankiwmicro6e.

OLIGOPOLY

Chad Mcdermott/Dreamstime.com

Learning Objectives

In this chapter, you will...

- See what market structures lie between monopoly and competition

- Examine what outcomes are possible when a market is an oligopoly

- Learn about the prisoners' dilemma and how it applies to oligopoly and other issues

- Consider how competition laws try to foster competition in oligopolistic markets

If you go to a store to buy hockey skates, it is likely that you will come home with one of two brands: Nike–Bauer or Reebok–CCM. These two companies make almost all of the skates sold in Canada. Together these firms determine the quantity of skates produced and, given the market demand curve, the price at which skates are sold.

The market for hockey skates is an example of an **oligopoly**. The essence of an oligopolistic market is that there are only a few sellers. As a result, the actions of any one seller in the market can have a large impact on the profits of all the other sellers. Oligopolistic firms are interdependent in a way that competitive firms are not. Our goal in this chapter is to see how this interdependence shapes the firms' behaviour and what problems it raises for public policy.

The analysis of oligopoly offers an opportunity to introduce **game theory**, the study of how people behave in strategic situations. By "strategic," we mean a situation in which a person, when choosing among alternative courses of action, must consider how others might respond to the action that person takes. Strategic thinking is crucial not only in checkers, chess, and tic-tac-toe but in many business decisions. Because oligopolistic markets have only a small number of firms, each firm must act strategically. Each firm knows that its profit depends not only on how much it produces but also on how much the other firms produce. In making its production decision, each firm in an oligopoly should consider how its decision might affect the production decisions of all the other firms.

Game theory is not necessary for understanding competitive or monopoly markets. In a market that is either perfectly competitive or monopolistically competitive, each firm is so small compared to the market that strategic interactions with other

oligopoly
a market structure in which only a few sellers offer similar or identical products

game theory
the study of how people behave in strategic situations

firms are not important. In a monopolized market, strategic interactions are absent because the market has only one firm. But, as we will see, game theory is useful for understanding oligopolies and many other situations in which a small number of players interact with one another. Game theory helps explain the strategies that people choose, whether they are playing hockey or selling hockey skates.

MARKETS WITH ONLY A FEW SELLERS

Because an oligopolistic market has only a small group of sellers, a key feature of oligopoly is the tension between cooperation and self-interest. Oligopolists are best off when they cooperate and act like a monopolist—producing a small quantity of output and charging a price above marginal cost. Yet because each oligopolist cares about only its own profit, there are powerful incentives at work that hinder a group of firms from maintaining the cooperative outcome.

A Duopoly Example

To understand the behaviour of oligopolies, let's consider an oligopoly with only two members, called a *duopoly*. Duopoly is the simplest type of oligopoly. Oligopolies with three or more members face the same problems as oligopolies with only two members, so we do not lose much by starting with the case of duopoly.

Imagine a town in which only two residents—Jack and Jill—own wells that produce water safe for drinking. Each Saturday, Jack and Jill decide how many litres of water to pump, bring the water to town, and sell it for whatever price the market will bear. To keep things simple, suppose that Jack and Jill can pump as much water as they want without cost. That is, the marginal cost of water equals zero.

Table 17.1 shows the town's demand schedule for water. The first column shows the total quantity demanded, and the second column shows the price. If the two well owners sell a total of 10 L of water, water goes for $110 per litre. If they sell a

TABLE 17.1

The Demand Schedule for Water	Quantity (in litres)	Price	Total Revenue (and total profit)
	0	$120	$ 0
	10	110	1100
	20	100	2000
	30	90	2700
	40	80	3200
	50	70	3500
	60	60	3600
	70	50	3500
	80	40	3200
	90	30	2700
	100	20	2000
	110	10	1100
	120	0	0

total of 20 L, the price falls to $100 per litre. And so on. If you graphed these two columns of numbers, you would get a standard downward-sloping demand curve.

The last column in Table 17.1 shows the total revenue from the sale of water. It equals the quantity sold times the price. Because there is assumed to be no cost to pumping water, the total revenue of the two producers equals their total profit.

Let's now consider how the organization of the town's water industry affects the price of water and the quantity of water sold.

Competition, Monopolies, and Cartels

Before considering the price and quantity of water that would result from the duopoly of Jack and Jill, let's discuss briefly what the outcome would be if the water market was either perfectly competitive or monopolistic. These two polar cases are natural benchmarks.

If the market for water was perfectly competitive, the production decisions of each firm drive price equal to marginal cost. In the market for water, marginal cost is zero. Thus, under competition, the equilibrium price of water would be zero, and the equilibrium quantity would be 120 L. The price of water would reflect the cost of producing it, and the efficient quantity of water would be produced and consumed.

Now consider how a monopoly would behave. Table 17.1 shows that total profit is maximized at a quantity of 60 L and a price of $60 per litre. A profit-maximizing monopolist, therefore, would produce this quantity and charge this price. As is standard for monopolies, price would exceed marginal cost. The result would be inefficient, because the quantity of water produced and consumed would fall short of the socially efficient level of 120 L.

What outcome should we expect from our duopolists? One possibility is that Jack and Jill get together and agree on the quantity of water to produce and the price to charge for it. Such an agreement among firms over production and price is called **collusion**, and the group of firms acting in unison is called a **cartel**. Once a cartel is formed, the market is in effect served by a monopoly, and we can apply our analysis from Chapter 15. That is, if Jack and Jill were to collude, they would agree on the monopoly outcome because that outcome maximizes the total profit that the producers can get from the market. Our two producers would produce a total of 60 L, which would be sold at a price of $60 per litre. Once again, price exceeds marginal cost, and the outcome is socially inefficient.

A cartel must agree not only on the total level of production but also on the amount produced by each member. In our case, Jack and Jill must agree how to split the monopoly production of 60 L. Each member of the cartel will want a larger share of the market because a larger market share means larger profit. If Jack and Jill agreed to split the market equally, each would produce 30 L, the price would be $60 per litre, and each would get a profit of $1800.

The Equilibrium for an Oligopoly

Oligopolists would like to form cartels and earn monopoly profits, but that is often not possible. As we discuss later in this chapter, competition laws prohibit explicit agreements among oligopolists as a matter of public policy. In addition, squabbling among cartel members over how to divide the profit in

collusion
an agreement among firms in a market about quantities to produce or prices to charge

cartel
a group of firms acting in unison

the market sometimes makes agreement among them impossible. Let's therefore consider what happens if Jack and Jill decide separately how much water to produce.

At first, one might expect Jack and Jill to reach the monopoly outcome on their own, because this outcome maximizes their joint profit. In the absence of a binding agreement, however, the monopoly outcome is unlikely. To see why, imagine that Jack expects Jill to produce only 30 L (half of the monopoly quantity). Jack would reason as follows:

"I could produce 30 L as well. In this case, a total of 60 L of water would be sold at a price of $60 per litre. My profit would be $1800 (30 L × $60 per litre). Alternatively, I could produce 40 L. In this case, a total of 70 L of water would be sold at a price of $50 per litre. My profit would be $2000 (40 L × $50 per litre). Even though total profit in the market would fall, my profit would be higher, because I would have a larger share of the market."

Of course, Jill might reason the same way. If so, Jack and Jill would each bring 40 L to town. Total sales would be 80 L, and the price would fall to $40. Thus, if the duopolists individually pursue their own self-interest when deciding how much to produce, they produce a total quantity greater than the monopoly quantity, charge a price lower than the monopoly price, and earn total profit less than the monopoly profit.

Although the logic of self-interest increases the duopoly's output above the monopoly level, it does not push the duopolists to reach the competitive allocation. Consider what happens when each duopolist is producing 40 L. The price is $40, and each duopolist makes a profit of $1600. In this case, Jack's self-interested logic leads to a different conclusion:

"Right now, my profit is $1600. Suppose I increase my production to 50 L. In this case, a total of 90 L of water would be sold, and the price would be $30 per litre. Then my profit would be only $1500. Rather than increasing production and driving down the price, I am better off keeping my production at 40 L."

The outcome in which Jack and Jill each produce 40 L looks like some sort of equilibrium. In fact, this outcome is called a *Nash equilibrium*. (It is named after economic theorist John Nash, whose life was portrayed in the book and movie *A Beautiful Mind*.) A **Nash equilibrium** is a situation in which economic actors interacting with one another each choose their best strategy given the strategies the others have chosen. In this case, given that Jill is producing 40 L, the best strategy for Jack is to produce 40 L. Similarly, given that Jack is producing 40 L, the best strategy for Jill is to produce 40 L. Once they reach this Nash equilibrium, neither Jack nor Jill has an incentive to make a different decision.

This example illustrates the tension between cooperation and self-interest. Oligopolists would be better off cooperating and reaching the monopoly outcome. Yet because they pursue their own self-interest, they do not end up reaching the monopoly outcome and maximizing their joint profit. Each oligopolist is tempted to raise production and capture a larger share of the market. As each of them tries to do this, total production rises, and the price falls.

At the same time, self-interest does not drive the market all the way to the competitive outcome. Like monopolists, oligopolists are aware that increases in the amount they produce reduce the price of their product. Therefore, they stop short of following the competitive firm's rule of producing up to the point where price equals marginal cost.

Nash equilibrium
a situation in which economic actors interacting with one another each choose their best strategy given the strategies that all the other actors have chosen

In summary, *when firms in an oligopoly individually choose production to maximize profit, they produce a quantity of output greater than the level produced by monopoly and less than the level produced by competition. The oligopoly price is less than the monopoly price but greater than the competitive price (which equals marginal cost).*

Quantity   Price

1. Competition   1. Monopoly
2. Oligopoly   2. Oligopoly
3. Monopoly   3. Competition
                      (= MC)

How the Size of an Oligopoly Affects the Market Outcome

We can use the insights from this analysis of duopoly to discuss how the size of an oligopoly is likely to affect the outcome in a market. Suppose, for instance, that John and Joan suddenly discover water sources on their property and join Jack and Jill in the water oligopoly. The demand schedule in Table 17.1 remains the same, but now more producers are available to satisfy this demand. How would an increase in the number of sellers from two to four affect the price and quantity of water in the town?

If the sellers of water could form a cartel, they would once again try to maximize total profit by producing the monopoly quantity and charging the monopoly price. Just as when there were only two sellers, the members of the cartel would need to agree on production levels for each member and find some way to enforce the agreement. As the cartel grows larger, however, this outcome is less likely. Reaching and enforcing an agreement becomes more difficult as the size of the group increases.

If the oligopolists do not form a cartel—perhaps because the competition laws prohibit it—they must each decide on their own how much water to produce. To see how the increase in the number of sellers affects the outcome, consider the decision facing each seller. At any time, each well owner has the option to raise production by 1 litre. In making this decision, the well owner weighs two effects:

1. *The output effect:* Because price is above marginal cost, selling 1 more litre of water at the going price will raise profit.
2. *The price effect:* Raising production will increase the total amount sold, which will lower the price of water and lower the profit on all the other litres sold.

If the output effect is larger than the price effect, the well owner will increase production. If the price effect is larger than the output effect, the owner will not raise production. (In fact, in this case, it is profitable to reduce production.) Each oligopolist continues to increase production until these two marginal effects exactly balance, taking the other firms' production as given.

Now consider how the number of firms in the industry affects the marginal analysis of each oligopolist. The larger the number of sellers, the less concerned each seller is about its own impact on the market price. That is, as the oligopoly grows in size, the magnitude of the price effect falls. When the oligopoly grows very large, the price effect disappears altogether, leaving only the output effect. That is, the production decision of an individual firm no longer affects the market price. In this extreme case, each firm takes the market price as given when deciding how much to produce. It increases production as long as price is above marginal cost.

We can now see that a large oligopoly is essentially a group of competitive firms. A competitive firm considers only the output effect when deciding how much to produce: Because a competitive firm is a price taker, the price effect is absent. Thus, *as the number of sellers in an oligopoly grows larger, an oligopolistic market looks more and more like a competitive market. The price approaches marginal cost, and the quantity produced approaches the socially efficient level.*

This analysis of oligopoly offers a new perspective on the effects of international trade. Imagine that Toyota and Honda are the only automakers in Japan, Volkswagen and BMW are the only automakers in Germany, and Ford and General Motors are the only automakers in Canada. If these nations prohibited international trade in autos, each would have an auto oligopoly with only two members, and the market outcome would likely depart substantially from the competitive ideal. With international trade, however, the car market is a world market, and the oligopoly in this example has six members. Allowing free trade increases the number of producers from which each consumer can choose, and this increased competition keeps prices closer to marginal cost. Thus, the theory of oligopoly provides another reason, in addition to the theory of comparative advantage discussed in Chapter 3, why all countries can benefit from free trade.

QuickQuiz   If the members of an oligopoly could agree on a total quantity to produce, what quantity would they choose? • If the oligopolists do not act together but instead make production decisions individually, do they produce a total quantity more or less than in your answer to the previous question? Why?

THE ECONOMICS OF COOPERATION

As we have seen, oligopolies would like to reach the monopoly outcome, but doing so requires cooperation, which at times is difficult to maintain. In this section we look more closely at the problems people face when cooperation is desirable but difficult. To analyze the economics of cooperation, we need to learn a little about game theory.

A particularly important "game" is called the **prisoners' dilemma.** This game provides insight into the difficulty of maintaining cooperation. Many times in life, people fail to cooperate with one another even when cooperation would make them all better off. An oligopoly is just one example. The story of the prisoners' dilemma contains a general lesson that applies to any group trying to maintain cooperation among its members.

prisoners' dilemma
a particular "game" between two captured prisoners that illustrates why cooperation is difficult to maintain even when it is mutually beneficial

The Prisoners' Dilemma

The prisoners' dilemma is a story about two criminals who have been captured by the police. Let's call them Bonnie and Clyde. The police have enough evidence to convict Bonnie and Clyde of the minor crime of carrying an unregistered gun, so that each would spend a year in jail. The police also suspect that the two criminals have committed a bank robbery together, but they lack hard evidence to convict them of this major crime. The police question Bonnie and Clyde in separate rooms, and they offer each of them the following deal:

"Right now, we can lock you up for one year. If you confess to the bank robbery and implicate your partner, however, we'll give you immunity and you can go free. Your partner will get 20 years in jail. But if you both confess to the crime, we won't need your testimony and we can avoid the cost of a trial, so you will each get an intermediate sentence of eight years."

If Bonnie and Clyde, heartless bank robbers that they are, care only about their own sentences, what would you expect them to do? Would they confess or remain silent? Figure 17.1 shows their choices. Each prisoner has two strategies: confess

FIGURE 17.1

Bonnie's Decision

		Confess	Remain Silent
Clyde's Decision	**Confess**	Bonnie gets 8 years / Clyde gets 8 years	Bonnie gets 20 years / Clyde goes free
	Remain Silent	Bonnie goes free / Clyde gets 20 years	Bonnie gets 1 year / Clyde gets 1 year

The Prisoners' Dilemma

In this game between two criminals suspected of committing a crime, the sentence that each receives depends both on his or her decision whether to confess or remain silent and on the decision made by the other.

or remain silent. The sentence each prisoner gets depends on the strategy he or she chooses and the strategy chosen by his or her partner in crime.

Consider first Bonnie's decision. She reasons as follows: "I don't know what Clyde is going to do. If he remains silent, my best strategy is to confess, since then I'll go free rather than spending a year in jail. If he confesses, my best strategy is still to confess, since then I'll spend 8 years in jail rather than 20. So, regardless of what Clyde does, I am better off confessing."

In the language of game theory, a strategy is called a **dominant strategy** if it is the best strategy for a player to follow regardless of the strategies pursued by other players. In this case, confessing is a dominant strategy for Bonnie. She spends less time in jail if she confesses, regardless of whether Clyde confesses or remains silent.

Now consider Clyde's decision. He faces exactly the same choices as Bonnie, and he reasons in much the same way. Regardless of what Bonnie does, Clyde can reduce his time in jail by confessing. In other words, confessing is also a dominant strategy for Clyde.

In the end, both Bonnie and Clyde confess, and both spend eight years in jail. Yet, from their standpoint, this is a terrible outcome. If they had *both* remained silent, both of them would have been better off, spending only one year in jail on the gun charge. By each pursuing his or her own interests, the two prisoners together reach an outcome that is worse for each of them.

You might have thought that Bonnie and Clyde would have foreseen this situation and planned ahead. But even with advance planning, they would still run into problems. Imagine that, before the police captured Bonnie and Clyde, the two criminals had made a pact not to confess. Clearly, this agreement would make them both better off *if* they both live up to it, because they would each spend only one year in jail. But would the two criminals in fact remain silent, simply because they had agreed to? Once they are being questioned separately, the logic of self-interest takes over and leads them to confess. Cooperation between the two prisoners is difficult to maintain, because cooperation is individually irrational.

dominant strategy
a strategy that is best for a player in a game regardless of the strategies chosen by the other players

Oligopolies as a Prisoners' Dilemma

What does the prisoners' dilemma have to do with markets and imperfect competition? It turns out that the game oligopolists play in trying to reach the monopoly outcome is similar to the game that the two prisoners play in the prisoners' dilemma.

Consider again the choices facing Jack and Jill. After prolonged negotiation, the two suppliers of water agree to keep production at 30 litres so that the price will be kept high and together they will earn the maximum profit. After they agree on production levels, however, each of them must decide whether to cooperate and live up to this agreement or to ignore it and produce at a higher level. Figure 17.2 shows how the profits of the two producers depend on the strategies they choose.

Suppose you are Jack. You might reason as follows: "I could keep production low at 30 litres as we agreed, or I could raise my production and sell 40 litres. If Jill lives up to the agreement and keeps her production at 30 litres, then I earn profit of $2000 with high production and $1800 with low production. In this case, I am better off with high production. If Jill fails to live up to the agreement and produces 40 litres, then I earn $1600 with high production and $1500 with low production. Once again, I am better off with high production. So regardless of what Jill chooses to do, I am better off reneging on our agreement and producing at a high level."

Producing 40 litres is a dominant strategy for Jack. Of course, Jill reasons in exactly the same way, and so both produce at the higher level of 40 litres. The result is the inferior outcome (from Jack's and Jill's standpoints) with low profits for each of the two producers.

This example illustrates why oligopolies have trouble maintaining monopoly profits. The monopoly outcome is jointly rational for the oligopoly, but each oligopolist has an incentive to cheat. Just as self-interest drives the prisoners in the prisoners' dilemma to confess, self-interest makes it difficult for the oligopoly to maintain the cooperative outcome with low production, high prices, and monopoly profits.

FIGURE 17.2

Jack and Jill's Oligopoly Game

In this game between Jack and Jill, the profit that each earns from selling water depends on both the quantity he or she chooses to sell and the quantity the other chooses to sell.

Jack's Decision

	Sell 40 L	Sell 30 L
Sell 40 L	Jack gets $1600 profit / Jill gets $1600 profit	Jack gets $1500 profit / Jill gets $2000 profit
Sell 30 L	Jack gets $2000 profit / Jill gets $1500 profit	Jack gets $1800 profit / Jill gets $1800 profit

Jill's Decision

Case Study

OPEC AND THE WORLD OIL MARKET

Our story about the town's market for water is fictional, but if we change water to crude oil, and Jack and Jill to Iran and Iraq, the story is quite close to being true. Much of the world's oil is produced by a few countries, mostly in the Middle East. These countries together make up an oligopoly. Their decisions about how much oil to pump are much the same as Jack and Jill's decisions about how much water to pump.

The countries that produce most of the world's oil have formed a cartel, called the Organization of the Petroleum Exporting Countries (OPEC). As originally formed in 1960, OPEC included Iran, Iraq, Kuwait, Saudi Arabia, and Venezuela. In 2010, Qatar, Indonesia, Libya, the United Arab Emirates, Algeria, Nigeria, Ecuador, and Angola were also members. These countries control more than three-fourths of the world's oil reserves. Like any cartel, OPEC tries to raise the price of its product through a coordinated reduction in quantity produced. OPEC tries to set production levels for each of the member countries.

The problem that OPEC faces is much the same as the problem that Jack and Jill faced in our scenario. The OPEC countries would like to maintain a high price of oil, but each member of the cartel is tempted to increase its production in order to get a larger share of the world total profit. OPEC members frequently agree to reduce production but then cheat on their agreements.

OPEC was most successful at maintaining cooperation and high prices in the period from 1973 to 1985. The price of crude oil rose from US$3 per barrel in 1972 to US$11 in 1974 and then to US$35 in 1981. But in the early 1980s member countries began arguing about production levels, and OPEC became ineffective at maintaining cooperation. By 1986 the price of crude oil had fallen back to US$13 per barrel.

In recent years, the members of OPEC have continued to meet regularly, but the cartel has been far less successful at reaching and enforcing agreements. Although the price of oil rose significantly in 2007 and 2008, the primary cause was increased demand in the world oil market, in part from a booming Chinese economy, rather than restricted supply. While this lack of cooperation among OPEC nations has hurt the profits of the oil-producing nations, it has benefited consumers around the world. ●

Other Examples of the Prisoners' Dilemma

We have seen how the prisoners' dilemma can be used to understand the problem facing oligopolies. The same logic applies to many other situations as well. Here we consider two examples in which self-interest prevents cooperation and leads to an inferior outcome for the parties involved.

FIGURE 17.3

An Advertising Game

In this game between firms selling similar products, the profit that each earns depends on both its own advertising decision and the advertising decision of the other firm.

Advertising When two firms advertise to attract the same customers, they face a problem similar to the prisoners' dilemma. For example, consider the decisions facing two beer companies, Molson and Labatt. If neither company advertises, the two companies split the market. If both advertise, they again split the market, but profits are lower, since each company must bear the cost of advertising. Yet if one company advertises while the other does not, the one that advertises attracts customers from the other.

Figure 17.3 shows how the profits of the two companies depend on their actions. You can see that advertising is a dominant strategy for each firm. Thus, both firms choose to advertise, even though both firms would be better off if neither firm advertised.

Common Resources In Chapter 11 we saw that people tend to overuse common resources. One can view this problem as an example of the prisoners' dilemma.

Imagine that two oil companies—Shell and Esso (Imperial Oil)—own adjacent oil fields. Under the fields is a common pool of oil worth $12 million. Drilling a well to recover the oil costs $1 million. If each company drills one well, each will get half of the oil and earn a $5 million profit ($6 million in revenue minus $1 million in costs).

Because the pool of oil is a common resource, the companies will not use it efficiently. Suppose that either company could drill a second well. If one company has two of the three wells, that company gets two-thirds of the oil, which yields a profit of $6 million. The other company gets one-third of the oil, for a profit of $3 million. Yet if each company drills a second well, the two companies again split the oil. In this case, each bears the cost of a second well, so profit is only $4 million for each company.

Figure 17.4 shows the game. Drilling two wells is a dominant strategy for each company. Once again, the self-interest of the two players leads them to an inferior outcome.

FIGURE 17.4

A Common-Resources Game

In this game between firms pumping oil from a common pool, the profit that each earns depends on both the number of wells it drills and the number of wells drilled by the other firm.

The Prisoners' Dilemma and the Welfare of Society

The prisoners' dilemma describes many of life's situations, and it shows that cooperation can be difficult to maintain, even when cooperation would make both players in the game better off. Clearly, this lack of cooperation is a problem for those involved in these situations. But is lack of cooperation a problem from the standpoint of society as a whole? The answer depends on the circumstances.

In some cases, the noncooperative equilibrium is bad for society as well as the players. For example, in the common-resources game in Figure 17.4, the extra wells dug by Shell and Esso are pure waste. Society would be better off if the two players could reach the cooperative outcome.

By contrast, in the case of oligopolists trying to maintain monopoly profits, lack of cooperation is desirable from the standpoint of society as a whole. The monopoly outcome is good for the oligopolists, but it is bad for the consumers of the product. As we first saw in Chapter 7, the competitive outcome is best for society because it maximizes total surplus. When oligopolists fail to cooperate, the quantity they produce is closer to this optimal level. Put differently, the invisible hand guides markets to allocate resources efficiently only when markets are competitive, and markets are competitive only when firms in the market fail to cooperate with one another.

Similarly, consider the case of the police questioning two suspects. Lack of cooperation between the suspects is desirable because it allows the police to convict more criminals. The prisoners' dilemma is a dilemma for the prisoners, but it can be a boon to everyone else.

Why People Sometimes Cooperate

The prisoners' dilemma shows that cooperation is difficult. But is it impossible? Not all prisoners, when questioned by the police, decide to turn in their partners in crime.

Cartels sometimes do manage to maintain collusive arrangements, despite the incentive for individual members to defect. Very often, the reason that players can solve the prisoners' dilemma is that they play the game not once but many times.

To see why cooperation is easier to enforce in repeated games, let's return to our duopolists, Jack and Jill, whose choices were given in Figure 17.2. Jack and Jill would like to agree to maintain the monopoly outcome in which each produces 30 L. Yet if Jack and Jill are to play this game only once, neither has any incentive to live up to this agreement. Self-interest drives each to renege and choose the dominant strategy of 40 L.

Now suppose that Jack and Jill know that they will play the same game every week. When they make their initial agreement to keep production low, they can also specify what happens if one party reneges. They might agree, for instance, that once one of them reneges and produces 40 L, both of them will produce 40 L forever after. This penalty is easy to enforce because if one party is producing at a high level, the other has every reason to do the same.

The threat of this penalty may be all that is needed to maintain cooperation. Each person knows that defecting would raise his or her profit from $1800 to $2000. But this benefit would last for only one week. Thereafter, profit would fall to $1600 and stay there. As long as the players care enough about future profits, they will choose to forgo the one-time gain from defection. Thus, in a game of repeated prisoners' dilemma, the two players may well be able to reach the cooperative outcome.

Case Study

THE PRISONERS' DILEMMA TOURNAMENT

Imagine that you are playing a game of prisoners' dilemma with a person being "questioned" in a separate room. Moreover, imagine that you are going to play not once but many times. Your score at the end of the game is the total number of years in jail. You would like to make this score as small as possible. What strategy would you play? Would you begin by confessing or remaining silent? How would the other player's actions affect your subsequent decisions about confessing?

Repeated prisoners' dilemma is quite a complicated game. To encourage cooperation, players must penalize each other for not cooperating. Yet the strategy described earlier for Jack and Jill's water cartel—defect forever as soon as the other player defects—is not very forgiving. In a game repeated many times, a strategy that allows players to return to the cooperative outcome after a period of noncooperation may be preferable.

To see what strategies work best, political scientist Robert Axelrod held a tournament. People entered by sending computer programs designed to play repeated prisoners' dilemma. Each program then played the game against all the other programs. The "winner" was the program that received the fewest total years in jail.

The winner turned out to be a simple strategy called *tit-for-tat*. According to tit-for-tat, a player should start by cooperating and then do whatever the other player did last time. Thus, a tit-for-tat player cooperates until the other player defects; he then defects until the other player cooperates again. In other words, this strategy starts out friendly, penalizes unfriendly players, and forgives them if warranted. To Axelrod's surprise, this simple strategy did better than all the more complicated strategies that people had sent in.

The tit-for-tat strategy has a long history. It is essentially the biblical strategy of "an eye for an eye, a tooth for a tooth." The prisoners' dilemma tournament suggests that this may be a good rule of thumb for playing some of the games of life. ●

QuickQuiz   Tell the story of the prisoners' dilemma. Prepare a table showing the prisoners' choices and explain what outcome is likely. ● What does the prisoners' dilemma teach us about oligopolies?

PUBLIC POLICY TOWARD OLIGOPOLIES

One of the ten principles of economics in Chapter 1 is that governments can sometimes improve market outcomes. The application of this principle to oligopolistic markets is, as a general matter, straightforward. As we have seen, cooperation among oligopolists is undesirable from the standpoint of society as a whole because it leads to production that is too low and prices that are too high. To move the allocation of resources closer to the social optimum, policymakers should try to induce firms in an oligopoly to compete rather than cooperate. Let's consider how policymakers do this and then examine the controversies that arise in this area of public policy.

Restraint of Trade and the Competition Act

Freedom to make contracts is an essential part of a market economy. Businesses and households use contracts to arrange mutually advantageous trades, relying on the court system to enforce those contracts. Yet for many years, Canadian judges have refused to enforce agreements that restrain trade among competitors (reducing quantities and raising prices, or price-fixing) as being against the public interest.

Canada's Competition Act codifies and reinforces this policy. Section 45(1) of the act states:

Every one who conspires, combines, agrees or arranges with another person
(a) to limit unduly the facilities for transporting, producing, manufacturing, supplying, storing or dealing in any product,
(b) to prevent, limit or lessen, unduly, the manufacture or production of a product or to enhance unreasonably the price thereof,
(c) to prevent or lessen, unduly, competition in the production, manufacture, purchase, barter, sale, storage, rental, transportation or supply of a product, or in the price of insurance on persons or property, or
(d) to otherwise restrain or injure competition unduly,
is guilty of an indictable offence and liable to imprisonment for a term not exceeding five years or to a fine not exceeding ten million dollars or both.

The Competition Act contains both civil and criminal provisions. As we discussed in Chapter 15, the Competition Bureau is responsible for enforcing the act. The bureau may refer criminal cases to the Attorney General of Canada and civil cases to the Competition Tribunal. Mergers, also discussed in Chapter 15, are governed by the civil provisions of the act. Conspiracies in restraint of trade, such as those described in section 45(1), above, fall under the criminal provisions of the act.

Other activities that are subject to criminal prosecution include bid-rigging, price discrimination, resale price maintenance, and predatory pricing. Bid-rigging occurs when potential bidders agree with other bidders to refrain from bidding on contracts, or rig bids in advance. Price discrimination occurs when a supplier charges different prices for similar quantities of goods sold to firms that compete with one another. Resale price maintenance occurs when a supplier "requires" retailers to sell its product at a specified (or minimum or maximum) price. Predatory pricing involves selling products at unreasonably low prices for the purpose of eliminating or substantially reducing competition. Criminal proceedings must be initiated by the commissioner, but individuals who have been harmed by criminal offences can sue for civil damages. These and other provisions of the Competition Act are used to prevent firms in oligopolistic industries from acting either individually or together in ways that make markets less competitive.

Controversies over Competition Policy

Over time, much controversy has centred on the question of what kinds of behaviour the competition laws should prohibit. Most commentators agree that price-fixing agreements among competing firms should be illegal. Yet the competition laws have been used to condemn some business practices whose effects are not obvious. Here we consider three examples.

Resale Price Maintenance

One example of a controversial business practice is *resale price maintenance,* also called *fair trade.* Imagine that Superduper Electronics sells DVD players to retail stores for $300. If Superduper requires the retailers to charge customers $350, it is said to engage in resale price maintenance. Any retailer that charged less than $350 would have violated its contract with Superduper.

At first, resale price maintenance might seem anticompetitive and, therefore, detrimental to society. Like an agreement among members of a cartel, it prevents the retailers from competing on price. For this reason, the courts have often viewed resale price maintenance as a violation of the competition laws.

Yet some economists defend resale price maintenance on two grounds. First, they deny that it is aimed at reducing competition. To the extent that Superduper Electronics has any market power, it can exert that power through the wholesale price, rather than through resale price maintenance. Moreover, Superduper has no incentive to discourage competition among its retailers. Indeed, because a cartel of retailers sells less than a group of competitive retailers, Superduper would be worse off if its retailers were a cartel.

Second, economists believe that resale price maintenance has a legitimate goal. Superduper may want its retailers to provide customers with a pleasant showroom and a knowledgeable sales force. Yet, without resale price maintenance, some customers would take advantage of one store's service to learn about the DVD player's special features and then buy the item at a discount retailer that does not provide this service. To some extent, good service is a public good among the retailers that sell Superduper products. As we discussed in Chapter 11, when one person provides a public good, others are able to enjoy it without paying for it. In this case, discount retailers would free-ride on the service provided by other retailers, leading to less service than is desirable. Resale price maintenance is one way for Superduper to solve this free-rider problem.

The example of resale price maintenance illustrates an important principle: *Business practices that appear to reduce competition may in fact have legitimate purposes.* This principle makes the application of the competition laws all the more difficult. The economists, lawyers, and judges in charge of enforcing these laws must determine what kinds of behaviour public policy should prohibit as impeding competition and reducing economic well-being. Often that job is not easy.

Predatory Pricing   Firms with market power normally use that power to raise prices above the competitive level. But should policymakers ever be concerned that firms with market power might charge prices that are too low? This question is at the heart of a second debate over competition policy.

Imagine that a large airline, call it Coyote Air, has a monopoly on some route. Then Roadrunner Express enters and takes 20 percent of the market, leaving Coyote with 80 percent. In response to this competition, Coyote starts slashing its fares. Some competition analysts argue that Coyote's move could be anticompetitive: The price cuts may be intended to drive Roadrunner out of the market so Coyote can recapture its monopoly and raise prices again. Such behaviour is called *predatory pricing.*

Although predatory pricing is a common claim in competition suits, some economists are skeptical of this argument and believe that predatory pricing is rarely, and perhaps never, a profitable business strategy. Why? For a price war to drive out a rival, prices have to be driven below cost. Yet if Coyote starts selling cheap tickets at a loss, it had better be ready to fly more planes, because low fares will attract more customers. Roadrunner, meanwhile, can respond to Coyote's predatory move by cutting back on flights. As a result, Coyote ends up bearing more than 80 percent of the losses, putting Roadrunner in a good position to survive the price war. As in the old Roadrunner–Coyote cartoons, the predator suffers more than the prey.

Economists continue to debate whether predatory pricing should be a concern for anticompetition policymakers. Various questions remain unresolved. Is predatory pricing ever a profitable business strategy? If so, when? Are the courts capable of telling which price cuts are competitive and thus good for consumers and which are predatory? There are no simple answers.

Tying   A third example of a controversial business practice is *tying.* Suppose that Makemoney Movies produces two new films—*Ironman* and *Hamlet.* If Makemoney offers theatres the two films together at a single price, rather than separately, the studio is said to be tying its two products.

The practice of tying is banned under the civil provisions of the Competition Act. The commonly used justification for the ban goes as follows: Imagine that *Ironman* is a blockbuster, whereas *Hamlet* is an unprofitable art film. By tying, the studio could use the high demand for *Ironman* to force theatres to buy *Hamlet*. It seems that the studio could use tying as a mechanism for expanding its market power.

Many economists are skeptical of this argument. Imagine that theatres are willing to pay $20 000 for *Ironman* and nothing for *Hamlet*. Then the most that a theatre would pay for the two movies together is $20 000—the same as it would pay for *Ironman* by itself. Forcing the theatre to accept a worthless movie as part of the deal does not increase the theatre's willingness to pay. Makemoney cannot increase its market power simply by bundling the two movies together.

Why, then, does tying exist? One possibility is that it is a form of price discrimination. Suppose there are two theatres. City Theatre is willing to pay $15 000

IN THE NEWS

BID-RIGGING IN SEWERS IS DIRTY BUSINESS

Another type of noncompetitive business practice is known as bid-rigging. *Bid-rigging occurs when several parties agree to a predetermined set of bids on a contract to give the appearance of a competitive bidding process. It is a form of price-fixing and collusion that is illegal in most countries, including Canada. This article discusses a recent bid-rigging case in Canada. It also illustrates the prisoners' dilemma at work, as firms involved in a bid-rigging collusion have an incentive to rat out their co-conspirators.*

Bid-Rigging Firm Rats Out Others; Company Pleads Guilty

One of six companies accused of being involved in a bid-rigging scheme to win provincial and municipal sewer service contracts in the Montreal region ratted out the others. Another company or individual whose identity is secret tipped off the federal Competition Bureau to the cartel in the first place.

And that's nearly always the way the Competition Bureau uncovers cartels and manages to file charges, it turns out.

MSC Rehabilitation Inc. pleaded guilty in Quebec Superior Court on Tuesday for its role in the bid-rigging cartel on 12 calls for tenders, including three in Montreal boroughs.

The company's guilty plea to a single charge is part of a leniency agreement MSC Rehabilitation has in exchange for providing evidence of the bid-rigging scheme to the Competition Bureau, bureau spokesperson Alexa Keating said on Wednesday. The company received a $75,000 fine and no charges were laid against company officials.

The bureau also laid a combined 156 charges against five other companies and their owners or presidents: Canalisation Nord Americaine Ltee, Groupe Esthetix, Colmatec Inc., Chalifoux Sani Laurentides Inc. and Kelly Sani-Vac Inc. They have yet to appear in court.

In all, the bid-rigging case involves 37 calls for tender in 2008 and 2009, and $3.3 million worth of sewer cleaning and maintenance contracts awarded by island

and off-island municipalities, Montreal boroughs and Transport Quebec.

The Competition Bureau offers immunity to anyone who alerts the authorities to a scheme they were involved in that had gone undetected, and leniency to anyone who subsequently steps forward and cooperates with the Competition Bureau's investigation, as was the case with MSC Rehabilitation.

Source: "Firm turns on bid-rig partners; Leniency deal brings information; five other companies face 156 charges in wide-ranging case on sewer tenders" by Linda Gyulai, *Montreal Gazette*, November 24, 2011, p. A4. Material reprinted with the express permission of: The Gazette, a division of Postmedia Network Inc.

for *Ironman* and $5000 for *Hamlet.* Country Theatre is just the opposite: It is willing to pay $5000 for *Ironman* and $15 000 for *Hamlet.* If Makemoney charges separate prices for the two films, its best strategy is to charge $15 000 for each film, and each theatre chooses to show only one film. Yet if Makemoney offers the two movies as a bundle, it can charge each theatre $20 000 for the movies. Thus, if different theatres value the films differently, tying may allow the studio to increase profit by charging a combined price closer to the buyers' total willingness to pay.

Tying remains a controversial business practice. The commonly heard argument that tying allows a firm to extend its market power to other goods is not well founded, at least in its simplest form. Yet economists have proposed more elaborate theories for how tying can impede competition. Given our current economic knowledge, it is unclear whether tying has adverse effects for society as a whole.

Case Study

THE MICROSOFT CASE

The most important and controversial anticompetition case in recent years has been the U.S. government's suit against Microsoft Corporation, filed in 1998. Certainly, the case did not lack drama. It pitted one of the world's richest men (Bill Gates) against one of the world's most powerful regulatory agencies (the U.S. Justice Department). Testifying for the government was a prominent economist (MIT professor Franklin Fisher). Testifying for Microsoft was an equally prominent economist (MIT professor Richard Schmalensee). At stake was the future of one of the world's most valuable companies (Microsoft) in one of the economy's fastest-growing industries (computer software).

"Me? A monopolist? Now just wait a minute. . . ."

A central issue in the Microsoft case involved tying—in particular, whether Microsoft should be allowed to integrate its Internet browser into its Windows operating system. The government claimed that Microsoft was bundling these two products together to expand the power it had in the market for computer operating systems into an unrelated market (for Internet browsers). Allowing Microsoft to incorporate such products into its operating system, the government argued, would deter other software companies such as Netscape from entering the market and offering new products.

Microsoft responded by pointing out that putting new features into old products is a natural part of technological progress. Cars today include stereos and air conditioners, which were once sold separately, and cameras come with built-in flashes. The same is true with operating systems. Over time, Microsoft has added many features to Windows that were previously stand-alone products. This has made computers more reliable and easier to use because consumers can be confident that the pieces work together. The integration of Internet technology, Microsoft argued, was the natural next step.

One point of disagreement concerned the extent of Microsoft's market power. Noting that more than 80 percent of new personal computers use a Microsoft operating system, the government argued that the company had substantial monopoly power, which it was trying to expand. Microsoft replied that the software market is always changing and that Microsoft's Windows was constantly being challenged by competitors, such as the Apple Mac and Linux operating systems. It also argued that the low price it charged for Windows—about $50 at that time, or only 3 percent of the price of a typical computer—was evidence that its market power was severely limited.

Like many large anticompetition suits, the Microsoft case became a legal morass. In November 1999, after a long trial, Judge Penfield Jackson ruled that Microsoft had great monopoly power and that it had illegally abused that power. In June 2000, after hearings about possible remedies, he ordered that Microsoft be broken up into two companies—one that sold the operating system and one that sold applications software. A year later, an appeals court overturned Jackson's breakup order and handed the case to a new judge. In September 2001, the Justice Department announced that it no longer sought a breakup of the company and wanted to settle the case quickly.

A settlement was finally reached in November 2002. Microsoft accepted some restrictions on its business practices. The government accepted that a browser would remain part of the Windows operating system. But the settlement did not end Microsoft's anticompetition troubles. In recent years, the company has contended with several private anticompetition suits, as well as suits brought by the European Union alleging a variety of anticompetitive behaviours. ●

QuickQuiz   What kind of agreement is illegal for businesses to make? • Why are the competition laws controversial?

CONCLUSION

Oligopolies would like to act like monopolies, but self-interest drives them closer to competition. Thus, oligopolies can end up looking either more like monopolies or more like competitive markets, depending on the number of firms in the oligopoly and how cooperative the firms are. The story of the prisoners' dilemma shows why oligopolies can fail to maintain cooperation, even when cooperation is in their best interest.

Policymakers regulate the behaviour of oligopolists through the anticompetition laws. The proper scope of these laws is the subject of ongoing controversy. Although price-fixing among competing firms clearly reduces economic welfare and should be illegal, some business practices that appear to reduce competition may have legitimate if subtle purposes. As a result, policymakers need to be careful when they use the substantial powers of the anticompetition laws to place limits on firms' behaviour.

SUMMARY

- Oligopolists maximize their total profits by forming a cartel and acting like a monopolist. Yet, if oligopolists make decisions about production levels individually, the result is a greater quantity and a lower price than under the monopoly outcome. The larger the number of firms in the oligopoly, the closer the quantity and price will be to the levels that would prevail under perfect competition.

- The prisoners' dilemma shows that self-interest can prevent people from maintaining cooperation, even when cooperation is in their mutual interest. The logic of the prisoners' dilemma applies in many situations, including advertising, common-resource problems, and oligopolies.

- Policymakers use the anticompetition laws to prevent oligopolies from engaging in behaviour that reduces competition. The application of these laws can be controversial, because some behaviour that may seem to reduce competition may in fact have legitimate business purposes.

KEY CONCEPTS

oligopoly, p. 371
game theory, p. 371
collusion, p. 373

cartel, p. 373
Nash equilibrium, p. 374

prisoners' dilemma, p. 376
dominant strategy, p. 377

QUESTIONS FOR REVIEW

1. If a group of sellers could form a cartel, what quantity and price would they try to set?

2. Compare the quantity and price of an oligopoly to those of a monopoly.

3. Compare the quantity and price of an oligopoly to those of a competitive market.

4. How does the number of firms in an oligopoly affect the outcome in its market?

5. What is the prisoners' dilemma, and what does it have to do with oligopoly?

6. Give two examples other than oligopoly that show how the prisoners' dilemma helps to explain behaviour.

7. What kinds of behaviour do the competition laws prohibit?

8. What is resale price maintenance, and why is it controversial?

PROBLEMS AND APPLICATIONS

1. *The New York Times* (Nov. 30, 1993) reported that "the inability of OPEC to agree last week to cut production has sent the oil market into turmoil . . . [leading to] the lowest price for domestic crude oil since June 1990."
   a. Why were the members of OPEC trying to agree to cut production?
   b. Why do you suppose OPEC was unable to agree on cutting production? Why did the oil market go into "turmoil" as a result?

   c. The newspaper also noted OPEC's view "that producing nations outside the organization, like Norway and Britain, should do their share and cut production." What does the phrase "do their share" suggest about OPEC's desired relationship with Norway and Britain?

2. A large share of the world supply of diamonds comes from Russia and South Africa. Suppose that the marginal cost of mining diamonds is

constant at $1000 per diamond, and the demand for diamonds is described by the following schedule:

Price	Quantity
$8000	5 000
7000	6 000
6000	7 000
5000	8 000
4000	9 000
3000	10 000
2000	11 000
1000	12 000

a. If there were many suppliers of diamonds, what would be the price and quantity?

b. If there was only one supplier of diamonds, what would be the price and quantity?

c. If Russia and South Africa formed a cartel, what would be the price and quantity? If the countries split the market evenly, what would be South Africa's production and profit? What would happen to South Africa's profit if it increased its production by 1000 while Russia stuck to the cartel agreement?

d. Use your answer to part (c) to explain why cartel agreements are often not successful.

3. This chapter discusses companies that are oligopolists in the market for the goods they sell. Many of the same ideas apply to companies that are oligopolists in the market for the inputs they buy.

a. If sellers who are oligopolists try to increase the price of goods they sell, what is the goal of buyers who are oligopolists?

b. National Hockey League team owners have an oligopoly in the market for hockey players. What is the owners' goal regarding players' salaries? Why is this goal difficult to achieve?

c. Hockey players went on strike in 2004 because they would not accept the salary cap that the owners wanted to impose. If the owners were already colluding over salaries, why did the owners feel the need for a salary cap?

4. Consider trade relations between Canada and Mexico. Assume that the leaders of the two countries believe the payoffs to alternative trade policies are as follows:

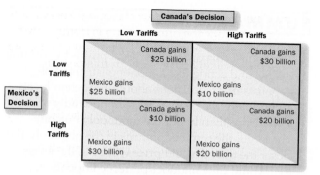

a. What is the dominant strategy for Canada? For Mexico? Explain.

b. Define *Nash equilibrium*. What is the Nash equilibrium for trade policy?

c. In 1993, Parliament ratified the North American Free Trade Agreement (NAFTA), in which Canada, the United States, and Mexico agreed to reduce trade barriers simultaneously. Do the perceived payoffs shown here justify this approach to trade policy?

d. Based on your understanding of the gains from trade (discussed in Chapters 3 and 9), do you think that these payoffs actually reflect a nation's welfare under the four possible outcomes?

5. Suppose that you and a classmate are assigned a project on which you will receive one combined grade. You each want to receive a good grade, but you also want to do as little work as possible. The decision box and payoffs are as follows:

Assume that having fun is your normal state, but having no fun is as unpleasant as receiving a grade that is two letters lower.

a. Write out the decision box that combines the letter grade and the amount of fun you have into a single payoff for each outcome.

b. If neither you nor your classmate knows how much work the other person is doing, what is the likely outcome? Does it matter whether you are likely to work with this person again? Explain your answer.

6. The chapter described an advertising game between Molson and Labatt. Suppose the federal government is considering a law prohibiting beer commercials on television.
   a. Would you expect the beer companies to oppose this law? Why?
   b. Would you expect beer company profits to rise or fall? Why?

7. Farmer Singh and Farmer Vu graze their cattle in the same field. If there are 20 cows grazing in the field, each cow produces $4000 of milk over its lifetime. If there are more cows in the field, then each cow can eat less grass, and its milk production falls. With 30 cows in the field, each produces $3000 of milk; with 40 cows, each produces $2000 of milk. Cows cost $1000 apiece.
   a. Assume that Farmer Singh and Farmer Vu can each purchase either 10 or 20 cows, but that neither knows how many the other is buying when she makes her purchase. Calculate the payoffs of each outcome.
   b. What is the likely outcome of this game? What would be the best outcome? Explain.
   c. There used to be more common fields than there are today. Why? (For more discussion of this topic, reread Chapter 11.)

8. Little Kona is a small coffee company that is considering entering a market dominated by Big Brew. Each company's profit depends on whether Little Kona enters and whether Big Brew sets a high price or a low price:

Big Brew threatens Little Kona by saying, " If you enter, we're going to set a low price, so you had better stay out." Do you think Little Kona should believe the threat? Why or why not? What do you think Little Kona should do?

9. Jeff and Steve are playing tennis. Every point comes down to whether Steve guesses correctly whether Jeff will hit the ball to Steve's left or right. The outcomes are:

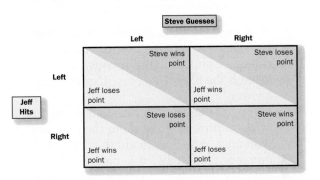

Does either player have a dominant strategy? If Jeff chooses a particular strategy (Left or Right) and sticks with it, what will Steve do? Can you think of a better strategy for Jeff to follow?

10. Let's return to the chapter's discussion of Jack and Jill's water duopoly (page 372). Suppose that Jack and Jill are at the duopoly's Nash equilibrium (total production of 80 L) when a third person, John, discovers a water source and joins the market as a third producer.
    a. Jack and Jill propose that the three of them continue to produce a total of 80 L, splitting the market three ways. If John agrees to this, how much profit will he make?
    b. After agreeing to the proposed deal, John is considering increasing his production by 10 L. If he does, and Jack and Jill stick to the agreement, how much profit will John make? What does this tell you about the proposed agreement?
    c. What is the Nash equilibrium for this market with three producers? How does it compare to the Nash equilibrium with two producers?

11. You and a classmate are assigned a project on which you will receive one combined grade. You each want to receive a good grade, but you

also want to avoid hard work. In particular, here is the situation:

- If both of you work hard, you both get an A, which gives each of you 40 units of happiness.
- If only one of you works hard, you both get a B, which gives each of you 30 units of happiness.
- If neither of you works hard, you both get a D, which gives each of you 10 units of happiness.
- Working hard costs 25 units of happiness.

a. Draw a 2 × 2 decision box for you and your classmate and fill in the payoffs.

b. What is the likely outcome? Explain your answer.

c. If you get this classmate as your partner on a series of projects throughout the year, rather than only once, how might that change the outcome you predicted in part (b)?

d. Another classmate cares more about good grades: He gets 50 units of happiness from

a B, and 80 units of happiness from an A. If this classmate was your partner (but your preferences were unchanged), how would your answers to parts (a) and (b) change? Which of the two classmates would you prefer as a partner? Would he also want you as a partner?

12. Two athletes of equal ability are competing for a prize of $10 000. Each is deciding whether to take a dangerous performance-enhancing drug. If one athlete takes the drug and the other does not, the one who takes the drug wins the prize. If both or neither take the drug, they tie and split the prize. Taking the drug involves health risks that are equivalent to a loss of X dollars.

a. Draw a 2 × 2 decision box describing the decisions the athletes face and fill in the payoffs.

b. For what X is taking the drug the Nash equilibrium?

c. Does making the drug safer (that is, lowering X) make the athletes better or worse off? Explain.

http:// For more study tools, please visit www.nelson.com/mankiwmicro6e.

THE ECONOMICS OF LABOUR MARKETS

6

THE MARKETS FOR THE FACTORS OF PRODUCTION

whethervain/iStockphoto

Learning Objectives

In this chapter, you will...

- Analyze the labour demand of competitive, profit-maximizing firms
- Consider the household decisions that lie behind labour supply
- Learn why equilibrium wages equal the value of the marginal product of labour
- Consider how the other factors of production—land and capital—are compensated
- Examine how a change in the supply of one factor alters the earnings of all the factors

When you finish school, your income will be determined largely by the kind of job you take. If you become a computer programmer, you will earn more than if you become a gas station attendant. This fact is not surprising, but it is not obvious why it is true. No law requires that computer programmers be paid more than gas station attendants. No ethical principle says that programmers are more deserving. What then determines which job will pay you the higher wage?

Your income, of course, is a small piece of a larger economic picture. In 2011, the total income of all Canadian residents was about $1.7 trillion. People earned this income in various ways. Workers earned about three-fourths of it in the form of wages and fringe benefits. The rest went to landowners and to the owners of *capital*—the economy's stock of equipment and structures—in the form of rent, profit, and interest. What determines how much goes to workers? To landowners? To the owners of capital? Why do some workers earn higher wages than others, some landowners higher rental income than others, and some capital owners greater profit than others? Why, in particular, do computer programmers earn more than gas station attendants?

The answers to these questions, like most in economics, hinge on supply and demand. The supply and demand for labour, land, and capital determine the prices paid to workers, landowners, and capital owners. To understand why some people have higher incomes than others, therefore, we need to look more deeply at the markets for the services they provide. That is our job in this and the next two chapters.

factors of production
the inputs used to produce goods and services

Derived Demand =

A firm's demand for a factor of production is a derived demand from its decision to supply a good in another market

This chapter provides the basic theory for the analysis of factor markets. As you may recall from Chapter 2, the **factors of production** are the inputs used to produce goods and services. Labour, land, and capital are the three most important factors of production. When a computer firm produces a new software program, it uses programmers' time (labour), the physical space on which its offices sit (land), and an office building and computer equipment (capital). Similarly, when a gas station sells gas, it uses attendants' time (labour), the physical space (land), and the gas tanks and pumps (capital).

In many ways factor markets resemble the goods markets we have analyzed in previous chapters, but they are different in one important way: The demand for a factor of production is a *derived demand*. That is, a firm's demand for a factor of production is derived from its decision to supply a good in another market. The demand for computer programmers is inextricably tied to the supply of computer software, and the demand for gas station attendants is inextricably tied to the supply of gasoline.

In this chapter we analyze factor demand by considering how a competitive, profit-maximizing firm decides how much of any factor to buy. We begin our analysis by examining the demand for labour. Labour is the most important factor of production, for workers receive most of the total income earned in the Canadian economy. Later in the chapter, we will see that our analysis of the labour market also applies to the markets for the other factors of production.

The basic theory of factor markets developed in this chapter takes a large step toward explaining how the income of the Canadian economy is distributed among workers, landowners, and owners of capital. Chapter 19 will build on this analysis to examine in more detail why some workers earn more than others. Chapter 20 will examine how much inequality results from this process and then consider what role the government should and does play in altering the distribution of income.

THE DEMAND FOR LABOUR

Labour markets, like other markets in the economy, are governed by the forces of supply and demand. This is illustrated in Figure 18.1. In panel (a) the supply and demand for apples determine the price of apples. In panel (b) the supply and demand for apple pickers determine the price, or wage, of apple pickers.

As we have already noted, labour markets are different from most other markets because labour demand is a derived demand. Most labour services, rather than being final goods ready to be enjoyed by consumers, are inputs into the production of other goods. To understand labour demand, we need to focus on the firms that hire the labour and use it to produce goods for sale. By examining the link between the production of goods and the demand for labour, we gain insight into the determination of equilibrium wages.

The Competitive, Profit-Maximizing Firm

Let's look at how a typical firm, such as an apple producer, decides what quantity of labour to demand. The firm owns an apple orchard and each week must decide how many apple pickers to hire to harvest its crop. After the firm makes its hiring decision, the workers pick as many apples as they can. The firm then sells the apples, pays the workers, and keeps what is left as profit.

FIGURE 18.1

The Versatility of Supply and Demand

The basic tools of supply and demand apply to goods and to labour services. Panel (a) shows how the supply and demand for apples determine the price of apples. Panel (b) shows how the supply and demand for apple pickers determine the wage of apple pickers.

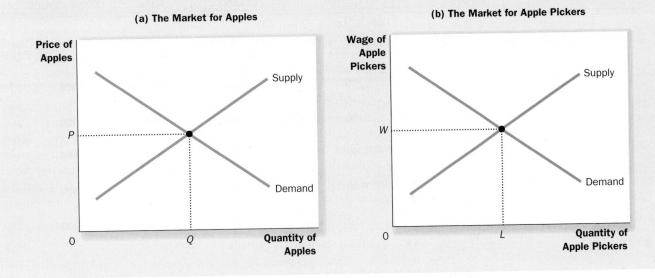

(a) The Market for Apples

(b) The Market for Apple Pickers

We make two assumptions about our firm. First, we assume that our firm is *competitive* both in the market for apples (where the firm is a seller) and in the market for apple pickers (where the firm is a buyer). A competitive firm is a price taker. Because there are many other firms selling apples and hiring apple pickers, a single firm has little influence over the price it gets for apples or the wage it pays apple pickers. The firm takes the price and the wage as given by market conditions. It has to decide only how many workers to hire and how many apples to sell.

Second, we assume that the firm is *profit-maximizing*. Thus, the firm does not directly care about the number of workers it has or the number of apples it produces. It cares only about profit, which equals the total revenue from the sale of apples minus the total cost of producing them. The firm's supply of apples and its demand for workers are derived from its primary goal of maximizing profit.

The Production Function
and the Marginal Product of Labour

To make its hiring decision, the firm must consider how the size of its workforce affects the amount of output produced. In other words, it must consider how the number of apple pickers affects the quantity of apples it can harvest and sell. Table 18.1 gives a numerical example. In the first column is the number of workers. In the second column is the quantity of apples the workers harvest each week.

These two columns of numbers describe the firm's ability to produce. As we noted in Chapter 13, economists use the term **production function** to describe

production function
the relationship between the quantity of inputs used to make a good and the quantity of output of that good

TABLE 18.1

How the Competitive Firm Decides How Much Labour to Hire

Labour	Output	Marginal Product of Labour	Value of the Marginal Product of Labour	Wage	Marginal Profit
L (number of workers)	Q (bushels per week)	$MPL = \Delta Q/\Delta L$ (bushels per week)	$VMPL = P \times MPL$	W	$\Delta Profit = VMPL - W$
0	0				
		100	$1000	$500	$500
1	100				
		80	800	500	300
2	180				
		60	600	500	100
3	240				
		40	400	500	−100
4	280				
		20	200	500	−300
5	300				

the relationship between the quantity of the inputs used in production and the quantity of output from production. Here the "input" is the apple pickers and the "output" is the apples. The other inputs—the trees themselves, the land, the firm's trucks and tractors, and so on—are held fixed for now. This firm's production function shows that if the firm hires 1 worker, that worker will pick 100 bushels of apples per week. If the firm hires 2 workers, the two workers together will pick 180 bushels per week, and so on.

Figure 18.2 graphs the data on labour and output presented in Table 18.1. The number of workers is on the horizontal axis, and the amount of output is on the vertical axis. This figure illustrates the production function.

One of the ten principles of economics introduced in Chapter 1 is that rational people think at the margin. This idea is the key to understanding how firms decide what quantity of labour to hire. To take a step toward this decision, the third column in Table 18.1 gives the **marginal product of labour**, the increase in the amount of output from an additional unit of labour. When the firm increases the number of workers from 1 to 2, for example, the amount of apples produced rises from 100 to 180 bushels. Therefore, the marginal product of the second worker is 80 bushels.

Notice that as the number of workers increases, the marginal product of labour declines. As you may recall from Chapter 13, this property is called **diminishing marginal product**. At first, when only a few workers are hired, they can pick the low-hanging fruit. As the number of workers increases, additional workers have to climb higher up the ladders to find apples to pick. Hence, as more and more workers are hired, each additional worker contributes less to the production of apples. For this reason, the production function in Figure 18.2 becomes flatter as the number of workers rises.

marginal product of labour
the increase in the amount of output from an additional unit of labour

diminishing marginal product
the property whereby the marginal product of an input declines as the quantity of the input increases

FIGURE 18.2

The Production Function

The production function is the relationship between the inputs into production (apple pickers) and the output from production (apples). As the quantity of the input increases, the production function gets flatter, reflecting the property of diminishing marginal product.

The Value of the Marginal Product and the Demand for Labour

Our profit-maximizing firm is concerned more with money than with apples. As a result, when deciding how many workers to hire to pick apples, the firm considers how much profit each worker would bring in. Because profit is total revenue minus total cost, the profit from an additional worker is the worker's contribution to revenue minus the worker's wage.

To find the worker's contribution to revenue, we must convert the marginal product of labour (which is measured in bushels of apples) into the *value* of the marginal product (which is measured in dollars). We do this using the price of apples. To continue our example, if a bushel of apples sells for $10 and if an additional worker produces 80 bushels of apples, then the worker produces $800 of revenue.

The **value of the marginal product** of any input is the marginal product of that input multiplied by the market price of the output. The fourth column in Table 18.1 shows the value of the marginal product of labour in our example, assuming the price of apples is $10 per bushel. Because the market price is constant for a competitive firm, the value of the marginal product (like the marginal product itself) diminishes as the number of workers rises. Economists sometimes call this column of numbers the firm's *marginal revenue product*: It is the extra revenue the firm gets from hiring an additional unit of a factor of production.

Now consider how many workers the firm will hire. Suppose that the market wage for apple pickers is $500 per week. In this case, as you see in Table 18.1, the first worker that the firm hires is profitable: The first worker yields $1000 in revenue, or $500 in profit. Similarly, the second worker yields $800 in additional revenue, or $300 in profit. The third worker produces $600 in additional revenue,

value of the marginal product
the marginal product of an input times the price of the output

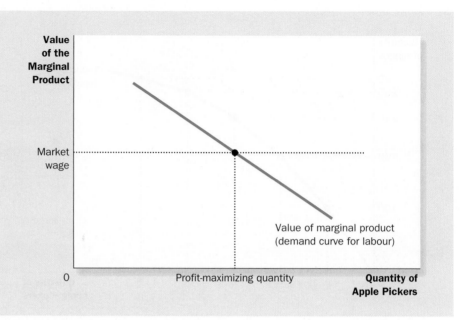

FIGURE 18.3

The Value of the Marginal Product of Labour

This figure shows how the value of the marginal product (the marginal product times the price of the output) depends on the number of workers. The curve slopes downward because of diminishing marginal product. For a competitive, profit-maximizing firm, this value-of-marginal-product curve is also the firm's labour demand curve.

or $100 in profit. After the third worker, however, hiring workers is unprofitable. The fourth worker would yield only $400 of additional revenue. Because the worker's wage is $500, hiring the fourth worker would mean a $100 reduction in profit. Thus, the firm hires only three workers.

It is instructive to consider the firm's decision graphically. Figure 18.3 graphs the value of the marginal product. This curve slopes downward because the marginal product of labour diminishes as the number of workers rises. The figure also includes a horizontal line at the market wage. To maximize profit, the firm hires workers up to the point where these two curves cross. Below this level of employment, the value of the marginal product exceeds the wage, so hiring another worker would increase profit. Above this level of employment, the value of the marginal product is less than the wage, so the marginal worker is unprofitable. Thus, *a competitive, profit-maximizing firm hires workers up to the point where the value of the marginal product of labour equals the wage.*

Having explained the profit-maximizing hiring strategy for a competitive firm, we can now offer a theory of labour demand. Recall that a firm's labour demand curve tells us the quantity of labour that a firm demands at any given wage. We have just seen in Figure 18.3 that the firm makes that decision by choosing the quantity of labour at which the value of the marginal product equals the wage. As a result, *the value-of-marginal-product curve is the labour demand curve for a competitive, profit-maximizing firm.*

What Causes the Labour Demand Curve to Shift?

We now understand the labour demand curve: It reflects the value of the marginal product of labour. With this insight in mind, let's consider a few of the things that might cause the labour demand curve to shift.

INPUT DEMAND AND OUTPUT SUPPLY: TWO SIDES OF THE SAME COIN

In Chapter 14 we saw how a competitive, profit-maximizing firm decides how much of its output to sell: It chooses the quantity of output at which the price of the good equals the marginal cost of production. We have just seen how such a firm decides how much labour to hire: It chooses the quantity of labour at which the wage equals the value of the marginal product. Because the production function links the quantity of inputs to the quantity of output, you should not be surprised to learn that the firm's decision about input demand is closely linked to its decision about output supply. In fact, these two decisions are two sides of the same coin.

To see this relationship more fully, let's consider how the marginal product of labour (MPL) and marginal cost (MC) are related. Suppose an additional worker costs $500 and has a marginal product of 50 bushels of apples. In this case, producing 50 more bushels costs $500; the marginal cost of a bushel is $500/50, or $10. More generally, if W is the wage, and an extra unit of labour produces MPL units of output, then the marginal cost of a unit of output is $MC = W/MPL$.

This analysis shows that diminishing marginal product is closely related to increasing marginal cost. When our apple orchard becomes crowded with workers, each additional worker adds less to the production of apples (MPL falls). Similarly, when the apple firm is producing a large quantity of apples, the orchard is already crowded

with workers, so it is more costly to produce an additional bushel of apples (MC rises).

Now consider our criterion for profit maximization. We determined earlier that a profit-maximizing firm chooses the quantity of labour so that the value of the marginal product ($P \times MPL$) equals the wage (W). We can write this mathematically as

$$P \times MPL = W$$

If we divide both sides of this equation by MPL, we obtain

$$P = W/MPL$$

We just noted that W/MPL equals marginal cost MC. Therefore, we can substitute to obtain

$$P = MC$$

This equation states that the price of the firm's output is equal to the marginal cost of producing a unit of output. *Thus, when a competitive firm hires labour up to the point at which the value of the marginal product equals the wage, it also produces up to the point at which the price equals marginal cost.* Our analysis of labour demand in this chapter is just another way of looking at the production decision we first saw in Chapter 14.

The Output Price   The value of the marginal product is marginal product times the price of the firm's output. Thus, when the output price changes, the value of the marginal product changes, and the labour demand curve shifts. An increase in the price of apples, for instance, raises the value of the marginal product of each worker who picks apples and, therefore, increases labour demand from the firms that supply apples. Conversely, a decrease in the price of apples reduces the value of the marginal product and decreases labour demand.

Technological Change   Between 1961 and 2011, the amount of output a typical Canadian worker produced in an hour rose by about 125 percent. Why? The most important reason is technological progress: Scientists and engineers are constantly figuring out new and better ways of doing things. This has profound implications for the labour market. Technological advance typically raises the marginal product of labour, which in turn increases the demand for labour, which in turn shifts the labour demand curve to the right.

It is also possible for technological change to reduce labour demand. The invention of a cheap industrial robot, for instance, could conceivably reduce the marginal product of labour, shifting the labour demand curve to the left. Economists call this *labour-saving* "technological change." History suggests, however, that most technological progress is instead *labour-augmenting*. Such technological advance explains persistently rising employment in the face of rising wages: Even though wages (adjusted for inflation) increased by over 100 percent during the last half-century, firms nonetheless increased by over 50 percent the amount of labour they employed.

The Supply of Other Factors   The quantity available of one factor of production can affect the marginal product of other factors. A fall in the supply of ladders, for instance, will reduce the marginal product of apple pickers and thus the demand for apple pickers. We consider this linkage among the factors of production more fully later in the chapter.

QuickQuiz   Define *marginal product of labour* and *value of the marginal product of labour*. • Describe how a competitive, profit-maximizing firm decides how many workers to hire.

THE SUPPLY OF LABOUR

Having analyzed labour demand in detail, let's turn to the other side of the market and consider labour supply. A formal model of labour supply is included in Chapter 21, where we develop the theory of household decision making. Here we discuss briefly and informally the decisions that lie behind the labour supply curve.

The Tradeoff between Work and Leisure

One of the ten principles of economics in Chapter 1 is that people face tradeoffs. Probably no tradeoff is more obvious or more important in a person's life than the tradeoff between work and leisure. The more hours you spend working, the fewer hours you have to watch TV, enjoy dinner with friends, or pursue your favourite hobby. The tradeoff between labour and leisure lies behind the labour supply curve.

Another of the ten principles of economics is that the cost of something is what you give up to get it. What do you give up to get an hour of leisure? You give up an hour of work, which in turn means an hour of wages. Thus, if your wage is $15 per hour, the opportunity cost of an hour of leisure is $15. And when you get a raise to $20 per hour, the opportunity cost of enjoying leisure goes up.

= ↑ wages
↑ Q supplied

The labour supply curve reflects how workers' decisions about the labour–leisure tradeoff respond to a change in that opportunity cost. An upward-sloping labour supply curve means that an increase in the wage induces workers to increase the quantity of labour they supply. Because time is limited, more hours of work means that workers are enjoying less leisure. That is, workers respond to the increase in the opportunity cost of leisure by taking less of it.

It is worth noting that the labour supply curve need not be upward sloping. Imagine you got that raise from $15 to $20 per hour. The opportunity cost of leisure is now greater, but you are also richer than you were before. You might decide that with your extra wealth you can now afford to enjoy more leisure. That is, at the higher wage, you might choose to work fewer hours. If so, your labour supply curve would slope backward. In Chapter 21, we discuss this possibility in terms of conflicting effects on your labour supply decision (called *the income and substitution effects*). For now, we ignore the possibility of backward-sloping labour supply and assume that the labour supply curve is upward sloping.

What Causes the Labour Supply Curve to Shift?

The labour supply curve shifts whenever people change the amount they want to work at a given wage. Let's now consider some of the events that might cause such a shift.

Changes in Tastes   In 1950, 34 percent of working-age women were employed at paid jobs or looking for work. In 2011, the number had risen to 62 percent. There are, of course, many explanations for this development, but one of them is changing attitudes toward work. A generation or two ago, it was the norm for women to stay at home while raising children. Today, family sizes are smaller, and more mothers choose to work. The result is an increase in the supply of labour.

Changes in Alternative Opportunities   The supply of labour in any one labour market depends on the opportunities available in other labour markets. If the wage earned by pear pickers suddenly rises, some apple pickers may choose to switch occupations. The supply of labour in the market for apple pickers falls.

Immigration   Movement of workers from region to region, or country to country, is an obvious and often important source of shifts in labour supply. When immigrants come to Canada, for instance, the supply of labour in Canada increases and the supply of labour in the immigrants' home countries contracts. In fact, much of the policy debate about immigration centres on its effect on labour supply and, thereby, equilibrium in the labour market.

QuickQuiz   Who has a greater opportunity cost of enjoying leisure—a janitor or a brain surgeon? Explain. Can this help explain why doctors work such long hours?

EQUILIBRIUM IN THE LABOUR MARKET

So far we have established two facts about how wages are determined in competitive labour markets:

$$W = MPL$$

1. The wage adjusts to balance the supply and demand for labour.
2. The wage equals the value of the marginal product of labour.

At first, it might seem surprising that the wage can do both these things at once. In fact, there is no real puzzle here, but understanding why there is no puzzle is an important step to understanding wage determination.

FIGURE 18.4

Equilibrium in a Labour Market

Like all prices, the price of labour (the wage) depends on supply and demand. Because the demand curve reflects the value of the marginal product of labour, in equilibrium, workers receive the value of their marginal contribution to the production of goods and services.

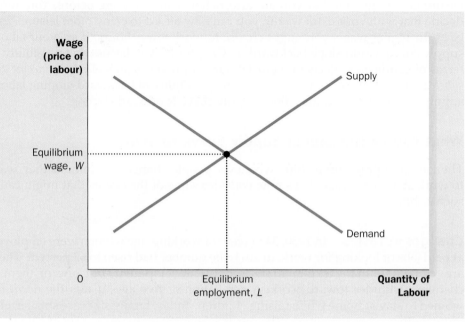

Figure 18.4 shows the labour market in equilibrium. The wage and the quantity of labour have adjusted to balance supply and demand. When the market is in this equilibrium, each firm has bought as much labour as it finds profitable at the equilibrium wage. That is, each firm has followed the rule for profit maximization: It has hired workers until the value of the marginal product equals the wage. Hence, the wage must equal the value of the marginal product of labour once it has brought supply and demand into equilibrium.

This brings us to an important lesson: *Any event that changes the supply or demand for labour must change the equilibrium wage and the value of the marginal product by the same amount, because these must always be equal.* To see how this works, let's consider some events that shift these curves.

Shifts in Labour Supply

Suppose that immigration increases the number of workers willing to pick apples. As Figure 18.5 shows, the supply of labour shifts to the right from S_1 to S_2. At the initial wage W_1, the quantity of labour supplied now exceeds the quantity demanded. This surplus of labour puts downward pressure on the wage of apple pickers, and the fall in the wage from W_1 to W_2 in turn makes it profitable for firms to hire more workers. As the number of workers employed in each apple orchard rises, the marginal product of a worker falls, and so does the value of the marginal product. In the new equilibrium, both the wage and the value of the marginal product of labour are lower than they were before the influx of new workers.

An episode in Israel illustrates how a shift in labour supply can alter the equilibrium in a labour market. During most of the 1980s, many thousands of Palestinians regularly commuted from their homes in the Israeli-occupied West Bank and Gaza Strip to jobs in Israel, primarily in the construction and agriculture

FIGURE 18.5

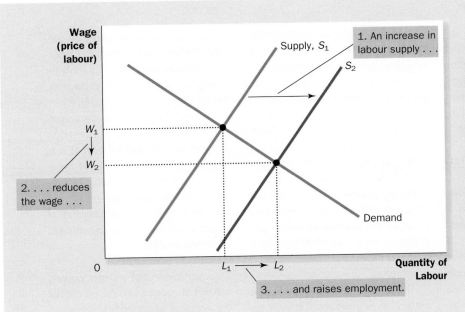

A Shift in Labour Supply

When labour supply increases from S_1 to S_2, perhaps because of an immigration of new workers, the equilibrium wage falls from W_1 to W_2. At this lower wage, firms hire more labour, so employment rises from L_1 to L_2. The change in the wage reflects a change in the value of the marginal product of labour: With more workers, the added output from an extra worker is smaller.

industries. In 1988, however, political unrest in these occupied areas induced the Israeli government to take steps that, as a by-product, reduced this supply of workers. Curfews were imposed, work permits were checked more thoroughly, and a ban on overnight stays of Palestinians in Israel was enforced more rigorously. The economic impact of these steps was exactly as theory predicts: The number of Palestinians with jobs in Israel fell by half, while those who continued to work

IN THE NEWS

DEMOGRAPHICS AND LABOUR MARKETS

As the following article discusses, recent graduates face mounting challenges in the labour market due to demographics and just plain bad luck.

Generation Unlucky

By Tim Shufelt

Graduating members of the Millennial Generation find themselves leaving the comforts of campus for what seems,

by historical standards, the bleakest of futures: limited job prospects, prohibitive housing prices, schizophrenic financial markets, the ravages of a global recession and one giant bill from decades of excess.

Landing that first career position has never been easy. But the labour force's youngest cohort seems to have some legitimate grievances.

Older workers are clinging to their jobs longer, eating up available salary and squeezing the job market from the top. That's exacerbating competition for junior vacancies, which high youth unemployment indicates are already in short supply.

When Boomers eventually do leave their jobs en masse, the capacity of the workforce to finance those retirements will be tested.

And the dwindling of defined-benefit pension plans will make it more difficult for Millennials to save for their own retirements, which can't even begin until they reconcile their record-high student debt loads.

Having enjoyed a stretch of relative economic prosperity, Boomers are now committing younger generations to a fate of austerity and stagnancy—an intergenerational transfer dubbed "fiscal child abuse" by one pundit.

Is this the unluckiest generation? [A]ccording to research . . . graduating into a recession can have permanent consequences for income and job quality.

"There is a risk that the longer it takes, the more their skills depreciate, and the less attractive they are to employers," said Philip Oreopoulos, labour economist at the University of Toronto and co-author of a study analyzing the incomes of a large number of Canadian graduates over a 20-year period.

The central finding of the much-cited study: Luck matters.

Those unlucky enough to graduate into a recession face an average initial income shortfall of almost 10%. It takes an average of 10 years after graduation to overcome the initial damages.

"They're significant and real and long-term," Mr. Oreopoulos said. "For some people, there are lifetime effects."

While contending with the effects of a recessionary employment market, what's

known interchangeably as Generation Y, the Millennial Generation or the Echo Boomers also must wrestle with a macroeconomic albatross that could persist long into their working lives.

More and more, Baby Boomers are indicted by analysts as having handed off to future taxpayers a monumental bill for years of unsustainable finances.

Through their control of politics and elections, Boomers "have rationally chosen a path of more consumption today at the expense of future generations," Jason Hsu, chief investment officer at Research Affiliates, said in a recent report.

The resulting "new normal" he envisions features "an extended period of lower economic and return expectations for the aging and debt-ridden developed world."

. . . .

Compound that with the effect of changing demographics, particularly the retirement cycle of the Boomers, and a substantial increase in the tax burden seems inescapable.

In developed countries, the support ratio of working-age adults per retiree was 5.3 to 1 in 1970, Mr. Hsu said. By 2050, that ratio is expected to fall to 2 to 1. In the United States, there will be "10 new retirees for each new entrant to the workforce," he said.

"Not only does the future appear unenviably poor in aggregate, it also appears predictably unproductive," he concluded.

Entitlement programs in the United States, including Social Security and Medicare, need profound reform to avoid a drastic increase to the taxes of the future American workers. In *The Coming Generational Storm*, Laurence Kotlikoff and Scott Burns likened the trend to fiscal child abuse.

Canada's public pensions, by contrast, are fairly well-funded. But retirement security is no less a concern for younger and future entrants to the workforce.

Between 1991 and 2009, the proportion of Canadian employees covered by a private pension plan fell from 45% to 33%. Of those, about 75% are members of defined-benefit plans. But the discrepancy between the public and private sectors is vast, with only 56% of private-sector pension members covered by defined benefits.

. . . .

Unemployment of younger workers remains at about 14%, the product of the recession, which tends to disproportionately punish youth, as well as the unsteady recovery, during which older workers have postponed retiring.

Many workers near retirement saw the value of their investment portfolios sink over the past few years and decided to stay on the job to top up their savings, said Eric Cousineau, founder of OC Group, a human resources consultancy.

Meanwhile, just to rise to the point of zero net worth will take students years, given that student debt has soared over the past two decades.

For many, that will mean "postponement of milestones of life, like having children or owning a house," Paul Cappon, president of the Canadian Council on Learning, said in a document.

Source: "Generation Unlucky: From Boom to Gloom" by Tim Shufelt, *National Post*, October 15, 2011, p. F1. Material reprinted with the express permission of: National Post, a division of Postmedia Network Inc.

FIGURE 18.6

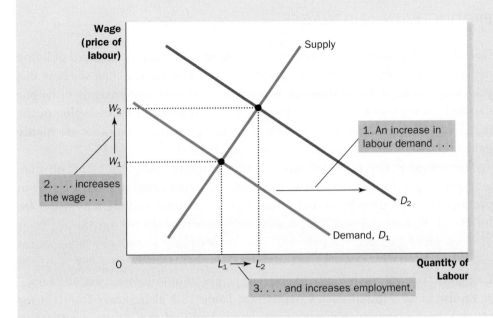

Wage (price of labour)

Supply

W_2

1. An increase in labour demand . . .

W_1

2. . . . increases the wage . . .

D_2

Demand, D_1

0

$L_1 \rightarrow L_2$

Quantity of Labour

3. . . . and increases employment.

A Shift in Labour Demand

When labour demand increases from D_1 to D_2, perhaps because of an increase in the price of the firms' output, the equilibrium wage rises from W_1 to W_2, and employment rises from L_1 to L_2. Again, the change in the wage reflects a change in the value of the marginal product of labour: With a higher output price, the added output from an extra worker is more valuable.

in Israel enjoyed wage increases of about 50 percent. With a reduced number of Palestinian workers in Israel, the value of the marginal product of the remaining workers was much higher.

Shifts in Labour Demand

Now suppose that an increase in the popularity of apples causes their price to rise. This price increase does not change the marginal product of labour for any given number of workers, but it does raise the *value* of the marginal product. With a higher price of apples, hiring more apple pickers is now profitable. As Figure 18.6 shows, when the demand for labour shifts to the right from D_1 to D_2, the equilibrium wage rises from W_1 to W_2, and equilibrium employment rises from L_1 to L_2. Once again, the wage and the value of the marginal product of labour move together.

This analysis shows that prosperity for firms in an industry is often linked to prosperity for workers in that industry. When the price of apples rises, apple producers make greater profit, and apple pickers earn higher wages. When the price of apples falls, apple producers earn smaller profit, and apple pickers earn lower wages. This lesson is well known to workers in industries with highly volatile prices. Workers in oil fields, for instance, know from experience that their earnings are closely linked to the world price of crude oil.

From these examples, you should now have a good understanding of how wages are set in competitive labour markets. Labour supply and labour demand together determine the equilibrium wage, and shifts in the supply or demand curve for labour cause the equilibrium wage to change. At the same time, profit maximization by the firms that demand labour ensures that the equilibrium wage always equals the value of the marginal product of labour.

Case Study

PRODUCTIVITY AND WAGES

One of the ten principles of economics in Chapter 1 is that our standard of living depends on our ability to produce goods and services. We can now see how this principle works in the market for labour. In particular, our analysis of labour demand shows that wages equal productivity as measured by the value of the marginal product of labour. Put simply, highly productive workers are highly paid, and less productive workers are less highly paid.

This lesson is key to understanding why workers today are better off than workers in previous generations. Table 18.2 presents some data on growth in productivity and growth in real wages in Canada (that is, wages adjusted for inflation). From 1961 to 2007, productivity as measured by output per hour of work grew 1.73 percent per year. Real wages grew at 1.67 percent—almost exactly the same rate, just as standard theory predicts. With a growth rate of 1.7 percent per year, productivity and real wages double about every 40 years.

Productivity growth varies over time. Table 18.2 also shows the data for several shorter periods that economists have identified as having very different productivity experiences. Around 1973, the Canadian economy experienced a significant slowdown in productivity growth that has lasted, to varying degrees, up to today. The cause of this productivity slowdown is not well understood. Moreover, it is evident that during this period of declining productivity, the link between productivity and real wages was broken. From 1981 to 2000, productivity growth outstripped real wage growth by a significant margin. From 2000 to 2007, the link was reestablished, although with real wage growth

TABLE 18.2

Productivity and Wage Growth in Canada

Time Period	Growth Rate of Productivity	Growth Rate of Real Wages
1961–2007	1.73%	1.67%
1961–1973	3.00	3.87
1973–1981	1.29	1.38
1981–1989	1.15	0.28
1989–2000	1.54	0.79
2000–2007	1.03	1.24

Note: Sub-periods are chosen to be cyclically neutral (peak to peak). Real wages and labour share are calculated with the labour compensation series from the *Canadian Productivity Accounts.*
Source: Reprinted by permission of the Centre for the Study of Living Standards.

MONOPSONY

On the preceding pages, we built our analysis of the labour market with the tools of supply and demand. In doing so, we assumed that the labour market was competitive. That is, we assumed that there were many buyers of labour and many sellers of labour, so each buyer or seller had a negligible effect on the wage.

Yet imagine the labour market in a small town dominated by a single large employer. That employer can exert a large influence on the going wage, and it may well use that market power to alter the outcome. Such a market in which there is a single buyer is called a *monopsony*.

A monopsony is in many ways similar to a monopoly (a market with one seller). Recall from Chapter 15 that a monopoly firm produces less of the good than would a competitive firm; by reducing the quantity offered for sale, the monopoly firm moves along the product's demand curve, raising the price and also its profits. Similarly, a monopsony firm in a labour market hires fewer workers than would a competitive firm; by reducing the number of jobs available, the monopsony firm moves along the labour supply curve, reducing the wage it pays and raising its profits. Thus, both monopolists and monopsonists reduce economic activity in a market below the socially optimal level. In both cases, the existence of market power distorts the outcome and causes deadweight losses.

This book does not present the formal model of monopsony because, in the real world, monopsonies are rare. In most labour markets, workers have many possible employers, and firms compete with one another to attract workers. In this case, the model of supply and demand is the best one to use.

slightly higher than productivity growth. The reasons for short-term differences between growth rates in productivity and real wages are not completely understood; however, the longer term relationship is quite stable and consistent with our theory. ●

QuickQuiz   How does an immigration of workers affect labour supply, labour demand, the marginal product of labour, and the equilibrium wage?

THE OTHER FACTORS OF PRODUCTION: LAND AND CAPITAL

We have seen how firms decide how much labour to hire and how these decisions determine workers' wages. At the same time that firms are hiring workers, they are also deciding about other inputs to production. For example, our apple-producing firm might have to choose the size of its apple orchard and the number of ladders to make available to its apple pickers. We can think of the firm's factors of production as falling into three categories: labour, land, and capital.

The meaning of the terms *labour* and *land* is clear, but the definition of *capital* is somewhat tricky. Economists use the term **capital** to refer to the stock of equipment and structures used for production. That is, the economy's capital represents the

capital
the equipment and structures used to produce goods and services

accumulation of goods produced in the past that are being used in the present to produce new goods and services. For our apple firm, the capital stock includes the ladders used to climb the trees, the trucks used to transport the apples, the buildings used to store the apples, and even the trees themselves.

Equilibrium in the Markets for Land and Capital

What determines how much the owners of land and capital earn for their contribution to the production process? Before answering this question, we need to distinguish between two prices: the purchase price and the rental price. The *purchase price* of land or capital is the price a person pays to own that factor of production indefinitely. The *rental price* is the price a person pays to use that factor for a limited period of time. It is important to keep this distinction in mind because, as we will see, these prices are determined by somewhat different economic forces.

Having defined these terms, we can now apply the theory of factor demand that we developed for the labour market to the markets for land and capital. The wage is, after all, simply the rental price of labour. Therefore, much of what we have learned about wage determination applies also to the rental prices of land and capital. As Figure 18.7 illustrates, the rental price of land, shown in panel (a), and the rental price of capital, shown in panel (b), are determined by supply and demand. Moreover, the demand for land and capital is determined just like the demand for labour. That is, when our apple-producing firm is deciding how much land and how many ladders to rent, it follows the same logic as when deciding how many workers to hire. For both land and capital, the firm increases the quantity hired until the value of the

FIGURE 18.7

The Markets for Land and Capital

Supply and demand determine the compensation paid to the owners of land, as shown in panel (a), and the compensation paid to the owners of capital, as shown in panel (b). The demand for each factor, in turn, depends on the value of the marginal product of that factor.

(a) The Market for Land

(b) The Market for Capital

factor's marginal product equals the factor's price. Thus, the demand curve for each factor reflects the marginal productivity of that factor.

We can now explain how much income goes to labour, how much goes to land-owners, and how much goes to the owners of capital. As long as the firms using the factors of production are competitive and profit-maximizing, each factor's rental price must equal the value of the marginal product for that factor. *Labour, land, and capital each earn the value of their marginal contribution to the production process.*

Now consider the purchase price of land and capital. The rental price and the purchase price are obviously related: Buyers are willing to pay more for a piece of land or capital if it produces a valuable stream of rental income. And, as we have just seen, the equilibrium rental income at any point in time equals the value of that factor's marginal product. Therefore, the equilibrium purchase price of a piece of land or capital depends on both the current value of the marginal product and the value of the marginal product expected to prevail in the future.

Linkages among the Factors of Production

We have seen that the price paid to any factor of production—labour, land, or capital—equals the value of the marginal product of that factor. The marginal product of any factor, in turn, depends on the quantity of that factor that is available. Because

WHAT IS CAPITAL INCOME?

Labour income is an easy concept to understand: It is the paycheque that workers get from their employers. The income earned by capital, however, is less obvious.

In our analysis, we have been implicitly assuming that households own the economy's stock of capital—ladders, drill presses, warehouses, and so on—and rent it to the firms that use it. Capital income, in this case, is the rent that households receive for the use of their capital. In this case, firms will rent capital up to the point where the value of the marginal product of the capital is equal to the rental rate.

This assumption simplified our analysis of how capital owners are compensated, but it is not entirely realistic. In fact, firms usually own the capital they use and, therefore, they receive the earnings from this capital. These earnings from capital, however, eventually are paid to households. Some of the earnings are paid in the form of interest to those households who have lent money to firms. Bondholders and bank

depositors are two examples of recipients of interest. This is the explicit opportunity cost of capital to the firm discussed in Chapter 13. Thus, when you receive interest on your bank account, that income is part of the economy's capital income.

In addition, some of the earnings from capital are paid to households in the form of dividends. Dividends are payments by a firm to the firm's shareholders. A shareholder is a person who has bought a share in the ownership of the firm and, therefore, is entitled to share in the firm's profits. A firm does not have to pay out all its earnings to households in the form of interest and dividends. Instead, it can retain some earnings within the firm and use these earnings to buy additional capital. Although these retained earnings are not paid to the firm's shareholders, the shareholders still benefit from them: Because retained earnings increase the amount of capital the firm owns, they tend to increase future earnings and, thereby, the value of the firm's stock. This is known as a *capital gain*. The earnings of shareholders therefore consist of the dividends they receive plus the capital gains on their shares. Dividing these earnings (dividends plus capital gains) by the purchase price of the shares determines the rate of return on the shares.

Capital markets are very complex. In particular, capital earnings, whether they are in the form of interest, dividends, or capital gains, are risky. However, if we abstract from these complexities (such as risk) we can see that the rate of return on shares must equal the interest rate on money loaned to the firm. If this was not the case, households would prefer to receive their earnings from capital completely in one form or the other. So, in what follows, we will simply refer to the interest rate.

In a sense, rather than renting capital to firms and receiving the capital income in the form of rental payments, households can be viewed as renting money to firms, which in turn use this money to purchase capital. The rental payments on this money take the form of interest, dividends, and capital gains.

What determines the interest rate (and the rate of return on shares)? The supply and demand of money invested in capital of course! Without going into details, the supply of household funds to firms to invest in capital is determined by the tradeoff that individuals are willing to make between consuming now versus saving and consuming in the future. After all, current saving is really just future consumption. Individuals are impatient and prefer current consumption over future consumption. In order to save their money to consume later, they require a rate of return on their money to compensate them for the delay; this is the interest rate.

The demand for money invested in capital is determined by profit-maximizing firms that invest in capital up to the point where the value of the marginal product is equal to the cost of capital. We typically think of the value of the marginal product of capital as being measured over a given period of time, say a year. In this case, it is important to measure the cost of capital over the same period. As discussed in Chapter 13, one component of the cost of capital is the opportunity cost of the forgone rate of return on the money used to purchase the capital. This forgone rate of return is the interest rate. But, in Chapter 13 we simplified things by assuming that this was the only opportunity cost of investing in capital. In fact, there is another component to the cost of capital. Equipment and structures owned by firms wear out as it is used or becomes obsolete due to technological innovations. This reduces the value of the capital. This reduction in the value of the capital over time due to wear and tear and obsolescence is called *depreciation*. Depreciation is another component of the cost of capital. The *depreciation rate* is the annual rate at which capital depreciates.

With this in mind, now consider a profit-maximizing firm considering how much capital to purchase. The value of the marginal product of capital can be written as ($P \times MPK$), where P is the price of the additional output produced by an incremental unit of capital and MPK is the marginal product of that capital (economists, somewhat strangely, use the letter K to denote capital). As discussed above, the opportunity cost of capital consists of two components: the interest rate and the depreciation rate. Let P_K be the purchase price of a unit of capital, i the interest rate, and d the depreciation rate on that capital. A profit-maximizing firm thus demands capital up to the point where the value of the marginal product is equal to the opportunity cost of capital, or

$$P \times MPK = P_K \times (i + d)$$

For example, say the purchase price of a machine used in production is $300 000; this is P_K. If the interest rate (i) is 5 percent and the depreciation rate on the capital (d) is also 5 percent, the opportunity cost of capital (the right-hand side of the above equation) is $30 000 ($300 000 $\times$ (0.05 + 0.05) = $30 000). A profit-maximizing firm will purchase additional machines up to the point where the value of purchasing another (the value of the marginal product) is just equal to $30 000 per year.

These institutional details are interesting and important, but they do not alter our conclusion about the income earned by the owners of capital. Capital is paid according to the value of its marginal product, regardless of whether this income is transmitted to households in the form of interest, dividends, or capital gains.

of diminishing marginal product, a factor in abundant supply has a low marginal product and thus a low price, and a factor in scarce supply has a high marginal product and a high price. As a result, when the supply of a factor falls, its equilibrium factor price rises.

When the supply of any factor changes, however, the effects are not limited to the market for that factor. In most situations, factors of production are used together in a way that makes the productivity of each factor dependent on the quantities of the other factors available to be used in the production process. As a result, a change in the supply of any one factor alters the earnings of all the factors.

For example, suppose a hurricane destroys many of the ladders that workers use to pick apples from the orchards. What happens to the earnings of the various factors of production? Most obviously, the supply of ladders falls and, therefore, the equilibrium rental price of ladders rises. Those owners who were lucky enough to avoid damage to their ladders now earn a higher return when they rent out their ladders to the firms that produce apples.

Yet the effects of this event do not stop at the ladder market. Because there are fewer ladders with which to work, the workers who pick apples have a smaller marginal product. Thus, the reduction in the supply of ladders reduces the demand for the labour of apple pickers, and this causes the equilibrium wage to fall.

This story shows a general lesson: An event that changes the supply of any factor of production can alter the earnings of all the factors. The change in earnings of any factor can be found by analyzing the impact of the event on the value of the marginal product of that factor.

QuickQuiz   What determines the income of the owners of land and capital? How would an increase in the quantity of capital affect the incomes of those who already own capital? How would it affect the incomes of workers?

CONCLUSION

This chapter explained how labour, land, and capital are compensated for the roles they play in the production process. The theory developed here is called the *neoclassical theory of distribution*. According to the neoclassical theory, the amount paid to each factor of production depends on the supply and demand for that factor. The demand, in turn, depends on that particular factor's marginal productivity. In equilibrium, each factor of production earns the value of its marginal contribution to the production of goods and services.

The neoclassical theory of distribution is widely accepted. Most economists begin with the neoclassical theory when trying to explain how the Canadian economy's $1.7 trillion of income is distributed among the economy's various members. In the following two chapters, we consider the distribution of income in more detail. As you will see, the neoclassical theory provides the framework for this discussion.

Even at this point you can use the theory to answer the question that began this chapter: Why are computer programmers paid more than gas station attendants? It is because programmers can produce a good of greater market value than can a gas station attendant. People are willing to pay dearly for a good computer game, but they are willing to pay little to have their gas pumped and their windshield washed. The wages of these workers reflect the market prices of the goods or services they produce. If people suddenly got tired of using computers and decided to spend more time driving, the prices of these goods and services would change, and so would the equilibrium wages of these two groups of workers.

SUMMARY

- The economy's income is distributed in the markets for the factors of production. The three most important factors of production are labour, land, and capital.

- The demand for factors, such as labour, is a derived demand that comes from firms that use the factors to produce goods and services. Competitive, profit-maximizing firms hire each factor up to the point at which the value of the marginal product of the factor equals its price.

- The supply of labour arises from individuals' tradeoff between work and leisure. An upward-sloping labour supply curve means that people

respond to an increase in the wage by enjoying less leisure and working more hours.

- The price paid to each factor adjusts to balance the supply and demand for that factor. Because factor demand reflects the value of the marginal product of that factor, in equilibrium, each factor is compensated according to its marginal contribution to the production of goods and services.

- Because factors of production are used together, the marginal product of any one factor depends on the quantities of all factors that are available. As a result, a change in the supply of one factor alters the equilibrium earnings of all the factors.

KEY CONCEPTS

factors of production, p. 396
production function, p. 397
marginal product of
    labour, p. 398

diminishing marginal
    product, p. 398
value of the marginal
    product, p. 399

capital, p. 409

QUESTIONS FOR REVIEW

1. Explain how a firm's production function is related to its marginal product of labour, how a firm's marginal product of labour is related to the value of its marginal product, and how a firm's value of marginal product is related to its demand for labour.

2. Give two examples of events that could shift the demand for labour.

3. Give two examples of events that could shift the supply of labour.

4. Explain how the wage can adjust to balance the supply and demand for labour while simultaneously equalling the value of the marginal product of labour.

5. If the population of Canada suddenly grew because of a large immigration, what would happen to wages? What would happen to the rents earned by the owners of land and capital?

PROBLEMS AND APPLICATIONS

1. Suppose that the prime minister proposes a new law aimed at reducing heath care costs: All Canadians are to be required to eat one apple daily.
   a. How would this apple-a-day law affect the demand and equilibrium price of apples?
   b. How would the law affect the marginal product and the value of the marginal product of apple pickers?

    c. How would the law affect the demand and equilibrium wage for apple pickers?

2. Show the effect of each of the following events on the market for labour in the computer manufacturing industry.
   a. The government buys personal computers for all college and university students.
   b. More postsecondary students major in engineering and computer science.

c. Computer firms build new manufacturing plants.

3. Your enterprising uncle opens a sandwich shop that employs 7 people. The employees are paid $6 per hour, and a sandwich sells for $3. If your uncle is maximizing his profit, what is the value of the marginal product of the last worker he hired? What is that worker's marginal product?

4. Suppose a freeze in British Columbia destroys part of the apple crop.
   a. Explain what happens to the price of apples and the marginal product of apple pickers as a result of the freeze. Can you say what happens to the demand for apple pickers? Why or why not?
   b. Suppose the price of apples doubles and the marginal product falls by 30 percent. What happens to the equilibrium wage of apple pickers?
   c. Suppose the price of apples rises by 30 percent and the marginal product falls by 50 percent. What happens to the equilibrium wage of apple pickers?

5. During the 1980s and 1990s Canada experienced a significant inflow of capital from other countries.
   a. Using a diagram of the Canadian capital market, show the effect of this inflow on the rental price of capital in Canada and on the quantity of capital in use.
   b. Using a diagram of the Canadian labour market, show the effect of the capital inflow on the average wage paid to Canadian workers.

6. Suppose that labour is the only input used by a perfectly competitive firm that can hire workers for $50 per day. The firm's production function is as follows:

Days of Labour	Units of Output
0	0
1	7
2	13
3	19
4	25
5	28
6	29

Each unit of output sells for $10. Plot the firm's demand for labour. How many days of labour should the firm hire? Show this point on your graph.

7. This chapter has assumed that labour is supplied by individual workers acting competitively. In some markets, however, the supply of labour is determined by a union of workers.
   a. Explain why the situation faced by a labour union may resemble the situation faced by a monopoly firm.
   b. The goal of a monopoly firm is to maximize profits. Is there an analogous goal for labour unions?
   c. Now extend the analogy between monopoly firms and unions. How do you suppose that the wage set by a union compares to the wage in a competitive market? How do you suppose employment differs in the two cases?
   d. What other goals might unions have that make unions different from monopoly firms?

8. Leadbelly Co. sells pencils in a perfectly competitive product market and hires workers in a perfectly competitive labour market. Assume that the market wage rate for workers is $150 per day.
   a. What rule should Leadbelly follow to hire the profit-maximizing amount of labour?
   b. At the profit-maximizing level of output, the marginal product of the last worker hired is 30 boxes of pencils per day. Calculate the price of a box of pencils.
   c. Draw a diagram of the labour market for pencil workers (as in Figure 18.4) next to a diagram of the labour supply and demand for Leadbelly Co. (as in Figure 18.3). Label the equilibrium wage and quantity of labour for both the market and the firm. How are these diagrams related?
   d. Suppose some pencil workers switch to jobs in the growing computer industry. On the side-by-side diagrams you prepared in part (c), show how this change affects the equilibrium wage and quantity of labour for both the pencil market and for Leadbelly. How does this change affect the marginal product of labour at Leadbelly?

9. Smiling Cow Dairy can sell all the milk it wants for $4 a litre, and it can rent all the robots it

wants to milk the cows at a capital rental price of $100 a day. It faces the following production schedule:

Number of Robots	Total Product
0	0 litres
1	50
2	85
3	115
4	140
5	150
6	155

a. In what kind of market structure does the firm sell its output? How can you tell?

b. In what kind of market structure does the firm rent robots? How can you tell?

c. Calculate the marginal product and the value of the marginal product for each additional robot.

d. How many robots should the firm rent? Explain.

10. The nation of Ectenia has 20 competitive apple orchards, which sell apples at the world price of $2. The following equations describe the production function and the marginal product of labour in each orchard:

$$Q = 100L - L^2$$

$$MPL = 100 - 2L$$

where Q is the number of apples produced in a day, L is the number of workers, and MPL is the marginal product of labour.

a. What is each orchard's labour demand as a function of the daily wage W? What is the market's labour demand?

b. Ectenia has 200 workers who supply their labour inelastically. Solve for the wage W. How many workers does each orchard hire? How much profit does each orchard owner make?

c. Calculate what happens to the income of workers and orchard owners if the world price of apples doubles to $4.

d. Now suppose the price of apples is back at $2, but a hurricane destroys half the orchards. Calculate how the hurricane affects the income of each worker and of each remaining orchard owner. What happens to the income of Ectenia as a whole?

http:// For more study tools, please visit www.nelson.com/mankiwmicro6e.

EARNINGS AND DISCRIMINATION

19

whethervain/iStockphoto

Learning Objectives

In this chapter, you will...

- Examine how wages compensate for differences in job characteristics

- Learn and compare the human-capital and signalling theories of education

- Examine why in some occupations a few superstars earn tremendous incomes

- Learn why wages rise above the level that balances supply and demand

- Consider why it is difficult to measure the impact of discrimination on wages

- See when market forces can and cannot provide a natural remedy for discrimination

- Consider the debate over comparable worth as a system for setting wages

In Canada today, the typical physician earns about $200 000 per year, the typical police officer about $50 000, and the typical farm worker about $20 000. These examples illustrate the large differences in earnings that are so common in our economy. They also explain why some people live in mansions, ride in limousines, and vacation on the French Riviera, while other people live in small apartments, ride the bus, and vacation in their own backyards.

Why do earnings vary so much from person to person? Chapter 18, which developed the basic neoclassical theory of the labour market, offers an answer to this question. There we saw that wages are governed by labour supply and labour demand. Labour demand, in turn, reflects the marginal productivity of labour. In equilibrium, each worker is paid the value of his or her marginal contribution to the economy's production of goods and services.

This theory of the labour market, although widely accepted by economists, is only the beginning of the story. To understand the wide variation in earnings that we observe, we must go beyond this general framework and examine more precisely what determines the supply and demand for different types of labour. That is our goal in this chapter.

SOME DETERMINANTS OF EQUILIBRIUM WAGES

Workers differ from one another in many ways. Jobs also have differing characteristics—both in terms of the wage they pay and in terms of their nonmonetary attributes. In this section we consider how the characteristics of workers and jobs affect labour supply, labour demand, and equilibrium wages.

Compensating Differentials

When a worker is deciding whether to take a job, the wage is only one of many job attributes that the worker takes into account. Some jobs are easy, fun, and safe; others are hard, dull, and dangerous. The better the job as gauged by these nonmonetary characteristics, the more people there are who are willing to do the job at any given wage. In other words, the supply of labour for easy, fun, and safe jobs is greater than the supply of labour for hard, dull, and dangerous jobs. As a result, "good" jobs will tend to have lower equilibrium wages than "bad" jobs.

For example, imagine you are looking for a summer job in a local beach community. Two kinds of jobs are available. You can take a job as a beach-badge checker, or you can take a job as a garbage collector. The beach-badge checkers take leisurely strolls along the beach during the day and check to make sure the tourists have bought the required beach permits. The garbage collectors wake up before dawn to drive dirty, noisy trucks around town to pick up garbage. Which job would you want? Most people would prefer the beach job if the wages were the same. To induce people to become garbage collectors, the town has to offer higher wages to garbage collectors than to beach-badge checkers.

Economists use the term **compensating differential** to refer to a difference in wages that arises from nonmonetary characteristics of different jobs. Compensating differentials are prevalent in the economy. Here are some examples:

compensating differential
a difference in wages that arises to offset the nonmonetary characteristics of different jobs

- Coal miners are paid more than other workers with similar levels of education. Their higher wage compensates them for the dirty and dangerous nature of coal mining, as well as the long-term health problems that coal miners experience.
- Workers who work the night shift at factories are paid more than similar workers who work the day shift. The higher wage compensates them for having to work at night and sleep during the day, a lifestyle that most people find undesirable.
- Professors are paid less than lawyers and doctors, who have similar amounts of education. Professors' lower wages compensate them for the great intellectual and personal satisfaction that their jobs offer. (Indeed, teaching economics is so much fun that it is surprising that economics professors are paid anything at all!)

Human Capital

As we discussed in the previous chapter, the word *capital* usually refers to the economy's stock of equipment and structures. The capital stock includes the farmer's tractor, the manufacturer's factory, and the teacher's chalkboard. The essence of capital is that it is a factor of production that itself has been produced.

There is another type of capital that, while less tangible than physical capital, is just as important to the economy's production. **Human capital** is the accumulation of investments in people. The most important type of human capital is education. Like all forms of capital, education represents an expenditure of resources at one point in time to raise productivity in the future. But, unlike an investment in other forms of capital, an investment in education is tied to a specific person, and this linkage is what makes it human capital.

human capital
the accumulation of investments in people, such as education and on-the-job training

Not surprisingly, workers with more human capital on average earn more than those with less human capital. University graduates in Canada, for example, earn about 60 percent more than workers who end their education with a high-school diploma. This large difference has been documented in many countries around the world. It tends to be even larger in less-developed countries, where educated workers are in scarce supply.

It is easy to see why education raises wages from the perspective of supply and demand. Firms—the demanders of labour—are willing to pay more for the highly educated because highly educated workers have higher marginal products. Workers—the suppliers of labour—are willing to pay the cost of becoming educated only if there is a reward for doing so. In essence, the difference in wages between highly educated workers and less educated workers may be considered a compensating differential for the cost of becoming educated.

Case Study
THE VALUE OF SKILLS

"The rich get richer and the poor get poorer." Like many adages, this one is not always true, but has been in Canada in recent years. We'll talk more about income distribution in the next chapter, but at this point we will address what many feel is an important determinant of the distribution of income in an economy: the wage gap between workers with high skills and workers with low skills. Numerous studies have documented and tried to explain movements in this wage gap, or "premium," over time.

Figure 19.1 shows the ratio of the median earnings of university graduates to the median earnings of high-school graduates without any additional education; the data are for males in Canada and the United States from 1980 to 2007. The figure shows that in the United States the ratio has grown steadily over time. In 1980, U.S. university graduates earned about 40 percent more than high-school graduates; in 2007 they earned about 80 percent more. The situation has been somewhat different in Canada. Although the relative wages of Canadian university graduates are clearly higher than the wages of high-school graduates, the wage premium has not grown over time. In 1980, Canadian university graduates earned about 60 percent more than high-school graduates; in 2007, they earned about 53 percent more.

What explains these different trends in the earnings gap between skilled and unskilled workers? No one knows the full explanation, but economists have proposed various hypotheses. One explanation relies on the supply and demand of

FIGURE 19.1

Ratio of Earnings of Male University Graduates to Male High-School Graduates, 1980–2007

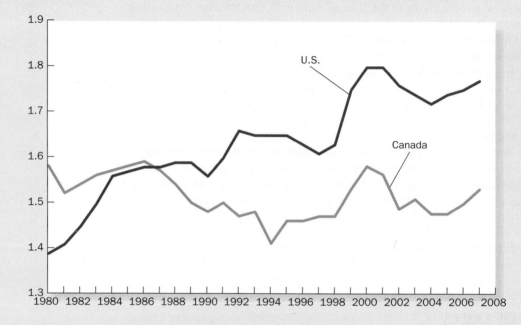

Sources: Adapted from J. Burbidge, L. MaGee, and A. Robb, "The Education Premium in Canada and the United States," *Canadian Public Policy,* Vol. XXVII, No. 2, 2002; authors calculations based on Statistics Canada, Education Indicators in Canada: An International Perspective, Catalogue no. 81-604-X, 2010; and U.S. Bureau of Labor Statistics.

skilled labour relative to the supply and demand of unskilled labour in the two countries to explain differences in relative wages.

One explanation for the rising wage premium in the United States is that demand for skilled labour there increased more quickly than the relative supply. With the relative demand curve for skilled labour shifting outward faster than the relative supply curve, there has been a corresponding increase in relative wages, which in turn has contributed to greater wage inequality in the United States.

Economists have offered two hypotheses for the U.S. trend. The first explanation is that international trade has increased the relative demand for skilled labour. In recent years, the amount of trade between the United States and other countries has increased dramatically. Because unskilled labour is plentiful and cheap in many foreign countries, the United States tends to import goods produced with unskilled labour and to export goods produced with skilled labour. Thus, the expansion in international trade has increased the domestic (relative) demand for skilled labour.

The second hypothesis is that changes in technology have altered the relative demand for skilled and unskilled labour. Consider the growing use of computers.

Computers raise the demand for skilled workers who can use the new machines and reduce the demand for unskilled workers whose jobs are replaced by computers. For example, many companies now rely more on computer databases and less on filing cabinets to keep business records. This change raises the demand for computer programmers and reduces the demand for filing clerks. Thus, with increased computerization, the demand for skilled labour rises and the demand for unskilled labour falls.

Economists have found it difficult to gauge the validity of these two hypotheses. It is possible, perhaps even likely, that both are true: Increasing international trade and technological change may both be responsible for the growing U.S. wage gap.

But why haven't we observed a similar increase in the relative earnings of Canadian skilled workers? Canada's trade with other countries has also grown significantly, and Canadian companies have access to the same technologies as U.S. companies. Yet the wage gap in Canada has remained relatively constant over time. Are Canadian labour markets not subject to similar influences?

Several possible explanations have been offered. One possibility is that in Canada the supply of skilled labour relative to unskilled labour has increased at about the same rate as the relative demand. As a result, the gap between the earnings of skilled workers and the earnings of unskilled workers has remained roughly unchanged over this 27-year period. On the other hand, in the United States, the relative supply of skilled labour has not kept up with the rise in relative demand, which explains the increase in the earnings of skilled workers relative to those of unskilled workers in the United States.

Another explanation is that Canadian companies have lagged U.S. companies in investment in capital equipment over this period. If investment in equipment makes skilled workers relatively more productive than unskilled workers, this too could explain the relatively flat skill premium in Canada relative to the United States. ●

Ability, Effort, and Chance

Why do NHL hockey players get paid more than those in the minor leagues? Certainly, the higher wage is not a compensating differential. Playing in the NHL is not a less pleasant task than playing in the minor leagues; in fact, the opposite is true. The NHL does not require more years of schooling or more experience. To a large extent, players in the NHL earn more just because they have greater natural ability.

Natural ability is important for workers in all occupations. Because of heredity and upbringing, people differ in their physical and mental attributes. Some people are strong, others weak. Some people are smart, others less so. Some people are outgoing, others awkward in social situations. These and many other personal characteristics determine how productive workers are and, therefore, play a role in determining the wages they earn.

Closely related to ability is effort. Some people work hard, others are lazy. We should not be surprised to find that those who work hard are more productive and earn higher wages. To some extent, firms reward workers directly by paying people on the basis of what they produce. Salespeople, for instance, are often paid as a percentage of the sales they make. At other times, hard work is rewarded less directly in the form of a higher annual salary or a bonus.

Chance also plays a role in determining wages. If a person attended a trade school to learn how to repair televisions with vacuum tubes and then found this skill was made obsolete by the invention of solid-state electronics, he or she would end up earning a low wage compared to others with similar years of training. The low wage of this worker is due to chance—a phenomenon that economists recognize but do not shed much light on.

How important are ability, effort, and chance in determining wages? It is hard to say, because ability, effort, and chance are hard to measure. But indirect evidence suggests that they are very important. When labour economists study wages, they relate a worker's wage to those variables that can be measured—years of schooling, years of experience, age, and job characteristics. Although all of these measured variables affect a worker's wage as theory predicts, they account for less than half of the variation in wages in our economy. Because so much of the variation in wages is left unexplained, omitted variables, including ability, effort, and chance, must play an important role.

Case Study

THE BENEFITS OF BEAUTY

People differ in many ways. One difference is in how attractive they are. The actress Keira Knightley, for instance, is a beautiful woman. In part for this reason, her movies attract large audiences. Not surprisingly, the large audiences mean a large income for Knightley.

How prevalent are the economic benefits of beauty? Labour economists Daniel Hamermesh and Jeff Biddle tried to answer this question in a study published in the December 1994 issue of *The American Economic Review*. Hamermesh and Biddle examined data from surveys of individuals in the United States and Canada. The interviewers who conducted the survey were asked to rate each respondent's physical appearance. Hamermesh and Biddle then examined how much the wages of the respondents depended on the standard determinants—education, experience, and so on—and how much they depended on physical appearance.

Hamermesh and Biddle found that beauty pays. People who are deemed to be more attractive than average earn 5 percent more than people of average looks. People of average looks earn 5 to 10 percent more than people considered less attractive than average. Similar results were found for men and women.

What explains these differences in wages? There are several ways to interpret the "beauty premium."

Good looks pay.

Tony Marsh/Reuters/Corbis

One interpretation is that good looks are themselves a type of innate ability determining productivity and wages. Some people are born with the attributes of a movie star; other people are not. Good looks are useful in any job in which workers present themselves to the public—such as acting, sales, and waiting on tables. In this case, an attractive worker is more valuable to the firm than an unattractive worker. The firm's willingness to pay more to attractive workers reflects its customers' preferences.

A second interpretation is that reported beauty is an indirect measure of other types of ability. How attractive a person appears depends on more than just heredity. It also depends on dress, hairstyle, personal demeanour, and other attributes that a person can control. Perhaps a person who successfully projects an attractive image in a survey interview is more likely to be an intelligent person who succeeds at other tasks as well.

A third interpretation is that the beauty premium is a type of discrimination, a topic to which we return later. ●

An Alternative View of Education: Signalling

Earlier we discussed the human-capital view of education, according to which schooling raises workers' wages because it makes them more productive. Although this view is widely accepted, some economists have proposed an alternative theory, which emphasizes that firms use educational attainment as a way of sorting between high-ability and low-ability workers. According to this alternative view, when people earn a college or university degree, for instance, they do not become more productive, but they do *signal* their high ability to prospective employers. Because it is easier for high-ability people to earn a college or university degree than it is for low-ability people, more high-ability people get postsecondary degrees. As a result, it is rational for firms to interpret a postsecondary degree as a signal of ability.

The signalling theory of education is similar to the signalling theory of advertising discussed in Chapter 16. In the signalling theory of advertising, the advertisement itself contains no real information, but the firm signals the quality of its product to consumers by its willingness to spend money on advertising. In the signalling theory of education, schooling has no real productivity benefit, but the worker signals his innate productivity to employers by his willingness to spend years at school. In both cases, an action is being taken not for its intrinsic benefit but because the willingness to take that action conveys private information to someone observing it.

Thus, we now have two views of education: the human-capital theory and the signalling theory. Both views can explain why better-educated workers tend to earn more than less-educated workers. According to the human-capital view, education makes workers more productive; according to the signalling view, education is correlated with natural ability. But the two views have radically different predictions for the effects of policies that aim to increase educational attainment. According to the human-capital view, increasing educational levels for all workers would raise all workers' productivity and thereby their wages. According to the signalling view, education does not enhance productivity, so raising all workers' educational levels would not affect wages.

Most likely, truth lies somewhere between these two extremes. The benefits to education are probably a combination of the productivity-enhancing effects of human capital and the productivity-revealing effects of signalling. The open question is the relative size of these two effects.

The Superstar Phenomenon

Although most actresses earn very little and often have to take other jobs to support themselves, Canadian actress Ellen Page has earned millions of dollars making movies. Similarly, although most people who play hockey do it for free as a hobby, Sidney Crosby earns millions as an NHL hockey player. Ellen Page and Sidney Crosby are superstars in their fields, and their great public appeal is reflected in high incomes.

Why do Ellen Page and Sidney Crosby earn so much? It is not surprising that there are differences in incomes within occupations. Good carpenters earn more than mediocre carpenters, and good plumbers earn more than mediocre plumbers. People vary in ability and effort, and these differences lead to differences in income. Yet the best carpenters and plumbers do not earn the many millions that are common among the best performers and athletes. What explains the difference?

To understand the tremendous incomes of Ellen Page and Sidney Crosby, we must examine the special features of the markets in which they sell their services. Superstars arise in markets that have two characteristics:

1. Every customer in the market wants to enjoy the good supplied by the best producer.
2. The good is produced with a technology that makes it possible for the best producer to supply every customer at low cost.

If Ellen Page is one of the best actresses around, then everyone will want to see her next movie; seeing twice as many movies by an actress half as good is not a good substitute. Moreover, it is *possible* for everyone to enjoy the acting of Ellen Page. Because it is easy to make multiple copies of a movie, Ellen Page can provide her service to millions of people simultaneously. Similarly, because hockey games are broadcast on television, millions of fans can enjoy the extraordinary athletic skills of Sidney Crosby.

We can now see why there are no superstar carpenters and plumbers. Other things equal, everyone prefers to employ the best carpenter, but a carpenter, unlike an actress, can provide his services to only a limited number of customers. Although the best carpenter will be able to command a somewhat higher wage than the average carpenter, the average carpenter will still be able to earn a good living.

Above-Equilibrium Wages: Minimum-Wage Laws, Unions, and Efficiency Wages

Most analyses of wage differences among workers are based on the equilibrium model of the labour market—that is, wages are assumed to adjust to balance labour supply and labour demand. But this assumption does not always apply. For some workers, wages are set above the level that brings supply and demand into equilibrium. Let's consider three reasons why this might be so.

One reason for above-equilibrium wages is minimum-wage laws, as we first saw in Chapter 6. Most workers in the economy are not affected by these laws because their equilibrium wages are well above the legal minimum. But for some workers, especially the least skilled and least experienced, minimum-wage laws raise wages above the level they would earn in an unregulated labour market.

A second reason that wages might rise above their equilibrium level is the market power of labour unions. A **union** is a worker association that bargains with employers over wages and working conditions. Unions often raise wages above the level that would prevail without a union, perhaps because they can threaten to withhold labour from the firm by calling a **strike**. Studies suggest that union workers earn about 10 to 20 percent more than similar nonunion workers.

A third reason for above-equilibrium wages is suggested by the theory of **efficiency wages.** This theory holds that a firm can find it profitable to pay high wages because doing so increases the productivity of its workers. In particular, high wages may reduce worker turnover, increase worker effort, and raise the quality of workers who apply for jobs at the firm. If this theory is correct, then some firms may choose to pay their workers more than they would normally earn.

Above-equilibrium wages, whether caused by minimum-wage laws, unions, or efficiency wages, have similar effects on the labour market. In particular, pushing a wage above the equilibrium level raises the quantity of labour supplied and reduces the quantity of labour demanded. The result is a surplus of labour, or unemployment. The study of unemployment and the public policies aimed to deal with it is usually considered a topic within macroeconomics, so it goes beyond the scope of this chapter. But it would be a mistake to ignore these issues completely when analyzing earnings. Although most wage differences can be understood while maintaining the assumption of equilibrium in the labour market, above-equilibrium wages play a role in some cases.

union
a worker association that bargains with employers over wages and working conditions

strike
the organized withdrawal of labour from a firm by a union

efficiency wages
above-equilibrium wages paid by firms in order to increase worker productivity

QuickQuiz   Define *compensating differential* and give an example. • Give two reasons why more-educated workers earn more than less-educated workers.

THE ECONOMICS OF DISCRIMINATION

Another source of differences in wages is discrimination. **Discrimination** occurs when the marketplace offers different opportunities to similar individuals who differ only by race, ethnic group, sex, age, or other personal characteristics. Discrimination reflects some people's prejudice against certain groups in society. Although discrimination is an emotionally charged topic that often generates heated debate, economists try to study the topic objectively in order to separate myth from reality.

discrimination
the offering of different opportunities to similar individuals who differ only by race, ethnic group, sex, age, or other personal characteristics

Measuring Labour-Market Discrimination

How much does discrimination in labour markets affect the earnings of different groups of people? This question is important, but answering it is not easy.

It might seem natural to gauge the amount of discrimination in labour markets by looking at the average wages of different groups. For example, Canadian studies show that women who are members of ethnic minorities receive lower wages than white women and that men who are members of ethnic minorities are paid less than white men. The average wage of female workers is about 80 percent of the average wage of male workers. Studies have found that Aboriginal people living off reserves earn about 10 percent less than non-Aboriginal people. There is also some evidence that earnings differences exist among workers of different language origins. In particular, some studies find a significant unilingual-francophone earnings disadvantage, although more recent evidence suggests that the size of the disadvantage is decreasing. These wage differentials are sometimes presented as evidence that many employers discriminate against minority groups and women.

Yet there is a potential problem with this inference. Even in a labour market that is free of discrimination, different people earn different wages. People differ in the amount of human capital they have and in the kinds of work they are able and willing to do. People also differ in the amount of experience they have and the extent to which that experience is continuous or uninterrupted. The wage differences we observe in the economy may be, to a large extent, attributable to the determinants of equilibrium wages we discussed in the previous section. Simply observing differences in wages among broad groups—minorities and nonminorities, women and men—does not prove that employers discriminate.

Consider, for example, the role of human capital. The proportion of individuals with high-school, college, and university degrees differs substantially across various groups. For example, the proportion of white males and females with high-school, college, and university degrees in Canada exceeds the proportion of Aboriginal people with these degrees. Moreover, a greater proportion of males than females have college and university degrees, although this is changing as more females than males are now enrolled in Canadian universities. With the sizable wage gap between skilled and unskilled labour discussed earlier in this chapter, no doubt some of the wage differences between groups can be attributed to differences in education levels.

Differences in human capital may themselves be a function of discrimination of a more subtle form. "Pre-market differences" in productive characteristics, such as schooling, may be influenced by various social factors, and these social influences may themselves be the result of systemic pre-market discrimination that affects people's choices and opportunities. For example, for many years schools directed girls away from science and math courses even though these subjects may have had greater value in the marketplace than some of the alternatives.

Human capital acquired in the form of job experience can also help explain wage differences. In particular, women tend to have less job experience on average than men. One reason is that female labour-force participation has increased over the past several decades. Because of this historic change, the average female worker today is younger than the average male worker. In addition, women are more likely to interrupt their careers to raise children. For both reasons, the experience of the average female worker is less than the experience of the average male worker. (Of course, this still doesn't explain the wage gap between women and men of the same age and with the same experience.)

Yet another source of wage differences is compensating differentials. Men and women do not always choose the same type of work, and this fact may help explain some of the earnings differential between men and women. For example, women are more likely to be administrative assistants, and men are more likely to be truck drivers. The relative wages for these jobs depend in part on the working conditions of each job. Because these nonmonetary aspects are hard to measure, it is difficult to gauge the practical importance of compensating differentials in explaining the wage differences that we observe.

In the end, the study of wage differences among groups does not establish any clear conclusion about the prevalence of discrimination in Canadian labour markets. Most economists believe that some of the observed wage differentials are attributable to discrimination, but there is no consensus about how much. The only conclusion about which economists are in consensus is a negative one: *Because the differences in average wages among groups in part reflect differences in human capital and job characteristics, they do not by themselves say anything about how much discrimination there is in the labour market.*

Discrimination by Employers

Let's now turn from measurement to the economic forces that lie behind discrimination in labour markets. If one group in society receives a lower wage than another group, even after controlling for human capital and job characteristics, who is to blame for this differential?

The answer is not obvious. It might seem natural to blame employers for discriminatory wage differences. After all, employers make the hiring decisions that determine labour demand and wages. If some groups of workers earn lower wages than they should, then it seems that employers are responsible. Yet many economists are skeptical of this easy answer. They believe that competitive, market economies provide a natural antidote to employer discrimination. That antidote is called the *profit motive.*

Imagine an economy in which workers are differentiated by their hair colour. Blondes and brunettes have the same skills, experience, and work ethic. Yet, because of discrimination, employers prefer not to hire workers with blonde hair. Thus, the demand for blondes is lower than it otherwise would be. As a result, blondes earn a lower wage than brunettes.

How long can this wage differential persist? In this economy, there is an easy way for a firm to beat out its competitors: It can hire blonde workers. By hiring blondes, a firm pays lower wages and thus has lower costs than firms that hire brunettes. Over time, more and more "blonde" firms enter the market to take advantage of this cost advantage. The existing "brunette" firms have higher costs and, therefore, begin to lose money when faced with the new competitors. These losses induce the brunette firms to go out of business. Eventually, the entry of blonde firms and the exit of brunette firms cause the demand for blonde workers to rise and the demand for brunette workers to fall. This process continues until the wage differential disappears.

Put simply, business owners who care only about making money are at an advantage when competing against those who also care about discriminating. As a result, firms that do not discriminate tend to replace those that do. In this way, competitive markets have a natural remedy for employer discrimination.

Case Study

EXPLAINING THE GENDER WAGE GAP

Table 19.1 illustrates ratios of female-to-male wages in Canada by selected occupation groups for 1997 and 2010. Over all occupations, the ratio increased slightly from 1997 to 2010, from 83 to 87. This was also true for different occupations. There was also quite a bit of variation across occupations, with a low of 76 in sales in 2010 and a high of 96 in clerical occupations.

As discussed previously, unadjusted (gross) data can be misleading. The size and variability of the earnings gap across age groups, educational levels, and occupations suggest that many factors are at work, and it is important to attempt to identify and control for those factors. Economists typically do this by using data on individual workers and accounting for individual characteristics that would be expected to influence earnings: education, experience, occupation or industry, hours of work, and so on. Statistical techniques are then used to divide the gross female–male earnings gap into two components: the part that is explained by differences in individual worker characteristics, and the part that is unexplained. The unexplained component is typically attributed to discrimination.

An example of this approach, based on a Statistics Canada study, is shown in Table 19.2. This table shows the percentage of the female–male wage gap that is explained by differences in various worker characteristics and the percentage that is then left unexplained. Fifty-one percent of the wage gap is unexplained and could therefore be attributed to discrimination of some kind. Of the factors that help to explain the wage gap, the most important are the industry that a person works in, the person's occupation, and his or her full-year, full-time equivalent (FYFTE) on-the-job experience. ●

TABLE 19.1

Ratio of Female-to-Male Wages by Occupation, 1997 and 2010

Occupation	1997	2010
All occupations	83	87
Management	78	84
Clerical	90	96
Sciences	85	89
Teachers	88	94
Sales	74	76
Construction	75	81

Source: Adapted from Statistics Canada, CANSIM database www5.statcan.gc.ca/cansim, Table 282-0070.

TABLE 19.2

Factors Explaining Gap	Fraction of Gap Explained
Education	4.5
FYFTE*	10.1
Tenure	2.8
Age of youngest family member	0.7
Marital status	0.8
Part-time status	3.6
Region	0.0
Urban size	−0.6
Union status	0.8
Firm size	0.9
Duties	4.3
Influence on budget and staffing decisions	1.3
Industry	11.2
Occupation	8.6
Total explained	49.0
Total unexplained	51.0

*FYFTE is full-year, full-time equivalent experience.

Fraction of the Female-to-Male Wage Gap Explained by Various Factors

Source: Adapted from Statistics Canada, Analytical Studies Branch Research Paper Series: The Persistent Gap: New Evidence on the Canadian Gender Wage Gap 11F0019MWE 2001157 no. 157, released January 20, 2001.

IN THE NEWS

LANGUAGE AND WAGES IN CANADA

In this article, the author (who is an economist at McGill University) discusses some research on the wage gap between anglophones and francophones. The conclusion? It's complicated . . . .

While Francophones Get Richer, Anglophones Get Poorer

By William Watson

What is now almost official history in this province is that Bill 101 . . . righted historic wrongs by increasing the demand for French-speaking workers and closing the wage gap between English- and French-speakers in Quebec, mainly by raising the wages of historically underpaid francophones.

A new study by David Albouy, a young Franco-American economist who was an undergraduate at McGill University and is now teaching at the University of Michigan, suggests the official history isn't quite right. It seems the wage gap was closed more by lowering the relative wages of Quebec anglophones than raising those of Quebec francophones, who weren't actually that badly off to begin with.

Albouy uses census data to look at the employment income of males 20 to 59 who worked full time. Unlike other researchers, who typically compared anglo and franco Quebecers, he divides wage-earners into four groups:

anglophones and francophones both inside and outside Quebec. That lets him see how Quebec wage rates compared with those in the rest of the country.

His results are intriguing. In 1970, Quebec francophones averaged $16.40 an hour (measured in the purchasing power of year-2000 dollars). That was only three per cent less than francophones in the rest of the country, who averaged $16.90 an hour. The similarity suggests Canadian labour markets were pretty integrated and francophone Quebecers didn't regard themselves as stuck in Quebec, an argument often used to rationalize lower wages here than elsewhere.

In 1970, however, anglophones in the rest of the country averaged $18.70 an hour, 11 per cent more than non-Quebec francophones and 14 per cent more than Quebec francophones. How come? Could be differences in education or experience. Could be the usefulness of English in the world market. Could be simple, old-fashioned discrimination. The raw data don't say.

Quebec anglophones are the real surprise. In 1970, they made $22.20 an hour, fully 35 per cent more than Quebec francophones, a gap that prompts thoughts of Westmount Rhodesians, "speak white!" and all the rest.

But it was also 19 per cent more than anglophones in the rest of the country. How was it that Quebec anglophones had such an advantage over English-speakers in other provinces? And if the pickings were so easy in anglo Quebec, why didn't anglos from the rest of the country come here and drive down anglo wages?

What happened after 1970? In relative terms, Quebec anglophones got hammered. Their average wages in 2000 were $22.30, still the highest in the country, but only 10 cents more than in 1970. By contrast, non-Quebec anglophones had risen to $21.90, non-Quebec francophones to $21.20, and Quebec francophones to $20.60. Wage differences essentially collapsed. There was only an eight-per-cent difference between top and bottom, vs. 35 per cent in 1970.

Why did Quebec's anglophones still lead the pack, despite all that has happened over the last three decades? Very likely because they were much better educated than the other three groups. In 2000, fully 24 per cent held at least a bachelor's degree. That compares with just 17 per cent of anglos outside Quebec and just 15 per cent of francophones in Quebec.

In fact, if you control for differences in education, in 2000 there was an unexplained wage gap favouring Quebec francophones. Yes, they made less on average than anglos, but, given their lower average education, they made more than they "should have"—about four per cent more. That's a big change since 1970, when they made almost 14 per cent less than expected, given their education and experience.

It's always tempting to ascribe wage differences that differences in education, training, experience can't explain to discrimination. But it's probably not wise. Wages may depend on more things than even the smartest economists, like Albouy, can squeeze into their equations. There might not have been discrimination in favour of anglos in 1970 and there might not be discrimination against them now.

What is clear is that for whatever reason, the big losers in Quebec, relatively speaking, over the last three decades have been anglophones.

Source: "While francophones get richer, anglophones get poorer; New study by a Franco-American challenges some old myths about Quebec" by William Watson, *Montreal Gazette*, October 16, 2007, page A19. Material reprinted with the express permission of: The Gazette, a division of Postmedia Network Inc.

Discrimination by Customers and Governments

The profit motive is a strong force acting to eliminate discriminatory wage differentials, but there are limits to its corrective abilities. Here we consider two of the most important limits: *customer preferences* and *government policies.*

To see how customer preferences for discrimination can affect wages, consider again our imaginary economy with blondes and brunettes. Suppose that restaurant owners discriminate against blondes when hiring servers. As a result, blonde servers earn lower wages than brunette servers. In this case, a restaurant could open up with blonde servers and charge lower prices. If customers cared only about the quality and price of their meals, the discriminatory firms would be driven out of business, and the wage differential would disappear.

On the other hand, it is possible that customers prefer being served by brunettes. If this preference for discrimination is strong, the entry of blonde restaurants need not succeed in eliminating the wage differential between brunettes and blondes. That is, if customers have discriminatory preferences, a competitive market is consistent with a discriminatory wage differential. An economy with such discrimination would contain two types of restaurants: Blonde restaurants hire blondes, have lower costs, and charge lower prices. Brunette restaurants hire brunettes, have higher costs, and charge higher prices. Customers who did not care about the hair colour of their servers would be attracted to the lower prices at the blonde restaurants. Bigoted customers would go to the brunette restaurants. They would pay for their discriminatory preference in the form of higher prices.

Another way for discrimination to persist in competitive markets is for the government to mandate discriminatory practices. If, for instance, the government passed a law stating that blondes could wash dishes in restaurants but could not work as servers, then a wage differential could persist in a competitive market. For example, before South Africa abandoned its system of apartheid, blacks were prohibited from working in some jobs. Discriminatory governments pass such laws to suppress the normal equalizing force of free and competitive markets.

To sum up: *Competitive markets contain a natural remedy for employer discrimination. The entry into the market of firms that care only about profit tends to eliminate discriminatory wage differentials. These wage differentials persist in competitive markets only when customers are willing to pay to maintain the discriminatory practice or when the government mandates it.*

Case Study

DISCRIMINATION IN SPORTS

As we have seen, measuring discrimination is difficult. To determine whether one group of workers is discriminated against, a researcher must correct for differences in productivity between that group and other workers in the economy. Yet, in most firms, it is difficult to measure a particular worker's contribution to the production of goods and services.

One type of firm in which measurement is easier is the sports team. Professional teams have many objective measures of productivity. In baseball, for example, we can measure a player's batting average, home runs, stolen bases, and so on. In hockey, we can measure a player's goals, assists, and plus–minus statistics.

Economists focus on three main types of potential discrimination in sports: (1) salary discrimination; (2) position segregation, where certain positions are systematically assigned to certain groups; and (3) hiring, or entry, discrimination, where only the most productive elements of the discriminated group are hired.

U.S. studies have tended to focus on wage discrimination on racial grounds. These studies suggest that racial discrimination has indeed existed in sports teams, and that much of the blame may lie with customers. For example, a study published in the *Journal of Labor Economics* in 1988 (6:1) found that black basketball players earned 20 percent less than white players of comparable ability. The study also found that attendance at basketball games was larger for teams with a greater proportion of white players. A similar situation also existed for baseball players, although more recent studies of salaries have found no evidence of discriminatory wage differentials. One interpretation of these findings is that customer discrimination makes black players less profitable than white players for team owners. In the presence of such customer discrimination, a discriminatory wage gap can persist, even if team owners care only about profit.

A series of studies that appeared in *Canadian Public Policy* between 1987 and 1995 examined the existence of discrimination against francophone hockey players in the NHL. Early work focused on hiring discrimination. Using various performance measures for NHL players, it was determined that francophone players are underrepresented in the NHL and have tended to outperform their anglophone counterparts. One interpretation of this evidence is that francophones have been subjected to hiring discrimination. As a result of discrimination, francophones must outperform anglophones by a significant margin to get into the league in the first place.

Subsequent studies have questioned this interpretation. For example, an alternative interpretation is that the inability of marginal francophone players to communicate well in English impedes their ability to adapt to the needs of the team. Thus, for marginal players, selecting partially on the basis of language maximizes the success of the team both on and off the ice.

Other work has emphasized differences in playing styles between junior hockey teams in Quebec (the primary providers of francophone players to the NHL) and junior hockey teams in English-speaking provinces. In particular, the Quebec-based teams tend to favour smaller players with offensive abilities, whereas NHL teams tend to favour bigger players with defensive abilities, especially for marginal or "role" players. This suggests that the underrepresentation of francophones in the NHL is not due to hiring discrimination but to different preferences in playing styles. Yet another study, using updated data, has found no evidence of either hiring or wage discrimination against francophones.

A recent salvo in the debate introduces the role of the location of NHL cities. The premise of this study is that the historic tensions between English Canadians and French Canadians suggests that francophones playing for teams based in English Canada may face salary discrimination, while francophones playing for teams based in the United States, where no such tensions exist, do not. Using this approach, the study finds evidence that francophones playing in English Canada do indeed suffer significant salary discrimination. ●

QuickQuiz   Why is it hard to establish whether a group of workers is being discriminated against? • Explain how profit-maximizing firms tend to eliminate discriminatory wage differentials. • How might a discriminatory wage differential persist?

CONCLUSION

In competitive markets, workers earn a wage equal to the value of their marginal contribution to the production of goods and services. Many things, however, affect the value of the marginal product. Firms pay more for workers who are more talented, more diligent, more experienced, and more educated because these workers are more productive. Firms pay less to those workers against whom customers discriminate because these workers contribute less to revenue.

The theory of the labour market we have developed in the previous two chapters explains why some workers earn higher wages than other workers. The theory does not say that the resulting distribution of income is equal, fair, or desirable in any way. That is the topic we take up in Chapter 20.

SUMMARY

- Workers earn different wages for many reasons. To some extent, wage differentials compensate workers for job attributes. Other things equal, workers in hard, unpleasant jobs get paid more than workers in easy, pleasant jobs.

- Workers with more human capital get paid more than workers with less human capital. The return to accumulating human capital is high and has increased over the past two decades.

- Although years of education, experience, and job characteristics affect earnings as theory predicts, there is much variation in earnings that cannot be explained by things that economists can measure. The unexplained variation in earnings is largely attributable to natural ability, effort, and chance.

- Some economists have suggested that more-educated workers earn higher wages not because education raises productivity but because workers with high natural ability use education as a way to signal their high ability to employers. If this signalling theory is correct, then increasing the educational attainment of all workers would not raise the overall level of wages.

- Wages are sometimes pushed above the level that brings supply and demand into balance. Three reasons for above-equilibrium wages are minimum-wage laws, unions, and efficiency wages.

- Some differences in earnings are attributable to discrimination on the basis of race, sex, or other factors. Measuring the amount of discrimination is difficult, however, because one must correct for differences in human capital and job characteristics.

- Competitive markets tend to limit the impact of discrimination on wages. If the wages of a group of workers are lower than those of another group for reasons not related to marginal productivity, then nondiscriminatory firms will be more profitable than discriminatory firms. Profit-maximizing behaviour, therefore, can reduce discriminatory wage differentials. Discrimination persists in competitive markets, however, if customers are willing to pay more to discriminatory firms or if the government passes laws requiring firms to discriminate.

KEY CONCEPTS

compensating differential, p. 418
human capital, p. 419

union, p. 425
strike, p. 425

efficiency wages, p. 425
discrimination, p. 425

QUESTIONS FOR REVIEW

1. Why are coal miners paid more than other workers with similar amounts of education?

2. In what sense is education a type of capital?

3. How might education raise a worker's wage without raising the worker's productivity?

4. What conditions lead to economic superstars? Would you expect to see superstars in dentistry? In economics? Explain.

5. Give three reasons why a worker's wage might be above the level that balances supply and demand.

6. What difficulties arise in deciding whether a group of workers has a lower wage because of discrimination?

7. Do the forces of economic competition tend to exacerbate or ameliorate discrimination on the basis of race?

8. Give an example of how discrimination might persist in a competitive market.

PROBLEMS AND APPLICATIONS

1. University and college students sometimes work as summer interns for private firms or the government. Many of these positions pay little or nothing.
   a. What is the opportunity cost of taking such a job?
   b. Explain why students are willing to take these jobs.
   c. If you were to compare the earnings later in life of workers who had worked as interns and those who had taken summer jobs that paid more, what would you expect to find?

2. As explained in Chapter 6, a minimum-wage law distorts the market for low-wage labour. To reduce this distortion, some economists advocate a two-tiered minimum-wage system, with a regular minimum wage for adult workers and a lower, "sub-minimum" wage for teenaged workers. Give two reasons why a single minimum wage might distort the labour market for teenaged workers more than it would the market for adult workers.

3. A basic finding of labour economics is that workers who have more experience in the labour force are paid more than workers who have less experience (holding constant the amount of formal education). Why might this be so? Some studies have also found that experience at the same job (called *job tenure*) has an extra positive influence on wages. Explain.

4. At some colleges and universities, economics professors receive higher salaries than professors in some other fields.
   a. Why might this be true?
   b. Some other colleges and universities have a policy of paying equal salaries to professors in all fields. At some of these schools, economics professors have lighter teaching loads than professors in some other fields. What role do the differences in teaching loads play?

5. Sara works for Steve, whom she dislikes because of his snobbish attitude. Yet when she looks for other jobs, the best she can do is find a job paying $10 000 less than her current salary. Should she take the job? Analyze Sara's situation from an economic point of view.

6. Imagine that someone offers you a choice: You could spend four years studying at the world's best university, but you would have to keep your attendance there a secret. Or you could be awarded an official degree from the world's best university, but you couldn't actually attend. Which choice do you think would enhance your future earnings more? What does your answer say about the debate over signalling versus human capital in the role of education?

7. When recording devices were first invented almost 100 years ago, musicians could suddenly supply their music to large audiences at low cost. How do you suppose this development affected the income of the best musicians? How do you suppose it affected the income of average musicians?

8. A case study in this chapter described how customer discrimination in sports seems to have an important effect on players' earnings. Note that this is possible because sports fans know the players' characteristics, including their race. Why is this knowledge important for the existence of discrimination? Give some specific examples of industries where customer discrimination is and is not likely to influence wages.

9. Suppose that all young women were channelled into careers as secretaries, nurses, and teachers; at the same time, young men were encouraged to consider these three careers and many others as well.
   a. Draw a diagram showing the combined labour market for secretaries, nurses, and teachers. Draw a diagram showing the combined labour market for all other fields. In which market is the wage higher? Do men or women receive higher wages on average?
   b. Now suppose that society changed and encouraged both young women and young men to consider a wide range of careers. Over time, what effect would this change have on the wages in the two markets you illustrated in part (a)? What effect would the change have on the average wages of men and women?

10. This chapter considers the economics of discrimination by employers, customers, and governments. Now consider discrimination by workers. Suppose that some brunette workers did not like working with blonde workers. Do you think this worker discrimination could explain lower wages for blonde workers? If such a wage differential existed, what would a profit-maximizing entrepreneur do? If there were many such entrepreneurs, what would happen over time?

http://   For more study tools, please visit www.nelson.com/mankiwmicro6e.

INCOME INEQUALITY AND POVERTY

Learning Objectives

In this chapter, you will...

- Examine the degree of economic inequality in our society
- Consider some problems that arise when measuring economic inequality
- See how political philosophers view the government's role in redistributing income
- Consider the various policies aimed at helping poor families escape poverty

"The only difference between the rich and other people," Mary Colum once said to Ernest Hemingway, "is that the rich have more money." Maybe so. But this claim leaves many questions unanswered. The gap between rich and poor is a fascinating and important topic of study—for the comfortable rich, for the struggling poor, and for the aspiring and worried middle class.

From the previous two chapters you should have some understanding about why different people have different incomes. A person's earnings depend on the supply and demand for that person's labour, which in turn depend on natural ability, human capital, compensating differentials, discrimination, and so on. Because labour earnings make up about three-fourths of the total income in the Canadian economy, the factors that determine wages are also largely responsible for determining how the economy's total income is distributed among the various members of society. In other words, they help determine who is rich and who is poor.

In this chapter we discuss the distribution of income—a topic that raises some fundamental questions about the role of economic policy. One of the ten principles of economics in Chapter 1 is that governments can sometimes improve market outcomes. This possibility is particularly important when considering the distribution of income. The invisible hand of the marketplace acts to allocate resources efficiently, but it does not necessarily ensure that resources are allocated fairly. As a result, many economists—although not all—believe that the government should redistribute income to achieve greater equality. In doing so, however, the government runs into another of the ten principles of economics: People face tradeoffs. When the government enacts policies to make the distribution of income more equitable, it distorts incentives, alters behaviour, and makes the allocation of resources less efficient.

Our discussion of the distribution of income proceeds in three steps. First, we assess how much inequality there is in our society. Second, we consider some different views about what role the government should play in altering the distribution of income. Third, we discuss various public policies aimed at helping society's poorest members.

THE MEASUREMENT OF INEQUALITY

We begin our study of the distribution of income by addressing four questions of measurement:

1. How much inequality is there in our society?
2. How many people live in poverty?
3. What problems arise in measuring the amount of inequality?
4. How often do people move among income classes?

These measurement questions are the natural starting point from which to discuss public policies aimed at changing the distribution of income.

Canadian Income Inequality

Imagine that you lined up all of the families in the economy according to their annual family income. Then you divided the families into five equal groups: the bottom fifth, the second fifth, the middle fifth, the fourth fifth, and the top fifth. Table 20.1 shows the average income for each of these groups as well as the share of total income that each group of families received in Canada in 2010.

These numbers give us a way of gauging how the economy's total income is distributed. If income were equally distributed across all families, each one-fifth of families would receive one-fifth (20 percent) of income. If all income were concentrated among just a few families, the top fifth would receive 100 percent and the other fifths would receive 0 percent. The actual economy, of course, is between these two extremes.

Using family income before taxes and transfers as the income measure, Table 20.1 shows that in 2010, the bottom fifth of all families received 2.1 percent of all market income and the top fifth of all families received 52 percent. In

TABLE 20.1

Distribution of Market Income in Canada, 2010	Group	Average Annual Family Income in Group	% of Total Canadian Market Income
Source: Statistics Canada, Market, Total and After-Tax Income, by Economic Family Type and After-Tax Income Quintiles, 2010, constant dollars, annual (CANSIM Table 202-0701), Ottawa: Statistics Canada, 2012. Reproduced and distributed on an "as is" basis with the permission of Statistics Canada.	Bottom Fifth	$ 6 700	2.1
	Second Fifth	23 100	7.3
	Middle Fifth	45 400	14.3
	Fourth Fifth	77 000	24.3
	Top Fifth	164 900	52.0

FIGURE 20.1

Income Distribution in Canada, 1976–2010

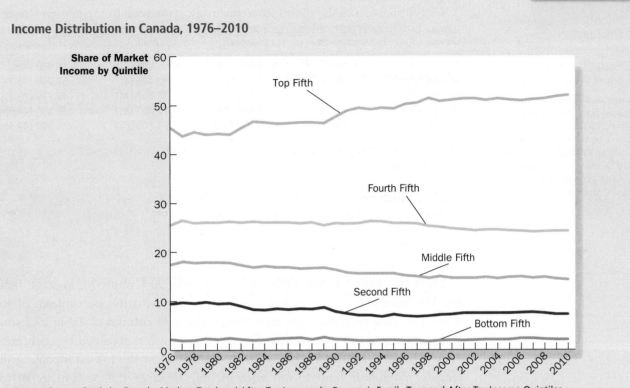

Source: Source: Statistics Canada, Market, Total and After-Tax Income, by Economic Family Type and After-Tax Income Quintiles, 2010, constant dollars, annual (CANSIM Table 202-0701), Ottawa: Statistics Canada, 2012.

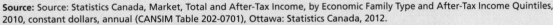

other words, even though the top and bottom fifths include the same number of families, the top fifth has about 25 times as much income as the bottom fifth.

Figure 20.1 shows the distribution of income over time, from 1976 to 2010. As can be seen, the share of market income (before taxes and transfers) earned by the top 20 percent in Canada increased over this period, from about 45 percent in 1976 to 52 percent in 2010. This came primarily at the expense of the so-called "middle class," represented by the middle 60 percent of the income distribution; the share of the lowest 20 percent stayed roughly constant at 2 percent.

Case Study

INCOME REDISTRIBUTION IN CANADA

Various government policies are specifically designed to redistribute income. One way that governments do this is via income tax and transfer programs, which are not taken into account in Table 20.1. Table 20.2 shows how these two programs affect the distribution of income in Canada. Note that an unattached individual is considered to be a family unit.

TABLE 20.2

Distribution of Income in Canada, including Transfers and Income Taxes (percentage shares in parentheses), 2010

Source: Author calculations adapted from Statistics Canada, Market, Total and After-Tax Income, by Economic Family Type and After-Tax Income Quintiles, 2010, constant dollars, annual (CANSIM Table 202-0701), Ottawa: Statistics Canada, 2012.

Group	Average Family Market Income	Average Transfers Received	Average Income Taxes Paid	Average Income after Transfers and Taxes
Bottom Fifth	$ 6 700 (2.1)	$ 8 800 (19)	$ 900 (2)	$ 15 000 (4.8)
Second Fifth	23 100 (7.3)	12 000 (26)	2 400 (4)	32 700 (10.7)
Middle Fifth	45 400 (14.3)	10 500 (23)	6 200 (11)	49 700 (16.2)
Fourth Fifth	77 000 (24.3)	8 900 (19)	12 400 (21)	73 500 (24.0)
Top Fifth	164 900 (52.0)	6 300 (13)	35 700 (62)	135 500 (44.3)

The first column in the table replicates Table 20.1, showing average family market income for each group and (in parentheses) the percentage of total market income received from that group. The next column of Table 20.2 shows the average amount of government monetary transfers received by each group. As can be seen from the table, with the exception of the lowest income group, transfer payments tend to fall with income, as does the percentage of total payments received.

Another way the government redistributes income is through the tax system. Income taxes play a particularly important role in this regard. As can be seen from the table, average income taxes paid increased markedly with income. The richest income group paid an average of $35 700 in income taxes, accounting for over 60 percent of income taxes paid, while the lowest income group paid an average of $900 in taxes, accounting for 2 percent of income taxes.

The final column of the table shows the average income for each group after transfers and income taxes, which is computed by adding transfers to market income and subtracting income taxes. Note that the distribution of after-tax/transfer income is more equal, although the highest income group still accounts for about 44 percent of income. Also, note that for the bottom three income groups (representing the lowest 60 percent of family income earners), their income after transfers and taxes is greater than their market income. In contrast, for the highest income groups (the richest 40 percent of income earners), combined income taxes and transfers lower their income.

Another way of measuring income inequality is by calculating the Gini coefficient (named after the Italian statistician Corrado Gini). The Gini coefficient is a widely used measure of inequality that calculates the extent to which the distribution of income among individuals within a country deviates from a perfectly equal distribution. A Gini coefficient of 0 represents perfect equality (that is, every person in society has the same amount of income). In this case, each of the five income groups in the previous tables, each representing 20 percent of the population, would earn 20 percent of income. A Gini coefficient of 1 represents perfect inequality (that is, one person has all the income and the rest of society has none). So, the higher the Gini coefficient, the less equal the income distribution.

Figure 20.2 presents the Gini coefficient for Canada from 1976 to 2010. Gini coefficients for both market income and after-tax/transfer income are illustrated. As we would expect, the Gini coefficient for after-tax/transfer income is lower than the Gini coefficient for market income, because the tax/transfer system redistributes income from higher income groups to lower income groups. So the distribution of after-tax/transfer income is more equal than the distribution of market income. However, both Gini coefficients are increasing over time, which indicates that the distribution of both types of income in Canada has become less equal over this period.

It is also interesting to consider the extent of redistribution due to the tax and transfer system. This can be done by calculating what is known as the "R-factor" (R is for redistribution). The R-factor is the percentage difference between the Gini coefficient based on market income and the coefficient based on after-tax/transfer income. Thus, it is the difference between the Gini coefficients for market income and after-tax/transfer income, divided by the Gini coefficient for market income. An increase of the R-factor indicates an increase in redistribution through the tax/transfer system.

FIGURE 20.2

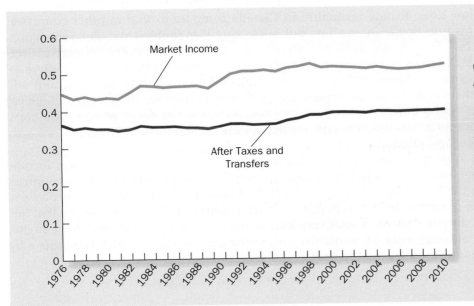

Gini Coefficients, Market and After-tax/Transfer Income, 1976–2010.

Source: Statistics Canada, Market, Total and After-Tax Income, by Economic Family Type and After-Tax Income Quintiles, 2010, constant dollars, annual (CANSIM Table 202-0701), Ottawa: Statistics Canada, 2012. Reproduced and distributed on an "as is" basis with the permission of Statistics Canada.

FIGURE 20.3

Redistribution in Canada (the R-Factor), 1976–2010

Source: Author calculations adapted from Statistics Canada, Market, Total and After-Tax Income, by Economic Family Type and After-Tax Income Quintiles, 2010, constant dollars, annual (CANSIM Table 202-0701), Ottawa: Statistics Canada, 2012.

The R-factor from 1976 to 2010 for Canada is shown in Figure 20.3. Over this period it is evident that the amount of redistribution in the Canadian tax/transfer system increased, as the R-factor increased from about 18.5 in 1976 to about 23.7 in 2010. However, from the mid-1990s to the mid-2000s, the degree of redistribution declined somewhat from its peak of 28.7 in 1994. This coincides with a period of fiscal consolidation on the part of both the federal and provincial governments, which saw transfers decline. There are signs of a modest increase in redistribution over the past couple of years of the sample. ●

Income Inequality around the World

How does income inequality in Canada compare to that in other countries? This question is interesting, but answering it is problematic. For some countries, data are not available. Even when they are, not every country collects data in the same way; for example, some countries collect data on individual incomes, whereas other countries collect data on family incomes, and still others collect data on expenditure rather than income. As a result, whenever we find a difference between two countries, we can never be sure whether it reflects a true difference in the economies or merely a difference in the way data are collected.

With this warning in mind, consider Figure 20.4, which compares income inequality in 13 selected countries using Gini coefficients. Of the 13 countries in the figure, the most equal (with the lowest Gini coefficient) is Sweden and the most unequal is South Africa. Of the countries in the figure, we see that inequality in Canada is relatively low, as most of the other countries have higher Gini coefficients. Of particular note is the United States, which has quite a bit more income inequality than Canada.

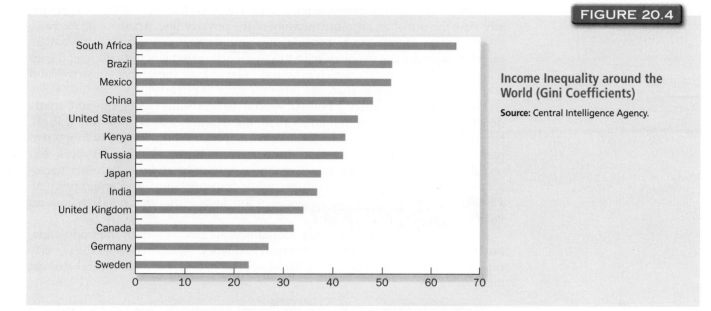

FIGURE 20.4

Income Inequality around the World (Gini Coefficients)

Source: Central Intelligence Agency.

The Poverty Rate

In assessing income inequality in Canada, we may be interested not only in the distribution of income but also in the number of Canadians living in poverty. Being relatively worse off is different from living in poverty, and government policies regarding income distribution should recognize the distinction.

The **poverty rate** is the percentage of the population with family income below the poverty line. The **poverty line** is the level of family income below which a family is considered poor. Unfortunately, the poverty line is not a well-defined concept. Indeed, unlike the United States but like most other nations, Canada does not have an official measure of the poverty line.

Statistics Canada does, however, produce an annual estimate called the *low-income cutoff* (LICO), which has been widely used as a measure of the "official" poverty line in Canada. The LICO is calculated as the level of income at which a household of a given size in a community with a given population spends 20 percent more than average on food, shelter, and clothing. Canadian families spend an average of about 43 percent of their income on these three goods. Thus, families that spend more than 63 percent of their income on food, clothing, and shelter fall under the LICO. In 2010, the poverty rate in Canada using the (after tax) LICO approach was 9 percent.

As Statistics Canada is always quick to point out, the problem with using the LICO as a measure of poverty is that it is a relative measure that is defined in relation to average income. Critics claim that relative measures such as the LICO provide a means of gauging the extent of income inequality, not the extent of poverty. Although the extent of income inequality in the country is an important consideration, it is not the same thing as poverty. It is possible for a country to have a great deal of income inequality but not to have any citizens living in poverty.

poverty rate
the percentage of the population whose family income falls below an absolute level called the *poverty line*

poverty line
an absolute level of income set by the federal government for each family size, below which a family is deemed to be in poverty

To overcome the limitations of relative measures such as the LICO, some people advocate the use of an absolute measure of the poverty line. An absolute measure involves measuring the cost of acquiring essential goods and services, or what are called *basic needs*. The problem with this approach is that it is difficult to come up with a list of basic needs, which is bound to be at least somewhat subjective and arbitrary (but no more so than any other measure of poverty).

The federal government's Human Resources and Skills Development Canada developed such a measurement, called the Market Basket Measure (MBM), based on the cost of goods and services needed for a typical family of four—two parents and two children—to eat a nutritious diet, buy clothing for work and social occasions, house themselves in their community, and pay for other necessary expenditures, such as furniture, public transportation, and entertainment. For 2007, using the MBM, the incidence of low income among Canadian families with children was 10.1 percent.

Poverty is an economic malady that affects all groups within the population, but it does not affect all groups with equal frequency. Table 20.3 shows the poverty rates for several groups using the MBM approach, and it reveals several striking facts:

- Poverty is correlated with ethnicity. Recent immigrants are more than twice as likely to live in poverty than is the general population, as are aboriginals living off-reserve.
- Poverty is high for the work-limited disabled. Almost one-third of the work-limited disabled live in poverty.
- Families headed by a single parent are about 2.5 times as likely to live in poverty than the average, and unattached individuals are more than 3 times more likely to be poor than average.

These three facts have described Canadian society for many years, and they show which people are most likely to be poor.

Problems in Measuring Inequality

Although data on the income distribution and the poverty rate help to give us some idea about the degree of inequality in our society, interpreting these data is

TABLE 20.3

Who Is Poor?

This table shows that the poverty rate varies greatly among different groups within the population.

Source: Low Income in Canada 2000–2007 Using the Market Based Measure, Incident of Low Income table (percent) URL: http:www.hrsdc.gc.ca/eng/publications_resources/research/categories/inclusion/2009/sp-909-07-09/tableIncidence.shtml Human Resources and Skills Development Canada, 2009. Reproduced with the permission of the Minister of Public Works and Government Services Canada, 2012.

Group	Poverty Rate
All persons	10.1%
Single persons	26.6
Unattached individuals (45–64)	32.8
Work-limited disabled	32.5
Recent immigrants	22.3
Off-reserve aboriginals	22.1
Children	11.9

not as straightforward as it might first appear. The data are based on households' annual incomes. What people care about, however, is not their incomes but their ability to maintain a good standard of living. For various reasons, data on the income distribution and the poverty rate give an incomplete picture of inequality in living standards. We examine these reasons below.

In-Kind Transfers   Measurements of the distribution of income and the poverty rate are based on families' *money* income. Through various government programs, however, the poor receive many nonmonetary items, including food, housing vouchers, and other services. Transfers to the poor given in the form of goods and services rather than cash are called **in-kind transfers**. Standard measurements of the degree of inequality do not take account of these in-kind transfers.

> **in-kind transfers**
> transfers to the poor given in the form of goods and services rather than cash

Because in-kind transfers are received mostly by the poorest members of society, the failure to include in-kind transfers as part of income greatly affects the measured poverty rate. Unfortunately, it is difficult to obtain data on the value of these in-kind transfers.

The important role of in-kind transfers makes evaluating changes in poverty more difficult. Over time, as public policies to help the poor evolve, the composition of assistance between cash and in-kind transfers changes. Some of the fluctuations in the measured poverty rate, therefore, reflect the form of government assistance rather than the true extent of economic deprivation.

The Economic Life Cycle   Incomes vary predictably over people's lives. A young worker, especially one in school, has a low income. Income rises as the worker gains maturity and experience, peaks at around age 50, and then falls sharply when the worker retires at around age 65. This regular pattern of income variation is called the **life cycle**.

> **life cycle**
> the regular pattern of income variation over a person's life

Because people can borrow and save to smooth out life cycle changes in income, their standard of living in any year depends more on lifetime income than on that year's income. The young often borrow, perhaps to go to school or to buy a house, and then repay these loans later when their incomes rise. People have their highest saving rates when they are middle-aged. Because people can save in anticipation of retirement, the large declines in incomes at retirement need not lead to similar declines in the standard of living.

This normal life cycle pattern causes inequality in the distribution of annual income, but it does not represent true inequality in living standards. To gauge the inequality of living standards in our society, the distribution of lifetime incomes is more relevant than the distribution of annual incomes. Unfortunately, data on lifetime incomes are not readily available. When looking at any data on inequality, however, it is important to keep the life cycle in mind. Because a person's lifetime income smooths out the highs and lows of the life cycle, lifetime incomes are surely more equally distributed across the population than are annual incomes.

Transitory versus Permanent Income   Incomes vary over people's lives not only because of predictable life cycle variation but also because of random and transitory forces. One year, freezing rain may damage maple trees in Quebec, causing the income of Quebec maple syrup producers to decline temporarily. Over time the damaged trees will recover, and the incomes of maple syrup producers will rise again.

Just as people can borrow and lend to smooth out life cycle variations in income, they can borrow and lend to smooth out transitory variation in income. When maple syrup producers have a good year, they would be foolish to spend all of their additional income. Instead, they will likely save some of it against a "rainy day." Similarly, they respond to temporarily low incomes by drawing on their savings or by borrowing.

To the extent that a family saves and borrows to buffer itself from transitory changes in income, these changes do not affect its standard of living. A family's ability to buy goods and services depends largely on its **permanent income**, which is its normal, or average, income.

permanent income
a person's normal income

To gauge inequality of living standards, the distribution of permanent income is more relevant than the distribution of annual income. Although permanent income is hard to measure, it is an important concept. Because it excludes transitory changes in income, permanent income is more equally distributed than is current income.

Economic Mobility

People sometimes speak of "the rich" and "the poor" as if these groups consisted of the same families year after year. In fact, this is not at all the case. Economic mobility, the movement of people among income classes, is substantial in the Canadian economy. Movements up the income ladder can be due to good luck or hard work, and movements down the ladder can be due to bad luck or laziness. Some of this mobility reflects transitory variation in income, while some reflects more persistent changes in income.

A key measure of economic mobility is intergenerational mobility, which concerns the persistence of economic success from generation to generation. Three Canadian economists (Miles Corak, Lori Curtis, and Shelly Phipps) have sought to measure and compare the amount of intergenerational mobility across countries. This is a difficult task that is fraught with measurement problems, but one way of doing this is to calculate the intergenerational elasticity of earnings between fathers and sons (comparable calculations for daughters and mothers are not possible, given data limitations). The intergenerational elasticity measures the percentage change in the earnings of sons divided by the percentage change in the earnings of their fathers. The lower the intergenerational elasticity, the lower the extent to which economic outcomes are transmitted across generations and the higher the degree of economic mobility.

Corak, Curtis, and Phipps have assembled comparable estimates of the intergenerational elasticity of earnings between fathers and sons for several high-income countries. These estimates are shown in Figure 20.5. As can be seen from the figure, there is a wide variation in the degree of intergenerational mobility across the countries. The United Kingdom, Italy, and the United States exhibit a relatively low degree of economic mobility, while in Denmark, Norway, Finland, and Canada, intergenerational economic mobility is much higher. In Canada, the intergenerational elasticity of income between fathers and sons is only 0.19, which means that a 10 percent increase in the earnings

FIGURE 20.5

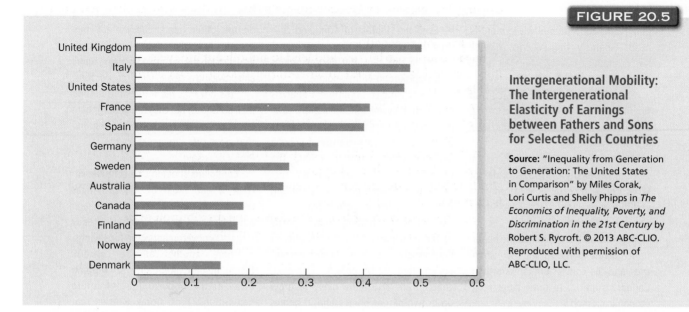

**Intergenerational Mobility:
The Intergenerational
Elasticity of Earnings
between Fathers and Sons
for Selected Rich Countries**

Source: "Inequality from Generation
to Generation: The United States
in Comparison" by Miles Corak,
Lori Curtis and Shelly Phipps in *The
Economics of Inequality, Poverty, and
Discrimination in the 21st Century* by
Robert S. Rycroft. © 2013 ABC-CLIO.
Reproduced with permission of
ABC-CLIO, LLC.

of a father is associated with only a 1.9 percent increase in the earnings of the
son. This suggests a very high degree of economic mobility across generations.
In the United States, on the other hand, the elasticity is 0.50—a 10 percent
increase in father earnings is associated with a 5 percent increase in son
earnings.

QuickQuiz   What does the poverty rate measure? • Describe three potential
problems in interpreting the measured poverty rate.

IN THE NEWS

THE AMERICAN DREAM IS IN CANADA

*The so-called American dreams—"from shirtsleeves to shirtsleeves in three generations"—is
much more likely in Canada than in the United States.*

**In Canada, Unlike the U.S., the
American Dream Lives On**

By Barrie McKenna

We know the gap between rich and poor
in Canada is large and growing.

One need look no further than
Attawapiskat and other northern com-
munities for evidence that not all
Canadians are living the dream.

But income disparity shouldn't be
confused with equality of opportunity.

And guess what? Canada is a world
leader in economic mobility, right up
there with Denmark, Norway and other
Scandinavian countries.

A recent front-page story in *The New
York Times* highlighted new research

that "turns conventional wisdom on its head"—namely, that Americans enjoy less economic mobility than their peers in, gasp, Canada.

Yes, the U.S. is richer, but it's also significantly more unequal, and a lot less mobile. Inequality is inherited, much like hair and eye colour.

The conclusion is based partly on the work of University of Ottawa professor Miles Corak, a social policy economist and former director of family and labour research at Statistics Canada.

Prof. Corak has quantified the opportunity divide between the two countries and his conclusions are startling. Canadians are up to three times more economically mobile than Americans, and it's almost entirely due to the conditions faced by those living at the very top and bottom of society, according to a new study he co-authored: Economic Mobility, Family Background, and the Well-Being of Children in the United States and Canada.

"What distinguishes the two countries is what's happening at the tails," Prof. Corak explained in an interview. "Rich kids grow up to be rich adults and poor kids stay poor. In Canada, that's not so much the case."

The American dream that anyone can rise from humble beginnings to vast wealth has become a myth. And as the gap between rich and poor widens, the middle class is shrinking.

For now, at least, the dream of upward mobility in Canada is still alive. Canadians can thank a legacy of sound public policy and a more progressive tax system.

Even the poorest of Canadian children have access to good schools, quality health care and decent homes (Attawapiskat notwithstanding).

A new Finance Department analysis found that seven million mainly low-income Canadians out of 24 million tax filers got a net cash transfer from the federal income tax regime in 2008. The Child Tax Credit, for example, has successfully mitigated poverty by shifting federal tax dollars to poor families.

The labour market, thanks partly to the paid parental leave benefits of Employment Insurance, likewise encourages parents to be parents. Canadian children are also more likely to grow up in two-parent homes and in homes where at least one parent works part-time to provide home care.

Compare that to the United States, where schools are financed primarily by wildly variable local property taxes rather than state income taxes. Neighbourhoods with low home values and marginal businesses have underfunded and failing schools, which become magnets for perpetual failure.

But it's a country of extremes, and life is good if you're at the top in the United States. A child's chance of staying at the wealth pinnacle is much greater than in Canada.

The divergence of opportunity in the U.S. grows even more pronounced with higher education. Tuition fees, which can easily run into the tens of thousands of dollars per year, essentially put the best schools out of reach for many Americans. Wealthy Americans,

on the other hand, can literally buy opportunity for their children, paying their way through the best colleges, hiring tutors and providing access to family connections.

"It's not that the fathers are getting their sons jobs, but they are getting them into the right college and networks, and that pays off a lot more in the U.S.," Prof. Corak said.

Canadians shouldn't be complacent. Ottawa and most of the provinces are running large budget deficits, and education and health care are already targets as governments hunt for savings.

There's another cause for concern. Rising income inequality is chipping away at the opportunities of future generations. Prof. Corak worries that wealthy Canadians may be forming exclusionary institutions in a drift toward Americanization. It's reflected in increasingly polarized cities such as Toronto, where neighbourhoods are becoming more sharply divided along income and ethnic lines, he said.

The dream of upward mobility may be alive for the current crop of young Canadians.

That dream is an essential component of a healthy economy, and policy makers should ensure it's passed on to future generations.

THE POLITICAL PHILOSOPHY OF REDISTRIBUTING INCOME

We have just seen how the economy's income is distributed and have considered some of the problems in interpreting measured inequality. This discussion was *positive* in the sense that it merely described the world as it is. We now turn to the *normative* question facing policymakers: What should the government do about economic inequality?

This question is not just about economics. Economic analysis alone cannot tell us whether policymakers should try to make our society more egalitarian. Our views on this question are, to a large extent, a matter of political philosophy. Yet because the government's role in redistributing income is central to so many debates over economic policy, here we digress from economic science to consider a bit of political philosophy.

Utilitarianism

A prominent school of thought in political philosophy is **utilitarianism**. The founders of utilitarianism are the English philosophers Jeremy Bentham (1748–1832) and John Stuart Mill (1806–1873). To a large extent, the goal of utilitarians is to apply the logic of individual decision making to questions concerning morality and public policy.

The starting point of utilitarianism is the notion of **utility**—the level of happiness or satisfaction that a person receives from his or her circumstances. Utility is a measure of well-being and, according to utilitarians, is the ultimate objective of all public and private actions. The proper goal of the government, they claim, is to maximize the sum of utility of everyone in society.

The utilitarian case for redistributing income is based on the assumption of *diminishing marginal utility*. It seems reasonable that an extra dollar of income to a poor person provides that person with more additional utility than does an extra dollar to a rich person. In other words, as a person's income rises, the extra well-being derived from an additional dollar of income falls. This plausible assumption, together with the utilitarian goal of maximizing total utility, implies that the government should try to achieve a more equal distribution of income.

The argument is simple. Imagine that Peter and Paul are the same, except that Peter earns $80 000 and Paul earns $20 000. In this case, taking a dollar from Peter to pay Paul will reduce Peter's utility and raise Paul's utility. But, because of diminishing marginal utility, Peter's utility falls by less than Paul's utility rises. Thus, this redistribution of income raises total utility, which is the utilitarian's objective.

At first, this utilitarian argument might seem to imply that the government should continue to redistribute income until everyone in society has exactly the same income. Indeed, that would be the case if the total amount of income—$100 000 in our example—were fixed. But, in fact, it is not. Utilitarians reject complete equalization of incomes because they accept one of the ten principles of economics presented in Chapter 1: People respond to incentives.

utilitarianism
the political philosophy according to which the government should choose policies to maximize the total utility of everyone in society

utility
a measure of happiness or satisfaction

To take from Peter to pay Paul, the government must pursue policies that redistribute income, such as the Canadian income tax and welfare system. Under these policies, people with high incomes pay high taxes, and people with low incomes receive income transfers. Yet, if the government takes away additional income a person might earn through higher income taxes or reduced transfers, both Peter and Paul have less incentive to work hard. As they work less, society's income falls, and so does total utility. The utilitarian government has to balance the gains from greater equality against the losses from distorted incentives. To maximize total utility, therefore, the government stops short of making society fully egalitarian.

A famous parable sheds light on the utilitarian's logic. Imagine that Peter and Paul are thirsty travellers trapped at different places in the desert. Peter's oasis has much water; Paul's has little. If the government could transfer water from one oasis to the other without cost, it would maximize total utility from water by equalizing the amount in the two places. But suppose that the government has only a leaky bucket. As it tries to move water from one place to the other, some of the water is lost in transit. In this case, a utilitarian government might still try to move some water from Peter to Paul, depending on how thirsty Paul is and how leaky the bucket is. But, with only a leaky bucket at its disposal, a utilitarian government will not try to reach complete equality.

Liberalism

liberalism
the political philosophy according to which the government should choose policies deemed to be just, as evaluated by an impartial observer behind a "veil of ignorance"

A second way of thinking about inequality might be called **liberalism**. Philosopher John Rawls develops this view in his book *A Theory of Justice*. This book was first published in 1971, and it quickly became a classic in political philosophy.

Rawls begins with the premise that a society's institutions, laws, and policies should be just. He then takes up the natural question: How can we, the members of society, ever agree on what justice means? It might seem that every person's point of view is inevitably based on that person's particular circumstances—whether he or she is talented or less talented, diligent or lazy, educated or less educated, born to a wealthy family or a poor one. Could we ever *objectively* determine what a just society would be?

To answer this question, Rawls proposes the following thought experiment. Imagine that before any of us is born, we all get together in the beforelife (the pre-birth version of the afterlife) for a meeting to design the rules that will govern society. At this point, we are all ignorant about the station in life each of us will end up filling. In Rawls's words, we are sitting in an "original position" behind a "veil of ignorance." In this original position, Rawls argues, we can choose a just set of rules for society because we must consider how those rules will affect every person. As Rawls puts it, "Since all are similarly situated and no one is able to design principles to favor his particular conditions, the principles of justice are the result of fair agreement or bargain." Designing public policies and institutions in this way allows us to be objective about what policies are just.

Rawls then considers what public policy designed behind this veil of ignorance would try to achieve. In particular, he considers what income distribution a person would consider fair if that person did not know whether he or she would end up at the top, bottom, or middle of the distribution. Rawls argues that a person in the original position would be especially concerned about the possibility of being at the *bottom* of the income distribution. In designing public policies, therefore, we should aim to raise the welfare of the worst-off person in society. That is, rather than maximizing the sum of everyone's utility, as a utilitarian would do, Rawls would maximize the minimum utility. Rawls's rule is called the **maximin criterion**.

maximin criterion
the claim that the government should aim to maximize the well-being of the worst-off person in society

Because the maximin criterion emphasizes the least fortunate person in society, it justifies public policies aimed at equalizing the distribution of income. By transferring income from the rich to the poor, society raises the well-being of the least fortunate. The maximin criterion would not, however, lead to a completely egalitarian society. If the government promised to equalize incomes completely, people would have no incentive to work hard, society's total income would fall substantially, and the least fortunate person would be worse off. Thus, the maximin criterion still allows disparities in income, because such disparities can improve incentives and thereby raise society's ability to help the poor. Nonetheless, because Rawls's philosophy puts weight on only the least fortunate members of society, it calls for more income redistribution than does utilitarianism.

Rawls's views are controversial, but the thought experiment he proposes has much appeal. In particular, this thought experiment allows us to consider the redistribution of income as a form of *social insurance*. That is, from the perspective of the original position behind the veil of ignorance, income redistribution is like an insurance policy. Homeowners buy fire insurance to protect themselves from the risk of their housing burning down. Similarly, when we as a society choose policies that tax the rich to supplement the incomes of the poor, we are all insuring ourselves against the possibility that we might have been a member of a poor family. Because people dislike risk, we should be happy to have been born into a society that provides us with this insurance.

It is not at all clear, however, that rational people behind the veil of ignorance would truly be so averse to risk as to follow the maximin criterion. Indeed, because a person in the original position might end up anywhere in the distribution of outcomes, he or she might treat all possible outcomes equally when designing public policies. In this case, the best policy behind the veil of ignorance would be to maximize the average utility of members of society, and the resulting notion of justice would be more utilitarian than Rawlsian.

Libertarianism

A third view of inequality is called **libertarianism**. The two views we have considered so far—utilitarianism and liberalism—both view the total income of society as a shared resource that a social planner can freely redistribute to achieve some social goal. By contrast, libertarians argue that society itself earns no income—only individual members of society earn income. According to libertarians, the government should not take from some individuals and give to others in order to achieve any particular distribution of income.

libertarianism
the political philosophy according to which the government should punish crimes and enforce voluntary agreements but not redistribute income

For instance, philosopher Robert Nozick writes the following in his famous 1974 book *Anarchy, State, and Utopia:*

We are not in the position of children who have been given portions of pie by someone who now makes last minute adjustments to rectify careless cutting. There is no *central* distribution, no person or group entitled to control all the resources, jointly deciding how they are to be doled out. What each person gets, he gets from others who give to him in exchange for something, or as a gift. In a free society, diverse persons control different resources, and new holdings arise out of the voluntary exchanges and actions of persons.

Whereas utilitarians and liberals try to judge what amount of inequality is desirable in a society, Nozick denies the validity of this very question.

The libertarian alternative to evaluating economic *outcomes* is to evaluate the *process* by which these outcomes arise. When the distribution of income is achieved unfairly—for instance, when one person steals from another—the government has the right and duty to remedy the problem. But, as long as the process determining the distribution of income is just, the resulting distribution is fair, no matter how unequal.

Nozick criticizes Rawls's liberalism by drawing an analogy between the distribution of income in society and the distribution of grades in a course. Suppose you were asked to judge the fairness of the grades in the economics course you are now taking. Would you imagine yourself behind a veil of ignorance and choose a grade distribution without knowing the talents and efforts of each student? Or would you ensure that the process of assigning grades to students is fair without regard for whether the resulting distribution is equal or unequal? For the case of grades at least, the libertarian emphasis on process over outcomes is compelling.

Libertarians conclude that equality of opportunities is more important than equality of incomes. They believe that the government should enforce individual rights to ensure that everyone has the same opportunity to use his or her talents and achieve success. Once these rules of the game are established, the government has no reason to alter the resulting distribution of income.

QuickQuiz   Pam earns more than Pauline. Someone proposes taxing Pam in order to supplement Pauline's income. How would a utilitarian, a liberal, and a libertarian evaluate this proposal?

POLICIES TO REDUCE POVERTY

As we have just seen, political philosophers hold various views about what role the government should take in altering the distribution of income. Political debate among the larger population of voters reflects a similar disagreement. Despite these continuing debates, however, most people believe that, at the very least, the government should try to help those most in need. According to a popular metaphor, the government should provide a "safety net" to prevent any citizen from falling too far.

Poverty is one of the most difficult problems that policymakers face. Poor families are more likely than the overall population to experience homelessness, drug dependency, domestic violence, health problems, teenage pregnancy, illiteracy, unemployment, and low educational attainment. Members of poor families are both more likely to commit crimes and more likely to be victims of crimes. Although it is hard to separate the causes of poverty from the effects, there is no doubt that poverty is associated with various economic and social ills.

Suppose that you were a policymaker in the government, and your goal was to reduce the number of people living in poverty. How would you achieve this goal? Here we consider some of the policy options that you might consider. Although each of these options does help some people escape poverty, none of them is perfect, and deciding which is best is not easy.

Minimum-Wage Laws

Laws setting a minimum wage that employers can pay workers are a perennial source of debate. Advocates view the minimum wage as a way of helping the working poor without any cost to the government. Critics view it as hurting those it is intended to help.

The minimum wage is easily understood using the tools of supply and demand, as we first saw in Chapter 6. For workers with low levels of skill and experience, a high minimum wage forces the wage above the level that balances supply and demand. It therefore raises the cost of labour to firms and reduces the quantity of labour that those firms demand. The result is higher unemployment among those groups of workers affected by the minimum wage. Although those workers who remain employed benefit from a higher wage, those who might have been employed at a lower wage are worse off.

The magnitude of these effects depends crucially on the elasticity of demand. Advocates of a high minimum wage argue that the demand for unskilled labour is relatively inelastic, so that a high minimum wage depresses employment only slightly. Critics of the minimum wage argue that labour demand is more elastic, especially in the long run when firms can adjust employment and production more fully. They also note that many minimum-wage workers are teenagers from middle-class families, so that a high minimum wage is imperfectly targeted as a policy for helping the poor.

Welfare

One way to raise the living standards of the poor is for the government to supplement their incomes. The primary way in which the government does this is through the welfare system. **Welfare** is a broad term that encompasses various government programs. In Canada, welfare programs are the responsibility of provincial/territorial governments, which receive some help in funding the programs from the federal government.

welfare
government programs that supplement the incomes of the needy

The features of welfare programs and the levels of benefits vary significantly across Canada. However, the programs share some common features. Most programs distinguish between people who are considered employable and those who are not. People who are considered employable typically receive lower benefits. Individuals who are not considered employable, families with dependent children, and individuals with disabilities receive higher benefits.

A common criticism of welfare programs is that they reduce the incentive to work. One way in which they do this is by reducing welfare benefits when an individual earns other income. In the past many provinces/territories reduced welfare payments dollar for dollar when an individual earned other income. This resulted in a marginal tax rate on earned income of 100 percent. This reduces the incentive for welfare recipients to find work to supplement their welfare cheques, and results in what many refer to as a "welfare trap." In response to this criticism, many provinces and territories have lowered the implicit tax-back rates on welfare benefits, but they are still very high—in excess of 70 percent in most provinces/territories.

Negative Income Tax

Whenever the government chooses a system to collect taxes, it affects the distribution of income. This is clearly true in the case of a progressive income tax, whereby high-income families pay a larger percentage of their income in taxes than do low-income families. As we discussed in Chapter 12, equity across income groups is an important criterion in the design of a tax system.

negative income tax
a tax system that collects revenue from high-income households and gives transfers to low-income households

Many economists have advocated supplementing the income of the poor using a **negative income tax**. According to this policy, every family would report its income to the government. High-income families would pay a tax based on their incomes. Low-income families would receive a subsidy. In other words, they would "pay" a "negative tax."

For example, suppose the government used the following formula to compute a family's tax liability:

$$\text{Taxes owed} = (1/3 \text{ of income}) - \$10\,000$$

In this case, a family that earned $60 000 would pay $10 000 in taxes, and a family that earned $90 000 would pay $20 000 in taxes. A family that earned $30 000 would owe nothing. And a family that earned $15 000 would "owe" −$5000. In other words, the government would send this family a cheque for $5000.

Under a negative income tax, poor families would receive financial assistance without having to demonstrate need. The only qualification required to receive assistance would be a low income. Depending on one's point of view, this feature can be either an advantage or a disadvantage. On the one hand, a negative income tax does not encourage illegitimate births and the breakup of families, as critics of the welfare system believe current policy does. On the other hand, a negative income tax would subsidize those who are simply lazy and, in some people's eyes, undeserving of government support.

In-Kind Transfers

Another way to help the poor is to provide them directly with some of the goods and services they need to raise their living standards. For example, charities provide the needy with food, shelter, and children's toys for special occasions. In Canada, in-kind transfers supplied by the government include subsidized housing and daycare. Publicly funded health care, financed by income taxes and payroll taxes, can also be thought of as an in-kind transfer to the poor.

Is it better to help the poor with these in-kind transfers or with direct cash payments? There is no clear answer.

Advocates of in-kind transfers argue that such transfers ensure that the poor get what they need most. Among the poorest members of society, alcohol and drug addiction is more common than it is in society as a whole. By providing the poor with food and shelter, society can be more confident that it is not helping to support such addictions. This is one reason why in-kind transfers are more politically popular than cash payments to the poor.

Advocates of cash payments, on the other hand, argue that in-kind transfers are inefficient and disrespectful. The government does not know what goods and services the poor need most. Many of the poor are ordinary people down on their luck. Despite their misfortune, they are in the best position to decide how to raise their own living standards. Rather than giving the poor in-kind transfers of goods and services that they may not want, it may be better to give them cash and allow them to buy what they think they need most.

Employment Insurance

Employment Insurance (EI) is one way the government provides some income support to people who find themselves temporarily out of work.

EI is available to workers who lose their jobs through no fault of their own; those who quit their jobs for no good reason or who are fired for cause receive no benefits. To qualify for EI, people must have worked a certain number of hours since their last spell of unemployment. Benefit levels are set at 55 percent of the individual's previous salary, up to a maximum equal to the average industrial wage. Unemployed workers can receive benefits for a maximum of 45 weeks.

There is ongoing debate in Canada on whether the EI system should be organized along the principles of an insurance program, or whether it should be operated as simply an income-transfer program. Those who argue that the EI system should embody insurance principles focus on various features of the current system. The EI system is funded from payroll taxes paid by both employees and employers. The payroll tax rates are the same for employees and employers in all industries, even though some industries and occupations have a much higher risk of unemployment than others. The construction industry, for example, tends to be both cyclical and seasonal. As a result, construction workers are more likely to be laid off than, say, university professors. Yet if a construction worker earns the same salary as a university professor, the construction worker and her employer will pay the same amount in EI payroll taxes as the university professor and his employer.

This equality in payroll tax payments contravenes one of the most important principles of insurance: High-risk individuals should pay higher insurance premiums than low-risk individuals. For example, young, single males pay much higher car insurance premiums than older, married males because they are more likely to have a car accident; similarly, people with poor driving records pay higher premiums than people with good driving records.

IN THE NEWS

EI AND WORK INCENTIVES

Government programs designed to address poverty may also reduce the incentive to work. The following article explains how this can happen.

EI Claimants Bough Out

By David Johnston

The economy is going from bad to worse on the Gaspé peninsula, but people aren't grasping at straws just yet. In fact, they're grasping at Christmas-tree branches, and it's putting money in people's pockets.

In recent weeks, 250 people have been out in the woods, snipping small branches off balsam fir trees and hauling them to a new company that makes Christmas wreaths and other festive products.

When the company, WreathsPlus, was founded last fall in the industrial park outside the town of Gaspé, people took notice. New businesses are rare in the region, and seasonal workers who hadn't worked enough during the summer to get Employment Insurance over the winter saw an opportunity to qualify.

And so WreathsPlus had no trouble finding workers when it opened for a two-month production run last fall. Even

Emploi-Québec got in the act, agreeing to pay half the wages of 40 of the 70 original workers, under a job-training scheme.

The provincial subsidy was good for WreathsPlus, good for the workers, and even good for the government, as it helped the 40 qualify for Employment Insurance and kept them from falling onto welfare rolls.

But then something remarkable happened: The wreaths the workers made sold like mad. Wholesalers loved them. This year, they put in orders for tens of thousands of them, as well as for other related balsam and cedar decorative products.

And so when three WreathsPlus facilities in Gaspé, Murdochville, and Rivière au Renard opened last month for another two-month run, there was work for 170 people, not just 70.

That's when the trouble started. Try as it did, the company could find only 150 people willing to work, even though the region's official unemployment rate is 19 percent, the highest in

Quebec. The problem, said WreathsPlus co-owner Bruce Jones, is that most of the people he tried to recruit said they'd already qualified for EI and didn't want to work. WreathsPlus had outgrown the local economy's demand for EI qualifying weeks. . . .

WreathsPlus's seasonal production employees earn a minimum wage of $6.90 per hour, plus a small bonus that sees the most productive earn $8.50 per hour. This compares with the $7.10 per hour for people on EI, when you consider that the average Quebec EI recipient received a weekly cheque of $284.

People on EI would be looking at a 20-cent-per-hour pay cut if they went out to work for WreathsPlus instead of staying at home.

And so it is that one of the fastest-growing companies in the Gaspé faces an unofficial labour shortage.

Source: David Johnston, "EI Claimants Bough Out," *The Montreal Gazette*, November 11, 2000, p. A19.

In effect, EI provides an implicit wage subsidy to industries that employ workers with a high risk of unemployment. In the absence of EI, construction workers would demand higher wages to compensate them for the higher risk of unemployment (recall our discussion of compensating differentials in Chapter 19). However, in the presence of EI, construction companies can pay their workers relatively lower wages because EI benefits provide a cushion if workers are laid off: Workers do not demand as much to compensate them for the risk of unemployment because their income will not fall by as much. For this reason, it is argued that EI payroll tax rates should be experience-rated. Under an experience-rated system, EI payroll tax rates would be higher in industries with a high risk of unemployment than in industries with a low risk of unemployment. Experience rating, it is claimed, would make the EI system more like true insurance and eliminate the implicit wage subsidies granted to some industries under the current system.

Not only is there currently no experience rating of EI in Canada, but some aspects of the EI system actually act as a sort of negative experience rating. For example, EI qualifying periods are shorter and benefit periods are longer in areas with persistently high unemployment rates. Sound insurance principles would require that workers in areas with high unemployment rates pay higher payroll taxes or receive lower benefits than workers in areas with low unemployment rates. However, by reducing the qualifying period and lengthening the benefit period in regions with high unemployment, the EI system does just the opposite. In this regard, the EI system acts as an income-transfer system to regions with high unemployment.

The debate over how closely the EI system in Canada should reflect insurance principles is a complicated and ongoing one.

QuickQuiz   List three policies aimed at helping the poor, and discuss the pros and cons of each.

CONCLUSION

People have long reflected on the distribution of income in society. Plato, the ancient Greek philosopher, concluded that in an ideal society the income of the richest person would be no more than four times the income of the poorest person. Although the measurement of inequality is difficult, it is clear that our society has much more inequality than Plato recommended.

One of the ten principles of economics discussed in Chapter 1 is that governments can sometimes improve market outcomes. There is little consensus, however, about how this principle should be applied to the distribution of income. Philosophers and policymakers today do not agree on how much income inequality is desirable, or even whether public policy should aim to alter the distribution of income. Much of public debate reflects this disagreement. Whenever taxes are raised, for instance, lawmakers argue over how much of the tax hike should fall on the rich, the middle class, and the poor.

Another of the ten principles of economics is that people face tradeoffs. This principle is important to keep in mind when thinking about economic inequality. Policies that penalize the successful and reward the unsuccessful reduce the incentive to succeed. Thus, policymakers face a tradeoff between equality and efficiency. The more equally the pie is divided, the smaller the pie becomes. This is the one lesson concerning the distribution of income about which almost everyone agrees.

SUMMARY

- Data on the distribution of income show wide disparity in our society. The richest fifth of families earns about 25 times as much income as the poorest fifth.

- Because in-kind transfers, the economic life cycle, transitory income, and economic mobility are so important for understanding variation in income, it is difficult to gauge the degree of inequality in our society using data on the distribution of income in a single year. When these other factors are taken into account, they tend to suggest that economic well-being is more equally distributed than is annual income.

- Political philosophers differ in their views about the role of government in altering the distribution of income. Utilitarians (such as John Stuart Mill) would choose the distribution of income to maximize the sum of utility of everyone in society. Liberals (such as John

Rawls) would determine the distribution of income as if we were behind a "veil of ignorance" that prevented us from knowing our own stations in life. Libertarians (such as Robert Nozick) would have the government enforce individual rights to ensure a fair process but then not be concerned about inequality in the resulting distribution of income.

- Various policies aim to help the poor— minimum-wage laws, welfare, negative income taxes, and in-kind transfers. Although each of these policies helps some families escape poverty, they also have unintended side effects. Because financial assistance declines as income rises, the poor often face effective marginal tax rates that are very high. Such high effective tax rates discourage poor families from escaping poverty on their own.

KEY CONCEPTS

poverty rate, p. 443
poverty line, p. 443
in-kind transfers, p. 445
life cycle, p. 445

permanent income, p. 446
utilitarianism, p. 449
utility, p. 449
liberalism, p. 450

maximin criterion, p. 451
libertarianism, p. 451
welfare, p. 453
negative income tax, p. 454

QUESTIONS FOR REVIEW

1. Does the richest fifth of the Canadian population earn four, eight, or twenty-five times the income of the poorest fifth?

2. How does the extent of income inequality in Canada compare to that of other nations around the world?

3. What groups in the population are most likely to live in poverty?

4. When gauging the amount of inequality, why do transitory and life cycle variations in income cause difficulties?

5. How would a utilitarian, a liberal, and a libertarian determine how much income inequality is permissible?

6. What are the pros and cons of in-kind (rather than cash) transfers to the poor?

7. Describe how antipoverty programs can discourage the poor from working. How might you reduce this disincentive? What are the disadvantages with your proposed policy?

PROBLEMS AND APPLICATIONS

1. By most measures, over the past 20 years, income inequality in the United States has increased relative to income inequality in Canada. Some factors that may explain this difference were discussed in Chapter 19. What are they?

2. What do you think would happen to wage rates in the construction industry if Canada introduced full experience rating to the EI system? Explain.

3. Economists often view life cycle variation in income as one form of transitory variation in income around people's lifetime, or permanent, income. In this sense, how does your current income compare to your permanent income? Do you think your current income accurately reflects your standard of living?

4. The chapter discusses the importance of economic mobility.
   a. What policies might the government pursue to increase economic mobility *within* a generation?
   b. What policies might the government pursue to increase economic mobility *across* generations?
   c. Do you think we should reduce spending on current welfare programs in order to increase spending on programs that enhance economic mobility? What are some of the advantages and disadvantages of doing so?

5. Consider two communities. In one community, ten families have incomes of $100 each and ten families have incomes of $20 each. In the other community, ten families have incomes of $200 each and ten families have incomes of $22 each.
   a. In which community is the distribution of income more unequal? In which community is the problem of poverty likely to be worse?
   b. Which distribution of income would Rawls prefer? Explain.
   c. Which distribution of income do you prefer? Explain.

6. This chapter uses the analogy of a "leaky bucket" to explain one constraint on the redistribution of income.
   a. What elements of the Canadian system for redistributing income create the leaks in the bucket? Be specific.
   b. Do you think that the NDP or Conservative political parties generally believe that the bucket used for redistributing income is more leaky? How does that belief affect their views about the amount of income redistribution that the government should undertake?

7. Suppose there are two possible income distributions in a society of ten people. In the first distribution, nine people would have incomes of $30 000 and one person would have an income of $10 000. In the second distribution, all ten people would have incomes of $28,000.
   a. If the society had the first income distribution, what would be the utilitarian argument for redistributing income?
   b. Which income distribution would Rawls consider more equitable? Explain.
   c. Which income distribution would Nozick consider more equitable? Explain.

8. Most measures of the poverty rate do not include the value of in-kind transfers in family income. Yet the value of in-kind transfers can be substantial. An example of an in-kind transfer is a housing subsidy. Let's say that the value of the housing subsidy is $5000 for each recipient family.
   a. If the government gave each recipient family an amount of cash equal to $5000 instead of the housing subsidy, do you think that most of these families would spend an additional $5000 on housing? Why or why not?
   b. How does your answer to part (a) affect your view about whether we should determine the poverty rate by valuing in-kind transfers at the price the government pays for them? Explain.
   c. How does your answer to part (a) affect your view about whether we should provide assistance to the poor in the form of cash transfers or in-kind transfers? Explain.

9. Suppose that a family's tax liability equalled its income multiplied by one-half, minus $10 000. Under this system, some families would pay

taxes to the government, and some families would receive money from the government through a "negative income tax."

a. Consider families with pre-tax incomes of $0, $10 000, $20 000, $30 000, and $40 000. Make a table showing pre-tax income, taxes paid to the government or money received from the government, and after-tax income for each family.

b. What is the marginal tax rate in this system? (See Chapter 12 if you need to review the definition of marginal tax rate.) What is the maximum amount of income at which a family *receives* money from the government?

c. Now suppose that the tax schedule is changed, so that a family's tax liability equals its income multiplied by one-quarter, minus $10 000. What is the marginal tax rate in this new system? What is the maximum amount of income at which a family receives money from the government?

d. What is the main advantage of each of the tax schedules discussed here?

10. John and Jeremy are utilitarians. John believes that labour supply is highly elastic, whereas Jeremy believes that labour supply is quite inelastic. How do you suppose their views about income redistribution differ?

http://   For more study tools, please visit www.nelson.com/mankiwmicro6e.

TOPICS FOR FURTHER STUDY

7

THE THEORY OF CONSUMER CHOICE

21

Sean Gladwell/GetStock.com

Learning Objectives

In this chapter, you will...

- See how a budget constraint represents the choices a consumer can afford

- Learn how indifference curves can be used to represent a consumer's preferences

- Analyze how a consumer's optimal choices are determined

- See how a consumer responds to changes in income and changes in prices

- Decompose the impact of a price change into an income effect and a substitution effect

- Apply the theory of consumer choice to three questions about household behaviour

When you walk into a store, you are confronted with thousands of goods that you might buy. Because your financial resources are limited, you cannot buy everything that you want. You therefore consider the prices of the various goods being offered for sale and buy a bundle of goods that, given your resources, best suits your needs and desires.

In this chapter we develop the theory that describes how consumers make decisions about what to buy. So far in this book, we have summarized consumers' decisions with the demand curve. As we have seen, the demand curve for a good reflects consumers' willingness to pay for it. When the price of a good rises, consumers are willing to pay for fewer units, so the quantity demanded falls. We now look more deeply at the decisions that lie behind the demand curve. The theory of consumer choice presented in this chapter provides a more complete understanding of demand, just as the theory of the competitive firm in Chapter 14 provides a more complete understanding of supply.

One of the ten principles of economics discussed in Chapter 1 is that people face tradeoffs. The theory of consumer choice examines the tradeoffs that people face in their role as consumers. When a consumer buys more of one good, he can afford less of other goods. When he spends more time enjoying leisure and less time working, he has lower income and can afford less consumption. When he spends more of his income in the present and saves less of it, he must accept a lower level of consumption in the future. The theory of consumer choice examines how consumers facing these tradeoffs make decisions and how they respond to changes in their environment.

After developing the basic theory of consumer choice, we apply it to three questions about household decisions. In particular, we ask:

1. Do all demand curves slope downward?
2. How do wages affect labour supply?
3. How do interest rates affect household saving?

At first, these questions might seem unrelated. But, as we will see, we can use the theory of consumer choice to address each of them.

THE BUDGET CONSTRAINT: WHAT THE CONSUMER CAN AFFORD

Most people would like to increase the quantity or quality of the goods they consume—to take longer vacations, drive fancier cars, or eat at better restaurants. People consume less than they desire because their spending is *constrained*, or limited, by their income. We begin our study of consumer choice by examining this link between income and spending.

To keep things simple, we examine the decision facing a consumer who buys only two goods: Pepsi and pizza. Of course, real people buy thousands of different kinds of goods. Yet assuming there are only two goods greatly simplifies the problem without altering the basic insights about consumer choice.

We first consider how the consumer's income constrains the amount he spends on Pepsi and pizza. Suppose that the consumer has an income of $1000 per month and that he spends his entire income each month on Pepsi and pizza. The price of a litre of Pepsi is $2, and the price of a pizza is $10.

The table in Figure 21.1 shows some of the many combinations of Pepsi and pizza that the consumer can buy. The first line in the table shows that if the consumer spends all his income on pizza, he can eat 100 pizzas during the month, but he would not be able to buy any Pepsi at all. The second line shows another possible consumption bundle: 90 pizzas and 50 L of Pepsi. And so on. Each consumption bundle in the table costs exactly $1000.

The graph in Figure 21.1 illustrates the consumption bundles that the consumer can choose. The vertical axis measures the number of litres of Pepsi, and the horizontal axis measures the number of pizzas. Three points are marked on this figure. At point A, the consumer buys no Pepsi and consumes 100 pizzas. At point B, the consumer buys no pizza and consumes 500 L of Pepsi. At point C, the consumer buys 50 pizzas and 250 L of Pepsi. Point C, which is exactly at the middle of the line from A to B, is the point at which the consumer spends an equal amount ($500) on Pepsi and pizza. Of course, these are only three of the many combinations of Pepsi and pizza that the consumer can choose. All the points on the line from A to B are possible. This line, called the **budget constraint**, shows the consumption bundles that the consumer can afford. In this case, it shows the tradeoff between Pepsi and pizza that the consumer faces.

budget constraint
the limit on the consumption bundles that a consumer can afford

FIGURE 21.1

The Consumer's Budget Constraint

The budget constraint shows the various bundles of goods that the consumer can afford for a given income. Here the consumer buys bundles of Pepsi and pizza. The table and graph show what the consumer can afford if his income is $1000, the price of Pepsi is $2 per litre, and the price of a pizza is $10.

Litres of Pepsi	Number of Pizzas	Spending on Pepsi	Spending on Pizza	Total Spending
0	100	$ 0	$1000	$1000
50	90	100	900	1000
100	80	200	800	1000
150	70	300	700	1000
200	60	400	600	1000
250	50	500	500	1000
300	40	600	400	1000
350	30	700	300	1000
400	20	800	200	1000
450	10	900	100	1000
500	0	1000	0	1000

The slope of the budget constraint measures the rate at which the consumer can trade one good for the other. Recall from the appendix to Chapter 2 that the slope between two points is calculated as the change in the vertical distance divided by the change in the horizontal distance (rise over run). From point A to point B, the vertical distance is 500 L, and the horizontal distance is 100 pizzas. Thus, the slope is 5 L per pizza. (Actually, because the budget constraint slopes downward, the slope is a negative number. But for our purposes we can ignore the minus sign.)

Notice that the slope of the budget constraint equals the *relative price* of the two goods—the price of one good compared to the price of the other. A pizza costs 5 times as much as a litre of Pepsi, so the opportunity cost of a pizza is 5 L of Pepsi. The budget constraint's slope of 5 reflects the tradeoff the market is offering the consumer: 1 pizza for 5 L of Pepsi.

QuickQuiz   Draw the budget constraint for a person with income of $1000 if the price of Pepsi is $5 per litre and the price of a pizza is $10. What is the slope of this budget constraint?

PREFERENCES: WHAT THE CONSUMER WANTS

Our goal in this chapter is to see how consumers make choices. The budget constraint is one piece of the analysis: It shows what combination of goods the consumer can afford given his income and the prices of the goods. The consumer's choices, however, depend not only on his budget constraint but also on his preferences regarding the two goods. Therefore, the consumer's preferences are the next piece of our analysis.

Representing Preferences with Indifference Curves

The consumer's preferences allow him to choose among different bundles of Pepsi and pizza. If you offer the consumer two different bundles, he chooses the bundle that best suits his tastes. If the two bundles suit his tastes equally well, we say that the consumer is *indifferent* between the two bundles.

Just as we have represented the consumer's budget constraint graphically, we can also represent his preferences graphically. We do this with indifference curves. An **indifference curve** shows the various bundles of consumption that make the consumer equally happy. In this case, the indifference curves show the combinations of Pepsi and pizza with which the consumer is equally satisfied.

Figure 21.2 shows two of the consumer's many indifference curves. The consumer is indifferent among combinations A, B, and C because they are all on the same curve. Not surprisingly, if the consumer's consumption of pizza is reduced, say from point A to point B, consumption of Pepsi must increase to keep him equally happy. If consumption of pizza is reduced again, from point B to point C, the amount of Pepsi consumed must increase yet again.

The slope at any point on an indifference curve equals the rate at which the consumer is willing to substitute one good for the other. This rate is called the **marginal rate of substitution** (*MRS*). In this case, the marginal rate of substitution measures how much Pepsi the consumer requires in order to be compensated for a one-unit reduction in pizza consumption (as indicated by the numeral "1" in

indifference curve
a curve that shows consumption bundles that give the consumer the same level of satisfaction

marginal rate of substitution
the rate at which a consumer is willing to trade one good for another

FIGURE 21.2

The Consumer's Preferences

The consumer's preferences are represented with indifference curves, which show the combinations of Pepsi and pizza that make the consumer equally satisfied. Because the consumer prefers more of a good, points on a higher indifference curve (I_2 here) are preferred to points on a lower indifference curve (I_1). The marginal rate of substitution (MRS) shows the rate at which the consumer is willing to trade Pepsi for pizza.

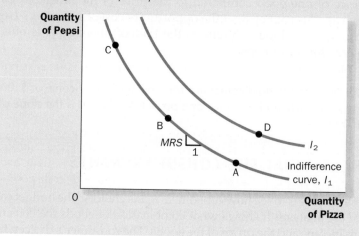

Figure 21.2). Notice that because the indifference curves are not straight lines, the marginal rate of substitution is not the same at all points on a given indifference curve. The rate at which a consumer is willing to trade one good for the other depends on the amounts of the goods he is already consuming. That is, the rate at which a consumer is willing to trade pizza for Pepsi depends on whether he is hungrier or thirstier, which in turn depends on how much pizza and Pepsi he is consuming.

The consumer is equally happy at all points on any given indifference curve, but he prefers some indifference curves to others. Because he prefers more consumption to less, higher indifference curves are preferred to lower ones. In Figure 21.2, any point on curve I_2 is preferred to any point on curve I_1.

A consumer's set of indifference curves gives a complete ranking of the consumer's preferences. That is, we can use the indifference curves to rank any two bundles of goods. For example, the indifference curves tell us that point D is preferred to point A because point D is on a higher indifference curve than point A. (That conclusion may be obvious, however, because point D offers the consumer both more pizza and more Pepsi.) The indifference curves also tell us that point D is preferred to point C because point D is on a higher indifference curve. Even though point D has less Pepsi than point C, it has more than enough extra pizza to make the consumer prefer it. By seeing which point is on the higher indifference curve, we can use the set of indifference curves to rank any combinations of Pepsi and pizza.

Four Properties of Indifference Curves

Because indifference curves represent a consumer's preferences, they have certain properties that reflect those preferences. Here we consider four properties that describe most indifference curves:

- *Property 1: Higher indifference curves are preferred to lower ones.* People usually prefer more of something to less of it. This preference for greater quantities is reflected in the indifference curves. As Figure 21.2 shows, higher indifference curves represent larger quantities of goods than lower indifference curves. Thus, the consumer prefers being on higher indifference curves.
- *Property 2: Indifference curves are downward sloping.* The slope of an indifference curve reflects the rate at which the consumer is willing to substitute one good for the other. In most cases, the consumer likes both goods. Therefore, if the quantity of one good is reduced, the quantity of the other good must increase in order for the consumer to be equally happy. For this reason, most indifference curves slope downward.
- *Property 3: Indifference curves do not cross.* To see why this is true, suppose that two indifference curves did cross, as in Figure 21.3. Then, because point A is on the same indifference curve as point B, the two points would make the consumer equally happy. In addition, because point B is on the same indifference curve as point C, these two points would make the consumer equally happy. But these conclusions imply that points A and C would also make the consumer equally happy, even though point C has more of both goods. This contradicts our assumption that the consumer always prefers more of both goods to less. Thus, indifference curves cannot cross.
- *Property 4: Indifference curves are bowed inward.* The slope of an indifference curve is the marginal rate of substitution—the rate at which the consumer is willing to

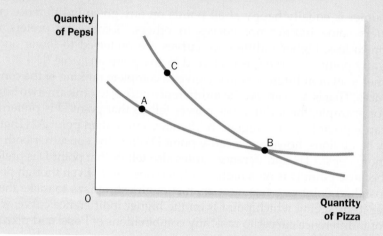

FIGURE 21.3

The Impossibility of Intersecting Indifference Curves

A situation like this can never happen. According to these indifference curves, the consumer would be equally satisfied at points A, B, and C, even though point C has more of both goods than point A.

trade off one good for the other. The marginal rate of substitution (*MRS*) usually depends on the amount of each good the consumer is currently consuming. In particular, because people are more willing to trade away goods that they have in abundance and less willing to trade away goods of which they have little, the indifference curves are bowed inward. As an example, consider Figure 21.4. At point A, because the consumer has a lot of Pepsi and only a little pizza, he is very hungry but not very thirsty. To induce the consumer to give up 1 pizza, the consumer has to be given 6 L of Pepsi: The marginal rate of substitution is 6 L per pizza. By contrast, at point B, the consumer has little Pepsi and a lot of pizza, so he is very thirsty but not very hungry. At this point, he would be willing to give up 1 pizza to get 1 L of Pepsi: The marginal rate of substitution is 1 L per pizza. Thus, the bowed shape of the indifference curve reflects the consumer's greater willingness to give up a good that he already has in large quantity.

Two Extreme Examples of Indifference Curves

The shape of an indifference curve tells us about the consumer's willingness to trade one good for the other. When the goods are easy to substitute for each other, the indifference curves are less bowed; when the goods are hard to substitute, the indifference curves are very bowed. To see why this is true, let's consider the extreme cases.

Perfect Substitutes
Suppose that someone offered you bundles of nickels and dimes. How would you rank the different bundles?

Most likely, you would care only about the total monetary value of each bundle. If so, you would judge a bundle based on the number of nickels plus twice

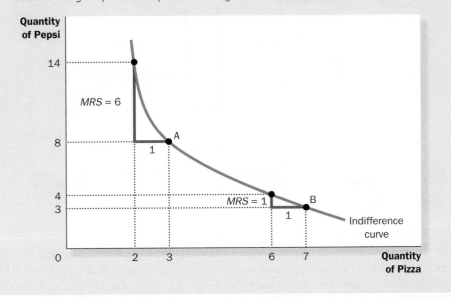

FIGURE 21.4

Bowed Indifference Curves

Indifference curves are usually bowed inward. This shape implies that the marginal rate of substitution (MRS) depends on the quantity of the two goods the consumer is consuming. At point A, the consumer has little pizza and much Pepsi, so he requires a lot of extra Pepsi to induce him to give up one of the pizzas: The marginal rate of substitution is 6 L of Pepsi per pizza. At point B, the consumer has much pizza and little Pepsi, so he requires only a little extra Pepsi to induce him to give up one of the pizzas: The marginal rate of substitution is 1 L of Pepsi per pizza.

the number of dimes. In other words, you would always be willing to trade 1 dime for 2 nickels, regardless of the number of nickels and dimes in the bundle. Your marginal rate of substitution between nickels and dimes would be a fixed number: 2.

We can represent your preferences about nickels and dimes with the indifference curves in panel (a) of Figure 21.5. Because the marginal rate of substitution is constant, the indifference curves are straight lines. In this extreme case of straight indifference curves, we say that the two goods are **perfect substitutes**.

Perfect Complements   Suppose now that someone offered you bundles of shoes. Some of the shoes fit your left foot, others your right foot. How would you rank these different bundles?

In this case, you might care only about the number of pairs of shoes. In other words, you would judge a bundle based on the number of pairs you could assemble from it. A bundle of 5 left shoes and 7 right shoes yields only 5 pairs. Getting 1 more right shoe has no value if there is no left shoe to go with it.

We can represent your preferences for right and left shoes with the indifference curves in panel (b) of Figure 21.5. In this case, a bundle with 5 left shoes and 5 right shoes is just as good as a bundle with 5 left shoes and 7 right shoes. It is also just as good as a bundle with 7 left shoes and 5 right shoes. The indifference curves, therefore, are right angles. In this extreme case of right-angle indifference curves, we say that the two goods are **perfect complements**.

perfect substitutes
two goods with straight-line indifference curves

perfect complements
two goods with right-angle indifference curves

FIGURE 21.5

Perfect Substitutes and Perfect Complements

When two goods are easily substitutable, such as nickels and dimes, the indifference curves are straight lines, as shown in panel (a). When two goods are strongly complementary, such as left shoes and right shoes, the indifference curves are right angles, as shown in panel (b).

In the real world, of course, most goods are neither perfect substitutes (like nickels and dimes) nor perfect complements (like right shoes and left shoes). More typically, the indifference curves are bowed inward, but not so bowed as to become right angles.

QuickQuiz   Draw some indifference curves for Pepsi and pizza. Explain the four properties of these indifference curves.

OPTIMIZATION: WHAT THE CONSUMER CHOOSES

The goal of this chapter is to understand how a consumer makes choices. We have the two pieces necessary for this analysis: the consumer's budget constraint and the consumer's preferences. Now we put these two pieces together and consider the consumer's decision about what to buy.

The Consumer's Optimal Choices

Consider once again our Pepsi and pizza example. The consumer would like to end up with the best possible combination of Pepsi and pizza—that is, the combination on the highest possible indifference curve. But the consumer must also end up on or below his budget constraint, which measures the total resources available to him.

Figure 21.6 shows the consumer's budget constraint and three of his many indifference curves. The highest indifference curve that the consumer can reach

FIGURE 21.6

The Consumer's Optimum

The consumer chooses the point on his budget constraint that lies on the highest indifference curve. At this point, called the optimum, *the marginal rate of substitution equals the relative price of the two goods. Here the highest indifference curve the consumer can reach is I_2. The consumer prefers point A, which lies on indifference curve I_3, but the consumer cannot afford this bundle of Pepsi and pizza. By contrast, point B is affordable, but because it lies on a lower indifference curve, the consumer does not prefer it.*

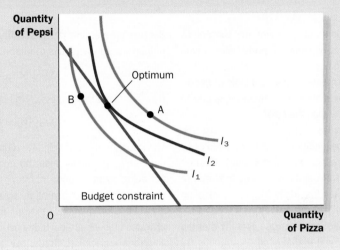

(I_2 in the figure) is the one that just barely touches the budget constraint. The point at which this indifference curve and the budget constraint touch is called the *optimum*. The consumer would prefer point A, but he cannot afford that point because it lies above his budget constraint. The consumer can afford point B, but that point is on a lower indifference curve and, therefore, provides the consumer less satisfaction. The optimum represents the best combination of consumption of Pepsi and pizza available to the consumer.

Notice that, at the optimum, the slope of the indifference curve equals the slope of the budget constraint. We say that the indifference curve is *tangent* to the budget constraint. The slope of the indifference curve is the marginal rate of substitution between Pepsi and pizza, and the slope of the budget constraint is the relative price of Pepsi and pizza. Thus, *the consumer chooses consumption of the two goods so that the marginal rate of substitution equals the relative price.*

In Chapter 7 we saw how market prices reflect the marginal value that consumers place on goods. This analysis of consumer choice shows the same result in another way. In making his consumption choices, the consumer takes as given the relative price of the two goods and then chooses an optimum at which his marginal rate of substitution equals this relative price. The relative price is the rate at which the *market* is willing to trade one good for the other, whereas the marginal rate of substitution is the rate at which the *consumer* is willing to trade one good for the other. At the consumer's optimum, the consumer's valuation of the two goods (as measured by the marginal rate of substitution) equals the market's valuation (as measured by the relative price). As a result of this consumer optimization, market prices of different goods reflect the value that consumers place on those goods.

UTILITY: AN ALTERNATIVE WAY TO DESCRIBE PREFERENCES AND OPTIMIZATION

We have used indifference curves to represent the consumer's preferences. Another common way to represent preferences is with the concept of *utility*. Utility is an abstract measure of the satisfaction or happiness that a consumer receives from a bundle of goods. Economists say that a consumer prefers one bundle of goods to another if one provides more utility than the other.

Indifference curves and utility are closely related. Because the consumer prefers points on higher indifference curves, bundles of goods on higher indifference curves provide higher utility. Because the consumer is equally happy with all points on the same indifference curve, all these bundles provide the same utility. You can think of an indifference curve as an "equal-utility" curve.

The *marginal utility* of any good is the increase in utility that the consumer gets from an additional unit of that good. Most goods are assumed to exhibit *diminishing marginal utility*: The more of the good the consumer already has, the lower the marginal utility provided by an extra unit of that good.

The marginal rate of substitution between two goods depends on their marginal utilities. For example, if the marginal utility of good X is twice the marginal utility of good Y, then a person would need 2 units of good Y to compensate for losing 1 unit of good X, and the marginal rate of substitution equals 2. More generally, the marginal rate of substitution (and thus the slope of the indifference curve) equals the marginal utility of one good divided by the marginal utility of the other good.

Utility analysis provides another way to describe consumer optimization. Recall that at the consumer's optimum, the marginal rate of substitution equals the ratio of prices. That is,

$$MRS = P_X / P_Y$$

Because the marginal rate of substitution equals the ratio of marginal utilities, we can write this condition for optimization as

$$MU_X / MU_Y = P_X / P_Y$$

Now rearrange this expression to become

$$MU_X / P_X = MU_Y / P_Y$$

This equation has a simple interpretation: At the optimum, the marginal utility per dollar spent on good X equals the marginal utility per dollar spent on good Y. (Why? If this equality did not hold, the consumer could increase utility by spending less on the good that provided lower marginal utility per dollar and more on the good that provided higher marginal utility per dollar.)

When economists discuss the theory of consumer choice, they might express the theory using different words. One economist might say that the goal of the consumer is to maximize utility. Another economist might say that the goal of the consumer is to end up on the highest possible indifference curve. The first economist would conclude that at the consumer's optimum, the marginal utility per dollar is the same for all goods, whereas the second would conclude that the indifference curve is tangent to the budget constraint. In essence, these are two ways of saying the same thing.

How Changes in Income Affect the Consumer's Choices

Now that we have seen how the consumer makes the consumption decision, let's examine how consumption responds to changes in income. To be specific, suppose that income increases. With higher income, the consumer can afford more of both goods. The increase in income, therefore, shifts the budget constraint outward, as in Figure 21.7. Because the relative price of the two goods has not changed, the slope of the new budget constraint is the same as the slope of the initial budget constraint. That is, an increase in income leads to a parallel shift in the budget constraint.

FIGURE 21.7

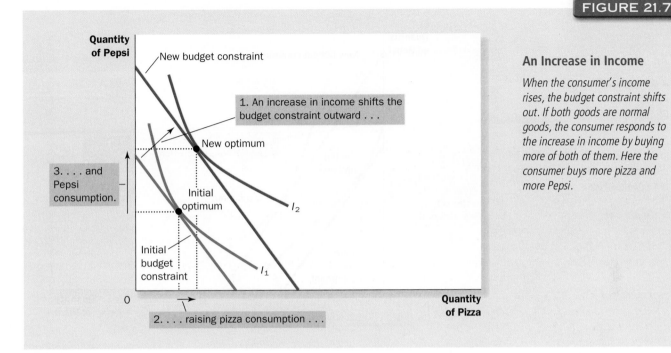

An Increase in Income

When the consumer's income rises, the budget constraint shifts out. If both goods are normal goods, the consumer responds to the increase in income by buying more of both of them. Here the consumer buys more pizza and more Pepsi.

The expanded budget constraint allows the consumer to choose a better combination of Pepsi and pizza. In other words, the consumer can now reach a higher indifference curve. Given the shift in the budget constraint and the consumer's preferences as represented by his indifference curves, the consumer's optimum moves from the point labelled "Initial optimum" to the point labelled "New optimum."

Notice that, in Figure 21.7, the consumer chooses to consume more Pepsi and more pizza. Although the logic of the model does not require increased consumption of both goods in response to increased income, this situation is the most common one. As you may recall from Chapter 4, if a consumer wants more of a good when his income rises, economists call it a **normal good**. The indifference curves in Figure 21.7 are drawn under the assumption that both Pepsi and pizza are normal goods.

Figure 21.8 shows an example in which an increase in income induces the consumer to buy more pizza but less Pepsi. If a consumer buys less of a good when his income rises, economists call it an **inferior good**. Figure 21.8 is drawn under the assumption that pizza is a normal good and Pepsi is an inferior good.

Although most goods are normal goods, there are some inferior goods in the world. One example is bus rides. High-income consumers are more likely to own cars and less likely to ride the bus than low-income consumers. Bus rides, therefore, are an inferior good.

normal good
a good for which, other things equal, an increase in income leads to an increase in demand

inferior good
a good for which, other things equal, an increase in income leads to a decrease in demand

How Changes in Prices Affect the Consumer's Choices

Let's now use this model of consumer choice to consider how a change in the price of one of the goods alters the consumer's choices. Suppose, in particular, that the

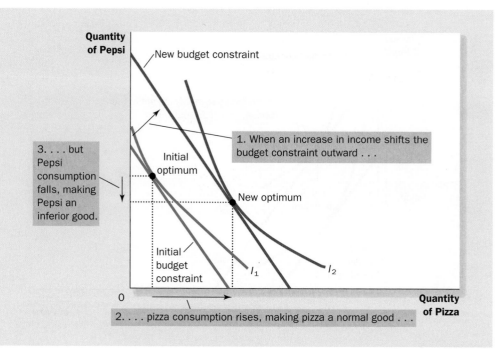

FIGURE 21.8

An Inferior Good

A good is an inferior good if the consumer buys less of it when his income rises. Here Pepsi is an inferior good: When the consumer's income increases and the budget constraint shifts outward, the consumer buys more pizza but less Pepsi.

3. . . . but Pepsi consumption falls, making Pepsi an inferior good.

1. When an increase in income shifts the budget constraint outward . . .

New budget constraint

Initial optimum

New optimum

Initial budget constraint

2. . . . pizza consumption rises, making pizza a normal good . . .

price of Pepsi falls from $2 to $1 per litre. It is no surprise that the lower price expands the consumer's set of buying opportunities. In other words, a fall in the price of any good shifts the budget constraint outward.

Figure 21.9 considers more specifically how the fall in price affects the budget constraint. If the consumer spends his entire $1000 income on pizza, then the price of Pepsi is irrelevant. Thus, point A in the figure stays the same. Yet if the consumer spends his entire income of $1000 on Pepsi, he can now buy 1000 rather than only 500 L. Thus, the end point of the budget constraint moves from point B to point D.

Notice that in this case the outward shift in the budget constraint changes its slope. (This differs from what happened previously when prices stayed the same but the consumer's income changed.) As we have discussed, the slope of the budget constraint reflects the relative price of Pepsi and pizza. Because the price of Pepsi has fallen to $1 from $2, while the price of pizza has remained at $10, the consumer can now trade a pizza for 10 L rather than 5 L of Pepsi. As a result, the new budget constraint is more steeply sloped.

How such a change in the budget constraint alters the consumption of both goods depends on the consumer's preferences. For the indifference curves drawn in this figure, the consumer buys more Pepsi and less pizza.

Income and Substitution Effects

The impact of a change in the price of a good on consumption can be decomposed into two effects: an **income effect** and a **substitution effect**. To see what these two

income effect
the change in consumption that results when a price change moves the consumer to a higher or lower indifference curve

substitution effect
the change in consumption that results when a price change moves the consumer along a given indifference curve to a point with a new marginal rate of substitution

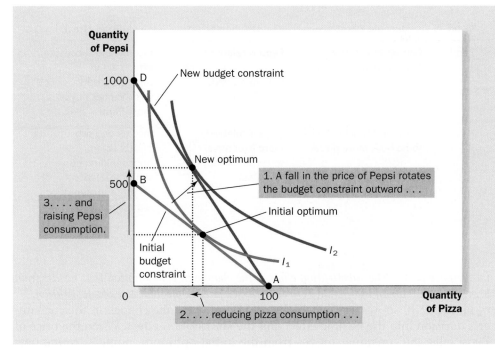

FIGURE 21.9

A Change in Price

When the price of Pepsi falls, the consumer's budget constraint shifts outward and changes slope. The consumer moves from the initial optimum to the new optimum, which changes his purchases of both Pepsi and pizza. In this case, the quantity of Pepsi consumed rises, and the quantity of pizza consumed falls.

effects are, consider how our consumer might respond when he learns that the price of Pepsi has fallen. He might reason in the following ways:

- "Great news! Now that Pepsi is cheaper, my income has greater purchasing power. I am, in effect, richer than I was. Because I am richer, I can buy both more Pepsi and more pizza." (This is the income effect.)
- "Now that the price of Pepsi has fallen, I get more litres of Pepsi for every pizza that I give up. Because pizza is now relatively more expensive, I should buy less pizza and more Pepsi." (This is the substitution effect.)

Which statement do you find more compelling?

In fact, both of these statements make sense. The decrease in the price of Pepsi makes the consumer better off. If Pepsi and pizza are both normal goods, the consumer will want to spread this improvement in his purchasing power over both goods. This income effect tends to make the consumer buy more pizza and more Pepsi. Yet, at the same time, consumption of Pepsi has become less expensive relative to consumption of pizza. This substitution effect tends to make the consumer choose more Pepsi and less pizza.

Now consider the end result of these two effects. The consumer certainly buys more Pepsi, because the income and substitution effects both act to raise purchases of Pepsi. But it is ambiguous whether the consumer buys more pizza, because the income and substitution effects work in opposite directions. This conclusion is summarized in Table 21.1.

We can interpret the income and substitution effects using indifference curves. *The income effect is the change in consumption that results from the movement to a higher*

TABLE 21.1

Income and Substitution Effects When the Price of Pepsi Falls

Good	Income Effect	Substitution Effect	Total Effect
Pepsi	Consumer is richer, so he buys more Pepsi.	Pepsi is relatively cheaper, so consumer buys more Pepsi.	Income and substitution effects act in same direction, so consumer buys more Pepsi.
Pizza	Consumer is richer, so he buys more pizza.	Pizza is relatively more expensive, so consumer buys less pizza.	Income and substitution effects act in opposite directions, so the total effect on pizza consumption is ambiguous.

indifference curve. The substitution effect is the change in consumption that results from being at a point on an indifference curve with a different marginal rate of substitution.

Figure 21.10 shows graphically how to decompose the change in the consumer's decision into the income effect and the substitution effect. When the price of Pepsi falls, the consumer moves from the initial optimum, point A, to the new optimum, point C. We can view this change as occurring in two steps. First, the consumer moves *along* the initial indifference curve I_1 from point A to point B. The consumer is equally happy at these two points, but at point B, the marginal rate of substitution reflects the new relative price. (The dashed line through point B

FIGURE 21.10

Income and Substitution Effects

The effect of a change in price can be broken down into an income effect and a substitution effect. The substitution effect—the movement along an indifference curve to a point with a different marginal rate of substitution—is shown here as the change from point A to point B along indifference curve I_1. The income effect—the shift to a higher indifference curve—is shown here as the change from point B on indifference curve I_1 to point C on indifference curve I_2.

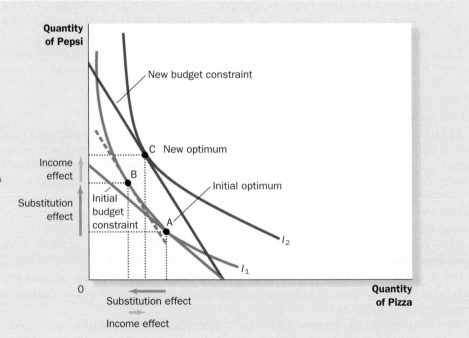

reflects the new relative price by being parallel to the new budget constraint.) Next, the consumer *shifts* to the higher indifference curve I_2 by moving from point B to point C. Even though point B and point C are on different indifference curves, they have the same marginal rate of substitution. That is, the slope of the indifference curve I_1 at point B equals the slope of the indifference curve I_2 at point C.

Although the consumer never actually chooses point B, this hypothetical point is useful to clarify the two effects that determine the consumer's decision. Notice that the change from point A to point B represents a pure change in the marginal rate of substitution without any change in the consumer's welfare. Similarly, the change from point B to point C represents a pure change in welfare without any change in the marginal rate of substitution. Thus, the movement from A to B shows the substitution effect, and the movement from B to C shows the income effect.

Deriving the Demand Curve

We have just seen how changes in the price of a good alter the consumer's budget constraint and, therefore, the quantities of the two goods that he chooses to buy. The demand curve for any good reflects these consumption decisions. Recall that a demand curve shows the quantity demanded of a good for any given price. We can view a consumer's demand curve as a summary of the optimal decisions that arise from his budget constraint and indifference curves.

For example, Figure 21.11 considers the demand for Pepsi. Panel (a) shows that when the price of a litre falls from $2 to $1, the consumer's budget constraint shifts outward. Because of both income and substitution effects, the consumer increases

FIGURE 21.11

Deriving the Demand Curve

Panel (a) shows that when the price of Pepsi falls from $2 to $1, the consumer's optimum moves from point A to point B, and the quantity of Pepsi consumed rises from 250 L to 750 L. The demand curve in panel (b) reflects this relationship between the price and the quantity demanded.

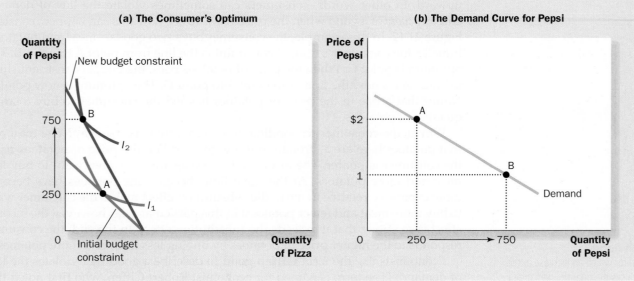

his purchases of Pepsi from 250 L to 750 L. Panel (b) shows the demand curve that results from this consumer's decisions. In this way, the theory of consumer choice provides the theoretical foundation for the consumer's demand curve.

It may be comforting to know that the demand curve arises naturally from the theory of consumer choice, but this exercise by itself does not justify developing the theory. There is no need for a rigorous, analytic framework just to establish that people respond to changes in prices. The theory of consumer choice is, however, very useful in studying various decisions that people make as they go about their lives, as we see in the next section.

QuickQuiz   Draw a budget constraint and indifference curves for Pepsi and pizza. Show what happens to the budget constraint and the consumer's optimum when the price of pizza rises. In your diagram, decompose the change into an income effect and a substitution effect.

THREE APPLICATIONS

Now that we have developed the basic theory of consumer choice, let's use it to shed light on three questions about how the economy works. These three questions might at first seem unrelated. But because each question involves household decision making, we can address it with the model of consumer behaviour we have just developed.

Do All Demand Curves Slope Downward?

Normally, when the price of a good rises, people buy less of it. Chapter 4 called this usual behaviour the *law of demand*. This law is reflected in the downward slope of the demand curve.

As a matter of economic theory, however, demand curves can sometimes slope upward. In other words, consumers can sometimes violate the law of demand and buy *more* of a good when the price rises. To see how this can happen, consider Figure 21.12. In this example, the consumer buys two goods—meat and potatoes. Initially, the consumer's budget constraint is the line from point A to point B. The optimum is point C. When the price of potatoes rises, the budget constraint shifts inward and is now the line from point A to point D. The optimum is now point E. Notice that a rise in the price of potatoes has led the consumer to buy a larger quantity of potatoes.

Why is the consumer responding in a seemingly perverse way? The reason is that potatoes here are a strongly inferior good. When the price of potatoes rises, the consumer is poorer. The income effect makes the consumer want to buy less meat and more potatoes. At the same time, because the potatoes have become more expensive relative to meat, the substitution effect makes the consumer want to buy more meat and fewer potatoes. In this particular case, however, the income effect is so strong that it exceeds the substitution effect. In the end, the consumer responds to the higher price of potatoes by buying less meat and more potatoes.

Giffen good
a good for which an increase in the price raises the quantity demanded

Economists use the term **Giffen good** to describe a good that violates the law of demand. (The term is named for economist Robert Giffen, who first noted this

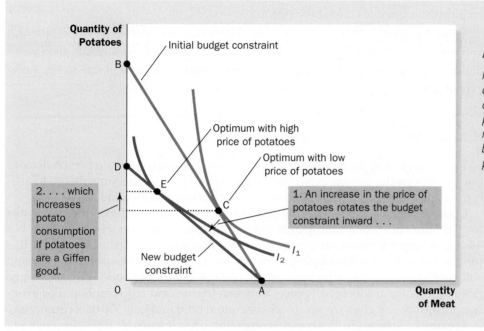

FIGURE 21.12

A Giffen Good

In this example, when the price of potatoes rises, the consumer's optimum shifts from point C to point E. In this case, the consumer responds to a higher price of potatoes by buying less meat and more potatoes.

possibility.) In this example, potatoes are a Giffen good. Giffen goods are inferior goods for which the income effect dominates the substitution effect. Therefore, they have demand curves that slope upward.

Case Study

THE SEARCH FOR GIFFEN GOODS

Have any actual Giffen goods ever been observed? Some historians suggest that potatoes were a Giffen good during the Irish potato famine of the nineteenth century. Potatoes were such a large part of people's diet that when the price of potatoes rose, it had a large income effect. People responded to their reduced living standard by cutting back on the luxury of meat and buying more of the staple food of potatoes. Thus, it is argued that a higher price of potatoes actually raised the quantity of potatoes demanded.

A study by Robert Jensen and Nolan Miller has produced similar but more concrete evidence for the existence of Giffen goods. These two economists conducted a field experiment for five months in the Chinese province of Hunan. They gave randomly selected households vouchers that subsidized the purchase of rice, a staple in local diets, and used surveys to measure how consumption of rice responded to changes in the price. They found strong evidence that poor households exhibited Giffen behaviour. Lowering the price of rice with the subsidy voucher caused households to reduce their consumption of rice, and removing the subsidy had the opposite effect.

Jensen and Miller wrote, "To the best of our knowledge, this is the first rigorous empirical evidence of Giffen behavior."

Thus, the theory of consumer choice allows demand curves to slope upward, and sometimes that strange phenomenon actually occurs. As a result, the law of demand we first saw in Chapter 4 is not completely reliable. It is safe to say, however, that Giffen goods are very rare. ●

How Do Wages Affect Labour Supply?

So far we have used the theory of consumer choice to analyze how a person decides how to allocate his income between two goods. We can use the same theory to analyze how a person decides to allocate his time between work and leisure.

Consider the decision facing Sally, a freelance software designer. Sally is awake for 100 hours per week. She spends some of this time enjoying leisure—riding her bike, watching television, studying economics, and so on. She spends the rest of this time at her computer developing software. For every hour she spends developing software, she earns $50, which she spends on consumption goods. Thus, her wage ($50) reflects the tradeoff Sally faces between leisure and consumption. For every hour of leisure she gives up, she works one more hour and gets $50 of consumption.

Figure 21.13 shows Sally's budget constraint. If she spends all 100 hours enjoying leisure, she has no consumption. If she spends all 100 hours working, she earns a weekly consumption of $5000 but has no time for leisure. If she works a normal 40-hour week, she enjoys 60 hours of leisure and has weekly consumption of $2000.

Figure 21.13 uses indifference curves to represent Sally's preferences for consumption and leisure. Here consumption and leisure are the two "goods" between which Sally is choosing. Because Sally always prefers more leisure and more consumption, she prefers points on higher indifference curves to points on lower ones. At a wage of $50 per hour, Sally chooses a combination of consumption and leisure

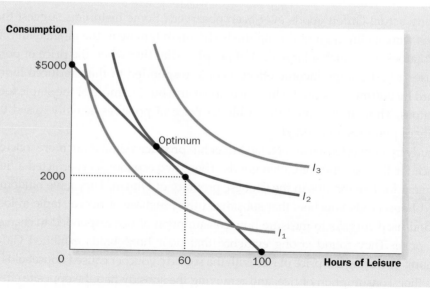

FIGURE 21.13

The Work–Leisure Decision

This figure shows Sally's budget constraint for deciding how much to work, her indifference curves for consumption and leisure, and her optimum.

represented by the point labelled "Optimum." This is the point on the budget constraint that is on the highest possible indifference curve, which is curve I_2.

Now consider what happens when Sally's wage increases from \$50 to \$60
per hour. Figure 21.14 shows two possible outcomes. In each case, the budget

FIGURE 21.14

An Increase in the Wage

The two sets of panels of this figure show how a person might respond to an increase in the wage. The graphs on the left show the consumer's initial budget constraint BC_1 and new budget constraint BC_2, as well as the consumer's optimal choices over consumption and leisure. The graphs on the right show the resulting labour supply curve. Because hours worked equal total hours available minus hours of leisure, any change in leisure implies an opposite change in the quantity of labour supplied. In panel (a), when the wage rises, consumption rises and leisure falls, resulting in a labour supply curve that slopes upward. In panel (b), when the wage rises, both consumption and leisure rise, resulting in a labour supply curve that slopes backward.

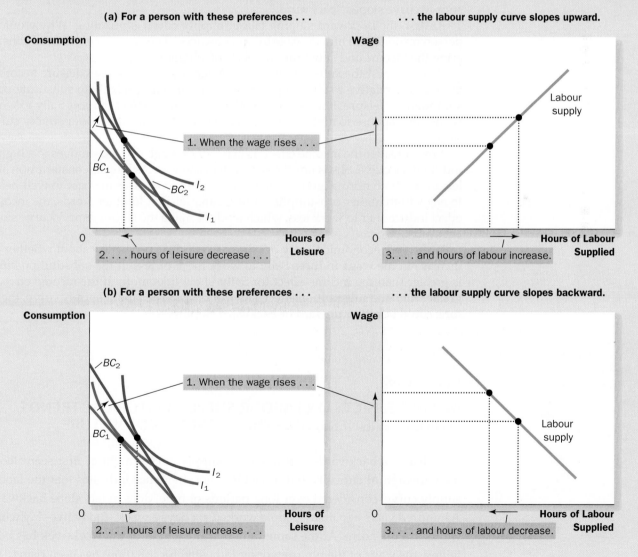

(a) For a person with these preferences . . .   **. . . the labour supply curve slopes upward.**

1. When the wage rises . . .

2. . . . hours of leisure decrease . . .   3. . . . and hours of labour increase.

(b) For a person with these preferences . . .   **. . . the labour supply curve slopes backward.**

1. When the wage rises . . .

2. . . . hours of leisure increase . . .   3. . . . and hours of labour decrease.

constraint, shown in the left-hand graph, shifts outward from BC_1 to BC_2. In the process, the budget constraint becomes steeper, reflecting the change in relative price: At the higher wage, Sally gets more consumption for every hour of leisure that she gives up.

Sally's preferences, as represented by her indifference curves, determine the resulting responses of consumption and leisure to the higher wage. In both panels, consumption rises. Yet the response of leisure to the change in the wage is different in the two cases. In panel (a), Sally responds to the higher wage by enjoying less leisure. In panel (b), Sally responds by enjoying more leisure.

Sally's decision between leisure and consumption determines her supply of labour because the more leisure she enjoys, the less time she has left to work. In each panel, the right-hand graph in Figure 21.14 shows the labour supply curve implied by Sally's decision. In panel (a), a higher wage induces Sally to enjoy less leisure and work more, so the labour supply curve slopes upward. In panel (b), a higher wage induces Sally to enjoy more leisure and work less, so the labour supply curve slopes "backward."

At first, the backward-sloping labour supply curve is puzzling. Why would a person respond to a higher wage by working less? The answer comes from considering the income and substitution effects of a higher wage.

Consider first the substitution effect. When Sally's wage rises, leisure becomes more costly relative to consumption, and this encourages Sally to substitute consumption for leisure. In other words, the substitution effect induces Sally to work harder in response to higher wages, which tends to make the labour supply curve slope upward.

Now consider the income effect. When Sally's wage rises, she moves to a higher indifference curve. She is now better off than she was. As long as consumption and leisure are both normal goods, she tends to want to use this increase in well-being to enjoy both higher consumption and greater leisure. In other words, the income effect induces her to work less, which tends to make the labour supply curve slope backward.

In the end, economic theory does not give a clear prediction about whether an increase in the wage induces Sally to work more or less. If the substitution effect is greater than the income effect for Sally, she works more. If the income effect is greater than the substitution effect, she works less. The labour supply curve, therefore, could be either upward or backward sloping.

Case Study

INCOME EFFECTS ON LABOUR SUPPLY: HISTORICAL TRENDS, LOTTERY WINNERS, AND THE CARNEGIE CONJECTURE

The idea of a backward-sloping labour supply curve might at first seem like a mere theoretical curiosity, but in fact it is not. Evidence indicates that the labour supply curve, considered over long periods of time, does in fact slope backward. A hundred years ago many people worked six days a week. Today five-day workweeks are the norm. At the same time that the length of the workweek has been falling, the wage of the typical worker (adjusted for inflation) has been rising.

Here is how economists explain this historical pattern: Over time, advances in technology raise workers' productivity and, thereby, the demand for labour. This increase in labour demand raises equilibrium wages. As wages rise, so does the reward for working. Yet rather than responding to this increased incentive by working more, most workers choose to take part of their greater prosperity in the form of more leisure. In other words, the income effect of higher wages dominates the substitution effect.

Further evidence that the income effect on labour supply is strong comes from a very different kind of data: winners of lotteries. Winners of large prizes in a lottery see large increases in their incomes and, as a result, large outward shifts in their budget constraints. Because the winners' wages have not changed, however, the *slopes* of their budget constraints remain the same. There is, therefore, no substitution effect. By examining the behaviour of lottery winners, we can isolate the income effect on labour supply.

The results from studies of lottery winners are striking. Of those winners who win more than $50 000, almost 25 percent quit working within a year, and another 9 percent reduce the number of hours they work. Of those winners who win more than $1 million, almost 40 percent stop working. The income effect on labour supply of winning such a large prize is substantial.

Similar results were found in a study, published in the May 1993 issue of the *Quarterly Journal of Economics,* of how receiving a bequest affects a person's labour supply. The study found that a single person who inherits more than $150 000 is four times as likely to stop working as a single person who inherits less than $25 000. This finding would not have surprised the nineteenth-century American industrialist Andrew Carnegie. Carnegie warned that "the parent who leaves his son enormous wealth generally deadens the talents and energies of the son, and tempts him to lead a less useful and less worthy life than he otherwise would." That is, Carnegie viewed the income effect on labour supply to be substantial and, from his paternalistic perspective, regrettable. During his life and at his death, Carnegie gave much of his vast fortune to charity. ●

"*No more 9-to-5 for me.*"

How Do Interest Rates Affect Household Saving?

An important decision that every person faces is how much income to consume today and how much to save for the future. We can use the theory of consumer choice to analyze how people make this decision and how the amount they save depends on the interest rate their savings will earn.

Consider the decision facing Sam, a worker planning ahead for retirement. To keep things simple, let's divide Sam's life into two periods. In the first period, Sam is young and working. In the second period, he is old and retired. When young, Sam earns $100 000. He divides this income between current consumption and saving. When he is old, Sam will consume what he has saved, including the interest that his savings have earned.

Suppose that the interest rate is 10 percent. Then, for every dollar that Sam saves when young, he can consume $1.10 when old. We can view "consumption when

IN THE NEWS

BACKWARD-SLOPING LABOUR SUPPLY IN KIRIBATI

In the island nation of Kiribati, when the coconut industry pays more, people spend less time working (picking coconuts) and more time enjoying leisure (fishing).

Reef Conservation Strategy Backfires

By Richard Harris

Aid organizations concerned about overfishing on tropical reefs often try to encourage fishermen out of their boats by offering them better-paying jobs on shore. But this strategy actually may make matters worse.

Take, for example, the story of Kiribati, an island nation in the central Pacific. Kiribati (pronounced KIR-a-bahs) has a simple economy. People either catch fish or they pick coconuts from their trees and produce coconut oil. Sheila Walsh, a postdoctoral researcher at Brown University, says most people do a bit of each.

The Kiribati government was concerned about overfishing. So it came up with a plan: It would subsidize the coconut oil industry.

"The thought was that by paying people more to do coconut agriculture, they would do less fishing," says Walsh. "And this would fulfill two goals: One, they would reduce overfishing; and two, people would be better off. They would have higher incomes."

Walsh wanted to know whether this plan was working, and the government invited her to study the issue. So, as part of her graduate work at the Scripps Institution of Oceanography, she flew to Kiribati to interview fishermen.

"And it turned out that, actually, the result of paying people more to do coconut agriculture was to increase fishing," she says. In fact, fishing increased by a startling 33 percent. The reef fish population dropped by an estimated 17 percent, putting the whole ecosystem at risk.

"It was a bit of a surprise, and we were wondering: What's going on here?"

The answer was simplicity itself. Walsh's study concludes that people earned more money making coconut oil, which meant they could work less to support themselves. And they spent their new leisure time fishing.

"It hit us like a bumper sticker saying—a bad day fishing is better than a good day working. And that's sort of the story here," Walsh says.

It turns out she had stumbled into a universal truth about fishing: Fishermen aren't just in it for the money. Anthropologist Richard Pollnac of the University of Rhode Island says, just think of those snazzy sport-fishing excursions.

"People pay big money to go sports-fishing," he notes. There aren't very many occupations that people will actually pay money to do in their leisure time, he says.

So fishing as an occupation provides psychic benefits, as well as money. Pollnac argues that not just individuals but whole cultures get hooked on the thrill of being out on the water, and the gamble of coming back with either a boatload or empty-handed. . . .

Walsh says she's trying to help the government figure out how to fix the problem of overfishing, which they'd accidentally made worse. Maybe, she says, the government can create new jobs out on the water by hiring the fishermen to patrol newly created nature preserves.

Source: ©2009 National Public Radio, Inc. NPR® news report titled "Reef Conservation Strategy Backfires," by Richard Harris was originally published on November 18, 2009, and is used with permission of NPR.

young" and "consumption when old" as the two goods that Sam must choose between. The interest rate determines the relative price of these two goods.

Figure 21.15 shows Sam's budget constraint. If he saves nothing, he consumes $100 000 when young and nothing when old. If he saves everything, he consumes nothing when young and $110 000 when old. The budget constraint shows these and all the intermediate possibilities.

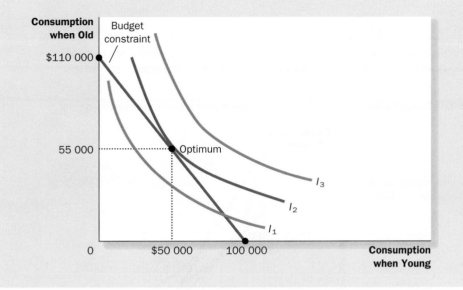

The Consumption–Saving Decision

This figure shows the budget constraint for a person deciding how much to consume in the two periods of his life, the indifference curves representing his preferences, and the optimum.

Figure 21.15 uses indifference curves to represent Sam's preferences for consumption in the two periods. Because Sam prefers more consumption in both periods, he prefers points on higher indifference curves to points on lower ones. Given his preferences, Sam chooses the optimal combination of consumption in both periods of life, which is the point on the budget constraint that is on the highest possible indifference curve. At this optimum, Sam consumes $50 000 when young and $55 000 when old.

Now consider what happens when the interest rate increases from 10 percent to 20 percent. Figure 21.16 shows two possible outcomes. In both cases, the budget constraint shifts outward and becomes steeper. At the new higher interest rate, Sam gets more consumption when old for every dollar of consumption that he gives up when young.

The two panels show different preferences for Sam and the resulting response to the higher interest rate. In both cases, consumption when old rises. Yet the response of consumption when young to the change in the interest rate is different in the two cases. In panel (a), Sam responds to the higher interest rate by consuming less when young. In panel (b), Sam responds by consuming more when young.

Sam's saving, of course, is his income when young minus the amount he consumes when young. In panel (a), consumption when young falls when the interest rate rises, so saving must rise. In panel (b), Sam consumes more when young, so saving must fall.

The case shown in panel (b) might at first seem odd: Sam responds to an increase in the return to saving by saving less. Yet this behaviour is not as peculiar as it might seem. We can understand it by considering the income and substitution effects of a higher interest rate.

Consider first the substitution effect. When the interest rate rises, consumption when old becomes less costly relative to consumption when young. Therefore, the substitution effect induces Sam to consume more when old and less when young. In other words, the substitution effect induces Sam to save more.

FIGURE 21.16

An Increase in the Interest Rate

In both panels, an increase in the interest rate shifts the budget constraint outward. In panel (a), consumption when young falls, and consumption when old rises. The result is an increase in saving when young. In panel (b), consumption in both periods rises. The result is a decrease in saving when young.

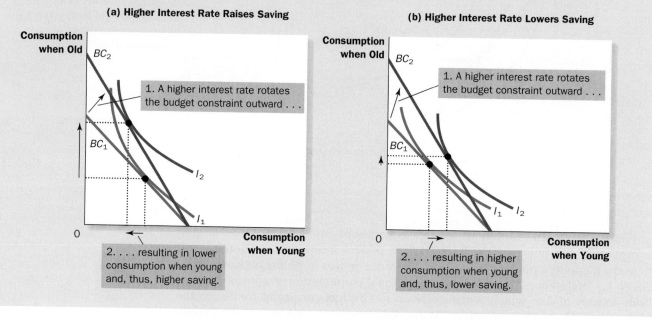

(a) Higher Interest Rate Raises Saving

Consumption when Old

BC_2

1. A higher interest rate rotates the budget constraint outward . . .

BC_1

I_2

I_1

0

Consumption when Young

2. . . . resulting in lower consumption when young and, thus, higher saving.

(b) Higher Interest Rate Lowers Saving

Consumption when Old

BC_2

1. A higher interest rate rotates the budget constraint outward . . .

BC_1

I_1 I_2

0

Consumption when Young

2. . . . resulting in higher consumption when young and, thus, lower saving.

Now consider the income effect. When the interest rate rises, Sam moves to a higher indifference curve. He is now better off than he was. As long as consumption in both periods consists of normal goods, he tends to want to use this increase in well-being to enjoy higher consumption in both periods. In other words, the income effect induces him to save less.

The end result, of course, depends on both the income and substitution effects. If the substitution effect of a higher interest rate is greater than the income effect, Sam saves more. If the income effect is greater than the substitution effect, Sam saves less. Thus, the theory of consumer choice says that an increase in the interest rate could either encourage or discourage saving.

Although this ambiguous result is interesting from the standpoint of economic theory, it is disappointing from the standpoint of economic policy. It turns out that an important issue in tax policy hinges in part on how saving responds to interest rates. Some economists have advocated reducing the taxation of interest and other capital income, arguing that such a policy change would raise the after-tax interest rate that savers can earn and would thereby encourage people to save more. Other economists have argued that because of offsetting income and substitution effects, such a tax change might not increase saving and could even reduce it. Unfortunately, research has not led to a consensus about how interest rates affect saving. As a result, there remains disagreement among economists about whether changes in tax policy aimed to encourage saving would, in fact, have the intended effect.

QuickQuiz   Explain how an increase in the wage can potentially decrease the amount that a person wants to work.

CONCLUSION: DO PEOPLE REALLY THINK THIS WAY?

The theory of consumer choice describes how people make decisions. As we have seen, it has broad applicability. It can explain how a person chooses between Pepsi and pizza, work and leisure, consumption and saving, and on and on.

At this point, however, you might be tempted to treat the theory of consumer choice with some skepticism. After all, you are a consumer. You decide what to buy every time you walk into a store. And you know that you do not decide by writing down budget constraints and indifference curves. Doesn't this knowledge about your own decision making provide evidence against the theory?

The answer is no. The theory of consumer choice does not try to present a literal account of how people make decisions. It is a model. And, as we first discussed in Chapter 2, models are not intended to be completely realistic.

The best way to view the theory of consumer choice is as a metaphor for how consumers make decisions. No consumer (except an occasional economist) goes through the explicit optimization envisioned in the theory. Yet consumers are aware that their choices are constrained by their financial resources. And, given those constraints, they do the best they can to achieve the highest level of satisfaction. The theory of consumer choice tries to describe this implicit, psychological process in a way that permits explicit, economic analysis.

The proof of the pudding is in the eating. And the test of a theory is in its applications. In the last section of this chapter we applied the theory of consumer choice to three practical issues about the economy. If you take more advanced courses in economics, you will see that this theory provides the framework for much additional analysis.

SUMMARY

- A consumer's budget constraint shows the possible combinations of different goods he can buy given his income and the prices of the goods. The slope of the budget constraint equals the relative price of the goods.
- The consumer's indifference curves represent his preferences. An indifference curve shows the various bundles of goods that make the consumer equally happy. Points on higher indifference curves are preferred to points on lower indifference curves. The slope of an indifference curve at any point is the consumer's marginal rate of substitution—the rate at which the consumer is willing to trade one good for the other.

- The consumer optimizes by choosing the point on his budget constraint that lies on the highest indifference curve. At this point, the slope of the indifference curve (the marginal rate of substitution between the goods) equals the slope of the budget constraint (the relative price of the goods).
- When the price of a good falls, the impact on the consumer's choices can be broken down into an income effect and a substitution effect. The income effect is the change in consumption that arises because a lower price makes the consumer better off. The substitution effect is the change in consumption that arises because a price change

encourages greater consumption of the good that has become relatively cheaper. The income effect is reflected in the movement from a lower to a higher indifference curve, whereas the substitution effect is reflected by a movement along an indifference curve to a point with a different slope.

- The theory of consumer choice can be applied in many situations. It can explain why demand curves can potentially slope upward, why higher wages could either increase or decrease the quantity of labour supplied, and why higher interest rates could either increase or decrease saving.

KEY CONCEPTS

budget constraint, p. 464
indifference curve, p. 466
marginal rate of
  substitution, p. 466

perfect substitutes, p. 469
perfect complements, p. 469
normal good, p. 473
inferior good, p. 473

income effect, p. 474
substitution effect, p. 474
Giffen good, p. 478

QUESTIONS FOR REVIEW

1. A consumer has income of $3000. Wine costs $3 per glass, and cheese costs $6 per kilogram. Draw the consumer's budget constraint. What is the slope of this budget constraint?

2. Draw a consumer's indifference curves for wine and cheese. Describe and explain four properties of these indifference curves.

3. Pick a point on an indifference curve for wine and cheese and show the marginal rate of substitution. What does the marginal rate of substitution tell us?

4. Show a consumer's budget constraint and indifference curves for wine and cheese. Show the optimal consumption choice. If the price of wine is $3 per glass and the price of cheese is

$6 per kilogram, what is the marginal rate of substitution at this optimum?

5. A person who consumes wine and cheese gets a raise, so his income increases from $3000 to $4000. Show what happens if both wine and cheese are normal goods. Now show what happens if cheese is an inferior good.

6. The price of cheese rises from $6 to $10 per kilogram, while the price of wine remains $3 per glass. For a consumer with a constant income of $3000, show what happens to consumption of wine and cheese. Decompose the change into income and substitution effects.

7. Can an increase in the price of cheese possibly induce a consumer to buy more cheese? Explain.

PROBLEMS AND APPLICATIONS

1. Jennifer divides her income between coffee and croissants (both of which are normal goods). An early frost in Brazil causes a large increase in the price of coffee in Canada.
   a. Show the effect of the frost on Jennifer's budget constraint.
   b. Show the effect of the frost on Jennifer's optimal consumption bundle, assuming that the substitution effect outweighs the income effect for croissants.
   c. Show the effect of the frost on Jennifer's optimal consumption bundle, assuming that

the income effect outweighs the substitution effect for croissants.

2. Compare the following two pairs of goods:
   - Coke and Pepsi
   - Skis and ski bindings

   In which case do you expect the indifference curves to be fairly straight, and in which case do you expect the indifference curves to be very bowed? In which case will the consumer respond more to a change in the relative price of the two goods?

3. Mario consumes only cheese and crackers.
   a. Could cheese and crackers both be inferior goods for Mario? Explain.
   b. Suppose that cheese is a normal good for Mario while crackers are an inferior good. If the price of cheese falls, what happens to Mario's consumption of crackers? What happens to his consumption of cheese? Explain.

4. Jim buys only milk and cookies.
   a. In 2012, Jim earns $100, milk costs $2 per litre, and cookies cost $4 per dozen. Draw Jim's budget constraint.
   b. Now suppose that all prices increase by 10 percent in 2013 and that Jim's salary increases by 10 percent as well. Draw Jim's new budget constraint. How would Jim's optimal combination of milk and cookies in 2013 compare to his optimal combination in 2012?

5. Consider your decision about how many hours to work.
   a. Draw your budget constraint assuming that you pay no taxes on your income. On the same diagram, draw another budget constraint assuming that you pay a 15 percent tax.
   b. Show how the tax might lead to more hours of work, fewer hours, or the same number of hours. Explain.

6. Sarah is awake for 100 hours per week. Using one diagram, show Sarah's budget constraints if she earns $6 per hour, $8 per hour, and $10 per hour. Now draw indifference curves such that Sarah's labour supply curve is upward sloping when the wage is between $6 and $8 per hour, and backward sloping when the wage is between $8 and $10 per hour.

7. Draw the indifference curve for someone deciding how much to work. Suppose the wage increases. Is it possible that the person's consumption would fall? Is this plausible? Discuss. (Hint: Think about income and substitution effects.)

8. The welfare system provides income to some needy families. Typically, the maximum payment goes to families that earn no income; then, as families begin to earn income, the welfare payment declines gradually and eventually disappears. Let's consider the possible effects of this program on a family's labour supply.
   a. Draw a budget constraint for a family assuming that the welfare system did not exist. On the same diagram, draw a budget constraint that reflects the existence of the welfare system.
   b. Adding indifference curves to your diagram, show how the welfare system could reduce the number of hours worked by the family. Explain, with reference to both the income and substitution effects.
   c. Using your diagram from part (b), show the effect of the welfare system on the well-being of the family.

9. Economist George Stigler once wrote that, according to consumer theory, "if consumers do not buy less of a commodity when their incomes rise, they will surely buy less when the price of the commodity rises." Explain this statement.

10. A college student has two options for meals: eating at the dining hall for $6 per meal, or eating a Cup O' Soup for $1.50 per meal. His weekly food budget is $60.
   a. Draw the budget constraint showing the tradeoff between dining hall meals and Cups O' Soup. Assuming that he spends equal amounts on both goods, draw an indifference curve showing the optimum choice. Label the optimum as point A.
   b. Suppose the price of a Cup O' Soup now rises to $2. Using your diagram from part (a), show the consequences of this change in price. Assume that our student now spends only 30 percent of his income on dining hall meals. Label the new optimum as point B.
   c. What happened to the quantity of Cups O' Soup consumed as a result of this price change? What does this result say about the income and substitution effects? Explain.
   d. Use points A and B to draw a demand curve for Cup O' Soup. What is this type of good called?

11. Consider a couple's decision about how many children to have. Assume that over a lifetime a couple has 200 000 hours of time to either work or raise children. The wage is $10 per hour. Raising a child takes 20 000 hours of time.

a. Draw the budget constraint showing the tradeoff between lifetime consumption and number of children. (Ignore the fact that children come only in whole numbers!) Show indifference curves and an optimum choice.

b. Suppose the wage increases to $12 per hour. Show how the budget constraint shifts. Using income and substitution effects, discuss the impact of the change on number of children and lifetime consumption.

c. We observe that, as societies get richer and wages rise, people typically have fewer children. Is this fact consistent with this model? Explain.

12. Five consumers have the following marginal utility of apples and pears:

	Marginal Utility of Apples	Marginal Utility of Pears
Jerry	12	6
George	6	6
Elaine	6	3
Kramer	3	6
Newman	12	3

The price of an apple is $2, and the price of a pear is $1. Which, if any, of these consumers are optimizing over their choice of fruit? For those who are not, how should they change their spending?

13. You consume only soda and pizza. One day, the price of soda goes up, the price of pizza goes down, and you are just as happy as you were before the price changes.
a. Illustrate this situation on a graph.

b. How does your consumption of the two goods change? How does your response depend on income and substitution effects?
c. Can you afford the bundle of soda and pizza you consumed before the price changes?

14. State whether each of the following statements is true or false. Explain your answers.
a. "All Giffen goods are inferior goods."
b. "All inferior goods are Giffen goods."

15. Daniel is a diligent student who loves getting As, but he also loves watching movies. Daniel is awake for 100 hours each week, and studying and watching movies are his only two activities. Daniel must study for 20 hours per week for each A he earns. Each movie is 2 hours long.
a. Draw Daniel's budget constraint that shows the tradeoff between the number of As he can receive and the number of movies he can watch. Assuming that he is happiest when he earns three As, draw an indifference curve that marks his optimal choice of studying and movie watching. How many movies does he watch each week?

With a new semester beginning, Daniel decides to get his difficult requirements out of the way. Each class now requires him to study for 25 hours per week to get an A.
b. Draw the new budget constraint on your graph. Show one possible outcome on your diagram. How will the relative strengths of the income and substitution effects determine whether Daniel makes better or worse grades and whether he watches more or fewer movies?

http:// For more study tools, please visit www.nelson.com/mankiwmicro6e.

22

FRONTIERS OF MICROECONOMICS

Sean Gladwell/GetStock.com

Learning Objectives

In this chapter, you will...

- Learn how to examine problems caused by asymmetric information

- Examine the market solutions to asymmetric information

- Consider why democratic voting systems may not represent the preferences of society

- Realize why people may not always behave as rational maximizers

Economics is a study of the choices that people make and the resulting interactions they have with one another. This study has many facets, as we have seen in the preceding chapters. Yet it would be a mistake to think that all the facets we have seen make up a finished jewel, perfect and unchanging. Like all scientists, economists are always on the lookout for new areas to study and new phenomena to explain. This final chapter on microeconomics offers an assortment of three topics at the discipline's frontier to see how economists are trying to expand their understanding of human behaviour and society.

The first topic is the economics of *asymmetric information*. In many different situations, some people are better informed than others, and the imbalance in information affects the choices they make and how they deal with one another. Thinking about this asymmetry can shed light on many aspects of the world, from the market for used cars to the custom of gift-giving.

The second topic we examine in this chapter is *political economy*. Throughout this book we have seen many examples in which markets fail and government policy can potentially improve matters. But "potentially" is a necessary qualifier: Whether this potential is realized depends on how well our political institutions work. The field of political economy applies the tools of economics to understand the functioning of government.

The third topic in this chapter is *behavioural economics*. This field brings some of the insights from psychology into the study of economic issues. It offers a view of human behaviour that is more subtle and complex than that found in conventional economic theory, a view that may be more realistic.

This chapter covers a lot of ground. To do so, it offers not a full helping of these three topics but, instead, a taste of each. One goal is to show a few of the directions economists are heading in their effort to expand knowledge of how the economy works. Another goal is to whet your appetite for more courses in economics.

ASYMMETRIC INFORMATION

"I know something you don't know." This statement is a common taunt among children, but it also conveys a deep truth about how people sometimes interact with one another. Many times in life, one person knows more about what is going on than another. A difference in access to relevant knowledge is called an *information asymmetry*.

Examples abound. A worker knows more than his employer about how much effort he puts into his job. A seller of a used car knows more than the buyer about the car's condition. The first is an example of a *hidden action*, whereas the second is an example of a *hidden characteristic*. In each case, the party in the dark (the employer, the car buyer) would like to know the relevant information, but the informed party (the worker, the car seller) may have an incentive to conceal it.

Because asymmetric information is so prevalent, economists have devoted much effort in recent decades to studying its effects. And, indeed, the 2001 Nobel Prize in economics was awarded to three economists (George Akerlof, Michael Spence, and Joseph Stiglitz) for their pioneering work on this topic. Let's discuss some of the insights that this study has revealed.

Hidden Actions: Principals, Agents, and Moral Hazard

moral hazard
the tendency of a person who is imperfectly monitored to engage in dishonest or otherwise undesirable behaviour

agent
a person who is performing an act for another person, called the *principal*

principal
a person for whom another person, called the *agent*, is performing some act

Moral hazard is a problem that arises when one person, called the **agent**, is performing some task on behalf of another person, called the **principal**. If the principal cannot perfectly monitor the agent's behaviour, the agent tends to undertake less effort than the principal considers desirable. The phrase *moral hazard* refers to the risk, or "hazard," of inappropriate or otherwise "immoral" behaviour by the agent. In such a situation, the principal tries various ways to encourage the agent to act more responsibly.

The employment relationship is the classic example. The employer is the principal, and the worker is the agent. The moral-hazard problem is the temptation of imperfectly monitored workers to shirk their responsibilities. Employers can respond to this problem in various ways:

- *Better monitoring:* Parents hiring nannies have been known to plant hidden video cameras in their homes to record the nanny's behaviour when the parents are away. The aim is to catch irresponsible behaviour.
- *High wages:* According to *efficiency-wage theories* (discussed in Chapter 19), some employers may choose to pay their workers a wage above the level that balances supply and demand in the labour market. A worker who earns an above-equilibrium wage is less likely to shirk, because if she is caught and fired, she might not be able to find another high-paying job.

- *Delayed payment:* Firms can delay part of a worker's compensation, so if the worker is caught shirking and is fired, he suffers a larger penalty. One example of delayed compensation is the year-end bonus. Similarly, a firm may choose to pay its workers more later in their lives. Thus, the wage increases that workers get as they age may reflect not just the benefits of experience but also a response to moral hazard.

Employers can use any combination of these various mechanisms to reduce the problem of moral hazard.

There are many other examples of moral hazard beyond the workplace. A homeowner with fire insurance will likely buy too few fire extinguishers because

CORPORATE MANAGEMENT

Much production in the modern economy takes place within corporations. Like other firms, corporations buy inputs in markets for the factors of production and sell their output in markets for goods and services. Also, like other firms, they are guided in their decisions by the objective of profit maximization. But a large corporation has to deal with some issues that do not arise in, say, a small family-owned business.

What is distinctive about a corporation? From a legal standpoint, a corporation is an organization that is granted a charter recognizing it as a separate legal entity, with its own rights and responsibilities, distinct from those of its owners and employees. From an economic standpoint, the most important feature of the corporate form of organization is the separation of ownership and control. One group of people, called the *shareholders*, own the corporation and share in its profits. Another group of people, called the *managers*, are employed by the corporation to make decisions about how to deploy the corporation's resources.

The separation of ownership and control creates a principal–agent problem. In this case, the shareholders are the principals, and the managers are the agents. The chief executive officer and other managers are in the best position to know the business opportunities that are available, and they are charged with the task of maximizing profit for the shareholders. But ensuring that they carry out this task is not always easy. The managers may have goals of their own, such as taking life easy, having a plush office and a private jet, throwing lavish parties, or enjoying the prestige of presiding over a large business empire. The managers' goals may not always coincide with the goal of profit maximization.

The corporation's board of directors is responsible for hiring and firing top management. The board monitors the managers' performance, and it designs their compensation packages. These packages often include incentives aimed at aligning the interest of shareholders with the interest of management. Managers might be given bonuses based on performance or options to buy the company's stock, which are more valuable if the company performs well.

Note, however, that the directors are themselves agents of the shareholders. The existence of a board overseeing management only shifts the principal–agent problem. The issue then becomes how to ensure that the board of directors fulfills its own legal obligation of acting in the best interest of the shareholders. If the directors become too friendly with management, they may not provide the required oversight.

The corporation principal–agent problem has been in the news in recent years. The top managers of several prominent companies, such as Enron, Tyco, and WorldCom, were found to be engaging in activities that enriched themselves at the expense of their shareholders. In these cases, the actions were so extreme that they were criminal, and the corporate managers were not just fired but also sent to prison. In some cases, shareholders sued directors for failing to monitor management sufficiently.

Fortunately, criminal activity by corporate managers is rare. But in some ways, it is only the tip of the iceberg. Whenever ownership and control are separated, as they are in most large corporations, there is an inevitable tension between the interests of shareholders and the interests of management.

the homeowner bears the cost of the extinguisher while the insurance company receives much of the benefit. A family may live near a river with a high risk of flooding because the family enjoys the scenic views, while the government bears the cost of disaster relief after a flood. Many regulations are aimed at addressing the problem: An insurance company may require homeowners to buy fire extinguishers, and the government may prohibit building homes on land with high risk of flooding. But the insurance company does not have perfect information about how cautious homeowners are, and the government does not have perfect information about the risk that families undertake when choosing where to live. As a result, the problem of moral hazard persists.

Hidden Characteristics: Adverse Selection and the Lemons Problem

adverse selection
the tendency for the mix of unobserved attributes to become undesirable from the standpoint of an uninformed party

Adverse selection is a problem that arises in markets where the seller knows more about the attributes of the good being sold than the buyer does. As a result, the buyer runs the risk of being sold a good of low quality. That is, the "selection" of goods being sold may be "adverse" from the standpoint of the uninformed buyer.

The classic example of adverse selection is the market for used cars. Sellers of used cars know their vehicles' defects while buyers often do not. Because owners of the worst cars are more likely to sell them than are the owners of the best cars, buyers are apprehensive about getting a "lemon." As a result, many people avoid buying vehicles in the used-car market. This lemons problem can explain why a used car only a few weeks old sells for thousands of dollars less than a new car of the same type. A buyer of the used car might surmise that the seller is getting rid of the car quickly because the seller knows something about it that the buyer does not.

A second example of adverse selection occurs in the labour market. According to another efficiency-wage theory, workers vary in their abilities, and they may know their own abilities better than do the firms that hire them. When a firm cuts the wage it pays, the more talented workers are more likely to quit, knowing they are better able to find other employment. Conversely, a firm may choose to pay an above-equilibrium wage to attract a better mix of workers.

A third example of adverse selection occurs in markets for insurance. For example, buyers of life insurance know more about their own health problems than do insurance companies. Because people with greater hidden health problems are more likely to buy life insurance than are other people, the price of life insurance reflects the costs of a sicker-than-average person. As a result, people in average health may be discouraged from buying life insurance by the high price.

When markets suffer from adverse selection, the invisible hand does not necessarily work its magic. In the used-car market, owners of good cars may choose to keep them rather than sell them at the low price that skeptical buyers are willing to pay. In the labour market, wages may be stuck above the level that balances supply and demand, resulting in unemployment. In insurance markets, buyers with low risk may choose to remain uninsured because the policies they are offered fail to reflect their true characteristics. Advocates of government-provided insurance sometimes point to the problem of adverse selection as one reason not to trust the private market to provide the right amount of insurance on its own.

Signalling to Convey Private Information

Although asymmetric information is sometimes a motivation for public policy, it also motivates some individual behaviour that otherwise might be hard to explain. Markets respond to problems of asymmetric information in many ways. One of them is **signalling**, which refers to actions taken by an informed party for the sole purpose of credibly revealing his private information.

signalling
an action taken by an informed party to reveal private information to an uninformed party

We have seen examples of signalling in previous chapters. As we saw in Chapter 16, firms may spend money on advertising to signal to potential customers that they have high-quality products. As we saw in Chapter 19, students may earn postsecondary and postgraduate degrees to signal to potential employers that they are high-ability individuals. Recall that the signalling theory of education contrasts with the human-capital theory, which asserts that education increases a person's productivity, rather than merely conveying information about innate talent. These two examples of signalling (advertising, education) may seem very different, but below the surface they are much the same: In both cases, the informed party (the firm, the student) uses the signal to convince the uninformed party (the customer, the employer) that the informed party is offering something of high quality.

What does it take for an action to be an effective signal? Obviously, it must be costly. If a signal were free, everyone would use it, and it would convey no information. For the same reason, there is another requirement: The signal must be less costly, or more beneficial, to the person with the higher-quality product. Otherwise, everyone would have the same incentive to use the signal, and the signal would reveal nothing.

Consider again our two examples. In the advertising case, a firm with a good product reaps a larger benefit from advertising because customers who try the product once are more likely to become repeat customers. Thus, it is rational for the firm with the good product to pay for the cost of the signal (advertising), and it is rational for the customer to use the signal as a piece of information about the product's quality. In the education case, a talented person can get through school more easily than a less talented one. Thus, it is rational for the talented person to pay for the cost of the signal (education), and it is rational for the employer to use the signal as a piece of information about the person's talent.

The world is replete with instances of signalling. Magazine ads sometimes include the phrase "as seen on TV." Why does a firm selling a product in a magazine choose to stress this fact? One possibility is that the firm is trying to convey its willingness to pay for an expensive signal (a spot on television) in the hope that you will infer that its product is of high quality. For the same reason, graduates of elite schools are always sure to put that fact on their résumés.

Case Study

GIFTS AS SIGNALS

A man is debating what to give his girlfriend for her birthday. "I know," he says to himself, "I'll give her cash. After all, I don't know her tastes as well as she does, and with cash, she can buy anything she wants." But when he hands her the money, she is offended. Convinced he doesn't really love her, she breaks off the relationship.

"Now we'll see how much he loves me."

Thinkstock

screening

an action taken by an uninformed party to induce an informed party to reveal information

What's the economics behind this story?

In some ways, gift-giving is a strange custom. As the man in our story suggests, people typically know their own preferences better than others do, so we might expect everyone to prefer cash to in-kind transfers. If your employer substituted merchandise for your paycheque, you would likely object to the means of payment. But your reaction is very different when someone who (you hope) loves you does the same thing.

One interpretation of gift-giving is that it reflects asymmetric information and signalling. The man in our story has private information that the girlfriend would like to know: Does he really love her? Choosing a good gift for her is a signal of his love. Certainly, picking out a gift has the right characteristics to be a signal. It is costly (it takes time), and its cost depends on the private information (how much he loves her). If he really loves her, choosing a good gift is easy because he is thinking about her all the time. If he doesn't love her, finding the right gift is more difficult. Thus, giving a gift that suits the girlfriend is one way for him to convey the private information of his love for her. Giving cash shows that he isn't even bothering to try.

The signalling theory of gift-giving is consistent with another observation: People care most about the custom when the strength of affection is most in question. Thus, giving cash to a girlfriend or boyfriend is usually a bad move. But when students receive a cheque from their parents, they are less often offended. The parents' love is less likely to be in doubt, so the recipient probably won't interpret the cash gift as a signal of lack of affection. ●

Screening to Uncover Private Information

When an informed party takes actions to reveal his private information, the phenomenon is called *signalling*. When an uninformed party takes actions to induce the informed party to reveal private information, the phenomenon is called **screening**.

Some screening is common sense. A person buying a used car may ask that it be checked by an auto mechanic before the sale. A seller who refuses this request reveals his private information that the car is a lemon. The buyer may decide to offer a lower price or to look for another car.

Other examples of screening are more subtle. For example, consider a firm that sells car insurance. The firm would like to charge a low premium to safe drivers and a high premium to risky drivers. But how can it tell them apart? Drivers know whether they are safe or risky, but the risky ones won't admit to it. A driver's history is one piece of information (which insurance companies in fact use), but because of the intrinsic randomness of car accidents, history is an imperfect indicator of future risks.

The insurance company might be able to sort out the two kinds of drivers by offering different insurance policies that would induce them to separate themselves. One policy would have a high premium and cover the full cost of any accidents that occur. Another policy would have low premiums but would have, say, a $1000 deductible. (That is, the driver would be responsible for the first $1000 of damage, and the insurance company would cover the remaining risk.) Notice that the deductible is more of a burden for risky drivers because they are more likely to have an accident. Thus, with a large enough deductible, the low-premium policy with a deductible would attract the safe drivers, while the high-premium policy without a deductible would attract the risky drivers. Faced with these two policies, the two kinds of drivers would reveal their private information by choosing different insurance policies.

Asymmetric Information and Public Policy

We have examined two kinds of asymmetric information—moral hazard and adverse selection. And we have seen how individuals may respond to the problem with signalling or screening. Now let's consider what the study of asymmetric information suggests about the proper scope of public policy.

The tension between market success and market failure is central in microeconomics. We learned in Chapter 7 that the equilibrium of supply and demand is efficient in the sense that it maximizes the total surplus that society can obtain in a market. Adam Smith's invisible hand seemed to reign supreme. This conclusion was then tempered with the study of externalities (Chapter 10), public goods (Chapter 11), imperfect competition (Chapters 15 through 17), and poverty (Chapter 20). These examples of market failure showed that government can sometimes improve market outcomes.

The study of asymmetric information gives us new reason to be wary of markets. When some people know more than others, the market may fail to put resources to their best use. People with high-quality used cars may have trouble selling them because buyers will be afraid of getting a lemon. People with few health problems may have trouble getting low-cost health insurance because insurance companies lump them together with those who have significant (but hidden) health problems.

Asymmetric information may call for government action in some cases, but three facts complicate the issue. First, as we have seen, the private market can sometimes deal with information asymmetries on its own, using a combination of signalling and screening. Second, the government rarely has more information than the private parties. Even if the market's allocation of resources is not first-best, it may be second-best. That is, when there are information asymmetries, policymakers may find it hard to improve upon the market's admittedly imperfect outcome. Third, the government is itself an imperfect institution—a topic we take up in the next section.

QuickQuiz A person who buys a life insurance policy pays a certain amount per year and receives for his family a much larger payment in the event of his death. Would you expect buyers of life insurance to have higher or lower death rates than the average person? How might this be an example of moral hazard? Of adverse selection? How might a life insurance company deal with these problems?

Case Study

ASYMMETRIC INFORMATION AND THE 2007–09 FINANCIAL CRISIS

In 2007, the world economy entered an economic and financial contraction, the likes of which had not been experienced since the Great Depression of the 1930s. Dubbed by many as the *Second Great Contraction* (the first being the Great Depression), the resulting worldwide recession left virtually no country unscathed. Canada entered recession in the fourth quarter of 2008 and emerged in the third quarter of 2009. While Canada weathered the storm much better than many other countries, over this period, gross domestic product (the total value of goods and services produced in Canada) fell by over 7 percent.

It is widely agreed that the Second Great Contraction started as a financial crisis, triggered by the subprime mortgage market in the United States. Subprime mortgages are risky mortgages issued to individuals with poor credit histories who have a high probability of default. As the crisis spread across financial institutions around the world, credit dried up and countries entered a severe recession. At the time this book was written, it seemed that the world, and in particular Canada, was slowly emerging from the recession; however, the effects of the crisis are expected to last for a long time.

While analysis of the crisis is complex, and indeed is ongoing, the presence of asymmetric information in financial markets is thought by many economists to have been an important factor exacerbating the crisis.

Indeed, the presence of asymmetric information explains in large part the very existence of financial intermediaries, such as banks. While banks offer many services—a place to safely keep your funds, along with their many other useful functions—in large part, they exist because of their ability to reduce the risks associated with asymmetric information. For example, borrowers know more about their financial condition and ability to repay loans than lenders do, which can give rise to both adverse selection (where those least able to pay back a loan are more likely to seek a loan) and moral hazard (where borrowers engage in excessive risk-taking). This makes lending money directly to borrowers a risky proposition. Banks and other financial intermediaries possess specialized expertise in analyzing and assessing risk and in monitoring lenders, which reduces both adverse selection and moral hazard in financial markets. That is why you might be more inclined to give your money to a bank, which in turn lends the money to consumers and companies, rather than lending the money directly to borrowers yourself.

While the underlying causes of the financial crisis are still being debated, some economists have argued that, leading up to the crisis, the financial sector did not manage very well the risks associated with asymmetric information. The argument is that the emergence of several innovations in the financial sector and the growth of so-called "shadow banking institutions" (such as investment banks and hedge funds), which were heavily involved in them, resulted in a weakening of the traditional assessment and monitoring activities of financial institutions.

One such innovation, called *securitization* or *asset-backed securities*, involves the bundling together of loans, such as mortgages, into a security that is then sold to a third party, who can in turn sell it to another party or bundle it with other securities to form yet another security, and on and on. In the recent financial crisis, as the mortgages underlying these securities became farther removed from the original face-to-face lender–borrower arrangement, it is argued that the problem of asymmetric information concerning the risk associated with the underlying assets became worse. Many of these asset-backed securities were backed by high-risk subprime mortgages.

Leading into the crisis, investment banks such as Bear Stearns and Lehman Brothers in the United States were heavily involved in asset-backed securities. Investment banks are nondeposit-taking institutions that underwrite and trade securities, and issue financial advice to companies and governments, among other things. These institutions are not subject to the same regulatory scrutiny as deposit-taking banks. In 2008, after receiving an emergency loan from the U.S. Federal Reserve (the U.S. central bank), Bear Stearns was bought by JPMorgan Chase for a fraction of its pre-crisis value; Lehman Brothers went bankrupt. The collapse of Bear Stearns and Lehman Brothers has come to epitomize the financial crisis.

It has also been argued that financial institutions faced strong incentives to engage in risky behaviour because of the nature of the compensation schemes for their employees: a type of moral hazard. For example, financial sector bonuses tied to returns with no downside in the event of default encouraged riskier and riskier behaviour on the part of employees. As a result of this, some analysts have called for greater, and better, regulation of financial institutions, their activities, and their compensation schemes.

Finally, it has also been strongly suggested that the reaction of governments to the crisis—and in particular the bailout of financial institutions and, in the United States and Canada, car manufacturers—generated a type of moral hazard. The idea here is that knowing that the government will bail you out gives you little incentive to manage your risks prudently. The unprecedented government bail-outs associated with the crisis may thus have set the stage for problems down the road as companies and financial institutions that are considered "too big to fail" engaged in riskier behaviour.

The repercussions of the financial and economic crisis are likely to be long-lasting. While there is some disagreement over the form that subsequent policies should take to minimize the chance of similar events in the future, an understanding of the role of asymmetric information will be front and centre. •

POLITICAL ECONOMY

As we have seen, markets left on their own do not always reach a desirable allocation of resources. When we judge the market's outcome to be either ineffi-cient or inequitable, there may be a role for the government to step in and improve the situation. Yet before we embrace an activist government, we need to consider one more fact: The government is also an imperfect institution. The field of *political economy* (sometimes called the field of *public choice*) applies the methods of economics to study how government works.

The Condorcet Voting Paradox

Most advanced societies rely on democratic principles to set government policy. When a city is deciding between two locations to build a new park, for example, we have a simple way to choose: The majority gets its way. Yet, for most policy

TABLE 22.1

The Condorcet Paradox

If voters have these preferences over outcomes A, B, and C, then in pairwise majority voting, A beats B, B beats C, and C beats A.

	Voter Type		
	Type 1	Type 2	Type 3
Percentage of electorate	35	45	20
First choice	A	B	C
Second choice	B	C	A
Third choice	C	A	B

issues, the number of possible outcomes far exceeds two. A new park, for instance, could be placed in many possible locations. In this case, as the eighteenth-century French political theorist Marquis de Condorcet famously noted, democracy might run into some problems trying to choose one of the outcomes.

For example, suppose there are three possible outcomes, labelled A, B, and C, and there are three voter types with the preferences shown in Table 22.1. The mayor of our town wants to aggregate these individual preferences into preferences for society as a whole. How should she do it?

At first, she might try some pairwise votes. If she asks voters to choose first between B and C, voter types 1 and 2 will vote for B, giving B the majority. If she then asks voters to choose between A and B, voter types 1 and 3 will vote for A, giving A the majority. Observing that A beats B, and B beats C, the mayor might conclude that A is the voters' clear choice.

But wait: Suppose the mayor then asks voters to choose between A and C. In this case, voter types 2 and 3 vote for C, giving C the majority. That is, under pairwise majority voting, A beats B, B beats C, and C beats A. Normally, we expect preferences to exhibit a property called *transitivity:* If A is preferred to B, and B is preferred to C, then we would expect A to be preferred to C. The **Condorcet paradox** is that democratic outcomes do not always obey this property. Pairwise voting might produce transitive preferences for a society, depending on the pattern of individual preferences, but as our example in the table shows, it cannot be counted on to do so.

One implication of the Condorcet paradox is that the order in which things are voted on can affect the result. If the mayor suggests choosing first between A and B and then comparing the winner to C, the town ends up choosing C. But if the voters choose first between B and C and then compare the winner to A, the town ends up with A. And if the voters choose first between A and C and then compare the winner to B, the town ends up with B.

There are two lessons to be learned from the Condorcet paradox. The narrow lesson is that when there are more than two options, setting the agenda (that is, deciding the order in which items are voted) can have a powerful impact on the outcome of a democratic election. The broad lesson is that majority voting by itself does not tell us what outcome a society really wants.

Condorcet paradox
the failure of majority rule to produce transitive preferences for society

Arrow's Impossibility Theorem

Since political theorists first noticed Condorcet's paradox, they have spent much energy studying voting systems and proposing new ones. For example, as an alternative to pairwise majority voting, the mayor of our town could ask each voter to rank the possible outcomes. For each voter, we could give 1 point for last place, 2 points for second to last, 3 points for third to last, and so on. The outcome that receives the most total points wins. With the preferences in Table 22.1, outcome B is the winner. (You can do the arithmetic yourself.) This voting method is called a *Borda count*, for the eighteenth-century French mathematician and political scientist who devised it. It is often used in polls that rank sports teams.

Is there a perfect voting system? Economist Kenneth Arrow took up this question in his 1951 book, *Social Choice and Individual Values*. Arrow started by defining what a perfect voting system would be. He assumes that individuals in society have preferences over the various possible outcomes: A, B, C, and so on. He then assumes that society wants a voting scheme to choose among these outcomes that satisfies several properties:

- *Unanimity:* If everyone prefers A to B, then A should beat B.
- *Transitivity:* If A beats B, and B beats C, then A should beat C.
- *Independence of irrelevant alternatives:* The ranking between any two outcomes A and B should not depend on whether some third outcome C is also available.
- *No dictators:* No person always gets his or her way, regardless of everyone else's preferences.

These all seem like desirable properties for a voting system to have. Yet Arrow proved, mathematically and incontrovertibly, that *no voting system can satisfy all of these properties*. This amazing result is called **Arrow's impossibility theorem**.

The mathematics needed to prove Arrow's theorem is beyond the scope of this book, but we can get some sense of why the theorem is true from a couple of examples. We have already seen the problem with the method of majority rule. The Condorcet paradox shows that majority rule fails to produce a ranking among the outcomes that always satisfies transitivity.

As another example, the Borda count fails to satisfy the independence of irrelevant alternatives. Recall that, using the preferences in Table 22.1, outcome B wins with a Borda count. But suppose that suddenly C disappears as an alternative. If the Borda count method is applied only to outcomes A and B, then A wins. (Once again, you can do the arithmetic on your own.) Thus, eliminating alternative C changes the ranking between A and B. The reason for this change is that the result of the Borda count depends on the number of points that A and B receive, and the number of points depends on whether the irrelevant alternative, C, is also available.

Arrow's impossibility theorem is a deep and disturbing result. It doesn't say that we should abandon democracy as a form of government. But it does say that, no matter what voting scheme society adopts for aggregating the preferences of its members, in some way it will be flawed as a mechanism for social choice.

Arrow's impossibility theorem
a mathematical result showing that, under certain assumed conditions, there is no scheme for aggregating individual preferences into a valid set of social preferences

The Median Voter Is King

Despite Arrow's theorem, voting is how most societies choose their leaders and public policies, often by majority rule. The next step in studying government is

FIGURE 22.1

The Median Voter Theorem: An Example

This bar chart shows how 100 voters' most-preferred budget is distributed over five options, ranging from zero to $20 billion. If society makes its choice by majority rule, the median voter (who here prefers $10 billion) determines the outcome.

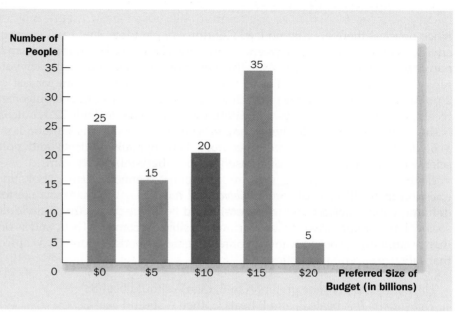

median voter theorem
a mathematical result showing that if voters are choosing a point along a line and each voter wants the point closest to his most preferred point, then majority rule will pick the most preferred point of the median voter

to examine how governments run by majority rule work. That is, in a democratic society, who determines what policy is chosen? In some cases, the theory of democratic government yields a surprisingly simple answer.

Let's consider an example. Imagine that society is deciding on how much money to spend on some public good, such as the CBC. Each voter has his own most preferred budget, and he always prefers outcomes closer to his most preferred value to outcomes further away. Thus, we can line up voters from those who prefer the smallest budget to those who prefer the largest. Figure 22.1 is an example. Here there are 100 voters, and the budget size varies from zero to $20 billion. Given these preferences, what outcome would you expect democracy to produce?

According to a famous result called the **median voter theorem**, majority rule will produce the outcome most preferred by the median voter. The *median voter* is the voter exactly in the middle of the distribution. In this example, if you take the line of voters ordered by their preferred budgets and count 50 voters from either end of the line, you will find that the median voter wants a budget of $10 billion. By contrast, the average preferred outcome (calculated by adding the preferred outcomes and dividing by the number of voters) is $9 billion, and the modal outcome (the one preferred by the greatest number of voters) is $15 billion.

The median voter rules the day because his preferred outcome beats any other proposal in a two-way race. In our example, more than half of the voters want $10 billion or more, and more than half want $10 billion or less. If someone proposes, say, $8 billion instead of $10 billion, everyone who prefers $10 billion or more will vote with the median voter. Similarly, if someone proposes $12 billion instead of $10 billion, everyone who wants $10 billion or less will vote with the median voter. In either case, the median voter has more than half of the voters on his side.

What about the Condorcet voting paradox? It turns out that when the voters are picking a point along a line and each voter aims for his own most preferred point, the Condorcet paradox cannot arise. The median voter's most preferred outcome beats all challengers.

One implication of the median voter theorem is that if each of two political parties is trying to maximize its chance of election, they will both move their positions toward the median voter. Suppose, for example, that the Liberal party advocates a budget of $15 billion, while the Conservative party advocates a budget of $10 billion. The Liberal position is more popular in the sense that $15 billion has more proponents than any other single choice. Nonetheless, the Conservative party gets more than 50 percent of the vote: It will attract the 20 voters who want $10 billion, the 15 voters who want $5 billion, and the 25 voters who want zero. If the Liberals want to win, they will move their platform toward the median voter. Thus, this theory can explain why the parties in a two-party system are similar to each other: They are both moving toward the median voter.

Another implication of the median voter theorem is that minority views are not given much weight. Imagine that 40 percent of the population wants a lot of money spent on the national parks, and 60 percent wants nothing spent. In this case, the median voter's preference is zero, regardless of the intensity of the minority's view. Such is the logic of democracy. Rather than reaching a compromise that takes into account everyone's preferences, majority rule looks only to the person in the exact middle of the distribution.

Politicians Are People, Too

When economists study consumer behaviour, they assume that consumers buy the bundle of goods and services that gives them the greatest level of satisfaction. When economists study firm behaviour, they assume that firms produce the quantity of goods and services that yields the greatest level of profits. What should they assume when they study people involved in the practice of politics?

Politicians also have objectives. It would be nice to assume that political leaders are always looking out for the well-being of society as a whole, that they are aiming for an optimal combination of efficiency and equity. Nice, perhaps, but not realistic. Self-interest is as powerful a motive for political actors as it is for consumers and firm owners. Some politicians, motivated by desire for reelection, are willing to sacrifice the national interest to solidify their base of voters. Other politicians are motivated by simple greed. If you have any doubt, you should look at the world's poor nations, where corruption among government officials is a common impediment to economic development.

This book is not the place to develop a theory of political behaviour. That topic is best left to the political scientists. But when thinking about economic policy, remember that this policy is made not by a benevolent king, but by real people with their own all-too-human desires. Sometimes they are motivated to further the national interest, but sometimes they are motivated by their own political and financial ambitions. We shouldn't be surprised when economic policy fails to resemble the ideals derived in economics textbooks.

QuickQuiz   A school district is voting on the school budget and the resulting student–teacher ratio. A poll finds that 35 percent of the voters want a ratio of 9:1, 25 percent want a ratio of 10:1, and 40 percent want a ratio of 12:1. What outcome would you expect the district to end up with?

BEHAVIOURAL ECONOMICS

Economics is a study of human behaviour, but it is not the only field that can make that claim. The social science of psychology also sheds light on the choices that people make in their lives. The fields of economics and psychology usually proceed independently, in part because they address a different range of questions. But recently a field called *behavioural economics* has emerged in which economists are making use of basic psychological insights. Let's consider some of these insights here.

People Aren't Always Rational

Economic theory is populated by a particular species of organism, sometimes called *Homo economicus.* Members of this species are always rational. As firm managers, they maximize profits. As consumers, they maximize utility (or, equivalently, pick the point on the highest indifference curve). Given the constraints they face, they rationally weigh all the costs and benefits and always choose the best possible course of action.

Real people, however, are *Homo sapiens.* Although in many ways they resemble the rational, calculating people assumed in economic theory, they are far more complex. They can be forgetful, impulsive, confused, emotional, and shortsighted. These imperfections of human reasoning are the bread-and-butter of psychologists, but until recently, economists have neglected them.

Herbert Simon, one of the first social scientists to work at the boundary of economics and psychology, suggested that humans should be viewed not as rational maximizers but as *satisficers.* Rather than always choosing the best course of action, they make decisions that are merely good enough. Similarly, other economists have suggested that humans are only "near rational" or that they exhibit "bounded rationality."

Studies of human decision making have tried to detect systematic mistakes that people make. Here are a few of the findings:

- *People are overconfident.* Imagine that you were asked some numerical questions, such as the number of African countries in the United Nations, the height of the tallest mountain in North America, and so on. Instead of being asked for a single estimate, however, you were asked to give a 90 percent confidence interval—a range such that you were 90 percent confident the true number falls within it. When psychologists run experiments like this, they find that most people give ranges that are too small: The true number falls within their intervals far less than 90 percent of the time. That is, most people are too sure of their own abilities.
- *People give too much weight to a small number of vivid observations.* Imagine that you are thinking about buying a car of brand X. To learn about its reliability, you read *Consumer Reports,* which has surveyed 1000 owners of car X. Then you run into a friend who owns car X, and she tells you that her car is a lemon. How do you treat your friend's observation? If you think rationally, you will realize that she has increased your sample size only from 1000 to 1001, which does not provide much new information. But because your friend's story is so vivid, you may be tempted to give it more weight in your decision making than you should.
- *People are reluctant to change their minds.* People tend to interpret evidence to confirm beliefs they already hold. In one study, subjects were asked to read and evaluate a research report on whether capital punishment deters crime.

After reading the report, those who initially favoured the death penalty said they were more sure in their view, and those who initially opposed the death penalty also said they were more sure in their view. The two groups interpreted the same evidence in exactly opposite ways.

Think about decisions you have made in your own life. Do you exhibit some of these traits?

A hotly debated issue is whether deviations from rationality are important for understanding economic phenomena. An intriguing example arises in the study of tax-advantaged retirement savings accounts that some firms offer their workers. In some firms, workers can choose to participate in the plan by filling out a simple form. In other firms, workers are automatically enrolled and can opt out of the plan by filling out a simple form. It turns out many more workers participate in the second case than in the first. If workers were perfectly rational maximizers, they would choose the optimal amount of retirement saving, regardless of the default offered by their employer. In fact, workers' behaviour appears to exhibit substantial inertia. Understanding their behaviour seems easier once we abandon the model of rational man.

Why, you might ask, is economics built on the rationality assumption when psychology and common sense cast doubt on it? One answer is that the assumption, even if not exactly true, is still a good approximation. For example, when we studied the differences between competitive and monopoly firms, the assumption that firms rationally maximize profit yielded many important and valid insights. Recall from

IN THE NEWS

BEHAVIOURAL ECONOMICS AND FACEBOOK

This article was written prior to the Facebook initial public offering (IPO) of its stock on Friday, May 18, 2012. It proved to be remarkably prescient. The IPO price was $38. On the Friday of the IPO, the stock reached as high as $45, but closed at roughly the IPO price of $38. On the following Monday, the decline began, as the stock closed at just over $34. At the time of writing (September 5, 2012), the stock was trading at $18.58.

Facebook IPO Meets Behavioral Economics

By John Wasik

You may be smitten with the Facebook story and debating whether or not to buy stock when the company goes public. But if you haven't studied the history of IPOs, you may be jumping into the purchase with unrealistic expectations and flawed biases.

While many of those allocated shares early on will likely prosper—or be able to sell quickly at a profit after an immediate run-up—the rest of us might not fare as well.

The company may raise up to $10.6 billion, an amount that would beat the debuts of tech giant Google Inc. while giving it a total stock market value that exceeds Amazon.com. Facebook has indicated an initial public offering (IPO) per-share range of $28 to $35, pegging the potential value of the company at $77 billion to $96 billion.

But when an IPO scores big on its first day, data shows that's not a leading indicator as to how it performs in the future.

"With the exception of IPOs from 1999–2000, there is no reliable relation between first-day returns and the subsequent three-year return," says Jay Ritter, a professor of finance at the University of Florida who has been studying IPO results and updates a database on their performance.

Even if Facebook soars immediately to a market cap of $150 billion or more, there are warning signs ahead, says Ritter: "further upside potential is severely limited."

And if Facebook grows significantly over time, like Apple? Just based on the historical record of IPOs, there are no guarantees.

Looking at three-year buy-and-hold periods, and comparing them to the larger market, IPO investors made a meager market-adjusted total return of 2 percent from 2001-2010, reports Ritter.

Going back even further, the buy-and-holders did much worse with IPOs when compared to the larger market, as measured by the S&P 500 index including dividends and capital gains. They lost almost 32 percent from 1999-2000; dropped 34 percent from 1995-1998; and declined almost 23 percent from 1980–1989. Remember, these were the golden-fleece days of IPOs, which peaked at 675 offerings in 1996. All told, IPO holders lost about 20 percent in market-adjusted returns from 1980 through 2010, Ritter found.

That then brings us into the realm of behavioral economics, an emerging science that examines how irrational and overconfident we can be. We all love a good story—especially about the stocks that we buy. That hard-wired predilection, though, may prevent us from analyzing past history and accepting the reality that many tech stocks are duds down the road (Pets.com ring a bell?).

I asked Prof. Daniel Kahneman, Nobel laureate in economics and author of the classic "Thinking Fast and Slow" about how investors should regard a new stock like Facebook. While he declined to predict how the company will fare, he suggested looking at the histories of previous stock offerings and their competitors.

In his research, Prof. Kahneman, one of the godfathers of behavioral economics, has discovered that not only do investors tend to be overconfident about their investment choices, they make decisions too quickly based on intuition, which is often wrong. We may fixate upon a number—such as a stock price—and "anchor" it in our minds as something that's obtainable, even though it may be unrealistic. Then we may fool ourselves into thinking that we can predict how well a stock or the general market may do. On top of that, most of us are born optimists.

"People don't know the boundaries of their expertise," Kahneman said. "We live in a subjective world and can't separate what we can forecast from what we can't."

To make our decision making even more complicated, a part of our brains

Kahneman calls "System One" creates a "coherent" view of an event that suppresses any ambiguities or other interpretations.

In the case of Facebook, the story of a Harvard undergrad creating a tech colossus has a satisfactory sweetness to it. There's no question that Facebook is one of the most-anticipated public offerings in recent memory. With 900 million signed up to the service and growing—I'm an avid user—it's undeniably one of the most powerful and addictive forms of social media on the planet. Founder Mark Zuckerberg may be our era's Alexander Graham Bell.

But what about the competition? Can the company sustain its growth and gain advertising? Skepticism often gets sidetracked when System One is ruling.

Ultimately, though, despite their magical powers, tech stocks are subject to the laws of supply and demand, earnings, competition and ever-fickle market sentiment. If we can look ourselves in the mirror and admit that, then having honest face time with a Facebook purchase may erase some future worry lines.

Chapter 2 that economic models are not meant to replicate reality but are supposed to show the essence of the problem at hand as an aid to understanding.

Another reason that economists so often assume rationality may be that economists are themselves not rational maximizers. Like most people, they are overconfident, and they are reluctant to change their minds. Their choice among alternative theories of human behaviour may exhibit excessive inertia. Moreover, economists may be content with a theory that is not perfect but is good enough. The model of rational man may be the theory of choice for a satisficing social scientist.

People Care About Fairness

Another insight about human behaviour is best illustrated with an experiment called the *ultimatum game*. The game works like this: Two volunteers (who are otherwise strangers to each other) are told that they are going to play a game and could win a total of $100. Before they play, they learn the rules. The game begins with a coin flip, which is used to assign the volunteers to the roles of player A and player B. Player A's job is to propose a division of the $100 prize between himself and the other player. After player A makes his proposal, player B decides whether to accept or reject it. If he accepts it, both players are paid according to the proposal. If player B rejects the proposal, both players walk away with nothing. In either case, the game then ends.

Before proceeding, stop and think about what you would do in this situation. If you were player A, what division of the $100 would you propose? If you were player B, what proposals would you accept?

Conventional economic theory assumes in this situation that people are rational wealth-maximizers. This assumption leads to a simple prediction: Player A should propose that he gets $99 and player B gets $1, and player B should accept the proposal. After all, once the proposal is made, player B is better off accepting it as long as he gets something out of it. Moreover, because player A knows that accepting the proposal is in player's B interest, player A has no reason to offer him more than $1. In the language of game theory (discussed in Chapter 17), the 99–1 split is the Nash equilibrium.

Yet when experimental economists ask real people to play the ultimatum game, the results are very different from this prediction. People in the role of player B usually reject proposals that give them only $1 or a similarly small amount. Knowing this, people in the role of player A usually propose giving player B much more than $1. Some people will offer a 50–50 split, but it is more common for player A to propose giving player B an amount such as $30 or $40, keeping the larger share for himself. In this case, player B usually accepts the proposal.

What's going on here? The natural interpretation is that people are driven in part by some innate sense of fairness. A 99–1 split seems so wildly unfair to many people that they reject it, even to their own detriment. By contrast, a 70–30 split is still unfair, but it is not so unfair that it induces people to abandon their normal self-interest.

Throughout our study of household and firm behaviour, the innate sense of fairness has not played any role. But the results of the ultimatum game suggest that perhaps it should. For example, in Chapters 18 and 19 we discussed how wages were determined by labour supply and labour demand. Some economists have suggested that the perceived fairness of what a firm pays its workers should also enter the picture. Thus, when a firm has an especially profitable year, workers (like player B) may expect to be paid a fair share of the prize, even if the standard equilibrium does not dictate it. The firm (like player A) might well decide to give workers more than the equilibrium wage for fear that the workers might otherwise try to punish the firm with reduced effort, strikes, or even vandalism.

People Are Inconsistent over Time

Imagine some dreary task, such as doing your laundry, shovelling snow off your driveway, or filling out your income tax forms. Now consider the following questions:

1. Would you prefer (A) to spend 50 minutes doing the task immediately or (B) to spend 60 minutes doing the task tomorrow?
2. Would you prefer (A) to spend 50 minutes doing the task in 90 days or (B) to spend 60 minutes doing the task in 91 days?

When asked questions like these, many people choose B to question 1 and A to question 2. When looking ahead to the future (as in question 2), they minimize the amount of time spent on the dreary task. But faced with the prospect of doing the task immediately (as in question 1), they choose to put it off.

In some ways, this behaviour is not surprising: Everyone procrastinates from time to time. But from the standpoint of the theory of rational man, it is puzzling. Suppose that, in response to question 2, a person chooses to spend 50 minutes in 90 days. Then, when the 90th day arrives, we allow him to change his mind. In effect, he then faces question 1, so he opts for doing the task the next day. But why should the mere passage of time affect the choices he makes?

Many times in life, people make plans for themselves, but then they fail to follow through. A smoker promises herself that she will quit, but within a few hours of smoking her last cigarette, she craves another and breaks her promise. A person trying to lose weight promises that he will stop eating dessert, but when the waiter brings the dessert cart, the promise is forgotten. In both cases, the desire for instant gratification induces the decision maker to abandon his own past plans.

Some economists believe that the consumption–saving decision is an important instance where people exhibit this inconsistency over time. For many people, spending provides a type of instant gratification. Saving, like passing up the cigarette or the dessert, requires a sacrifice in the present for a reward in the distant future. And just as many smokers wish they could quit and many overweight individuals wish they ate less, many consumers wish they saved more. According to one survey, more than 50 percent of Canadians were concerned that they were not saving enough for retirement.

An implication of this inconsistency over time is that people should try to find ways to commit their future selves to following through on their plans. A smoker trying to quit may throw away her cigarettes, and a person on a diet may put a lock on the refrigerator. What can a person who saves too little do? He should find some way to lock up his money before he spends it. Some retirement accounts, such as retirement saving plans, do exactly that. A worker can agree to have some money taken out of his paycheque before he ever sees it. The money is deposited in an account that can be used before retirement only with a penalty. Perhaps that is one reason why these retirement accounts are so popular: They protect people from their own desires for instant gratification.

QuickQuiz   Describe at least three ways in which human decision making differs from that of the rational individual of conventional economic theory.

CONCLUSION

This chapter has examined the frontier of microeconomics. You may have noticed that we have sketched out ideas rather than fully developing them. This is no accident. One reason is that you might study these topics in more detail in advanced courses. Another reason is that these topics remain active areas of research and, therefore, are still being fleshed out.

To see how these topics fit into the broader picture, recall the ten principles of economics from Chapter 1. One principle states that markets are usually a good way to organize economic activity. Another principle states that governments can sometimes improve market outcomes. As you study economics, you can more fully appreciate the truth of these principles as well as the caveats that go with them. The study of asymmetric information should make you more wary of market outcomes. The study of political economy should make you more wary of government solutions. And the study of behavioural economics should make you wary of any institution that relies on human decision making—including both the market and the government.

If there is a unifying theme to these topics, it is that life is messy. Information is imperfect, government is imperfect, and people are imperfect. Of course, you knew this long before you started studying economics, but economists need to understand these imperfections as precisely as they can if they are to explain, and perhaps even improve, the world around them.

SUMMARY

- In many economic transactions, information is asymmetric. When there are hidden actions, principals may be concerned that agents suffer from the problem of moral hazard. When there are hidden characteristics, buyers may be concerned about the problem of adverse selection among the sellers. Private markets sometimes deal with asymmetric information with signalling and screening.

- Although government policy can sometimes improve market outcomes, governments are themselves imperfect institutions. The Condorcet paradox shows that majority rule fails to produce transitive preferences for society, and Arrow's impossibility theorem shows that no

voting scheme will be perfect. In many situations, democratic institutions will produce the outcome desired by the median voter, regardless of the preferences of the rest of the electorate. Moreover, the individuals who set government policy may be motivated by self-interest rather than the national interest.

- The study of psychology and economics reveals that human decision making is more complex than is assumed in conventional economic theory. People are not always rational, they care about the fairness of economic outcomes (even to their own detriment), and they can be inconsistent over time.

KEY CONCEPTS

moral hazard, p. 492
agent, p. 492
principal, p. 492
adverse selection, p. 494

signalling, p. 495
screening, p. 496
Condorcet paradox, p. 500

Arrow's impossibility
 theorem, p. 501
median voter theorem, p. 502

QUESTIONS FOR REVIEW

1. What is moral hazard? List three things an employer might do to reduce the severity of this problem.

2. What is adverse selection? Give an example of a market in which adverse selection might be a problem.

3. Define *signalling* and *screening,* and give an example of each.

4. What unusual property of voting did Condorcet notice?

5. Explain why majority rule respects the preferences of the median voter rather than the average voter.

6. Describe the ultimatum game. What outcome from this game would conventional economic theory predict? Do experiments confirm this prediction? Explain.

PROBLEMS AND APPLICATIONS

1. Each of the following situations involves moral hazard. In each case, identify the principal and the agent, and explain why there is asymmetric information. How does the action described reduce the problem of moral hazard?
   a. Landlords require tenants to pay security deposits.
   b. Firms compensate top executives with options to buy company stock at a given price in the future.
   c. Car insurance companies offer discounts to customers who install antitheft devices in their cars.

2. Suppose that the Live-Long-and-Prosper Life Insurance Company charges $5000 annually for an insurance policy. The company's president suggests that the company raise the annual price to $6000 in order to increase its profits. If the firm followed this suggestion, what economic problem might arise? Would the firm's pool of customers tend to become more or less healthy on average? Would the company's profits necessarily increase?

3. A case study in this chapter describes how a boyfriend can signal to a girlfriend that he loves her by giving an appropriate gift. Do you think saying "I love you" can also serve as a signal? Why or why not?

4. Some AIDS activists believe that life insurance companies should not be allowed to ask applicants if they are infected with the HIV virus that causes AIDS. Would this rule help or hurt those who are HIV-positive? Would it help or hurt those who are not HIV-positive? Would it exacerbate or mitigate the problem of adverse selection in the market for life insurance? Do you think it would increase or decrease the number of people without life insurance? In your opinion, would this be a good policy?

5. The government is considering two ways to help the needy: giving them cash, or giving them free meals at soup kitchens. Give an argument for giving cash. Give an argument, based on asymmetric information, for why the soup kitchen may be better than the cash handout.

6. Ken walks into an ice-cream parlour.

   WAITER: We have vanilla and chocolate today.
   KEN: I'll take vanilla.
   WAITER: I almost forgot. We also have strawberry.
   KEN: In that case, I'll take chocolate.

   What standard property of decision making is Ken violating? (Hint: Reread the section on Arrow's impossibility theorem.)

7. Why might a political party in a two-party system choose not to move toward the median voter? (Hint: Think about abstentions from voting and political contributions.)

8. Two ice-cream stands are deciding where to locate along a one-kilometre beach. Each person sitting on the beach buys exactly one ice-cream cone per day from the stand nearest to him. Each ice-cream seller wants the maximum number of customers. Where along the beach will the two stands locate?

9. After a widely reported earthquake in British Columbia, many people call their insurance company to apply for earthquake insurance. Might this reaction reflect some deviation from rationality? Discuss.

10. Three friends are choosing a restaurant for dinner. Here are their preferences:

	Rachel	Ross	Joey
First choice	Italian	Italian	Chinese
Second choice	Chinese	Chinese	Mexican
Third choice	Mexican	Mexican	French
Fourth choice	French	French	Italian

a. If the three friends use a Borda count to make their decision, where do they go to eat?
b. On their way to their chosen restaurant, they see that the Mexican and French restaurants are closed, so they use a Borda count again to decide between the remaining two restaurants. Where do they decide to go now?
c. How do your answers to parts (a) and (b) relate to Arrow's impossibility theorem?

11. Three friends are choosing a TV show to watch. Here are their preferences:

	Chandler	Phoebe	Monica
First choice	Dexter	Glee	House
Second choice	Glee	House	Dexter
Third choice	House	Dexter	Glee

a. If the three friends try using a Borda count to make their choice, what would happen?
b. Monica suggests a vote by majority rule. She proposes that first they choose between

Dexter and Glee, and then they choose between the winner of the first vote and House. If they all vote their preferences honestly, what outcome would occur?
c. Should Chandler agree to Monica's suggestion? What voting system would he prefer?
d. Phoebe and Monica convince Chandler to go along with Monica's proposal. In round one, Chandler dishonestly says he prefers Glee over Dexter. Why might he do this?

12. Five roommates are planning to spend the weekend in their dorm room watching movies, and they are debating how many movies to watch. Here is their willingness to pay:

	Quentin	Spike	Ridley	Martin	Steven
First film	$14	$10	$8	$4	$2
Second film	12	8	4	2	0
Third film	10	6	2	0	0
Fourth film	6	2	0	0	0
Fifth film	2	0	0	0	0

Buying a DVD costs $15, which the roommates split equally, so each pays $3 per movie.
a. What is the efficient number of movies to watch (that is, the number that maximizes total surplus)?
b. From the standpoint of each roommate, what is the preferred number of movies?
c. What is the preference of the median roommate?
d. If the roommates held a vote on the efficient outcome versus the median voter's preference, how would each person vote? Which outcome would get a majority?
e. If one of the roommates proposed a different number of movies, could his proposal beat the winner from part (d) in a vote?
f. Can majority rule be counted on to reach efficient outcomes in the provision of public goods?

http:// For more study tools, please visit www.nelson.com/mankiwmicro6e.

GLOSSARY

ability-to-pay principle the idea that taxes should be levied on a person according to how well that person can shoulder the burden (p. 264)

absolute advantage the comparison among producers of a good according to their productivity (p. 55)

accounting profit total revenue minus total explicit cost (p. 278)

adverse selection the tendency for the mix of unobserved attributes to become undesirable from the standpoint of an uninformed party (p. 494)

agent a person who is performing an act for another person, called the *principal* (p. 492)

Arrow's impossibility theorem a mathematical result showing that, under certain assumed conditions, there is no scheme for aggregating individual preferences into a valid set of social preferences (p. 501)

average fixed cost fixed costs divided by the quantity of output (p. 451)

average revenue total revenue divided by the quantity sold (p. 297)

average tax rate total taxes paid divided by total income (p. 263)

average total cost total cost divided by the quantity of output (p. 284)

average variable cost variable costs divided by the quantity of output (p. 284)

benefits principle the idea that people should pay taxes based on the benefits they receive from government services (p. 264)

budget constraint the limit on the consumption bundles that a consumer can afford (p. 464)

budget deficit an excess of government spending over government receipts (p. 257)

budget surplus an excess of government receipts over government spending (p. 257)

business cycle fluctuations in economic activity, such as employment and production (p. 15)

capital the equipment and structures used to produce goods and services (p. 409)

cartel a group of firms acting in unison (p. 373)

circular-flow diagram a visual model of the economy that shows how dollars flow through markets among households and firms (p. 24)

club goods goods that are excludable but not rival (p. 237)

Coase theorem the proposition that if private parties can bargain without cost over the allocation of resources, they can solve the problem of externalities on their own (p. 229)

collusion an agreement among firms in a market about quantities to produce or prices to charge (p. 373)

common resources goods that are rival in consumption but not excludable (p. 237)

comparative advantage the comparison among producers of a good according to their opportunity cost (p. 55)

compensating differential a difference in wages that arises to offset the nonmonetary characteristics of different jobs (p. 418)

competitive market a market in which there are many buyers and many sellers so that each has a negligible impact on the market price (p. 296)

complements two goods for which an increase in the price of one leads to a decrease in the demand for the other (p. 73)

Condorcet paradox the failure of majority rule to produce transitive preferences for society (p. 500)

constant returns to scale the property whereby long-run average total cost stays the same as the quantity of output changes (p. 289)

consumer surplus a buyer's willingness to pay minus the amount the buyer actually pays (p. 150)

corrective taxes taxes enacted to correct the effects of negative externalities (p. 220)

cost the value of everything a seller must give up to produce a good (p. 155)

cost–benefit analysis a study that compares the costs and benefits to society of providing a public good (p. 241)

cross-price elasticity of demand a measure of how much the quantity demanded of one good responds to a change in the price of another good, computed as the percentage change in quantity demanded of the first good divided by the percentage change in the price of the second good (p. 107)

deadweight loss the fall in total surplus that results from a market distortion, such as a tax (p. 451)

demand curve a graph of the relationship between the price of a good and the quantity demanded (p. 70)

demand schedule a table that shows the relationship between the price of a good and the quantity demanded (p. 69)

diminishing marginal product the property whereby the marginal product of an input declines as the quantity of the input increases (p. 280)

discrimination the offering of different opportunities to similar individuals who differ only by race, ethnic group, sex, age, or other personal characteristics (p. 425)

diseconomies of scale the property whereby long-run average total cost rises as the quantity of output increases (p. 289)

dominant strategy a strategy that is best for a player in a game regardless of the strategies chosen by the other players (p. 377)

economic profit total revenue minus total cost, including both explicit and implicit costs (p. 278)

economics the study of how society manages its scarce resources (p. 4)

economies of scale the property whereby long-run average total cost falls as the quantity of output increases (p. 289)

efficiency the property of a resource allocation of maximizing the total surplus received by all members of society (p. 160)

efficiency wages above-equilibrium wages paid by firms in order to increase worker productivity (p. 425)

efficient scale the quantity of output that minimizes average total cost (p. 286)

elasticity a measure of the responsiveness of quantity demanded or quantity supplied to one of its determinants (p. 98)

equilibrium a situation in which the price has reached the level where quantity supplied equals quantity demanded (p. 79)

equilibrium price the price that balances quantity supplied and quantity demanded (p. 451)

equilibrium quantity the quantity supplied and the quantity demanded at the equilibrium price (p. 79)

equity the fairness of the distribution of well-being among the members of society (p. 160)

excludability the property of a good whereby a person can be prevented from using it (p. 236)

explicit costs input costs that require an outlay of money by the firm (p. 277)

exports goods and services produced domestically and sold abroad (p. 60)

externality the uncompensated impact of one person's actions on the well-being of a bystander (p. 12)

factors of production the inputs used to produce goods and services (p. 396)

fixed costs costs that do not vary with the quantity of output produced (p. 282)

free rider a person who receives the benefit of a good but avoids paying for it (p. 238)

game theory the study of how people behave in strategic situations (p. 371)

Giffen good a good for which an increase in the price raises the quantity demanded (p. 478)

horizontal equity the idea that taxpayers with similar abilities to pay taxes should pay the same amount (p. 451)

human capital the accumulation of investments in people, such as education and on-the-job training (p. 419)

implicit costs input costs that do not require an outlay of money by the firm (p. 277)

imports goods and services produced abroad and sold domestically (p. 60)

incentive something that induces a person to act (p. 8)

income effect the change in consumption that results when a price change moves the consumer to a higher or lower indifference curve (p. 474)

income elasticity of demand a measure of how much the quantity demanded of a good responds to a change in consumers' income, computed as the percentage change in quantity demanded divided by the percentage change in income (p. 107)

indifference curve a curve that shows consumption bundles that give the consumer the same level of satisfaction (p. 466)

inferior good a good for which, other things equal, an increase in income leads to a decrease in demand (p. 473)

inflation an increase in the overall level of prices in the economy (p. 14)

in-kind transfers transfers to the poor given in the form of goods and services rather than cash (p. 445)

internalizing the externality alter incentives so that people take account of the external effects of their actions (p. 217)

law of demand the claim that, other things equal, the quantity demanded of a good falls when the price of the good rises (p. 69)

law of supply the claim that, other things equal, the quantity supplied of a good rises when the price of the good rises (p. 75)

law of supply and demand the claim that the price of any good adjusts to bring the quantity supplied and the quantity demanded for that good into balance (p. 81)

liberalism the political philosophy according to which the government should choose policies deemed to be just, as evaluated by an impartial observer behind a "veil of ignorance" (p. 450)

libertarianism the political philosophy according to which the government should punish crimes and enforce voluntary agreements but not redistribute income (p. 451)

life cycle the regular pattern of income variation over a person's life (p. 445)

lump-sum tax a tax that is the same amount for every person (p. 263)

macroeconomics the study of economy-wide phenomena, including inflation, unemployment, and economic growth (p. 29)

marginal changes small incremental adjustments to a plan of action (p. 7)

marginal cost the increase in total cost that arises from an extra unit of production (p. 284)

marginal product the increase in output that arises from an additional unit of input (p. 280)

marginal product of labour the increase in the amount of output from an additional unit of labour (p. 398)

marginal rate of substitution the rate at which a consumer is willing to trade one good for another (p. 466)

marginal revenue the change in total revenue from an additional unit sold (p. 298)

marginal tax rate the extra taxes paid on an additional dollar of income (p. 263)

market a group of buyers and sellers of a particular good or service (p. 68)

market economy an economy that allocates resources through the decentralized decisions of many firms and households as they interact in markets for goods and services (p. 10)

market failure a situation in which a market left on its own fails to allocate resources efficiently (p. 12)

market power the ability of a single economic actor (or small group of actors) to have a substantial influence on market prices (p. 12)

maximin criterion the claim that the government should aim to maximize the well-being of the worst-off person in society (p. 451)

median voter theorem a mathematical result showing that if voters are choosing a point along a line and each voter wants the point closest to his most preferred point, then majority rule will pick the most preferred point of the median voter (p. 502)

microeconomics the study of how households and firms make decisions and how they interact in markets (p. 29)

monopolistic competition a market structure in which many firms sell products that are similar but not identical (p. 352)

monopoly a firm that is the sole seller of a product without close substitutes (p. 320)

moral hazard the tendency of a person who is imperfectly monitored to engage in dishonest or otherwise undesirable behaviour (p. 492)

Nash equilibrium a situation in which economic actors interacting with one another each choose their best strategy given the strategies that all the other actors have chosen (p. 374)

natural monopoly a monopoly that arises because a single firm can supply a good or services to an entire market at a smaller cost than could two or more firms (p. 322)

negative income tax a tax system that collects revenue from high-income households and gives transfers to low-income households (p. 454)

normal good a good for which, other things equal, an increase in income leads to an increase in demand (p. 473)

normative statements claims that attempt to prescribe how the world should be (p. 30)

oligopoly a market structure in which only a few sellers offer similar or identical products (p. 352)

opportunity cost whatever must be given up to obtain some item (p. 55)

perfect complements two goods with right-angle indifference curves (p. 469)

perfect substitutes two goods with straight-line indifference curves (p. 469)

permanent income a person's normal income (p. 446)

positive statements claims that attempt to describe the world as it is (p. 30)

poverty line an absolute level of income set by the federal government for each family size, below which a family is deemed to be in poverty (p. 443)

poverty rate the percentage of the population whose family income falls below an absolute level called the *poverty line* (p. 443)

price ceiling a legal maximum on the price at which a good can be sold (p. 122)

price discrimination the business practice of selling the same good at different prices to different customers (p. 334)

price elasticity of demand a measure of how much the quantity demanded of a good responds to a change in the price of that good, computed as the percentage change in quantity demanded divided by the percentage change in price (p. 98)

price elasticity of supply a measure of how much the quantity supplied of a good responds to a change in the price of that good, computed as the percentage change in quantity supplied divided by the percentage change in price (p. 108)

price floor a legal minimum on the price at which a good can be sold (p. 122)

principal a person for whom another person, called the *agent*, is performing some act (p. 492)

prisoners' dilemma a particular "game" between two captured prisoners that illustrates why cooperation is difficult to maintain even when it is mutually beneficial (p. 376)

private goods goods that are both excludable and rival in consumption (p. 236)

producer surplus the amount a seller is paid for a good minus the seller's cost (p. 155)

production function the relationship between the quantity of inputs used to make a good and the quantity of output of that good (p. 279)

production possibilities frontier a graph that shows the combinations of output that the economy can possibly produce given the available factors of production and the available production technology (p. 26)

productivity the quantity of goods and services produced from each hour of a worker's time (p. 13)

profit total revenue minus total cost (p. 276)

progressive tax a tax for which high-income taxpayers pay a larger fraction of their income than do low-income taxpayers (p. 265)

property rights the ability of an individual to own and exercise control over scarce resources (p. 12)

proportional tax a tax for which high-income and low-income taxpayers pay the same fraction of income (p. 265)

public goods goods that are neither excludable nor rival (p. 236)

quantity demanded the amount of a good that buyers are willing and able to purchase (p. 69)

quantity supplied the amount of a good that sellers are willing and able to sell (p. 75)

rational people people who systematically and purposefully do the best they can to achieve their objectives (p. 7)

regressive tax a tax for which high-income taxpayers pay a smaller fraction of their income than do low-income taxpayers (p. 265)

rival in consumption the property of a good whereby one person's use diminishes other people's use (p. 236)

scarcity the limited nature of society's resources (p. 4)

screening an action taken by an uninformed party to induce an informed party to reveal information (p. 496)

shortage a situation in which quantity demanded is greater than quantity supplied (p. 80)

signalling an action taken by an informed party to reveal private information to an uninformed party (p. 495)

strike the organized withdrawal of labour from a firm by a union (p. 425)

substitutes two goods for which an increase in the price of one leads to an increase in the demand for the other (p. 72)

substitution effect the change in consumption that results when a price change moves the consumer along a given indifference curve to a point with a new marginal rate of substitution (p. 474)

sunk cost a cost that has already been committed and cannot be recovered (p. 303)

supply curve a graph of the relationship between the price of a good and the quantity supplied (p. 76)

supply schedule a table that shows the relationship between the price of a good and the quantity supplied (p. 75)

surplus a situation in which quantity supplied is greater than quantity demanded (p. 80)

tariff a tax on goods produced abroad and sold domestically (p. 195)

tax incidence the manner in which the burden of a tax is shared among participants in a market (p. 133)

total cost the market value of the inputs a firm uses in production (p. 276)

total revenue (for a firm) the amount a firm receives for the sale of its output (p. 276)

total revenue (in a market) the amount paid by buyers and received by sellers of a good, computed as the price of the good times the quantity sold (p. 101)

Tragedy of the Commons a parable that illustrates why common resources get used more than is desirable from the standpoint of society as a whole (p. 243)

transaction costs the costs that parties incur in the process of agreeing and following through on a bargain (p. 230)

union a worker association that bargains with employers over wages and working conditions (p. 425)

utilitarianism the political philosophy according to which the government should choose policies to maximize the total utility of everyone in society (p. 449)

utility a measure of happiness or satisfaction (p. 449)

value of the marginal product the marginal product of an input times the price of the output (p. 399)

variable costs costs that do vary with the quantity of output produced (p. 283)

vertical equity the idea that taxpayers with a greater ability to pay taxes should pay larger amounts (p. 265)

welfare government programs that supplement the incomes of the needy (p. 453)

welfare economics the study of how the allocation of resources affects economic well-being (p. 149)

willingness to pay the maximum amount that a buyer will pay for a good (p. 150)

world price the price of a good that prevails in the world market for that good (p. 191)

INDEX

(4,6)

SUGGESTIONS FOR SUMMER READING

IF YOU ENJOYED THE ECONOMICS COURSE THAT YOU HAVE JUST FINISHED, YOU MIGHT LIKE TO READ ABOUT ECONOMIC ISSUES IN THE FOLLOWING BOOKS:

PAUL BLUSTEIN

The Chastening: Inside the Crisis That Rocked the Global Financial System and Humbled the IMF
New York: Public Affairs, 2001

A journalist tells the story of how economic policymakers around the world muddled through the financial crisis of the late 1990s.

WILLIAM BREIT AND BARRY T. HIRSCH

Lives of the Laureates
Cambridge, MA: MIT Press, 2004

Eighteen winners of the Nobel Prize in economics offer autobiographical essays about their life and work.

DIANE COYLE

Sex, Drugs & Economics
New York: Texere, 2002

Basic economics applied to a wide range of sometimes unconventional topics.

JOHN CROW

Making Money: An Insider's Perspective on Finance, Politics, and Canada's Central Bank
Etobicoke, ON: John Wiley & Sons, 2002

Part memoir, part history, part analysis of major monetary policy issues, *Making Money* brings to life the inner workings and the politics of the Bank of Canada.

AVINASH DIXIT AND BARRY NALEBUFF

Thinking Strategically: A Competitive Edge in Business, Politics and Everyday Life
New York: Norton, 1991

This introduction to game theory discusses how all people—from corporate executives to criminals under arrest—should, and do, make strategic decisions.

WILLIAM EASTERLY

The Elusive Quest for Growth: Economists' Adventures and Misadventures in the Tropics
Cambridge, MA: MIT Press, 2001

A World Bank economist examines the many attempts to help the world's poorest nations and why they have so often failed.

MILTON AND ROSE FRIEDMAN

Free to Choose
New York: Harcourt Brace, 1979

Two economists argue that society should rely less on the government and more on the free market.

ROBERT L. HEILBRONER

The Worldly Philosophers
New York: Touchstone, 1953; revised 1999

A classic introduction to the lives, times, and ideas of the great economic thinkers, including Adam Smith, David Ricardo, and John Maynard Keynes.

JOHN HELLIWELL

Globalization and Well-Being
Vancouver: UBC Press, 2003

This text is essential reading for all those trying to think their way through the welter of conflicting assertions about what is left for national policies in today's world.

DOUGLAS A. IRWIN

Free Trade under Fire
Princeton, NJ: Princeton University Press, 2005

An economist sheds some light on the debate over globalization.

PAUL KRUGMAN

Peddling Prosperity
New York: Norton, 1994

A survey of the evolution of economic ideas and policy, with an emphasis on macroeconomics and international trade.